Principles of Law Office Management

CONCEPTS AND APPLICATIONS

Principles of Law Office Management

CONCEPTS AND APPLICATIONS

Eileen P. Rosenberg
Professor of Management, Elms College
Founder and former director of Elms Paralegal Institute

West Publishing Company
Minneapolis/St. Paul   New York   Los Angeles   San Francisco

Production Credits
Text Design: LightSource Images
Artwork: Randy Miyake
Composition: Parkwood Composition Services, Inc.

West's Commitment to the Environment
In 1906, West Publishing Company began recycling materials left over from the production of books. This began a tradition of efficient and responsible use of resources. Today, up to 95 percent of our legal books and 70 percent of our college and school texts are printed on recycled, acid-free stock. West also recycles nearly 22 million pounds of scrap paper annually—the equivalent of 181,717 trees. Since the 1960s, West has devised ways to capture and recycle waste inks, solvents, oils, and vapors created in the printing process. We also recycle plastics of all kinds, wood, glass, corrugated cardboard, and batteries, and have eliminated the use of styrofoam book packaging. We at West are proud of the longevity and the scope of our commitment to the environment.

Production, Prepress, Printing and Binding by West Publishing Company.

 PRINTED ON 10% POST CONSUMER RECYCLED PAPER

COPYRIGHT © 1993 By WEST PUBLISHING COMPANY
610 Opperman Drive
P.O. Box 64526
St. Paul, MN 55164-0526

All rights reserved

Printed in the United States of America

00 99 98 97 96 95 94 93   8 7 6 5 4 3 2 1 0

Library of Congress Cataloging-in-Publication Data
Rosenberg, Eileen Popkoski, 1938–
    Principles of law office management : concepts and applications / Eileen P. Rosenberg.
      p.   cm.
    Includes index.
    ISBN 0-314-01359-8 (hard : acid-free)
    1. Law offices—United States. I. Title.
KF318.R67 1993
340'.068—dc20

93-9794
CIP

To my husband Victor, with love and appreciation. Without his thoughtful caring, support, understanding, and in-house counsel, all my dreams would still be dreams.

Brief Contents

PART ONE — Managerial Concepts — 1

Chapter 1	Managerial Perspectives	2
Chapter 2	Planning and Decision Making	38
Chapter 3	Organizing and Organizations	80
Chapter 4	Directing: Authority, Power, and Politics	115
Chapter 5	Controlling: Resources, Time, and Growth	143

PART TWO — Managerial Applications — 183

Chapter 6	Managing Financial Resources	184
Chapter 7	Managing Human Resources	213
Chapter 8	Supervision	247
Chapter 9	Leadership	270
Chapter 10	Groups and Group Dynamics	294
Chapter 11	Motivation	319
Chapter 12	Communications	345
Chapter 13	Change, Conflict, and Stress	373
Chapter 14	Clients and Marketing	404
Chapter 15	Ethical Responsibilities	434

Contents

		Preface	13
PART ONE		**Managerial Concepts**	1
Chapter 1		**Managerial Perspectives**	2
		Law Office Management	5
		What Is a Manager?	11
		A Manager's Challenges	14
		The Four Basic Managerial Functions	18
		Managerial Levels, Skills, and Roles	20
		Successful Law Office Managers of the Future	24
		Questions for Discussion and Review	28
		Experiential Exercises	28
Special Focus		*Contributions to Management Theory*	*33*
Chapter 2		**Planning and Decision Making**	38
		Planning	40
		Kinds of Plans	42
		Steps in the Planning Process	49
		The Nature of Decisions	54
		Steps in the Decision Process	54
		Factors That Influence Decision Quality	60
		Involvement in Planning and Decision Making	64
		Techniques for Group Involvement	68
		Barriers to Planning and Decision Making	71
		Law Firm Retreats	72
		Questions for Discussion and Review	75
		Experiential Exercises	76
Chapter 3		**Organizing and Organizations**	80
		The Importance of Organizing	82
		The Architecture of Organizations	83
		The Four Activities of Organizing	88
		Division of Labor	88
		Departmentalization and Organizational Design	90
		Coordinating Elements of Organizing	94
		Control Elements in Organizing	97
		Contemporary Organizational Designs	100
		Organizational Culture	105
		Characteristics of Successful Organizations in the 1990s	109
		Questions for Discussion and Review	112
		Experiential Exercises	112
Chapter 4		**Directing: Authority, Power, and Politics**	115
		Authority	118
		Delegation	119
		Power	122
		Sources of Power	123
		Influence	126
		Managerial Power Strategies	127
		Politics	131
		Empowerment	133
		Questions for Discussion and Review	135
		Experiential Exercises	136

Chapter 5	Controlling: Resources, Time, and Growth	143
	The Nature of Control	145
	Areas of Control	147
	The Control Process	170
	Workers and Controls	171
	Measuring Effectiveness	172
	Crisis Management	173
	Time Management	174
	Controlling Growth	177
	Questions for Discussion and Review	179
	Experiential Exercises	179

PART TWO Managerial Applications 183

Chapter 6	Managing Financial Resources	184
	Keeping Track of Finances	186
	Operating Budgets	187
	The Steps in the Budgetary Process	190
	The Revenue Stream	195
	The Value of Time	200
	Management Financial Reporting	201
	Areas of Financial Management	204
	Profitability	207
	Questions for Discussion and Review	209
	Experiential Exercises	209

Chapter 7	Managing Human Resources	213
	The Human Resource Process	216
	The Major Activities of Human Resource Managers	217
	Legal Constraints	232
	Evaluating Human Resources	240
	Questions for Discussion and Review	242
	Experiential Exercises	242

Chapter 8	Supervision	247
	Challenges of Supervision in the 1990s	249
	Supervision in the Professional Setting	251
	Being a Supervisor	252
	Effective Supervision	255
	Styles of Supervision	255
	Performance Appraisals	258
	Appraisal Tools and Techniques	260
	Employee Discipline	262
	Questions for Discussion and Review	267
	Experiential Exercises	267

Chapter 9	Leadership	270
	The Search for Leadership	273
	Law Firm Managers and Leadership	275
	What Makes a Leader?	276
	Leadership Theories	277
	Meeting the Challenges of Law Firm Leadership	288
	Questions for Discussion and Review	290
	Experiential Exercises	290

Chapter 10	Motivation	294
	Motivation in the Law Firm	296
	Performance and Individual Differences	300
	Behind the Scenes: The Motivational Framework	303
	Theories of Motivation	305
	Goal Setting as a Motivational Strategy	312
	New Motivational Tools	313
	Questions for Discussion and Review	314
	Experiential Exercises	314

Chapter 11	Groups and Group Dynamics	319
	Groups and the Organization	321

CONTENTS

	The Formation and Effects of Groups	323
	The Structure of Work Groups	327
	Group Roles	328
	Group Norms and Status	328
	Group Cohesiveness	331
	Managers and Groups	334
	Group Status in the Law Firm	336
	Questions for Discussion and Review	340
	Experiential Exercises	340
Chapter 12	**Communications**	**345**
	Communications and the Legal Profession	348
	The Communication Process	349
	Persuasiveness of Communications	353
	Writing Effectively	356
	Speaking Effectively	358
	Listening Effectively	360
	Communication in the Law Firm	362
	Barriers to Good Communication	364
	Improving Communication	365
	How to Run Successful Meetings	366
	Questions for Discussion and Review	370
	Experiential Exercises	371
Chapter 13	**Change, Conflict, and Stress**	**373**
	Change	376
	Theories of Change	379
	Bringing about Effective Change	382
	Conflict	384
	Stress	390
	Effects of Stress	395
	Differences in Responses to Stress	396
	Coping with Stress	398
	Questions for Discussion and Review	399
	Experiential Exercises	399
Chapter 14	**Clients and Marketing**	**404**
	Marketing and the Legal Profession	406
	Marketing	409
	Personal Selling	412
	Public Relations	414
	Advertising	416
	Practice Development	418
	Clients	420
	Building Firm-Wide Involvement in Marketing	427
	Creative Marketing Approaches	428
	Questions for Discussion and Review	429
	Experiential Exercises	430
Chapter 15	**Ethical Responsibilities**	**434**
	Managerial Ethics	436
	Good People	438
	Good Lawyers	440
	The Laws of Lawyering	442
	ABA Model Rules of Professional Conduct	443
	The Good Manager	447
	Good Law Firms	452
	Ethical Choices	454
	Ethical Dilemmas	456
	Questions for Discussion and Review	459
	Experiential Exercises	459
Glossary		461
Endnotes		474
Name Index		495
Subject Index		499

Preface

Life has always been complicated and challenging for legal professionals. Today, the demands have intensified. In a volatile economy and a crowded field, competitiveness means survival. Clients have become careful consumers. The complications of practice have exploded. New technology, new structures, new specializations, and new processes have invaded the workplace of the legal professional. These challenges are not unique to the practice of law, however. All businesses, to a greater or lesser degree, are faced with finding competitive advantages, but other businesses have long since recognized the contributions of professional management. The business of law has now acknowledged that it, too, needs the expertise of specialized management. The 1991 ABA conference blamed "unsound management practices" for the "Emerging Crisis in the Quality of Lawyer's Health and Lives":

> The concept many lawyers have of a profession—which excludes the relevance and validity of business principles—actually compounds the problem. Professionals are not trained as managers and are not schooled in business practices. Indeed, law schools in the past have resisted increasing the amount of skills provided, let alone business training. Without the necessary training, and with a reluctance to follow the advice of business "professionals," law firm managers have not viewed the firm as a business, except in the most obvious and basic way—as a source of economic profit...
>
> Thus, the true problem is that many firms are run on management principles that are not only antithetical to the conduct of the business of law as a profession, but also unsound under modern business management theory. The failure to treat lawyers and support staff as an investment in human capital, to be nurtured and developed to their maximum potential, violates both concepts. Many law firm managers in the 1980s resembled not the enlightened corporate executive or professional, but rather the industrial manager in the early years of the industrial revolution.[1]

This text pays attention to the fact that the management in the law firm has unique challenges because of the roles nonlawyers have in an organization of professionals. Although most lawyers recognize the need for more professional approaches to practice management, they continue to deliberate the presence of nonlawyers in the inner sanctum. Management of the law firm, whether by lawyers or nonlawyers, is not simply "overseeing." It is a unique kind of service to professionals that provides support for the proper functioning of all that helps the professional do his or her job. It demands a special understanding of planning, organizing, directing, and controlling within the law firm professional environment. This kind of management can not be learned just by applications. It demands a depth of substantive preparation that integrates practical applications with the richness of today's management theory. A well-managed firm, whose respect for its members works hand in hand with high standards, can better serve its clients and itself.

I wrote this text based on the philosophy that today's law firm managers must be trained for more than the lean and mean aspects of administrative fundamentals. They must learn that management is a portable skill, a highly complicated people-process. The newest paralegal coordinator to the most senior executive administrator all rely on an understanding of workers that is rooted in the richness of management theories. This text intends to help those who are new in the field of

---

[1] "The Underlying Problem—Unsound Management Practices," from the ABA report of "At the Breaking Point: A National Conference on The Emerging Crisis in the Quality of Lawyers' Health and Lives—Its Impact of Law Firms and Client Services," The American Bar Association (1991): 12.

law understand what professional management is like for those who practice law. Many courses in law office management believe in a "nuts and bolts" variety of office practice, emphasizing the "how-to's" of office administration, but this work recognizes the fact that management not only consists of practical applications but also of the larger aspects of management that affect peoples' lives. It will provide students with practical applications as well as with the same kind of substance and depth as is provided for students of business management in the best of programs at our national colleges and universities, who have long benefitted from management courses that focus on both people *and* processes.

Many share with me the conviction that education does not limit aspirations but encourages them, helps us believe in our dreams, and giving us ways to feed and nourish them and turn them into realities. The intent of *Principles of Law Office Management: Concepts and Applications* is to help newcomers in the field understand the challenges ahead, to encourage the aspirations of students, and to provide life-long tools for becoming effective managers. Some students may become managers in that field, serving as paralegal coordinators, supervisors or administrators. Some may eventually head departments, offices, or even firms. And others may decide not to become part of management at all. All, including this last group, by learning what is involved in law office management, will have greater respect for the field of management. Because of that, they will be better team players, an invaluable asset for all law firms. Students will learn that the managerial challenge encompasses and yet surpasses the skills of filling out forms and mastering filing systems. They will gain additional respect for the operations and procedures of the law firm. They will have some understanding of how successful management is all about working with people, enabling them to give their best.

This text targets college level students with interests in the field of law. Paralegal students, in particular, will learn more about law offices and the practice of law, but the text will also be useful to all those who want to learn more about management in law firm settings, including law students who want to know more about the field and those who are changing careers.

Legal managers, as our newest professionals, will benefit from the perspective that comes from understanding up-to-date research and its applications. The legal community will be able to have additional confidence in the specialized contributions of these managers who will have earned the right, through successful use of thorough preparation, to true respect and acceptance. A "good" manager can help bring about the best of human dignity and respect in the fair exchanges between employer and worker. In understanding that balance, the best of management theory makes sense.

ORGANIZATION OF THE TEXT

The framework of this text has two major parts. Part One explores the principal managerial challenges of the law firm. It first provides an overview of management, from its historic origins to contemporary schools of thought. It traces the development of law firm management in particular, looking at the career of the legal administrator. It then devotes one chapter to each of the four principal managerial activities: planning, organizing, directing and controlling.

Part Two examines managerial applications of these concepts for the law firm. Management of the law firm's Financial Resources is followed by chapters on Human Resources, and Supervision. Part Two then explores law firm issues as Leadership, Groups and Group Dynamics, Motivation, Communications, and Change, Conflict and Stress. This section concludes with two indispensable areas for management in today's law firm, a chapter addressing Clients and Marketing followed by a chapter on Ethical Responsibilities.

Each chapter is written as a self-contained section so that the instructors can select the materials that are the most critical for their students. The content of the text is designed to give a complete, concise, and timely overview of contemporary management for legal settings.

TO THE STUDENT

Right now, you may not be sure where you are going to work, especially if you are a beginner in the field of law. Some of you may choose careers in a law office that develop from a career specialty, as secretarial, paralegal, computer technology, marketing, finance or accounting, or even library science. If you are a paralegal, over 95% of you will be working with lawyers throughout your paralegal careers. Others among you may be among the vast numbers who are changing career paths. You have many experiences from other sectors, as in business and government. You are now ready to translate your specialized skills into the law office management.

You will all need to know a great deal about the settings where lawyers practice law. There are many different kinds of law offices, differing in size from a handful of individuals to one of the newer international mega-firms. When you complete this text, you will know much about how those firms are managed. You will learn about the challenges managers have. You will know about the structures and processes that hold law firms together as effective groups of workers. Other courses will teach you what the law is. This course will teach you about the **structures** within which law is practiced and about working with the **people** who fill those structures.

There are two main reasons for you to study law office management. First, law isn't practiced in a vacuum. The more you know about how the dimensions and the diversity of people, places and things interact in order to practice law, the more you will feel at ease in the law practice setting. You will be better able to use all the skills you have learned in preparation for working there. This will help you become a better practicing paralegal, a better professional. If you are not management-bound, you will learn how the system works and the importance of each person in the system. Most of all, you will learn enough about the challenges of law firm managers to become a "team player," a vital and contributing member.

Secondly, some of you may eventually become managers, as legal administrators, legal assistant managers, and coordinators. This book will help you learn the basics for that career path. If management is part of your career planning, this text will provide you with more than the forms and functions of a law firm. It will give you some of the thinking that has gone into being a successful manager. Whatever your professional and personal choices are, understanding management will help you understand yourself, your co-workers and your organization, and that is a very marketable commodity.

CHAPTER FEATURES

The following summarizes the features found in the text:

- **Learning Objectives.** At the beginning of each chapter is a highlighted list of the basic learning objectives of the chapter. It will read, "After completing this chapter, you should be able to:" This will give students an overview of what is to follow.
- **Focus from the Field** presents the view of practitioners, through interviews, comments and observations. At the beginning of each chapter, there is a glimpse into some facet of management, as it applies to law. Hearing from those who have "been there" is often reassuring and always rewarding.
- **In the News.** These are excerpts from current literature and periodicals. Each example follows the themes of the chapter and will give students a feel for the realities they will be encountering in the law firm setting. These materials are drawn from sources such as *The Wall Street Journal, Legal Administrator, The National Law Journal, California Law Business, The New York Times,* and several other contemporary and appropriate management sources.
- **Another Look** gives brief, "real life" excerpts from contemporary business literature, case study vignettes and close-ups. This feature contributes a fresh look at some of the different views managers can have about some basic issues and questions that will aid in discussing them.
- **Terminology.** The vocabulary of business is a tool for managers. The terminology that is the most useful is highlighted in the text. It reappears in a glossary at the end of the text where you will find a concise definition and a reference to the page where each term was originally explained. This will give students an additional opportunity to review their meanings and to refer to them in their original context.
- **Experiential Exercises.** Materials for self-assessment, questionnaires, and other similar materials appear at the end of each chapter. Students will be able to see their own particular strengths, interests, and styles. They also serve as suggestions for class activities and learning experiences that will help students become involved in thinking through managerial theory.
- **Questions for Discussion and Review.** Additional questions are provided at the end of each chapter as a basis for thoughtful discussion or review.

SUPPLEMENTS

The following supplements are available with the text:

- The **instructor's manual** provides instructors with sample class syllabi and suggestions for student projects and term papers. In addition, each chapter in the manual contains:
  - Learning Objectives
  - Chapter Summary
  - Teaching suggestions
  - A Lecture Outline
  - Answers to the Questions for Discussion and Review
  - Notes on the Experiential Exercises
  - Additional "Special Focus" articles
  - Additional Experiential Exercises and Another Look features
- The **test bank** includes over 80 questions for each chapter in a variety of formats including true/false, multiple choice, matching and essay.
- The **WESTEST Computerized Testing** program offers the complete test bank on disk.
- The **transparency masters** consist of over 50 figures for use as overheads, including figures taken from the text and additional figures created by the author.
- **The student study guide,** prepared by Anneta Buster of Brown Mackie College, includes a variety of review questions which help students test their knowledge of chapter concepts and terminology. In addition, practice exercises are included for each chapter. These exercises provide hypothetical scenarios designed to help students apply chapter concepts to the law office setting. (For student purchase.)

ACKNOWLEDGMENTS AND CREDITS

The author would like to acknowledge all those who have helped in the preparation of this text: the members of ALA and LAMA who assisted with suggestions and the original survey; the law firm of Robinson, Donovan, Madden & Barry and its senior partners, especially Attorney Victor Rosenberg, for sharing what they have learned; and the legal administrators who first taught law office management at Elms College: Pat Hourihan, Dick LeMoine, Gail Suchy, Hal Cort, and Jane Henley. Appreciation is also given the legal managers who participated in the interviews for the text, to Peter Raven-Hansen of George Washington University Law School for his help and support, to the reference room librarians at the Jupiter, Florida branch of the Palm Beach Libraries, and to all those who assisted with materials and permissions. The author owes thanks to her Elms College Department of Management colleagues Bill Donovan and Dr. David Kimball, to Dr. Jean LaLiberte for her review of marketing, and to a vast number of wonderful students, who have encouraged and helped in many ways.

Thanks is also due to the team of national reviewers for their insight and honesty, including: Anneta A. Buster, Brown Mackie College; Dolores Grissom, Samford University; Melvin Hartley, Fayetteville Technical Community College; John Medbury, Anna Maria College; Kathryn Myers, St. Mary-of-the-Woods College; Kathleen Reed, University of Toledo Community and Technical College; Dr. George D. Schrader, Auburn University at Montgomery; and Ardye Stephens, University of West Florida.

Finally I would like to thank Judy Raimondi for her work on the interviews of legal managers, the business and paralegal students who have assisted with both the testbank and the instructor's manual, and Elizabeth Hannan, Patricia Bryant, Sandra Gangelhoff, and Kim Kaliszewski at West Publishing.

PART ONE

Managerial Concepts

CHAPTER 1

Managerial Perspectives

LEARNING OBJECTIVES

After completing this chapter, you should be able to:

- Understand the changes that have taken place in the legal profession and the need for professional approaches to management;
- Define management and explain why management is important to society and to individuals;
- Explain the development of law office management and discuss why the practice of law is both a business and a profession;
- List and define the four major managerial responsibilities and the skills needed at each of the three levels of management;
- Explore the roles of the manager; and
- Discuss future challenges for legal managers.

Ellen Bump, a newly appointed paralegal coordinator, works for the Springfield, Massachusetts firm of Robinson, Donovan, Madden & Barry, P.C. She began with the firm as a secretary in 1977. After obtaining a Certificate of Advanced Paralegal Studies in 1984, Ellen was promoted to the position of paralegal. In 1990, Ellen received her bachelor of arts in business management. She then developed and submitted a proposal for a new position of paralegal coordinator to the firm's managing partners. The firm readily accepted Ellen's proposal and appointed her to the new position. She is now supervising more than a dozen paralegals.

FOCUS FROM THE FIELD

Ellen C. Bump: Challenges for a New Manager

What new challenges did your role as paralegal coordinator bring?

Before I was appointed manager, we [the paralegals] floundered around without having anyone to go to directly with any problems, suggestions, or advice on how to handle certain situations. I think that I give them a person to come to, and I have the ability to speak directly with the executive committee if need be or to speak with the associate managers. Also, the firm wanted to make sure that the paralegals were being utilized as much as they ought to be, because a lot of times we were finding that the paralegals were doing things that the clerical people should have been doing and it was just easier to have a paralegal do it. As a result, work that the paralegal was doing was not billable to the client and our profitability was going down. We just needed someone to go to the attorneys and say, "This is how you have to use us. This is how you should not use us."

What do you think makes a good manager?

One of the main things that I have come across in this new position is that you have to listen and you have to get both sides to the story or the problem. You can't just have somebody come in angry about something and assume that's exactly what happened. I think that it helps to know where to go with particular problems. You have to backtrack and follow through to find out what really happened. You have to get the facts, because people are emotional when they get angry and they don't always see the clear picture. I think that you also have to be open to new ideas and not think that you have all of the answers. That's one of my main goals—not to become dictatorial in my position but to try to get suggestions from the paralegals and try to implement as many ideas as possible that would make their jobs easier and would also benefit the firm. My initial tendency was that anything the paralegals wanted, I wanted them to have because I wanted them to be completely satisfied with their jobs. But I also had to recognize that I had to look at the firm as a whole. What the paralegals may want is not necessarily best for the firm.

Where do you feel you've been successful?

It's much too soon to know any successes, but creating and obtaining the position itself was certainly a success. I finished with my bachelor's degree in June and it took me from June to September to put together a written proposal for this job and to present it to the managing partner. I suppose it is a success because I agonized long and hard over how to present it and what goals I wanted for the paralegals and for the firm.

Where do you think your biggest challenges will be?

Getting the attorneys to adjust their thinking and educating them on the proper use [of paralegals]. I am in the process of putting together a manual of responsibilities for individual paralegals. We have estate probate paralegals and drafting paralegals. We also have real estate paralegals, an environmental law and land use paralegal, and the litigation paralegals. Each one of them has a specific function to perform for the benefit of the attorneys; I am simply listing them. It [the manual] will also serve as an educational tool for the attorneys.

What is it like being a legal assistant manager?

I like it. It's something I've been working toward for many years. As soon as I began working on my bachelor's degree in management, I knew that this was something that I wanted to do. I'm very glad to be doing it. Frankly, it's somewhat scary and a little lonely. I have no one on my level to go to with a problem. I have to go to an associate manager or the managing partner, and they've been helpful. I expect I'll be making some mistakes as I learn.

What are some of the most common mistakes managers make?

I hate to keep going back to it but not listening is a big problem. Also, accepting advice from those who know more than you do. You need to accept advice and follow it even if sometimes it goes against what you really want to do, because it comes from people with far more experience than you. Delegating is another problem. In my present position and before also, my job was to delegate assignments to the litigation paralegals. I found that if it was a really boring assignment, I would feel bad about giving it to someone and keep it myself. You're not supposed to do that. You're supposed to delegate as much as you can to people but I tend to want to keep people interested. I'm trying to change that. Delegating is a problem.

What advice do you have for those thinking about becoming law office managers?

Learn some people skills before you take it on. Also, don't give up the fight if it's something that you really want. They have always treated me so well at the firm. To go to the partners with my proposal for the position felt pushy and that's just not my nature. But I am convinced that if I hadn't done it, I would be waiting and waiting and getting more and more frustrated. Be aggressive but be prepared. I think that it would help to become familiar with the profession in your community. Know which other offices have managers, know who to talk to, know how paralegals are utilized in the community. You can't just narrow your focus to the one firm; you have to have a knowledge of the community. I also think that you need to have experience as a paralegal. I don't think that you can just come into a position as a manager without having first done the work yourself.

An effective organization is a living thing: An organization *is* its people. People breathe life and purpose and energy into an organization. An organization has a manner, spirit, tempo, nature, character. It has moods, joys, fears, and sorrows. But most important of all, an effective organization has a purpose that is shared by its members and to which they willingly commit their efforts. People working together can do almost anything.
(James Hayes, *Memos for Management*)[1]

CHAPTER 1 / MANAGERIAL PERSPECTIVES

> **T**he management of creative workers has become the most critical area faced by managements in both the private and public sectors ... The quality and extent of what is accomplished in the foreseeable future have become a function of the ability of managements to harness and channel the efforts of creative workers. The difference in success between one effort and another, one organization and another, depends on whether management understands the differences between the management of professional activities and the management relevant to the assembly line.
> (Albert Shapero, *Managing Professional People*)[2]
>
> **A**s the legal profession marches toward the 21st century, likely scenarios for the law practice of the future keep apace. On the horizon are ever greater financial pressures on lawyers, more sophisticated and global clients, and practitioners who demand more out of their jobs and personal lives.
> (Thomas F. Gibbons, *"Law Practice in 2001"*)[3]

LAW OFFICE MANAGEMENT

You are likely studying the principles of law office management in order to learn about this new branch of management or more specifically, how you can focus your efforts toward a new career as a law office manager. In this book, you will learn about the responsibilities of those who wear the many different hats of the many kinds of managers in a law office. What brought about this new career? What forms does management take—both within and outside of the legal office? What can you do and learn to best prepare yourself for this field? What challenges are ahead? How important is this career to the legal profession?

> No job is more vital to our society than that of the manager. It is the manager who determines whether our social institutions serve us well or whether they squander our talents and resources. It is time to strip away the folklore about managerial work, and time to study it realistically so that we can begin the difficult task of making significant improvements in its performance.[4]

To appreciate the importance of law office managers, whether you make management one of your career choices or not, it would be worthwhile to understand the development of this career.

Changing Times

Lawyering, until the most recent times, has been a profession consisting of individual performers, and the delivery of legal services to society has been organizationally simple.

The legal profession, like much of the rest of American society, was transformed between the 1870s and the 1920s. The law partnership was basically a nineteenth century creation, which began simply as working arrangements between two or more persons. Even by the turn of the century, the range of clients' problems became too complex for any one person to provide all the expertise.[5]

The worldwide changes that occurred in labor and industry between the late 1800s and the early 1900s also brought unsurpassed change to the profession of law. These seeds were planted as far back as the 1880s, when the legendary Boston attorney and later United States Supreme Court Justice Louis D. Brandeis, urged his colleagues to recognize the business aspects of the law profession. He was among the first to encourage changes that would render the practice of law a profitable business. He himself "epitomized the emerging industrial lawyer," developing his own firm as a "vertically organized, specialized law firm" with a concentration on corporate law. Brandeis became a staunch advocate of large-scale law firms, noting that they "offered the best chances for monetary and professional success."[6] He was among the first to openly advocate and utilize solid recruiting practices, incorporating the basic principles of management into his own law practice. He scouted actively for bright young prospects who could add to the bench strength of his firm and hired beginners that he could quickly invite into partnerships. As legal scholar Gerard Gawalt notes, Brandeis's "policy was to hire as salaried assistants Harvard Law School graduates who stood high in their class." When these same young associates complained about his receiving all the credit for their work, he explained his views:

IN THE NEWS

Paths to a New Career

The previous decade saw a dramatic change in the role of the average American law firm administrator.

"In the past," says Elizabeth Kalb, administrator at New York's Summit Rovins & Feldesman and newly elected president of the Association of Legal Administrators, "we would concentrate on time sheets, hiring secretaries, making sure there's paper in the men's room. Now we're involved in senior level financial management. We're creating a culture at the firm. And we're involved in marketing, communications and practice management development. We're not just managing strategies. We're creating them."

In many firms, even the title of the job has changed—from office manager or director of administration to law office administrator, executive director, chief operating officer, or, in some firms, chief executive officer.

"The position of the law office administrator has been evolving in the direction of greater responsibility and a stronger role," notes John F. Coburn, vice president at the Cambridge Mass., consulting firm of Gray-Judson & Howard Inc. Mr. Coburn recently completed a study of what he calls "the new breed" of law office administrators. "That evolution has been geometric, starting in the 1960s. By the year 2000, firms will be seeing the administrator as being as important as any other human being in the firm. When asked, 'Which person could you least afford to lose?' many firms will say 'the administrator.'"

"That evolution accelerated in the 1980s," adds Daniel De-Lucchio, principal at Altman & Weil, "when the profit squeeze really began to be felt in the law firms. All the economic, profit and competition pressures hit home then. And the firms came to realize that the only way they could stay profitable was if the firms were run as businesses."

Notes John Walker, managing partner at Los Angeles' Latham & Watkins, "The position has changed as firms have changed. It has been increasingly important, especially for the larger firms, to have someone more competent and more experienced in business in these positions. Someone to whom the lawyers will cede power."

Mr. Coburn sees three major reasons for the expanding responsibilities of office administrators. First, he says, "The complexity and size of law firms has caused an increasing need to treat the firms as businesses. Second, the increasingly competitive nature of the legal profession requires someone in the organization to run it efficiently. And third, lawyers are not good at administering and managing. These people need to spend time rainmaking and delivering legal services. The firm can't afford to have its most valuable people" bogged down in nuts-and-bolts items.

"This is a belated and painful recognition by law firms," Mr. Coburn adds. "Some firms still don't believe it."

For the firms that do recognize the need for business professionals in the position, says Sylvia Lurie, the ALA's communications director, "The job description has changed dramatically. The new one focuses more on 'big picture' and high-level responsibilities within traditional operations management areas, such as finance, systems and technology, human resources, etc.

The organization of large offices . . . must result in the greatest efficiency to clients and the greatest success to the individual members both pecuniary and in reputation. . . . In such an organization, the place of each man must be found—not prescribed. The advantage of the large field is that every man has the opportunity of trying himself at everything or anything—and by the natural law comes to do those things that on the whole he does most effectively.[7]

By the 1890s, his financial success was legendary. "Law is getting to be 'more and more like a business,'" the contented Brandeis noted in 1905.[8] Brandeis, who believed strongly that a well-run business of law could benefit society, might aptly be called the first "true pioneer of modern forms of law firm organization."[9] Large law firms emerged around Brandeis's time, at the turn of the century, and have steadily evolved into what some today perceive as "law factories."[10] As far back as the 1930s, most lawyers still practiced alone or with only one partner, but the leaders of the profession no longer enjoyed uncomplicated practices. The majority of outstanding lawyers were found in large firms.[11] Still, by the mid-sixties, there were only slightly more than fifty law firms that had more than fifty lawyers. Even so, on the seventy-fifth

IN THE NEWS (continued)

And it adds more responsibilities in practice management areas, including marketing and plannings."

The list of responsibilities seems almost endless. According to Ms. Lurie, administrators commonly manage all the business functions of the office; prepare all financial plans and analyses; manage, screen and hire all nonlegal personnel; oversee the law library; monitor continuing legal education for legal staff; maintain and continually refine equipment, paying particular attention to new technology, including computer hardware and software; and oversee billing and collections. In some firms, the administrator is involved in marketing and practice development as well.

"The role in individual law firms varies all over the block," says Paul Bellows of the Atlanta consulting firm Sherry & Bellows. "But, generally, the role today is much more consequential."

Perhaps typical of the expanded role are the duties of John Gerhardt, managing director at Nixon, Hargrave, Devans & Doyle in Rochester, N.Y. Mr. Gerhardt reports, "I have overall responsibility for managing the business aspects of the firm, for long-range planning, for evaluation of business opportunities, mergers and lateral partners. I negotiate deals on the part of the firm." He adds, "Technology is a big part of my responsibility."

According to Jack Vaughan, administrative partner at Houston's Fulbright & Jaworski, "The job has become more financial in nature. It's much more sophisticated than it ever has been. I'm responsible for all financial planning, short-term and long-term. Part of that includes studying client profitability, and the profitability of offices and individuals."

As the responsibilities and job description changed, so has the description of the people hired as administrators. "There is no single model from which we evolved," says Summit Rovins' Ms. Kalb. "We range from the secretary who's been promoted to the paralegal to the office manager to very high-level CEOs."

In the 1970s, adds Mr. Bellows, "administrators were more likely to come out of the military." Today, administrators at the larger firms, particularly, are more likely to be former executives in large corporations or accounting firms. Mr. Gerhardt, for instance, is a former general manager of the northeast region of Mobil Chemical's plastics division. Mr. Vaughan was a partner with one of the big accounting firms.

"The profession has matured," says Mr. DeLucchio. "Administrators now are very professional. In the past, the proficient, professional executive secretary would increasingly be given more responsibility, eventually becoming an office manager. But firms now feel they've outgrown their own people."

This evolution has had a great impact on many in the profession— not the least of which is the added power and prestige. "When I first started, we were implementers of other people's decisions," says Ms. Kalb. "Now, administrators are the partners of the partners of the firm."

Margaret Cronin Fisk, "Dramatic Changes in Field," *National Law Journal: NLJ Special Legal Administrators Issue* (April 1990): 1, 3. Reprinted with permission.

---

anniversary of the founding of the American Bar Association, the *ABA Journal* commented on the vast changes in the legal profession since the early 1900s: "The organized bar at the beginning of this century was collegial and tight-knit, regarding itself as a learned profession rather than a business"; ethnic and minority groups were not welcomed; and women were barred from law schools.

Since then, the doors to the profession have swung open more widely, as dramatic changes transformed the practice of law. It was a period that gave us the rise of the megafirms and intensified competition for law school admission; complex litigation and alternate dispute resolution; lawyer advertising and liability for legal malpractice; and an end to recommended fee schedules and the beginning of probono.

Some things changed a good deal. By the 1940s, attendance at American Bar Association-approved law schools replaced apprenticeships as the paths to a legal career. A profession of mostly general practitioners became highly specialized because of economic necessity.[12]

Initial forms of law practice management, necessitated by growing firms, have assumed greater importance with economic threats, such as the increasing number of lawyers, price resistance to exorbitant fees, mergers, and bankruptcies.

Seeking New Answers

By the early part of the century, law practices had begun to seek new ways to manage the practice of law, yet it was not until the late sixties that firms delegated management tasks to nonlawyers. "What you saw," says Jerry Brown, former president of the Association of Legal Administrators, "was a lot of firms bringing in people to handle the back room operations—to do the accounting."[13] In many firms, those lawyers who seem most able to run the organization were and still are asked to assume management responsibilities, although they were—and are—likely to have little or no specialized training in management. Many lawyers believe the solution to effective management is the creation of management teams. Law firm committees are often responsible for different management functions and responsibilities. In many law firms, as happens everywhere, management is haphazard. Even very successful firms have been run through a seat-of-the-pants, gut-level management style. Today's competitive market has been changing all that. Though the business of law is still in transition, law firms everywhere now seem to acknowledge that, without good management, even the most talented legal professionals will only sit on the sidelines. Over the past twenty years, "the nonlawyer role in administration has grown and areas of responsibility given to administrators have mushroomed." Today's firms, somewhat accustomed to "the administrator's presence," seemed more to appreciate the vital role that an administrator can play.[14]

Your interest in the practice of law likely has exposed you to many of the changes that have affected law firms. Today, according to an ABA survey, the median law firm size is now eight lawyers. Nearly one-quarter of American lawyers work in firms that billed between $1 million and $3 million in 1985. The number of firms with 100 or more lawyers has increased from only four in 1960 to well over 200 today. In just the last five years, the number of firms comprising more than 200 lawyers has increased nearly four-fold, to about seventy. According to the recently adopted American Bar Association report on professionalism, firms of more than 300 lawyers are not uncommon. Many of these firms have multistate offices as well as international ones. Twenty-five years ago, firms of such size and geographic diversity were simply nonexistent.[15]

Is all of today's best legal work done in mega-firms? The answer is a resounding no. Many talented lawyers are found in solo practice or small firms, at times simply because of their area of practice or the size of the community in which they work or, at other times, because of a basic belief that "small is beautiful." The sole practitioner is a kindred spirit to the small business entrepreneur who trades freedom for long hours and many unshared responsibilities. The law firm best known to many clients is not the one that projects a corporate image, but the firm that employs one or two lawyers and, frequently, a support staff of legal assistants and paralegals. These firms, too, practice the "business of law." The large firms, however, now utilize a multitiered structure. Many nonlawyer managerial personnel now address the additional needs of growing firms. Some of these new positions include personnel managers, legal assistant managers, and marketing directors. Meanwhile, the need for professional management increases as law firms continue to grow. The result? Law firms now acknowledge that the professional manager of professional settings is a role that has long been necessary. Those within firms generally agree that "comprehensive management of the firm's professional side is a new, challenging, long overdue phase of management,"[16] brought about by technological developments, economic demands, and changes within the legal profession itself.

Technological Developments

Advances in technology create ripples throughout society. Yesterday's high tech—"the telephone, the typewriter, and possibly the female stenographer typist"[17]—made the proliferation of large law firms possible. Such innovations spelled the end of the old-style law office. New equipment and new legal support staff were added to the management responsibilities of the sole practitioner or the managing partner. Coordinating work within expanding firms became more complex, often beyond the scope of lawyers untrained as managers, and was decidedly not a cost-efficient use of an attorney's time.

Economic Demands

One of the major forces for change in the practice of law is economic reality. In particular, the economic changes of the 1960s and the more recent threats of the early 1990s have forced attorneys to become better managers. The struggle for economic survival, intensified by an attitude of competition within the legal industry, has caused law firms to seek more professional and more proven management methods from business and traditional industry. With over "800,000 licensed lawyers in the U.S., 1 for every 300 Americans,"[18] a survival-of-the-fittest mentality has evolved, intensified by the expanding use of advertising to promote legal services. Law firms have come to terms with their needs for new management philosophies and structures. As John Naisbitt and Patricia Aburdene, well-known observers of managerial trends in all fields, have pointed out, "Corporations that cling to the outdated philosophy and structure of the old industrial era will become extinct in this new information society."[19] Law firms in general have been forced to abandon outdated methods and to make the managerial, structural, and procedural changes they need to survive. The contributions of professional management have become as critical to law firms as those of lawyers (see Figure 1–1).

FIGURE 1–1
Job Descriptions for Legal Administrators and Other Law Firm Administrative Personnel

PRINCIPAL ADMINISTRATOR
Partner-level chief business executive of the firm who is responsible for business management. This individual participates in policy-making and planning decisions in the areas of finance, personnel, and general administration.

ADMINISTRATIVE OFFICE MANAGER
Chief administrator who reports to and assists a supervising lawyer or committee responsible for the firm's business management.

BRANCH OFFICE MANAGER
Administrator of the second or succeeding locations of a multi-office firm. This individual is responsible for those aspects of the firm's business management assigned to that office.

ACCOUNTING MANAGER
Directly responsible for performing the firm's accounting function. This individual supervises staff and maintains equipment. (The principal administrator sometimes performs these tasks.)

ACCOUNTING SUPERVISOR
Directly supervises the accounting staff and the accounting department's operations.

INFORMATION SERVICES MANAGER/LIBRARIAN
Organizes and maintains staff information and resources. This includes the library, past work, and electronic research.

LEGAL ASSISTANT MANAGER
Administers the firm's legal assistant program.

COMPUTER SYSTEM MANAGER
Operates and maintains the firm's computers.

MARKETING ADMINISTRATOR
Responsible for the firm's marketing and related activities.

OFFICE SERVICES MANAGER
Supervises the firm's auxiliary support services. These include messengers, receptionists, telephone operators, supply clerks, and copy center personnel.

PERSONNEL MANAGER
Responsible for all personnel matters involving support staff. Administers the process of hiring, assigning, supervising, training, evaluating, maintaining personnel records, and salary administration.

RECRUITMENT ADMINISTRATOR
Coordinates the firms' professional staff recruitment program. This may include new associate orientation and the summer clerk program.

DOCUMENT PRODUCTION MANAGER
Duties include hiring, training, and evaluating personnel assigned to individual lawyers as well as those working in a word processing center or secretarial pool. This position serves a training and quality control function.

SOURCE: Association of Legal Administrators, *1990 ALA Compensation Survey*. Adapted with permission.

ANOTHER LOOK

Nonlawyer Partners? Now?

WASHINGTON, March 1, 1990—"The District of Columbia Court of Appeals adopted a ruling today that will allow nonlawyers to become partners in Washington law firms, the first time it will be permitted anywhere in the nation. The rule, which will take effect in January, comes after many years of debate on the subject in many states and before such forums as the American Bar Association." (Neil A. Lewis)

This ruling opens the door to the use of in-house professionals, such as physicians, accountants and engineers. From within law firms, they will add their expertise to the delivery of legal services. Previously, in 1983, the ABA had rejected a proposal that would allow law firms to use nonlegal professionals for legal services. Many law firms had been establishing subsidiaries in order to utilize the services of lobbyists, economists, and investment counselors. Opponents still fear that firms will lose their focus and turn into "variety stores" of professional services.

SOURCE: Neil A. Lewis, "Non-Lawyers to Be Partners in Firms in Nation's Capitol," *The New York Times* (2 March 1990): B8.

1. How can a law firm most effectively bundle together professional services?
2. What benefits does using nonlegal professionals offer law firms? What disadvantages?
3. How would a law firm benefit from having a professional CEO as partner?

Changes in the Profession

Each organization, especially those, like the law profession, that undergo significant changes, learns to adapt through trial and error. For each subsequent generation, each organization develops new approaches to its unique problems. We can trace many changes in the practice of law to increasing industrialization and urbanization and to ever-expanding corporations. Corporate growth has led to international structures that have blurred geopolitical boundaries. Floods of new legislation, prevailing attitudes about litigation as an institutional weapon, and the ever-increasing complexity of rules and regulations have also played major roles. In a few short decades, numerous new legal specializations have appeared, such as environmental law, computer law, products liability, professional malpractice, the constitutionality of nuclear war, and a new form of family law that focuses on biological issues of childbearing, parenting, and custody rights. New kinds of career decisions are available: new types and levels of partnerships, shared attorney positions, part-time attorneys, and creative contract arrangements are no longer unusual. New forms of practice and new organizational structures are increasingly common, from satellite firms to national and international firms. One of the more significant recent changes in the profession, bound to trigger further transformation in the practice of law, is that of sharing full executive level managerial responsibilities with nonlawyers. Previously, most attorneys believed that they were not only responsible for managing their law practices but also that they had to *be* the managers, a belief that reflected the conviction that they, as lawyers, had an obligation to preserve the integrity of the profession.[20] Even the management of law firms was a privileged inner sanctum. This tenet still raises many issues for the legal profession. However, though the profession of lawyering maintains its sacrosanct aura, a March 1990 decision in the Washington, D.C., area has opened the doors for nonlawyer partners (see Another Look, below).[21] Still, the ruling has made some people—including ethics experts—uneasy. Those who oppose the measure believe that opening law firms to nonlawyer partners would "jeopardize client confidentiality, encourage the unauthorized practice of law and lead to the improper solicitation of clients." Its proponents, on the other hand, point out that safeguards, based on existing models, could provide guidelines for handling nonlawyer experts and other members of a support staff. In addition, easing the restrictions on nonlawyer partners might increase a firm's ability to offer a package of services based on clients' needs. These service clusters might consist of environmental, financial, architectural, or even public relations advice, enhanced by legal expertise. At present, however, the scope is much narrower: in the minds of many, the "sole purpose" of partnership is still to "provide legal services to clients."[22]

A Business or a Profession?

What does the law office novice need to know? You should keep in mind that the practice of law is a service business; its intangible products arise from very real and tangible settings. Lawyers are true professionals, and these individuals who deliver legal services have long been concerned over the issue of law as a business. This conundrum appears to be deeply rooted in legal tradition. In the early 1900s, Elihu Root, a Boston lawyer and the first American Bar Association president, urged his colleagues to treat their profession with the same kind of managerial approach used by business and industry. The success of Root's practice helped many to accept his advice, just as the successes of firms today inspire confidence in treating law like a business. Through the years, however, debate over the "business of law" has continued to disturb many lawyers. To understand the reasons for their discomfort necessitates examining the development of current law firm structures. Students who are just beginning to contemplate the business side of the practice of law should soon be aware that not all professionals are comfortable mixing business with professionalism. As recently as the April 1991 ABA National Conference, "At the Breaking Point," lawyers argued from both sides of the business/professionalism split. Some lamented how a "bottom-line mentality" has affected the profession while others maintained that "profit has always been a factor in the practice of law. It is elitist to say law is not a business. The better a firm runs its business, the better it is able to serve paying clients, take *pro bono* cases, and improve the lives of its staff." Despite their differences, the ABA conference participants agreed that professionalism and business are not mutually exclusive, and they found common ground in the well-known definition of a profession as a group that works together "in pursuing a learned art as a common calling in the spirit of public service—no less a public service because it may incidentally be a means of livelihood."[23]

WHAT IS A MANAGER?

A **manager** is a person assigned responsibility for the management process, who by organizing and directing the efforts of others and by allocating resources helps an organization to reach its goals. Management, even according to its dictionary definition, implies careful, tactful treatment of others.[24] Managers need to be more than organizational technicians, especially in places that depend on the individual efforts of their people, as do law firms.

> The real leadership problems of our institutions—the getting things done, the implementation, the evolving of a consensus, the making of the right decisions at the right time with the right people—is where the action is. Although we as a society haven't learned to give much credit to managers, I hope we can move toward recognizing that managerial and leadership jobs are among the most critical tasks of our society. As such, they deserve the professional status that we give to our more traditional fields of knowledge...[25]

Peter Drucker, one of the most prolific writers on management, observes that society today "has become a society of organizations," with organizations performing "social tasks," those activities that provide goods and services to people. Drucker believes that management careers in professional settings, where the services offered are highly specialized, provide the greatest opportunities for educated people.[26] Law firm management in particular offers the satisfaction of getting things done by orchestrating the efforts of others in a unique and rewarding setting.

Management and Administration

People often use the terms administration and management interchangeably, though the words are actually far from synonymous. An administrator is one who is of service, who "ministers" or serves, carrying out orders and filling requests on behalf of others. In its strictest interpretation, administration is the process of ministering according to predetermined structures and processes, such as rules, regulations, and procedures. Management, on the other hand, is an activity similar to but broader than administration. In addition to ministering according to an organization's structures and processes, management also takes part in the planning, organizing, directing, and controlling that becomes part of those structures and processes. As the challenges of management are better met by those who believe in the "professional integrity of the specialized career of management, so will there be a growth in respect for what good professional management can accomplish."[27] Managers operate at all levels of an organization. Organizations no longer simply allocate responsibility between managers and administrators. Rather, they need to designate as a manager anyone, at any level, who has been delegated the responsibility and the authority for reaching organizational objec-

IN THE NEWS

A New Career

There is a new type of business executive in growing demand—the law firm administrator—and management recruiters are having a field day filling requests for such nonlegal expertise.

In the old days, even as recently as the 1960's and 1970's, law firms usually assigned one partner to spend part or all of his or her time managing the organization's business. The duties included sending out bills and collecting payments, buying equipment ranging from law books to paper clips, and managing the nonlegal staff.

Today, computer-age complexities have increasingly caught up with law firms. Many already use computer terminals for word processing, research and accounting. Teleconferencing is also on the rise to speed communication and reduce travel, as is the use of electronic mail.

Paralegals handle technical preparation and provide the fast footwork often needed to make filings with courts, thereby freeing lawyers for higher-billing activities.

Cutting costs has become vastly more significant because many clients have protested high legal fees. Some corporations have increased inside legal staffs to save money.

And relaxed rules on advertising have helped to lure many individual clients away to law firms that proclaim services at low, stated fees for simple matters like wills, uncontested divorces, home buying, and advice.

Lawyers have also found competition getting fiercer, especially among younger lawyers. In fact, there is such a surplus of lawyers that many have had to take jobs in other fields, such as banking, insurance and government.

Some law firms have gone out of business or have been forced into mergers, resulting in a trend toward bigger firms with many branches.

Some firms have been able to remain relatively small by presenting themselves as legal boutiques—specialists in space age law, environmental law, energy law, maritime law, international law and the like.

These factors and others have necessitated the use of strategic planning and more business-like procedures within law firms.

Meyer Haberman, president of Interquest Inc., a management recruiting firm that specializes in staffing law firms, reported that more and more firms had been asking him to find them business managers.

"Law firm business management involves people management," he said. "It is not good if the prospective managers have worked only with numbers."

Backgrounds can vary widely, with managers coming from accounting, data processing, the military and finance, Mr. Haberman said, adding that "what he lacks in background the manager can bring in, such as getting computer experts to help computerize the office." A master of business administration

---

tives. Whenever anyone is given "formal authority over an organizational unit," management expert Henry Mintzberg writes, he or she becomes a manager. "From formal authority comes status, which leads to various interpersonal relations, and from this comes access to information."[28] Given this combination of authority, relationships, and access, the manager can use the results of his or her managerial efforts to benefit the organization as a whole, whether he or she holds responsibility for a subunit or for the entire organization.

Managerial Orchestration

What do managers do? Drucker notes that a manager is like the "conductor of a symphony orchestra, through whose effort, vision, and leadership, individual instrumental parts that are so much noise by themselves become the living whole of music. But the conductor has the composer's score; he is only the interpreter. The manager is both composer and conductor."[29] However, the manager's role as conductor is hardly easy: the audience may see—or hear—harmonious results but it is often while "the orchestra members are having various personal difficulties, stage hands are moving music stands, alternating excessive heat and cold are creating audience and instrument problems, and the sponsor of the program is insisting on irrational changes in the program."[30]

Managing in Professional Settings

In hearing and watching performances of music greats, such as Leonard Bernstein conducting at Tanglewood

CHAPTER 1 / MANAGERIAL PERSPECTIVES

IN THE NEWS (continued)

degree is helpful but not necessary, he said.

"It's a difficult job, the pace is frenetic and the manager has to take a lot of abuse and punishment," Mr. Haberman continued. "The rule of thumb is that the first administrator of a law firm is never successful because he's a guinea pig."

Talking about the increasing requests for law firm managers, another management recruiter, William K. Zinke, said: "I guess I should throw in another factor—recognition on the part of lawyers that they were not trained to be business managers, they are not good at it, nor interested, and therefore it is more cost-effective for the firm to hire one outside."

Mr. Zinke, president of Human Resource Services Inc., said: "In the 60's and certainly in the 70's law firms began to realize the need for real managers, perhaps giving them different titles like director of administration. Now the titles have gone up a notch to something like executive director. They even have an Association of Legal Administrators, which is not just window trimming but evidence of the increasing importance of the business managers."

He confirmed that pay ranges widely, from perhaps $25,000 a year for a part-time administrator at a small firm to more than $300,000 paid by one of the nation's largest law firms, Skadden, Arps, Slate, Meagher & Flom, which has 350 lawyers.

"I helped a firm with fewer than 30 lawyers hire a business manager in the $50,000 to $60,00 range," Mr. Zinke said. "I would say a firm with 25 lawyers should consider a business administrator. When you get to the 35- to 40-lawyer range, I would think it was even more important, and at 50 there is no question that a business administrator is needed."

"One way to be effective as a manager," Mr. Zinke continued, "is to insure that opportunities are not missed by the lawyers due to lack of business knowledge." He cited one law firm that learned that telephone charges billable to clients for long-distance calls had not been updated for many years. "The firm was losing money on its phone calls," he said.

The business manager must not accept second-class treatment, Mr. Zinke said, but should insist he be considered as a professional peer.

Mr. Zinke added that some law firms were also looking for controllers, another indication of the growing need for more businesslike management at such firms.

Elizabeth Fowler, "Wanted: Law Firm Managers," *New York Times* (21 March 1984). Copyright © 1984/89 by The New York Times Company. Reprinted by permission.

in the Berkshires of Massachusetts or Dave Brubeck and his talented sons sharing their musical exuberance, the analogy of how managers conduct organizational activities holds true. The excitement and challenge of producing a first-class performance depends on untold hours of planning, organizing, directing, and controlling the work of talented professionals. The improvisational jazz of a Brubeck family performance is a fitting analogy for an organization of professionals such as lawyers. Each individual has unique preparations to make, but the work of the whole depends on the intensity, quality, and quantity—and even the enthusiasm—of each member's performance. In a Brubeck performance, each player becomes a composer and conductor; each shares in the spotlight. But the concept of management as a *task* remains: that role reflects principles that are universally applicable whether the manager in question is a jazz musician or the member of a professional organization. In every setting, managerial tasks are similar; conversely, each role a manager assumes differs from setting to setting and from day to day. The professional setting called a law firm presents special challenges for a manager. A manager does not simply take charge of professionals. "No one really directs partners in a law firm. You can urge and nudge and try to influence, but they are not directed," comments a former law firm chief executive. "You have owner-operators. The real test is how you keep them informed about their firm, but keep them from tinkering . . . You must always try to enhance the institutional focus of lawyers. What matters is not just their practice, but how that practice integrates with the overall firm."[31] This is much like the Brubeck analogy: the manager attempts to bring out the best of the professional energy in the members who comprise the organization. The excitement and challenge managers feel in working successfully with highly trained and educated professionals was revealed in a survey of law firm administrators: when asked what they liked the most about their jobs, their almost-unanimous response was "The variety!" Managers spoke of the breadth of their responsibilities and the need for skills in working with people who, by the nature of their profession, are usually creative, intelligent, and articulate. After the diversity of tasks, the law practice managers spoke of the interpersonal aspects that appealed to them, including the challenge of working with the many kinds of individuals who populate the law practice setting. The process of management can draw from the same rich body of experience, research, and common sense that provides material for all the literature on its applications. What is the manager's primary task? Contemporary management writers Naisbitt and Aburdene believe that "the manager's role is to create a nourishing environment for personal growth, in addition to the opportunity to contribute to the growth of the institution." [32]

Management: An Art, a Science, or a Profession?

Both businesspeople and business writers have long debated whether or not effective management can be learned. Some maintain that good managers are those who simply possess an innate talent for the job. These observers call management an art. Others say that management, a body of mostly scientific knowledge, is a valid field of study in and of itself; they believe management is a science. In addition, many argue as to whether or not management is a profession.

Management as an Art

The art of management is a common idea. As an art, management can lift the human spirit, providing perspective and vision, enriching the lives of an organization's members. When asked his views on the "art" of being the boss, J. Paul Getty said that management was a field that could not be "systemized, learned or practiced according to formula." With many others, he believed management to be "an art—even a creative art." [33]

Management as a Science

Management was never considered a scientific branch of knowledge until the late 1900s, when management theorists and efficiency experts began to examine the complex work settings brought about by changes in industry and technology. Science is often defined as a body or area of knowledge, based on theories that have grown out of observations that have been hypothesized, researched, and proven as valid. Much management theory is based on economics, mathematics, sociology, psychology, social psychology, organizational behavior, and many other sciences, depending on the nature of the managerial setting. While the art of management responds to human needs and values, the science of management blends an organization's resources to produce tangible results.

Management as a Profession

Given the ideas presented in this chapter, profession can be defined as an occupation distinguished by the advanced education and self-regulation of its members. For example, according to these standards, lawyers, doctors, and accountants are often described as professionals. However, the common understanding of the term "professional" has come to include nearly any career that demands much education and dedication, as well as high standards of performance. This can easily be said of many managers. The second "Another Look" feature in this chapter will help you to decide whether, according to these criteria, management truly is a profession.

A MANAGER'S CHALLENGES

We were not all born to be managers. Some of us will be content with being lawyers—or paralegals—or computer specialists—or any one of many choices. As a student, you are probably wondering what lies ahead, not only in terms of your life in general but in terms of a career. Knowing what management is all about and what makes a good manager will be valuable for you whether you become a manager or not. Recall your very first look at a law office. You perhaps saw people working, a waiting area, phones, doors, desks, and equipment. Then you learned that law offices were more than personnel, furniture, offices, and machines. You learned about the different roles that people played. You recognized the different functions that took place in the different work areas and spaces. You began to understand how the interaction among people is the secret to an organization's success. You discovered that a law firm office swarms with activity: client reception, conferences, word processing, record keep-

TABLE 1–1
Are Managers True Professionals? Some Analytical Arguments

Characteristics of Professionals	Are Managers Professionals?	Or Are Managers Non-Professionals?
Expertise Specialized and extensive education and training are required.	Managers need a broad range of specialized training, as currently prescribed by the AACSB.	Managers do not need special degrees or education.
Autonomy Professionals are independent, able to make many of their own decisions in the service of clients.	No one has complete autonomy, but managers require independence and authority to make decisions.	Managers do not have true autonomy, since they serve "shareholders" and must answer to them.
Specialized Body of Learning Professionals must master a set body of learning before offering services.	The AACSB has developed a specific core of learning for the managerial degree.	No fully agreed-upon specialized body of learning is required in order to be a manager.
Collegial Maintenance of Standards Professionals are dedicated to their work and are concerned about its quality. They themselves set standards, policing and enforcing the conduct of the members of their profession.	Accreditation by a degree-granting college partially serves this same function.	Managers have no specific accrediting body or licensing board.
Identification Professionals strongly identify with the group of others who occupy that profession.	Managers acquire professional identity through a variety of organizations, such as the AMA, the ALA, and LAMA.	There are too many managerial associations for managers to claim strong affiliations.
Ethics There are standards for conduct for each professional field. Most stress conduct that is neither self-serving nor emotional.	While there is as yet no specific code of ethics for managers, AACSB schools and others are establishing a core of ethical practices for managers.	Managers do not have a special code of ethics.

1. Discuss whether or not lawyers meet all the characteristics for a profession. Do paralegals? Do legal secretaries?
2. Using the pros and cons given above, discuss whether or not managers should be called professionals. Be prepared to share your views with the class.

SOURCE: Based on S. Kerr, M. A. Von Glinow, and J. Schriesheim, "Issues in the Study of 'Professionals' in Organizations: The Case of Scientists and Engineers," *Organizational Behavior and Human Performance* 18 (1977): 329–345; and Edgar Schein, "Management Education: Some Troublesome Realities and Possible Remedies," *Journal of Management Development* 7 (1988): 5–15.

ing, accounting and finance procedures, research, secretarial and support staff work, paralegal and attorney duties. All of these activities revolve around the simple but profoundly complicated service of interpreting laws. The more you recognize law offices as places where professionals, paraprofessionals, and support personnel work together to provide this service, the more you will understand how singularly challenging it is to plan, organize, direct, and control the processes that transpire in those settings. You will learn that management is more than office administration. It is the challenge of working with people.

Understanding Management

Understanding management is not easy, whether you look at it from the top of an organization or from the bottom.

> Despite its critical importance, its high visibility and its spectacular rise, management is the least known and the least understood of our basic institutions. Even people in a business often don't understand the full scope of what management is all about. Once management is considered apart from what we see as "authority," it is not easy for the ordinary worker to be sure of what the full responsibility of management is all about. It is hard to be sure of what management does and what it is supposed to be doing, how it acts and why, and whether it does a good job or not.[34]

Because all organizations exist for specific reasons and because each organization in its own way delivers a product or a service that individuals or groups in society need or want, the ultimate success or survival of any organization depends on two factors: on being needed by society and on its ability to reach its goals effectively and efficiently. These two factors represent the challenge of management. Still, it is "hard to be sure of what management does and what it is supposed to be doing, how it acts and why, and whether it does a good job or not."[35] Most experts agree on the three characteristics of management: (1) It is a process, a continuing and overlapping series of activities; (2) it exists in order to reach organizational goals; and (3) it reaches these goals by drawing on personal skills and training to work with and through people while using organizational resources. **Management** is the continuing activity of using the organization's resources in working with people, through the processes of planning, organizing, directing, and controlling in order to reach organizational objectives. The **primary responsibility of management** is to ensure that the organization does what it needs to do in order to reach its objectives.

Understanding Organizations

Consisting of a group of people who work together toward specific goals, an **organization** is formally defined as a social system that is unified by a specific goal and is held together by the combination of the roles and activities of its members.

> Management is tasks. Management is a discipline. But management is also people. Every achievement of management is an achievement of a manager. Every failure is the failure of a manager. *People* manage rather than "forces" or "facts." The vision, dedication, and integrity of managers determine whether there is management or mismanagement.[36]

A person who works alone can freely decide what goals are important and how to reach them. When others are involved, issues of coordination, agreement and mutual consideration arise. People working together need a process that links their efforts and focuses these efforts on common goals. Usually, people can accomplish much more by working together than by working alone, and generally accepted beliefs in the usefulness of basic management principles commonly guide such concerted activity. This belief is known as the **universality of management,** the conviction that the same basic guidelines for organizational processes and structures are useful everywhere. One of these universal ideas is that people fulfill a wide variety of roles in each organization, contributing in some way or another. You yourself may choose to contribute as part of clerical support services or as a paralegal, or you may see your present decision as one step out of several on a career ladder. You may perhaps begin as a paralegal, then take on the responsibilities of a senior paralegal, a paralegal coordinator, a paralegal supervisor, or a legal assistant manager. You may subsequently be ready for other responsibilities and challenges. You may have a long-range career goal, perhaps that of litigation manager or office manager. You may contribute your talents as a personnel manager or firm administrator, or as a director of administration. You may have decided to formally study law and work as an attorney, or you may be thinking about one of a wide range of other career options now available in the law firm and in law firm management. No matter what level of work or managerial responsibility you choose, you will be only as effective as your ability to build on the simplest management principle of all: the universal need to work together. Even the responsibilities for resolving the human tensions and struggles that arise naturally within any organization fall to the manager. It is the effective manager who realizes that workers, out of their basic self-esteem, are there to contribute, to "invest in work." It is the enlightened manager who understands the role that basic human dignity plays and knows that workers develop strong commitment to organizations, sometimes in spite of tremendous odds.[37] Above all, it is the role of the successful manager to ensure the success of both the organization and the individual employees under his or her supervision.

Understanding the Importance of Management

Management's **primary purpose** is to help an organization reach its objectives both effectively and efficiently. In our **economic system**, every organization offers a service or product to society. In order to make its service or product available, each organization must perform specific jobs. Law firms offer the service of law, choosing from many forms of practice. Like other organizations, many law firms depend on their managers to help determine goals, to help to develop a strategy for reaching them, and to assist in making those goals a reality.

Managing Professionals

Managing an organization of professionals presents a special challenge. The term "professional," though used freely, in most people's minds connotes a certain prestige. While doctors, engineers, scientists, accountants, college professors, and lawyers are generally considered the primary groups of professionals, **professionals** in general are those individuals whose careers call for intellectual expertise, relative autonomy in decision making, and commitment to a field that is governed collegially, according to the agreed-upon ethical standards of its members. Professional work carries a certain social importance, and professionals must therefore operate with a high degree of personal responsibility. Not only are they required to take full responsibility for their own work but also for the work of those who assist them. Another side of this responsibility is that professionals may completely identify with what they accomplish. Such personal identification differs significantly from the impersonal atmosphere of other settings, such as in manufacturing or service occupations. In the United States, the work force consists largely of knowledge workers—those who consider their knowledge to be their contribution to the work site—and their number grows daily. Managers who understand the nature and management of professional activities will be more effective managers in professional settings.[38] No matter what the organizational level or the form of the organization itself, managing an organization or professionals is decidedly more distinctive and more challenging than management within any other setting.

Managerial Responsibilities

Management within a professional setting must be appropriately suited to the uniqueness of the profession. Failure to customize management styles guarantees ineffectiveness and inefficiency. This is one reason why today's law practice is now validating the role of professional management. During the past few decades, law firms have increasingly accepted the specialized know-how that professional managers can offer, perceiving such knowledge as the best way to provide high-quality legal service to a very complex and demanding society (see Figure 1–2). Nonetheless, despite their working within a professional setting, managers who customize their management style for particular professional organizations still begin with the three main tasks of all management. They must help their organizations in reaching objectives, in being efficient, and in being effective.

Reaching Objectives

Objectives are the ends or goals that a person or group wishes to accomplish. Management helps an organization to reach its particular set of goals by influencing the actions of its members.[39] Although organizational goals differ, one objective is essential to the survival of all organizations: profit.

Being Efficient

The ability to obtain organizational objectives using the least amount of organizational resources, **efficiency** reflects a positive ratio of outputs to inputs, the achieving of goals through the best use of time, money, and people.

Being Effective

Effectiveness is the ability to reach intended results by determining appropriate objectives and accomplishing them. As Peter Drucker has commented, "The pertinent question is not how to do things right, but how to find the right things to do, and to concentrate resources and efforts on them."[40] Managers achieve effectiveness by using the most appropriate resources to reach each organizational objective.

FIGURE 1–2
Career Opportunities in Legal Administration

ADMINISTRATOR

Five-attorney law firm in Clearwater, Florida, seeks legal administrator with strong management experience. BA degree required and MBA preferred. Strong personnel skills essential. Excellent benefits. Salary commensurate with experience. Please respond to: (Blind Box #W) ALA, 175 East Hawthorn Parkway, Suite 325, Vernon Hills, IL 60061–1428.

OFFICE MANAGER

Kansas City law firm seeks experienced office manager. Strong personnel skills and prior law firm experience a must. No accounting experience necessary. Salary negotiable, good fringe benefits. Send resume to: Niewald, Waldeck, Norris & Brown, 2500 Commerce Tower, 911 Main Street, Kansas City, MO 64105.

FIRM ADMINISTRATOR/BOOKKEEPER

Established (40+ yrs.) seven (7) lawyer firm in Bethlehem, PA, seeks a law firm administrator/bookkeeper. Firm has high litigation (primarily defense). Candidate must have strong bookkeeping skills & preferably some experience as administrator. Knowledge of PCs a plus. Responsibilities include overseeing support staff of 9 and all administrative functions of firm incl. payroll, time & billing, A/R, A/P, personnel & computer (PC) generated management reports. Allentown/Bethlehem/Easton area (Lehigh Valley) is 2 hrs. west of NYC and 1 hr. north of Phila. Salary commensurate w/experience. Send resume w/salary reqmt. to: Paul J. Schoff, Esq., Margolis, Smith, Baker & Schoff, P.C., P.O. Box 2728, Lehigh Valley, PA 18001–2728.

LEGAL ADMINISTRATOR

Mid-size law firm in Dayton, Ohio, seeking experienced Legal Administrator. Administrative authority for financial and personnel management, information systems and facilities. Financial background with ability to analyze financial statements essential. Personnel experience and ability to handle support staff and office services. Familiarity with personal computers and information systems for professional offices a plus. Forward resume WITH base salary requirement in confidence to our consultants. Altman & Weil, Inc., P.O. Box 472, Dept. 1322, Ardmore, PA 19003.

LEGAL ADMINISTRATOR

Knoxville, TN, based 100+ attorney law firm with six offices seeks Legal Administrator with 10+ years of legal and/or corporate management experience; legal and multi-office experience preferred. Job description includes management of professional staff in human resources, information systems, finance, recruiting and office administration. Reply in confidence to Attn: N. Fountain, P.O. Box 1792, Knoxville, TN 37902.

OFFICE ADMINISTRATOR

Thirty-five attorney firm seeks administrator experienced in all aspects of law office management, including human resources, accounting, budgeting & cost controls and computer systems management. Resume and salary requirements to Gerald Gaffaney at Mariscal, Weeks, McIntyre and Friedland P.A., 201 W. Coolidge, Phoenix, AZ 85013.

SOURCE: ALA News (September/October 1989): 68. Adapted with permission.

THE FOUR BASIC MANAGERIAL FUNCTIONS

Do you remember playing "statues" when you were young, becoming absolutely still at the order to "freeze"? Try now to imagine a motionless law firm. All the right resources are available. All the best-qualified personnel are on board. All the perfect clients are ready to be helped. What is needed to set these right components in motion? The answer is management: the driving, energizing force in all organizations. Managers provide the stimulus that enables others to get the organization's job done. To do this, they draw on the resources each organization uses. First, managers rely on the organization's human resources: its competent and skilled workers. Secondly, they depend on its financial resources, including the revenues, capital, or the ability to obtain financing. Third, they require physical resources: tangible goods and properties, such as the materials, equipment, offices, and supplies the organization needs. What managers actually do with these resources ultimately falls within **four basic managerial functions:** planning, organizing, directing, and controlling, which coordinate all the activities

These are some of the feeders of managerial failures:
1. Insensitivity to others: an abrasive, intimidating, bullying style.
2. Cold, aloof, arrogant.
3. Betrayal of trust.
4. Overly ambitious.
5. Specific performance problems with the business.
6. Overmanaging: inability to delegate or build a team.
7. Unable to staff effectively.
8. Unable to think strategically.
9. Unable to adapt to boss with different style.
10. Overdependent on advocate or mentor.

SOURCE: David A. Whetten and Kim S. Cameron, *Developing Managerial Skills* (Glenview, Illinois: Scott, Foresman and Company, 1984): 15.

ANOTHER LOOK
Why Do Some Managers Fail?

1. List the "failure feeders" of an ineffective manager you've known.
2. What good characteristics did they have?
3. What other attributes do you think would contribute to a manager's ineffectiveness?

---

of an organization. We can analyze the activities of management from many other perspectives, but this long-established classification clearly describes what managers do. No matter the size or the nature of an organization, managers must perform these basic operations that transform the organization from a static collection of people and things to a dynamic entity.

Planning

Planning is the process of determining the future of an organization by establishing its goals and objectives and by formulating strategies to achieve them. Planning is the primary managerial function; the other three functions incorporate planning. The planning function varies, depending on the level of management; the nature of the organization, including the complexity of its resources; the scope of plans; and the time involved.

Organizing

Organizing is the process of allocating resources and work tasks so that the organization can reach its objectives efficiently and effectively. It is deciding what needs to be done and by whom.

Directing

Directing is the process of staffing, influencing, and leading employees so that they attain organizational goals. Through directing, managers shape worker activity. It is the process of ensuring that the organization moves toward its goals and objectives.

FIGURE 1–3
The Four Managerial Functions

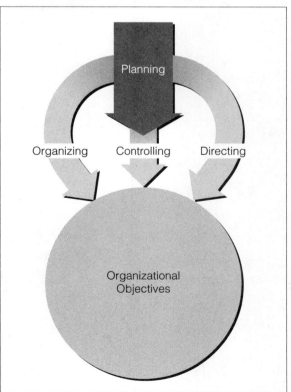

Controlling

Controlling is the process of regulating and overseeing activities to ensure quality performance and end results. Managers exercise control by establishing standards, monitoring the work group's progress toward those standards, and then measuring results by comparing them to expectations and taking corrective actions, if needed.

MANAGERIAL LEVELS, SKILLS, AND ROLES

Although all managers at all levels participate in the four basic managerial functions, different managers spend a different amount of time on each activity. Organizations differ as well, particularly law practice settings, which now range from solo practices to international corporate structures. Responsibilities for the management function vary greatly, and as they become larger and more complex, organizations need various levels of management to fulfill differing managerial responsibilities.

Managerial Levels

The level of management depends on the manager's position in the organizational hierarchy, as shown in Figure 1–4. The hierarchical pyramid splits into four basic divisions: upper management, middle management, supervisory management, and nonmanagerial supervised employees.

Upper Management

Managers at the **upper management** level formulate major policies, decide future strategies, and make the organization's most important decisions. In addition, they oversee those who perform specialized functions. In many law firms, top management often holds exclusive power to oversee the attorneys. This power may be delegated to an executive committee, commonly composed of senior partners and usually headed by a managing partner. The managing partner's responsibility is to function as a collegial CEO. In legal settings, as in many other organizational settings, power and responsibility are concentrated at the top. Management at this level is executive in nature. In a law firm, top

FIGURE 1–4
Managerial Levels

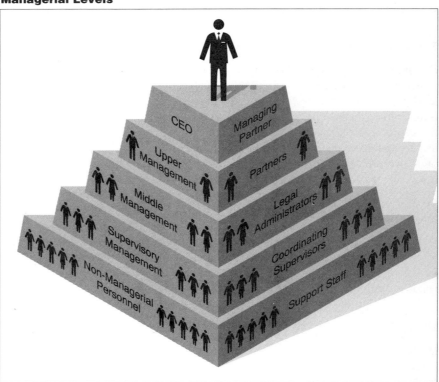

management consists of the firm's owners, those who are its equity partners.

Middle Management

Managers at the **middle management** level are responsible for subordinates in various areas. They are also accountable to upper-level management. In a law practice setting, middle managers may include managing directors, directors of administration, directors of special professional services, financial managers, vice-presidents or directors of various areas (such as general litigation, claims, finances, or human resources), department chairs, legal administrators, and law office managers. Middle management positions are not always identifiable by title. One should be cautious when determining the level of management solely according to a position's title. The level of authority and responsibility and reporting expectations are better indicators of hierarchical level. A manager who is vice president of marketing, with one or two subordinates, is at a different level of middle management than an individual bearing the title of Law Office Manager, who may be responsible for all support staff and non-attorney personnel. Middle managers, who interpret and implement policies, decisions, and directives of top management, often actually influence decisions more than top-level managers, due to timing, focus, and proximity to the issues, and an informed, up-to-date expertise. Whatever his or her title, a middle manager must be allowed the power and responsibility to reach the objectives of top management.

Supervisory Management

Supervisory or first-level managers are the next largest managerial group. **Supervisory management,** as shown on the second step of the pyramid in Figure 1–4, directly oversees those who perform specific functions at the firm's work sites. Supervisory managers in law practice settings may include paralegal coordinators, legal assistant managers, legal assistant supervisors, case managers, general supervisors, and office managers. First-level managers are delegated the responsibility and authority to coordinate the contributions of a group of workers. They direct, supervise, and work closely with those for whom they are responsible. To assist workers and to set standards for quality, supervisory managers are expected to understand the work of their supervisees, and they are responsible for many short-term operative decisions (see Figure 1–5).

FIGURE 1–5
A Morning in the Life of a Paralegal Coordinator

7:30	Arrive and review the day's appointments and activities. Organize priorities for the day.
7:45	Arrange for coverage for a paralegal who just called in sick.
7:48	Talk to executive director about the luncheon with United Way committee; set up a meeting date to review the law firm personnel brochure with the executive director and the marketing coordinator.
8:00	Meet with the real estate paralegals about registry procedures.
9:00	Write up and follow through on results of client relations meeting; have a draft drawn up of paralegals' suggestions.
10:25	Spend unscheduled time with a paralegal who wants to arrange additional vacation time the following week.
10:45	Review time slips with executive director and bookkeeper.
12:00	Spend time reviewing completeness of paralegal time slips.
12:30	Luncheon meeting: United Way Community Endeavors Committee.

Nonmanagerial Positions

The base of most organizational pyramids is composed of nonmanagerial employees. Support staff is usually the largest group of employees in most organizations. In legal settings, this group may consist of receptionists, secretaries, legal assistants, and other personnel, such as couriers, maintenance personnel, library assistants, and all other employees who perform specific tasks for the organization. Their responsibilities primarily include their own performance, and their expected contributions to the organization are clearly defined.

Managerial Skills

Though managers at all levels need the same basic sets of skills, each level makes different demands, as shown in Figure 1–6. Managerial skills can be grouped into technical skills, interpersonal skills, and conceptual skills.

FIGURE 1-6
Percentages of Skills Needed at Three Managerial Levels

	Conceptual	Interpersonal	Technical
UPPER-LEVEL	39.4%	42.7	17.9
MIDDLE-LEVEL	22.8	42.4	34.8
FIRST-LEVEL	12.0	37.7	50.3

SOURCE: Based on Thomas L. Wheelen and J. David Hunger, "Skills of an Executive," a paper presented to the Academy of Management, Kansas City, Mo., August 1976.

Technical Skills

Technical skills, which reflect the ability to utilize job-related knowledge, are skills and proficiencies that a manager needs for the work that he or she must do. The closer a manager is to the performance of isolated tasks, the more specific task-related knowledge he or she needs in order to be an effective manager. For instance, a first-level or supervisory manager, such as a coordinator of litigation paralegals, must have mastered the paralegal's role in the litigation process. In supervising, the coordinator needs to set standards and to ensure that his or her paralegals meet these expectations. Upper-level managers, however, may have mastered a variety of skills that they can apply to the task of management. Their general expertise in multiple areas increases their managerial effectiveness.

Conceptual Skills

Conceptual skills reflect the ability to observe, think, conclude, determine, and envision. Managers with strong conceptual skills perceive an organization as a whole rather than as a collection of parts. All managers need the ability to conceptualize. It becomes increasingly important the higher a manager is in the managerial hierarchy. Upper level managers, more than all others, must deal with histories and *past* cultures, *present* policies and results, and *future* consequences, strategies, and planning. Organizations need top-level managers to integrate and understand the complexities of internal and external events to project and to anticipate, and to plan future directions.

Interpersonal Skills

This last set of skills is essential to managers at all levels. **Interpersonal skills** enable managers to understand others, to value others, and to inspire them to contribute to the organization. Managers use these human skills in working with people within the organization—including peers, superiors, and subordinates—and those outside the organization, such as clients and professional colleagues. Those who possess effective interpersonal skills are better able to (1) minimize and resolve conflict, (2) bring about cohesive and cooperative efforts, (3) build group effort, (4) communicate, and (5) lead.

At the lower levels of management, technical and human skills are most essential. By comparison, middle-level managers make more use of conceptual and human skills, while managers at the uppermost levels of management are likely to concentrate on conceptual skills (see Figure 1–6).

Managerial Roles[41]

People in organizations expect to see their managers communicating information, making decisions, and being helpful when there are needs to be taken care of. Henry Mintzberg, a well-known expert on what managers do, observes that each manager functions as a kind of "nerve center in an information-processing network." Even in team management, or in management by committee, people cannot "share a single management position unless they act as one entity." He describes ten inseparable managerial roles that a manager cannot delegate to others unless the manager participates in a complete sharing of information with the delegate and thus reintegrates the ten roles. According to Mintzberg, as managers plan, organize, direct, and control, they fulfill their duties in any of three ways: through interpersonal roles, through informational roles, and through decisional roles.

FIGURE 1-7
The Manager as Nerve Center

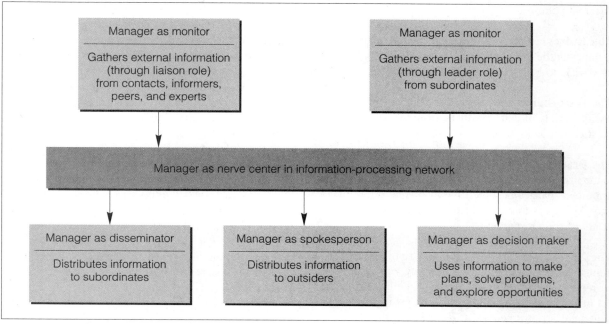

SOURCE: Figure from *The Nature of Managerial Work* by Henry Mintzberg. Copyright © 1973 by Henry Mintzberg. Reprinted by permission of HarperCollins Publishers.

Interpersonal Roles

Through **interpersonal roles,** managers fulfill their responsibility to act with, for, and on behalf of others. Such roles include the following:

The Figurehead. As figureheads, managers become the focus of respect, taking part in ceremonies and rituals and representing the law firm at external functions. A good manager understands the public aspect of the role, realizing that a certain status and responsibility accompany the position.

The Leader. Because he or she is responsible for individuals in the law firm, whether this responsibility extends to the entire staff or to people within individual departments or subunits, the manager must assume the role of leader, the person who most strongly influences others.

The Liaison. The manager, in working with others, is expected to make contacts with peers and superiors, as well as with his or her subordinates. This linkage with others in the law firm is essential to the flow of information within the organization.

Informational Roles

Informational roles entail controlling, disseminating, and processing useful information. Managers, as information processors, are always attuned to any possible source of information, using as many channels as possible to boost the accuracy and quantity of data that will help to get the job done.

The Monitor. The monitor gathers information, using this information for the advantage of the law firm.

The Disseminator. As **disseminator,** the manager increases the usefulness of the information he or she gathers by sharing it with the right personnel.

The Spokesperson. Managers must act on behalf of others, usually their subordinates and their firms. They represent, inform, and influence, addressing audiences in both public and private arenas.

Decisional Roles

Through **decisional roles,** a manager enacts his or her responsibility to make effective decisions. Decisions are the actions that propel the law firm in particular directions; for managers, these actions fall into four different patterns:

The Entrepreneur. As those most responsible for results that the firm achieves, managers attempt to find new ways to better these results.

The Disturbance Handler. Managers must resolve a wide variety of daily conflicts, from the trivial to the most consequential events in the firm.

The Resource Allocator. Of the resources available to the firm, those of time and energy often are the most important, particularly the time available to the manager. Managers are expected to determine the allocation of all a firm's resources.

The Negotiator. This last role is a routine one, and a manager may accomplish it in many ways, such as by representing employees' needs to the law firm and the firm's needs to its employees, suggesting mutually beneficial arrangements, and working with others to resolve conflicts, grievances, and crises (see Figure 1–7 on page 23 for a summary of Mintzberg's description of managerial roles).

SUCCESSFUL LAW OFFICE MANAGERS OF THE FUTURE

Jobs used to be simpler. Evaluating results and delegating responsibility was once less complicated. Within organizations that depend on today's technology, management presents a whole new set of challenges. Management consultant Robert Heller has noted that "in these bygone, good old days, you could safely leave the control and ordering to somebody else—the Man, the Boss. . . ." Now, he observes, each manager needs to be "a Supermanager—the boss of bosses. . . . Technology, innovation, marketing, organization, financial structure, productivity, futurology, turnarounds, etc., etc.—all the large words that used to belong exclusively to the large men in the large corporations now belong to almost everybody. To that extent, we're all bosses now." [42] What trends will law firm administrators face in the years ahead? John Coburn, vice president of the consulting firm of Gray-Judson, conducted in-depth interviews with fifteen legal administrators from some of the country's larger firms. From his study, Coburn projected trends in legal administration activities:

The law firm administrator of the 1990s will be one of the most valuable and influential members of the firm, viewed by the partners as being on a par with the firm's senior partners and rainmakers. These administrators will be leaders of their firms and will be the virtual equivalent of partners in terms of status and compensation. They will be involved in areas that would be unthinkable today, including lateral recruiting, partner compensation, practice area development and overall firm strategy. A large percentage will be recruited from executive positions in business and industry and will carry titles as "managing director," "chief operating officer" and even "chief executive officer."

The better known administrators of the 1990s will be recruited actively within the legal community and will move from firm to firm to pursue new managerial challenges and financial rewards. Firms encountering difficulty will tend to bring in strong executives and give them far-reaching power to deal with the situation. In some cases, these individuals will actually be credited with "saving the firm." [43]

Law practice managers, says Coburn, will hold more responsibilities, playing an increased role in governance and leadership. They will exercise more professional discretion and autonomy and will be increasingly responsible for those critical areas that are directly linked to a firm's profitability. In addition, other studies show that managers of the future, in all fields, will need to be more solidly prepared—more educated, more perceptive, more capable of integrating complexity. This complexity will increase the importance of managers: turbulence needs to be harnessed by someone who can anticipate, manage, and benefit from change. Experienced managers who see John Coburn's broad continuum of a law office manager's duties are not surprised (see Figure 1–8). Neither are they surprised at the high turnover that occurs among law firm managers. Failure is not unusual, but it is not always the legal administrator's fault. Instead, several prominent consultants attribute such failure to "the unwillingness or inability of the law firm to accept the basic concept of a 'nonlawyer' involved in areas the lawyers consider their own." [44]

Professional Associations

New professional associations have been created to assist and support law office managers. Among these organizations is the Association of Legal Administrators, begun in 1971. It now numbers over 7,500 mem-

How does one break into management? Career path planning requires an active approach to making things happen, as Ellen Bump did, in the Focus from the Field at the start of this chapter. Her firm, Robinson, Donovan, Madden & Barry, is a small, respected law firm which, like many throughout the country, has dealt with issues of growth. The 24-attorney firm dates back to the 1800s, when its first lawyer, George Robinson, served as one of Massachusetts' earliest governors. He became known for his successful and trendsetting defense of the now-legendary Lizzie Borden. Like many of today's firms, it has benefited from the specialized contributions of paralegals. The following memo from Peter Kehoe, executive director of administration at Robinson, Donovan, Madden & Barry, announces Ellen Bump's promotion to paralegal coordinator.

ANOTHER LOOK

A New Manager in the Making

November 6, 1990

TO: ALL ATTORNEYS AND PARALEGALS
FROM: PETER KEHOE
SUBJECT: PARALEGAL UTILIZATION AND MANAGEMENT

The Executive Committee has established a new position within the firm under the heading of Paralegal Managers. Our primary goal is effective use of attorney time, substituting paralegals for lawyers in executing those tasks which can be accomplished using paralegal skills. In order to accomplish this goal, it is necessary to establish minimal professional requirements for paralegals, to increase the visibility and professional recognition of professional paralegals, and to enhance all paralegals' personal motivation and job satisfaction. The National Association of Legal Assistants has defined the position, in major part: "Under the supervision of a lawyer, the legal assistant shall apply knowledge of law and legal procedures in rendering direct assistance to lawyers, clients, and courts. . ." Paralegals are recognized by the firm as professionals. They should be treated so as to salary and benefits. We understand that a conscious choice has been made by most paralegals to pursue that profession, not to attend law school. It is the firm's goal to hire paralegals for the long term. Training is important to all these goals. Its main purpose will be to increase billable time, increase efficiency, increase productivity and to improve attitudes, working relationships, and motivation. To accomplish these objectives, the firm is establishing the position of paralegal manager. The Paralegal Manager will standardize and monitor our practices with regard to delegating work to paralegals so as to increase their productivity.

Ellen Bump has been appointed to this position by the Executive Committee. She has been appointed to this position effective November 8, 1990. I am sure Ellen will appreciate your assistance and support as she assumes the challenges and responsibilities of her new position.

Adapted with the permission of Robinson, Donovan, Madden, & Barry, P.C. Springfield, MA 01115.

---

1. What benefits will the paralegal manager position offer the firm?
2. Describe this firms' attitudes toward its paralegals and their value to the organization.

---

bers in all states, extends to seven Canadian provinces and eight foreign countries, and shows a 10 percent growth in membership annually. Over 90 percent of ALA administrators are employed in law firms, and the rest work within corporate and government settings. Over 30 percent of its members serve as legal administrators in firms of 1 to 14 lawyers, 32 percent in firms with 15 to 49 lawyers, and 29 percent in firms that number over 50 lawyers.[45] Seeking to "enhance the competence of the legal administrator and the legal

FIGURE 1–8
The Continuum of Administrator Responsibilities

Accounting/Bookkeeping
Space, Real Estate
Data Processing
Word Processing, Production
Support Staff Management
Profitability Analysis
Purchasing
Budgeting
Vendor Relations
Billing, Collections
Purchasing
Committee Management
Non-Lawyer Training
Client Relationships
Policies and Procedures
Utilization
Information Systems
Diversification
Leverage Management
Branching
Communications
Competitor Analysis
Case Staffing
Practice Development
Marketing
Lawyer Recruiting
Mergers & Acquisitions
Public Relations
Strategic Planning
Lawyer Utilization
Partner Compensation
Lawyer Evaluation
Quality Control

SOURCE: Adapted with permission from John F. Coburn, "The Legal Administrator of the 1990's: A New Breed," *Legal Economics* (January/February 1989).

management team,"[46] the ALA opens its membership to those who carry responsibilities in general management, financial management, human resource management, systems management, facilities management, and practice management. Members of the association include executive directors, directors of administrative services, directors of administration, administrators, directors of finance and administration, directors of finance, business managers, and many others. A second association, the Legal Assistant Management Association, is a national group created in 1984 to meet the needs of first-level supervisors. Its surge in membership evidences the growth in this field. As the number of legal assistants increases, the need for first-level supervisory managers also grows, providing a new level of legal managerial career that is both productive and profitable for law firms. Legal assistant managers serve many first-level functions, and the membership of their namesake association includes legal assistant supervisors, paralegal managers, paralegal coordinators, administrative managers, executive assistants, and managers, supervisors, and coordinators of various departments or divisions, such as litigation, corporate law, criminal law, and real estate.

Future Challenges

To many legal professionals, accepting a nonlawyer professional as CEO is still a shaky proposition. Many years of tradition and self-regulation reinforce the legal profession's resistance to change. Past changes in the organizational structure of law firms have not always been smooth. Many first-hire administrators stay only briefly in their new firms, unable to meet the firms' expectations which are still ambiguous and often conflicting. Through such difficulties, firms are learning the importance of clear, accurate, and complete job descriptions for administrators. They have also learned that the component most critical to the success of any manager is the law firm's strong commitment to the value of a legal administrator. Many lawyers are reluctant to hire for jobs they believe themselves competent to perform, but, many lawyers have realized a simple fact: The time they spend on administrative tasks cuts into the time they could better spend practicing law.[47]

In *Megatrends,* James Naisbitt predicts the major trends that all managers will face. These trends include the change from an industrial to an informational society, an emphasis on high tech, a more global economy, a long-term focus in business and industry, and increasingly decentralized organizational structures.[48] Naisbitt suggests that the labor pool will change as well, providing fewer qualified workers in specialized areas. Managers will need to deal with many human issues in the workplace, such as AIDS, drugs, and health care. More women will enter the work force, as two-career families continue to be the answer to meeting economic demands. Workers and managers alike will struggle with societal issues, such as ethics, environmental concerns, and increasing internationalization. Our economy will continue to favor service industries; in these fields, the traditional top-down style of the managerial hierarchy increasingly will give way to more collaborative work styles once allowed only to professionals. Walter Kiechell, writer and editor at *Fortune* magazine, has projected that "the ideal for the year 2000 is the concept of self-management. This model holds that the person who knows best what it takes to motivate himself or herself is that person. Likewise, the person who knows best how to do a job is the person who performs it. A manager's job will be to give workers all of the resources and tools they need to do their job—and then get out of their way so that they can do it."[49] A manager will need to be well prepared to understand the worker, the organization, and how to make the most of their mutual dependence.

Pieces of a Puzzle

We are still learning how people can maximize their work contributions. In many ways, management study is still relatively new and mysterious. What are the current approaches to management? In a special focus section at the end of this chapter, we will examine some of the most important contributions to management theory, beginning with contributions from days long gone by and concluding with several contemporary approaches, including the management science approach, the contingency or situationalist approach, and the behavioral scientist approach. Management expert Harold Koontz compared the multitude of managerial approaches to a jungle, citing what he called "the confusion among intelligent managers arising from the wide differences in findings and opinions among academic experts."[50] Koontz believed that management experts were describing management like the three blind men of the Hindu proverb, who described an elephant, each basing his description on only part of the whole animal. Pushing for a more cohesive field of study, Koontz stressed the need for a clearer understanding, while recognizing that management is too broad and too challenging to allow for a single best approach. However, it is easy to be optimistic, along with Koontz, that someday our image of management, like the image of the elephant, will be more cohesive.[51]

Few can see the whole picture in terms of managerial theory: how all the pieces create an effective manager. Many questions remain. Do happy workers make good workers, do good workers make happy workers, or does a successful and profitable organization either keep workers good, in the sense of being effective, or happy, in the sense of fitting into the organization and believing that they contribute to its success? Many popular works on management try to solve these management mysteries, and many provide solid insights. We should remember, however, that a valuable idea is much smaller than a valuable theory. In terms of contemporary works, we must remember that no matter how profound and aesthetically pleasing they may be, they represent passing notions, not reliable theory. Until ideas are openly proposed and tested, they remain only conjectures or guesses. Very few contemporary management theories have been thoroughly researched, and even existing theories have their limitations. Because management itself is such a complex field, this is not surprising. As onlookers trying to understand management or as participants in the field, we are all still students of management and of life itself. The best that we can do is to study the ideas now available and to remain open to future ones.

ANOTHER LOOK

Lincoln and Management Styles*

The creaky office in the front room on the second floor in Hoffman's Row, at 109 North Fifth Street, Springfield, Illinois, in which Stuart and Lincoln conducted their partnership (the site now designated by a bronze marker), was anything but pretentious. The few items of furniture, consisting of a small couch, a chair, a wooden bench, "a feeble attempt at a book-case," and a table which answered the purpose of a desk, bore little resemblance to each other. The physical appearance of "Office No. 4" was not untypical of the law offices of that year of grace. To the lawyer of today, accustomed to all the conveniences of the modern law factory, with its sleek, almost treadmill efficiency, it is hard to conceive of a time when the typewriter and all the other time- and labor-saving devices were unknown. The paperwork of lawyers was onerous in those days, since it had to be done laboriously by pen.

The original office, from all accounts an incredibly dingy place even for a pioneer law office, consisted of a single room, which overlooked Hoffman's Row; in the center of the room stood a long table, 10' by 3', with a smaller one at the end. In a corner stood a desk containing the law firm's papers; a bookcase against the wall held some law books and miscellaneous other volumes. The couch and a tall, unblackened stove were the only other articles of any consequence in this room which, from the standpoint of appointments, was destitute of legitimate claims to be called an office (where Lincoln ate meager lunches of cheese and crackers . . .). The physical appearance of untidiness was only matched by the antique methods the partners pursued in keeping records. Like Lincoln, Herndon was lacking in all the qualities of a businessman. For several years (1845–47) Herndon, one of whose duties was to keep the books of the partnership, maintained a combination daybook and fee book in rather desultory fashion. It listed the cases (or, to be exact, some of the cases) which the partners handled in Springfield and in the adjoining counties of Logan, Menard, and Christian, and the fees charged. This book, entirely in Herndon's fairly good handwriting, contains 125 numbered cases (1,2,3, etc.) of the two-year period before Lincoln went to Congress.

With the passing years, the partners came to rely increasingly on even such haphazard records as Herndon kept in the early stages of the partnership. Cash fees were usually split on the spot, so to speak. . . . Wrote Herndon, "Lincoln would collect monies due us and our fees on the circuit and divide it, putting his half in his pocketbook and using it as he wanted to; he would wrap my half up in a roll, putting my name on a slip of paper and then, wrapping it, the slip, around the roll of money and then, putting it in his pocketbook and when he came home he would come to the office and hand me my money."

Case files of the firm were nonexistent; pleadings, correspondence and papers were generally in a state of chaos. Of a system in filing there was none. Lincoln's capacious stovepipe hat, with its wide sweatband, very often served the purpose of a filing cabinet. Herndon wrote of it: "This hat of Lincoln's—a silk plug—was an extraordinary receptacle. It was his desk and his memorandum book . . . where he carried quite all his plunder, checkbook for the bank account, letters answered and unanswered, handkerchief, etc." At other times, when he had finished with legal papers, Lincoln would put them away in places known only to himself. After his death, Herndon discovered a bundle of papers with the notation in Lincoln's hand: "When you can't find it anywhere else, look in this."

*John J. Duff, *Lincoln: A Prairie Lawyer* (New York: Rinehart & Co., Inc., 1960).

1. In terms of law office management and organization, what has not changed since Lincoln's time?
2. What contemporary office practices would have helped Lincoln and his partners?

CHAPTER 1 / MANAGERIAL PERSPECTIVES

QUESTIONS FOR DISCUSSION AND REVIEW

1. What is management and why is it important?
2. Why is business important as a social organization?
3. How is the practice of law both a business and a profession?
4. How has the career of the legal administrator evolved?
5. Is what makes a good manager the same as what makes a good administrator?
6. Compare the four major managerial responsibilities of a paralegal coordinator to those of a firm's top legal administrator. Contrast the mix of skills needed at each of those two levels of management.
7. If you had to decide whether management is truly an art, a science, or a profession, which of the three would you choose? Explain your views.
8. Does studying the past have any true value for the law firm?
9. Debate the pros and cons of ensuring that each member of a law firm understands what management is, what it does, and what it is supposed to be.
10. In the Special Focus section, select one or two contributors to management theory and discuss how their theories apply to the law firm setting.
11. After reading the Special Focus section, create your own set of "Ten Commandments of Management Theories for the Law Firm," based on the theories you find most suitable for law practice settings.

EXPERIENTIAL EXERCISES

I. What Kind of Manager Will You Be?* Assessing Your Own Management Skills

If you have never held any managerial positions, management skills may seem far removed from your list of talents. However, most of us learn management in many ways, often through our everyday dealings with others. Even if you are an experienced manager, this assessment exercise will give you feedback on your management style.

Rate yourself according to the following characteristics. The closer you place a check to a characteristic, the more indicative it is of you. Rate yourself as you are, not as you would like to be or would like others to *think* you are!

1. Prefer to work with others / Prefer to work alone
2. Often seek leadership opportunities / Often avoid leadership opportunities
3. Assertive / Not assertive
4. Priorities well established / Priorities not yet well established
5. Inclined to take pleasure from others' successes / Inclined to be jealous of others' successes

---

*Reprinted, by permission of the publisher, from "Improving Managerial Effectiveness Through Model-Based Training," by Jerry I. Porras and B. Anderson, in *Organizational Dynamics* (Spring 1981): 72. Copyright © 1981 by ANACOM, a division of American Management Association, New York. All rights reserved.

PART 1 / MANAGERIAL CONCEPTS

−2   6. Inclined to let others do their own thing   ___:_1_:___:___:___   Have strong desire to influence others

+2   7. Generally unwilling to take responsibility for what others do   ___:___:___:_1_:___   Generally willing to take responsibility for others' behavior

4   8. Inclined to exercise power or authority   _1_:___:___:___:___   Not inclined to exercise power or authority

4   9. Easily identify with others' feelings   _1_:___:___:___:___   Experience difficulty identifying with others' feelings

+4   10. Have trouble making decisions   ___:___:___:___:_1_   Have no trouble making decisions

+4   11. Inclined to be upset and anxious at having lots of time demands   ___:___:___:___:_1_   Have no difficulty tolerating numerous time demands

+4   12. Inclined to leave things as they are, even when dissatisfied   ___:___:___:___:_1_   Inclined to suggest and initiate change when needed

+4   13. Do not control the use of my time   ___:___:___:___:_1_   Largely control the use of my time

      14. Feel that I know myself intimately   _1_:___:___:___:___   Feel frequently out of touch with myself

4   15. Can generally find all needed information prior to making decisions   _1_:___:___:___:___   Frequently have difficulty obtaining information needed to make a decision

−2   16. Not very competitive   ___:_1_:___:___:___   Very competitive

+4   17. Uncomfortable when distinctive or singled out   ___:___:___:___:_1_   Enjoy being distinctive or singled out

4   18. Have little trouble being criticized   _1_:___:___:___:___   Bothers me a lot to be criticized

0   19. Generally rebel against authority   ___:___:_1_:___:___   Generally obey authority

4   20. Self-confident   _1_:___:___:___:___   Not self-confident

+4   21. Have trouble expressing myself verbally   ___:___:___:___:_1_   Generally do well expressing myself verbally

4   22. Trusted by others   _1_:___:___:___:___   Often distrusted by others

+4   23. Uncomfortable giving straightforward negative feedback to others   ___:___:___:___:_1_   No trouble giving straightforward negative feedback to others

24. Have few or no close interpersonal relationships   ___:___:___:_|_:___   Have many close interpersonal relationships   +4
25. High need to achieve   ___:_|_:___:___:___   Low need to achieve   2
26. Have a strong desire to exercise power   ___:_|_:___:___:___   Not interested in pursuing positions of power   2
27. Able to effectively resolve disagreements to the satisfaction of both parties   _|_:___:___:___:___   Have difficulty resolving disagreements to the satisfaction of both parties   4
28. Can absorb criticism without becoming defensive   _|_:___:___:___:___   Become very defensive when criticized   4
29. Likely to assume a leadership role in a group when a formal leader has not been appointed   _|_:___:___:___:___   Inclined to let others assume a leadership role in a group   4
30. Feel comfortable giving formal presentations or talks   _|_:___:___:___:___   Have great difficulty giving a formal presentation or talk   4

II. What do Managers *Really* Do? Interviewing Those in the Field

Arrange to meet with a legal administrator in your community. Using the outline below,* prepare your own interview script. Assure the administrator of confidentiality and be sure not to use names or sources in class. Write a follow-up thank you to your interviewee, remembering the value of his or her time and the gift he or she has freely given you and your class. Present a summary of what you have learned about law office management in class, including accurate information on the manager's title, job responsibilities, and career path.
a. Describe a typical day at the law firm.
b. What are your most time-consuming activities?
c. What are the most critical problems you face as a manager?
d. What are the most critical skills a law firm manager needs?
e. What are the major causes of failure for legal administrators?
f. Why is there so much turnover in your field?
g. If you could design a college course to help students become successful law office managers, what would the course include?

---

*From DEVELOPING MANAGEMENT SKILLS by David A. Whetten and Kim S. Cameron. Copyright © 1984 by Scott, Foresman and Company. Reprinted by permission of HarperCollins Publishers.

h. On a scale of 1 (rarely) to 10 (constantly), can you rate the extent to which you use the following skills or behaviors during your workday?

____ Managing personal stress
____ Managing time
____ Setting goals
____ Making individual decisions
____ Recognizing/defining problems
____ Using verbal communication skills
____ Delegating
____ Motivating others
____ Managing conflict
____ Interviewing
____ Gaining and using power
____ Orchestrating change
____ Appraising others' performance
____ Facilitating group decision making
____ Listening
____ Disciplining others
____ Achieving self-awareness
____ Empathizing
____ Team building
____ Solving problems
____ Conducting meetings
____ Negotiating

III. Modern Bureaucracy*

Some people respond well to some of the elements that Max Weber idealized for his bureaucratic organization. The following questionnaire will indicate your own acceptance and comfort with contemporary bureaucratic principles. Circle the number that best indicates your agreement with each statement.

4 = Strongly agree
3 = Agree
2 = Disagree
1 = Strongly disagree

1. Goal setting should be a method for putting into practice the organization's strategic plan.   4 3 2 1
2. Training and development activities should provide a forum for instructing organization members in important policies and procedures.   4 3 2 1
3. Roles and responsibilities in an organization should be determined on the basis of tasks and situations.   4 3 2 1
4. Performance appraisals should be used to give rewards or administer sanctions, based on an individual's work activity.   4 3 2 1
5. The organizational chart should provide a simplified but helpful structure for examining and understanding the organization.   4 3 2 1
6. Problem solving should be a step-by-step rational process to resolve organizational issues.   4 3 2 1
7. Conflict should be best dealt with through rational examination of the issues and resolution by higher authority.   4 3 2 1
8. Strategic planning should be aimed at developing clear action plans that are recognized and understood by everyone.   4 3 2 1

---

*SOURCE: M. Sashkin and W. C. Morris, *Experiencing Management,* 10–17. Copyright © 1987, by Addison-Wesley Publishing Company, Inc., Reading, Massachusetts. Reprinted with permission of the publisher.

9. Decision making should involve an accepted, rational sequence of steps that, if followed, will lead to a sound conclusion.   4 3 2 1
10. Career planning should help the organization set up stable long-range plans based on the most efficient use of individuals' talents.   4 3 2 1
11. People should be motivated to achieve by concrete rewards for performance.   4 3 2 1
12. The most important function of organizational communication should be the development of a shared understanding of the nature of the organization.   4 3 2 1
13. Meetings should be forums for organized discussion and, as appropriate, decision making.   4 3 2 1
14. Clear rules and policies should be the basis for running a smoothly functioning organization.   4 3 2 1
15. Promotions should be ways of recognizing effective task performance and rationally using human resources to the organization's best advantage.   4 3 2 1

IV. Are You Ready for the Real World?

What does it take to be a manager in a law office setting? Hardly a world for the weak, law firm management thrusts managers into a world filled with unique career demands, an environment for those who are ready to meet the challenges of working with legal professionals.

1. Compile a list of the positive traits you associate with lawyers (such as intelligent, hardworking, confident, resolute, determined) and a list of their negative traits (such as stubborn, egotistical, arrogant, demanding, hard to work with).
2. Using these two lists, discuss those traits that would help an attorney to excel in the practice of law.
3. Label each of the traits you discussed in step 2 with an S or a U, to indicate whether or not you think that trait would help you to be a SUCCESSFUL or UNSUCCESSFUL law office manager. Discuss your choices.

SPECIAL FOCUS

Contributions to Management Theory

Building on the Past

The pressured and dynamic activities of a law firm may seem light years away from the staid and rational body of knowledge called management theory, yet understanding management theory has much to offer successful legal practices. Ever since people began to make collaborative or group efforts, learning how to manage well—no matter in what setting—has been of interest to many. In learning about management in the law firm setting, experts from the past might seem out of place, but law firm management theory is not and never will be a totally new creation, having emerged from the management wisdom of many settings, not just that of the practice of law. The Another Look feature that follows offers a glimpse at the "management" style of one of the greats of the legal profession, Abraham Lincoln. The excerpt could depict many lawyers, of Lincoln's era and even of today! Lincoln, like many other lawyers, relied on the services of a partner. His interests in politics and law became manageable only after he established multisite offices with local attorneys, an arrangement that had—and still has—its difficulties. Delivery of legal services in Lincoln's day, as it is for some now, did not merely consist of a knowledge of the law. Some may conclude that law practice management has not progressed noticeably since Lincoln's time and that the need for management concepts transcends time and place. Effective management solutions, no matter when they come about, are of great value. Many principles that worked successfully centuries ago may still have merit today. Some of these processes have cut across cultures and time and technological lines. To understand management well, it is useful as well as enriching to understand its roots. Although many theories have proved successful, here we will focus our overview on the contributions of (1) the ancients, (2) the forerunners of management theory, (3) the classical management contributors, (4) the human relationist school, (5) the management scientists and (6) the situationalists.

The Ancients[52]

Early records describe the accomplishments of the Sumerians, the Egyptians, the Babylonians, and other ancient civilizations, as well as those of Moses and the Hebrews. The wonders of the world could not have been built without superb skills. The Great Wall of China and the Pyramids were accomplishments that must have taken extraordinary managerial talent. As far back as 5000 B.C., the Sumerians devised accurate and complex accounting methods; around 4000 B.C., the Egyptians developed their own system for planning, organizing, and controlling, relying on their managerial skills for the construction of massive monuments and building projects which required staggering amounts of raw material and labor; and documents from 1100 B.C. describe how the Chinese used the four managerial functions of planning, organizing, directing, and controlling. The Greeks, around 400 B.C, were known to have advocated a scientific approach to work, considering management a special and separate art. Pericles spoke of a worker's individual dignity and merit, urging employers to recognize each worker's uniqueness and commitment to the organization and to allow workers to maintain a balance between work and nonwork activities.[53] Even Biblical accounts, such as those detailing the life of Moses,[54] acknowledge the need for managerial skills. Later, the early Romans accomplished masterful management through effective communications and centralized control. Later, during medieval times, one outstanding managerial accomplishment was that of an Italian shipbuilding business called the Arsenal of Venice, located on the shores of the Adriatic Sea. Its records show phenomenal productivity and expertise accomplished through standardized production, assembly lines, inventory systems, and elaborate and accurate accounting procedures for tracking costs and revenues. Management at the Arsenal promulgated employee-centered policies that seem farsighted even today, featuring an exceptional benefits package that included such job perks as afternoon wine-breaks, for which management provided only the best of wines![55] Years later, a Florentine statesman named Nicolo Machiavelli wrote his masterpiece on managerial and political savvy, titled *The Prince*. Machiavelli believed that effective managers base decisions on expediency, that political principles equal power principles, and that all that matters is accomplishing what one sets out to do. Still used to defend what many view as manipulative managerial practices, Machiavellian writings argue the legitimacy of any measure that leads to the personal and political power one needs to control one's rivals and subordinates. Though many other historic records document past managerial accomplishments, the few presented above provide us a brief glimpse at the foundations on which modern management studies are based.

Forerunners of Management Theory[56]

Of early management writings, only a handful of the best have survived. Among the works that have stood the test of time are those of English statesman Sir Thomas More, author of *Utopia*, a scenario for the ideal social organization; those of Scottish economist Adam Smith, most notably *The Wealth* of Nations, which suggested methods for developing thriving private enterprises; and the writings of British socialist and industrialist Robert Owen, who developed a management philosophy that stressed workers' rights, exceptional for its day. For many reasons, Owen is known as the forerunner of the human relations approach. A fourth outstanding contributor from the past was a Cambridge University professor named Charles Babbage, who described principles of management in what is known as the first scholarly treatise on management: On the Economy of Machinery and Manufacturing. Babbage's most noteworthy contribution, as a writer and mathematician, included the development of the differential calculating machine, a predecessor of the modern computer. Because of this, Babbage is credited with being the father of modern computer concepts. He also encouraged businesspeople to learn from others in their fields. Your specialized course in law office management is in keeping with his advice!

The Classicists

The classical approach to management is the name given to the first efforts in the nineteenth century to develop a body of managerial studies. The approach came as a response to the unprecedented changes brought by the Industrial Revolution. The economic system had changed dramatically. New inventions and new discoveries resulted in entirely new work structures. Workers themselves were beginning to be more conscious of their rights as individuals. **Classical management** was based on a concern for productivity that sought the most effective and efficient ways to run organizations. The classicists are usually grouped into three schools of thought: (1) scientific management, (2) administrative management, and (3) bureaucracy.

Classical Scientific Management. Emphasizing efforts to increase worker efficiency, those who used the scientific approach to management developed their findings from observations, hypotheses, tests, and experiments. Significant contributors to **scientific management** included Frederick Taylor and a husband-wife team, Frank and Lillian Gilbreth.

Frederick Taylor (1856–1915) began his career as a machine shop laborer at Midvale Steel Works in Philadelphia, Pennsylvania. A few years later, after being promoted to gang boss, Taylor went through three years of bitter conflict with his men, who resented his zeal at trying to get them to do a fair day's work for their pay. Frustrated with worker sabotage and grumbling, he was convinced that both management and labor had to undergo a "mental revolution" that would work to improve the system for everyone's benefit. Taylor's personal anguish, which he experienced both as a manager and as a worker, motivated his efforts: he wanted workers to have "security, acceptance from others and justice . . . through a concrete, predictable system of scientific management." What he encouraged now seems like a list of basic requirements: division of work; standardization; rest breaks; an efficient arrangement of equipment and work areas; incentive wages based on the piece system; and a differential rate system that would offer a higher rate of pay to workers who performed exceptionally well. Taylor's **time studies** were not only the basis for time standards and piece rates, but also provided models for improved work methods.[57] In sum, Taylor's management theories promoted these concepts: (1) efficiency studies, (2) careful recruiting and selection procedures, (3) improved interpersonal relations, and (4) the effective division of labor.[58] Taylor's scientific approach to improving production and efficiency standards, first published in 1911, continues to influence management studies today. As one of the most successful scientific management experts, Taylor has won the title of "Father of Scientific Management."

Frank and Lillian Gilbreth (1868–1924); (1878–1972). If you have seen the classic movie Cheaper by the Dozen (or have read the book on which it is based), you'll find it easier to appreciate this husband and wife team. Providing what might be called a zanier look at scientific management, the film not only depicts the Gilbreth's efforts to raise twelve children (!) but the Gilbreth brood's willing—and sometimes not-so-willing participation in their father's efficiency studies! While Frank Gilbreth used his **motion studies** to analyze the different motions used to perform any task, in 1915, Lillian Moller Gilbreth became the first woman in the United States to receive a doctoral degree. Her dissertation, "The Psychology of Management," was one of the first texts to emphasize management psychology. While her husband's work continued to focus on efficiency, hers concentrated on human variables such as fatigue and motivation. She also contributed to the growing field of personnel management, studying the implications of selection, placement, and training issues.[59]

Classical Administrative Management. The second school of classical thought, **administrative management,** emphasizes using the principles and procedures that work best for *each* organization, focusing on the administrative *process* within the organization. Those who advocated administrative management believed that the management function could not be limited to one phase or aspect of management. This comprehensive view of management was based on the belief that in addition to one best way of performing tasks, there is one best way to manage an organization. Among the major contributors to this school of thought were college academics and successful executives of major companies, including Henri Fayol, Mary Parker Follett, and Chester Barnard.

Henri Fayol (1841–1925). Henri Fayol, a French engineer and geologist who later became a leading executive, was one of the leading contributors to administrative management. In 1916, Fayol published his Administration Industrielle et Generale, promoting the idea that management could be analyzed and taught. According to Fayol, any prosperous operation depended not only on its top management, but on management at all levels. Because of the richness and scope of his thinking, Fayol is known as the pioneer of administrative management. He suggested that the management process consisted of "The Five Basic Rules," basic tasks similar to the four traditional functions of management we discussed earlier. Also promoting a conviction that management principles were universally true, Fayol developed "Fourteen Principles of Management" to be used as *guidelines* for the five basic rules of management—not, as he wrote, as rigid rules for the mindless.

Mary Parker Follett (1868–1933). Mary Parker Follett approached management with the insight of a political and social philosopher, insisting on the need for an administrative overview. Resembling contemporary management sermons, Follett's progressive observations promoted business as "services" and profits as belonging to the "common good," a managerial profit-sharing idea that saw workers partaking of financial and human successes at work.[60] Follett's *Dynamic Organization* championed the need for managers to be aware of three work site issues: workers' organizational consent, community, and an integration of interests. Follett defined **organizational consent** as the voluntary give and take that occurs between workers and managers in meeting the constant challenges of everyday work life. Strongly rooted in an early career in social work and community service, her ideas stress a concept that seems instinctive today: that management cannot remain effective without willing riders on its bandwagon. Follett also stressed a larger vision for managers, believing that both employers and workers are part of an organizational community, a collegial, volunteer relationship offering mutual benefits. She believed that conflicts at work are reconcilable only through dialogue and direct communication and that the major task of management is to enable people at all levels of the organization to *cooperate* in reaching organizational goals, a coordination of effort and mutual answering of needs that Follett called an **integration of interests.**

Chester I. Barnard (1886–1961). Executive Chester Barnard, former president of New Jersey Telephone, based his original and effective views in *The Functions of the Executive* on his experiences as a CEO. Barnard described the organization as a social system where the executive was the key to success, where cooperation was essential, and where activities required careful and strategic coordination. Envisioning organizations as positively functioning interpersonal systems where social forces interact, Barnard maintained that the executive's most critical role is to preserve equilibrium in informal as well as formal organizational systems, shaping the organization's objectives so that workers can contribute their best performance. Organizations only work well, Barnard wrote, when management both cooperates with and cultivates an ethical attitude toward workers, instead of relying utterly on authority. Management may achieve such cooperation through effective organizational communications, which are a manager's primary function—not a surprising view for the historically successful CEO of a telephone company to take![61]

Classical Bureaucratic Focus. The third school of thought is that of **bureaucracy,** a form of management that focuses on organizational structure and the use of carefully determined roles, regulations, and functions to help the organization to run smoothly.

Max Weber (1864–1920), a German sociologist and economist, advocated bureaucracy as a way to ensure fair treatment for workers. Weber proposed establishing management systems that would allow large organizations to function equitably, efficiently, and consistently, basing his ideas on the efficiency of the nineteenth-century German political structure, a system he admired greatly. To bring about his ideal of fairness, Weber depicted a bureaucratic system controlled by regulations and rules, not by the personalities of its members. Convinced that the limitations of bureaucracy stemmed from flaws in establishing its rules and regulations, Weber believed that the key to organizational effectiveness was based on the three legitimate sources of authority: sources established on rational, traditional, or charismatic grounds. For example, rational authority legitimately belonged to those given the job to command. Weber stressed the chain of command and opposed undermining the authority of any supervisor at any level. Though today, we tend to recognize only the negative connotations of *bureaucracy,* the bureaucratic ideal offered advantages as well as disadvantages. In Weber's system, bureaucracy represented an organizational Eden that treated people at all levels fairly and divided work according to the special talents of workers. In such a setting, authority was clearly defined, all employees respected the organizational hierarchy, the rights and duties of employees were clearly established, and specific procedures guided the performance of all activities. Selected and advanced according to their technical competence, workers understood that work was primarily economic, not social. However, although Weber intended only positive outcomes for bureaucracy, the negatives surrounding its rules and rigidity outweighed its efficient and fair intentions. The extensive record keeping and paperwork needed to ensure impartiality and accountability became bureaucracy's most memorable feature, the "red tape" that strangled Weber's ideal. The system that encouraged impersonalization and conformity was, not surprisingly, highly unpopular with workers who already felt alienated. Loyalty, concern for coworkers, initiative, and group efforts were hardly hallmarks of the individual in the bureaucratic organization.[62]

The Human Relationalists

In the early 1920s, management studies began to gain acceptance as tools for learning about running effective organizations. A few colleges and universities began to teach management. This led to an enriched understanding of the field, through a blending of social sciences, psychology, economics, and mathematics. **Human relations management** emphasizes the productivity that the respectful and equitable treatment of workers can produce. Notable contributions to this approach include the Hawthorne Studies and the work of Rensis Likert, as well as that of many other writers who focused on the role of the individual in the organization.

The Hawthorne Studies. In an attempt to contribute to this new field, a group of university professors, including F. J. Roethlisberger, William J. Dickson, and Elton Mayo, were invited to conduct scientific studies at an actual worksite. The Chicago-based Western Electric Company wanted to see how Taylor's first principle of scientific management ("Division of Work," which promotes worker specialization as the most efficient way to use skills and talents) applied to workers in the real world. Interested in determining the working environment that would encourage work performance while minimizing fatigue, Western Electric encouraged the professors to study the effect of working conditions on plant production at the company's Hawthorne Works. The original study considered variables such as temperature, rest periods, working hours, and other working conditions. At the heart of today's most influential management thinking, the Hawthorne Studies became the basis for many subsequent studies that have concentrated on the correlation between human variables and positive work performance. During the years 1924–32, three different Hawthorne Studies actually took place: (1) the Illumination Experiment, (2) the Relay Assembly Room Test Experiments, and (3) the Bank Wiring Room Experiment. From each study came new findings. The researchers first learned that productivity was linked to workers' awareness of being part of an experiment. This is called the **Hawthorne effect,** now known as the tendency of individuals to increase their efforts when they receive favorable treatment or attention. The researchers also discovered that interpersonal factors were very important to workers and that the researchers' presence had led to a new working atmosphere, one in which the workers enjoyed respect and attention. Last, the researchers learned that money was not the only motivator in group work: the workers at the Hawthorne plant had developed stronger norms based on group acceptance and preserving respect within the work group. Such findings led to a new emphasis on the value of investing in an organization's human capital.

Rensis Likert (1903–). Rensis Likert, who directed the University of Michigan's Institute of Social Research, also conducted many studies on the role of employee-management interaction in the workplace. Likert showed how supportive relationships, as contrasted with threatening supervision, were valuable not only to the workers' sense of well-being but increased productivity as well. Likert developed organization profiles by formulating sets of characteristics and contrasting participative organizations with hierarchically controlled ones. Likert also developed communication models that were based on "linkage," the networks or communication patterns within organizations.[63]

Humanist Writings

New insight into worker motivation led to a series of studies that focused on the person, the worker. These works included the writings of Chris Argyris, author of *The Individual and the Organization*,[64] and William Foote Whyte, author of *Money and Motivation* and *Men at Work.* There are many noteworthy contributors, whose works we will examine later in the chapter on motivation, who also studied how effective organizations treat their members. These researchers and management experts were now examining the meaning of work, motivation, and dignity.[65]

Management Scientists

The **management science** approach, dating from the 1950s and 1960s, was greatly influenced by military studies conducted during World War II, when many of the country's leading scientists were involved in operations research. Their goal was to master the complexity of the military's operational problems. Based on the these studies that employed the scientific method, management science remains an approach based on the collection and use of quantifiable data. It relies on (1) making observations, (2) formulating hypotheses, (3) careful deductions, and (4) repeated testing. Though mathematical models first served to accommodate multiple variables and to address economic implications, the use of computers later facilitated these studies. Current applications for scientific management include sophisticated mathematically based managerial tools such as inventory control models, network models, and probability models.

Situationalists: Contingency Management

The **contingency management school,** also known as the situationalist school, stresses the need for managers to adapt to the situations and forces that are unique to each organization. This school of thought reinforces the idea that no two law firms are alike: the kind of management large suburban firms thrive on will not work for small-town firms. All management equals the process of adaptation, all organizations face different contingencies, and all managerial decisions must be considered in light of unique internal and external organizational factors. Concerned with responding to such variables, the contingency approach is most appropriate for managerial activities that involve working with people, such as leadership or motivation.

CHAPTER 2

Planning and Decision Making

LEARNING OBJECTIVES

After completing this chapter, you should be able to:

- Explain what planning is and why it has primacy over all other management functions;
- Identify the kinds of plans and their uses;
- Understand the power of strategic planning for the law firm;
- Explain and apply the seven steps in the planning process;
- Understand the nature of decision making and the steps in the decision-making process;
- Understand the importance of and the dilemmas involved in participative management;
- Discuss the advantages and disadvantages of group decision making;
- Explain the benefits of divergent and creative thinking and how to encourage it; and
- Explain what is involved in successful law firm retreats.

Joel Rose is president of Joel A. Rose & Associates, a management consulting firm to the legal profession, in Philadelphia, Pennsylvania. With over twenty-four years of experience in consulting, Mr. Rose has lectured for associations such as the American Bar Association. A prolific writer, he has published articles in such publications as The Practical Lawyer *and* The National Law Journal.

FOCUS FROM THE FIELD

Joel Rose: Planning—Meeting Professional, Ethical, and Economic Needs

Is law practice management too fluid a field for long-term planning?

I think that in today's legal environment, from both the business side and the economic side, a firm must participate in some type of long-term planning or the firm will be hurting very badly. A law firm must continually develop to maintain or enlarge its client base. In today's environment, a firm needs to produce a quality legal service and it has to be provided in a prompt and fair manner to both the client and the firm. The firm must also be able to provide an opportunity for partners and associates to achieve their own personal, professional, and economic objectives. Unless there is some planning involved, I think that a firm can lose its position in the marketplace. However, a firm should not attempt to plan more than three years. There are some critical examples for a longer term of planning, such as space requirements of the firm or retirement of a partner. These issues are important ones that cannot be thought out overnight. With these exceptions, to develop a long-term plan covering five to ten years would be a foolish exercise.

What role should clients play in planning?

My perception of the long-term planning process involves not only reviewing trends of financial and management information over a certain period, but also a reasonably candid discussion with the firm's top clients. The discussion should determine what those clients' plans are. The firm should also develop a "partnership" arrangement with the clients so that the firm understands the clients' needs. Part of the planning process will include approaches to satisfy the clients' needs. So, clients have a particularly important role in this as it relates to long-term planning for marketing services. We survey our top clients to find out how the firm has been providing services. These discussions are important because they help us to correct problems that may be eroding the relationship between the client and the firm. There are many firms that sit in a vacuum and decide what to do and how to do it. I think that this is a very narrow view. Clients have a key role in the planning process.

What do you see as the biggest challenge in this area?

I think that the biggest challenge in the planning process is the implementation of the plan. It's very important to discuss with the partners and the associates the approaches or strategies to be used to obtain desired objectives. Once you've accomplished that, the plan is only as good as its implementation. That is where the biggest problems occur—whether or not the attorneys are really committed to this plan. Ongoing assessment should be made to determine the most appropriate strategy to be followed. The implementation must be monitored to assess how effectively the plan is being implemented and corrective action must be taken as required. In my opinion, the implementation of the plan and the follow-up to the implementation are the most difficult and challenging parts of the planning process.

How can partners and other members of the law firm participate in the planning process?

Partners, associates, and paralegals can and should contribute in terms of providing information about the planning process itself. They have an active role in providing information as to their level of satisfaction with the firm—whether or not the firm is meeting with their professional, ethical and economic needs. They may wish the firm to aspire to a level that it is not at. A major area of partner impact has to do with the evaluation of the firm's strengths as well as its weaknesses. I think that once partners have an opportunity to participate in the planning process they sense that they can shape the direction that the firm will take. Then, hopefully, they will be buying into the planning process. If the planning process involves what the partners want, then the implementation phase can be somewhat easier. Unless attorneys are involved in this, there is little reason for them to become involved in the planning process.

And now Alice found herself in a dark forest with nowhere to go.... Looking about, she was startled to see a Cheshire Cat sitting on a bough of a tree grinning down at her.... "Cheshire Puss," she began timidly, "would you tell me which way I can go from here?"
"That depends on where you want to get to," said the Cat.
"I don't much care," Alice answered. And the Cheshire Cat responded,
"Then, it really doesn't matter much, does it?"
(Lewis Carroll, *Alice in Wonderland*)[1]

Planning is the most enjoyable thing I do in my professional life. Planning is fun, as much as anything, because it is crucial. Planning is what management is all about for, as Mr. Peter Drucker and other students of management have observed, *I can do nothing about yesterday, almost nothing about today, but at least a little about tomorrow, more about next week and plenty about next year.* Planning is synonymous with the future and that's where people with intelligence, skills and perception will spend their time and effort.
(Guy P. French, "The Payoff from Planning")[2]

Individually and collectively, privately and professionally, we shape our lives by the decisions we make and by the skill, energy and persistence with which we put them into effect. If we aspire to live better lives, then we must learn to make better decisions and to implement them more effectively. But no matter what daring or courage we bring to the making of a decision, or how great the drive and determination with which we carry it out, that decision can only be as good as the thinking, the decision-thinking, leading up to it. The single most important step we can take to improve the quality of our decisions is, therefore, to improve the quality of the thinking which precedes them.
(Ben Heirs, *The Professional Decision Thinker*)[3]

PLANNING

Planning, as Alice learned from the Cheshire Cat, is caring about where you want to go. As she found out, planning also implies that you know both where you are and where you've come from. A law firm that understands that planning means caring about what happens to it knows how to manage responsively and responsibly. A law firm that plans well can shape and direct its future, deciding in advance what it will do.

While planning is a critical yet relatively simple management device, it can sometimes become quite complex. Its definitions are many, but they all share these three elements: a sense of **purpose,** a sense of **direction,** and a **process** for reaching the organization's goals. The primary management function, **planning** involves evaluating information, assessing future outcomes, and selecting a course of action that will enable the organization to reach its objectives. Enabling managers to direct and shape the future, planning is the most crucial part of the management process. Good management thinks ahead. Unlike Alice, it has a sense of where it is going, and it cares.

What Is Planning?

Planning is:

> "The process of determining how the management system will reach its objectives." (Certo)[4]
>
> "The process of setting objectives and determining what should be done to accomplish them." (Schermerhorn)[5]
>
> "A dynamic process that uses the best historical data available, coupled with a detailed definition of the present environment and added to an evaluation of alternative futures to arrive at an optimum solution." (Lowe)[6]
>
> "Choosing a course of action and deciding in advance what is to be done, in what sequence, when, and how." (Megginson, Mosely, and Pietri)[7]
>
> "The process through which managers determine goals and devise the means for utilizing resources to accomplish them.... The process of analyzing the environment, setting objectives, and designing courses of action to achieve them." (Baird, Post, and Mahon)[8]
>
> "Determining the direction of a business by establishing objectives and by designing and implementing the strategies necessary to achieve those objectives." (Pearce and Robinson)[9]

Primacy of Planning

Planning is basic to the management process. It is the principal activity upon which all other managerial activities—organizing, directing, and controlling—are based (see Figure 2–1). It is possible to organize, direct, and control without any formal plan or direction in mind. But if you want to have any consistency of direction, any smoothly operating departments, any unity of purpose, or any organizational commitment, you need to plan. As management writer William Anthony observes:

> Top managers usually have a vision of where they would like to take the company. It may only be a mental vision, but it is, nevertheless, a vision. They clearly see where they want to go and how they wish to get there. This vision serves as an overall road map or plan of operation.[10]

By articulating and sharing this vision through use of the planning process, managers can help organizations transform dreams and wishes into success:

> Strong leaders articulate direction and save the organization from change via "drift." They create a vision of a possible future that allows themselves and others to see more clearly the steps to take, building on present capacities and strengths, on the results of Force A and Force B, to get there."[11]

We cannot overstate the value of effective planning. No matter how successfully law firms got by in the past by simply letting things happen, modern competition and economic restraints will not allow a contemporary law firm to survive without at least basic planning and goal setting.[12]

Sense of Direction and Purpose

What does planning accomplish? For one thing, it helps a law firm to cope with the basic questions of organizational life: Who are we? Why are we here? Where are we going? Organizations differ widely in their attitudes toward the future. Some law firms, for example, are *reactive*, responding out of need and pressure and operating at the mercy of their environment. Others are more *proactive*, using planning to create a solid basis for their actions. These firms set goals that help them to respond to the demands of their environment in a creative and dynamic way. Today's marketplace, one adviser writes, "makes it an absolute imperative for every law firm, no matter what its size, to implement an effective planning process."[13] Most lawyers are so involved with the pressures of the present that planning comes last on their list of priorities. It is not unusual to hear lawyers assert that they cannot plan the long-term growth of a law firm, claiming that it's impossible to project growth for the upcoming year, much less future growth. Though no planner can truly predict the future, planners can and should be responsive and ready for the possibilities that the future brings. They can shape the organization's response to the future, minimizing its mistakes and augmenting its opportunities. We could ask again: What does planning accomplish? All planning ultimately serves two purposes: protection and affirmation. Planning is "protective when it reduces the uncertainties that are part of business conditions"; it becomes "affirmative when it leads to increased organizational success. In itself, planning is strong evidence of the health of an organization."[14]

Planning Styles

There are two approaches to planning: directionless vision and directed vision. Directionless vision is a tool

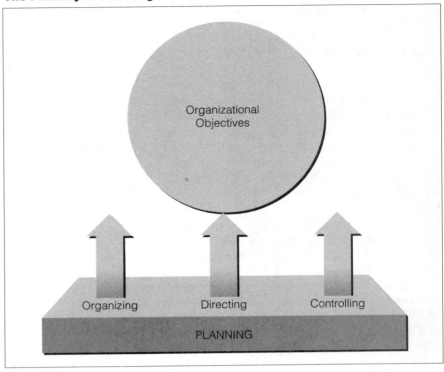

FIGURE 2-1
The Primacy of Planning

for the manager who does not plan, but who tries desperately to see a way out of the dark. This manager spends his or her time reacting to crises, responding to the unexpected, resolving and smoothing conflicts, and trying to control turmoil, a technique often called the fire-fighter approach to management. The second approach to planning is that of directed vision. Though a manager who uses this approach will still need to deal with the unexpected, even when his or her planning is as effective as possible, this same manager will minimize the time he or she spends resolving crises and will build on a shared sense of direction. This common vision (1) will help to coordinate the operations of all aspects of the organization, (2) will lead to a sense of unity and purpose within each worker and each unit, (3) will minimize lost time and energy, (4) will create an efficient use of resources, (5) will reduce guesswork, and, above all, (6) will help the entire organization to look to the future with hope. If a law firm knows where it wants to go, workers sense the stability and face the future with confidence. If all levels of the management team, from executive partner to paralegal coordinator to support staff supervisor, share in determining the firm's future, the trip ahead will be smoother. Involvement in decision making fosters a stronger ownership of goals at all levels, as well as agreement on the issues that matter. Planning improves the quality of all decisions, at all levels.

KINDS OF PLANS

Planning constitutes a framework that supports all other processes throughout the organization. In this text, we will examine two basic categories of plans: strategic plans and operational plans, which include both single-use plans and standing plans.

Strategic Plans

The long-range plans that determine the overall direction of an organization, **strategic plans** describe the law firm's very nature and purpose for existing. Providing a focus for the organization's other plans, they help the law firm to articulate what it considers important:

Karl Weick observes that:

Plans are important in organizations, but not for the reasons people think.... Plans are symbols, advertisements, games, and excuses for interactions. They are *symbols* in the sense that when an organization does not know how it is doing or knows that it is failing, it can signal a different message to observers.... [P]lans are *advertisements* in the sense that they are often used to attract investors to the firm.... Plans are *games* because they are often used to test how serious people are about the programs they advocate.... Finally, plans become *excuses for interaction* in the sense that they induce conversations among diverse populations about projects that may have been low priority items.

SOURCE: Karl Weick, as quoted in Rosabeth Moss Kanter, *The Change Masters* (New York: Simon & Schuster, Inc., 1983): 296.

ANOTHER LOOK

What Plans Really Are

1. What is Weick implying about plans? What organizational purposes do plans serve?
2. Can plans also be toys? riddles? group trophies?
3. Are there any other purposes that plans can serve, such as personal needs or group agendas?

[L]awyers, by and large, care about more than money and will continue to do so. They will care about friendship among partners, about the firm's commitment to quality work, about the firm's professional reputation, about the firm's and their commitment to community activities, and about the other intangibles that go with being a lawyer and glue together the institution that is their law firm.[15]

Strategic plans include the mission, or *why* the organization exists; its goals and objectives, or *what* the organization identifies as its aims or purposes; and *when, where,* and *how*: the organization's specific strategies and the means through which it intends to reach its goals.

Mission

The mission statement of an organization is its single most important document. A **mission statement** is the written description of the organization's main purpose for existing, an overview of what the law firm considers to be of value. A primary meaning of the term *mission,* often a word that carries religious connotations, is a "sending out or being sent out with the authority to perform a special duty."[16] In contemporary management, adhering to the organization's mission represents the most important goal of decision making. Because its mission statement describes the organization's special task or purpose, the statement provides a focus for all other decisions the organization makes. The mission statement receives support from the organization's **goals,** which are its broad, long-term targets, and its **objectives,** which represent specific short-range targets.

Components of the Mission Statement. A mission statement conveys three important messages about an organization. A firm's mission statement, above all, articulates its purpose, stating why the organization is venturing into the economic world. Second, the statement differentiates the firm, disclosing its uniqueness by describing the specific function it is to perform. Third, the statement stakes out the firm's territory, delineating the area that the firm claims as its operational turf. Without a comprehensive and clear mission statement, a law firm cannot develop any planning; for unless its members can agree about the core reason for the law practice's existence, they can develop no consistent vision for the future. The Another Look on page 46 presents the criteria for an effective mission statement.

Characteristics of the Mission Statement. A well-written law firm mission statement has specific characteristics: (1) it is brief, often no more than a few paragraphs in length; (2) it is all-encompassing, focusing on the central purpose of the organization; (3) it accurately describes the services that the firm currently provides, identifying the categories of law practice that the firm comprises; (4) it states the market that the firm is to serve, whether its members practice individual law or represent corporations through local, regional, or international bases; (5) it articulates what makes the

ANOTHER LOOK

Long-Range Planning Is Necessary

Long-range planning is becoming a critical duty for today's law firm administrator, especially at larger firms such as 200-lawyer Lewis, D'Amato, Brisbois & Bisgaard, and 500-plus-attorney Latham & Watkins.

Richard Macumber, chief operations officer of Los Angeles-based Lewis D'Amato, believes the planning "process is as valuable—if not more valuable—than the actual plan itself."

That's because it forces the firm to think about "where it's been, where it is today and where it's going," he says.

Mr. Macumber has been with Lewis D'Amato for 15 months. He also has held executive director positions at the Century City firm of Weissburg & Aronson; at what is now the West Los Angeles firm of Haight, Brown & Bonesteel; and at the L.A. firms of Overton, Lyman & Prince and McKenna, Conner & Cuneo.

"During that time," he says, "I have seen the role of administrative director gravitate from what was originally a personnel, facilities and purchasing function, to one of planning, finance and systems technology."

Most law firms can benefit from instituting a three- to five-year plan, he explains. "Then the administrator's main job is to coordinate and facilitate."

At Lewis D'Amato, a planning committee—comprised of partners at various levels throughout the firm but heavily weighted toward senior partners—meets on a regular basis. "Before I arrived," Mr. Macumber recalls, "Bob [founding partner Robert F. Lewis] had an uncanny feel for what ought to be done and how to make things happen. There were procedures, but they were all in his head. So one of my duties has been to put the planning function on a more formal basis."

The firm is still working on its first formal plan, which, according to Mr. Macumber, will deal with a wide variety of issues. "Along with the standard projections for marketing and staffing, strategic planning forces us to think about clients needs and how to respond to them. And we also think about growth and what we have to do to remain competitive. We want to make sure we're current in the right legal areas."

One problem that Lewis D'Amato shares with other firms doing long-range planning is finding time to have meetings. "We have all-day meetings, and it's tough getting together," he notes. "We've tried it on Saturdays, Friday nights, and Saturday mornings. The meetings work best on a Saturday, although occasionally we have to take a weekday." He says the planning committee avoids day-to-day issues and tries to deal with the major problems.

"Of course," he adds, "We're all at the mercy of the market. We're client-driven. And in that situation, the best-laid plans, as they say, often go astray."

Along with keeping the planning sessions on course, Mr. Macumber points out that the administrative director must be a political animal. "The key to success is political savvy. You can't ever forget that it's the partners' firm.

"Some administrators get carried away and forget that we are laymen and civilians, regardless of our experience in another industry," he notes. "No matter what credentials someone might bring to the job, it is still an uphill proposition. You must be able to walk a tightrope between proposing ideas that you think would be good for the firm, while at the same time keeping aware of diplomacy and the political requirements.

"And we can never forget that we are both a business and a profession. We're a profession first. But we have to operate in a businesslike fashion or we won't survive long enough to serve the client needs."

That same administrative philosophy is maintained in each of Lewis D'Amato's other offices—San Diego, Santa Ana and San Francisco. Mr. Macumber points out that each office has an administrator who has "a certain amount of autonomy, but also has to satisfy the judgment of the partners in that office."

At Latham & Watkins, the Los Angeles-based firm has a national office division headed by John F. Walker Jr., who also is managing partner of the entire firm. Latham has offices located in Chicago, New York, Washington, D.C., San Diego and Orange County, in addition to Los Angeles, with a seventh office slated to open today in San Francisco.

Each office has a managing partner who has a straight-line reporting relationship to Mr. Walker, says Doug Benson, the firm's executive director. Likewise, each has an administrative manager who reports to that office's managing partner and also to Mr. Benson.

Before joining Latham & Watkins four years ago, Mr. Benson was a partner with Touche Ross & Company in its managing consulting division, so dealing with long-range planning issues is second nature to him. With 560 lawyers, several widespread offices and some 1,200 support staff, his executive director position "has become almost a chief operating officer role," he explains.

As such, long-range planning is a regular agenda item. Representatives from all the offices serve on the planning committee, and their input is always being evaluated and worked into the planning process.

Mr. Benson points out that a major part of his job is to keep tabs on the firm's financial condition. "Making financial projections is just as hard—or just as easy—as it is for any other business. Since we're primarily a firm that does work for businesses, as opposed to individuals, a lot of our long-range strategy comes from watching carefully what's happening in government and society and business in general.

"For instance, several years ago we accurately foresaw the increase in environmental work, and now we have a large and talented environmental practice."

The recent crash and burn of the junk-bond market was not a surprise to the firm. "We didn't predict it," he says, "but we have a number of M&A clients, so we knew the market volume was down."

He adds, "With a long-range plan, even though you sometimes can't react as fast as you might want, at least you're not blindsided."

SOURCE: Ron Smith, "Long-Range Planning Is Necessary," *California Law Business* (2 April 1990): 20. Reprinted with permission of *California Law Business*.

---

1. Why might a five-year long-range plan be more effective than a ten-year one? (Think of a few real-life "unpredictables" that support your answer—for example, specific technologies or business conditions that differ greatly from those of ten years ago.)
2. How might long-range planning in a firm that specializes in individual law differ from long-range planning in a firm like Mr. Benson's, that works mostly for businesses?

---

firm unique, giving the organization rationale, which explains its particular contribution and, hence, why the organization should continue to exist.[17]

The Purpose of Mission Statements. Why do law firms actually exist? A mission statement helps a law firm to explain—to itself and to others—what the firm is all about. Some law firms say that their primary purpose is to make a profit by the practice of law. Other firms believe that profit is a byproduct of providing services and that all enterprises have profit as a principal goal by their very presence in the economic system. To such firms, the purpose of making a profit goes without saying, since profit is essential to survival. Where a particular firm stands in the classic debate over law as a business versus law as a profession is

ANOTHER LOOK

Criteria for an Effective Mission Statement

What should a mission statement propose?
- It should offer organizational directions that can be used to measure progress.
- It should provide a vision of the organization that shows how it is clearly different from all others.
- It should define the business and operating domain within which the organization will function.
- It should offer relevancy to all of the organization's key shareholders.
- It should be exciting and inspiring.

Though mission statements are normally the result of a long process, they usually express the essence of an organization briefly and concisely.

SOURCE: Russell L. Ackoff, *Management in Small Doses* (New York: John Wiley & Sons, 1986): 38–42.

---

1. Contact individual partners in law firms in your area. Ask them for information on their mission statements. What criteria seem most valid for law firms?
2. Which criterion seems the easiest to provide for in a mission statement? Which might be the hardest?
3. Write a brief mission statement for an ideal law firm. Critique the statement as objectively as you can, commenting on its strengths and weaknesses.

---

sometimes apparent in the wording of its mission statement.

Because the other plans formulated within a law firm fall under the mission statement's broad terms, we might identify a mission statement as the umbrella objective of a law firm. Figure 2–2 offers an example of a mission statement for a law firm: "To provide quality access to the system of justice through excellence and integrity of professional services to our clients in Western Massachusetts." From this broad statement, a firm could establish general goals for areas such as these: how to provide high-quality, timely service; expectations for growth and profit; and a range of projections for an increase in market share. For each of these areas, the firm could then establish more specific, more attainable, and more measurable objectives—for example, formulating for service goal objectives that concern the timeliness, competency, and courtesy of the law firm's service providers. The firm could also formulate objectives for growth and profit, basing these objectives on the establishment of a new practice area. Objectives could also reflect the firm's wish to establish more positive and visible public relations, to increase its use of marketing, or to boost community awareness of individual lawyers.

Goals and Objectives

As we saw, goals are the broad, long-term aims of an organization, whereas objectives are its specific, short-range targets. People often use the terms *goals* and *objectives* interchangeably, but there is a useful distinction. In managerial settings, *goal* describes the end result the organization wants to achieve, just as the goal of a trip or a game marks the point at which the trip ends or the game is won. *Objectives,* by comparison, are the intermediary steps or decisions involved in achieving a final goal. They are similar to the stopovers on a trip or to the downs of a football game that may lead to the winning score. Some possible goals for law firms would include more desirable end results in areas such as growth, recognition through reputation, image, status, areas of practice, professional collaboration, specialized services, and client services. In later sections, you will learn more about managing by objectives and how to integrate organizational goals with individual ones.

Strategies

In planning, the word *strategies* carries two sets of meanings. The simpler meaning refers to *strategies* as an artful or skillful means of achieving goals. The more complex meaning is used in connection with strategic planning: a **strategy** is the critical plan that describes how an organization will fulfill its mission and reach its objectives. There are two kinds of strategies: explicit and implicit.

FIGURE 2–2
Sample Mission Statement, Goals, and Objective Areas

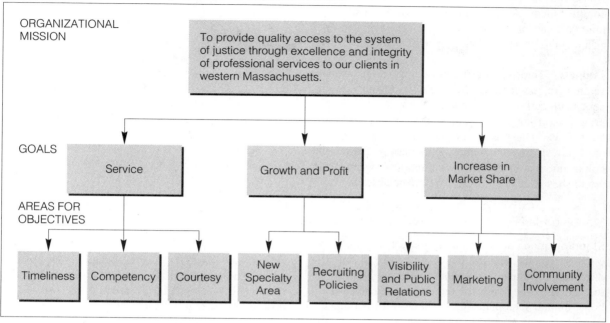

Explicit Strategy. An **explicit strategy** is a formally defined and articulated written plan that consists of the long-term objectives of the firm. It describes how the firm will achieve those objectives so that it can fulfill its mission.

Implicit Strategy. A law firm may also have an implicit strategy. An **implicit strategy** is an informally developed plan that responds to the firm's mission. Implicit strategies are the unwritten plans for reaching goals. Addressing objectives that are mutually agreed on and understood, they result not from a formal planning process but, rather, from shared understandings and consensus on ideas communicated over time.

Operational Plans

Operational plans are short-term or standing plans for the day-to-day, monthly, or yearly operation of an organization. To simplify your understanding of the categories and types of plans, the term *operational plans* in this text refers both to single-use and standing plans.

Single-Use Plans

Operational plans designed to achieve specific purposes for specified or limited amounts of time, **single-use plans** describe the procedures that organization members will use during specific activities or events. They include programs, projects, and budgets.

Programs. **Programs** are large-scale single-use plans designed to achieve a specific goal. In developing programs, planners need to establish the following:

- those who are responsible for the planning,
- the specific actions that the program is to accomplish,
- the timeline for completing the program, and
- effective reporting mechanisms for evaluating the program's degree of success.

A law firm might establish a special program to build customer relations, stressing that each member of the organization employ courtesy and consideration during each client interaction. Such a program would involve all levels of management. A paralegal coordinator, for instance, might work closely with his or her paralegals to help them become more client-conscious, thereby helping them to contribute toward reaching the firm's customer relations goal.

Projects. Smaller in scale than programs, **projects** are another form of a single-use plan. Designed to reach a specific goal, projects are usually completed by teams whose members often develop a sense of mutual accomplishment. A legal administrator, for example, might ask personnel from all parts of the firm to work as a team to produce an employee manual.

Budgets. **Budgets** are single-use financial plans that summarize the moneys allocated for resources and personnel, outlining expenditures for specific projects, programs, or lengths of time, such as a twelve-month budget year. Budgets are not manacles or constraints on behavior: they are simply guidelines. A plan with dollar amounts, a budget is a numerical system that establishes in advance the use of financial resources.

Standing Plans

Standing plans are operational plans that remain in effect for a considerable amount of time. Used as standards for procedures or decisions, they usually describe the actions to be taken for regularly occurring situations, though such plans may also describe actions to be taken in rare events. Plans generally considered to be long-standing include **policies,** which describe the general rules and principles that the firm will follow in taking action; **procedures,** which detail the actions that the firm will take during typical situations; **rules and regulations,** which specify the actions or behaviors required (or prohibited) in specific situations; and **practices,** which reflect traditional methods for handling specific circumstances.

Policies. **Policies** are standing plans that provide management with broad guidelines for making decisions and for acting in accordance with an organization's goals. An organization's members should take care to word policies as clearly as possible, so that they can easily recognize and rework or remove policies that become obsolete. Policies are used in many functional areas, including finances, personnel, public relations, marketing, and ethics. Some examples of policies appropriate for law firms might include a ''Firm Policy on Charitable Contributions,'' a ''Law Office Policy on Solicitation for Charitable Causes,'' a ''Statement on Confidentiality of Client Services,'' and ''Law Office Guidelines for Involvement in Community Activities.''

Procedures. **Procedures** are detailed guidelines for performing regularly occurring actions, though they may also be established for rare and extraordinary events, such as emergencies. Procedures describe in detail actions to be taken and the sequence for taking them. This means that a procedure tells you what to do and the order in which to do it. Some procedures, called standard operating procedures (sometimes referred to as SOPs), describe a firm's *accepted* operational procedures, such as the standard methods for opening client files or entering client bar codes for all transactions and support services. Some areas in which a law firm would use procedures include the following: billing, collection, hiring, and new staff orientation. Procedures are usually written in chronological order to ensure that organization members properly perform all the necessary aspects of a task. Written procedures eliminate ambiguity and reduce potential confusion and anxiety as well.

Rules and Regulations. **Rules and regulations** are written standing plans for specific actions that either are required or prohibited under certain conditions.

Practices. **Practices** are a form of rules; they may or may not be written. They are the accepted and usual ways of handling specific problems or situations, reflecting traditional interpretations of how things should be done.

Figure 2–3 summarizes strategic and operational plans.

Goals and Objectives

The basic components of the planning process are goals and objectives. **Goals** describe long-term directions,

FIGURE 2–3
Strategic and Operational Plans

TYPES OF STRATEGIC PLANS
Mission
Objectives
Strategies

TYPES OF OPERATIONAL PLANS

Single-Use Plans	Standing Plans
■ Nonrecurring	■ Recurring
■ Short-run, short term	■ Long-range, long-term
Programs	Policies
Projects	Procedures
Budgets	Practices
	Rules
	Regulations

whereas **objectives** are short-term targets that the organization establishes to help it reach its goals. There are two major types of goals and objectives: individual and organizational.

Individual Objectives

Long before workers become part of any organization, they have developed individual goals. Each has personal goals as well as professional goals. There are many possible goals for people to select. The objectives that help workers to attain their goals may include professional and personal development, professional opportunity, respect, affiliation, peer acceptance, autonomy and validation, and salary increases and satisfaction. Some of these areas may benefit just the individual; others may benefit just the organization; and some may benefit both.

Organizational Objectives

Organizational objectives are concerned with three basic areas: profitability, effectiveness, and efficiency. Management expert Peter Drucker warns that an organization that emphasizes only profitability objectives jeopardizes its survival. Organization members who seek nothing but immediate monetary rewards will tend to overlook what happens to profit in the long-term.

Figure 2–4 summarizes Drucker's eight recommended goal-setting areas for law firms. Note that the first five goal areas relate to a firm's operation; the last three are more subjective.

Goal Integration

Ideally, **goal integration** represents a harmonious overlapping of individual goals and organizational goals. However, not all individual goals are compatible with organizational goals. For example, a paralegal in a law firm who seeks to increase his or her time for travel and personal development fosters a personal goal that is incompatible with the law firm's goal of increasing productivity through more carefully monitored vacation schedules. Individual and organizational goals can overlap, though, becoming mutually beneficial. For instance, flextime may help an employee to reach a personal goal of spending more time on family needs and may also help the organization to increase productivity through better use of employee time, less of which will be needed for phone calls home or for taking personal sick days to care for family members. Figure 2–5 illustrates the overlap between organizational and individual goals.

STEPS IN THE PLANNING PROCESS

Effective planning requires taking an unbiased look at the past, analyzing the present, and carefully considering all of the alternatives that are open to the organization. Experts generally agree on a series of steps for a successful planning process that encourages participation at all levels of the organization.[18] These steps involve (1) assessing the present, (2) determining goals and objectives, (3) identifying available options, (4) se-

FIGURE 2–4
Goals for Law Firms

---

1. Market Standing: where the firm would like to be in relation to its competitors.
2. Innovation: which new ideas, technologies, and practice areas will encourage new ways of operating.
3. Productivity: the results that members of the firm can show.
4. Physical and Financial Resources: how best to acquire, use, and maintain capital and monetary resources.
5. Profitability: expectations for rates of growth and financial results.
6. Manager Performance and Development: clearly articulated performance levels for managerial productivity and growth.
7. Worker Performance and Attitude: measurable goals for the contributions of firm members, as well as concern for developing and maintaining a positive and productive attitude within each member.
8. Social Responsibility: statements and actions that indicate the organization's responsibilities to its clients and to society.[18]

SOURCE: Peter F. Drucker, *The Practice of Management* (New York: Harper & Row, 1954): 62–65, 126–29.

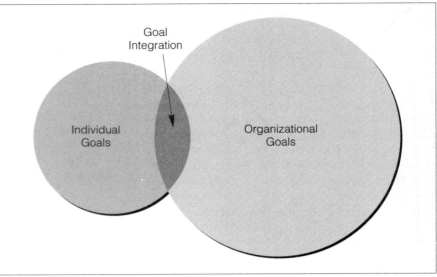

FIGURE 2-5
Goal Integration

lecting the best alternative, (5) implementing the plan, and (6) evaluating the results.

Assess the Present

When beginning the planning process, you must first look at what is happening within your organization and assess its present realities, gathering information sufficient to support the plan you wish to develop. This is the "doing your homework" part of the planning process.

Determine a Goal

Determining your final goal is the next step in planning. Just as planning a trip is impossible unless you know your final destination, a plan for the law firm requires a target. When traveling, you must have a clear idea of your destination before you can determine stopovers along the way. In planning, the same is true: you must first know where the firm wishes to go. This is goal setting. In order to determine goals, planners must be able to answer these questions: Who do we want to be? Where do we want to go? What do we want to do? Figure 2-6 summarizes seven trends that will shape future law firm goals, as well as the working atmosphere within law firms themselves.

Identify Alternatives

Your next step is to generate all the possible forms your plan might take. By determining all the possible alternatives the firm can choose in order to reach its goals, you increase its options and, therefore, its chances of success.

Select the Best Alternative

The next step in planning is to choose the best possible alternative. To do this, you must ask three critical questions about each alternative:

Is It Acceptable?

Six factors can limit the acceptability of some alternatives:

Political Limitations. Some alternatives will never fly for a very simple reason: some partners would never accept them.

Legal Limitations. Some alternatives obviously—or not-so-obviously—fail to reflect current laws and regulations.

Human Limitations. Some alternatives aren't feasible given the numbers and abilities of available personnel.

FIGURE 2-6
Seven Trends That Will Affect Future Law Firm Goals

1. A Global Economy
   The world will continue to shrink, creating greater demands for international practice and bilingual members within law firms.
2. A Goodbye to Authoritarian Styles
   New management styles at law firms will at long last see the necessity for "webs" of workers, teams that replace the old hierarchy.
3. A Concern for the Environment
   The need to save Mother Earth from continued ravaging will increase the need for environmental law as well as conscientious use of the earth's resources.
4. An Emphasis on Keeping Clients
   The knowledge that acquiring new clients costs ten times more than retaining established ones (plus the fact that future clients as *consumers* will expect more) will result in intense competition that centers on client service.
5. An Older Society
   Over 76 million baby boomers will enter middle age in the next ten years, bringing a resurgence of age activism, social concerns, and increased emphasis on estate planning.
6. An Increased Dependence on Technology
   Few law firms will be able to survive without the increased and expert use of technology in all areas.
7. An Emphasis on the Person
   As high tech increases, so does the need for high touch. Self-serving will be out, and new work styles, new considerations, and new approaches—based on a genuine respect for the person—will be in.

SOURCE: Based on John Naisbitt and Patricia Aburdene, *Megatrends 2000: Ten New Directions for the 1990s* (New York: William Morrow and Company, 1990); and "What Areas Are Hot Now? The Answer All Depends . . ." *National Law Journal* (September 1990).

Physical Limitations. Available facilities and space may dictate options.

Technological Limitations. The firm may be unwilling or unable to make a long-term commitment to upgrading its technical resources or the technical skills of its staff.

Economic Limitations. Is the alternative affordable? The financial and human resource costs may be prohibitive.[19]

What Effects Will It Have?

After exploring the factors that might limit its acceptability, planners should then consider the effects of an alternative by picturing both a best-case scenario, and a worst-case scenario.

Is It Appropriate?

In selecting the best alternative, planners should ask if it is consistent with the organization's mission and goals. Should the alternative selected not be consistent with the overall direction of the organization, the plan may represent a side trip that impairs the organization's long-term effectiveness.

Implement the Plan

Once you have determined the alternative to be selected, you must then put the plan into action. To do so, consider these questions:

- What needs to be done?
- Who will do it?
- What time frame will we establish?
- What specific results do we hope for?

When you and the others involved in the process have agreed on the answers, you are ready to activate the plan.

Evaluate the Results

You must not overlook this important final step: the need to evaluate the plan. When you establish the timing for your plan, you should schedule in periodic evaluation as a critical part of the planning process. Do not wait to evaluate only at the end. Performing evaluations along the way will provide you with the feedback you need to adjust your plan. A final and decisive assessment will then reveal whether or not you have reached your objectives. Figure 2–7 summarizes the steps in the planning process.

Avoiding Failure

The possibility of failure haunts every planning process. Organization members may not understand the steps involved in the process, or they may collect data insufficient to formulate a workable plan. The organization may confuse financial projections with planning or, in starting formal planning, may undertake too much at once. The lion's share of blame often falls on management. Managers may not understand the overall nature of the planning process; they may fail to become involved in the process; or management may simply fail to use the plans that the process produces.[20] The Another Look that follows offers eight suggestions for law firms undertaking the planning process.

FIGURE 2–7
Steps in the Planning Process

Step 1
Assess the Organization's Present State.
1. Strengths and weaknesses
2. Opportunities and threats
3. Current environment

Step 2
Set Goals and Objectives.
1. Who do we want to be?
2. Where do we want to go?
3. What do we want to do?

Step 3
Identify Alternatives. What available options will help us meet these goals?

Step 4
Choose the Best Alternative. Is the plan:
1. Challenging enough?
2. Realistic enough?
3. Complete enough?
4. Consistent with organization's mission and goals?

Step 5
Implement the Plan.
1. What needs to be done?
2. Who will do it?
3. When?
4. What specific results do we hope for?

Step 6
Evaluate.
1. What has been effective?
2. What do we need to correct?
3. What changes should we make?
4. What opportunities can we build on?

Law firms first need to decide what they are, who they are and where they want to go, says Blane R. Prescott of Hildebrandt Inc., a New Jersey-based management consultant firm for attorneys.

The buzz-words in that area are "long-range planning" and "strategic planning." But there are problems there, too.

"A lot of firms have never done any long-range planning, and don't know how to plot a course for their future and pursue plans that will really benefit them. They end up with wish lists instead of plans," says Mr. Prescott, who works out of Hildebrandt's Walnut Creek office.

He lists eight rules firms should consider before launching a strategic plan or long-range planning project:

- Avoid lofty goals such as becoming the best firm in the city or state. "You can't measure them and there is no way of knowing when you achieve them. Goals need to be realistic," he says.
- Choose goals that can be measured through achievement.
- Make sure the goals are client-driven. For instance, a firm says it wants to get into environmental law without considering its clients' need in that area. "A firm needs to make a proactive effort to solicit opinions from its clients. Ask them what is going to happen to their business, other practice areas they need, other areas of legal expertise they will require. You'll find that most businesses are used to doing some form of long-range planning and are very receptive about being asked about them."
- Do not overlook the need to improve just the quality of your services. The most successful firms in the 1990s will be the ones known for delivering high quality work that is cost-effective, according to Mr. Prescott. Long-range planning should include putting new procedures in place that benefit the client.
- Make realistic financial projections, but not beyond five years. "Firms too frequently make the mistake of assuming they will continue to grow at a rapid rate without realizing that if they do, the profits are going to fall—because they're going to have to make more people partners. Firms should determine what changes need to be made right now so they can maintain profitability three and four years down the road," he says.
- Assess the impact of losing a major client. The top 10 clients generate anywhere from 25 to 35 percent of most firms' revenues, he says. The firms should consider what could happen, where they would put their attorneys, and whether they are over-dependent in one practice area.
- Ask for associates' input. "They're the ones most affected by long-range plans. Involve them in the process if for no reason other than psychological. If you go to your associates and say, 'Here's our long-range plan,' I guarantee they will be upset," he warns.
- Develop a timetable. A lot of firms go off on a planning retreat and set a bunch of goals, he notes, only to repeat the process the next year. They fail to assign responsibilities or set a timetable. He suggests at least setting a date for the management committee to make recommendations.

The KISS (Keep It Simple, Stupid) method is the polestar for writing a long-range plan, says Mr. Prescott. "You see a lot of firms coming up with a 100-page book that sits on the shelf and nobody knows what to do with it. The best long-range plans are around five pages, with particular people assigned responsibilities."

SOURCE: Lowell Forte, "Eight Rules That Firms Should Keep in Mind," *California Law Business* (2 April 1990): 20. Reprinted with permission of *California Law Business*.

ANOTHER LOOK

Eight Rules That Firms Should Keep in Mind

1. Which of these eight rules would be easiest to implement? Most difficult?
2. Formulate three to five rules for dealing with law firm plans that are already underway.
3. In terms of plan evaluations, comment on the following statement: "If it's not broken, don't fix it." Should a law firm ever establish a cutoff point for evaluating its plans? Why? Why not?

THE NATURE OF DECISIONS

Definition

A **decision** is a choice made from two or more considered alternatives, even alternatives as simple as those involved in deciding whether or not to decide. Decisions are the basic unit of all organizational activity. Everything an organization member does is the result of some form of decision. Herbert Simon, who received a Nobel Prize for his work on decision making, believes that a manager's job is synonymous with decision making.[21] Decisions permeate every managerial task, from deciding which paralegal will handle a new case to deciding what to write on staff evaluations. Indeed, decisions are an integral part of every job in the law firm. Just as love is said to make the world go round, decisions fuel and drive the organization.

Basic Managerial Activity

Within an organization, decisions are not limited to the planning function. Managerial decisions are part of all basic managerial areas: organizing, directing, and controlling as well as planning. Managers are responsible for making decisions on whatever falls within their responsibility. Peter Drucker explains that "the end products of managers' works are decisions and actions."[22] Decision making is the most important recurring responsibility within a law firm. Even in our personal lives, we constantly need to make decisions. Choices occur on a regular basis, from selecting items off a restaurant menu to making decisions on lifetime commitments. In making a decision, we choose from the options available to us in order to resolve the issues confronting us. Making a choice can result in far-reaching or even irrevocable consequences.[23] To make a good decision—as managers, as other organization members, or simply as people—we must think of its potential results. We must consider its possible consequences and the commitments it might entail, particularly when others are involved. When accountability is likely to be high, being skilled at decision making is an enviable talent.

Significance Level

The significance level of any decision, depends on three factors: first, the number of organization members it will affect; second, its costs in terms of money, time and energy, and key personnel; and third, its projected long-term effects on the organization. Some experts suggest three additional factors: the amount of time a decision takes to make, the proportion of the organization that it will affect, and the organizational functions on which it focuses.[24] Law firm personnel, particularly higher-level managers must be "able to shoulder accountability for a range of decisions that must be made on behalf of the firm." They need to decide, for example, what changes are necessary in the firm's practice areas and in its computer software, what health benefit packages to offer, and how to allot secretarial and support staff services.[25] However, although upper-level managers must be able to assume calculated risks and drive the decision-making process, middle managers and supervisory managers also are accountable for decisions, even though their decisions affect fewer people directly, are not as costly, and have less impact on the organization as a whole. Members at any level who understand and master decision making are the keys to an effectively run law firm.

STEPS IN THE DECISION PROCESS

There are seven steps in making effective decisions: (1) looking at the goals of the organization, (2) identifying the problems, (3) asking the right questions, (4) considering the consequences, (5) making the decision, (6) implementing the decision, and (7) evaluating the decision. We will examine these steps more closely in the following paragraphs.

Peter Kehoe has been executive director of administration for the law firm of Robinson, Donovan, Madden and Barry, P.C., since 1988. Mr. Kehoe previously served as chief of USAF Airman Personnel Programs, retiring as a colonel in 1979. He then became director of administration for Booze, Allen and Hamilton, an Atlanta-based consulting firm, before developing his interests in the area of law office management.

FOCUS FROM THE FIELD

Peter Kehoe: One Key Point— Our Responsibility of Service to the Client

Is decision making easier or harder in a law firm?

It's no different in terms of management concepts. Decision making is a process that must be implemented in any organization. Decision making is a follow-up to problem solving. In the law firm environment, the kind of persons that you're dealing with bring an awful lot of credentials to the table, whether it's the managing partner or the committee chair. They supply part of the process that makes the job much easier for people in my position. Too many times we forget that there are different levels of decision making. Those various levels must be considered as part of the overall management scheme. My firm's built-in executive decision-making process is in the form of the executive committee. This committee is comprised of three senior attorneys whom I work with to resolve many policy issues. It's our responsibility to ensure that the proper decisions are made.

Are there any special barriers or restraints to effective decision making in law firms?

There are certain tradeoffs. In a few offices, you find that you have several people who have equal say in the operation of the firm. By working closely through the executive committee process, there is very little controversy. Through communication and explanation of where we want to go as a firm, it's very easy to make sure that everyone has input.

In what kinds of decision making can you involve other members of the firm?

For example, we're in the throes of a marketing effort. Marketing is fairly new to the legal environment. As you establish certain elements of a marketing program, you realize that marketing is every attorney's responsibility. For that matter, it's the responsibility of every employee of the firm to assure that we not only have the proper perception of the community and of what we stand for but also that the community knows what our responsibilities are to it. The feeling that we have as a law firm is that it is everyone's responsibility to be involved in the day-to-day activities in terms of making it a better place to work.

What do you think are the most common reasons for poor decisions?

I would go back to the process itself. We don't take enough time doing our homework. You want to gather the facts relating to a particular subject and be in a position to do some analysis before the decision is presented to the policymakers.

Can someone learn effective decision making?

I come from a school of thought where you must realize that all the elements of management have to be addressed. I encourage all people to take at least the basic courses in management, where subjects like decision-making will be addressed. When you come into the legal environment, you can't overlook the fact that a law firm is a business. You must become knowledgeable of the managing process so that it becomes part of your management style. People like Ellen Bump, our paralegal

> coordinator, have done it right. In terms of their first love, they've decided it's the law. But at the same time, they realize that there are other things that they can contribute to the firm, like management. I'm trying to make a contribution by articulating to our people how this firm, like any law firm, has a human side. It is operated on a day-to-day basis. All our people understand that our most important decisions are based on one key point: our responsibility of service to the client.

Looking at the Goals

In beginning the decision-making process, you establish parameters—usually the organization's goals—within which you must make the decision. This ensures that decision will be correct for the organization.

Identifying the Problem

Next, you need to clarify the need for a decision, determining what the problem is and distinguishing the problem from its symptoms.

The Problem

Knowing clearly what a problem represents is important. It is easy to underestimate the gravity of a problem. Management writer Chester Barnard has observed that managers usually become aware of organizational problems in three ways: through orders issued by their own supervisors, through situations that their subordinates bring to their attention, and through the performance of their regular activities.[26]

The Symptoms

Focusing on the symptoms of a problem rather than its cause is a common error. It is also a common mistake to confuse problems with their solutions. Members of a law firm often fail to see past the symptoms to the root of a problem. Managers, for instance, see turnover as a problem. Seeing turnover as the symptom of a greater problem, the effective manager asks the questions that will reveal the core of the trouble, such as why so many secretaries have left, why they take positions for less pay in other firms, why the remaining secretarial staff spends so much time complaining, and why they never seem to willingly put in overtime. That turnover is not the true problem is obvious, even to the untrained eye.

Asking the Right Questions

The next step involves asking the questions that will generate feasible potential solutions, all of which must be realistic. There are several possible sources for workable alternatives. First, experience is a good teacher. Here, the most experienced decision makers have an undeniable advantage, especially if they have dealt with similar issues in the past. Secondly, other organization members can provide information and insight. The decision maker, especially a managerial decision maker, may turn to many people, whether they are managers, respected workers, or other key individuals. Groups such as task forces and committees, particularly those whom the decision will affect, have the potential for providing workable solutions and alternatives. Lastly, decision makers can benefit from exchanges with outside sources, such as members in other organizations, professional contacts, associations, and professional literature. Any source of relevant knowledge will provide a foundation for more effective decisions.[27]

Considering the Consequences

In selecting among alternatives, you need to ask not only what alternative is good or what an alternative is worth, but what the consequences of an alternative will be. You should list your every available option and carefully consider any limitations that might weigh against its use.

Making the Decision

Only after evaluating all available alternatives should you actually make the decision. Though the preceding steps may take considerable time, the time involved is far less important than accurately processing the information that will lead to the decision. Mark McCormack, author of *What They Don't Teach You at Harvard Business School,* comments:

CHAPTER 2 / PLANNING AND DECISION MAKING

Managers in law firms of every size must make decisions on many of the same issues: What new office automation will benefit the firm? How much space will the firm need in three, five, or ten years? Who will have which office in the new space?

The firm's management group—regardless of its composition—must decide whether and how others will be involved in the decision-making process. The "group" may be the senior partner in a firm of three lawyers, the managing partner and the administrator in a firm of fifty lawyers, or a management or executive committee of five partners and the administrator in a firm of 500.

The question of involvement will arise whether it is a firm policy-making decision or a firm management decision. Should associates be involved in a decision about office location? Should staff be involved in technology decisions? There is no one "right" way to answer these questions. What works in one firm may not work in another. What makes a decision "right" is whether it accomplishes its intended goals and whether others in the firm accept it. If, according to these criteria, the decision is "wrong," the results are poorer future decisions and unnecessary friction and morale problems.

SOURCE: Carol F. Phillips, "Issues at Firms: Avoiding the Wrong Choices," *National Law Journal* (8 May, 1989): 23.

ANOTHER LOOK

Avoiding the Wrong Choices

---

1. As a manager in a law firm, how might you go about involving others in the decision-making process? What personal traits do you have that would make involving others especially easy or especially difficult?
2. Your firm is considering the purchase of one of several new computer software packages. Whose advice should receive more weight: that of an administrator who for years has overseen the costs of implementing automation or that of a new paralegal who happens to be a computer whiz?

The people I respect the most in business are all instant decision makers. They don't need to know every "knowable" fact first. They accept that they are going to make their share of wrong decisions and are self-confident enough to know that most of the time they are going to make the right one.... Facts are a decision maker's tools, but (1) they won't take the place of intuition, (2) they won't make the decision for you, and (3) they are only as useful as your ability to interpret them.[28]

You should not fear making intuitive decisions. Intuition—the sudden insight that imparts sense to problems that had seemed insurmountable—has been the most obvious cause of some great scientific discoveries, some extraordinary inventions, and some brilliant managerial decisions.[29] Moving from thought to action is what counts. One must know when to make the decision. The *imperfection of closure* often accompanies "moving" on a decision. A decision maker must accept the idea that he or she cannot always have all the data involved, all the appropriate people, or generate every possible alternative. Most managers know that the imperfection of closure is better than no decision at all. McCormack believes that competent decision making results from a manager's reliance on his or her intuitive good sense and an instinctive ability to foresee a decision's effects on the organization. The competent decision maker recognizes every decision, the small as well as the large, as important, although he or she cannot possibly put the same amount of time and information into making each one. However, no decision should be carelessly made, and managerial effectiveness consists of making the countless little decisions well so that the same focus and care are at work when the big ones come. Figure 2-8 describes activities typical of an effective decision maker.

Implementing the Decision

Having selected an alternative, you next need to bring it to life by implementing it. Implementing a decision involves three phases:

IN THE NEWS

How Strategic Management Works in the Law Firm*

Until recently a healthy, growing economy left room for many law firms to prosper alongside each other. A profitable market position was available not only to the national "megafirm," but also the regional mid-size firm and the smaller boutique or general practice firms. Yet, how many of us have recently heard stories of mid-size firms seeking mergers as an answer to their ills; smaller firms which have dissolved or are coming to grips with a declining client base and an aging partnership; and mega-firms concerned with falling profitability and their inability to compete for global corporations? Perhaps the economy has finally caught up with law firms, or law firms economics have finally caught up with the economy.

Changes in the environment outside the law firm, as well as changes to the very fabric of the law firm structure, can either pose a great threat to a firm's very existence or, for those firms who can think strategically, provide great opportunities. For instance, corporations faced with a tougher economic environment and resulting cost constraints are already bringing more routine work inside and are expanding significant resources developing law departments oriented to excellence, or at least oriented to decreasing the costs associated with outside counsel. These law departments are challenging increases to their outside counsel's hourly rates and developing procedures which can be expected to greatly limit value billing.

The search for the competitive edge is the central operating task of our time. Like other business entities, law firms compete to sell their services to individuals and corporations and to attract the necessary talent and resources. The Managing Partners and Executive Directors of the 1990s will have to change their primary focus from a concern with efficiencies and budgets to one focusing on innovation, adaptability to change, creativity, and implementation. They must become strategic thinkers and leaders of their firm's planning process. If not, it becomes questionable whether their firms will be able to sustain profitability or, in some cases, even survive.

Managing the External Forces through Strategy

The term "strategic management" (not to be confused with strategic *marketing*) is relatively new to law firms. Partners are currently grappling with the following strategic issues:

- *"Are these really the practice areas we should be into in the 1990s...?"*
- *"Profits are down... maybe we should divest ourselves of some of our branches... perhaps we should expand into other markets..."*
- *"Competitors are beating us hands down, not only with today's services, but with new services that seem to have caught on..."*
- *"The business has turned into a price war... clients just go to the lowest priced firm..."*
- *"I want to get some direction*

*SOURCE: Robert E. Berkow, National Director of Legal Consulting for Ernst & Young, "Law Firms Look to Strategic Management for Direction," *Briefing for Legal Management* (Winter 1990), no. 29000. Copyright © 1990 by Ernst & Young. Reprinted by permission.

- Deciding who to involve in the implementation
- Deciding when implementation should occur
- Determining how to communicate the decision to the organization.[30]

Passing the Test

Like the last steps in strategic planning, the last step of the decision-making process entails determining whether the chosen alternative will pass the test—that is, does it work? Evaluating your decision involves two phases: feedback intervals and predetermined final review.

Feedback

At predetermined intervals you must gather feedback to see if the effects of your decision are matching your

IN THE NEWS (continued)

into this outfit so everyone knows where we're going... We've got to stop fighting fires and get on with our future..."

In the past, a more competitive environment forced management to look to increased efficiencies as a substitute for declining revenues or margins. Though internal operating improvements benefit a firm, they are often *not sufficient to offset the impact of changes in outside factors*—there are only so many cuts to the library budget that can be sustained without affecting the quality of information available and only so many times automation costs can be postponed without affecting operating efficiencies.

Many managers "firefought" by reacting to outside factors, such as rent increases and the loss of significant clients, as they occurred. They often failed to react to change if the implications of that change were not clear. As they dealt with strategic issues, many of them did so in a random reactive sense—without an overall plan to focus energies on the most significant issues. Today, law firm management must learn to recognize and prepare for change before it occurs.

The Concept

The pace of change and the intensity of competition calls for strategic management throughout the organization. Planning and implementation, both in terms of tactics and strategies, must be guided in the most critical long-term direction and yet be synergistic with short-term needs. To assure the best chance of achieving strategic goals, three cultural conditions must be fulfilled:

1. There must be a *shared vision* of the organization's ultimate goals.
2. There must be a *common understanding* of the organization's resources, of its competitive environment, and of the strategies adopted.
3. There must be *across-the-board acceptance* of the direction and urgency of the organization's strategic and operating plans.

Unless all three conditions are met, resources will not be applied or managed properly and successful implementation will not take place.

The Process

The process of developing a strategic management framework moves through three phases:

1. *Strategy Foundation,* during which the shared vision and "Strategic Excellence Positions" are developed. These Strategic Excellence Positions are the factors that clearly differentiate your firm from the competition in a way that is appropriate to the market. This differentiation generally is based on the quality and/or scope, efficiency, or timeliness of services provided.
2. *Strategic Development,* during which objectives are established and quantified, and strategies are formulated.
3. And most importantly, *Implementation,* during which programs, action plans, and operating procedures are designed to focus efforts of management on putting the strategies into effect, to achieve the organization's goals.

Every law firm has a strategy; some articulated, some not, some well-conceived, some not. The best of these strategies are formulated in written plans which can be communicated clearly and concisely. They are built upon a foundation of comprehensive basic analysis, sound strategic principles, and responsiveness to the patterns of change occurring around the firm.

While all three stages of the process are important, strategic planning must place the greatest efforts on implementation and developing a strategic plan.

---

expectations and to see whether the decision is really solving the problem. If the decision is not achieving its intended results, you should reexamine each step in the decision-making process and either modify the decision or seek an entirely different solution.

Final Review

At some time during the decision-making process, you must evaluate your decision. This evaluation can be a part of any annual review or can take place at a specifically determined time. You need to ask if the decision has had the effect you intended. If it has, you have made the right decision. If it has not, one of the first questions you should ask is this: Have I correctly made use of the decision making process?

FIGURE 2-8
Tasks of Effective Decision Makers

> As much as possible, the effective decision maker:
> - Surveys a wide range of objectives to be fulfilled, acknowledging the multiplicity of values that are at stake;
> - Canvasses many alternative courses of action;
> - Intensively searches for new information relevant to the alternatives;
> - Assimilates and takes account of new information or expert judgments, even those that differ from the initially preferred course of action;
> - Reconsiders the positive and negative consequences of alternatives originally regarded as unacceptable before making a final choice;
> - Carefully examines the possible risks as well as the potential advantages of the preferred alternative; and
> - Makes detailed provisions for implementing and monitoring the chosen course of action and devises contingency plans that may be required should the original plan fail.

SOURCE: Irving L. Janis and L. Mann. *Decision Making: A Psychological Analysis of Conflict, Choice, and Commitment* (New York: The Free Press, 1977): 10–14.

FACTORS THAT INFLUENCE DECISION QUALITY

Many factors influence our ability to make good decisions. Law firm members can increase their potential for effective decision making by avoiding the cognitive traps into which decision makers subconsciously fall, by being wary of conformity and appreciating divergent thinking, by realizing the advantages or disadvantages of their positions within the organizational group and by encouraging creativity.

Cognitive Traps

Many quirks in our cognitive processes can result in poor decisions. Some of us can easily relate to these traps. They include our (1) **bounded rationality,** (2) our personal limitations, (3) our confidence in our own **intuition,** and (4) cognitive flaws such as **perceptual errors** and **faulty reasoning.**

Bounded Rationality

Of all the snares that can trap us as decision makers, bounded rationality affects us the most. Describing the most individual of our limitations, **bounded rationality** defines the set of personal limitations within which we process information in making decisions, tending to prefer simplified responses instead of the more complex. Bounded rationality restricts decision making in several critical ways:

- First, decision making is not always an easy process. People have to be motivated in order to root out all the alternatives needed for good decisions. This is generally easier when the decision maker is dissatisfied with present conditions; bounded rationality, however, encourages complacency. Because bounded rationality results in our being more comfortable staying within the security of the status quo, only serious discord and conflict are able to jolt us enough to consider the new and untried.
- Second, decision makers tend to use the information that is most convenient, often choosing what is least costly in terms of time, energy, and resources.
- Third, the search for alternatives strongly reflects the decision maker's own needs, beliefs, values, attitudes, experiences, and training.[31] The more limited these factors, the more limited the alternatives.

Personal Limitations

The personal limitations within which we make decisions have three dimensions. The first limiting factor is our emotional repertoire—our sensitivity to and understanding of a wide range of emotions. The second

TABLE 2-1
Decision-Making Tendencies According to Personality Type

Personality Type	Decision-Making Tendency
Cautious or Conservative	■ Will be hesitant and slow to move
Impulsive	■ Will rush to decide without adequate facts or input ■ Will make hasty and imprudent decisions
Perfectionist	■ Will be afraid of making mistakes ■ Will tend to seek the flawless solution
Rigid	■ Will be hesitant to seek or adapt to changes
Pessimistic	■ Will assume the worst ■ Will tend to see only hopeless situations
Poor Risk-Takers	■ Will find it difficult to move on decisions ■ Will "pocket veto" the decisions of others by setting them aside ■ Will ignore suggestions until it is too late or until interest has waned
Highly Intelligent and Well-Educated	■ Will be more likely to overcome flaws in decision making ■ Will be more likely to identify problems ■ Will be more likely than the less educated to make effective decisions
Power Hungry	■ Will be less apt to allow others to participate in the decision-making process ■ Will make decisions based on control and the manipulation of others
Political	■ Will attempt to please the most important power holders
Emotional	■ Will let personal issues cloud their judgment
Low Self-Esteem	■ Will be hesitant and insecure ■ Will tend to be indecisive ■ Will be interested in seeing which way the wind blows ■ Will be more motivated by ego-enhancement than by the desire to make effective decisions

SOURCE: Based on Andrew J. DuBrin, R. Duane Ireland, and J. Clifton Williams, *Management and Organization* (Cincinnati: South-Western Publishing Co., 1989): 102–03.

factor involves our unique blend of attitudes and values. The third consists of our intellectual abilities, such as the skill with which we handle cognitive complexities. **Cognitive complexity** refers to the ability to assimilate complicated information when making a decision.[32] People who can integrate complexity can comprehend more information simultaneously and from different perspectives. However, although this ability to process substantial amounts of information should lead to more effective decisions, as yet little research has studied this theory. Table 2–1 lists eleven personality types and the effects (positive as well as negative) that each type will have on decision making.

Intuition[33]

Intuition is the "knowing or coming to decisions without the conscious use of information or logic." It is "the ability to identify good decisions through gut feelings." Intuition has its place. A manager, for example, who has internalized the organization's goals can "handle uncomplicated problems quite easily from instinct." Although many successful people in organizations refer to gut feelings, these intuitive beliefs are often combinations of experience and insight. Hard facts are important, but "scientific techniques cannot replace a manager's intuition in making a final decision." On the other hand, intuition can often lead to poor decisions if the decisions are complex. Decision makers increase their risks as well as their need for luck when acting solely on intuition.

Perceptual Errors and Faulty Reasoning

Perceptual errors and faulty reasoning come in many forms. Common perceptual errors include emotional appeal and selective perception; faulty reasoning includes stereotypes and generalizations. Many mistakes stem from the erroneous information we develop from our inferences, illusions, and our limited ability to predict outcomes. Experienced decision makers don't need to be reminded how easy it is to reach the wrong conclusions. We all need to be constantly on the lookout for the errors that occur in our thinking processes. Such an increased concern for accurate and unbiased information results in better decisions.

Limitations within Organizations

Not every poor decision is the result of blundering into a cognitive trap. Organizational limitations may harm a decision as well. James March and Herbert Simon, management writers, describe an organization as "a choosing, decision-making, problem-solving organism that can do one or a few things at a time, and that can attend to only a small part of the information recorded in its memory and presented by the environment."[34] If this description is valid, we can more easily understand why people in a law firm may make decisions based on limited information, inferences, speculation, and guesswork when information becomes scarce, costly to obtain, or seemingly incomprehensible or unpredictable.[35] Decision makers are only human, and their decisions are only as good as the resources—personal and organizational—available to them. The concept of bounded rationality reminds us of that.

Divergent Thinking

A decision-making factor far more positive than cognitive traps, **divergent thinking** is the ability to think in ways that deviate from the norm or from previously expressed or commonplace ideas. All of us have experienced group pressure and the results of differing from the majority. But, as management writer Harold Leavitt notes, "The fact that we have encountered it often doesn't make the pain and pressure any less. In fact, our experience has taught this so well that we can foretell early in the process what we will be in for if we buck the group." No one welcomes rejection, which is, despite our society's assertions to the contrary, a typical response to individuality and nonconformity.[36] Still, in organizations, diversity is more valuable than conformity.

> There is an old story at General Motors about Alfred Sloan. At a meeting with his key executives, Sloan proposed a controversial strategic decision. When asked for comments, each executive responded with supportive comments and praise. After announcing that they were all in apparent agreement, Sloan stated that they were not going to proceed with the decision. [Either his executives didn't know enough to point out potential downsides of the decision, or they were agreeing to avoid upsetting the boss and disrupting the cohesion of the group.] The decision was delayed until a debate could occur over the pros and cons.[37]

Group Factors

Just as personal factors may influence our decisions and divergent thinking can generate original alternatives, group factors can influence our approach to the decision-making process. These three characteristics most profoundly affect the decisions that a group's members—and, hence, the members of a law firm or any other organization—make: conformity, consensus, and disagreement.

Conformity

In many ways, society expects all of us to conform. **Conformity** is the attempt to maintain harmony in a group by expressing agreement with its opinions. American society claims it places a high value on nonconformity, praising rugged individualists and pioneers, but it is not at all unusual to pay the high price of non-acceptance or mistrust for nonconformity. Our society values getting along, especially with your bosses and colleagues, not the seeming trouble that nonconformity entails. Yet, managers should be suspicious of those who conform too easily and too willingly.

> People are often reluctant to report unpleasant facts, especially if they contradict the viewpoints of the boss . . . [You have to] do your own homework. Then keep in mind that many of the "facts" you read or may hear have filtered through various people trying to protect themselves, or sometimes, almost unconsciously, telling you what they think you want to hear. You have to make it clear in meetings that you're not going to shoot the messenger.[38]

Ben Heirs, author of *The Professional Decision Thinker,* asserts that "real debate between people with conflicting views is not just unavoidable, it is absolutely essential."[39] Decision makers who encourage diversity take risks. They also promote a decision-making process that utilizes the full scope of talent within the organization. Peter Drucker writes that the "understanding that underlies the right decision grows out of the clash and conflict of divergent opinions and out of the serious consideration of competing alternatives."[40] The job of the manager, he says, is "not to smooth over divergencies of opinion or to find acceptable compromises between opposing views . . . but rather to find a whole range of answers each of which will, if they are good ones, attract passionate support and, perhaps, equally strong opposition."[41] Most managers find it easier to foster and reward unanimity. Workers who comply are much more pleasant than those who don't. How does a manager become secure enough to encourage those who question and challenge? He or she must set the stage for forthright communications with all workers, with no glossing over issues. By advocating open discussions, by letting conflict surface, and by being flexible in selecting and adopting solutions, managers can create a climate where divergent thinking is not only allowed but appreciated and encouraged.

Consensus

Consensus is a form of decision making based on general agreement. Because it is a highly valued process in professional organizations, it is an important consideration for law firms. If the principal partners in particular are unaware of the value of consensus, the organizational structure can quickly deteriorate, even in the oldest and most established firms. Many who believe in participative management say that consensus is essential to decision making. Others say that governance by consensus equals governance by the least common denominator: if all areas of disagreement have been eliminated, the group must accept *what remains.* The area of agreement is often the narrow band in the middle, the snippet of argument that all can accept. By accepting only that which displeases no one, consensus ignores many effective solutions and possibilities. Consensus "merely requires the leader to find out what most people in the organization will accept."[42] In spite of these limitations, however, consensus is invaluable, particularly in law firms and other professional organizations. Consensual agreement is particularly "preferred for smaller, non-diversified, privately held firms" since "in more simple and stable markets" such firms may use consensus for most if not all of their decision making.[43] In law firms in general, the kind of partner-level decision making that comes about through consensus offers an obvious long-term advantage. However, consensus may not be as effective at other levels within the firm. It has been said that "in a large organization, 'good ideas have lots of foster parents, and the bad decisions produce lots of orphans.' Consensus, after all, is safer: The footprints are covered."[44]

Disagreement

In the decision-making process, moderate levels of conflict may help to increase interest and other productive behavior, encouraging participants in the process to obtain better information, to learn through discussing the decision with others, and to think systematically.[45] **Cognitive conflict** is a way to structure disagreement by encouraging different viewpoints and incorporating critical thinking into organizational decisions, especially those that involve the different ways in which people interpret problems or decisions. Programming disagreement is now advocated as an effective decision-making technique. Agreement typically suggests that those in agreement are satisfied and secure. When carefully examined, agreement may only represent the path of least resistance, not a quality decision. Members of a firm who try to structure conflict into the decision-making process can be assured that the resulting decision has been challenged at the right time and in the right place.

Creativity

"Managers—at least, the good ones—are creative all the time," writes Robert Kaplan, a management writer who sees the manager's ability to recognize and define problems as a creative art:

> Managers exhibit creativity in the way they arrange and rearrange, collect and disperse information, ideas, tasks, and people. . . . Like the jazz musician, effective managers play variations within a larger thematic framework; they improvise in dealing with problems and people. Ineffective managers replay the same tune, use the same instrument, operate in a narrow band, mentally and interpersonally.[46]

Creativity is a valuable planning and decision-making tool. What is creativity? Creativity is the ability to combine realities in new, appropriate, and inventive ways. Being innovative takes time and energy, and law firm members who are creative realize that creative contributions entail risks and anxiety. Creative ideas take preparation and time. They require an incubation period within an organization before they can emerge and gain acceptance. In order to be effective, creative ideas need to be accompanied by realistic insight.[47]

Myths about Creativity

There are many misconceptions about creative individuals in general. John Keil, in *The Creative Mystique: How to Manage It, Nurture It, and Make It Pay*, addresses some of the myths about creativity. Some people, he writes, erroneously believe that "creative people are sophisticated and worldly. They're cultured, well-read, and snobbish." Research shows that creative people are simply more curious than most individuals. Creative people are thought to be more intelligent than others, but researchers have found this to be untrue. The creative easily give the impression of great intelligence because of their wide interests and innate curiosity. Creative individuals are commonly thought to be disorganized. Researchers disagree: "One of the secrets of being a successful creative person is being able to organize one's thoughts." The creative are sometimes thought to be witty and seldom boring. Researchers on creativity remind us that there are all kinds of bores, even creative ones![48]

Successful Decisions and Creativity

Recent studies link creativity to managerial effectiveness. "Successful business people approach their problems creatively" and are "able to take criticism and pressure." They are flexible, able to work in any setting they choose, under any conditions. They are able to juggle tasks and projects.[49] As managers, creative people can become totally immersed in expressing their inner visions. They know that "their chief challenge is to organize familiar materials in a fresh way. They are curious, adventurous, experimental, willing to take risks, and they are absorbed in meeting the challenges of their working day."[50] Creative law firm members generate richer options when seeking alternatives for problems. In making decisions, this is indispensable; creativity is highly desirable, and managers should seek ways to release creative tendencies in themselves and in their colleagues. The Another Look that follows offers suggestions for unleashing creativity.

INVOLVEMENT IN PLANNING AND DECISION MAKING

Who is responsible for planning? Who may participate in important decisions? Both processes, in various ways, allow every individual in the firm to be involved. From support staff to partners, each has a role to play. The best planning and decision making emerges from a collective process that involves workers at appropriate levels at the right times and stages:

> [Organizations often have] the wrong sets of people participate in particular planning activities. Planning requires not only generation of information for making decisions, but decision making itself. The kinds of decisions and types of data needed should dictate the choice of who is involved in what aspects of planning within an organization.[51]

While determining who actually makes decisions is not always easy in most organizations, in law practice settings, the answer has traditionally been simple: partners make the decisions. However, as law practices increase in size and complexity, this answer will change. Decision makers will obtain input from the firm's stakeholders if they want the firm to benefit from a well-managed planning and decision-making process. Those who employ participative decision making will not do so simply out of enlightenment but to ensure the most successful results.

Managers and other members at different levels of the firm play different roles in the planning process. Table 2–2 summarizes the planning roles of managers; we will more closely examine these roles and the decisional roles of others in the law firm in the sections that follow.

The Role of Upper-Level Management

Top management—partners, owners, directors—should be most involved in planning and decision making for the entire organization. Planning for the organization's most critical decisions occurs at this level. Upper-level management is responsible for the policies and practices that shape the law firm's future. Plans of this nature are strategic, since they represent the firm's approach to the challenges that lie ahead. Top management always has the final responsibility for planning decisions. The more critical the planning is to the future of the organization, the more important it is that top management become closely involved. Those at the

1. Being Right. We learn that there's only one right answer, but the creative person knows there are often many right ways of doing and being. Look for plural answers.
2. Logic. Are logical thinking and critical thinking the same? Logic is valuable for decisions, but why should the best answers always need to be logical? Sometimes they are those that defy simple explanations. Too much logic can be a trap that short-circuits your thinking processes.
3. Rules. Following the rules leads to the straight and narrow, and may lead to a dead end as well. Creative people learn how to break out of expected patterns, asking why as well as why not.
4. Practicality. Sensible ideas aren't always the most serviceable and useful. Ask "What if" questions, break out of the tedious and humdrum, and try to find new and sometimes seemingly impractical stepping stones to new ways.
5. Fuzziness. The ambiguity of fuzzy thinking often is seen as a source of problems. Clear thinking and accurate communications help avoid conflict and confusion. But ambiguity can stimulate your imagination, forcing you to look at more than one meaning, more than one way, more than one answer.
6. Mistakes. You'll never make mistakes if you never try anything new. If you never risk, you never grow. Errors can be used as stepping stones. Our greatest failures can be used to help us start completely from scratch.
7. Play. Why not? Life should have moments of freedom to be and to experiment and to enjoy. We can play around with a new thought, toy with a new idea, have a little fun with a new approach. Play helps us look at life not just as win/lose, but win-some, lose-some, and start a new game.
8. Limits. Specialization is the basis of our careers. We are taught to avoid being "jack of all trades and master of none." One-track minds can result from too much specialization, though, as valuable as it is for success. We must learn to go outside our own territories. Hunt for new ideas by making excursions and exploring new territory. Widen your boundaries.
9. Foolishness. Who wants to look foolish? But foolishness can release us from our ego needs and our pompous ways, can help us look at life in silly but new ways, and can stimulate our creative juices.
10. Definitions. We limit ourselves by our self-concepts. Learn to define yourself as willing to risk new ways of being you. Think of yourself as alive and creative. Thinking helps make it so.

ANOTHER LOOK

Releasing the Power of Creativity

SOURCE: These techniques were originally described by Roger Van Oech in *A Whack on the Side of the Head* (New York: Warner Books, 1983). This presentation is based on the work of Roy J. Lewicki, Donald D. Bowen, Douglas T. Hall, and Francine S. Hall in *Experiences in Management and Organizational Behavior,* 3d ed. (New York: John Wiley & Sons, 1988): 96–97. Used by permission.

1. What triggers your creativity? Describe the time of day, environment, and situations that are likely to make you feel creative.
2. Would the time and situations you described in question 1 apply to a law office or other work setting? Why? Why not?
3. Using the ten-item list of suggestions, how would you go about releasing creativity in others? Describe one or two specific techniques you might try.

top are responsible for asking these important questions:

- What direction should the organization be taking?
- What direction is it presently taking?
- What forces might affect its present direction? and
- Is the direction appropriate?[52]

TABLE 2–2
Management Functions in the Planning Process

Level and Responsibility	Time	Scope	Planning Functions
Top Management ■ Managing Partners ■ Owners	Long-Range	Broad	1. Formulate strategies 2. Set policies 3. Allocate resources 4. Set long-term goals
Middle Management ■ All Attorneys ■ Associates ■ Departments or Divisions	Long & Mid-Range	Medium	1. Assist with strategic implementation 2. Set supportive policies, procedures, and budgets 3. Allocate and utilize resources
Low/Supervisory Management ■ Departments ■ Supportive Staff	Short-Term	Narrow	1. Set guidelines for work schedules 2. Allocate and utilize resources 3. Implement policies, procedures, and budgets

Those at the top are also responsible for encouraging positive organizational attitudes and commitment. If a law firm's staff does not validate planning by taking it seriously or fails to consider planning an activity vitally important to the organization's future, planning is bound to result in wasted time, misspent energy, and demoralization. Plans that receive lip service rather than respect and resources are doomed to failure.

The Role of Middle Management

Middle management is responsible for making decisions related to shorter-range goals and for offering and obtaining input on strategic plans to be approved by top management. Law firms have led the way in team management by forming partners into management committees that report to the full partnership. This format lends itself well to the planning function. Middle managers often can effectively utilize planning committees as part of a team approach to management.

The Role of Supervisory Management

Lower-level management develops plans for shorter-term objectives. These plans usually involve current operational needs and often reflect current budgetary allocations.

Participative Management

Current management thought stresses the need to involve in decision making those whom plans and decisions will affect. This practice has three advantages. First, it encourages and rewards involvement. Second, it emphasizes the importance of each individual in the organization. Third, it creates a healthier organization. Most decisions, including deciding who should be involved in the decision-making process, are made at the managerial level. Those at the top may have status and prestige, but results depend on those at all levels, even at the bottom.

How do managers set the stage for involving workers? Rosabeth Moss Kanter, well known for her perceptive views on management, makes this suggestion:

> [Starting with] local issues for specific, smaller groups makes the most sense. People might feel uninformed about macro-issues and thus threatened by having their opinions solicited. Or they might feel that one voice doesn't matter anyway. But when it comes to local issues, people can talk from their own experience, respond from their own needs. People are always experts on what touches them personally.

Besides, she claims, "actual involvement in a decision-making process on the job (obtaining and processing information, evaluating outcomes, defining action strategies) tends to teach people to articulate

TABLE 2-3
Advantages and Disadvantages of Group Decision Making

Advantages	**Disadvantages**
Time well spent; greater hold on alternatives and consequences	Time wasted; antipathy for members of the group and for the decision-making group process
Greater amount of information	Conflicting views
More approaches, insights	More confusion, opinions
Increased acceptance of outcomes; more interest and support for the task	Intensified battle lines, with hostility toward any outcome
Cohesiveness, team-building	Conformity, social pressures
Acceptance of different views; appreciation for divergence	Nonacceptance of divergent thinking
Positive long-term investment of time, featuring ownership of and commitment to results; fewer communication problems during implementation	Loss of time; a rush to produce solutions that leaves members feeling manipulated
Participation by mature professionals who honestly seek to contribute accurate information as well as their best judgment, creativity, commitment, and collaborative efforts	Control by individuals with personal political agendas who use subversive efforts, intimidation, emotional manipulation, self-serving statements, and nonrefutable "expertise"
Stimulation of ideas and interest	Power plays and growing tensions
Reinforcement of teamwork and group efforts	Reinforcement of interpersonal conflicts and antipathies that overflow into the work site

corporate goals."[53] Effective managers take **stakeholders**—all those who have a legitimate personal interest in the success of a company—into account.[54] Research emphasizes the close positive relationship between participation and commitment. In fact, as you have probably discovered, a worker who no longer senses that he or she makes a difference becomes alienated. Managers in law firms who are convinced of the client-driven nature of the organization recognize stakeholders as one of the elements most essential to the firm's success: *Every single product of the firm depends on the involvement of each of its members and his or her commitment to quality results.* Everyone, from the newest secretary, receptionist, or word processor to the most senior partner, affects how the firm reaches its goals. Managers who realize that decisions require commitment never take the compliance of lower-level members for granted. They know that their subordinates do not simply accept plans and decisions automatically. In a law firm, receptionists, secretaries, and other members of the support staff may structurally be at the bottom of the hierarchy, but they are generally closest to the consumer and the community. They are in an excellent position to observe problems and offer different viewpoints. Their involvement in decision making also frequently creates the commitment necessary for successful implementation.[55]

Involving others in decision making differs from individual decision making in that (1) the composition of the group will shape the outcomes, and (2) the dynamics of the group process, which include such factors as the group members' ability to communicate, the group's cohesiveness, and the forces that motivate the members, influence the decision process. But involving others, despite the unpredictability it adds to the process, holds many attractions. Several people will contribute more information than a single person, will represent a wider viewpoint and range of values, and will be more likely to commit themselves to a decision that they have helped to make. Table 2–3 summarizes the advantages and disadvantages of group involvement in decision making. The law office manager, especially, who realizes how much involving the organization's entire staff in any project would cost in terms of time and money, needs to be aware of the disadvantages and caveats of group decision making.

TECHNIQUES FOR GROUP INVOLVEMENT

There are many tools that law firm managers and members can use to improve the quality of their decisions. When involving members of the firm in the decision process is both appropriate and worthwhile, being at ease with these specialized techniques for group planning and decision making may prove invaluable. Though many sophisticated mathematical decision-making models are currently in vogue, there are also several approaches that law firm members can utilize, at any organizational level. They include (1) scenario building, (2) the Delphi method, (3) brainstorming, (4) nominal group technique, (5) the devil's advocate decision program, and (6) the dialectic decision method.

Scenario Building

Scenarios are projections of events that are likely to happen—or that may possibly happen—in the future. **Scenario building** involves painting a picture of what lies ahead. Forcing us to anticipate future events, alternative scenarios create in us a sense of results based on ''What if'' possibilities. There are computer programs that are helpful in developing contingency planning premises for finances and other quantifiable areas, as well as nonmathematical uses for scenario building that allow law firms to utilize their members' hypotheses about future conditions and how the organization will respond to such conditions. For example, a group that is participating in scenario building might attempt to answer questions such as ''What if paralegals were allowed to practice without attorney supervision?'' or ''What if non-attorney managers were full partners?''

Delphi Method

The **Delphi method** is a decision-making process that uses questionnaires to gather the written opinions of experts in a given field. Its name is derived from the ancient oracles of Apollo from the Greek city of Delphi, who were famous for their supposed ability to see the future. The contemporary Delphi method doesn't consult seers or oracles, but, by using the ideas of those who are considered experts, it helps organizations to predict what may lie ahead. Rand Corporation employees developed this technique as a way to obtain the collective wisdom, insights, and experiences of a large group of knowledgeable people. The objectivity of the written process encourages participants to respond fully and creatively, free from the usual restraints and pressures to conform characteristic of one-on-one or group interactions. The Delphi method is a highly structured tool that selects a group or panel of experts from both inside and outside the organization to give confidential answers to the same series of questions. Their answers, based on their perceptions of future happenings, are tabulated, and returned to all respondents, who may then provide additional input on the same questions, but only after seeing the opinions of the others. This process helps an organization to create a composite view of its future.

Steps in the Delphi Method

1. After clearly identifying the problem they wish to solve, decision makers within the law firm ask several experts to participate in the decision-making process. Each expert is asked to make a forecast on the topic in question.
2. The decision makers provide response sheets to each expert, who anonymously and independently provides answers, comments, and suggestions that center around an identical set of questions. The decision makers collect and study the responses.
3. The decision makers record, summarize, and reproduce all of the answers, comments, and suggestions and distribute copies of the summation to the same participants, who may then change or augment their original replies.
4. The participants, again in writing, evaluate and comment on the results of the first round of responses, and revise and adjust their own responses, if they believe it is valuable to do so.
5. The decision makers compile the replies generated in the preceding step and distribute a copy of these replies to each participant. The decision makers may repeat steps 4 and 5 until a clear consensus emerges or until they attain an acceptable level of agreement on the issues they are addressing.

CHAPTER 2 / PLANNING AND DECISION MAKING

The Advantages

The process is tenacious: decision makers ask, collect, sum up, return, and revise until they believe they have secured a common view.[56] This procedure can easily and creatively be adapted for the law setting. For example, a law firm might use the Delphi method to allow a select group within the firm to address certain issues without forcing the group's members to forfeit valuable time for other activities.

Brainstorming

Brainstorming is a decision-making technique that asks members of a group to generate as many ideas as they can on a given subject. Brainstorming sessions usually focus on specific problems or issues. Some topics are more suitable for the brainstorming technique than others—for example, the topics to be discussed at a professional retreat for paralegals, techniques for increasing support staff participation in client service, or methods for decreasing overtime expenses by 10 percent are all good brainstorming topics. Participants in the brainstorming process, who should receive the topics before they attend the brainstorming session, are instructed to suggest as many solutions as possible. The group critiques only the most plausible alternatives.

Rules for Brainstorming

There are four basic rules for brainstorming sessions:

- No criticism of any idea is allowed.
- Free association of ideas, the open expression of thoughts evoked by ideas already expressed, is encouraged. The more original and unique the ideas are, the better.
- The more ideas the participants can produce, the stronger their chances of producing a feasible alternative.
- Mental ''hitchhiking'' or ''piggybacking'' is encouraged, so that participants will build on one another's ideas, thereby generating more extensive and complex solutions.[57]

Buzz Sessions

Buzz sessions are brainstorming sessions usually involving larger groups that subdivide, brainstorm, and report their ideas back to the larger group. Like smaller-group brainstorming sessions, buzz sessions provide an easy way to generate new ideas and to involve participants in a nonthreatening group process. Although critics of the processes point out that group dynamics and pressures still operate during the sessions, such pressures do not seem to impair the quality—or the quantity—of ideas that brainstorming and buzz sessions produce.

Nominal Group Technique

Nominal group technique is a very effective decision-making tool. Because the participants in the process do much of their work individually, the group they comprise is nominal—that is, a group in name only. **Nominal group technique** obtains individual input as well as a group response on a particular topic from the same set of people. The nominal group process largely bypasses the political issues and pressures common in groups. It is similar to brainstorming in that NGT participants form a group to collect the solutions they arrive at individually. But it is like the Delphi technique in that NGT protects its participants from group biases, particularly at the beginning.[58]

Steps for Nominal Group Technique

Before the NGT process begins, participants, who are assigned to groups of no more than seven members, are presented with the issues to be discussed and receive directions and materials for recording their responses. The group selects a facilitator who is responsible for seeing (1) that the group follows the ground rules and (2) that all responses of the participants are recorded on a flip chart or an another easily visible device. The procedure is as follows:

1. The facilitator presents to the group the question or problem to be addressed and after the members clearly understand it, each writes a minimum of three possible solutions. This is done silently and may even be done before the group convenes.
2. The facilitator requests one idea at a time from each member and records each on the flip chart so that all can see. At this step, the facilitator enforces three ground rules:

   - No discussion is allowed.
   - Questions about any entry will be answered only at the end of the process.
   - Repeated ideas may be combined, but only if they are absolutely identical.

3. After all the ideas have been presented and recorded, the facilitator leads the group in a discussion to see if any idea requires clarification. At

this point, the group may combine similar ideas, but only with the approval of the original contributors. Each idea then receives a number, which leads to the next step.
4. The facilitator asks the group members to silently and independently rank the top five ideas, awarding a score of 5 to the idea they value most highly, a score of 4 to the next, and so on. Although the members generally rank five ideas, the number may vary according to the amount of time available.
5. After asking each member to read his or her rankings out loud, the facilitator records the rankings on the chart, next to each idea being considered.
6. The facilitator leads the group in an additional discussion on the top-ranking ideas, asking for comments, questions, and additional clarification.
7. The members again rank the ideas, selecting the three that they consider most valuable. The facilitator again tallies the rankings and the final group result is ready to be shared.

The Advantages

Nominal group technique provides an effective tool for gathering creative input—for example, for assessing the ideas of a top management group preparing a partners' retreat. It can also be used by departments, committees, support staff groups, or any other teams who need a process that leads to independent views and the full participation of their members. Though the nominal group technique works for groups of all sizes, it works best when the number of participants is limited to approximately seven. It can be used by larger groups if the facilitator can allow time for members' comments and questions and can tally rankings and process results efficiently.

Devil's Advocate Decision Program

The term devil's advocate dates back to medieval times when, in the course of church hearings for the canonization of a saint, a member of the clergy was assigned the role of official protagonist. During the proceedings, this "devil's advocate" attempted to uncover reasons for denying the candidate's canonization. A contemporary **devil's advocate decision program (DADP)** builds programmed conflict into the decision-making process by assigning one or more members of the group the task of pointing out all the weaknesses of a proposed solution to a problem.

The Procedure

The technique is simple:

1. The group proposes a course of action.
2. A devil's advocate (individual or group) is assigned to criticize the proposal; all participants must know that the role is legitimate and welcomed.
3. The devil's advocate presents an ongoing critique to the key decision makers.
4. The decision makers gather any additional information relevant to the issues.
5. The group adopts, modifies, or discontinues the proposed course of action.
6. The group monitors its decision.

The Advantages

The devil's advocate procedure is designed "to identify potential pitfalls and problems with a proposed course of action."[59] Using this strategy legitimizes divergent thinking and acknowledges the value of constructive disagreement.

The Dialectic Decision Method

Another process that helps groups to program conflict into the decision-making process is the dialectic decision method. The dialectic method, which traces its roots to the works of Plato and Aristotle, is based on the principle that every idea or event (called a thesis) has an opposite, called an antithesis. When using the **dialectic decision method,** decision makers propose a plan that allows advocates of different points of view to propose and discuss assumptions in support of their ideas. This process is well suited for the adversarial style of lawyering.

The Procedure

This process involves the following steps:

1. The decision-making group proposes a course of action.
2. The group identifies assumptions underlying the proposal.
3. Members generate a counterproposal based on opposite assumptions.
4. Advocates of each position present and debate the merits of their proposal before the group's key decision makers.

5. The group decides either to adopt one of the positions or to discuss another option, e.g., a compromise.
6. The group monitors its decision.[60]

The Advantages

While this last technique requires more individual expertise in debating styles and may dampen spontaneity, it can provide a disciplined structure for attacking decisions and coming up with results that are well thought out. Utilizing the method can be as simple as encouraging group members to poke holes in an idea or suggestion.

BARRIERS TO PLANNING AND DECISION MAKING

There are many barriers to effective planning and decision making, all well known to practicing managers and other members of law firms. The most common obstacle to planning, and the one with which we sympathize the most, is lack of time. Day-to-day pressures sap the energies of planners, who find that, compared to daily crises, planning is not high on the priority list. In addition, planning is costly. It tends to use up valuable resources, a tendency that pushes planning even lower on the priority list. Planning can also be hindered by external forces well beyond the control of even the most competent organization member. The economy, for example, is well beyond the control of any one individual, yet it is a powerful dictator of plans and decisions. Many organizations would prefer to believe that they survive best by not disturbing the status quo, but this belief is no longer as acceptable for law firms as it was in the sixties and seventies, when many firms prospered despite little formal planning.

> Most law practices were growing rapidly due to expanding demand for legal services, high profit margins, and relative stability. Furthermore, the legal profession, trained in the common-law tradition of case-by-case analysis, was accustomed to reacting to the needs of clients rather than managing their own business, and therefore, philosophically alien to the notion of planning.[61]

This alienation to planning is now a luxury that most firms can ill afford. In addition to time restraints, daily pressures, and external forces, decision makers face two other obstacles, often of their own making: poor attitudes about planning and the fear of making mistakes.

Attitudes

Other barriers to planning and decision making stem from a fear of change and the costs involved in the process of change. To many organization members, change may seem annoying or even frightening. For decision makers, change conjures up images of political pressures, perpetual complainers, and saboteurs, as well as images of mountains of paperwork, new conflicts and anxieties, and an additional barrage of communications. Positive attitudes promote a healthier climate for change, a climate that is critical to effective planning and decision making. According to Ben Heirs, who has written often on effective decision making, managers are responsible for creating "an atmosphere in which people feel positively encouraged to think out loud, and in which the thoughts they express are welcomed, respected, and taken seriously, even if some of them are badly articulated, half-formed, or even half-baked."[62] Growing evidence suggests that "conflict and dissent are what organizations really need to succeed. Corporate decisions should be made after thoughtful consideration of counterpoints and criticism."[63] Top managers who disparage the diversity, creativity, and time usage that are essential to effective decision making will need to learn tolerance and to realize that those labeled as organizational troublemakers often contribute the most valuable ideas to the organization's decisions.

Action and Imperfection

One of "the major causes of unsuccessful outcomes is one that is very much under the leader's control: *Poor quality of the decision making procedures used either to arrive at a new policy or to reaffirm the existing policy.*"[64] But if you prefer to be realistic, you should appreciate the fact that sometimes a perfect decision is impossible:

> No book, expert, or test can be used to find the "truth" in decision making. Bad outcomes can occur no matter what steps are taken. The best that a decision maker can do is follow steps that increase the prospects of understanding foreseeable risks and prepare for possible bad outcomes.[65]

Members of a law firm need to be patient during planning and decision making, acknowledging the flaws inherent within all human processes as well as their own limitations and bounded rationality. Poor decision-making strategies arise all too frequently and spontaneously. Those at a partners' meeting may vote on an issue without sufficiently sharing their views. A managing partner, pigeonholed at the firm picnic by an employee seeking a scheduling change, may make a unilateral decision that undermines present policies. An administrator may rush ahead and decide to purchase computer equipment without consulting those who will use it.[66] The results of these decisions will testify to the poor quality of the decision-making processes that produced them. In the long run, however, making no decision can sometimes be worse than making a poor one. As a new manager or as a member of the firm at any level, whether you are beginning as a receptionist, a supervisor, an associate, or an administrator of an office or the entire firm, you should develop a positive attitude toward making decisions and toward making mistakes! Each experience offers you the potential for enrichment. You will learn that many difficult decisions must be made with such imperfect information and such little time that mistakes are inevitable. Only those who delude themselves about their culpability, those who are too cautious to grow and to learn, and those who are dead never make mistakes. You cannot accomplish planning and decision making without taking risks. To accept your mistakes, to take responsibility for them, and to continue to make honest and informed efforts are the best contributions that you, whether as a manager or as any other member of the organization, can make to your firm.

LAW FIRM RETREATS

One of the major planning tools used by larger law firms throughout the country is the retreat, where partners, as the critical decision makers of the firm, set aside time from their practice, select another setting or environment, and in that alternate setting focus on the topic or topics they consider to be of utmost importance. Joel Rose observes that "in the law office context, [the retreat] is an opportunity for attorneys (whether partners only or . . . partners and associates) to meet away from the office and daily pressures of business to review and discuss issues concerning the firm.''[67] Over the past few years, law firms that once used this format exclusively to address partner issues now use the retreat format to allow members of departments within the firm to address the issues that are important to them. Groups of paralegals, for instance, can schedule time to be spent off-site working on areas of special interest, such as a proposal for a paralegal policy manual. Teams of attorneys and support staff can also use this format to work together with a special consultant to develop firm-wide programs in marketing, for example. Most law practices have little in-house time to devote to special issues. Time availability is, if not nonexistent, usually complicated by many uncontrollable external factors, such as the requirements of the court system and the urgency of clients' needs.

> [Retreats that are] properly planned and conducted, are invaluable happenings which may produce new business strategies, commit the organization to cohesive goals and objectives, or simply improve communications. When poorly conceived or improperly run, retreats are at best costly, time-consuming exercises and at worst actually can be counterproductive.[68]

There are several considerations to keep in mind when planning a retreat. Those who plan the exercise must have a clear view as to the retreat's purpose; should involve the partners or other participants in pre-determining a well-focused agenda; should be well prepared, providing complete data packets in advance; should establish ground rules beforehand, in an effort to preclude potential problems; and, finally, should select a suitable retreat facility.

Purpose

Retreats allow law firms to engage in the critical planning sessions that are part of the ordinary workday scheduling of other businesses. There are many reasons why this format is effective for law firms. Since the work week allows firm members little time to address mutual issues in-depth, the retreat can offer many benefits, such as social activities that reinforce positive coalitions. The retreat format encourages the use of a law-firm strength: collaborative approaches to decision making. Recognizing that time allocations and pressures differ enormously for professionals within an organization, the retreat allows for full collaboration between the firm's most important decision makers. It can be a powerful team-building tool, allowing participants time to develop supportive relationships and stronger alliances, if all goes well.

Realistically, the retreat format also has a downside. The time that the participants spend together and the issues they select may create difficulties. First, there is always an issue of personalities and working relationships. If a retreat is not carefully conducted, previously uneasy relationships that lasted only because the parties basically ignored one another may explode into non-

- Firm governance
- Policy determination and implementation
- Staffing
- Organization and management of substantive practice areas
- Business development
- Client relations
- Automation of processes
- Financial management
- Fees and billing
- Training of associates and key administrative personnel
- Space requirements
- Branch office operations
- Firm growth or contraction
- Decisions on newer practice areas[71]

ANOTHER LOOK

Issues Worth Retreating For

1. Ask an attorney how his or her law firm has organized a retreat.
2. Look for opinions on the kinds of retreats and topics that work and the kinds that should be avoided.
3. What kinds of topics do you think are unsuitable for a retreat?

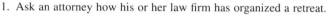

productive and unresolvable conflicts. Efforts to deal openly may so threaten participants with fragile egos that they leave the retreat resembling bundles of raw nerves. Second, time during the retreat must be well spent. Attorneys who have willingly given up the scarce time they ordinarily set aside for personal and family needs will not tolerate time-wasting.

Site Selection

Because the site selected for a retreat can influence its outcome, the selection should be carefully made. Off-site locations are preferable. During in-house retreats participants are prone to wander off to their offices or to other familiar haunts, particularly if discussions get heated up or become tiresome. Off-site locations allow the participants undisturbed time away from regular interruptions. Planners should choose facilities for their privacy and relatively quiet surroundings, for their good working arrangements, and for the availability of space that lends itself to easy communications. The ideal facility has an atmosphere conducive to positive feelings. It should help to make the retreat a rewarding and enjoyable experience for the participants, with as many amenities as the firm's budget and good sense allow!

Preparing the Agenda

To be "used as a forum for establishing goals, developing strategies, and addressing significant opportunities, problems, or concerns,"[69] the time spent at a retreat should be carefully allocated. All of the critical stakeholders must help to choose the topics for a retreat. Suitable areas include all long-term issues that require consensus, such as determining the firm's desired direction. Such issues would include decisions involving philosophy and goals, economic realities, financial data and management reports, governance issues, operational and practice management decisions, marketing, and practice development policies. Especially suitable for the retreat agenda are strategic planning areas, particularly those that concern growth, retrenchment, or maintaining the firm's present course. Other areas suitable for retreat planning might include space allocations, client services, general problems, and professional development, such as updating partners and associates on changes in the law. Correctly choosing agenda items for the retreat is critical. Planners should consult with senior participants, identify the issues to be studied, obtain input from all participants, confirm the agenda topic, and gather data on the topic, using questionnaires, if needed. While the final decision to include a topic falls to a retreat leader, whether that leader is senior partner, a consultant, or someone with special abilities in the particular area to be studied, the litmus test for an agenda item is determining whether or not "the particular issue requires discussion or decision by all attendees."[70] The above Another Look lists topics worthy of a retreat.

General Preparation[72]

Because retreats offer so much potential for planning and decision making, planners should spend considerable time and effort designing the retreat with the right members of the firm, surveying and getting feedback from members of the executive committee and other partners or participants whenever appropriate.

> The planners should review, tabulate and report on partners' comments and concerns to the executive committee to set an order of priority for those issues that will be discussed at the retreat. After selection of the subjects, the planners should draft a proposed agenda that will include dates and times for the meetings, locations, recommended retreat leaders and attendees. ... The proposed agenda should be discussed with the executive committee before distribution to the partners.[73]

Data Packets

The planners should prepare information packets containing background and financial data pertinent to the issues to be discussed, review these packets with the executive committee, and then distribute them to the retreat participants. Joel Rose advises giving participants a state-of-the-firm report that provides annual comparisons for practice area growth and contraction, revenues and expenses, lawyer and nonlawyer personnel ratios, equipment acquisitions, current space requirements, and the firm's success at business development.[74] Because the participants should not spend valuable group time doing what they can do individually in advance, they should receive their data packets well before the retreat. Schedules for events at the retreat should also be distributed in advance. Such schedules should include agenda topics; a schedule of activities for the entire retreat, listing times for arrival, formal meetings, presentations, meals, free time, and structured activities; and any other appropriate information, such as who to call with questions or complications when the best-laid plans go awry! The agenda should lead from general topics to more specific ones. For example, the participants should attend informational sessions and discuss broader conceptual issues before they discuss specific approaches for achieving results. In addition, the agenda should place neutral issues at the beginning of the retreat, saving any foreseeable hotly contested emotional issues for later.[75]

Ground Rules

Retreat planners are advised to establish and adhere to a set of ground rules, such as the list in Figure 2–9, which is based on ideas found in *Robert's Rules of Parliamentary Procedures.* Such rules, which should be established in advance in order to set expectations and limits for participants, may describe procedures for addressing sensitive issues (possibly through the use of a third party) or for smoothing communications among participants.

FIGURE 2–9
Ten Ground Rules for Law Firm Retreats

1. Set time limits for speakers.
2. Promote respect for and appreciation of divergent opinions.
3. Encourage the participants to admit and accept the right to disagree, thereby keeping the discussion orderly and calm.
4. Value disagreement as a contribution of honesty.
5. Stick to the agenda, limiting remarks to a current issue.
6. Never attack or belittle personalities, or allow any participant to do so.
7. Address the *issues* behind emotions and anger.
8. Provide for equal time, allowing those who haven't spoken to speak before someone who has already contributed speaks again.
9. Ensure that participants have equal opportunities to influence by allowing a speaker to address each question no more than twice, not counting brief comments or answers.
10. Encourage quieter participants by inviting them to speak, if others have dominated the discussion.

Potential Problems

Because of the intense interaction they promote, not all retreats are peaceful planning sessions. Some firms, as legal consultant Donald Akins observes, "have so many factions and frictions they are afraid to hold a retreat." Yet Akins believes that "when there are this many problems, it is only a matter of time before there is an explosion. A retreat could serve as a catalyst to addressing the real issues and improving lawyer relations."[76] In the energy of the retreat setting, all major or minor issues that have festered may break free like the swarm of evils from Pandora's box. Retreat planners need to be aware of this potential for conflict to be prepared to handle whatever conflicts arise. Unchecked, retreats can easily lead to nonproductive behavior and attitudes.

Hidden Agendas

Like any other group process, no matter how positive its potential outcomes might be, the retreat might elicit some negative behavior. Participants may have hidden agendas, using the retreat to sabotage firm members with whom they disagree, to push pet issues, or to belittle others as part of a power play or a personal vendetta. Others may dominate group discussions, causing uneven participation, creating frustration, and destroying group commitment. Problems may also arise if participants belittle the proceedings, telling the group that they are taking themselves too seriously, that there is not enough humor and too much gloom and pomposity, or that the discussion is focusing on negatives. Such comments are sometimes only efforts to subvert truly serious issues that represent an honest need to look realistically at negative data.

The Players

The key players in the firm must be present at the retreat. If they are not, the retreat process will be incomplete. However, some participants, legitimately or otherwise, may be unwilling to commit themselves to retreat plans, causing complications and delays.

Expectations

Some participants also may have unrealistic expectations, wanting miraculous results in return for the time they have invested in the retreat. (On the other hand, some participants may consider the retreat a perfect time for socializing.) A law firm cannot expect a retreat to solve all of its problems, especially those that have taken years to develop. Retreats cannot work miracles; they can simply help a firm to establish goals and directions for long-term ongoing processes. Consequently, the expectations of firm members should be realistic.

The Retreat Facilitator

Key planners should seriously consider who will moderate, lead, or facilitate group discussion at the retreat:

> Generally the senior or more influential partners ... may be elected to coordinate and serve as discussion leaders for specific topics during the retreat. They should be selected for leadership and communication skills, knowledge and insight about the firm, understanding and objectivity, and ability to generate and control discussions on specific topics.[77]

However, there may be advantages to selecting outside consultants for this role. Firms that appreciate the importance of retreats often ask a consultant to plan and conduct such activities. An experienced facilitator can bring a twofold benefit: an objectivity that remains clear even during heated discussions and an expertise in group dynamics, which may serve as a guide for honest and productive communications. An effective retreat facilitator can help to give members of the firm "an opportunity to review past performance, resolve current difficulties and plan for the future."[78]

QUESTIONS FOR DISCUSSION AND REVIEW

1. What distinguishes planning from decision making? Why is planning said to have primacy over the other three management functions?
2. Identify and explain the different types of plans. Give examples, based on a hypothetical law firm.
3. What are the qualifications and the characteristics of successful planners? What do you consider to be your strengths as a planner?
4. What distinguishes strategic planning from planning in general? Is one more important to the law firm than the other?
5. Explain the steps of the formal planning process.

Which step do you consider most important? Explain why.
6. What aspects of today's environment specifically affect law firms?
7. Some say planning is critical for a law firm's survival. Explain why you agree or disagree.
8. Think of a decision you have made recently and describe it in managerial terms.
9. Identify the steps in the decision-making process, commenting on the particular challenge each step might present to law firm management.
10. Discuss the importance of participative involvement in planning and decision making. Give examples that show when each of the following groups should be involved:
    a. Partners   d. Secretaries
    b. Associates   e. Support Staff
    c. Paralegals   f. Clients
11. Comment on the pros and cons of conformity and conflict in decision making. Which is the most beneficial to a law firm?
12. You are the paralegal coordinator of a large corporate law department. You believe the size of the organization presents a special challenge in terms of commitment and teamwork for the ten paralegals you supervise. What decision-making strategy would you use to explore this issue with them? Explain how it relates to your goals.
13. Outline the cognitive traps of decision making, using real life examples.
14. Identify one major issue facing law firms. Of the major decision-making techniques available to managers, which one do you think holds the most promise for involving others in the firm? Explain your choice.
15. Create a list of possible topics to be used as themes for a law firm retreat involving one of the following:
    a. Partners only
    b. Partners and associates
    c. Paralegals in a firm
    d. A team of attorneys, paralegals and appropriate support staff
    e. A corporate law department

    What elements are important in planning a law firm retreat? What role does site selection play? What aspects of this planning process do you believe to be most critical?

EXPERIENTIAL EXERCISES

I. Planning in the Law Firm

A. You are a member of an administrative team at Hubris, Hooper, and Happie, P.C. As a result of a decision made at an executive committee meeting this past week, you have all been asked to plan a one-day law firm retreat for the sixteen paralegals in the firm, to take place in six months. The suggested agenda is continuing professional development and evaluations, but the partners are also concerned that the time be spent to develop a spirit of teamwork as well.

1. How will you proceed with your plans?
2. What steps will you take to ensure a successful retreat? Prepare a time line.
3. Who will be involved at which steps in the planning process, and why?
4. Where will you hold the retreat? When? Why?
5. Suggest an agenda for the day.
6. What will you include in the data packet?

B. Your law firm has never used paralegals before. Over the years, it has added responsibilities to the work of its many secretaries, who have continued to learn and grow with the challenges. However, the firm, too, has grown. Its executive committee knows that you are not only interested in law office management but are also taking a course in the field. The committee suggests to you that you may be able to combine your knowledge of management with your beliefs about the value of paralegals to help the firm add a staff of paralegals. Using what you have learned in this chapter, describe the planning steps that would be necessary for adding this staff to the law firm.

CHAPTER 2 / PLANNING AND DECISION MAKING

C. The executive committee would like you to make a recommendation for one of the following:
a. Selecting a new computer system
b. Choosing a software program for timekeeping and billing
c. Improving the firm's filing systems
d. Updating and streamlining the firm's library system

II. Signs of the Times

You are paralegal coordinator for a ten-attorney firm, LaPlante, Waters, and Flourish, P.C., that specializes in real estate practice. You have been there ten years. Having seen its rapid growth in the past, you now see a dramatic drop. You know that this is a sign of the times, and that the economy has played havoc with your firm's practice. But you are still particularly concerned about the fifteen paralegals who work for you. You are facing serious retrenchment. What makes you more concerned is that, because the past years were so busy, you never developed an evaluation program for paralegals. There is no system in place. The executive committee has just asked you to develop one.

You are not sure where to begin. You know that your subordinates trust you and look to you for leadership. You understand their challenges, having begun as a paralegal yourself. Convinced that having them help develop the evaluation criteria and process with you will lead to better results, you prefer having them involved in the decision process.

1. The executive committee has just informed you that only ten paralegals will be needed for the next fiscal year. The managing partner is not fond of your wanting to involve the paralegals in establishing an evaluation system, believing that they should not be participating at this level of decision making. Convince Attorney LaPlante of the value of your idea by outlining for him and explaining to him how you will involve the paralegals in the decision-making process and how the firm will benefit from their involvement.
2. You have a meeting with your paralegal staff. Three of them do all the talking:
   a. Paralegal X: hardworking, dependable person who is very agreeable and backs up everything you say.
   b. Paralegal Y: an old-timer who has worked at the firm longer than you have, is not happy with life in general, has lost enthusiasm for the job, and who is negative and perhaps burned out.
   c. Paralegal Z: a newly hired rising star who is enthusiastic and eager to learn; a questioner, a thinker; not someone who "goes along to get along."

   When asked if they would be willing to work with you in developing the methods and criteria for the evaluation process, X says yes; Y says no; Z says maybe. Write a brief dialogue in which X, Y, and Z debate their positions.
3. Generate a list of the ten most important criteria for evaluating the performance of paralegals. With which criteria would X most strongly agree? Y? Z? With which would each disagree? Why?

III. How Creative Are You?*

In order to assess your own creative tendencies and preferences, complete the following exercise. After each statement, indicate the degree to which you agree or disagree by filling in the blank following each item based on this scale:

---

*Reprint by permission of the Putnam Publishing Group from "How Creative Are You?" by Eugene Raudsepp. Copyright © 1981 by Eugene Raudsepp.

A. If you strongly agree
B. If you agree
C. If you neither agree nor disagree, or simply don't know
D. If you strongly disagree
E. If you strongly disagree

Try to describe your attitudes and behaviors as accurately as possible.

1. I always work with a great deal of certainty that I'm following the correct procedures for solving a particular problem. ____
2. It would be a waste of time for me to ask questions if I had no hope of obtaining answers. ____
3. I feel that a logical, step-by-step method is best for solving problems. ____
4. I occasionally voice opinions in groups that seem to turn some people off. ____
5. I spend a great deal of time thinking about what others think of me. ____
6. I feel that I may have a special contribution to make to the world. ____
7. It is more important for me to do what I believe to be right than to try to win the approval of others. ____
8. People who seem uncertain about things lose my respect. ____
9. I am able to stick with difficult problems over extended periods of time. ____
10. On occasion I get overly enthusiastic about things. ____
11. I often get my best ideas when doing nothing in particular. ____
12. I rely on intuitive hunches and the feeling of "rightness" or "wrongness" when moving toward the solution of a problem. ____
13. When problem solving, I work faster when analyzing the problem and slower when synthesizing the information I've gathered. ____
14. I like hobbies that involve collecting things. ____
15. Daydreaming has provided the impetus for many of my more important projects. ____
16. If I had to choose, I would rather be a physician than an explorer. ____
17. I can get along more easily with people if we belong to about the same social and business class. ____
18. I have a high degree of aesthetic sensitivity. ____
19. Intuitive hunches are unreliable guides in problem solving. ____
20. I am much more interested in coming up with new ideas than I am in trying to sell them to others. ____
21. I tend to avoid situations in which I might feel inferior. ____
22. When I evaluate information, its source is more important to me than its content. ____
23. I like people who follow the rule "Business before pleasure." ____
24. Self-respect is much more important than the respect of others. ____
25. I feel that people who strive for perfection are unwise. ____
26. I like work in which I must influence others. ____

CHAPTER 2 / PLANNING AND DECISION MAKING

27. It is important for me to have a place for everything and everything in its place. _____
28. People who are willing to entertain "crackpot" ideas are impractical. _____
29. I enjoy fooling around with new ideas, even if there is no practical payoff. _____
30. When a certain approach to a problem doesn't work, I can quickly reorient my thinking. _____
31. I don't like to ask questions that show ignorance. _____
32. I am able to change my interests to pursue a job or career more easily than I can change a job to pursue my interests. _____
33. Inability to solve a problem is frequently due to asking the wrong questions. _____
34. I can frequently anticipate the solution to my problems. _____
35. It is a waste of time to analyze one's failures. _____
36. Only fuzzy thinkers resort to metaphors and analogies. _____
37. At times I have so enjoyed the ingenuity of a crook that I hoped he or she would go scot-free. _____
38. I frequently begin work on a problem that I can only dimly sense and not yet express. _____
39. I frequently forget things, such as names of people, streets, highways, small towns, etc. _____
40. I feel that hard work is the basic factor in success. _____
41. To be regarded as a good team member is important to me. _____
42. I know how to keep my inner impulses in check. _____
43. I am a thoroughly dependable and responsible person. _____
44. I resent things being uncertain and unpredictable. _____
45. I prefer to work with others in a team effort rather than alone. _____
46. The trouble with many people is that they take things too seriously. _____
47. I am frequently haunted by my problems and cannot let go of them. _____
48. I can easily give up immediate gain or comfort to reach the goals I have set. _____
49. If I were a college professor, I would rather teach factual courses than those involving theory. _____
50. I'm attracted to the mystery of life. _____

CHAPTER 3

Organizing and Organizations

LEARNING OBJECTIVES

After completing this chapter, you should be able to:

- Understand the importance of organizing and its four main activities;
- Describe the various kinds of organizational design;
- Identify the elements of control and coordination in organizing;
- Discuss the relationships among authority, delegation, and responsibility;
- Describe contemporary approaches to organizational design;
- Explore the elements and effects of organizational culture; and
- Identify characteristics of successful organizations of the 1990s.

Paul Morton, director of administration at the fifty-attorney law firm of Sherbourne, Powers & Needham in Boston, Massachusetts, has worked in legal administration for more than thirteen years. Mr. Morton initially managed a ten-attorney San Francisco firm while contemplating law school. He quickly discovered that he enjoyed the unique challenges of managing an organization as complex as a law firm. Mr. Morton has been an active member of the Association of Legal Administrators (ALA) for many years, serving as chapter president in Delaware and in Boston. Currently, Mr. Morton serves as education coordinator for ALA's Human Resources Section.

FOCUS FROM THE FIELD

Paul Morton: There Is No One Correct Organizational Design

How important is organizational structure to a law firm?

Organizational structure is extremely important to any law firm, regardless of size. As soon as a firm begins to define roles, it begins to establish an organizational structure. The delegation of responsibility within a law firm must be understood by all parties if a firm is to effectively meet the needs of its clients. A clear understanding of the organizational structure and its importance are really required to make the entity run effectively.

What changes are ahead for law firms in terms of organizational design?

It would depend, to a very large degree, on the size and personality of the firm. Across the board, we will continue to see the trend toward viewing the practice as a business. We will look for new ways to operate and expand our practices more effectively and efficiently. While in the 1980s we saw a heavier emphasis on the business side of practicing law, I think in the 1990s we will see a greater emphasis on some of the older values, including a focus on the quality of the service provided to the client. We will also see a new emphasis on quality-of-life issues, as attorneys strive to achieve a balance. These issues will be addressed by various management approaches. Law firms, and law firm management practices, evolve. Some are managed by dictators, others by a democratic committee approach. At various stages in their growth and development, firms will change from one approach to another, and often back again. There is no one correct organizational design for all firms; different styles are appropriate for different firms at different times. I doubt that we will see many truly new management styles; I do believe that we will see different firms trying alternative approaches to see what fits best.

What is the biggest challenge in the area of organization?

It has been said that managing lawyers is akin to herding cats. When you're dealing with individuals at all levels (professionals, staff, and management) who are extremely talented, bright, intellectual and demanding, it's a struggle to get them to work in a management structure which requires them to relinquish some independence. Keeping a group of attorneys focused on common goals, and pointing the firm in a given direction and keeping it there—as opposed to letting it evolve in a more haphazard manner—will be the biggest challenge.

How does the structure of law firms differ from other organizations?

Managing a group of professional service providers, whether they are doctors, lawyers or architects, is different from managing other types of organizations simply because of the product they offer—the talents of the staff. Lawyers are taught to question everything, to be aggressive and analytical. Many partners believe they have the right to question how everything in a firm is managed. While the basic organizational structure is not necessarily different (i.e., partnership, professional corporation), administrators often believe they have at least as many bosses as they have partners. Understanding this balance of power, and harnessing it within an organizational structure, is a critical challenge. Law firms have only recently become committed to being managed. This is the basic difference between law firms and other types of businesses, which have been managed since their inception.

What is the most important role that a law office manager or administrator should play?

The most important role an administrator can play is that of a leader, guide, counselor, and implementor. When an administrator is new to a firm, one of the most important things that should be done is to define the parameters of the position, to make sure that everyone understands what is expected. In many instances, much of the frustration administrators experience is caused by a disparity in expectations. Many attorneys do not understand the role of the administrator. The role can vary from firm to firm, and many people with the same title can have very different responsibilities. It's a wide-open spectrum. Ultimately, each administrator must develop his or her own style, and must ensure that his or her style is consistent with the style and goals of the firm.

Ours has become, for better or worse, a society of organizations. We are born in organizations and educated in organizations so that we can later work in organizations. At the same time, organizations can supply us and entertain us, they govern us and harass us (sometimes concurrently). Finally, we are buried by organizations. Yet aside from a small group of scholars called "organization theorists" who study them, and those managers inclined to look deeply into the subject of their management, few people really understand these strange collective beasts that so influence our daily lives.
(Henry Mintzberg, *Mintzberg on Management*)[1]

At first glance, hierarchy may be difficult to praise. Bureaucracy is a dirty word, even among bureaucrats, and in business, there is a widespread view that managerial hierarchy kills initiative, crushes creativity, and has therefore seen its day. Yet . . . properly structured, hierarchy can release energy and creativity, rationalize productivity, and actually improve morale.
(Elliot Jaques, "In Praise of Hierarchy")[2]

THE IMPORTANCE OF ORGANIZING

Organizing is the managerial activity that involves planning and deciding how to use resources to reach organizational goals. When performing this activity, managers choose the organizational structures that will provide the best use of resources and the most balanced relationships among tasks, activities, and people. In this chapter, we will examine the effects of how organizations are organized. We will look at members and their activities, and how they are arranged within an organization. In addition, we will examine the four activities that organizers use to divide the tasks, departmentalize the work, and coordinate and control the efforts of people within the organization. Ultimately, organizations are collections of people. The purposes, paths, and patterns of those individuals at work make up the organization. Workers need to be more than just present in the workplace; they need to share a common goal. Through their presence and their purposeful interactions, workers propel the organization in a common direction toward a desired destination. Organization theorist Saul Gellerman expresses the belief that "organization studies can be revealing exercises. After all, real organizations are not simply inanimate boxes on an organization chart; they consist of men and women with their own ambitions and vulnerabilities, and many of them have understandable tendencies to defend their own territories.''[3] Understanding basic concepts of organizations and organizing will help us to understand how this balance between personal ambition and organizational goals comes about. To organize, managers must first identify the activities that need to be performed. They must then identify the individuals and departments best suited to perform these activities, as well as the best methods of coordinating and controlling these tasks. Some definitions for organizing are seen below.

The following definitions provide four similar but subtly different glimpses at the concept of *organizing*:

> What managers do when they design, structure, and arrange the components of an organization's internal environment to facilitate attainment of organizational goals. (Dunham and Pierce)[4]
>
> The process of dividing work into manageable components and coordinating results to achieve a purpose. (Schermerhorn)[5]
>
> The process of defining the essential relationships among people, tasks, and activities in such a way that all the organization's resources are integrated and coordinated to accomplish its objectives effectively and efficiently. (Pearce and Robinson)[6]
>
> The formal structure of work ... Tasks must be assigned, so must responsibilities and authority; activities must be grouped together into departments and provision made for coordination. The extent and nature of delegation to different levels must be decided. The communications system must be devised. ... It must include the people who have to make the structure work as well as the formal structure itself. (Stewart)[7]

If we could accomplish what we wanted to without involving others—if workers were robots, for instance—organizing would be less challenging. But organizations exist to achieve what individuals cannot accomplish on their own. Although planning has primacy over all other managerial activities, organizing is the critical next step. Organizing activates plans, determining the mix between jobs and people and setting in motion activities essential to the organization's efforts to reach its goals effectively and efficiently. In the words of management writer Samuel Certo, ''Organizing creates and maintains relationships between all organizational resources by indicating which resources are to be used for specified activities, and when, where, and how the resources are to be used. A thorough organizing effort helps managers to minimize costly weaknesses, such as duplication of effort and idle organizational resources.''[8] In sum, organizing accomplishes the following:

- It improves the use of human and material resources, enabling the organization to efficiently reach its goals.
- Organizing allocates authority and responsibility so that the proper personnel are accountable for the progress and results of organizational activities.
- Organizing establishes formal channels for the flow of effective communications thereby minimizing conflict and preventing ambiguity.

THE ARCHITECTURE OF ORGANIZATIONS

Each organization has its own architecture, a structural style that results from a unique combination of two basic building blocks—people and tasks—and four basic building activities: division of labor, departmentalization, coordinating, and controlling. The design into which the organization assembles these blocks and activities affects the quality of work life within it. Every day, right around sunrise across the world, people rise to face another day, perform their morning rituals, and leave their homes, traveling, usually, to some organizational setting to participate in the activity we call ''work.'' Each of these workers contributes different skills and energies to tasks that are similar to or different from the tasks that coworkers perform, exercises differing degrees of authority and autonomy, and creates unique professional relationships with fellow workers. He or she works with superiors, peers, and subordinates in changing combinations of cooperation, coordination, and control. The organization's architecture consists of a relatively stable arrangement of these tasks, relationships, and divisions of labor. It influences how people contribute to the organization's goals.

The Concept of Organization

Organization exists in many forms. Sociologists say that we can classify organizations according to two factors: the needs they fulfill and the benefits that society derives from their existence. To fulfill human needs and offer general social benefits, there are formally established groups that include social and religious groups, associations, and educational and business institutions. There are also informal groups, such as family units, groups of friends, neighbors, cliques, and clubs. Even though people are most at ease when they are a part of such "a web of collectivized patterns,"[9] it is easy to take some of these life patterns for granted. For example, most people never question their proximity to and dependency on other people. This commonplace reliance on organizations results from our natural dependence on collaborative efforts and the relative stability and predictability that organizations offer. However, despite our natural affinity toward organizations, group life may present difficulties as well as benefits:

> Proximity and dependency, as conditions of social life, harbor the threats of human conflict, of capricious antisocial behavior, of the instability and unpredictability of human relationships, and of uncertainty about the very nature of the social structure and the roles it gives to its members . . .[10]

Compensating for or overcoming such problems presents a challenge for every organization, professional or social, formal or informal.

Having examined the concept, its benefits, and its challenges, we have yet to ask: What is an organization? A very formal definition might describe an **organization** as an identifiable social structure that engages in various activities for a particular purpose. A simpler definition might identify an organization as a collection of people who work together to achieve mutual goals. For the purposes of this text, organizations are *groups* of people who take part in *patterned activities* that lead toward a common *goal*. The following definitions contain these three elements:

> An organization is the arrangement of personnel for facilitating the accomplishment of some agreed-upon purpose through the allocation of functions and responsibilities. (John M. Gaus)[11]
>
> A system of consciously coordinated activities or forces of two or more persons. (Chester I. Barnard)[12]
>
> A formalized intentional structure of roles or positions. (Koontz and Weihrich)[13]
>
> Collective action in the pursuit of a common mission, a fancy way of saying that a bunch of people have come together under a common label ("General Motors," "Joe's Body Shop") to produce some product or service. (Henry Mintzberg)[14]

> An open social system that consists of the patterned activities of a group of people that tend to be goal-directed. (Katz and Kahn)[15]

Formal and Informal Organizations

Organizations, then, are people working together for a particular reason. However, such a formal definition largely overlooks the tensions, achievements, joys, and dramas that occur daily within an organization. "Formal structure describes only the organization's basic anatomy. Companies must also concern themselves with organizational physiology—the systems and relationships that allow the lifeblood of information to flow through the organization."[16] Many believe that you can't really understand the formal organization unless you know the informal one. What differentiates the two? The **formal organization** consists of the official structures, work divisions, and processes that enable the organization to reach its goals. In contrast, the **informal organization** consists of the unofficial structures, activity patterns, and processes that develop spontaneously, without formal planning. Despite their informal origins, these structures, patterns, and processes also influence how the organization reaches its goals. Within a law firm, this division into formal and informal characteristics has been likened to an "organizational iceberg" (see Figure 3–1 on page 85).[17]

The Formal Organization

Comprising the tip or the visible surface of the iceberg, the formal organization consists of the formally designed and officially acknowledged parts of the organization that show up on the organizational charts: the organization's structure; its hierarchy and the relationships that the hierarchy establishes; job titles and descriptions; the formal paths of communications and formal lines of authority; written plans, procedures, and policies; and any viable decisions that the organization has made public. The formal organization uses policies, traditions, rules, and regulations to enforce its norms, which it communicates through announcements, notices, memorandums, and other official forms of communication.

The Informal Organization

Every formal organization gives rise to an informal organization. Representing all that the formal organization does not dictate or decide, the informal orga-

FIGURE 3-1
The Organizational Iceberg

Formal Organization

Official structures

Work divisions

Organizational processes

The formally designed organization
- Structure
- Hierarchy and hierarchical levels
- Job titles and descriptions
- Span of control

Formal paths of communication
- Announcements, notices, and other vehicles for official communications

Formal lines of authority
- Written plans, procedures, policies, and decisions

Formal authority networks and power
- Position, authority, rewards, and punishment power

Informal Organization

Unplanned structures

Spontaneous patterns of activities and relationships

Affective and unofficial social processes

Informal and spontaneous structures
- Relationships, alliances, systems and networks

Informal communications
- Grapevine; perceptions based on feelings, needs, and wants

Informal lines of authority
- Power and influence from subunits, expertise, friendships, and alliances; perceptions of trust and openness

Informal authority network and power
- Abilities and motivational patterns; individual and group norms and values

SOURCE: Based on Samuel C. Certo, *Principles of Modern Management: Functions and Systems*, 3d ed. (Dubuque, Iowa: Wm. C. Brown Company, 1986): 270.

nization is the covert side of the organization. It consists of the patterns of interpersonal relationships; the power and influence of individuals, groups, or substructures; the norms and values of individuals and their work or social groups; perceptions of trust and openness; the feelings of individuals, as well as their perceived or real needs and wants; and the abilities and motivational patterns of the organization's members. Using the organization's grapevine to communicate information according to need and interest, the informal organization creates its own norms. Ideally, these norms support and enhance the organization's formal rules and regulations; however, in negative circumstances, informal norms can undermine the formal organization. Relationships in the informal organization arise spontaneously. Although they sometimes mirror formal relationships in the organization, such informal relationships develop outside the precepts of the organization's hierarchy. Feeding "a network of personal and social relationships not established or required by the organization but arising spontaneously as people associate with one another,"[18] the roots of these informal systems are embedded in the formal organization itself and are strengthened by the very formality of its structures.[19]

Formal and Informal Structures within the Law Firm

The formal and informal structures within a law firm are much like those in other organizations. The law firm's formal organization results in the power of position and authority, while the informal organization attempts, through the unceasing endeavors of its networks, alliances, and expertise, to redistribute and balance the overwhelming power of its formal counterpart. The formal organization rarely acknowledges or sanctions these attempts. The interaction between the two systems can be either positive or negative, since the informal organization can either support the firm and its policies or sabotage and diminish them. Within the law firm, as in all organizations, the formal organizational structure is based on the hierarchical structure; spinning off from the formal structure, the law firm's informal structure can take many often predictable forms: the four senior partners who have become closer through the years in their relationships as founding members, the groups of secretaries who meet regularly for lunch and for social exchanges, the firm's softball team, even the morning coffee break regulars. In addition, attorneys interact professionally and personally with others in the organization, attorneys and non-attorneys alike, creating a wide range of informal relationships. Technologically keen associates may enjoy the support of a computer users group with several of the firm's word processing staff. A junior partner may carpool with the librarian and a secretary. The managing partner may discover a willing and formidable racquetball opponent in a new paralegal. While relationships like these (and groups like those shown in Figure 3–2) never appear on organizational charts, they certainly influence how a law firm actually operates.

FIGURE 3–2
Informal Groups within a Law Firm

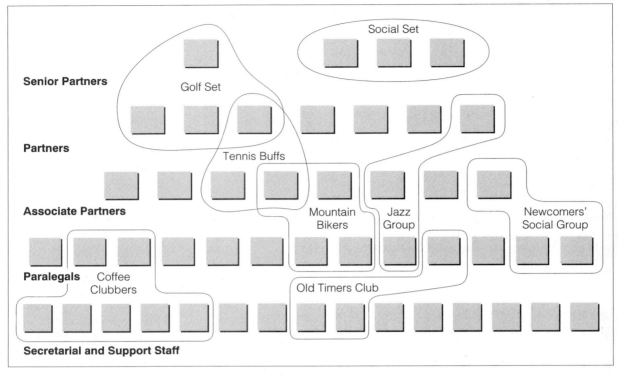

Organizations and People

Work is a central aspect of life, and people's motives for working range from basic economic survival to pure altruism. Most reasons for working include economic concerns, such as earning a living and being able to afford extras; the desire to meet social needs, such as the need to interact and to develop new friendships; the wish to increase social status, possibly through the prestige associated with a certain profession; and the need to build self-esteem by establishing an individual identity, through work which often reveals a person's values and through which the individual may make his or her most lasting contributions to society.[20] In the following sections, we will more closely examine the motives that compel people to work, as well as the motives behind workers' and organizations' behavior toward each other.

Psychological Contracts

No matter where you work, both you and your organization have expectations for how the other is to behave. Each of us operates under the terms of an unwritten **psychological organizational contract**:

> The organization does certain things to and for the employee and refrains from doing other things. It pays him, gives him status and job security, and does not ask him to do things too far removed from his job description. In exchange, the employee reciprocates by working hard, doing a good job, and refraining from criticizing the company in public and hurting its image . . . Both parties to the contract are guided by assumptions concerning what is fair and equitable.[21]

This contract does not require signatures. Rather, it represents an unspoken agreement between employer and worker in which both sides expect an exchange of contributions for inducements. The result is this: People contribute work to the organization in exchange for rewards, and the organization induces them to work by offering to reward them for that work. In turn, the organization has a right to expect dependable attendance, quality performance, and positive behaviors. The parties' expectations are contractual, and they achieve equity, or a state of equilibrium, if the organization's inducements are fairly equal to the worker's contributions.

> Inducements refer to all the rewards that accrue to individuals from working. One of the most important inducements is money in the form of wages, salaries, or benefits. Other inducements include satisfying work that creates feelings of fulfillment and involvement, friendly coworkers and supervisors who make life pleasant and meaningful, the opportunity to provide service to others and to society, and the opportunity for self-expression and economic security.[22]

Abuse of Organizations

Unfortunately, sometimes even despite the best inducements, employees can abuse an organization in a thousand different ways. Organizational energy can leak away through careless or unperformed work, use of the organization's time for loafing, or excessive socializing. Workers can also abuse organizations through *time theft*, the unauthorized use of extra personal time, the making of nonemergency personal phone calls outside of break periods, or the shortening of workdays through tardy arrivals, long lunches, and early departures. Stealing of time also includes overusing sick time and devising other creative justifications for nonproduction. *Communal entitlement*, the belief that the equipment and supplies of an organization are part of the contractual agreement, represents still another form of maltreatment. In law firms, especially, where quality supplies may be plentiful, workers may easily feel entitled to the occasional box of pens, a package of floppy or hard disks, or even a ream of laser-quality computer paper!

Abuse of Individuals

Everyone knows that organizations are powerful. They can use wages, benefits, working conditions, treatment, and job assignments to control workers. They can hire and fire. They can require employees to do much in the guise of "standard" job requirements. Workplace reality is sometimes far different from what we consider to be constitutional rights. Employers can demand loyalty, deny freedom of speech, and deprive workers of privacy and security rights. Even the lockers, desks, and files of workers may be subject to employer inspection or takeover.[23] Employers can make life very miserable, if they so choose, sometimes in attempts to force workers to leave.

For nonconforming workers who resist pressures to leave, work life can become unbearable. Workers often experience humiliating, unfair, and demeaning evaluation systems against which they may have little recourse. Supposedly in the name of professionalism, these same workers may succumb to pressures to work long hours of unpaid overtime. Some employers exploit job titles by endowing employees with designations that suggest executive, administrative, or professional positions, in order to strip them of their nonexempt status. Exempt employees are those workers who are not required to be paid overtime, according to the provisions of the federal government's Fair Labor Standards Act. According to the FLSA, employers need not pay overtime compensation to executive, administrative, and professional personnel, among others. Employers can withhold payment from workers, forcing them to seek legal help to receive the wages they have fairly earned. Some abuses are caused by the power-hungry and abrasive personalities of those in charge. Petty and arrogant dictators are not uncommon in any work setting. To ensure utter compliance, some employers threaten even the most cooperative workers with being fired or the first to go. When such threats become real, inequitable layoffs and terminations cause long-lasting repercussions in many lives. Unfortunately, many of these workplace horrors are not unheard of in law firms, where the additional stress of working with highly pressured professionals can take its toll.

> By definition, all organizations tramp on individuality and demand some sort of conformity in order to turn out uniform products—saved souls, Boy Scouts with merit and Merit Badges, or Compaq computers. All companies run over people to varying degrees and depending on rank in the firm . . .[24]

In many instances, however, an organization may maltreat individuals within it without any conscious intent to do so. By their very size and structure, organizations are superior to individuals, able to wield enormous power, which their employees feel in many ways. On the other hand, an organization is only as strong as the people—satisfied and productive or browbeaten and prone to excuses—that comprise it. Achieving mutual benefit becomes, for both, a search for equilibrium, a balance of organizational and individual power.

Tension between Individuals and Organizations

The tension involved in attaining this balance does not show up on any organizational charts. As a manager, however, you should be aware of this ongoing struggle, the press of the organization on the individual to conform and the effort of the individual to maintain his or her identity. Many writers have given considerable thought to the effects of organizations on employees. Chris Argyris, for instance, believes that mature individuals experience the greatest difficulty conforming to the demands of the organization.[25] Others, believing that relationships between people and organizations will always reflect conflict, are convinced that organizations dominate and diminish their workers simply because people are inherently cooperative, desirous of social approval, and eager not to disrupt the status quo.[26] Though most organizations will sincerely attempt to meet the needs of both mature and immature individuals, workplaces and their employees will always be striving to gain or preserve the necessary equity and equilibrium between worker contributions and organizational inducements and rewards. As a manager, you will quickly learn that this balance is never easily attained. It is one that frequently places professional and personal costs on workers and, ultimately, on the organization.

THE FOUR ACTIVITIES OF ORGANIZING

The building blocks of organizations are people and jobs. An organization is the structure that results from the pattern into which these blocks are assembled. Typically, each organization creates its structure through these four activities: division of labor, departmentalization, coordination, and control.

Division of Labor

Division of labor is the actual division of work into jobs that need to be done in the organization. Managers must first divide the organization's workloads into units or assignments that they could reasonably expect one person to complete. Division of work refers to the *task elements* in organizing.

Departmentalization

Departmentalization is the process of arranging work into clusters of activities based on the organization's divisions of work and people, otherwise known as its organizational design. Managers analyze the areas of work that are to be done, grouping them into meaningful units or sets of tasks. Departmentalization refers to the *structural elements* in organizing.

Coordination

Coordination is the process of ensuring, through the use of certain coordinating elements, that different organizational divisions function together smoothly. Utilizing concepts such as the unity of command, the scalar chain, and the span of management, managers attempt to arrange efficient and productive interactions between tasks and among people. Coordination refers to the use of these concepts to provide for the *coordinating elements* in organizing.

Control

Control is the regulation of activities and results through direction, guidance, and the successful distribution and use of authority. Through control elements, managers must determine who in each work group or unit will oversee work performance and ensure that the group is meeting its task or production goals. This distribution of *authority* provides for the *control elements* in organizing.[27]

Table 3–1 presents questions essential to these four activities, which we will discuss in detail in the following sections.

DIVISION OF LABOR

Dividing work into distinct job assignments is not new. Our earliest history is filled with examples of the division of labor. In 1776, Adam Smith designated a special chapter as "The Division of Labor" in his classic work, *The Wealth of Nations*. Smith wrote that, within society, each worker contributes some form of labor as an exchange, supplying others "abundantly with what they have occasion for, and they accommodate him as amply with what he has occasion for, and a general plenty diffuses itself through all the different ranks of society." In this process of exchange, each worker can play a different role.[28] The need to apportion work is at the foundation of all organizations, and is, in fact, the reason for organization.[29] To divide work effectively, managers must understand what the work entails. Researchers suggest five dimensions of work tasks: skill variety, task identity, task significance, autonomy, and feedback.[30]

CHAPTER 3 / ORGANIZING AND ORGANIZATIONS

TABLE 3–1
The Four Activities of Organizing

Activity	Element Involved	Questions To Be Decided
Division of Labor	Tasks	How should the work be divided? Who is best at each task?
Departmentalization	Structures	What structures will offer the greatest efficiency? effectiveness? motivation? Which arrangements of people (departments, units, teams) will represent the best groupings of work activities?
Authority	Control	Who will delegate work? Who will oversee the work? Who will control the outcomes?
Coordination ■ Unity of Command ■ The Scalar Chain ■ The Span of Management	Coordination	How will the work flow be coordinated? Which tasks and workers will be easier to coordinate? Which coordinating mechanisms will result in less conflict, more results? Who will report to whom? What is the chain of command?

Skill Variety

Skill variety is the range of skills that a worker needs to perform a job. A law firm's messenger uses one set of skills; a law firm marketing coordinator employs another.

Task Identity

Task identity is the degree to which the worker can identify the finished product as being completely his or hers. An attorney who is almost totally responsible for a particular case may completely identify with the work involved; this means that the attorney acknowledges near-full responsibility for the case as well. A group of paralegals in a real estate department who share responsibility for completing their duties also share task identity, as well as a sense of responsibility for their work.

Task Significance

Task significance is the importance of a task, as measured by the degree to which the task affects others, either within or outside of the organization. The tasks of a firm's executive director, for example, are much more significant than those of the firm's bookkeeper, though both sets of jobs are equally essential and are important in different ways.

Autonomy

Autonomy is the amount of independence with which the individual worker may plan, schedule, and complete his or her assigned work. The greater an employee's autonomy, the greater his or her responsibility. Secretaries and other support staff generally have little autonomy. Managing partners, on the other hand, have a great deal of autonomy, first as professionals and, second, as those in positions of power and influence.

Feedback

Feedback is a transfer of information that assesses employee or organizational effectiveness, work quality, and performance. Jobs differ greatly in degrees, kinds, and availability of feedback.

These five qualities just described differ from task to task. Professionals such as attorneys will perform jobs that are high in task significance, since these jobs affect the economic and personal well-being of many individuals. Attorneys' tasks also rank high in terms of autonomy. A lawyer's job requires both relative freedom and discretionary power. A receptionist, on the other hand, needs many interpersonal skills but only a limited—though important—range of other abilities, such as organizational skills. Each job embodies a unique mix of these five characteristics. Understanding the mix will not only help managers to design jobs that are appropriate to the organization, but will also help them to understand each job's motivational potential.

DEPARTMENTALIZATION AND ORGANIZATIONAL DESIGN

Structure

According to organizational theorist William Scott, structure "is the logical (and consistent) relationship of functions in an organization, arranged to accomplish the objectives of the organization efficiently. Structure implies system and pattern."[31] **Structuring** an organization is the process of establishing groupings and patterns of work relationships and then coordinating them with the organization's resources. **Restructuring,** on the other hand, is an effort to improve the organization by reorganizing or otherwise altering its structure. Organizational structures, like buildings, must be designed to facilitate the processes that are critical to meeting the organization's objectives. For many organizations today, "The real art and significance of managing groups of professionals, such as lawyers, consists of coping with doubts and uncertainties." The very structure of the law firm, for example, must be designed to accommodate rather than exacerbate those challenges.[32] The structure that an organization chooses should be appropriate to its field and the times, should be in keeping with its strategy and size, and should be based on the best use of its resources. But no matter how perfect the structure, the inefficient, ineffective, or inappropriate behavior of people within that structure can disrupt "the best laid organizational plans, and thwart the cleanness of the logical relationships found in the structure."[33] Finding the ideal structure means finding the structure that will elicit the best possible response from the elements that make the organization unique.

> There is, of course, no such thing as an "ideal" structure for any organization. Advantages must be paid for by accepting disadvantages. In decisions of this kind, one looks for the alternative with the greatest strategic advantages— that is, the one that serves the company's most critical long-range goals—and the fewest strategic disadvantages. Then one swallows the latter as the price of the former, and concentrates on making the most of those advantages.[34]

Organizational Design

Organizational design is the process of matching the form of the organization—its structure, resources, and organizational processes—to its function of responding to its basic mission and reaching its goals and objectives. Designing the organization leads to the creation of its structure. The **organizational structure** is the system of logical and appropriate uses for activities that enables the organization to meet its goals as it grows or declines. There are traditional approaches to organizing, as well as standard methods. While the structural approach must be appropriate to the organization, even one consisting of only two members, most approaches are simply logical divisions, based on the organization's levels and groupings of authority and tasks. The twentieth-century legal profession is undergoing a drastic change in structure:

> The ratio of associates to partners has multiplied, and firms have revived or created new categories of subordinates: the permanent associate, senior attorney, or salaried partner (who does not share profits); and the staff or contract attorney (who is hired annually and never considered for partnership). Firms also employ more paralegals and use computers to increase the productivity of clerical personnel, thereby reallocating significant amounts of legal work previously performed by lawyers. Many firms have diversified their services by hiring a variety of nonlawyer professionals (e.g., accountants, economists, scientists, psychologists). The size, internal differentiation, and stratification of these service enterprises demand more bureaucratic structures, often headed by nonlegal managers. Some firms have invested retained earnings in nonlegal enterprises (such as commerical real estate). And there even is talk of allowing nonlawyers to invest in firm equity, completing the structural homology between the large firm and the corporations it serves.[35]

In law firms, organizational design is not easy. Though the product of a law office is simply to provide the service of legal expertise, those who deliver that service usually develop direct and complex links to those who receive it.

> Unlike the more traditional (and frequently more stable) corporate structure, where the lines of responsibility and reporting relationships are more clearly delineated, the law firm model is replete with vague and ambiguous lines of reporting relationships.
>
> In addition to its rigid, segmented structure, law firm management has traditionally encouraged overspecializa-

The partnership structure has served the legal profession in three ways—governance, economics, and collegiality. . . . Bound in the partnership structure are many tenets of the canons of ethics. The partnership precludes sharing fees with nonlawyers, which would be fee splitting. The partnership prevents conflicts of interest by avoiding situations in which independence is jeopardized by serving those who might profit from that service, such as outside shareholders. The partnership, and its collegiality, sustains that isolation from corrupt sources that might injure independence and objectivity, the very essence of the lawyer's value to business and society.

The collegiality of the partnership flows to the governance and management of law firms in which partners select, from one of their own, a partner or partners who manage the firm and who function as chief executive officers. In larger firms, an executive committee of senior partners frequently functions as a board of directors. For generations, this has been the accepted mode, unaltered by even the professional corporation. . . . When all of these elements—the changing demands of collegiality, marketing, the economy, the growing complexity of the law firm—are added, the partnership structure begins to creak a little from antiquity and inadequacy.

(Bruce W. Marcus)

ANOTHER LOOK

Is The Partnership Structure an Anachronism?

SOURCE: Bruce W. Marcus, "Is the Partnership Structure an Anachronism?" *Legal Management* (November/December 1989): 32–35.

1. Of the three useful contributions of the partnership structure—governance, economics, and collegiality—which, if any, do you believe is most out-of-date and inappropriate?
2. Can collegiality truly exist in a for-profit organization?
3. Are today's attorneys too greedy for true partnerships? Explain.
4. What needs of contemporary professionals does the partnership structure still have the potential to fulfill?

---

tion by segregating professionals within the organization and by designing jobs requiring finer and finer segmentation of skills. Although perhaps poorly prepared to do so, lawyers will need to learn to accept the human aspects of organizational change, because many lawyers are now beginning to recognize that they need to be able to handle a broader variety of assignments if their firms are to compete successfully.[36]

Organizational Charts

Organizational charts are graphic representations that depict the levels of the managerial hierarchy and the roles and reporting relationships within an organization. Simple drawings that can easily be updated, organizational charts consist of lines and boxes that map out formal organizational relationships. An accurately delineated organizational chart eradicates confusion about (1) authority relationships (who reports to whom), (2) the level of managerial authority (who has authority over whom), (3) accountability and control (who is responsible for what), (4) decision responsibility (who should make the decisions), and (5) organizational structure (what the organization looks like). (This last feature is especially useful for analyzing complex organizations.) Figures 3–3a through 3–3d provide sample organizational charts for law firms of various sizes; Figure 3–3e illustrates the organizational chart of a law department within a large corporation.

Departmentalization

The most common method for delineating an organization's structure is to establish departments. **Departmentalization** is the process of organizing work into logical and appropriate divisions (1) by function or process; (2) by clients, the recipients of the organization's service; (3) by product, the service that an organization provides, and (4) by place or location. These four basic divisions can be interrelated. For ex-

FIGURE 3–3a
A Solo-Practitioner Law Firm

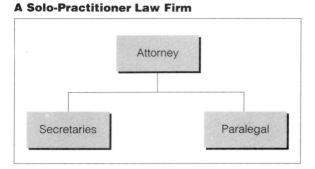

ample, a law firm may decide to base its structure on service, dividing its practice into the legal specializations it wishes to emphasize. On this basic structure, the firm may decide to superimpose a division based on its administrative processes. Within this division, the firm may create subdivisions in areas such as finance, marketing, and information services. However, departmentalization is trickier than it seems, and structural decisions like these are only uncomplicated on paper. In actuality, the process is rife with complications.[37] For instance, on the surface, the structural design of a law firm with branches in several cities may seem fairly uncomplicated. But if each branch benefits from practicing the same types of legal specializations, the firm must departmentalize accordingly, establishing subunits in areas such as real estate and bankruptcy law within each branch. Revealing inner workings of an organization, basic structural divisions help us to see not only how an organization apportions its activities but how management and other personnel fit in.

Departmentalization by Function

Departmentalization by function distributes activities according to the major categories of work in the organization. In most organizations, categories include finance, marketing, and production. In legal settings, the functional equivalent of production is that of legal activities.

Departmentalization by Service

Departmentalization by service distributes organizational resources according to the kind of service that the organization provides. In the manufacturing world, companies departmentalize by products; a law firm departmentalizes by dividing its product—the service it provides—into groupings of legal specialties, such as a litigation division, or by establishing sections based on a more specific practice, such as an environmental law department.

FIGURE 3–3b
A Small Law Firm (5–25 Attorneys)

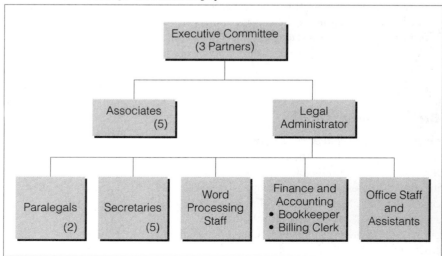

SOURCE: Printed with the permission of Hendel, Collins, & Newton, P. C., Springfield, Massachusetts.

CHAPTER 3 / ORGANIZING AND ORGANIZATIONS

FIGURE 3–3c
A Medium-Size Law Firm (25–50 Attorneys)

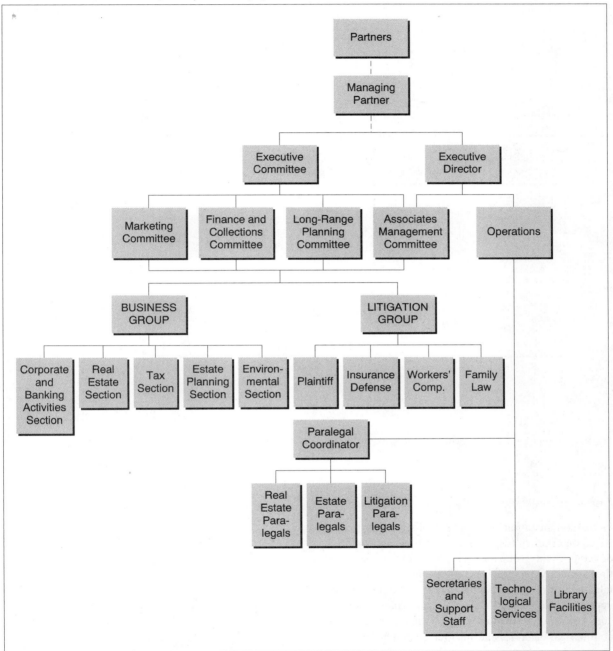

SOURCE: Printed with the permission of Robinson, Donovan, Madden & Barry, P.C., Springfield, Massachusetts.

FIGURE 3–3d
A Large Law Firm (50+ Attorneys)

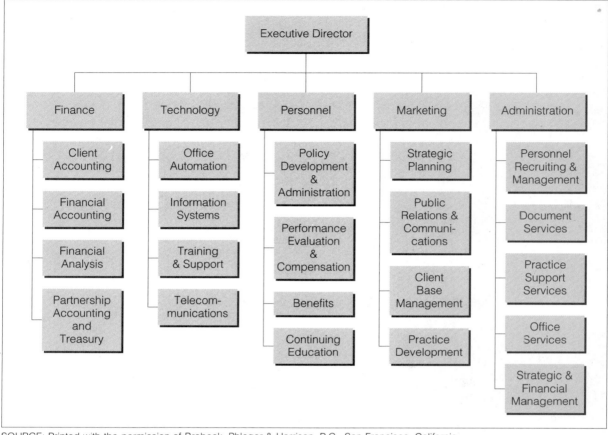

SOURCE: Printed with the permission of Brobeck, Phleger & Harrison, P.C., San Francisco, California.

Departmentalization by Clients

Departmentalization by clients establishes departments based on efficient response to clients' needs. As firms develop client groups whose needs can be best met through a concentrated use of resources, departmentalization by clients becomes an effective option. Some departments consist of a single client, such as a large corporation or individual clients, such as real estate, commercial banking, and insurance companies.

Departmentalization by Location

Departmentalization by location distributes the firm's activities according to where they are being performed. A firm that departmentalizes by location may establish branch offices in different cities, states, or countries, in an effort to maximize the efficient use of its resources.

Figure 3–4 presents an example of each of the four types of departmentalization.

COORDINATING ELEMENTS OF ORGANIZING

Coordination is the attempt to arrange and integrate organizational elements so that the organization functions efficiently. Management writer James Mooney, in *The Principles of Organization*, cites coordination—"the orderly arrangement of group effort to provide unity of purpose in the pursuit of a common purpose"—as the first rule in organizing.[38] But how does

FIGURE 3–3e
A Corporate Law Department

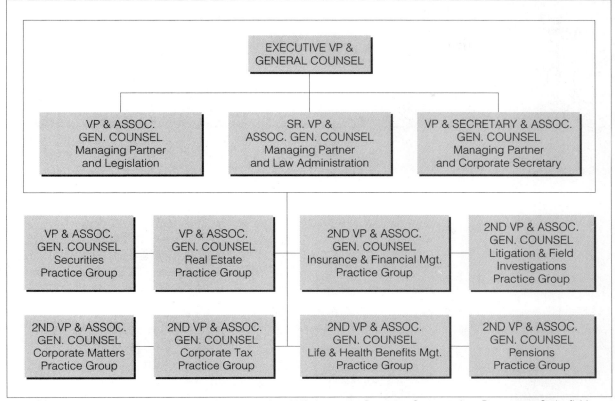

SOURCE: Printed with the permission of Massachusetts Mutual Life Insurance Company, Corporate Law Department, Springfield, Massachusetts. Courtesy of Attorney Thomas J. Finnegan, Jr., Vice President, Secretary, and Associate General Counsel.

this "orderly arrangement" come about? While we can accurately describe some organizations as tight ships, others seem to run miraculously on good will and chaos. Perfectly operating organizations are probably only found in such literary works as Sir Thomas More's *Utopia*. How do the members of an organization ensure that its structures will actually work? Coordination primarily involves three classic principles of management: unity of command, the scalar chain, and the span of management.

Unity of Command

Complaints about too many bosses are commonplace and well-justified. "Dual command . . . wreaks havoc in all concerns, large or small, in home and in state," Henri Fayol writes. "For any action whatsoever, an employee should receive orders from one superior only."[39] **Unity of command** indicates a system in which a subordinate receives orders from only one superior. However, such systems are rare. In many settings, workers must do their best to answer to several people. Obeying commands from two or more sources, is at times impossible: multiple orders may contradict each other or unfairly increase the recipient's work load. But, even though requiring an organization member to take orders from more than one superior may seem undesirable, in some settings, such as a law firm, where high-level specialization is the rule, such a situation may be unavoidable: there may need to be more than one source of authority. Still, law firms, like other organizations likely to exhibit a less-than-total unity of command, must take care to identify an ultimate authority to whom workers are most highly responsible and to whom they may go for guidance when multiple instructions conflict. As Herbert Simon has observed, "In case two authoritative commands conflict, there should be a single determinate person whom the subordinate is expected to obey."[40]

FIGURE 3-4
The Four Types of Departmentalization

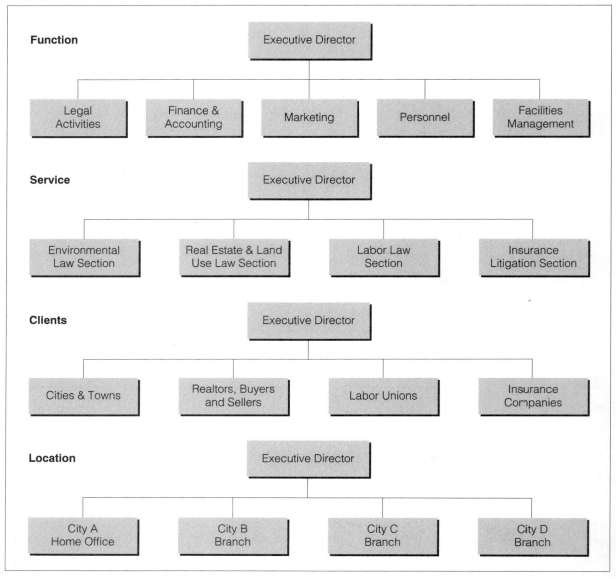

The Scalar Chain

The **scalar chain** describes the linkage of authority that begins at the top of the organizational hierarchy and descends, connecting positions throughout the organization like links in a chain. Henri Fayol describes the chain as the link of superiors ranging from the ultimate authority to the lowest ranks. The line of authority is the route followed—via every link in the chain—by all communications which start from or go to the ultimate authority."[41] The scalar chain is an inherent structural feature within all—or nearly all—organizations. James Mooney observes that "whenever we find an organization of even two people, related as superior and subordinate, we have the scalar principle." As an organization grows, the chain lengthens and subdelegation appears.[42]

Span of Management

The **span of management** defines the number of subordinates for whom a manager is responsible. The term differs from "span of control" in that control refers to only one function of management. Managers need to decide how many subordinates they can effectively manage. Opinions differ. Some management experts say that the ideal number of subordinates is four; by comparison, "at the lowest level of organization, where what is delegated is responsibility for specific tasks and not for the supervision of others, the number may be eight or twelve."[43] Still others suggest different numbers for what is possible or workable or effective; many different variables determine the span of management that is ideal for each organization or for each organizational department or subunit. The most important of these variables are the human ones. Managers must know the answers to these questions: How much can I rely on individual workers? How much close supervision do these workers need? What's the nature of our task? What kind of motivation is present? How much coordination and control does the job require? What results can I reasonably expect from these people? Answering such questions calls for a close and careful look at the complexity of human relationships and the demands of work. The ideal span of management is likely to be based on an "interplay of individual personality, informal groups, intraorganizational conflict, and the decision-making processes in the formal structure."[44]

However, ideals are one thing; reality is another. How many subordinates a manager can effectively manage is ultimately a very subjective decision. Three factors are likely to affect this decision. The first is ability. A talented manager who understands the organization and its people probably will opt for a wider span of management than someone who lacks managerial skill. The type of people and functions that the manager is to supervise represents the second factor. For instance, motivated, competent employees will make the management process far less demanding than those who are uncooperative or unproductive. The third factor involves the extent of communication. Workers performing a simple task nearby are likely to present less of a managerial challenge in terms of communication than workers performing a complex job in another building, another state, or another country. From these three determinants come two basic managerial spans: wide spans and narrow ones.

Wide Span

A wide span of management is one where the manager is responsible for many individuals. This results in a flat organizational structure with few managers and few managerial levels. An example of an organization that has a relatively flat hierarchical structure and a wide span of management would be a law firm in which a single attorney has built a solo practice with a group of paralegals, secretaries, a receptionist, and a bookkeeper. While there is but one level of management (the sole practitioner), there is a wide span of management, since almost a dozen people report directly to that manager. Flat organizational structures can encourage communication. They can be changed quickly, and they result in lower managerial costs.

Narrow Span

Requiring more managers and more hierarchical levels, a narrow span of management is one in which several managers are each responsible for several subordinates. This creates a tall organizational structure. There are countless examples of organizations possessing tall structures, many of which, from time to time, restructure or eradicate layers of management in attempts to streamline and increase their efficiency.

Figure 3–5 depicts the two basic spans of management.

CONTROL ELEMENTS IN ORGANIZING

We have looked at the structure, the architecture of the organization. As an architect's blueprint depends on construction to become real in terms of concrete and steel, an organization requires certain elements and processes to bring it to life. What processes drive the organization? What keeps each employee and unit portrayed on the organizational chart functioning as they were intended to do? "What it takes to get the organization up and running is essentially the same two things all vehicles need: a person in the driver's seat and a source of power."[45] Without the drivers, the organization goes nowhere; in control terms, these drivers come in many shapes and sizes. Talcott Parsons, who views organization from a sociological perspective, writes that

FIGURE 3-5
Spans of Management in the Law Firm

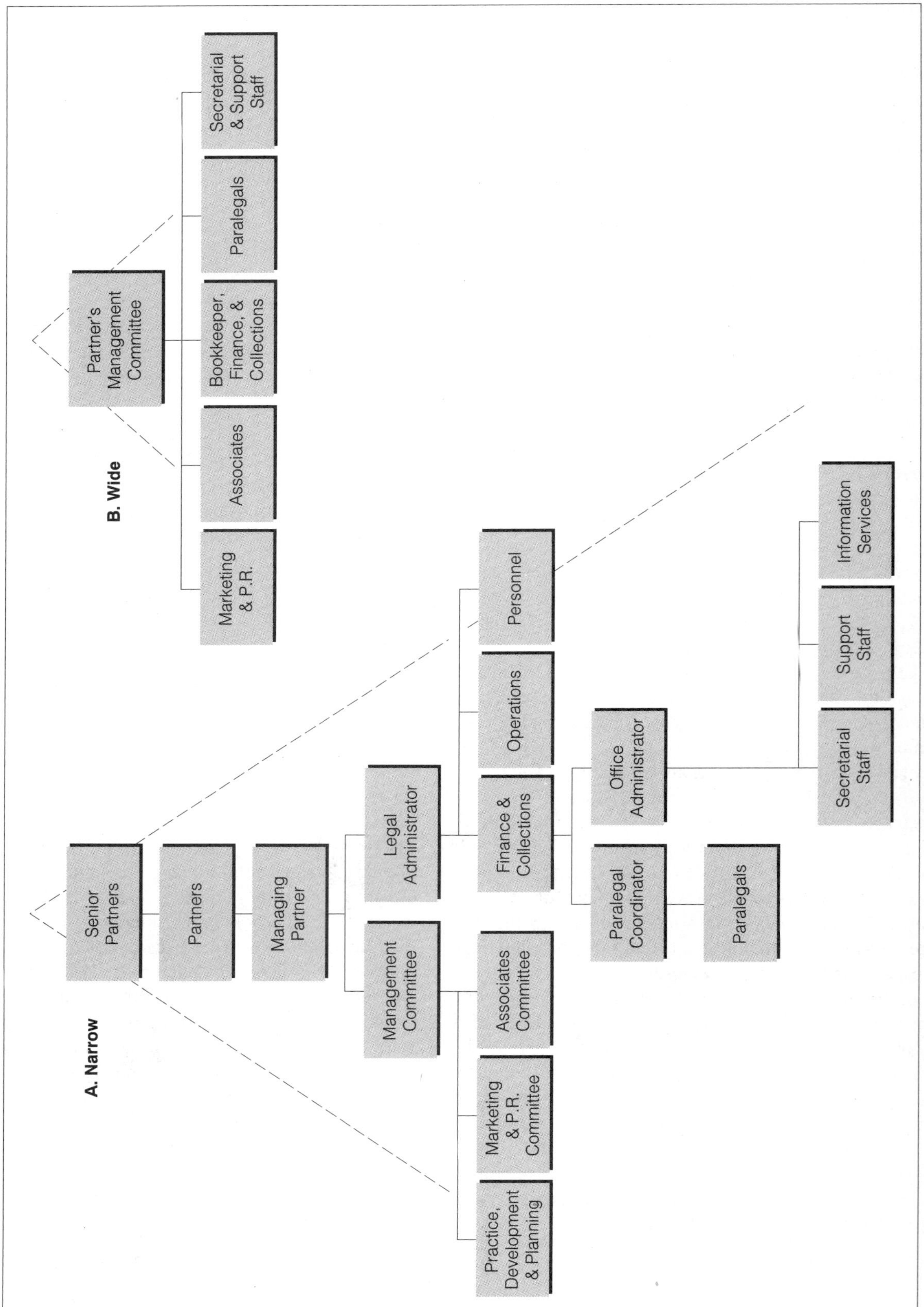

A. Narrow

- Senior Partners
- Partners
- Managing Partner
  - Management Committee
    - Practice, Development & Planning
    - Marketing & P.R. Committee
    - Associates Committee
  - Legal Administrator
    - Finance & Collections
      - Paralegal Coordinator
        - Paralegals
      - Office Administrator
        - Secretarial Staff
        - Support Staff
        - Information Services
    - Operations
    - Personnel

B. Wide

- Partner's Management Committee
  - Marketing & P.R.
  - Associates
  - Bookkeeper, Finance, & Collections
  - Paralegals
  - Secretarial & Support Staff

... we ordinarily think of the organization as having some kind of "management" or "administration"—a group of people carrying some kind of special responsibility for the organization's affairs, usually formulated as "policy formation" or "decision-making." Then under the control of this top group we would conceive of various operative groups arranged in a "line" formation down to the lowest in the line of authority. In a somewhat different relation we would also think of various groups performing "staff" functions, usually some kinds of experts who stand in an advisory capacity to the decision makers at the various levels, but who do not themselves exercise 'line" authority.[46]

This progression of responsibility becomes the art that accompanies the architecture: the control processes that consist of (1) authority, which allows its holder to legitimately require that each organizational component, whether human or inanimate fulfill its intended purpose; (2) delegation, which distributes authority; (3) responsibility; and (4) accountability.

Authority

Authority is having someone in the driver's seat. **Authority** is the legitimate right to tell other people what to do, to make decisions, and to use resources. Power and authority are often confused. Power, however, is the ability to exert influence and control, whereas authority is the formal right to do so. Without some form of authority, which Fayol identifies as "the right to give orders and the power to exact obedience,"[47] organizations would be unable to operate. The different levels of the organizational hierarchy call for different levels of authority and different amounts of responsibility. Like the owners of private businesses, who exercise complete control over their ventures,[48] the owners within a law firm, the partners, wield ultimate authority. Generally, however, the pattern of authority throughout the firm reflects either centralization or decentralization.

Centralization

Centralization places authority with the central figures in the hierarchy, reflecting a structure in which responsibility rests with the few, usually the higher-level managers, rather than with the many. In a highly centralized organization, top management makes all important decisions, and middle- and lower-level managers implement them.

Decentralization

Placing responsibility with many members of an organization rather than with just a few, **decentralization** diffuses authority throughout the organizational structure, even at the lowest levels where it allows lower-level managers to make those decisions that directly affect their subordinates. When authority is delegated, workers share power and enjoy a sense of ownership in the organization, which is likely to enhance their interest in the outcome of their contributions. Decentralization is the norm and is almost absolutely necessary in organizations where the environment is complex and uncertain; where the membership is composed of educated professionals, who demand more voice in decision making; or where most decisions are relatively minor.

Delegation

Delegation is the process of transferring authority by assigning tasks and the necessary authority to subordinates, who accept responsibility for those tasks. Although it is "a precarious venture that requires the continuous elaboration of formal mechanisms of coordination and control,"[49] delegation allows organizations to achieve more. It frees up managers' time for more critical activities. It can lead to positive attitudes in workers, such as a sense of ownership in results at both the departmental and organizational levels and allows them more experience in managerial activities. Delegation also can lead to collaboration between members at different levels, each sharing responsibilities and pulling together for overall team results. Organizations of professionals in particular need to delegate and decentralize in order to create the sense of respect and autonomy that their workers require. However, delegation is often a source of difficulty:

> [T]oo much or insufficient delegation can render an executive incapable of action. The failure to delegate responsibility and authority equally may result in frustration for the delegatee. Overlapping of authority often causes clashes in personality. Gaps in authority cause failures in getting jobs done, with one party blaming the other for shortcomings in performance.[50]

Although delegation is important, it is equally important for all workers within a firm to be able to assume responsibility. Mary Parker Follett, whom we met in the Special Focus section at the end of Chapter 1, believed that "the taking of responsibility, each according to his capacity, each according to his function in the whole . . ., this taking of responsibility is usually the most vital matter in the life of every human being, just as the allotting of responsibility is the most important part of business administration."[51]

Accountability

Accountability is being responsible for one's acts. Fayol notes that "responsibility is a corollary of authority; it is its natural consequence and essential counterpart, and wheresoever authority is exercised, responsibility arises."[52] A subordinate who receives the authority and power to perform an assigned task is obligated to perform that task acceptably.

Based on the work of Henri Fayol, Figure 3–6 presents a list of suggestions for organizations that reflect, among other things, accountability, coordination, and the unity of command.

CONTEMPORARY ORGANIZATIONAL DESIGNS

In the following sections, we will examine four approaches to organizational design that offer valuable structural alternatives to both small and large law firms: Rensis Likert's System 4, the matrix design, organic and mechanistic designs, and inverted hierarchical structures.

Likert's System 4

Rensis Likert, a well-known contributor to management thought, explored the relationship between organizational design and effective organizations while working as a social scientist at the University of Michigan. Deviating from the traditional hierarchical approach to organizational design, Likert isolated the features that he considered critical to organizations: leadership, motivation, communication, interaction, decision making, organizational goal setting, control, and performance goal setting. Likert's research led to four basic organizational designs that he referred to simply as Systems 1, 2, 3, and 4. System 4 has become the model for a highly enlightened but also productive and effective organization.

The human organization of a System 4 firm is made up of interlocking work groups with a high degree of group loyalty among the members and favorable attitudes and trust among peers, superiors, and subordinates. Consid-

FIGURE 3–6
Guidelines for Organizing the Law Firm

I.	Carefully prepare the operating plan.
II.	Organize the human and material aspects so that they are in keeping with the objectives, resources, and requirements of the firm.
III.	Set up a single, competent, energetic formal management structure.
IV.	Coordinate all efforts and activities.
V.	Make clear, distinct, and precise decisions.
VI.	Select the most appropriate personnel—the ablest workers and the most competent managers.
VII.	Define duties.
VIII.	Encourage initiative and responsibility.
IX.	Reward fairly and suitably.
X.	Use sanctions for faults and errors.
XI.	Maintain discipline.
XII.	Ensure that individual interests are in keeping with organizational ones.
XIII.	Recognize the unity of command.
XIV.	Promote both material and human coordination.
XV.	Institute and effect controls.
XVI.	Avoid regulations, red tape, and paperwork.

SOURCE: Adapted from Henri Fayol, General and Industrial Management, trans. Constance Storrs (London: Pitman Publishing, Ltd., 1949): 19–42.

eration for others and relatively high levels of skills in personal interaction, group problem solving, and other group functions also are present. These skills permit effective participation in decisions on common problems. Participation is used, for example, to establish organization objectives which are a satisfactory integration of the needs and desires of all the members of the organization and of persons functionally related to it. Members of the organization are highly motivated to achieve the organization's goals. High levels of reciprocal influence occur, and high levels of total coordinated influence are achieved in the organization. Communication is efficient and effective. There is a flow from one part of the organization to another of all the relevant information important for each decision and action. The leadership in the organization has developed a highly effective social system for interaction, problem solving, mutual influence, and organizational achievement. This leadership is technically competent and holds high performance goals.[53]

Characteristics of the Four Systems

Likert's four systems are based on factors such as an organization's attitudes toward its members, method of control, degree of authority, and its communication and decision-making styles:

System 1, the exploitive/authoritative style, resembles the bureaucratic organization. Its characteristics include downward communication, hostile attitudes, control through punishment, and highly centralized decision making.

System 2, the benevolent/authoritative style is, like System 1, highly centralized and authoritative, but slightly more benevolent and less hostile and punitive.

System 3, the consultative style, exhibits patterns of stronger communications that flow both ways, from the top down as well as from subordinates to top managers. The ideas and contributions of subordinates were considered, and authority was more decentralized.

System 4, the participative/group-oriented style, reflects a highly decentralized flow of authority and open communications and participation in the organizing process. It encourages high levels of mutual trust among all levels in the organization. Likert has suggested that System 4 is the ideal design for an effectively run organization.

Because their size allows them more opportunities to build close communication links with and to show an interest in and concern for their workers, smaller law firms adapt more easily to Likert's view of the ideal structure. However, because the law firm needs to produce timely, accurate, and complete work, it is difficult to convert managers—in large law firms in particular—to System 4 management, in spite of its high correlation with organizational success. Many managers simply demand more proof. As one supervisor commented, "This interest-in-people approach is alright, but it is a luxury. I've got to keep pressure on for production, and when I get production up, then I can afford to take time to show an interest in my employees and their problems." Such managers and their units, caught in a cycle of production pressure which lowers morale, which lowers productivity (which in turn increases production pressure), may never find the time. As Likert comments, "The belief that [System 4] is a luxury reveals true priorities, and those who share this view are not those likely to find high productivity in their own units."[54]

The Principle of Supportive Relationships

An organization reflects the **principle of supportive relationships** when its leadership and processes "ensure the maximum probability that in all interactions and in all relationships within the organization, each member, in the light of his or her background, values, desires, and expectations, will view the working experience as a supportive one which builds and maintains his or her own sense of personal worth and importance."[55] This principle is one of the key elements in a System 4 design. The greater an organization's success in following it, Likert believes, the greater will be the noneconomic forces motivating its members, leading to fuller cooperation in achieving organizational goals.

Linking Pin Roles

Linking pin roles are managerial communication roles that ensure the smooth flow of communications from one level of the hierarchy to another. In fulfilling these roles, managers become major channels in the linkage of communications, facilitating its open exchange. Whereas traditional organizational structures are based on interaction that flows from superiors to subordinates throughout the hierarchy, System 4 uses

ANOTHER LOOK

Likert Talks about Supportive Relationships

We all need sources of support. Likert calls this the "principle of supportive relationships," the need for members of an organization to be able to depend on one another as part of a team. Likert believes that the more fully this principle of supportive relationships is applied throughout the organization, the greater will be the extent to which (1) the motivational forces of all its members will be compatible and to which (2) these motivational forces will result in cooperative behaviors that focus on achieving organizational goals. Likert says it this way:

> The leadership and other processes of the organization must be such as to ensure a maximum probability that in all interactions and in all relationships within the organization, each member, in the light of his background, values, desires, and expectations, will view the experience as supportive and one which builds and maintains his personal sense of worth and importance.
>
> In applying this principle, the relationship between the superior and the subordinate is crucial. This relationship, as the principle specifies, should be one which is supportive and ego-building. The more often the superior's behavior is ego-building instead of ego-deflating, the better will be his effect on organizational performance... Both the behavior of the superior and the employee's perception of the situation must be such that the subordinate, in the light of his background, values, and expectations, sees the experience as one which contributes to his sense of personal worth and importance, one which increases and maintains his sense of significance and human dignity.

Rensis Likert, *New Patterns of Management* (New York: McGraw-Hill, 1961): 103.

1. Reword Likert's principle, making it as simple and as practical as possible. How does your interpretation differ from his? How is it similar?
2. What does Likert's thinking contribute to contemporary management thought?
3. Why are the subordinate's perceptions most important?
4. How does this kind of thinking relate to the "bottom line" in terms of productivity and profit?

---

an "overlapping group form of structure with each work group linked to the organization by means of persons who are members of more than one group. These individuals who hold overlapping group memberships are called 'linking pins.' "[56] This overlapping structure, which links communications throughout the organization, allows all those whom a decision will affect to take part in making it. It allows for group decision making and encourages participation in the decision-making process. Likert describes the benefits of such a system: "There is a minimum of idle talk. Communication is clear and adequately understood. Important issues are recognized and dealt with. The atmosphere is one of 'no-nonsense' with emphasis on high productivity, high quality, and low costs. Decisions are reached promptly, clear-cut responsibilities are established, and tasks are performed rapidly and productively." Likert reminds us, however, that the group decision-making method never exonerates a supervisor for the quality of a group's decision: "He is responsible for building his subordinates into a group that makes the best decisions and carries them out well. *The superior is accountable for all decisions, for their execution, and for the result.*"[56] Figure 3–7 illustrates Likert's linking pin structure.

One of the prominent features of the System 4 organizational design is its emphasis on high performance goals. But in order to meet these goals, an organization must first ensure that its employees share in the desire to meet them. Likert believes that employees want stable employment, job security, opportunities, acceptable or satisfactory compensation, and some pride in the firm they work for, its accomplishments, and its performance.

A firm must succeed and grow to provide its employees with what they want from a job: pride in the job and company, job security, adequate pay, and opportunities

FIGURE 3–7
Linking Pin Roles between Organizational Work Groups

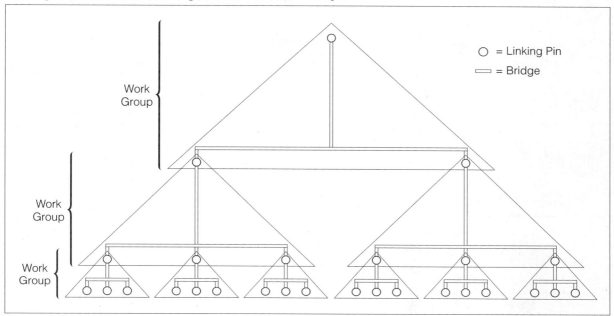

for promotion. Economic success is a 'situational requirement' which can only be met when the organization, its departments, and its members have high performance goals.[58]

It is not enough for the organization to have high goals; it must have the full support of each of its members as well. System 4 emphasizes supportive relationships, linking pin roles in communication for group decision making, and high performance standards. Because it integrates individual, departmental, and organizational goals, it is a useful model for law firms.

Matrix Design

A growing organization needs to hire additional people, to develop and fill new positions, and, of course, to add levels to its hierarchy. Within such an organization, coordination and control processes become more challenging and more complex. The "obvious organizational solution to strategies that required multiple, simultaneous management was the matrix structure," which became popular in the late 1970s and the early 1980s.[59] The **matrix organizational structure** combines functional and divisional forms of departmentalization to achieve better coordination and control. A matrix can be organized by divisional units, functional units, services, programs, or products. A law firm, for example, can use a matrix structure to organize itself according to the managerial functions that take place in each of its branches (its functional dimension) and then according to the branches themselves (its divisional dimension) (see Figure 3–8). Such a matrix has a dual chain of command, one for the overall organization and one for each law office or division within the firm. Some personnel have dual reporting relationships as well, a responsibility that links roles within the organization to produce a grid-like structure. Matrixes are useful for large organizations that are under internal pressure from critical sectors, that foster interdependence between units or departments, and that wish to employ efficiency and economies in the use of their resources.[60] In addition, organizations may use the matrix form to create multi-disciplinary teams to work on special projects. And since a dual focus is part of the matrix design, it can help a law firm with branch offices to respond to geographic problems such as distance and local community needs.

Advantages of the Matrix Structure

The matrix structure offers certain advantages:

Responsiveness. It enables a law firm to be more responsive to its immediate environment.

FIGURE 3–8
Matrix Organization Structure for a Multi-Branch Law Office

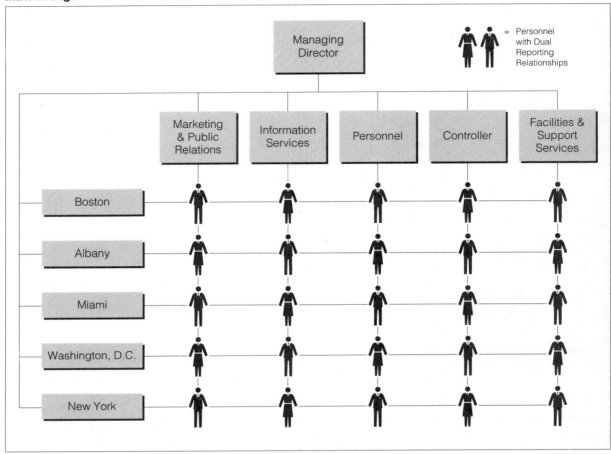

Resource Efficiencies. It provides an effective means for controlling the costs of client services while still providing access to greater resources.

Planning Benefits. The structure necessitates better and more concerted planning efforts for the entire firm. This leads to a more diverse planning process that increases the firm's chances of improving the efficiency of its operations.

Motivational Benefits. A matrix arrangement can also increase motivation, since it enables members to participate more fully in decision making and in other processes throughout the organization.

Increased Opportunities. The matrix structure increases opportunities for advancement, because it allows members to gain valuable managerial experience without weighting them down with full managerial responsibility.[61]

Disadvantages of the Matrix Structure

Despite its many benefits, a matrix can also create confusion, set the stage for power struggles, and place additional stress on organization members through its dual reporting requirements.[62] Coordinating needs and schedules may be difficult and time-consuming. Its parallel reporting relationships, which are effective for working with the diverse and sometimes conflicting needs of functional, product, and geographic management groups, can nonetheless lead to confusion; its multiple information channels, which allow managers to analyze the organization's environment, can result in a proliferation of communication and informational log jams; and its ability to create overlapping responsibilities, which allows subordinates greater responsibility and increases the organization's ability to respond to change, can lead to turf battles and engender ambiguity in terms of accountability.[63]

Organic and Mechanistic Organizations

In the early 1960s, two British researchers, Tom Burns and G. M. Stalker, described two opposing structures that they believed organizations utilized in order to exploit their human resources in the most efficient manner possible. Terming these organizational extremes **mechanistic** and **organic** management systems, Burns and Stalker were quick to point out that each is a valid structural option, appropriate for particular times and circumstances.[64]

An Organic Organization

An **organic organization** is a dynamic and responsive structure that can maximize the use of organizational processes and factors in both its internal and external environments.

A Mechanistic Organization

Resembling a bureaucracy, a **mechanistic organization** is a stable structure that consists of clear-cut divisions and roles, as specified by its well-defined rules, regulations, and hierarchical arrangements of responsibilities. In addition, a mechanistic organization relies on a strongly-protected chain of command.

Mechanistic management is likely an accurate way to describe present-day law firm management practices. Most law firm management centers on the mechanistic assumption that all knowledge about the activities of the firm and its tasks should be available only to the firm's partners and, in many firms, only the partners are involved in decisions.

Figure 3–9 compares mechanistic and organic organizational structure.

The Inverted Hierarchical Structure

Unlike traditional organizational charts, which normally trace authority as it descends through an organization, charts that depict an inverted hierarchy attempt to clarify the reporting relationships within the organization. This upside-down structure is popular among customer-driven companies, including Nordstrom and Dana, and Scandinavian Airlines, whose efforts to become client-oriented are described by its president, Jan Carlzon in *Moments of Truth*. Though inverted organizational structures may just be fantasies, in some managers' opinions, even client-driven organizations in particular must be responsive to those who ultimately determine their survival—the users of their services. Figure 3–10 applies the inverted hierarchical structure to a law firm.

ORGANIZATIONAL CULTURE

Just like people, organizations have reputations. Law firms are no exception. Well-established firms, like Nutter, McClennen & Fish of Boston, have created and reinforced their image over the years. Over time, a firm's actions, both behind its doors and in public, create for that firm a distinct character. Even smaller and less-established firms quickly develop identities: "That's the down-to-earth firm" or "That's the firm that hires barracudas." For better or for worse, people select symbols that come to represent the whole firm and with those symbols reduce the firm's reputation to a stereotype, most generally as a "good" firm or a "bad" one.

However, like paint or skin, reputation is just a surface covering. Through **image management,** the careful control of its external symbols, a law firm, like other organizations, may manipulate the public's perception of the firm and its actions. Behind the facade that the firm creates for the public exists a complex inner structure. Just as people consist of more than flesh, blood, and bone, organizations are dynamic entities composed of more than just hierarchies, departments, and organizational charts. The element that breathes unique life into an organization is its culture. **Organizational culture** is the perception of an organization that is formed by the shared beliefs and assumptions of its members. An organization's culture consists of enduring characteristics, created by all the experiences, stories, norms, traditions, beliefs, slogans, and values that its members have shared.[65] An organization's culture is the total of its past, its present, and where it wants to go. Including the formal as well as the informal organization, this culture encompasses the organization's business environment, its values—including the desire for success, its heroes, its day-to-day routines,

FIGURE 3-9
A Comparison of Organic and Mechanistic Organizations

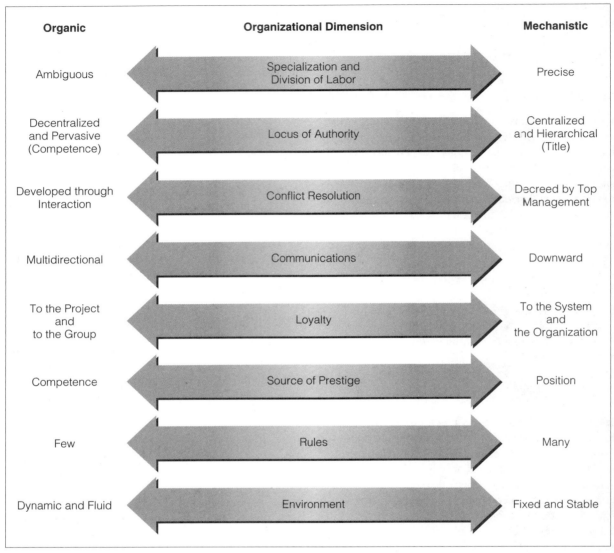

Elements of Culture

How does culture evolve in an organization? Just as groups of people in society develop powerful and complex cultures through conscious and unconscious decisions, organizations create their cultures through considerable effort and trial and error. The founders of an organization have a major impact on its early culture, and its methods of communicating values. Figure 3–11 depicts sources of culture within a law firm.

since no previous customs are around to dilute or otherwise modify their idea of what the organization should be. In the founders' hands, the culture is a clean slate: the small size that typically characterizes any new organization makes it easier for founders to impose their vision—and sometimes their biases—on all the organization's members.[66] Organizational culture is like a tapestry woven from the many meanings that the members hold in common about what the organization stands for and what it expects of them. There are five elements of culture in an organization:

FIGURE 3–10
The Inverted Hierarchical Structure in a Law Firm

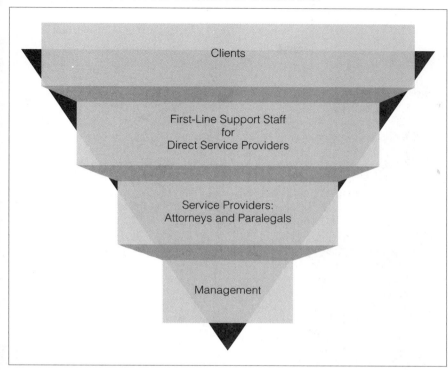

Environment

A firm's environment consists of its geographical, social, and political niche, the unique spot it occupies in the business world. Its fit within that niche depends on its particular practice of law and its service to society.

Values

Even a new firm possesses values. However, most evolve in the law firm over time, defining who and what is important, as well as what the firm's standards of achievement are.

Heroes

Organization members at all levels of the hierarchy who personify the organization's values become the firm's heroes, serving as examples for others.

Rites and Rituals

Procedures and routines that are part of everyday interactions become rituals. They are taken for granted, are unspoken, and usually remain unquestioned.

The Cultural Network

Each firm has its share of "storytellers, spies, priests, cabals, and whisperers" who communicate its culture through parables that bear messages of praise, disapproval, and identity.[67] Members also share understandings about the values, or *ethos*, of the law firm. They retell the stories, the legends of the firm, and share experiences that become common events for everyone. Those who fill this role create and enforce the firm's mythology. They shape norms, which become the generally accepted ways of doing business. They develop in-house jargon, which reinforces being part of the firm. They subliminally or overtly encourage other members to adopt the firm's attitude toward clients, file and record keeping, open doors, neat offices and desks, and even norms concerning interactions among personnel, such as relationships between secretaries and partners.

Consequences of Culture

A dominant culture, or a strong organizational culture, describes an organization in which the majority of members share the organization's most deeply rooted,

IN THE NEWS

Law Firms: Known by Their Reputations... and Their Cultures

After seven years of litigation, there is still some dispute over whether toxic solvents dumped at a tannery in Woburn, Mass., found their way into the municipal water supply and caused six deaths from leukemia. But there is no denying that bad karma from the case has seeped even further than the chemicals, crossing the Charles River and into Boston's blue-blooded bar.

Last July, Federal District Judge Walter Jay Skinner found that a lawyer for the tannery, Mary K. Ryan of Nutter, McClennen & Fish—the firm where Louis D. Brandeis wrote his famous briefs—had committed "deliberate misconduct" by hiding two reports from opposing counsel.

While chastising Ms. Ryan, who is a past president of the Women's Bar Association of Massachusetts, Judge Skinner cleared two lawyers with whom she had been working closely, Jerome P. Facher and Neil Jacobs of Hale & Dorr. Not only did he clear them; he extolled them, calling Mr. Facher "a tough but meticulously ethical advocate."

Not so long ago, even when Carl Yastrzemski was playing left field in Fenway Park, allegations of misbehavior in elite law firms were raised, and resolved, quietly. But at a time of heightened ethical scrutiny, Ms. Ryan has fought back in court. Seeking to overturn Judge Skinner's finding, she argues not only that she did nothing wrong, but that whatever she did, Hale & Dorr did too.

Nutter, McClennen's rebuttal on her behalf is couched in the most genteel terms; alleged discrepancies are "lapses in memory" rather than lies. "It is not Ms. Ryan's intention to turn her defense into an attack on other lawyers," said her own Brahmin lawyer, Paul B. Galvani of Ropes & Gray, in court papers. But before doing anything, he added, "she specifically sought and obtained" guidance from Mr. Facher and Mr. Jacobs, and "does not deserve to be singled out."

The two reports Ms. Ryan is said to have concealed turned up in 1987, shortly after Mr. Facher won an acquittal for Beatrice Foods, which owned the tannery from 1978 to 1983. Ms. Ryan acknowledged knowing about them but said she considered them both immaterial and privileged. The plaintiffs' lawyer, Jan Schlichtmann of Boston, whom one opposing lawyer described with admiration and annoyance as "a master at making

SOURCE: David Margolick, "At the Bar/In Which Boston Brahmin Law Firms Slug It Out. Genteely, of Course," *New York Times* (1 December 1989), p. B7. Copyright © 1989 by The New York Times Company. Reprinted with permission.

---

or core values. As management theorist Edgar Schein notes, "A strong culture is characterized by the organization's core values being intensely held, clearly ordered, and widely shared. The more members that accept the core values, agree on their order of importance, and are highly committed to them, the stronger the culture."[68] Because such commitment takes time to develop, cultures within older organizations are likely to be far more influential and powerful than cultures within relatively young organizations. Once established, culture affects many aspects of an organization, including those described in Table 3–2.

Kinds of Culture

The In the News article above gives us a glimpse at the cultures of several Boston law firms. While there are as many kinds of cultures as there are firms, organizations often have some cultural characteristics in common. One study suggests four distinct types of organizational culture. Most law firms may find a little of one or more of these cultures in their profiles:

Popular in firms that are on the firing line (such as those that specialize in criminal defense), the **macho/tough guy culture** rewards aggressive, hard-hitting behaviors and demands immediate results. Found in organizations with unpredictable demands, it provides a stage for those who love the spotlight, take risks, and succeed.

The **work-hard/play-hard culture**, common to high-profile firms (such as those that specialize in personal injury) thrives on activity, turning over a high volume of work and offering quick feedback.

IN THE NEWS (continued)

mountains out of molehills,'' moved to set aside the acquittal on the basis of attorney misconduct.

In hearings earlier this year, both Mr. Facher and Mr. Jacobs minimized their involvement with the reports and their role in secreting them. Later, though, Ms. Ryan laid out a detailed case, complete with 41 documents, in support of her claim.

Some Boston lawyers question the judge's decision to hit Ms. Ryan and hail Mr. Facher. They note that Mr. Facher went to Harvard Law School with the judge and has appeared often in his courtroom; Ms. Ryan is of another sex and a later era.

This might be your run-of-the-mill what-did-they-know-and-when-did-they-know-it dispute if any firm but Hale & Dorr were involved.

Nationally, Hale & Dorr has long been one of several archetypal Yankee law firms, the office of Joseph Welch of the Army-McCarthy hearings (''Have you no sense of decency, sir?'') and of James St. Clair, Richard M. Nixon's Watergate counsel.

In fact, every Boston Brahmin law firm has acquired its own distinctive stereotype. Foley, Hoag & Elliot caters to academics-in-exile, and Ropes & Gray is a place of preppy propriety. Even in this solemn group, Choate, Hall & Stewart is considered stuffy; Goodwin, Procter & Hoar no-nonsense. The firm long known as Gaston Snow & Ely Bartlett (and long derided as ''Ghastly Slow & Easily Beaten'') has a new name—Gaston, Snow, Beekman & Bogue—and a more modern image.

While perhaps the most successful of the bunch, Hale & Dorr also carries what is, at least locally, the harshest of labels: ''New York-style.'' It was the first to hire tough, non-Yankee (i.e., Irish and Jewish) litigators, as likely to have played hockey at Boston College as tennis at Harvard. Hale & Dorr represented Danny Ainge, the scrappy onetime Boston Celtic, but in a way, Danny Ainge also represented Hale & Dorr. That reputation is personified by the 63-year old Mr. Facher, an intense, irascible and invariably effective trial lawyer.

''Lawyers respect Hale & Dorr, but there's no love for them,'' said Jonathan Haar, who is writing a book about the Woburn case.

Next week's Massachusetts Lawyer's Weekly will have a letter from 23 lawyers in support of Ms. Ryan. No similar campaign is being mounted for Mr. Facher, a fact that neither surprises nor concerns him. ''When you have a firm that does difficult litigation rather than just rate-setting cases before the public utilities commission, that's been known from Welch to St. Clair to me and others,'' he said, ''you're going to pick up some resentment along the way.''

Filled with competitive activities that in the business world we would associate with high-power salespeople and their tactics, this climate is for active super-achievers. It is spawning law firms that emphasize strongly competitive practices, highly visible marketing, and well-distributed risks.

Often appearing in firms that require large contingency fees (such as those specializing in insurance company litigation), the **you-bet-your-company culture** relies on careful, detailed decision-making processes, based on expertise and substantial research. Found in slow-to-react, traditional law firms, this culture is also common in high-stakes, slow-feedback industries, such as architecture, where payoffs are large but sometimes infrequent.

Most often characterizing probate and other firms that specialize in estate work, the **process culture** focuses on technical and informational perfection, sometimes at the expense of results. Although this culture is fairly common in low-risk organizations that offer slow feedback, such as government, accounting, or financial services, it can throttle law firms, where timely action is imperative.[69]

CHARACTERISTICS OF SUCCESSFUL ORGANIZATIONS IN THE 1990s

Far from being untouchable havens for unchanging business practices, law firms, including legal corporate offices, will be unable to ignore the challenges facing

FIGURE 3–11
Sources of Culture within a Law Firm

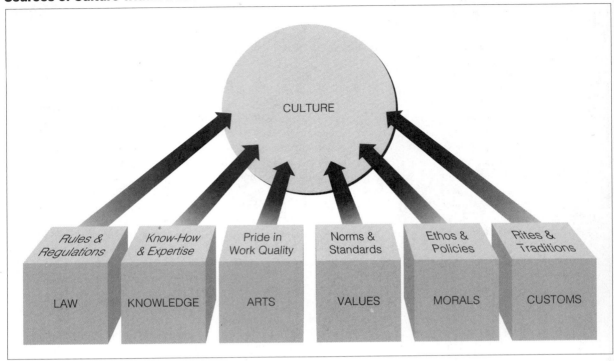

TABLE 3–2
Organizational Factors Affected by Culture

Individual Initiative	The degree to which the organization encourages responsibility, freedom, and independence.
Risk Tolerance	The manner in which the organization encourages and supports aggressiveness, risk taking, and innovation.
Direction	The clarity with which the organization conveys its expectations.
Integration	The degree of success with which the organization coordinates its efforts.
Management Support	The levels of clear communication, support, and assistance that management personnel offer subordinates.
Control	The types of governing mechanisms (such as rules, regulations, and close supervision) that the organization utilizes.
Identity	The amount of identification workers have with the organization.
Reward System	The method by which the organization allocates rewards, based on factors ranging from favoritism, seniority, and patronage to actual performance measures.
Conflict Tolerance	The organization's attitude toward divergent thinking, the expression of criticism, and outright conflict.
Communication Patterns	How the organization encourages communication flow and the degree to which it promotes open communication.

SOURCE: Based on George G. Gordon and W. M. Cummins, *Managing Management Climate* (Lexington, Mass.: Lexington Books, 1979); and Stephen P. Robbins, *Organization Theory: Structure, Design, and Applications*, 3d ed. (Englewood Cliffs, New Jersey: Prentice-Hall, Inc., 1990): 439.

all businesses in the 1990s. Tom Peters, who has written much on the challenges ahead for business, foresees changes that will affect the very structure and design of organizations. He predicts, for example, that the future will bring ''the end of hierarchy.'' Already, many businesses are flattening their layers of management, changing the pyramidal organization into a network without a clearly defined top or even a center. Peters foresees a shift from traditional business approaches to a client-centered concern that will be accompanied by a ''whole new idea of equality in relationships with outsiders.'' He envisions general industry copying the service organization's horizontal project orientation, learning a lesson from lawyer and other professional service providers who have ''traditionally used project teams'' and who ''are emerging as the best organizational models.'' He predicts a ''continuous-improvement-continuous-learning way of life,'' where each worker, as part of a self-management team, will be committed to ''better ways of doing things''; indeed, information technology will upend ''every organizational relationship.'' And all organizations will experience time-obsessed competition as part of their critical strategies for the nineties, striving to reduce the considerable percentage of time they waste when attempting to complete key projects. Time will be the key to achieving competitive superiority in the provision of law firm services. Says Peters, ''Every aspect of the organization structure and all processes have to be upended to accomplish this extreme variety of time-slashing.''[70]

Another observer notes that ''the new law firm structure resembles an organic family tree . . . Each law firm now varies according to firm size, growth patterns, partner relationships, client needs and the overall position of the law firm in the community. There is more pressure on associates and partners to be flexible and know what's going on.''[71]

And Rosabeth Moss Kanter warns of the downfalls for stable, traditional organizational structures as well as the potential dangers for fluid, entrepreneurial new designs:

> The traditional large, hierarchical corporation is not innovative or responsive enough; it becomes set in its ways, riddled with pecking-order politics, and closed to new ideas or outside influences. But the pure entrepreneurial firm—the fast-growing start-up—is not the answer, either; it is not always disciplined or cooperative enough to move from heady, spend-anything intervention to cost-effective production, and it can become closed in its own way, too

confident and too dependent on the magic of individual stars.[72]

From observations such as these, we may begin to form an image of the law firm of the near future. The successful structure will be flatter; populated by more autonomous units; oriented toward differentiation, producing high-quality, timely services and creating niche markets; will be quality- and service-conscious, more responsive, and faster at innovation; and, finally, a user of highly trained, flexible people as the principal means for adding value to its service. Law firm managers have a detailed road map for venturing into the organizational designs for the years ahead.[73] Figure 3–12 offers eight pieces of advice for firms seeking excellence in the 1990s and beyond.

FIGURE 3–12

Criteria for the Search for Excellence in the Law Firm

1. **A Bias for Action**
   Cultivate a preference for doing rather than dangling ideas through committees and analysis.

2. **Staying Close to the Customer**
   Learn about clients and how to cater to them.

3. **Autonomy and Entrepreneurship**
   Set up units of legal specialties or office activities that are encouraged to act independently and compete with each other.

4. **Productivity through People**
   Create in all law office workers the awareness that their best work is essential for everyone's success.

5. **Hands-On, Value-Driven**
   Insist that managing partners and firm leaders and managers keep in touch with the organization's mission, promoting a strong culture.

6. **"Stick to the Knitting"**
   Stay with the areas the firm knows best.

7. **Simple Form, Lean Staff**
   Use few administrative layers, keeping few people at the central activity and upper-level administrative levels of firm management.

8. **Simultaneously Loose-Tight Design**
   Foster a law firm climate that combines a commitment to its central values with tolerance for those who accept those values.

SOURCE: Adapted from Thomas Peters and Robert Waterman, Jr., *In Search of Excellence* (New York: Warner Books, 1982).

QUESTIONS FOR DISCUSSION AND REVIEW

1. Is being organized an inborn talent or a skill? How does being organized relate to the architecture or structuring of organizations?
2. Think of any poorly run organization you know. How are its problems linked to the four main activities involved in organizing?
3. What do authority, delegation, and responsibility have in common? How are they different?
4. Why is delegation difficult for new managers? Can managers over-delegate?
5. Describe an imaginary or a real law firm, explaining how it is either mechanistic or organic. Which form do you think is more effective as an organizational structure for a law firm?
6. Explain what an upside-down organization is. What advantages or disadvantages does the inverted hierarchy hold for law firms?
7. Using the five elements of culture, describe a law firm, college, or company you have experienced.

EXPERIENTIAL EXERCISES

I. Organizational Profiles*

On the opposite page is an outline of organizational characteristics based on the work of Rensis Likert. Choose an organization (for instance, a law firm where you have worked, an office where you have interned, a college or university you have attended, or any organization you may have experienced, even briefly) and, for each characteristic, check the area on the continuum that you believe best describes that organization. Then answer these questions:

1. What level of skills and knowledge does this organization expect its workers to contribute?
2. What effect does this expectation (and the degree to which it is fulfilled) appear to have on the organization's efficiency and effectiveness?

II. Designing Organizations

Windy, Erie, and O'Hare, P.C., is a law firm located in Chicago, with three branch offices in Terre Haute, Toledo, and Detroit. The firm consists of twelve partners, fourteen associates, one law firm administrator, ten paralegals, fourteen secretaries and word processors, one information services coordinator, one financial manager and a bookkeeper, and four receptionists, some of whom also assist with records and bookkeeping. There is an executive management committee consisting of three partners, and there are three lawyers' committees: finance, marketing and public relations, and long-range planning.

1. Design an organizational chart for the present firm. In what ways is the design organic or mechanistic?
2. Create an organizational chart as you might imagine the firm in five years. Is this design more or less mechanistic or organic than the design in question 1? Explain why.

---

*Rensis Likert, *The Human Organization* (New York: McGraw-Hill Book Company, 1967). Reprinted by permission.

	Organizational Variables	SYSTEM 1	SYSTEM 2	SYSTEM 3	SYSTEM 4
Leadership	How much confidence is shown in subordinates?	None	Condescending	Substantial	Complete
	How free do they feel to talk to superiors about their job?	Not at all	Not very	Rather free	Fully free
	Are subordinates' ideas sought and used, if worthy?	Seldom	Sometimes	Usually	Always
Motivation	Is predominant use made of 1 fear, 2 threats, 3 punishment, 4 rewards, 5 involvement?	1, 2, 3 occasionally 4	4, some 3	4, some 3 and 5	5, 4 based on group
	Where is responsibility felt for achieving organizational goals?	Mostly at top	Top and middle	Fairly general	At all levels
	How much cooperative teamwork exists?	None	Little	Some	Great deal
Communication	What is the direction of information flow?	Downward	Mostly downward	Down and up	Down, up and sideways
	How is downward communication accepted?	With suspicion	Possibly with suspicion	With caution	With a receptive mind
	How accurate is upward communication?	Often wrong	Censored for the boss	Limited accuracy	Accurate
	How well do superiors know problems faced by subordinates?	Know little	Some knowledge	Quite well	Very well
Decisions	At what level are decisions made?	Mostly at top	Policy at top, some delegation	Broad policy at top, more delegation	Throughout but well integrated
	Are subordinates involved in decisions related to their work?	Not at all	Occasionally consulted	Generally consulted	Fully involved
	What does decision-making process contribute to motivation?	Nothing, often weakens it	Relatively little	Some contribution	Substantial contribution
Goals	How are organizational goals established?	Orders issued	Orders, some comments invited	After discussion, by orders	By group action (except in crisis)
	How much covert resistance to goals is present?	Strong resistance	Moderate resistance	Some resistance at times	Little or none
Control	How concentrated are review and control functions?	Highly at top	Relatively highly at top	Moderate delegation to lower levels	Quite widely shared
	Is there an informal organization resisting the formal one?	Yes	Usually	Sometimes	No—same goals as formal
	What are cost, productivity, and other control data used for?	Policing, punishment	Reward and punishment	Reward, some self-guidance	Self-guidance, problem-solving

III. Supportive Relationships

In his ideal organizational design, System 4, Likert suggested that workers should determine the degree of support that is part of their relationships with their superiors. Select a superior you have or have had in the past. For each of the following questions, rate the degree of supportiveness of your relationship with that superior. Circle the number that best expresses your perception.

5 = Extremely strong
4 = Very strong
3 = Average
2 = Weak
1 = Very weak
0 = Nonexistent

____ 1. How do you rate the confidence you have in your boss?
____ 2. How do you rate the confidence he or she has in you?
____ 3. How do you rate the trust you have in your boss?
____ 4. How do you rate the trust he or she has in you?
____ 5. How do you rate your boss's interest in your achievements?
____ 6. How do you rate your boss's helping you in obtaining a good income?
____ 7. How do you rate your boss's efforts to understand your problems?
____ 8. How do you rate your boss's efforts to try to assist you in obtaining better income and benefits?
____ 9. How do you rate your boss's effect on your self-esteem?
____ 10. How do you rate your boss's active efforts to build you ego rather than deflate it?
____ 11. How do you rate your boss's respect for you?

Scoring: Add the numbers you have written before each item.

1. If your score is between 45 and 60, you have the ideal superior.
2. If your score is between 30 and 44, you must develop fortitude and personal motivational strengths.
3. If your score is between 15 and 29, you need to develop inner peace and support from outside sources.
4. If your score is between 0 and 14, you are a survivor! May you learn never to do unto others as they have done to you.

CHAPTER 4

Directing: Authority, Power, and Politics

LEARNING OBJECTIVES

After completing this chapter, you should be able to:

- Discuss the meanings of and relationships between authority, power, and politics;
- Understand the challenges of delegation and explain how to delegate successfully;
- Describe what power is, where power is found, and how power is used;
- Define the sources of personal and position power;
- Explain influence strategies and managerial and subordinate power strategies;
- Describe the role of politics in organizations, including the positive and negative results of political games and strategies; and
- Discuss the value of empowerment and the advantages of being empowered.

FOCUS FROM
THE FIELD

**Evelyn Murphy:
A Real Obligation
If You Are
at the Top**

Evelyn F. Murphy has been managing director of the Boston law firm of Brown, Rudnick, Freed and Gesmer since January 1991. The first woman in Massachusetts history to be elected to any statewide office, she has served as secretary of environmental affairs, secretary of economic affairs, and lieutenant governor of Massachusetts from 1987 to 1991. She holds a Ph.D. in economics from Duke University.

Was it difficult for you to delegate work at first?

It was not difficult for me. I have always relied on people working for me whom I felt had both the capacity to take on the responsibility of the work and in whom I placed a lot of trust and confidence. I find that it's important to give that authority to other people. It puts the pressure on them to be very careful in the quality of responses they give back. Over the years, particularly when I managed state government, I found that many of the technical staff would always know more than I did about the specific field of engineering and chemistry, and I relied on their knowledge but used my judgment as to how to use that information as the best collaboration of good staff work with the one person who has to be ultimately responsible.

Is it difficult managing attorneys?

I see it as a collaboration. They know more about the law and legal practice than I will ever know. I'm bringing my experience as a business/financial manager, as someone who as a political leader sees the larger issues in society, and as an economist—a Ph.D. economist—who sees the larger fiscal economic forces. So, what I see is a genuine collaboration of two different disciplines, those of an economist and of a lawyer, working together for the good of the firm and for the enhancement of a professional practice.

Are there positive attitudes about subordinates that their supervisors should have in order to delegate to them effectively?

I believe that the tone of any professional relationship is pretty much set by the person at the top. If you convey a tone of confidence, and a trust and a willingness to work with staff, the positive tone that you can set is infectious. It inspires a quality of work out of people which is far beyond what they will give if they're intimidated, if they feel they're going to be second-guessed. That tone is as important as any mechanical means that you have for delegating work.

Do you have any feedback mechanisms for making sure the responsibility is carried out?

I am confident enough about my own managerial skills and leadership to find it easy to delegate down responsibility and authority so that others get the practice and the experience of taking these things on. I think that's a very important part of bringing along other professionals. They've got to feel that kind of authority. They've got to feel that kind of responsibility. If you take it on yourself over and over again, the kind of professional training within a firm or within a governmental agency never happens.

Is there a specific behavior you are attentive to in your authority role?

Yes, I am very careful to be specific about the kind of items that come out of meetings and about who is responsible for follow-up. I am careful about scheduling appointments and report dates and having those happen so that people begin to see that there are deadlines that can be met and that everything is not infinitely flexible, and I'm also careful in a sort of routine fashion over months and years to make sure there's systematic follow-up on performance and on reviews so that things are not done in an ad hoc way.

So routine is very important?

Yes it is. You need a structure that people are comfortable with, that fits both the needs of the outside clients and the kind of rhythm and timing of a firm and its individual partners; but also it's important that everyone gets the same sense of expectations as to when reports and reviews and evaluations are going to be done.

What should supervisors be aware of in delegating work to others?

I think supervisors have to be careful to build on people's strengths and not reinforce weaknesses. I think supervisors have to set realistic deadlines and meet them, realistic in terms of what is expected from a client or some external force but also deadlines that the people who are going to have to meet them can meet. You have to be aware of not building in overexpectations. They must be realistic expectations for each individual. Then, you get the best performance out of people. And over the long term, you get the development of people's talents.

What is important to remember in one's use of power?

As a manager, I find it very important that when you have those top positions, that you exercise the power of the position to demonstrate some clear leadership to people who work for you. In fact, you have authority over people and what they're doing when they work for you, but the power side of it is to raise people's sights about what kind of contribution they are making, and someone with that power has an obligation to exercise it to the best of his or her judgment. Not to exercise it is I think to leave those who work with and for you in a more vulnerable position. So, there's a real obligation if you're at the top of anything, whether it's a secretary, an elected official, or at the top of a company, not just to manage but to lead and to set the direction, and to have people share that vision and to share that understanding about what kind of contribution they are making to society.

People who have never exercised power have all kinds of curious ideas about it. The popular notion of top leadership is a fantasy of capricious power: the top man presses a button and something remarkable happens; he gives an order as the whim strikes him, and it is obeyed. Actually, the capricious use of power is relatively rare except in some large dictatorships and some small family firms. Most leaders are hedged in by constraints—tradition, constitutional limitations, and realities of the external situation, rights and privileges of followers, the requirements of teamwork, and most of all, the inexorable demands of the large-scale organization, which does not operate on capriciousness. In short, most power is wielded circumspectly.
(John Gardner, "The Anti-Leadership Vaccine")[1]

. . . [**T**he little prince] plucked up his courage to ask the king a favor: "I should like to see a sunset . . . Do me that kindness . . . Order the sun to set." "If I ordered a general to fly from one flower to another like a butterfly, or to write a tragic drama, or to change himself into a sea bird, and if the general did not carry out the order he had received, which one of us would be in the wrong?" the king

> demanded. "The general or myself?" "You," said the little prince firmly. "Exactly. One must require from each the duty which each one can perform . . . I have the right to require obedience because my orders are reasonable." "Then my sunset?" the little prince reminded him . . . "You shall have your sunset. I shall command it. But, according to my science of government, I shall wait until conditions are favorable."
>
> (Saint-Exupéry, *The Little Prince*)[2]

AUTHORITY

In the excerpt above, Saint-Exupéry's little prince meets a king who claims he rules over everything, even the sun and the stars, simply by being wise enough to wait until the conditions are favorable. As a law firm manager, or even as an attorney or part of the firm's support staff, you will need similar wisdom when directing the efforts of others. Directing others requires an appreciation of power; knowing how to use power, in turn, requires you to understand the existing conditions within your firm. Power proliferates in legal settings, since power leads to influence, and persuasive influence is what makes successful lawyers. Law firms abound with the use of power. If you have worked in a law firm, you probably have found that the using and the holding and sharing of power permeates nearly every activity in the firm. Should power be studied as part of law office management? Is learning about the dynamics of power crucial? Harvard Business School graduate Mary Cunningham, who relates her much publicized career failure in the autobiographical *Powerplay,* believes so: "In business school, they taught us about cash flow, not about corporate politics; about return on equity, not about egos and pride." Because of her fall from the high executive ranks of the Bendix corporation, she discovered the hard way that learning about power "should have been every much a part of the curriculum as Production, Marketing, and Finance." [3]

There is one particular form of power that binds people together in the workplace, legitimizing the amount of influence some have over others: authority. Authority once originated in ownership: very simply, owners had the right to do as they chose with what they owned. Today, it is not so simple. Now focusing on the "assumptions about what actions management may take unilaterally and what actions should be open to influence by other stakeholders," [4] **authority** is the legitimate right, commonly reserved for managers, to command or influence, based on one's place in the hierarchy.

> The authoritarian relation between the one who commands and the one who obeys rests neither on common reason nor on the power of the one who commands; what they have in common is the hierarchy itself, whose rightness and legitimacy both recognize and where both have their predetermined stable place.[5]

Although most of us acknowledge that managerial authority directs and mandates in order to keep the needs of individuals and the needs of organizations in a productive balance, few of us give much serious thought to the right of those in authority to command, and we give even less thought to what the obligation to obey entails. Shoshana Zuboff, author of *The Smart Machine,* says that managers must have more than the right to command. They must establish credibility as well, developing "a context of belief that could legitimate and sustain the right to command." [6]

Professional organizations in particular are dynamic social exchanges whose workers realize their entitlement to respect and equity, especially in good economic times, when their skills and knowledge, though intangible, provide them with excellent commodities to offer in exchange for better salaries and other rewards. The psychological contract that exists between the organization and the individual encompasses all the terms for the entire set of expectations held by each side. It includes not only the basics, such as the pay and benefits each person may earn for the work he or she contributes, but "the whole pattern of rights and privileges" of the worker as well.[7] Questioning authority is an ongoing and unwritten part of that contractual exchange of inducements and contributions between individuals and organizations. If, when employees question authority, the answers do not provide them an equitable balance of power, the workers who can do so move on, seeking a workplace that will treat them decently. But no matter how independent workers are, no matter how able or willing they are to shake off organizational ties, authority is the most indispensable element of organizational life. Even an organization churning with politics and power abuses can still transform into authority whatever legitimate organizational power it possesses. As Abraham Zaleznik and Manfred Kets de Vries note,

> "Power" is an ugly word. It connotes dominance and submission, control and acquiescence, one man's will at the expense of another man's self-esteem ... Yet it is power, the ability to control and influence others, that provides the basis for the direction of organizations and for the attainment of social goals. Leadership is the exercise of power.[8]

Within the organization, a manager's **scope of authority** describes the range of requests that he or she legitimately can make, as well as the range of actions that he or she legitimately can perform.[9] Questions often arise concerning true justifiability of a manager's scope of authority:

> An executive can rightfully expect a supervisor to work hard and diligently; may he also influence the supervisor to spy on rivals, spend weekends away from home, join an encounter group? A coach can rightfully expect his players to execute specific plays; may he also direct their life styles outside the sport? A combat officer can rightfully expect his men to attack on order; may he also direct them to execute civilians whom he claims are spies? A doctor can rightfully order a nurse to attend a patient or observe an autopsy; may he order her to assist in an abortion against her will?[10]

Examining issues such as these will give you, as a future manager or member of a law firm, a better understanding of the legitimate scope of authority.

DELEGATION

"**Delegation** is the turning over of both the responsibility and the authority for doing a job to a subordinate who is held accountable for the performance of that job."[10] Assigning work to others is often difficult: experienced and inexperienced managers alike may tend to under- or over-delegate. The new paralegal coordinator, for example, anxious to stay on good terms with former coworkers, does not want to offend them by over-delegating. As a result, this new manager shelters subordinates by performing the harder tasks and ends up doing double duty. Some experienced managers, who are reluctant to accept the fact that their subordinates might make mistakes, also have a hard time delegating. These managers also experience difficulty in allowing their subordinates necessary access to power and resources. However, the failure to allow them such access is the failure to delegate; fearing the results of delegation or the process itself, some managers are content simply to oversee and to supervise.

Realistically, though, delegation can be a daunting task. For many managers, the most common dilemma of delegation is how to maintain responsibility for a task once it has been assigned to someone. Accountability, the assessment of how well workers do what they are asked to do, helps to resolve this dilemma. Although the subordinate is *always* held responsible for the outcome of a delegated task, the final responsibility, for both the task and the delegatee, rests with the delegator. Delegation never means abdication. The most difficult barrier that managers have to overcome is thinking that they are responsible for their subordinates' failures, rather than holding their subordinates accountable.

Successful Delegation

For managers to delegate successfully, they must be willing to take others' ideas seriously, have the insight to provide their subordinates with the right combination of free rein and support, be able to trust in the abilities of others and to allow people to grow and learn from their mistakes, without penalizing them for their failures or inadequacies.[12]

Steps in Delegating

There are four steps in delegating. First, you should begin by assigning the responsibility only to someone who is capable of doing what you ask. Second, you must communicate to the delegatee your expectations concerning what he or she needs to accomplish. Third, you must ensure that you have given the delegatee the authority he or she needs to meet these responsibilities. You may do this by providing him or her with the power and access that he or she will need within the organization to accomplish the task. Finally, you must establish a communications procedure by which the delegatee may report his or her progress and receive feedback, and, most importantly, you must hold that individual accountable for the task's success—or lack thereof.[13] Table 4–1 summarizes the steps in successful delegation.

Willingness of Subordinates

It is difficult to delegate to some subordinates. Some may show justifiable reluctance if they know that they will lack access to the right kinds of tools: the authority to work with others in doing what is asked, and the power to obtain the right resources for doing the job. In addition, if subordinates believe that their superior will not provide the guidance, communications, or support that they need, their reluctance is well founded. Some managers are known for delegating all their work to subordinates and taking credit for the outcomes. Subordinates must be able to see delegation as a legitimate and rational sharing of tasks, not as a lazy manager's technique for avoiding work.

What Cannot Be Delegated

Some aspects of a manager's work cannot be delegated. Conceptual planning is one such area, particularly when it constitutes part of a larger, perhaps organization-wide, plan. Subordinates should always be able to provide input during such planning, but control of the process must reside with the appropriate level of management. Resolving problems with morale is also nondelegable. Just as workers do not determine salary raises for their peers, they cannot resolve a coworker's dispute with the organization. Other work that cannot be delegated includes performance reviews for promotion or raises, direct assignments that the manager has received specifically from a superior, confidential work, and personal projects that would only waste a subordinate's time.

Weaknesses in Delegating

The often-heard complaint about not knowing how to delegate has many causes:

Insecurities

Some managers are uncertain of the range of their authority in delegating, not realizing that, in most organizations, managers must avoid doing *only* those things that their superiors specifically forbid. Other managers demonstrate a personal insecurity, an inability to trust the competence or motives of others. Still other managers, perceiving the giving of work to others as a sign of weakness or inability, fear being outdone by their subordinates. While such fears are not that unusual, a manager's being superior at every task is not nearly as important as his or her knowing how to develop the competencies of subordinates. Effective managers delight in the accomplishments of their subordinates. Seeing subordinates develop their talents is a valid aim for all managers, who should know that successful and appreciated workers are motivated to do their best for the organization.

TABLE 4–1
Steps in Successful Delegation

1. Assign the job clearly.
2. Communicate expectations for results.
3. Give the authority needed to fulfill the responsibilities:
   a. By allowing the necessary power.
   b. By providing access to the resources necessary to do the job.
4. Establish a communications system:
   a. To enable the delegatee to report and to receive feedback.
   b. To enable the delegator to hold the delegatee truly accountable.

Ego

The inability to delegate is also deeply rooted in ego-related needs. Some managers thrive on their reputations for achievement—and want to ensure that they reap these hard-earned rewards single-handedly. Operating under the motto "I can do it better myself," they emphasize being in charge, hoarding control and refusing to relinquish even a sliver of power.[14] Such managers are somehow convinced, often without solid evidence, that their results are unfailingly superior to those of others. Regardless, it is not an issue of who can do the job best but more a question of what is best for each person to do. A belief in long-term outcomes—rather than immediate results—is critical for managers and subordinates alike.

Planning Skills

The inability to plan causes many managers to forego delegation; in addition, most managers have genuine time pressures. They place delegating last on their list, not finding the time to teach others how to perform tasks; ironically, this time will remain unfound for managers who won't make delegation a priority. Those who do make delegating part of their managerial style find time to focus on larger issues of management, one of which is ensuring that others contribute their fair share.

Communication Skills

Poor communication skills cause many managers to be poor delegators. While managers are often adept at giving instructions for a delegated task, they frequently underestimate the importance of precisely expressing their expectations about how the job is to be performed. Subordinates working under ambiguous expectations can easily set off on the wrong track or be left stumbling about in the dark, unsure of what is really to be done.

Biases

Managers having biased or bigoted views may be reluctant to assign work to members of certain groups, basing such reluctance on the unfounded notion that someone is incapable of commitment, responsibility, or follow-through, or even is unable to perform the task itself. Instead of discussing the job with a possible delegatee, such managers decide a priori about the delegatee's competence, rather than validly assessing it.

Control Mechanisms

Managers also are often poor at establishing controls and scheduling follow-up sessions for work they have delegated. Delegating work is not a question of assigning a task and forgetting about it until the result appears, full-blown, on one's desk. A constant exchange of support, information, and feedback is an integral part of the delegation process.

Professional Guilt

Another common reason for the failure to delegate is a guilty fear of not having anything to do when the work is all delegated. Often this fear is based on a potential absence of work, not an actual one. A manager should be supervising people and resources; delegating represents a task, not the lack of one.

Impatience

Finally, some managers fail to delegate authority merely because of impatience.[15]

Taken together, these eight weaknesses represent a single idea: Any time that managers spend on jobs that subordinates could have performed is time taken away from their own job of managing, and is time lost for their organization.

> Many people, particularly those who are effective at accomplishing things, have an enormous sense of urgency, a tremendous drive to do things. They want things done "yesterday, if not before." Such people tend to be poor delegators of work, often doing the work themselves in the belief that this is the best way to ensure that it gets done. ... A sense of urgency is considered to be one of the essential attributes for a successful boss in our society. But it should be realized that there is a big difference between urgency and impatience: A sense of urgency means a real drive to get things done; impatience means unwillingness to accept the fact that getting them done does take time.[16]

Managers at all levels in a law firm, where time is a valuable commodity, can benefit from these understandings.

Managerial Delegation Styles

Law firm managers who delegate successfully trust their subordinates, becoming on-the-job teachers, coaches, communicators, and motivators. However, there are several managerial styles that inhibit successful delegation:[17]

The Protectors

Law firm managers who want to protect their subordinates from stress and failure, the protectors end up doing part of their subordinates' jobs.

The Abdicators

Abdicators, who fail to take responsibility for their subordinates' performance, often set themselves and their subordinates up for failure by providing too little authority for a delegated task, leading eventually to complete frustration and resentment.

The Predators

Delegating only parts of jobs, predators never allow the subordinate to experience the full range of responsibility that accompanies each task. The success of the jobs is often, at best, short-lived. When employees do not know exactly what to do or what is expected of them, it is almost impossible for them to do well.

The Stressors

The stressors force law firm employees to work under stress, in order to give them a "true" taste of the firing line, setting up unrealistic goals and experiences for them. Sometimes those who have been given too much responsibility experience difficulties with other workers who resent, resist, and undermine their efforts.

The Fire Fighters

These law firm managers insist on doing jobs themselves, rushing in to resolve crises and spending more time putting out fires than keeping the home fires burning productively.

POWER

To operate as social systems, as collections of people, all organizations rely on the paths, exchanges, and forces of power. As newspaper columnist James Kilpatrick once noted, "The name of the game is power. Nothing else. Who has power, how he gets it, how power is delegated, how power is restrained, how power is exercised—these are the questions that absorb us."[18] The tension that keeps the organization either in a positive and healthy flux or locked in a stalemate, power exists in the organization's formal and informal systems and in its network of professional and personal relationships. Both employers and employees wield power to maintain the balance of contributions and inducements. In his classic work, "The Concept of Power," Robert Dahl observes, "The concept of power is as ancient and ubiquitous as any that social theory can boast."[19]

Two of today's experts on power and leadership, Bennis and Nanus, write that power is one of the most familiar forces in the universe. They consider it the most basic social energy, saying that it has been given so many faces that we no longer can disassociate it from the connotations it has acquired through the years: avarice, insensitivity, cruelty, corruption. Power, they claim, is "the most necessary and most distrusted element exigent to human progress." Over the years, "Leaders have controlled, not organized, administered repression, not expression, held followers in arrestment rather than in evolution."[20] Americans in particular, observes David McClelland, a Harvard psychologist who has long researched power and influence, have a neurotic obsession with the misuse of power.[21] However, while some believe that too many people possess and ultimately abuse power, others maintain that the real problem, at least in organizations, is due less to an excess of power than to the fact that "too many people have too little power, especially people in leadership jobs."[22]

The Importance of Power in the Organization

Ideally, within organizations, power should be the reciprocal of leadership—what leaders receive from their followers in exchange for shouldering the responsibilities and tensions of leadership. Power, as Abraham Zaleznik suggests, enables leaders to transform their organizations. Those who choose careers in which they will exercise influence must understand beforehand the true nature of power and its potential for self-serving as well as for altruism. "It is no wonder, therefore," Zaleznik concludes, "that individuals who are highly motivated to secure and use power find a familiar and hospitable environment in business."[23] Professor John Kotter, who teaches a very successful course on power and influence to Harvard MBAs, seems to concur that power should be less a personal compulsion to control others than an organizational necessity to enable all members to perform well:

> ... the primary reason power dynamics emerge and play an important role in organizations is not necessarily because managers are power hungry, or because they want desperately to get ahead, or because there is an inherent conflict between managers who have authority and workers who do not. It is because the dependence inherent in managerial jobs is greater than the power or control given to the people in those jobs. Power dynamics, under these circumstances, are inevitable and are needed to make organizations function well.[24]

However, to some people, power itself, not the health of the organization, is the ultimate goal. Such people believe that power is vital to their success. Their compulsive need for professional power is simply an extension of their personal power needs. Others covet power in order to master lofty personal or professional goals. Finally, there are those who seek social power, using such power for the good of others.[25] Managers and those working in the law office should know the basic powerplays and players.

Definitions of Power

We usually consider **power** to be the ability to act, to do, to control, and to influence—in other words, the ability to accomplish what we want to accomplish. However, experts on power have many views on what power means to the organization. Organizational power is, among other things, the following:

> The ability to get things done, to mobilize resources, to get and use whatever it is that a person needs for the goals he or she is attempting to meet.... Power is the ability to *do* in the classic physical usage of power as energy, and thus it means having access to whatever is needed for the doing. (Kanter)[26]
>
> The probability that one actor in a social relationship will be in a position to carry out his own will, despite resistance, and regardless of the basis on which this probability rests. (Weber)[27]
>
> A force that results in behavior that would not have occurred if the force had not been present. (Mechanic)[28]
>
> The ability of one person or a group of persons to influence the behavior of others ... (Kaplan)[29]

The Flow of Power

We often think of the flow of organizational power in terms of a trickle-down theory, in which those at the top of an organization primarily allocate power and regulate its flow. The reality is that the flow of power is multi-directional. Rather than blindly believing in a top-down power flow, top management should be aware that they are involved in an uninterrupted and constantly changing power struggle—with others at the top as well as those at the bottom. No one is exempt from the fray; as Samuel Bacharach and Edward Lawler note, in their work *Power and Politics in Organizations*, "Individuals and subgroups within organizations are not passive recipients awaiting the downward trickle of power but rather are active participants mobilizing power for their own ends."[30] All law firm members participate in power activities, from the lowliest new hire to the most senior managing partner, and their participation splits the power flow into three distinct streams: a downward flow, which is the power managers use over subordinates; an upward flow, the power subordinates exercise over superiors; and a lateral flow, the exchanges of power between members and their peers. Given the right mix of personalities, needs, and drives, personnel at any level can create, enhance, control, and take power.

SOURCES OF POWER

Power arises from several different sources. The more sources you use, the greater your power. John French and Bertram Raven, who first defined the five basic sources of interpersonal power in 1959, suggested these distinct sources of power: legitimate power, reward power, coercive power, expert power, and referent power.[31] Management writers John Pearce and Richard Robinson have since suggested connection power and information power as additional power sources,[32] and a recent study further suggests collegiality as a source of power. The mix of power—its sources and its users—inevitably depends on many factors. Within law firms and other organizations, personal power is determined by two factors: position and personality characteristics.

Position Power

Position power results from the kinds of power that a person may attribute to his or her position in an organization: legitimate power, reward power, coercive power, and collegial power. For example, high-level managers may base their position power on their considerable ability to exercise reward and coercive power, whereas a paralegal's position power may arise solely from collegial power. Those at the top of the firm exercise considerable control over the development of their position power, frequently creating their own images of power and influence for those looking up from the bottom. McGill University professor Jay Conger, known internationally for his teachings on managerial leadership, reminds us that even the highest form of position power is not absolute:

> Such power exists in a vise of checks and constraints; it comes out of a system and the system, in turn, exacts a price... Power at the top is contingent upon conformity. Pressures to "fit in" also mean restraints on the unbridled exercise of power.[33]

In the following paragraphs, we will examine the four types of power that comprise position power.

Legitimate Power

Legitimate power is the form of power stemming from authority. The higher your position in the hierarchy, the greater your authority, and, therefore, the greater your legitimate power. Organization members most often exercise authority in the form of written or verbal requests, but, as we have seen, compliance is not necessarily automatic. People obey those in authority only if they believe that those who wield power have the right to make requests, give orders, or issue commands. Compliance is more likely if a power holder makes a request respectfully and politely rather than arrogantly; ensures that the request is within his or her scope of authority; and words the request clearly, concisely, and confidently. Polite requests are not to be confused with apologetic ones, which make the subordinate suspect that the requests are not worthy or legitimate and that compliance is not expected. Requests made in emergency or crisis situations demand an assertive delivery to guarantee immediate compliance. Even routine requests must be given confidently, in order to assure the subordinate of their legitimacy.[34]

Reward Power

A leader derives **reward power** from his or her ability to compensate subordinates who have complied with the leader's requests out of the belief that he or she is able to somehow reward them. Pay, promotion, and recognition are the traditional rewards managers offer subordinates for good performance and for their support and loyalty. While tangible rewards are always important to subordinates, the leader's personal appreciation and recognition are equally important.[35]

Coercive Power

Coercive power is based on a leader's ability to punish, thwart, and dismiss uncooperative, disloyal, or poorly performing subordinates. Workers sometimes obey because they realize that not to obey will lead to a wide range of punitive outcomes. Irate superiors may withhold promotions and pay raises. They can assign unfavorable or impossible work. They can also reprimand, offer public censure, or give others praise for the work that a worker in disfavor has done. Superiors can also humiliate, discredit, and berate noncomplying subordinates, or so intimidate those who want to stay out of trouble that they shun nonconformists. These behaviors are often sufficient to guarantee control, but all organization members know that the ultimate penalty is termination, one of the most powerful coercive tools of those in charge.

Collegial Power

Collegiality is a form of self-governance based on the equality that the members of a profession share as colleagues. In professional organizations such as law firms, **collegial power** constitutes a form of collective position power based on the shared authority of the organization's professional members. Professionalism, says Morgan McCall, writing on "Leadership and the Professional," is defined as a "function of expertise, autonomy, commitment, identification, ethics and collegial maintenance of standards."[36] Professionalism enhances collegial power, contributing to the governance system of law firms by building on partnership arrangements that channel collegial power through a system of committees. Governance of the law firm then becomes doubly binding and more powerful in that it couples collegial commitment with ownership commitment. A more hierarchical authority is then based on the group's authorization of one or more of its members, often on a rotating basis. In the highly competitive legal marketplace, where quick decisions are imperative, power and governance through collegiality may seem at first impractical, but the committee structure has many advantages. In all organizations, a committee is a "frequently used vehicle for coopting various internal interests and building legitimacy and support of decisions."[37] Making decisions through a committee structure leads to commitment for those decisions; and collegial power allows unparalleled participation in decision making. It enables each member to be involved in and to become committed to the issues that are critical to the firm.

Personal Power

We can attribute an organization member's other sources of power, including expert power, referent power, connection power, and information power, to what he or she does or is. These sources strengthen **personal power,** the power that results from an individual's personality. For instance, not all of a manager's power comes from the position power that accompanies the role. As John Kotter observes,

> To be able to plan, organize, budget, staff, control, and evaluate, managers need some control over the many people on whom they are dependent. Trying to control others solely by directing them and on the basis of power associated with one's position simply will not work—first,

because managers are always dependent on some people over whom they have no formal authority, and second, because virtually no one in modern organizations will passively accept and completely obey a constant stream of orders from someone just because he or she is the "boss."[38]

Referent Power

Those who are highly attractive and likable are apt to have more referent power. **Referent power** is based on associations with those who have personal magnetism, powerful or pleasing personalities, or enviable resources. People whom others find highly appealing are said to have a special gift, a *charisma,* by which they attract followers, inspire people, and win allies. Referent power reflects the desire to identify with someone who is admirable, enviable, and powerful. Our identifying with the rich and famous, with celebrities, or with those whom society most loves and respects leads to their being able to influence us. When we admire or like referent persons, the power holders, we look for their approval and acceptance. We may imitate them, using them as models. Leaders with high referent power influence people who accept and support them in order to be accepted by and identified with those leaders. Management consultant Rosabeth Moss Kanter observes, in addition, that "people get a sense of power themselves" when they enjoy "relatively close contact with sponsors (higher level people who confer approval, prestige, or backing)."[39] In this way, protégés benefit from referent power.[40] But highly referent leaders know that magnetism has a negative side as well. For one thing, it is difficult to find doting followers who are also independent thinkers. Devotees may be no more than *doppelgängers*—people who emulate the leader (sometimes down to hair and clothing styles!) and who speak only the words that he or she most wants to hear. "Yes men" in the truest sense of the term, doppelgängers form a close circle around a leader, ensuring their well-being through flattery and complete compliance. Ironically, more substantial followers may present problems of an opposite nature. Maintaining referent power requires energy and skill, especially with more discriminating followers. As researchers Gary Yukl and Tom Taber point out, highly referent leaders increase—and maintain—their power "by being considerate towards subordinates, showing concern for their needs and feelings, treating them fairly, and defending their interests when dealing with superiors and outsiders." But such a list of tasks requires a vast store of integrity and commitment, "and a leader who tries to appear friendly but who takes advantage of subordinates or fails to stick up for them will eventually find that his or her referent power has eroded away."[42]

Expertise Power

Expertise power is power based on superior knowledge or skills. Specialists enjoy the power of expertise. Their knowledge creates consultation opportunities for others, who accept the power holder's suggestions because they believe that he or she is more capable or more knowledgeable than they are. Computer experts, for example, can easily awe the less computer literate with a few swift computer commands. In this age of information, expertise in one's field is not only admirable but provides an essential advantage. Respect engenders power for the law firm member who can prove his or her competency as a professional.

Connection Power

Connection power is power based on a member's connections to, knowledge of, and positive relationships with people both inside and outside the organization. Followers respect the holder of connection power because they believe that he or she participates in relationships that will lead to additional resources, opportunities, and results, for them and for the organization. These relationships may also serve to further the power holder's causes within the organization by enabling the holder and his or her followers to bypass the hierarchy and to reflect the power that their sponsor holds.[43]

Information Power

Information power is power based on an individual's ability to share, conceal, or otherwise manipulate potentially valuable information. Such power draws its influence from the fact that others believe that the power holder possesses information that they need or want. Such information may reveal important communications or events; it may also consist of the gossip of an organization, which often contains details that may help superiors to better control or understand their people.

Total Power

Managers with strong position power and strong personal power establish high levels of organizational power. In mathematical terms, their total power is more the product of their position power and personal power than the sum of the two: in other words, position power × personal power = total power.[44] According to Rosabeth Moss Kanter, such a manager

- Is able to intercede favorably on behalf of someone having difficulties with the organization,
- Can get a talented subordinate a favorable placement,
- Gets approval for expenditures beyond the budget,
- Places items on the agenda at policy meetings,
- Has fast access to top decision makers,
- Has ongoing steady contact with top decision makers, and
- Has inside and early information about decisions and policy shifts.[45]

INFLUENCE

Influence is the ability to bring about change through the indirect use of power. Influencing is the process of offering power and other gifts in exchange for others' help in achieving a desired purpose. Such help may be willing or nearly inadvertent, depending on the subtlety of the influence process. Authority and influence are distinctly different. Authority flows downward; influence comes from the top as well as from subordinates, colleagues, or other sources. And although influence, like authority, represents a method of controlling others, influence may lead to more enduring changes.[46]

Influence Tactics

Access to power sources is not enough to explain why some leaders are more powerful than others. Power holders also must be able to choose and exercise the type of power that is appropriate to a given situation. A recent study, which asked people in organizations to describe how they induce others to do what they ask, defined five categories of influence tactics.[47] Corresponding to the five sources of power and influence described by French and Raven, these categories include legitimate requests, use of exchange tactics, pressure tactics and persistence, personal appeals through ingratiation or friendship, and skills of rational persuasion.

Legitimate Requests

Corresponding to the French and Raven category of legitimate power, a legitimate request is based on the power holder's role and the complier's view of the request as legitimate and in keeping with the rules, policies, and practices of the organization.

Exchange Tactics

A tool reflecting reward power, exchange tactics ask someone to do something while making an explicit or implicit promise of a reward.

Pressure Tactics and Persistence

An extension of coercive power, pressure tactics, which include persistent demands, threaten subordinates explicitly or implicitly with unpleasant consequences should they not comply.

Personal Appeals

A requester who makes a personal appeal, a reflection of referent power, either asks someone to do something out of personal friendship or secures a favor by ingratiating him- or herself to that person.

Rational Persuasion

Rational persuasion, which corresponds to expertise power, uses logical arguments and evidence to prove that a request is viable and capable of producing good results.[48] Strategies for persuasion, which is the process of influencing someone to do something by reasoning, urging, or inducement, include the law of reciprocity, manipulation, and ingratiation.

The Law of Reciprocity. Commonly called back-scratching, or palm-greasing, the **law of reciprocity** is the process of persuading someone to do something by appealing to his or her expectation of reciprocal exchanges from peers, superiors, or subordinates. Within organizations, this transfer of favors is a true—if sometimes ethically questionable—medium of exchange. Some favors are as personal and as simple as sending flowers on special occasions or out of appreciation for a valued relationship. Others are as personal as sympathy visits to funeral homes or as using one's power to take care of someone in the work setting. Organization members who understand the power of long-term investments in their colleagues and subordinates seek to reinforce professional ties, possibly by arranging to send an eager subordinate to a conference, by pulling a few strings in minor situations, or by otherwise enhancing coworkers' feelings of loyalty and dependence.[49] For reciprocity to be effective, the influencer needs to know that the person he or she wishes to influence is an ally, not an enemy. The influencer should know the potential ally's world, including his or her pressures, needs, goals, and sources of motivation. The more the influencer works with this person and encourages his or her trust, the easier the exchange—and future exchanges—will be.[50]

Manipulation. Although, ostensibly, Dale Carnegie's essential objective in *How to Win Friends and Influence People* was to teach people how to achieve cooperation through persuasion, not deception, at the heart of his approach is the belief that we can persuade others by discovering what motivates them and by using that something to manipulate them, if need be.[51] In many ways, this is simply an extension of the ideas of the sixteenth-century writer and politician Niccolo Machiavelli, who was quite possibly the master manipulator of all time. Machiavelli encouraged leaders to use craft and deceit for personal gains and, even more manipulatively, to use naked power to exert their wills: "One ought to be both feared and loved, but as it is difficult for the two to go together, it is much safer to be feared than loved . . . for love is held by a chain of obligation which, men being selfish, is broken whenever it serves their purpose; but fear is maintained by a dread of punishment which never fails."[52] At the end of this chapter, you will find a questionnaire that will measure your own Machiavellian tendencies. Organization members should be aware of the ethical issues involved in using manipulative strategies, especially those that are threatening or dishonest.

Ingratiation. **Ingratiation** is an attempt to benefit oneself by cultivating favor with powerful people or groups. Researcher Edward Jones suggests that those who ingratiate themselves are highly manipulative and are not highly skilled in any special field. They are more often found working for autocratic managers in settings where resources are scarce. The result of both individual style and organizational factors, ingratiation suggests a mechanism for coping with very powerful superiors, who create a climate that encourages compliant and subservient behaviors. Accordingly, ingratiation commonly employs flattery and a false display of sincerity. Known by many less-than-flattering names—bootlicking, among others—ingratiation is basically interpersonal manipulation, a form of reinforcement designed to shape positive perceptions of the flatterer. From Aesop's fable of the fox and the crow comes this moral: All flatterers exploit people who are foolish enough to listen to them. We should be aware of a very subtle and effective strategy for organizational ingratiation. It occurs when A, flattered manager, becomes less suspicious of the motives of B, a flatterer, because B is clever enough not to flatter A directly. Instead, B feeds the flattering comments to C, who, known for feeding information back to A, ends up delivering B's flattery more effectively than B could.[53]

MANAGERIAL POWER STRATEGIES

Does a manager need to be powerful? Can a manager afford not to understand the use of power? Because the very essence of a manager's job involves directing people within an organization, writes Andrew Pettigrew, researcher in the field of organizational behavior, each manager absolutely needs "an accurate perception of the power distribution in the social arena in which he lives." Understanding power becomes a prerequisite for the manager seeking support for his or her demands.[54] Each manager as well as each member of the law firm must know how to develop his or her position power and personal power.

Increasing Personal Power

To increase personal power, a manager can attempt to develop interpersonal ties that are built on a sense of mutual obligation. This helps workers to believe that it is acceptable to allow a manager to influence them, even through personal favors. Subordinates should have a basic trust in their managers, believing that they are worth working with and for. Managers can build this trust by quietly making their accomplishments known, by maintaining a good work record, and by building good personal press. A manager should reinforce perceptions that he or she has influence over resources; subordinates should realize that he or she has the power to share—or withhold—salaries, bonuses, and perks.[55] The manager should realize that subordinates seek other rewards as well, often in the form of respect and personal acknowledgment. This chapter's In the News article features John Kotter's sug-

IN THE NEWS

Insights for Managers

Managers can exert power in three directions: on their subordinates, on their superiors, and on their peers. To effectively use power, managers need to know how to exert influence in all three directions.

Influencing Subordinates.

Because supervisors have the legitimate right to hire, fire, and discipline subordinates, we often overestimate the power of supervisory jobs. What we typically overlook is the power that subordinates *as a group* have over their bosses. Subordinate power comes in many forms and is based on (1) skills that are difficult to replace quickly or easily, (2) specialized information and knowledge that others do not have, (3) good personal relationships that prevent a supervisor from reprimanding or replacing a subordinate without alienating other employees, and (4) the centrality of the subordinate's job, which may be critical to the performance of the supervisor's job.

The combination of these factors creates a situation in which the power of the subordinates is greater than the power of the supervisor despite the formal power that comes from the organization. Consequently, supervisors need to expand their power base beyond the legitimate power conferred by the organization. Effectively leading subordinates demands that supervisors bring additional sources of power to the job. The following suggestions have been made for supervisors to increase their clout during their early tenure as supervisors.

1. *Acquire the relevant interpersonal skills and abilities.* Being a good supervisor and successfully exerting power requires good interpersonal skills, persuasiveness, and the ability to identify and resolve conflicts quickly. Good verbal skills in listening and communicating are essential for influencing subordinates.

2. *Establish good working relationships.* Good working relationships are based on a combination of respect, admiration, obligation, and friendship. To be perceived as effective and a credible source of influence, supervisors need to maintain good relationships not only with subordinates but with superiors and others outside the chain of command.

3. *Acquire information.* Knowledge is power, but the most important knowledge in leadership jobs is detailed information about the social reality in which the job is embedded. Supervisors need to know who the relevant parties are, their different perspectives, and when these perspectives may be in conflict.

4. *Maintain a good track record.* Being perceived as a successful supervisor contributes to the supervisor's power position. A credible track record and the reputation it earns can help a supervisor obtain compliance in a fraction of the time that is required if credibility is lacking. Success breeds success, and the successful application of power in one situation increases the supervisor's potential power for the next occasion.

Influencing Superiors.

Successful employees need an effective boss to provide them with the necessary job opportunities, resources, organizational protection, and job security. Unfortunately, many employees do not feel they receive the support and encouragement they need to perform their jobs adequately. Even more serious is the fact that many employees think their supervisor is unfair, incompetent, biased, and unqualified to lead. These problems highlight

SOURCE: Reprinted with permission of The Free Press, a Division of Macmillan, Inc. from *POWER AND INFLUENCE: Beyond Formal Authority* by John P. Kotter. Copyright © 1985 by John P. Kotter.

---

gestions on how managers can increase their influence; law firm members in general may increase their personal power in many ways, possibly by

- Becoming acquainted with colleagues,
- Building on shared interests with coworkers,
- Respecting people's differences,
- Using reward power whenever possible,
- Inviting reciprocal influence, and
- Sharing information.[56]

Managers and other law firm members should be able to select and use strategies for increasing power that are appropriate to the levels of authority, the objectives, and the people involved. The Another Look which fol-

IN THE NEWS (continued)

the importance of being able to exert influence upward in the organization. They also explain why one of the most popular new courses at some universities is a course on boss management.

Although we typically think of power being exerted downward in an organization, it is equally important for subordinates to effectively exert power upwards. To obtain sufficient resources, support, and encouragement, subordinates must develop and maintain good working relationships with their superiors. The following principles have been suggested for developing good relationships with superiors and exerting upward influence.

1. Creative, competent subordinates take some of the load off their boss's shoulders. Effective subordinates solve problems rather than create them, and whenever possible they bring good news of successful solutions to the boss rather than failures and problems.
2. Change your boss's bad behavior with rewards. Catching your boss doing something good and rewarding this behavior is far more effective than criticizing or complaining. If your boss has traits you would like to change, reward positive behavior with thanks or sincere praise.
3. Look beyond the boundaries of your job description to let others benefit from your ideas and efforts. Bosses enjoy being told by outsiders that they have an exemplary subordinate: Take advantage of opportunities outside work to make yourself visible and manage your own public relations without devoting too much time and effort to it.
4. Recognized your boss's weaknesses and let them be your strengths. If the boss hates to attend meetings, offer to go instead and give a briefing later. If the boss hates to write reports, be a ghost writer and prepare a first draft. If the boss relates badly with certain people, perform those functions yourself that entail meeting these people. By becoming a representative of your boss, you will be given the knowledge and stature to do so properly.
5. Maintain a good working relationship by keeping the boss informed, behaving dependably and honestly, and using the boss's time and resources very selectively. Subordinates who are undependable, dishonest, or who waste their boss's limited time and energy are certain to destroy their relationship with their boss.

Influencing Peers.

Almost everyone in an organization depends on someone outside the formal chain of command. For example, supervisors depend upon the personnel department to screen new employees, while the personnel department depends on the supervisors to submit their staffing requirements. The success of most employees is influenced by how well they manage relationships outside the chain of command. Being able to influence one's peers often means the difference between effective and ineffective performance. Four suggestions have been offered for managing peer relationships.

1. Identify all the relevant lateral relationships both inside and outside the organization. This list represents the group of people whose performance and interactions must be monitored.
2. Assess who among these people may resist cooperation, why, and how strongly. This assessment will identify the leadership challenges and power struggles likely to occur.
3. Develop wherever possible a good relationship with these people to facilitate the communication, education, and negotiation processes required to reduce or overcome resistance. A good working relationship requires dependability and reciprocity from both parties.
4. When a good working relationship cannot be developed, some additional type of power intervention that is more subtle and more forceful should be developed to deal with the resistance.

---

lows presents ten familiar strategies for increasing personal power, both in the work setting and at home.

Increasing Position Power[57]

Although it draws primarily on the legitimate, reward, and coercive sources we examined earlier, position power may also gain strength from dimensions inherent in a position itself. The power of a given position increases in proportion to the degree to which it reflects each of these five qualities: centrality, criticality, flexibility, visibility, and relevance.

ANOTHER LOOK

Need More Personal Power?

1. Realistically assess the power you already have.
2. Gain the support of other people.
3. Develop expertise where others need help.
4. Create a need for your specialized resources.
5. Form a wide network of working relationships and make them known.
6. Hide the extent to which the responses of others reward or punish you.
7. Minimize the pain of criticism.
8. Learn as much as you can about the knowledge, understanding, attitudes, and motivations of those with whom you are trying to increase your power.
9. Ingratiate yourself.
10. Become a part of the group before initiating innovations.

SOURCE: W. Reichman and M. Levy, "Personal Power Enhancement: A Way to Execute Success," *Management Review* 6 (March 1977): 28–34.

1. What positive effects do you see for these suggestions? What, if any, negative ones?
2. List five of your own style strengths. Then formulate five specific strategies for increasing your personal power.
3. How can paralegals and support staff members of a law firm benefit from using personal power?

Centrality

A position that is central to the communications of an organization not only provides access to vital information but can allow the holder of such a position to regulate the flow of that information, deciding who receives it.

Criticality

A position that is critical to an organization's work flow occupies a strategic niche. How vital and how unique a position is determines its ability to influence the organization in its most important decision making.

Flexibility

Flexibility is another term for *discretion,* the amount of latitude an individual has "to improvise, to implement, and to demonstrate initiative."[58] A position that offers high flexibility presents few regulations, rules, or established routines for how work should be performed. The ability to use one's judgment in a position leads to increased power.

Visibility

Visibility is the degree to which the influential members of an organization notice work performance within a given position. Simply to perform well is not enough; results must be apparent to those at the top and convey a strong message of competence to those at the bottom as well. Given this dual obligation to evidence capability, managers and other law firm members should increase their visibility in as many ways as possible, such as by presenting reports in person, by ensuring that all of their papers have cover sheets that attest to the true source of the work, and by taking credit for all of their tasks, particularly before anyone else decides to do so! Nor should members overlook the importance of a strategic office location: a quiet, tucked-away office is good only for a hermit. Managers, especially, should occupy offices located in the heart of the action, tied to the firm's power network and central to its communications; merely by his or her presence in such a location, a manager can transmit a take-charge image to superiors and subordinates alike.

Relevance

Relevance reflects the relationship between a position's responsibilities and an organization's current priorities. A function that is immediately necessary to an organization acquires stature and importance. Those who function in such relevant positions are necessarily more powerful within their organization.[59]

The Language of Power

Within organizations, certain power symbols increase the visibility and reinforce the status of their holders.

1. Will fulfilling this request hurt this person psychologically, professionally, or physically?
2. Am I using more influence than is necessary to do my managerial job?
3. Am I using my power only for legitimate organizational reasons?
4. Do I have the valid right to have this person do something he or she would rather not do?
5. Is it a personal indulgence for me to have this person do what I am asking or is it for the good of the organization?
6. Does this request reflect ego or professional need?

SOURCE: Based on R. B. Dunham and J. L. Pierce, *Management* (Glenview, Ill.: Scott, Foresman and Company, 1989): 526–27.

ANOTHER LOOK

Am I Using Power Ethically?

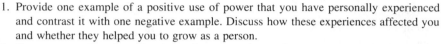

1. Provide one example of a positive use of power that you have personally experienced and contrast it with one negative example. Discuss how these experiences affected you and whether they helped you to grow as a person.
2. Suggest examples of positive uses of a manager's power.

Some of these symbols include the prestige offices and furnishings that convey to onlookers success and control. In large city firms, for example, the corner offices of senior partners reflect their occupants' high status, particularly if such offices are suites, with washrooms or other anterooms. Other examples include free (and nearby) parking, limousines, company cars, and private dining rooms or club memberships. While support staff often must resign themselves to standard-issue chairs and glimpses of windows, those at the top enjoy the law firm's many tactile symbols of importance, all designed to make organizational life more attractive and less spartan for the powerful.

Abuses of Power

We all fear the abuse of power, and, unfortunately, our fears are not unfounded. Some organization members treat their subordinates very poorly, fueling their personal power by minimizing others' self-confidence, by maximizing their subordinates' feelings of inadequacy, and by consciously depriving them of whatever power they may have. Such self-serving superiors may require subordinates to perform personal errands or assign them tasks with unreasonable deadlines or burdens. They hoard essential supplies, exact last-minute and late-night work, calling it the subordinate's professional responsibility, and abuse law firm privileges, sometimes by asking subordinates to type papers for family members or by using firm time for personal projects. Those who refuse to cooperate receive insignificant salary increases—or no increases at all; indeed, some power holders withhold justly earned employee salary increases while making lavish expenditures, ostensibly for the firm's sake, expecting both the firm and their subordinates to subsidize their expense accounts. Managers should constantly monitor their sensitivity to the ethical use of power; questions such as those in the following Another Look can alert a manager to any abusive tendencies in his or her power usage.

POLITICS

Within organizations, authority is socially acceptable, power has always been debatable, but politics raises even more questions. Oddly, although power and politics are everyday culprits behind many organizational decisions and behaviors, they form the focus of few management studies. Most managers admit that political behavior is commonplace, but think it more of a hindrance than a help.[60] However, in today's business world, most seem to understand that power and politics are essential for success and survival. Those who know how to "play the game" seem to outlast those who don't. Managers and other law firm members should be able to understand organizational politics, and benefit from taking part.

Politics is an exchange dimension of power built on transactions with stakeholders. More specifically, **politics** is the process of creating alliances, arranging obligations, manipulating others' behavior, exchanging influence, and engaging in other such activities in order to influence or attempt to influence for the purpose of protecting one's self-interests or promulgating one's version of organizational goals. An older and deceptively simple definition explains that politics is who gets what, when, and how.[61] "Politics," writes Jeffrey Pfeffer in *Power in Organizations,* "involves those activities taken within an organization to acquire, develop and use power and other resources to obtain one's preferred outcomes in a situation in which there is uncertainty or dissensus about choices." Pfeffer believes that all political activity exists to overcome some resistance or opposition.[62] Political efforts toward this end include minimizing, discrediting, controlling, and even denying that resistance and opposition exist. Using "intentional acts of influence to enhance or protect self-interests,"[63] those who engage in organizational politics create alliances, arrange obligations, purchase favors, and trade them, a process for reaching organizational goals that is considered not only normal but fair.

Political behavior increases for a number of reasons during times of organizational instability. Authoritarian organization members who like to take risks and who are highly controlling by nature automatically jockey for the most politically advantageous positions amid the uncertainty.[64] Workers who have high needs for power, autonomy, security, or status also vie for political influence.[65] However, the amount of political behavior within an organization also depends on specific situations as well as on the organization's culture. When resources are scarce, for instance, political activity increases, and when trust falls, political behavior rises.[66] Unfortunately, this increases managerial vulnerability as well. Managers amid instability must struggle with other would-be influencers to make their influence known, and they may even find themselves the target of political activity. When an organization's competitors are making dramatic moves, when the organization itself is feeling the impact from some new technology, or when it has undergone significant reductions in its revenues, political activity flourishes.[67] In such an uncertain climate, a manager can benefit from understanding the difference between power and politics, as well as the interactions that can help the manager to acquire power, transfer it, and use it.

Naiveté and Power

Pfeffer observes that students of management are often unaware of the sheer power of organizational politics; worse, they often receive no training that will prepare them for the political struggles within an organization. As David Whetton and Kim Cameron point out,

> Only the naive believe that the best recommendations always get selected, the most capable individuals always get the promotion, and the deserving units always get their fair share of the budget. These are political decisions heavily influenced by the interests of the powerful.[68]

In Pfeffer's opinion, preparation adequate to ensure the professional survival of a newly arrived member within an organization should include practical techniques for building and maintaining power.

Political Strategies

Political behavior assumes many faces in organizations. For example, management writer Stanley Young believes that we should distinguish beneficial political behaviors from those that are organizationally dysfunctional and even unethical. In addition to recognizing some routine but questionable behaviors for what they are, such as buck passing, withholding information, image building, and ingratiating oneself to one's superiors, we need to learn which behaviors are appropriate and productive.[69] Here are eight common political strategies, both positive and negative:[70]

Control the agenda and select the decision criteria. The person who controls the agenda primarily controls the meeting; he or she therefore, is able to determine discussion topics and to require the group to ignore issues that he or she considers distasteful or negative. Some subjects, however, are difficult or even impossible to disregard; such topics may incite a previously agreeable group to agenda mutiny.

Control access to information. We have seen how control of the information flow can equal power. There are also several ways to control information politically: by withholding negative details or anything else that would create a poor impression; by refusing to deny or confirm controversial issues; by avoiding contact with those who might ask for information that is more politically expedient to withhold; by being selective in the presentation of information; and by overwhelming others with irrelevant information. This last technique is particularly manipulative, since after your latest filibuster, you can boast about your genuine efforts to make the sharing of information a high priority.[71]

Use outside experts. Using the services of an outside expert can help to convince others of the value of ideas, even if these same others have heard the same message from inside sources and disbelieved it. However, this technique can backfire if insiders suspect—correctly—that the organization has brought in a consultant to lead groups to predetermined decisions, to serve managers' personal political agendas, or to perform repugnant tasks, such as terminating personnel or dissolving departments. Under these conditions, "experts" garner nothing more than cynicism and mistrust.[72]

Control access to influential people. One effective way of political control is to tightly regulate others' access to people with influence. To make these politically selective audiences look legitimate, those who are screening appointments may claim with regrets that the appointment book is filled, a seemingly legitimate excuse that the political screener often accompanies with an expression of sympathy for the overworked—and inaccessible—superior. Controlling access is a common and effective way of keeping another's influence to oneself.

Develop a base of support. In terms of ideas, quality is sometimes far less important than support. Those who want to see an organization use their ideas learn how to develop a base of support, sometimes indulging in horse trading, or reciprocal concessions, along the way.

Cultivate a favorable impression. Anyone who follows political campaigns knows the importance of impression management, the creation and maintenance of a candidate's positive image. People in organizations may formulate a positive image by wearing types, styles, and even colors of clothing associated with power and success; by putting the right spin on public information, events, and media coverage; by usurping credit for the success of others; and by associating oneself with any successful accomplishment.[73] Some workers expend much energy controlling how they are perceived by managers; they work at acclaiming their own accomplishments, at flattering superiors, at doing favors and kindnesses for them, and at agreeing with those in charge in order to gain their approval. These workers realize that decisions, such as promotions and pay increases, are shaped by managers' perceptions of workers.

Attack and blame others when things go wrong. Finding a scapegoat is a common tactic; finger-pointing implies that the "pointer" is not to blame! A very civilized and insidious way of attacking and blaming others is to speak of forgiveness and a lack of rancor toward them. By creating an image of kindness and tolerance for him- or herself, the forgiver induces others to ignore the question of guilt entirely.

Align with the powerful. Connecting oneself to the powerful is one of the world's oldest techniques for increasing political power. Peers as well as superiors may represent a source of power; for example, two subunits may join forces, thereby offering one another support.

EMPOWERMENT

Empowerment, the process of enabling and ennobling others, involves helping an individual to develop the power he or she needs to influence others, to function confidently and effectively within an organization, and to access the resources that he or she needs. Empowerment results in positive workers who believe in their ability to cope with the difficult people and situations that they encounter;[74] it ultimately results in a more effective organization. Contrary to the views of the power-hungry, sharing power benefits superiors as well as their subordinates.

Powerlessness

To understand empowerment, we must also understand the concept of powerlessness. Within organizations, the powerless frequently feel trapped. They often become victims, distrusting both their own and others' perceptions of their self-worth. Lacking control over even their immediate situation, they are unable to influence, to obtain the resources or support they need, to engage in the type of communication that would keep them informed and productive, or to provide input or to participate in the real workings of the organization. In terms of the organization itself, powerlessness, rather than enabling superiors to create a controlled and productive authoritarian structure, has many negative effects. Rosabeth Moss Kanter, who has written extensively on the effects of powerlessness on workers, notes that "in large organizations, at least, it is powerlessness that often creates ineffective people" who lack "control over their own fate and are dependent on others

ANOTHER LOOK

What Fosters Powerlessness?

THE ORGANIZATION ITSELF
Many changes and transitions
Mergers and acquisitions
Excessive competition
Impersonal bureaucratic climate
Poor communications
Highly centralized resources

THE QUALITY OF SUPERVISION
Authoritarian
Negative
Autocratic

THE REWARD SYSTEMS
Arbitrary allocations
Little incentive in terms of rewards
Poor linkage with competency
No linkage with innovation

THE JOB DESIGN
Excessive ambiguity
Lack of training and support
Unrealistic goals
Lack of necessary discretion
Low participation in job-related issues
Lack of needed resources
Lack of networking opportunities
Rigid work routines
Excessive rules and guidelines
Poor advancement and opportunity
Meaningless goals and tasks
Limited contact with senior management

SOURCE: Based on Jay A. Conger and R. N. Kanungo, "The Empowerment Process: Integrating Theory and Practice," *Academy of Management Review* (July 1988).

1. Which of these factors (if any) promote powerlessness within an organization to which you currently belong? How do they affect you personally, in terms of work quality and attitude?
2. Of the factors you mentioned in question 1, which do you think would be easiest to rectify? How might you transform these unpowering situations into empowering ones?

above them."[75] Such a situation is often self-perpetuating. Powerless people are "caught in a downward spiral." Their coping mechanisms are those "most likely to provoke resistance and further restriction of power or desultory management, and petty, dictatorial, rules-minded managerial styles."[76] The Another Look above lists the organizational factors most conducive to powerlessness.

Advantages of Being Empowered

Kanter observes that secure leaders "see empowering subordinates as a gain rather than a loss."[77] Empowerment restores workers to productive participation in the organization. It provides a sense of worth to individual employees, calling on them to become dynamically a part of the organization. Instilling such a sense of power, she writes, "is at the root of organizational effectiveness, especially during times of transition and transformation."[78]

Law firms can be at their productive best when subordinates believe that they share power and authority with their superiors.[79] Alfred Bandura, who has contributed much of the study on empowerment, suggests four empowerment strategies. First, he encourages those in authority to give workers positive emotional support in difficult times. Second, he recommends offering workers words of encouragement and positive persuasion. Third, Bandura advises managers to champion the firm's "success models," effective members with whom others can identify. Finally, he recommends that managers help workers to actually experience success in as many ways as possible.[80] Jay Conger, who also has written extensively on methods for empowering workers, suggests further that managers involve subordinates in developing their own work assignments, that they work to create a positive collaborative climate, that they reward their workers in visible and personal ways, and that they foster initiative and responsibility.[81] While some still skeptically regard empowerment as "only the latest managerial buzz word,"[82] many others, who wish to tap the best of the skills and competencies in a law office or in any other business setting, consider empowerment the key to unlocking effectiveness.

QUESTIONS FOR DISCUSSION AND REVIEW

1. How does power manifest itself in the law firm environment?
2. How is authority a form of power? Think of three authority figures you have known. Who, in your opinion, was most powerful? Least powerful? Discuss why.
3. What are the steps in successful delegation? Describe the different delegating styles and explain which style would be most suited for you, personally, as a law firm manager.
4. Discuss what power is and where it is found in organizations. Explain why some are more powerful than others, drawing examples from individuals you have known in legal setting.
5. What influence tactics have you seen in use? Which do work or might work for you?
6. What are the power strategies available to managers and to subordinates? How are they applicable to legal settings?
7. How can the use of power by subordinates strengthen or undermine a law firm? Discuss positive strategies that subordinates in a law office can use to exercise power.
8. People commonly complain about the politics plaguing many organizations. Choose a college, an office, or a social or professional group you have experienced and explain why you and others consider this organization to be political. What is the role of politics in this organization? Provide specific examples of political games and strategies, distinguishing any desirable, productive political behaviors from those that are organizationally dysfunctional or even unethical.
9. Define empowerment. Of what value is empowerment to subordinates in a law office? To women? To minorities? What advantages does empowerment offer organizations?
10. Discuss how subordinates in a law firm or in another organization you have experienced have coped with powerlessness. Provide specific examples of how they controlled their controllers, sabotaged operations, diminished the importance of work requests, poked fun at a superior, or employed any other methods of passive or active protest.
11. Discuss how you would delegate work to the following members of a law firm:
    a. A new paralegal who has great ambitions.
    b. A secretary who has been quite stressed and careless lately.
    c. A receptionist who sees you as a patsy.
    d. A paralegal who resents you and your new authority.
    e. An enthusiastic and hardworking team player.

EXPERIENTIAL EXERCISES

I. Sharing

You have just been made a new paralegal supervisor in the real estate department of your law office. Having always concentrated on doing your own job well, you now must oversee four other paralegals, some of whom are quite aggressive and outspoken about their work loads and scheduling needs. Using the steps suggested for delegating work to subordinates, discuss how you might handle each of the following situations.

1. You would like to assign Mary Mayes, 36, to work on a shopping mall transaction that will keep her in the office more than she is used to. Mary, who likes autonomy, will not be pleased about the new work, but she has the experience the job requires. You ask. She is negative and unwilling.
2. A particularly tedious research case has just been given to you to assign to your paralegals. You consult with the legal administrator, and together you decide that Bill Bonner, 27, is the best person for this job. Although Bill's schedule could best accommodate the work, you are concerned because he likes to run free and often fails to follow through on his tasks. You ask. He is belligerent, unwilling.
3. Carmen Belli, 31, has been making many errors lately with closing data. She thinks that she is overworked and that stress has been causing her to short-circuit. She asks you to do something about her assignments. You, however, believe that Carmen's "stress" results from the great deal of time that she spends talking about her new boyfriend and her social life. You need to assign additional work to her. You ask. She is outraged at your insensitivity.
4. Scotty Adams, 43 believes that she should have been made supervisor. You begin to realize that she has been working directly with the lawyers she wants to work with and has been ignoring your requests. When she does acknowledge your requests, she always seems willing to comply, but somehow, others end up with the work. Knowing that a showdown is probably inevitable, you ask Scotty to work on the deeds for the new properties the university is purchasing.

II. Empowerment Profile*

Understanding your preference for being powerful or powerless is the first step in understanding how others react to power. The following exercise will help you to assess your power tendencies. When you've responded to all of the items, total your **a** scores and **b** scores.

1. When I have to give a talk or write a paper, I . . .
    _____ a. Base the content of my talk or paper on my own ideas.
    _____ b. Do a lot of research, and present the findings of others in my paper or talk.

2. When I read something I disagree with, I . . .
    _____ a. Assume my position is correct.
    _____ b. Assume what's presented in the written word is correct.

---

*SOURCE: Pamela Cuming, "Empowerment Profile: Skill Preassessment," from *The Power Handbook* (Boston: CBI Publishers, 1980): 3–4. Copyright © 1980. Reprinted with permission from Van Norstrand Reinhold, New York.

CHAPTER 4 / DIRECTING: AUTHORITY, POWER, AND POLITICS

3. When someone makes me extremely angry, I . . .
   _____ a. Ask the other person to stop the behavior that is offensive to me.
   _____ b. Say little, not quite knowing how to state my position.

4. When I do a good job, it is important to me that . . .
   _____ a. The job represents the best I can do.
   _____ b. Others take notice of the job I've done.

5. When I buy new clothes, I . . .
   _____ a. Buy what looks best on me.
   _____ b. Try to dress in accordance with the latest fashion.

6. When something goes wrong, I . . .
   _____ a. Try to solve the problem.
   _____ b. Try to find out who's at fault.

7. As I anticipate my future, I . . .
   _____ a. Am confident I will be able to lead the kind of life I want to lead.
   _____ b. Worry about being able to live up to my obligations.

8. When examining my own resources and capacities, I . . .
   _____ a. Like what I find.
   _____ b. Find all kinds of things I wish were different.

9. When someone treats me unfairly, I . . .
   _____ a. Put my energies into getting what I want.
   _____ b. Tell others about the injustice.

10. When someone criticizes my efforts, I . . .
    _____ a. Ask questions in order to understand the basis for the criticism.
    _____ b. Defend my actions or decisions, trying to make by critic understand why I did what I did.

11. When I engage in an activity, it is very important to me that . . .
    _____ a. I live up to my own expectations.
    _____ b. I live up to the expectations of others.

12. When I let someone else down or disappoint them, I . . .
    _____ a. Resolve to do things differently next time.
    _____ b. Feel guilty, and wish I had done things differently.

13. I try to surround myself with people . . .
    _____ a. Whom I respect.
    _____ b. Who respect me.

14. I try to develop friendships with people who . . .
    _____ a. Are challenging and exciting.
    _____ b. Can make me feel a little safer and a little more secure.

15. I make my best efforts when . . .
    _____ a. I do something I want to do when I want to do it.

_____ b. Someone else gives me an assignment, a deadline, and a reward for performing.

16. When I love a person, I . . .
    _____ a. Encourage him or her to be free and choose for himself or herself.
    _____ b. Encourage him or her to do the same thing I do and to make choices similar to mine.

17. When I play a competitive game, it is important to me that I . . .
    _____ a. Do the best I can.
    _____ b. Win.

18. I really like being around people who . . .
    _____ a. Can broaden my horizons and teach me something.
    _____ b. Can and want to learn from me.

19. My best days are those that . . .
    _____ a. Present unexpected opportunities.
    _____ b. Go according to plan.

20. When I get behind in my work, I . . .
    _____ a. Do the best I can and don't worry.
    _____ b. Worry or push myself harder than I should.

_____ Total of all **a** scores.

_____ Total of all **b** scores.

III. Machiavellian Tendencies Questionnaire*

Although most of us see power as the ability to get things done and focus more on outcomes than on the methods we use, Machiavellianism—and the manipulation it implies—is far from dead. Use the following statements to assess your own Machiavellian tendencies. When you've answered all of the items, use the scoring directions below to interpret your responses.

SA = Strongly agree
A = Agree
N = Neither agree nor disagree
D = Disagree
SD = Strongly disagree

SD D N A SA   1. It's not uncommon for us to be good.

SD D N A SA   2. Humility is for the weak and unsuccessful.

SD D N A SA   3. We should never betray our best friends.

---

*SOURCE: Based on Richard Christie and Florence L. Geis, *Studies in Machiavellianism* (New York: Academic Press, 1970).

CHAPTER 4 / DIRECTING: AUTHORITY, POWER, AND POLITICS

SD D N A SA   4. It's better to be feared than loved.

SD D N A SA   5. Even the most talented among us should realize that skill and success are gifts.

SD D N A SA   6. Fair play and loyalty need to be put aside if they interfere with what needs to be done. We should be able to do whatever it takes to get our way.

SD D N A SA   7. Good people finish last.

SD D N A SA   8. Cheating, lying and dirty tricks are okay if the goal is important.

SD D N A SA   9. It is better to have people love you than be afraid of you.

SD D N A SA   10. You are foolish when you let yourself trust people completely.

SD D N A SA   11. The end never justifies the means we use to get there.

SD D N A SA   12. Everyone cheats and cuts corners; it's just a matter of being discovered.

SD D N A SA   13. It's the sign of a decent person to let your heart rule your head.

SD D N A SA   14. I never like to tell anyone my real reasons for doing things; it's better to keep them guessing.

SD D N A SA   15. What we need is more trust.

SD D N A SA   16. Good managers, in my book, always have to run a tight ship and crack the whip. People need to be kept in line.

SD D N A SA   17. Most people take pride in their work. They work hard, believing that it's the right thing to do.

SD D N A SA   18. It's only wisdom to stay on the good side of important people; flattery is always useful.

SD D N A SA   19. I'd rather be humble and honest than arrogant and successful.

SD D N A SA   20. The best way to work with people is to tell them what they want to hear, whether it's true or not.

Scoring: All of the even-numbered items indicate Machiavellian tendencies while all of the odd-numbered items reflect the opposite. For all answers to the odd-numbered items: SD = -5; D = -3; N = 0; A = $+3$; SA = $+5$. For all answers to the even-numbered items: SD = $+5$; D = $+3$; N = 0; A = -3; SA = -5. A high score indicates that you are a *High Mach:* You are pragmatic, using any means to accomplish your goals. You are manipulative and persuasive, and often exude confidence, eloquence, charm, and competence. Skilled at political maneuvers, you never let your heart rule your head, in spite of the impressions that you give. A low score identifies you as a *Low Mach;* congratulations! To protect yourself against *High Machs,* who flourish where others are afraid to challenge them, do not allow them to victimize you or others. Expose them to coworkers, describing how these *High Machs* have cheated and manipulated you or your colleagues. Value people more for what they *do,* not for what they *say* they will do. While they are preaching loyalty, fair play, and honesty, *High Machs* will be doing you in. Don't become irrational; *High Machs* thrive on powerful emotions, which they can use to distract and confuse you.[83]

IV. Charting Your DIP: The Delegation Inventory Profile

As a manager, how adept would you be at delegating tasks? For each item, circle the letter that best represents your views. The scoring directions that follow will help you to formulate your personal delegation skills profile.

SA = Strongly agree
A = Agree
N = Neither agree nor disagree
D = Disagree
SD = Strongly disagree

1. Emotional Security	SA A N D SD	1. I would like to allow subordinates to grow, even if their progress means that I eventually lose them.
	SA A N D SD	2. I think that a manager should always know more than subordinates.
	SA A N D SD	3. I believe that subordinates care about their work, even if they sometimes make mistakes.
2. Self-Esteem	SA A N D SD	4. Delegation is good, but I know that I could always do things better myself.
	SA A N D SD	5. I would be pleased by subordinates who could outperform me.
	SA A N D SD	6. If I were to give jobs to subordinates, I believe that I would never get the results I wanted.
3. Planning Skills	SA A N D SD	7. I firmly believe that I could find time to delegate and teach others what to do, if I wanted to.
	SA A N D SD	8. There's simply not enough time to delegate work properly.
	SA A N D SD	9. I believe that successful delegation means taking time to involve all workers fairly and effectively.

CHAPTER 4 / DIRECTING: AUTHORITY, POWER, AND POLITICS

4. Communication Skills	SA A N D SD	10. You shouldn't have to spend a lot of time talking to subordinates about how a task is to be done.
	SA A N D SD	11. I believe you should give clear and precisely worded expectations when delegating work.
	SA A N D SD	12. It's good for subordinates to be kept in the dark; it's their responsibility to ask their manager what he or she wants.
5. Tolerance	SA A N D SD	13. I would like to assess my workers' competencies and interests, either formally or informally.
	SA A N D SD	14. I believe that I would know ahead of time which workers would not be interested in new projects or specialties.
	SA A N D SD	15. I expect that my newer subordinates would always be much more willing to please than the old-timers.
6. Control	SA A N D SD	16. Once I give someone a job, it will be all theirs. I only want to see the end result.
	SA A N D SD	17. I think that a constant exchange of support, information, and feedback is all part of assigning jobs to workers.
	SA A N D SD	18. I wouldn't like my workers to bother me with progress reports concerning projects and special assignments.
7. Professional Guilt	SA A N D SD	19. As a manager, I will need to spend my time planning, supervising and coordinating.
	SA A N D SD	20. I would feel guilty and would worry about not having anything to do if I delegated work.
	SA A N D SD	21. Even after delegating all the work, I would have my own work to do ensuring that it was done well.
8. Patience	SA A N D SD	22. It takes too long to explain work; it gets done faster when you do it yourself.
	SA A N D SD	23. Getting things done will take time, whether my time or my subordinates'. You need to plan and be patient.
	SA A N D SD	24. It will be better for the organization when I do things my subordinates can do; it will take less time.

Scoring Directions

For each of the eight sections, use the scoring keys to add your scores. They will range from −15 to +15. Plot your scores on the grid below.

Scoring:
Even-numbered items: SA = −5; A = −3; N = 0; D = +3; and SD = +5.
Odd-Numbered items: SA = +5; A = +3; N = 0; D = −3; and SD = −5.

	−15 to −10	−9 to −4	−3 to +3	+4 to +9	+10 to +15
1. Emotional Security					
2. Self-Esteem					
3. Planning Skills					
4. Communication Skills					
5. Tolerance					
6. Control					
7. Sense of Responsibility					
8. Patience					

DIP Total Score	Impoverished Managerial Delegation Style: ___	Flimsy Managerial Delegation Style: ___	Indifferent Managerial Delegation Style: ___	Promising Managerial Delegation Style: ___	Praiseworthy Managerial Delegation Style: ___

CHAPTER 5

Controlling: Resources, Time, and Growth

LEARNING OBJECTIVES

After completing this chapter, you should be able to:

- Explain the nature of control and how it relates to other basic management activities;
- Identify and explain the four areas of control as they apply to law firms;
- Explain how the law firm controls its physical resources;
- Describe the systems that the firm uses to govern its information resources, including calendars, tickler systems, docket and records management and retrieval, and new matter forms and procedures;
- Explain how to handle client files and conflicts of interest;
- Identify and explain the characteristics of effective controls;
- Discuss resistance to control and ways of overcoming it;
- Describe the elements of crisis management;
- Explain how to develop effective time management strategies; and
- Discuss how growth affects people in a law firm.

FOCUS FROM THE FIELD

Anne Dodds: Varying Needs for Control

Anne Dodds, legal assistant administrator at the law firm of Carrington, Coleman, Sloman & Blumenthal in Dallas, Texas, has long been active in regional paralegal management associations and has recently served as national president of the Legal Assistant Management Association.

How do you train employees in the control process?

First of all, legal assistants that I hire have experience. I don't hire any legal assistants without experience. The requirement is that they have a bachelor's degree. Most of the legal assistants have certificates. I am kept aware of how their work is progressing. We have in-house programs and monthly legal assistant meetings, and I work with all of the legal assistants informally to communicate how we operate. Also, we have a case clerk program. In this program, I hire people with legal assistant certificates and the required educational degrees but no experience. Those people are very closely supervised by me and work under the direction of senior legal assistants and attorneys. Case clerks are in a different learning posture for about two years or until we feel that they are trained appropriately to move into the legal assistant positions. It takes time for someone to achieve a level of experience. So, many legal assistants in this firm have trained in clerk programs.

What are the critical areas in the control process?

I think that it's very important that I be plugged into the management structure of the firm and know what decisions are being made and why—that I be part of the decision-making process and be the primary person with input for the decisions that affect my department. Those decisions include salary setting, hiring procedures, reviews and evaluations, and determination of policy. All of these areas are important, and I am primarily responsible for them. I think that involvement in those areas is crucial to a program's development.

How much control is needed and desirable in a law firm?

Depending on the size of the firm and the size of the cases that attorneys and legal assistants work on, there are varying needs for control. I think that when you have many people working on a matter in a large firm, there needs to be a centralized form of docket control. There needs to be a way to manage the docket system throughout the firm. However, that will be different in different firms—some will want it controlled centrally and some will prefer an individual method. The amount of control is really dependent on the firm's attitude and environment. In this firm, we have a certain way of handling different matters, such as document control. The legal assistants are constantly educating the attorneys in this matter, and we have gotten to the point where legal assistants are primarily responsible for documents. Cases being different, we do not have a uniform method of control to be followed. Although control of these and other matters is important and necessary, we think that flexibility is extremely important also.

What are your primary responsibilities in this area?

People in supervisory positions have two responsibilities. I have a responsibility to represent the firm to the legal assistants, and I have a responsibility to represent the legal assistants to the firm. This means that you walk a tightrope. It's very important that the firm know that the supervisors have feelings of responsibility as to the well-being of the firm as a whole. However, the legal assistants also need to know that their well-being is considered important and foremost. Sometimes these responsibilities can appear to conflict, but, when analyzed, they do not. It is most important

> **T**hey *believed* in the customer. They *believed* in granting autonomy, room to perform. They *believed* in open doors, in quality. But they were stern disciplinarians, every one. They gave plenty of rope, but they accepted the chance that some of their minions would hang themselves. Loose-tight is about rope.
> (Peters and Waterman, *In Search of Excellence*)[1]
>
> **K**nowledge is a high-grade resource. And knowledge workers are expensive. Their placement is a key to their productivity. The first rule is that opportunities have to be staffed with people capable of running them and of turning them into results. To make knowledge workers productive requires constant attention to what management consulting firms and law firms call "assignment control." One has to know where the people who are capable of producing results in knowledge work—precisely because their results are so hard to measure.
> (Peter Drucker, "Managing the Knowledge Worker")[2]

THE NATURE OF CONTROL

Control has a special place in an organization. The idea of being out of control conjures images of explosively angry people, helplessness, and erratic behavior. Even growth has a downside when it is out of control. Law firms and other organizations need to contain and harness their growth—and the personnel and materials that such growth involves—if everyone is to benefit in the long run. **Control** is the power to direct, regulate, and coordinate the human and material resources within an organization. **Controlling** is the managerial activity that ensures that the organization consistently meets its objectives and that makes any changes necessary if it does not. Effective controlling leads to accuracy, timeliness, quality, and high performance—all essential for a law firm's survival, for its avoidance of malpractice, and for its profitability. The process of controlling entails using checks and balances to prevent undesired events from happening, such as missing court deadlines and trial dates, overlooking paralegal or clerical errors, or not noticing missing funds. Most of us are graduates of the School of Murphy's Law. Our experience has likely taught us that whatever can go wrong usually does. For any organization, the possibility of error is proportionate to the number of its employees and its size. Each employee and each task can go wrong in hundreds of ways, purposely or otherwise. Workers lose interest. Supplies can run out. Machines can break down. Deadlines can be missed, and court dates can pass unnoticed. Important information and documents may vanish. Bills go unsent and uncollected. Controlling means making sure that people in organizations do *what* is necessary, *when* it is necessary, and *how* it should be done.[3] Being in charge as a manager means being in control.

Levels of Management and Control

All managers find that the controlling function is an important part of their job. But the type of control they exercise depends on the level of their management position.[4]

Top Management

Top management is concerned with the direction of the organization and its effectiveness. In law firms, partners share this responsibility, using the control activities of long-range strategic planning to establish and evaluate overall firm objectives. In addition, they analyze and respond to financial data, such as profit and loss statements. To facilitate these control activities, a law firm's upper-level managers use reports and data usually prepared by those at the mid-management level. An example of such a report would be a monthly accounting that shows the firm's chargeable and nonchargeable hours, amounts billed, amounts collected, and the aging of accounts. Quarterly and annual reports prepared for financial analysis might include, in addition to profit and loss statements, balance sheets and additional time records. Besides using financial information as a basis for controls, partners, and other upper-level managers oversee, update, and approve all operational policies.

Middle Management

Middle managers participate in control activities that monitor the performance of those in the units that report to them. In law firms, the major control function of middle management is to prepare reports for those in upper-level management. Budget preparation and related activities are a major part of this feedback process, which keeps both upper- and middle-level management in touch with the more routine activities of the firm. Middle management sees that operational policies and procedures are in place and that the law firm's members observe them, that members consistently meet the firm's administrative standards by adhering to policies in areas such as calendaring, docket control, file and records management, and timekeeping. To document the progress of the departments and units that they oversee, middle managers prepare objective weekly or monthly reports, commonly obtaining input from subordinates in areas such as accounting and bookkeeping to help them in this task. As part of the control process, they attempt to correct problem areas before such areas require the attention of top management. **Management by exception** is the policy of bringing to upper-level managers only those problems significant enough to warrant their decisions.

Supervisory Management

Supervisory management is at the very heart of the control process. Management at this level functions close to the people who perform the firm's functional, facilitating, and maintenance tasks, monitoring not only their work methods but the kind of work each person produces. Supervisory management controls the implementation of operational plans at the worker-supervisor level, dealing directly with the many activities involved in calendaring, docket control, and file and records management, as well as with many other administrative procedures. Supervisors oversee work schedules, flow, output, and activities on a daily and weekly basis, or according to another system that the firm has determined. Management at this level benefits from the following:

- Up-close views of work habits and practices;
- An understanding of work load and the criteria that determine quality;
- Managerial skills sufficient to save upper management from wasting time on minor problems;
- The ability to instill a sense of team effort by being close to workers; and
- The ability to obtain, utilize, and convey accurate information.

The Relationship of Control to Other Management Functions

Controlling facilitates each of the other three principle management functions (see Figure 5–1).

Planning

Controlling is the counterpart of planning. Good planning makes controlling easier, and planning is incomplete without methods of governing its outcomes.

Organizing

Control oversees organizing and good organizing makes control easier. The more successfully the firm can organize itself—that is, give tasks to those best qualified to perform them, while creating optimal work-

FIGURE 5–1
The Relationship between Controlling and the Other Management Functions

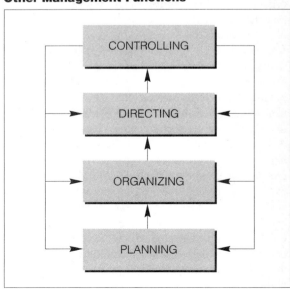

ing conditions—the less the firm will need to supervise those people or monitor the results of those tasks: the less it will need to control.

Directing

Controlling is the *guardian* for directing. Directors depend on a continuous flow of information that reveals whether or not the firm is meeting standards for production and performance. Control helps directors to determine how the directing process is progressing.

Controlling

Besides using control to facilitate the other managerial functions, managers initiate activities that monitor the effectiveness of their control processes and correct those processes when necessary.

Reasons for Control

Control leads to quality. It safeguards against irresponsibility and malpractice and helps the firm to deal with uncertainty.

Ensuring Quality

A firm that fails to establish methods for controlling the work that it does places its effectiveness and efficiency at stake. Without control, managers will at best see the firm maintain its status quo; at worst, they will have to confront the chaos of a firm that is out of control.

Avoiding Irresponsibility and Malpractice

Law firms are hardly immune from the threat they more commonly pose to others. They, too, are subject to litigation for malpractice. These legal challenges can come from many sources: from irate clients, from competitors, or from workers who believe they have been wronged. The more effective the firm's working policies and other controls are, the more the firm can assure itself of its members' compliance with legal and ethical standards. This lessens its susceptibility to lawsuits, which in turn helps to control its malpractice insurance costs.

Coping with Uncertainty and Complexity

By helping to integrate the many complex aspects of an organization, controlling helps the organization to center itself so that it can maintain its balance in the midst of the many challenges that it cannot control. Controlling offers the law firm stability for its future operations.

AREAS OF CONTROL

In a common misconception, people often think of *organizational control* as a synonym for *restriction*. However, Robert Waterman, widely recognized because of his classic work with Tom Peters, *In Search of Excellence*, writes that firms that are good at renewing themselves treat "facts as friends and financial controls as liberating." Managers in these firms enjoy having a handle on what is happening. They have an enormous hunger for the factual, says Waterman, seeing "information where others see only data." These managers utilize "comparisons, rankings, trends and any other way to combine the factual information that will make it useful to the firm,"[6] a process that also supports their efforts to keep the firm and its people on track.

The right kinds of controls are liberating because they lessen confusion and ambiguity, save time, safeguard against malpractice, and help the law firm to improve its service to clients. Through basic administrative **operational controls,** managers guide, monitor, and evaluate four types of resources within the firm: (1) financial resources, (2) human resources, (3) physical resources, and (4) information resources. Within each of these four areas, systems enable members of the firm to perform their jobs consistently and accurately. Charles Coulter, in commenting on the ALA's overview of management trends, elaborates on this idea:

> A system can be defined as a way of consistently producing an end result. A system is a process, method, or procedure that allows us to control the various tasks to be performed. In a law office and elsewhere, a system is a documented, logical method or way of handling transactions, procedures, or work flow to minimize waste, conserve professional time, and optimize productivity.[7]

A law firm documents its systems through a systems manual, a comprehensive collection of the firm's procedures, forms, and in-house rules. In addition, this manual should include an extensive overview of all of the firm's systems. First, the manual may describe controls for the following aspects of financial resources:

timekeeping practices and information; client billing and the collection of accounts receivable; accounting regulations; payment of bills; and areas such as marketing, for which the manual might detail policies for marketing practices, client entertainment, reimbursement procedures, and firm press releases. Second, in the area of human resources, the systems manual may include controls for all personnel policies and procedures, such as advertising and recruiting policies; interview and hiring procedures; new employee orientation expectations and responsibilities; job descriptions; evaluation practices and responsibilities; staff development and training policies; employee benefits; policies for vacations, overtime, sick days, absences, and lateness; and retirement and termination procedures. Next, in terms of physical resources, the firm's manual may describe policies and procedures for purchasing, equipment, inventory, asset control, supplies, and library acquisitions. A law firm's systems manual often gives the most extensive coverage to the fourth area, information resources. This is particularly helpful to newcomers to a firm, for the manual includes detailed descriptions of systems in areas ranging from mail and telephone procedures to confidentiality requirements. It often sets down procedures for activities such as dictation, typing, telephone communications, messages, and other office procedures, as well as procedures for client interactions and work assignments, new matter communications, docket management procedures, document creation, retrieval, and management regulations, all file procedures, including retention schedules, and requirements for file transfer and destruction. Finally, the systems manual can serve as a complete library of all the administrative forms in use at the firm.

Financial Resources Control

Used to project, estimate, and gauge the financial health and activities of the law firm, **financial resources control** is the process of using financial reports to ensure the effective use of the firm's capital. Control of financial resources, including billing and timekeeping, is the subject of Chapter 6.

Human Resources Control

Human resources control encompasses two topics: control of the human resource process, which consists of staffing, recruiting, and hiring (and which we will address in Chapter 7), and control of the supervision process, which involves supervising, evaluating, training, and improving worker performance (and which we will examine in detail in Chapter 8).

Physical Resources Control

Physical resources control oversees the use of the firm's material resources, including (1) its equipment, (2) its inventory of supplies, (3) its library, and (4) its use and upkeep of its space and facilities. In a larger firm, facilities management often is the exclusive role of a facilities manager.

Equipment

Overseeing the selection, upkeep, and use of equipment such as computers, telephones, and the machines used to facilitate administrative services, as well as arranging, recording, and maintaining maintenance or leasing contracts is a critical management responsibility. Firms commonly divide equipment control into telecommunications and general technology.

Telecommunications. Telecommunications management is at the core of a law firm's operations. Effective phone systems are one of the law firm's highest priorities. Many attorneys spend much of their day on the phone. The capabilities, upkeep, and efficiency of a firm's phone systems are a major part of the telecommunications aspect of the control process.

Technology. Computers and other technological equipment, such as modems, scanners, fax machines, and Local Area Network (LAN) systems bring demands similar to those in telecommunications management, but the presence of multiple users, whose skills often reveal a vast range of variation complicates the law firm's selection and use of computers considerably. Malfunctioning law firm systems cost serious setbacks and complications, the loss of time, and much frustration. Having knowledgeable personnel and effective maintenance procedures in place can help a firm to maintain control over trickier forms of technology. In the 1990s and beyond, the increasing use of computers and related equipment will mean increasing control challenges for law firm administrators. Among the technological developments creating new challenges and opportunities for law firms are the following:[8]

Integrated Hardware. Integrated hardware will consolidate the firm's information systems into a computerized network that comprises phone services, image reproduction, data control, document management, and video applications.

Integrated Software. Through the use of a central processing unit and common menus, those who manage the firm's software can provide all members of the law firm with open access to the firm's software applications. Table 5–1 lists basic law firm activities and computer activities that can facilitate these activities.

Work stations. Sixty-one percent of the lawyers in Chicago-Kent College of Law's 1991 Large Firm

TABLE 5–1
Law Firm Activities and Computer Applications

Activities	Applications
Accounting and Finance	Accounts receivable and accounts payable Calendar and billing (software such as Juris, CompuTrac, Timeslips, and Barrister) General ledger Integrated time and billing Payroll Tax and amortization programs
Support Services	Cost recovery systems and integrated time/expense programs Data bases Decisions support programs Spreadsheets Word processing
Legal Research	In-house reference searches using disks/CD ROM Information searches, utilizing on-line systems such as *Dialog* Medical/pharmaceutical data bases, such as *Medline, Toxline* or *Pharmaceutical News Index* On-line data bases, such as WESTLAW and LEXIS
Client Work and Billing	Bankruptcy support/filings Closing statements (settlement, foreclosure, and taxes) Collections Divorce settlements Estate planning (financial summaries, tax projections, and calculations) Litigation support Personal injury case management Probate support (reports, summaries, and schedules) Real estate (file, lender, and mortgage information) Tax preparation and planning programs
Data Base Management	Calendar and tickler files Calendaring and account inquiries Conflict-of-interest controls Docket management Document management and work product retrieval General management of cases and case status
Graphics and Visuals	Charts, slides, and video preparations Desktop publishing and promotions Graphics software for trial presentations
Housekeeping Functions & Communications	Computer linkage (communications with other computers) "Groupware" programs, designed for use by a network of users seeking similar applications Computer maintenance (such as anti-virus procedures, technical support, and functional analysis)

Survey reported having computers on or near their desks, compared to seven percent six years previously.[9] Computer use will soon permeate all levels of the law firm, and the PCs that members will use will be faster, more powerful and complex, and capable of far more applications than even their slightly older counterparts. Someone will need to research, schedule, and control this increased computer access and use—a control challenge that will more than likely fall to law firm administrators.

Fax Technology. The use of fax technology has spread so rapidly that few firms have learned how best to use this information tool. Proper use involves the reliable transmission of readable documents that are complete, unaltered, and authentic, and delivered in confidence to those for whom they are intended.[10]

Compact Disk Use. Compact disks, which provide an abundance of data storage, will lower the cost of storing data, provide easier access to data bases and research materials, and increase a firm's efficiency in controlling and accessing client information. CDs will also facilitate data-intensive computer applications such as docket management and conflict-of-interest searches.

Digital Dictation. One new technological application for law firms is digital dictation, a transcription system that replaces the standard analog cassette tape system with a device capable of converting digital codes with computer-like applications. The digital system works from a centralized unit that allows users to assign time priorities for dictations, to distribute work loads evenly among transcribers, to change the time status of materials (such as the date originated or the date due), to access dictation through phone lines, and to insert new materials anywhere in previously dictated materials without deleting. In addition, users can track time and costs by punching a client number into a keypad or by using a light pen capable of reading client and case bar codes.[11]

Administrative Services. The role of administrative services, which is, like facilities management itself, sometimes considered a distinct managerial role, oversees law firm areas such as the reproduction, facsimile, and supply center; the purchasing department; the mail room; delivery and messenger services; and, in some cases, housekeeping services. In addition to their roles as overseers, those who manage a firm's administrative services select computer, copy, dictation, transcription, and other equipment, studying current product reviews in order to select the vendors most appropriate to the firm's needs.

Inventory and Supplies Control

Inventory control sets standards for the quality, kinds, and amounts of supplies that the firm needs for its operations, provides feedback about the use of such supplies, and signals in advance the need for new supplies. Inventory control should also formulate mechanisms for slowing leakage, or workers' personal use of the firm's supplies, and for reordering items on a steady on-time, noncrisis basis, to avoid running out. Following just-in-time (JIT) inventory procedures minimizes storage costs, reduces the time that supply people spend writing up and placing orders, and lessens wastes—such as the reams of stationery that go unused because of capricious changes in a law firm's masthead!

The Law Firm Library

The law firm library was once a simple collection of books and reference documents. It, too, has undergone far-reaching changes. While many smaller firms still concentrate on keeping their print materials up-to-date and intact, using the most basic sign-out and control procedures, larger firms often use state-of-the art technology "to augment what is found within the library stacks."[12] Library information consulting firms exist solely to help law firms maximize one of their most valuable resources.

Library Systems. Those of us who have lent books to friends can sympathize (on a very small scale) with the law firm attempting to keep track of a costly collection of materials in constant need of updating. Control of a law firm's library is a continuing challenge. All members of the firm should follow library procedures in order to have full use of the firm's holdings, and policies should, among other things, control purchases of multiple copies of a given item and provide a method for recording all books the firm purchases and recognizing these books as part of the library's holdings, even those signed out by lawyers on a semipermanent basis. Using standard library procedures, the firm's library system should catalog all materials upon arrival, creating records to include in the firm's card catalog system, inventory, and annual report, and should prohibit the use of any newly arrived material until the library has properly received and recorded it. Bar coding provides an efficient method for tracking a library's inventory.[13] In addition, a firm should establish procedures for updating and weeding out library collections. Library routines vary greatly in law firms, ranging from simple shelving and storage, the filling out of book locator memo forms or cards, updating supplements, and summarizing available materials to the full-fledged services of professional librarians who specialize in information resources for the practice of law.

Technology for the Law Library. Current technology has made computer-assisted research conventional, based on the use of commercial data bases such as LEXIS and WESTLAW and similar products. Entire reference works are now available on compact disk. Computer data base management also allows a law firm library to inventory its holdings, to catalog information, to index firm briefs and memos, to create a firm form file bank, to track the firm's library purchases, and to recover costs by tracking charges for client services. Law firm libraries may be as simple as bookcases and shelves, but they may also contain reference and circulation areas; computer facilities; reading and work areas; seating; staff offices and stacks; on-line data base areas or rooms; microfilm and microfiche facilities and equipment; reference files and audiovisual equipment and materials; card catalogs and holdings; and dictation, telephone, and copy facilities.[14] Most law firms still encourage lawyers and paralegals to do book research first, emphasizing the cost-saving advantages of first becoming familiar with a legal issue through books, directories, digests, and encyclopedias before using the more costly services available through on-line data bases.[15]

The Library as a Clearinghouse. In some firms, libraries serve not only as research centers but act as clearinghouses for many other information management needs. Professional law librarians often see part of their role as being research brokers, who might assist firms by producing reference materials and extensive business information or up-to-date reports for newsletters or promotional work. In addition, a law librarian can help a firm to maintain an ''in-house work product or precedent file'' or an ''automated index of arbitrators,'' should the firm specialize in arbitration work. In addition, librarians may ''track and index continuing education programs, opposing counsel, legislation, administrative regulations, and biographies of attorneys in the firm.''[16] The library resource, if used to its full potential, can be an effective center for controlling the firm's information processing needs.

Space Planning

All the expansion and changes in law firms over the past decade or so have spotlighted the need for expertise in planning and allocating offices and space. In some firms, managers work with architects, designers, and contractors; in others, they are completely responsible for planning work stations and arranging work space and office changes, using prestige, status, and politics to resolve space allocation problems. Controlling space often comes down to controlling conflict and improving morale. What seems like a simple decision on space use, such as moving a secretary from one site in the office to another, can produce long-lasting complications and lower productivity. (Chapter 13 offers some suggestions for dealing with the changes involved in relocation.)

Information Resources Control

When legal administrators are asked what makes law office management so distinctly different, their answers commonly include the firm's need to control its information. The law firm builds its service to clients upon the information it possesses, its knowledge of the law, and its knowledge of clients. It relies on its ability to control and to use this information, and depends upon all of its members to adhere to the information resources systems it has established. The accounting and consulting firm of Holland Shipes Vann emphasizes the importance of controlling information within the law firm.

> Documentation is the key to combating disastrous administrative errors. You need to have the right documents and you need to make sure they're used properly. For example, you should have a standard client intake form to record information about every new client and every new client matter. Without a standard form, you will not, on a consistent basis, obtain all the information you need about every new client and every new matter for an existing client.[17]

Time controls are essential to the accurate, efficient use of information within a firm. Kline Strong and Arben Clark, whose classic text *Law Office Management* remains a standard reference, estimate that 45 percent of malpractice cases against lawyers could have been avoided through the use of some form of time controls, pointing out that "ironically, the more proficient a lawyer is, the more susceptible he may be to missing deadlines simply from the pressure of work."[18] Mary Ann Altman and Robert Weil, prominent law office management consultants, also believe that the law firm's customarily hectic pace has not only increased the number of missed deadlines but has swelled the number of law firm malpractice suits resulting from missing a statute of limitations or some other critical filing deadline.[19] Law firms need reliable and meticulous time controls, which are possible through the use of carefully kept (1) calendar and diaries, (2) work assignments, (3) tickler controls, (4) docket controls, (5) document management and retrieval systems, (6) records management, (7) conflict-of-interest controls, and (8) client files.

Calendars and Diaries

The firm should record each attorney and paralegal date or time obligation into a duplicate diary system, placing one copy with the docket clerk or the appropriate secretary and the other with the attorney or paralegal in question. Smaller firms may use wall calendars to track critical dates that apply to all firm members. Larger firms may use more elaborate systems, such as computer printouts, to record lawyer obligations.

Work Assignments

Work distribution and support systems are critical for efficient work flow. Theoretically, the balanced distribution of work between the attorneys and paralegals in a law firm will result in a consistently even caseload and relatively stable support staff demands for each case and client. This never happens. Law firms have both fat times and lean times, and distributing work evenly presents a continual challenge for managers. Uneven work assignments and responsibilities for attorneys and paralegals can create hard-to-resolve work inequities that leave some support personnel standing idle while others are swamped. In attempting to even out support staff work loads, managers should try to distinguish workers who are really under pressure from those who deserve acting awards for the creativity of their complaints.

Within a firm that assigns work to lawyers, paralegals, or clerks, a work assignment system that uses a standardized form can provide controls both for creating an even flow of work and obtaining accurate information about responsibilities. A *work assignment memo* should include client information; critical dates; directions for reporting and responsibility relationships; particular information about files, documents, and resources, if appropriate; and special instructions for the matter that is assigned. It is useful, for example, when the attorney assigning work expresses his or her expectations for how long the work should take. Knowing, as a paralegal, that you are to spend three hours on a matter—rather than a self-estimate of six hours, two days, or a week—allows you to schedule time for other projects and conveys the urgency of the matter at hand as well. Figure 5–2 presents a paralegal work assignment form.

Tickler or Monitor Controls

Perhaps the most critical controls in the law firm, tickler or monitor file systems help lawyers meet crucial deadlines and keep critical dates. A description of a firm's tickler system is required for most professional liability insurance.

Tickler Systems. Arranged by upcoming calendar dates a **tickler file** actively reminds law firm personnel of upcoming deadlines and the action required. The types of tickler systems in use include slip methods and perpetual calendar systems, file notation systems, and wall calendar systems; although computerized systems are available, a basic file card tickler system has long served the needs of many firms. In addition, lawyers' own calendars and diaries also serve as a backup system for dates, obligations, professional activities, and sometimes for billing and timekeeping information.

Many commercial forms and tickler file systems are currently available. Some commercial tickler forms have multi-part copies that are color-coded to serve as time reminders. A form in triplicate, for example, might have a golden top copy, to be delivered to the appropriate person one week in advance of any critical date, a middle copy of pink to be used three days before, and a bottom sheet of white or some other noticeable color to be distributed one day before the critical date. (Determining the lead time sufficient to complete required work—usually one to five days—is essential in establishing a tickler file system. In-house forms or simple file cards can be just as effective as commercial forms if a firm uses them consistently. The firm's filing system should keep tickler file reminder forms in a centralized tray or file folder envelope, or on three-by-

CHAPTER 5 / CONTROLLING: RESOURCES, TIME, AND GROWTH 153

FIGURE 5–2
Sample Paralegal Assignment Form

PARALEGAL ASSIGNMENT SHEET

ASSIGNED TO: _____   ASSIGNMENT DATE: _____
FROM: _____   DUE DATE: _____
FILE: _____   TASK DEGREE OF DIFFICULTY: _____
                                       (T1   T2   T3   T4)
                                       MAXIMUM AMOUNT OF TIME TO BE SPENT: _____
                                       REPORT BACK BY: _____
CLIENT #: _____   MATTER #: _____

TASK ASSIGNMENT

___ PREPARE COMPLAINT   ___ PREPARE ANSWER

DISCOVERY

___ PROPOUND INTERROGATORIES   ___ ANSWER INTERROGATORIES
___ DRAFT REQUEST FOR PRODUCTION   ___ ANSWER REQUEST FOR PRODUCTION
___ OBTAIN HOSPITAL RECORDS (RULE 13)   ___ OBTAIN MEDICALS
___ DETERMINE DAMAGES   ___ PREPARE SETTLEMENT BROCHURE
___ PREPARE MOTION TO _____
_____

WORKERS COMPENSATION

___ PREPARE CLAIM/APPEARANCE   ___ PREPARE DISCONTINUANCE
___ PREPARE PAYMENT W/O PREJUDICE _____
___ CALL DIA* RE _____
___ PREPARE LUMP SUM AGREEMENT _____

MISCELLANEOUS

___ SCHEDULE DEPOSITION OF _____
___ SCHEDULE IME** WITH _____
___ WRITE/CALL _____
_____

___ ORGANIZE FILE FOR TRIAL _____
_____

___ COPY CASE _____
_____

___ PREPARE _____
_____

RESEARCH - ISSUE _____
_____

ADDITIONAL INFORMATION:

0023Z

SOURCE: Reprinted with the permission of Robinson, Donovan, Madden & Barry, P.C., Springfield, Massachusetts.
* DIA: Division of Industrial Accidents.
**IME: Independent Medical Exam.

five-inch cards in a file box. The ticker file should be organized by months, days, and years, with the most recent date at the front of the file. Many experts in law firm administration suggest a five-year coverage for dates; others, three. In terms of specific advance preparation, the file should document individual dates, 1 through month's end, for the next two or three months. Whether customized or commercial, a tickler system should include the following information:

- Client name;
- Case;
- File/case number;
- Event/action/matter;
- Due and reminder dates;
- Date of event/appropriate statute of limitations, etc.;
- Responsible attorney;
- Other attorneys involved; and
- Date on which reminder was acknowledged.

Critical Dates. A tickler file may include dates such as the following:

- Client meeting dates;
- File delivery dates;
- Attorney obligations: court appearances, board of directors meetings, trustees meetings;
- Statute of limitations dates, renewal dates for judgments and licenses, corporation renewal dates, insurance coverage dates, copyright dates;
- Due dates for probate proceedings, closing dates for real estate matters, tax return dates;
- Review dates for wills and trusts; and
- Office dates: lease or insurance renewal dates, notary expiration dates, office meeting dates, office events, and staff and associate evaluation and review dates.

Tickler File Procedures. The firm's docket clerk, records coordinator, secretary, or some other responsible individual should pull reminders daily, first thing in the morning, and distribute them to the lawyers or their secretaries, who should, in turn, return data on any completed activities to this same person in order to update the system. The file tender should also pull any necessary files and give them to the lawyer or paralegal for whom they are intended. A computerized system can use printouts to yield updated information on obligations.

Figure 5–3 presents an example of a commercial tickler form.

The Docket and Docket Control

The word *docket* can refer to a list of cases pending in court, a summary of legal proceedings, or any list of tasks that a law firm needs to accomplish. A comprehensive overview of the time-dated obligations of the professionals in a firm, a **docket control system** monitors the law firm's deadlines, filing dates, and court dates. Docket control is imperative for timely follow-up, which is essential to survival within the time-intensive pressure of the legal field.

Docket Control Systems. Docket control systems, which can take the form of docket books, charts, index cards, or computer software, provide firm-wide information on all upcoming critical court dates, deadlines, and responsibilities. These systems may also serve as firm-wide monitoring and control systems and can aid in the equitable distribution of work assignments. Computerized calendar/docket systems are capable of providing information on attorney obligations, filing deadlines, scheduled appearances, lawyer and staff assignments, backup coverage and assistance, work-related appointments, warning dates, and even space utilization. Upper-level management, partners, the management committee, or the firm's subcommittees can call up reports covering a day, week, month, year, or any other time period for each attorney in the firm; the system can also generate similar reports for the entire firm or for specific departments or groups within it. Larger firms assign a **docket clerk** to oversee centralized calendar control.

Docket Control Procedures. For all time-dated obligations, the attorney responsible initiates a docket control memo or a similar form of notice. The attorney or his or her secretary gives the memo to the docket control clerk, secretary, receptionist, or some other support staff member responsible for docket control, who enters the information into the firm's docket control system and who later reminds the lawyer of the obligation in advance. Such reminders may occur only once or they may come in a series; in any case, they should allow the attorney sufficient time to prepare for the court appearance, deposition, or filing deadline in question. Some firms review such reminders at weekly planning meetings; larger firms may circulate this information.

The following paragraphs offer suggestions for an effective docket control system:

    Instantaneous Calendaring. The calendaring should be immediate and automatic. As soon as an appoint-

CHAPTER 5 / CONTROLLING: RESOURCES, TIME, AND GROWTH 155

FIGURE 5–3
Sample Three-Part Tickler Form

| CASE STYLE _____ | FILE NO. _____ |

☐ Review Only ☐ S/L
Action Required _____

First Reminder [   ]

Second Reminder _____

Attorney Handling _____

FIRST NOTICE
Order from ROSEMONT FORMS, INC., P.O. BOX 262, PETERSBURG, PA 16669, (814) 667-2580, (800) 544-4748 TICKLER (Form T-1)

| CASE STYLE _____ | FILE NO. _____ |

☐ Review Only ☐ S/L
Action Required _____

First Reminder [■■■■■■■■■■■]

Second Reminder [   ]

Attorney Handling _____

FINAL NOTICE
Order from ROSEMONT FORMS, INC., P.O. BOX 262, PETERSBURG, PA 16669, (814) 667-2580, (800) 544-4748 TICKLER (Form T-1)

| CASE STYLE _____ | FILE NO. _____ |

☐ Review Only ☐ S/L
Action Required _____

First Reminder _____

Second Reminder _____

Attorney Handling _____

LOCATOR COPY
Order from ROSEMONT FORMS, INC., P.O. BOX 262, PETERSBURG, PA 16669, (814) 667-2580, (800) 544-4748 TICKLER (Form T-1)

SOURCE: Reprinted with the permission of Rosemont Forms, Bryn Mawr, Pennsylvania.

ment has been made over the telephone, it should be calendared. All incoming and outgoing mail and other documentation should be checked for dates requiring lawyer action.

Backup Checks. Every system should have a double or even a triple check. For example, a lawyer and a secretary can check on each other through a duplicate system. A third person should be assigned to check each calendar in case both the lawyer and secretary are absent at the same time. (For this reason, notations must be legible.) The docket clerk should have a backup copy of the entire system. New employees should receive thorough training in the use of the docket control.

Generous Lead Time. The system should provide plenty of lead time to meet the requirements of each appointment. It may also provide a series of reminders as a deadline approaches.

Follow-up. The system should utilize a follow-up check—a method of recording that a tax return was filed or interrogatories answered on certain dates, for example—to ensure that the work has been done.[20]

Document Management and Retrieval

A **document retrieval system** consists of legal briefs, legal opinions, articles for publication, speeches, other memoranda of law, and any other work products that a firm can use to provide future legal services, as well as a document index that enables the firm members to access these products. Computerized systems help law firms to control the volume of written work they generate and to integrate past efforts into current operations. By creating "a data base of documents that is updated automatically every time a document is created, retrieved, edited, printed, archived, or deleted," these programs help a firm to keep "track of clients, matters, authors, secretaries, key words, and other relevant information."[21] However, while document management software can integrate multiple applications, including billing, time records, document histories, conflict searches, and document retention scheduling, many firms can still use basic noncomputerized systems to track the work they have already produced. One person in the firm should be primarily responsible for document management and retrieval; in larger firms, a records coordinator or law librarian may perform this duty.

Document Retrieval System Procedures. Any document retrieval system is based on the simple idea, "If you can't find it, it's no good." To establish a simple document index retrieval system, a firm might follow these steps:

1. Establish a centralized location for the system.
2. Formulate filing categories and write each category on a separate three-by-five-inch index card. A firm might file its documents according to index numbers, subject matter, attorney or author, the statutes involved, client, or date.
3. File documents in the system according to the categories established in step 2. A firm may file a document in one of two ways:

- By recording the document's file number on a *document index retrieval card* and returning the file to its location in the centralized client filing system, or
- By making a copy of the file, assigning the copy a sequential number, filing the copy in a special document index retrieval location, recording the sequential number on a document index retrieval card, and filing the card.

Figure 5–4 provides an example of a case index form that a law firm might use in a document index retrieval system.

Records Management

In the management of information, well-developed systems are critical. To be effective, a centralized information system must have a general index listing all of the information that it contains, based on case or clients; the system then breaks these categories down into subcategories, such as case type or the attorney responsible. Law firms usually use codes for categorizing client data, with the choice of code depending on the technology and preferences of the individual firm. A firm must monitor its information system continuously and thoroughly train its personnel to comply with the system's procedures, so that they can readily access, retrieve, and control the information necessary to the work of the firm and can help the firm to avoid the high costs of tracking down missing documents or files. Software programs, such as the many data base management programs on the market, can help law firms to establish codes and systems for easy information control and access. In the following paragraphs, we will examine four computer-assisted records management systems.

FIGURE 5–4
Sample Case Index Form

HOW TO USE THIS FORM: The white card is your active client index. File under the client's name. The blue card is your adverse party index. File under the adverse party name in a separate index tray. The buff copy is gummed and perforated. Use the top part as a file label and the lower part to head your accounting ledger, or paste the copy into the file folder for reference. Type client name in CAPS, adverse party in lower case. When the file closes, complete the white card and file in the closed client index. Use the blue card to calendar destruction.		
Client	Adverse Party	File No.
Address		Phones
Matter		Date Opened / Attorney Handling
Insurer/Forwarder		
Opposing Counsel		
Cross Index Names		
Memo		
Closed Date	Destroy Date	Closed Number
Client	Adverse Party	File No.

FORM D-46   CASE INDEX
REORDER FROM
ROSEMONT FORMS, INC., P.O. Box 262, Petersburg, PA 16669 • (800) 544-4748

SOURCE: Printed with the permission of Rosemont Forms, Bryn Mawr, Pennsylvania.

Automated Records Management Systems. An **automated records management system** provides an integrated technological approach to records management. For such a system, a law firm utilizes a data base program based on its storage and reporting needs and creates a basic computer file for each of its clients. With its records easily accessible within a reliable computer storage medium, the firm can make instant changes, additions, and deletions; easily conduct conflict-of-interest searches; print (with the proper software and a label printer) its own bar-code labels for its work products and files, client records, billing, and other information; and obtain data printouts (on the status of certain files, for example) by scanning bar codes with a light pen or other scanner.

Bar Codes. **Bar coding** is the process of assigning a file or other piece of data an identifying mark consisting of computer-readable lines similar to the universal product codes used on retail merchandise. By using bar-code labels, a firm can quickly access client and case records and can obtain immediate updates on the signed-out locations of files through the use of hand-held scanners.[22] Attorneys may scan their own offices, using light pens that are now standard desk equipment, while more compulsive legal administrators may send their underlings on file hunts—or go file hunting themselves! One bar-coding system, the portable computer-based *File Tracker*, works as follows:

1. The firm assigns a bar code and a client and case number to each new case, placing the bar code and number on file folders and other information access media, such as Rolodex® forms.
2. The firm enters full information concerning the case into the computer, using categories called "indexed fields." Using these fields, the firm can cross-index case information and conduct searches, such as those required for conflict-of-interest procedures.
3. The firm then bar codes strategic locations, such as attorney offices, file cabinets, the library, and conference rooms, and enters these codes in the computer.
4. The firm now can inventory its files and trace their movement by using a portable scanner to

IN THE NEWS

Hot Lines

Law firms have been slow to adapt to automation. With the exception of word processing, law firms have tended to rely on corporations and other businesses to test new applications before adopting them for their own use. Bar-code technology is one application that has been used heavily by other businesses and is just beginning to see wide acceptance in law offices of all sizes.

Bar codes are familiar to everyone. They are the graphic series of black and white lines of varying width that are ubiquitous on grocery-store products and on checks. The code represents an identification number that can be read by an optical character reader, often called a scanner. These codes are used to manage inventory and track the movement of specific items.

By creating a data base of the items to be tracked—such as library books, file folders, furniture or computer equipment—and assigning a unique bar code to each item, it becomes easy to track inventory and locate specific items.

As firms develop plans for managing, storing, retrieving and delivering information, they should consider the following applications for this technology: records management, library management, litigation support or document management, asset management, and mail management.

Possible Applications

Law firms are focusing increasingly on areas of potential exposure to liability. Many firms are beginning to examine the effect of inexact records management techniques in this context. Lost files mean lost information and jeopardy for client and firm. This concern, and the constant worry about containing administrative costs, are prompting firms to hire records management professionals to recommend and install more coherent file management solutions.

Bar coding physical files to monitor records circulation has proven to be a very effective method of preventing information loss. Once bar codes have been applied to the files and subfolders, the staff can use hand-held bar-code scanners to take frequent and fast inventories of records throughout the office. This technique greatly reduces the amount of time spent looking for lost files, and it diminishes the likelihood of losing important client information.

Firms have found that they must spend time evaluating and redesigning records management procedures to ensure that current and future needs are met by new systems. A correctly designed system, using bar-code technology, will provide firms with more efficient document handling, an automated rather than a manual master index, a more accurate index of files stored off-site and, most important, it gives the records staff the ability to be more responsive to attorneys' needs. The result is a records management system that reduces the firm's exposure to liability because of mismanaged records.

University and public libraries were the first to use bar-code technology to manage the circulation of books and journals. Most public library cards carry a bar code, and in many libraries every book has a bar code on the title page or back cover where the check-out card used to appear. As the cost of bar-code systems decreases and the size of law firm collections increases, law firm library managers will be able to justify the cost of installing these systems.

As firms evaluate the purchase and installation of automated library-management systems to manage cataloging, circulation, ordering, serials routing, interlibrary loans and binding, they also should be evaluating the possible savings available by integrating these applications with a bar-code system.

In litigation support, bar codes are being used to replace the Bates stamp to attach an identification number to documents and connect each document with detailed information about that document in the data base. Bar-code systems can be applied to full-text documents such as depositions and trial transcripts. These documents can be scanned into the data base or entered by loading diskettes supplied by a court reporter. Bar codes also can be applied to the indexes and abstracts of documents to locate document-specific information such as dates, authors, types of documents, recipients and subject terms assigned by case staffs.

Inventory control and asset management long have been a headache for law firms. Manually maintaining an accurate and current inventory is almost impossible. Obtaining serial numbers from equipment

SOURCE: Sandra S. Gold and Beth E. Chiaiese, "Bar-Coding Technology Comes to Law Offices," *The National Law Journal* (17 February 1992); 37, 39. Reprinted with permission.

IN THE NEWS (continued)

often is cumbersome. These numbers are usually attached to the equipment on tags in some inaccessible place, usually in unreadable, small characters. The usual result is an inaccurate list because of the difficulty of copying long numbers from the equipment to paper and then transferring the information to a data base.

With a system that uses bar codes, once the bar codes have been applied to the furniture or equipment, a hand-held scanner can be used to read the information, temporarily store the data in the scanner's memory and then load the data into the central data base. After office moves, a staff member can scan the bar codes and update the record of the location of equipment. Reports can be printed to show what each attorney and staff member has in his or her office. This information can then be used to establish insurance values and maintain up-to-date depreciation figures.

Law firms that use bar coding also can benefit from incentives offered to businesses by the U.S. Postal Service. Businesses that comply with post office procedures are given faster service and more discounts, and the benefits improve as businesses comply further with the procedures. Several factors, including in-house application of bar codes, affect the speed of processing mail through the system and the discount offered. It is to everyone's advantage to follow the procedures that allow the firm's mail to remain within the automated processing systems of the post office. Once a piece of mail is rejected and has to be handled manually, the cost and delivery time increase dramatically.

The post office system relies heavily on scanners that read ZIP codes and printers that print and apply bar codes representing those ZIP codes. The mail then is fed through a sorter that reads the code and sorts it by carrier route. Applying bar codes in-house will help speed the delivery of the firm's mail and qualify the firm for larger postal discounts than otherwise would be available.

Adopting bar-code technology in any or all of these applications will involve a number of expenses. Costs will depend on whether the application is networked or stand-alone; the size of the data base and the associated hard disk requirements; the quality of scanning and printing equipment; and the selected software.

There are many off-the-shelf software products available that may be appropriate for these applications. If the firm's procedures require a more unique approach, custom software may be necessary.

Hardware decisions should depend on the current configuration of hardware within the firm. If firm-wide standards exist, there is probably no reason to deviate for any of these applications. The type of printer selected should depend on the quality of labels desired. Laser printers or thermal-transfer printers are considered to produce the highest quality bar-code labels. Printers can cost from $300 for a dot-matrix printer to $30,000 or more for a printer that produces the bar-code label on a laminated strip that includes a color-coded client-matter number.

Bar-code labels should have a clear, crisp image that will not deteriorate after repeated scanning. They can be purchased pre-printed or printed in-house.

There is a variety of scanning equipment available, ranging from a light pen or wand to laser guns and intelligent scanners with greater memory capacity. The cost ranges from approximately $300 to $3,000.

It is likely that the largest expense in adopting bar-code technology for any of these applications will come with the conversion and implementation of the system. Producing and applying the bar codes and then entering the detailed data into the data base is a time-consuming task that involves many staff members. The cost will depend on the size of the collection to be entered, the time available to accomplish the conversion and the number of people working on the project.

Though the cost of purchasing hardware and software might seem to be high, if the same hardware and software can be used to develop systems for more than one application, bar-code technology may prove to be a very effective solution for controlling costs, improving accuracy and increasing productivity.

Bar-code technology is flexible, reliable and well-tested. It offers clear opportunities for enhanced accuracy of record-keeping in a variety of settings. It also offers some significant cost-control opportunities. But because initial costs can be substantial, the decision to adopt the technology will depend on a number of variables—chief among them the size of the law firm and the number of intended applications. In general, the technology will be most advantageous to firms that are able to make use of it for multiple functions.

scan the bar code of each location where files have been taken and the bar codes of the files in those locations.

5. Finally, the firm can generate reports that document missing files, conflict checks, case open and close dates, and the history of who has used files and for what length of time.

Expense Control and Recovery Systems. An **integrated expense control and recovery system** is an automated system that uses client codes such as the bar code to monitor the sources of service-related expenses. For example, when using the Equitrac system (shown in Figure 5–5), a firm can utilize codes such as bar codes to designate each client-related function, including phone calls, copy services, and postage costs. The firm can use the records that it documents through these bar codes to create item-specific client bills.

Optical Disk Filing Systems. One recent development is a self-contained desktop optical disk filing system that consists basically of a built-in scanner that converts documents to electronic data that the computer and its printer recognize and reproduce. The scanner, which can scan both sides of a document simultaneously, is combined with a screen-based program that provides a complete system for indexing, storing, cross-referencing, and locating documents, with built-in security protection for files and documents. One optical disk can store up to 13,000 documents, the rough equivalent of a six-drawer file.

Conflict-of-Interest Systems

The key to implementing the rules that govern conflicts of interest is an effective information system. Rules 1.7 and 1.9 of the Model Rules of Professional Conduct (which we will examine more closely in Chapter 15) prohibit firms from accepting any cases that will have an adverse effect on present or past cases, whether they involve the same matter or are seemingly unrelated. Law firms cannot offer their services to adversaries or potential adversaries at the same time. While avoiding conflicts of interest may not be difficult for smaller

FIGURE 5–5
Integrated Expense Control and Recovery System

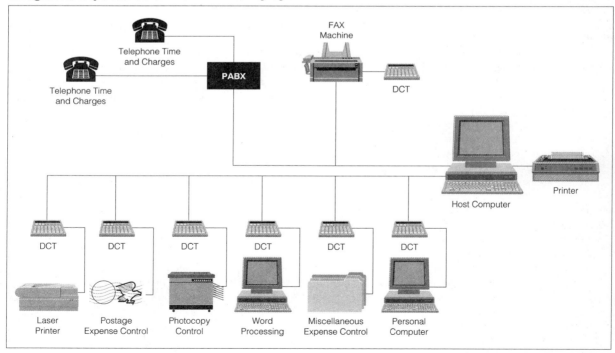

SOURCE: Reprinted through the courtesy of EQUITRAC, Coral Gables, FL. Copyright © 1990.

firms, larger, more complicated practices require more specialized conflict avoidance procedures.[23] The fact that a modern-day lack of client loyalty creates constantly changing client rosters within some firms makes avoiding conflicts of interest more difficult and the consequences for the failure to do so more serious.

Requirements. The minimum requirements for a system capable of locating conflicts of interest, writes nationally known legal ethicist Geoffrey Hazard, "are a 'new matter' form that every lawyer submits to a central source and an index system through which the central source can correlate clients and matters."[24] In smaller firms, index cards may still be sufficient, but larger firms are likely to require computer programs to facilitate central indexing, the search for conflicts and potential conflicts, correlation, and reporting. Computer systems still depend on human input, however, and the most effective legal manager cannot force attorneys to submit new matter sheets promptly. But a manager can distribute information in a timely fashion, focus the efforts of unintentionally negligent attorneys, and, through compliance and noncompliance reporting, document the behavior of those who are seriously negligent and uncooperative. Even a firm that has well-developed conflict-of-interest policies needs to carefully monitor information and records. Full staff compliance is critical. Chapter 15 will address the ethical issues that affect the management of law firms, including conflicts of interest.

Conflict-of-Interest Procedures. Before opening a file, accepting any case, or proceeding with any step within a case, a firm must first perform a conflict of interest search, checking and comparing information on the client with information on the adverse parties. If the client is a corporation, the search should seek possible conflicts of interests stemming from relationships between officers of any parent or subsidiary companies and members of the boards of directors and/or trustees. The person conducting the search should then note on a new matter form who was responsible for the conflict of interest search, when it was done, and, if the search uncovered any potential conflicts, how they were resolved.

Figures 5–6a through 5–6c present portions of a typical new matter form for a litigation department. Figure 5–6a represents the top page of the actual form, which contains two substantially similar pages for the firm's docket clerk and records department. Figure 5–6b presents case management and billing information areas from the fourth page of the actual form, and 5–6c shows the coding key for information entered on the form.

Client Files

An individual reference tool for each of a firm's clients, a client file includes billing information, fees charged, a history of the client's case or other work done for the client, a history of actions taken on the client's behalf, a written record of advice or counsel given, copies of communications, research reports and results, and any other data that affect the client. Effective records filing systems are vitally important to a law firm. Special insurance is available to help a firm protect and recreate its files, in case of a catastrophe. While organizing and locating necessary information sounds simple, in knowledge-based organizations, where words and documents proliferate, this is no easy task.

Client File Procedures. Whatever numeric or alphanumeric system a firm uses to impose order on its records, it should develop a master index to document all clients and adverse parties. (A master index is not necessary for straight alphabetical filing.) The firm should also establish procedures for organizing material within each client file. Papers should be punched and hung on metal fasteners within the file in reverse chronological order, the most recent date on top, so that attorneys and other personnel don't waste time shuffling through randomly arranged sheets. Pockets can be used to hold loose documents, and the firm should stamp the time and date on each document it receives—on the reverse side, to avoid marring important material on the front of the page. A secretary or a docket or file clerk should share with an attorney the responsibility for returning files; many larger firms request that files be returned to a central location, where a filing specialist will ensure that each file is intact and return it to its proper place. Filing systems in firms of all sizes should provide for after-hours access and procedures for handling mishaps, such as missing materials. A firm that is large enough might stress the importance of its records management system by assigning the control of filing responsibilities to a specific person or group.

New Matter Reports. Each time a client requests representation, a firm must process new matter information, and accurate handling of such information is essential to the firm's control of its work. A firm should

FIGURE 5–6a
Sample New Matter Form

[Form: Robinson Donovan Madden & Barry, P.C. — Initial Client Data Sheet, Litigation. Fields include Client No., Matter No., Entered Case Management, Docketed, Date File Opened; Client Information section with Client Name, D.O.B., P/D checkboxes, Address, S. Sec. No., Contact, Telephone, Fax, Existing Client Yes/No, Bill To, Employer, Insurer, Adjuster, Address, Insurers File No., Insurers Telephone No., D/L; Matter Information section with Case Name, Case Subject Matter, Statute of Limitations, Date Complaint Filed, Court/Administrative Body, Location, Immediate Action Needed, Responsible Attorney, Other Atty. Assigned, Paralegal Assigned; Adverse Party Information with Name, Address, Attorney, Address, Telephone; Additional Adverse Party(s) with Adverse Related Party and Relationship; Additional Client Party(s) Involved Include Subsidiaries, Parents and Related Corps. with Non Adverse Party and Relationship. Footer: "Complete Case Management/Billing Information on Part II. If more space is required attach additional sheet. File Copy."]

SOURCE: Figures 5–6a through 5–6c: Courtesy of Robinson, Donovan, Madden & Barry, P. C., Springfield, Massachusetts.

develop standard procedures, computerized or manual, for assimilating all new matter information, including client, case, and billing data, and for communicating this information to all of its members. Such communication can take place at regular weekly or periodic whole-firm or departmental planning meetings or through circulated memos or lists, with all attorneys receiving a controlled distribution list. Distributing new case and client information prevents initial conflict-of-interest problems, such as representing both the husband and wife in a divorce proceeding or representing the opposing side in a suit. Several computer

CHAPTER 5 / CONTROLLING: RESOURCES, TIME, AND GROWTH

FIGURE 5–6b
Case Management and Billing Information Areas of a Sample New Matter Form

CASE MANAGEMENT INFORMATION							
CASE DEGREE OF DIFFICULTY	CURRENT CASE STATUS (CHECK ONE)						
D1 MOST D2	NO SUIT	PLEADINGS	DISCOVERY	READY FOR TRIAL	APPEAL		DORMANT
D3 D4 LEAST	CONCILIATION	CONFERENCE	HEARING	REVIEW BOARD	LUMP SUM	§ 37	

BILLING INFORMATION						
BILL RATE SPECIFICATIONS	SET BILL RATE	SPECIAL BILL RATE				
CLIENT TYPE	DEPARTMENT	AREA OF LAW	BILL FORMAT	22 81 - STANDARD	523 81 - DETAILED	
BILLING FREQUENCIES						(YOU DEFINE CYCLE)
M - MONTHLY	Q - QUARTERLY	S - SEMI-ANNUAL	A - ANNUAL	C - UPON COMP.	Z -SPECIAL	

FIGURE 5–6c
Information Coding Key for Sample New Matter Form

CLIENT TYPES	DEPARTMENTS	DEGREES OF DIFFICULTY
1 INSURANCE 2 BANK 3 INDIVIDUAL 4 NON-PROFIT CORPORATION 5 CORPORATION 6 PARNERSHIP/ OTHER BUSINESSENTITY	1 BUSINESS/CORPORATE 2 ESTATE PLANNING/PROBATE 3 LITIGATION 4 REAL ESTATE 5 ADMINISTRATIVE ACTION 6 WORKER'S COMPENSATION 7 FAMILY LAW	D1 COMPLEX CASES, COMPLEX WORKER'S COMP CASES HIGH DAMAGES ($200,000 AND UP) D2 ROUTINE CASES, MODERATE DAMAGES ($25,000 TO $200,000) AND ROUTINE WORKER'S COMP CASES D3 ROUTINE DISTRICT COURT CASES, ARBITRATIONS D4 SMALL CLAIMS, SMALL ARBITRATIONS WC CASES ASSIGNED FOR LUMP SUM ONLY

AREAS OF LAW	
BUSINESS 11 CORPORATE ORGANIZATION 12 PARTNERSHIP 13 CORPORATE LEGAL FUNCTIONS 14 BUY-SELL AGREEMENTS 15 ACQUISITION AND SALES 16 BANK FINANCING ARRANGEMENTS 17 EMPLOYEE BENEFITS PLANS 18 PROFESSIONAL CORPORATION 20 ENVIRONMENTAL LAW 87 LOAN WORKOUT **TAX** 71 TAX PLANNING 72 INCOME TAX RETURNS 73 TAX LITIGATION 75 MUNICIPAL LAW 76 LABOR LAW 77 ADMINISTRATIVE LAW **BANK** 91 COMMERCIAL 92 TRUST 93 EXECUTIVE/ADMINISTRATIVE 94 INSTALLMENT 95 COMMERCIAL COLLECTION 96 CONSUMER COLLECTION 98 BANK OF BOSTON **REAL ESTATE** 21 RESIDENTIAL REP SELLER 22 RESIDENTIAL REP BUYER 23 RESIDENTIAL REP MORTGAGEE 24 COMMERCIAL TRANSACTION 25 LEASES/OPTIONS 26 REALTY TRUSTS AND PENSIONS 30 TITLE WORK 85 FORECLOSURE 86 REFINANCE	**ESTATE PLANNING/PROBATE** 31 DRAFT WILLS AND TRUSTS 32 DRAFT OTHER DOCUMENTS 33 TRUST ACCOUNT FOR BANK 34 PRIVATE FIDUCIARY ACCOUNTING & MANAGEMENT 35 ESTATE ADMINISTRATION (BANK) 36 ESTATE ADMINISTRATION (PERSONAL) 37 ADMINISTRATION (NON-PROBATE ESTATE) 38 OTHER (ESTATE PLANNING/PROBATE) 28 GUARDIANSHIPS/CONSERVATORSHIPS 29 FIDUCIARY DISPUTE RESOLUTION **FAMILY** 81 DIVORCE 82 ADOPTION/NAME CHANGE 83 MOD DECREE/CONTEMPT **LITIGATION/INSURANCE** 39 PRODUCTS LIABILITY 40 DENTAL MALPRACTICE 41 INSURANCE DEFENSE 42 INSURANCE SUBROGATION 43 THIRD PARTY WC RECOVERY 44 WORKMAN'S COMPENSATION DEFENSE 45 FIRE/CASUALTY LOSS 51 BUSINESS LITIGATION 52 LAND USE LITIGATION 53 PROBATE LITIGATION 54 DEFENSE (NON-INSURANCE) 55 BANKRUPTCY 56 CONTRACT LITIGATION 57 PROFESSIONAL LIABILITY 61 PLAINTIFF LITIGATION (PERSONAL INJURY) 62 PLAINTIFF WORKMAN'S COMPENSATION 63 COLLECTIONS LITIGATION 64 LAND DAMAGE LITIGATION 65 SOCIAL SECURITY BENEFITS LITIGATION 67 REAL ESTATE LITIGATION 68 DISCRIMINATION/WRONGFUL TERMINATION LITIGATION 69 MEDICAL MALPRACTICE 70 INSURANCE COVERAGE 78 ENVIRONMENTAL LITIGATION 79 CRIMINAL LAW 90 ARBITRATION 99 CHAPTER 93A 100 WC PROVIDE LIEN 103 NEGOTIATION OF SEVERANCE PACKAGE

programs can facilitate a firm's efforts to scan new information for potential conflicts of interest.

A new matter form should contain information such as the following:

The date on which the firm received the new matter.

Case name and number (the firm should reserve an area for a bar-code label, if necessary).

All attorney information, using initials or attorney code numbers, and including the attorney having primary responsibility, other attorney(s) involved, and the billing attorney.

The client's name and address, a notation indicating whether he or she is a new client or present client, and any organization information, if an organization is involved, including corporation, association, or partnership information, the name(s) and title(s) of the person(s) involved, and the names of affiliates, directors, and principal shareholders (needed for conflict-of-interest checks).

Additional client information, including spouse's name (if applicable), work information, any aliases by which the client is known, telephone information, and personal information appropriate to the case.

Type of case, describing the legal issues involved and the applicable statute of limitations, if any.

General nature of the client's needs, specifically describing the legal matter that the case involves and previous legal representation.

The name, address, and phone number of the opposing attorney.

The name, address, and phone number of the opposing party (whether case involves negotiation or litigation).

Other law firms involved.

Other relevant parties, e.g., insurers.

Billing information, including a client tax identification number; terms, the method of determining fees, and fee estimates; a discussion of fees and fee agreements; payment responsibility; billing schedule; and the identity of the person to whose attention the bill is to be sent, if the client is a large corporation or organization.

Notable interfirm relationships (e.g., whether a firm member is also a trustee of another firm).

Referral sources: Client's reasons for choosing the firm, including professional or personal referrals and effective advertising or marketing techniques.

Figures 5–7a through 5–7c present a client form and its accompanying matter form and conflict-of-interest check form.

Opening a File. After the firm completes a conflict-of-interest search concerning a new case, the records manager or other person responsible for such actions initiates the procedures necessary to open a file for the case, using the basic information from the new matters report.

Bookkeeping Information. The records manager sends information about the new case to the firm's bookkeeping personnel, providing them with client names and addresses; billing agreements (such as a set bill rate or a special bill rate); the billing format (for example, the firm's standard form or a more detailed one); fee estimates, if appropriate; information on when and where to bill, including the name of the person who is to receive the bill, if the client is an organization; and frequency of the billing cycles. At this time, the records manager might provide a photocopy of the new matters form to the bookkeeper, if it is the firm's policy to do so and if the new matters form that the firm uses does not automatically forward a special section to the bookkeeper.

Preparation of File Materials. The next step for the records manager is to prepare the actual file materials, using the firm's label-issuing procedures to generate simple, typed headers or to assign bar codes.

Client Data Base Information. Next, the records manager enters the client's name, address, phone, and client code information into the firm's client data base, which may range in sophistication from a computerized system that allows the firm to track sources, referrals, types of clients, and other information to a basic, typed communications file stored in a Rolodex®.

Tickler or Docket Control Entires. The lawyer responsible for the new case must provide all critical case-related dates on the new matter form, so that his or her secretary, the firm's docket control clerk, or another person assigned the task can enter them in the firm's tickler or docket control system.

Routing Codes. On the outside of each file folder, routing and action codes indicate the status of each

FIGURE 5–7a
Sample Client Form

```
CLIENT FORM
                        BULKLEY, RICHARDSON AND GELINAS

                                                                    NEW _____
                                                               ADDITION _____
                                                                 CHANGE _____

 1. Client No.         _____
 2. Client Name        _____
    (30 char.)
 3. Address 1          _____
    (30 char.)
 4. Address 2          _____
    (30 char.)
 5. Address 3          _____
    (30 char.)
 6. Address 4          _____
    (30 char.)
 7. Address 5          _____
    (30 char.)
 8. Address 6          _____
    (30 char.)
 9. Phone No.          (   ) _____
10. Originating Attorney      98
11. Print a Client/Matter Recap    Y ____  N  xx
12. Print One Matter/Page?         Y  xx   N ____
13. Alpha Sequence (6 char.)       _____
    (Defaults to first 6 characters of client name)
```

SOURCE: Figures 5–7a through 5–7c: Reprinted through the courtesy of Attorney Patrick J. Hourihan; Bulkley, Richardson and Gelinas, P.C., Springfield, Massachusetts.

file. If no notation appears, the records manager must return the file to the responsible attorney. An easy motto to remember is: "No due, no do." Table 5–2 explains three simple codes for indicating file activity.[25]

Kinds of Files. Law offices use three major categories of files. The most dominant type, client files, we have already examined. The second category, business files, may include personnel files, financial records, and vendor files. The third type encompasses personal files. An attorney's personal files, for instance, can consist of his or her records for service in community organizations, research files for articles that he or she has written, personal finance records, and favorite memorabilia, such as a business card from his or her first office. However, control over client files is the firm's main concern.

Filing Systems. A law firm bases its choice of a filing system on its needs and on the particular needs of its practice. While some firms opt for decentralized filing systems, such systems tend to breed complications; centralized systems make files easier to find by housing them in a single location. In addition, such systems make files easier to pull for docket control use. Within its system, a firm may arrange files according to one or a combination of five basic options: numerical order, alphabetical order, alphanumeric order, geographical divisions, and/or topical divisions. *Numeric filing* as-

FIGURE 5–7b
Sample Matter Form

MATTER FORM New ____
Addition ____
Change ____

Client: _____

1. Matter No. _____–_____
2. Description (25 char.) _____
3. Description (25 char) _____
4. Description (25 char) _____
5. Attention (25 char) _____
6. Title (25 char) _____
7. Your claim no. (25 char) _____
8. Date of Occurrence _____
9. Resp. Atty. _____
10. Assigned Atty. _____   23. Statement _____
11. Law Type _____   24. Past Due Y/N _____
12. Date Opened _____
13. Status (A/R) _____
14. Billable (Y/N) _____   25. Brief matter description:
15. Bill Frequency _____   _____
16. Billing Level Rate (1–6) _____   _____
17. Client Billed _____   _____
18. Add to Client Mailing List (Y/N) _____   _____
19. Fixed Amt. _____   _____
20. Fixed Type _____   _____
21. Contingency $ _____   _____
22. Contingency % _____   _____

Engagement Letter (Yes/No) If "No", explanation _____
_____
_____

_____
Responsible Attorney Signature

Matter Accepted _____
Area Coordinator/Managing Partner Signature

signs to each client and case a number based either on a date or a code; the system may use color coding to clarify the second type of number. *Alphabetical filing* simply arranges names alphabetically, while *alphanumeric filing* converts client names and cases to numeric codes which lend themselves to security coding, computer numbering, or bar coding. *Geographical organization* separates information by regions, satellite offices, cities, or branches. Finally, *topical* organization arranges records according to case type, specializations or divisions of legal practice, legal groups or teams of attorneys, or according to the firm's departmental or divisional structure. The following Another Look describes these five filing methods in more detail.

FIGURE 5–7c
Sample Conflict-of-Interest Check Form

CONFLICT OF INTEREST CHECK

The names of the following persons or entities have been checked through our open and closed file index for possible conflict of interest:

Name of Person/Entity　　　　　　Open File #　　　　　　Closed File #

_____
_____
_____
_____
_____
_____
_____
_____
_____
_____
_____
_____
_____
_____

Attach photocopies of cards.

Signature of Person Completing Conflict Check　　　　　　Date

TABLE 5–2
Routing Codes

Client File Code	Meaning
X CRC	Attorney CRC has finished with the file. Return to the central file.
7/25/93 CRC	Pull this file on 7/25/93 and deliver to CRC.
ABC	Deliver to firm member ABC. If no date notation, return to the lawyer who last used the file (in this case, CRC) for the appropriate notation.

File Circulation and Control. An effective file system is built on the basic premise that the files belong to the firm. They need to be centralized, they need to be controlled, and everyone is to follow the firm's procedures for using them. A firm that fails to enforce filing etiquette invites frustration, or even chaos, duplicates efforts, and wastes time.

Sign-out and Return Procedures. Even the simplest file circulation system should include sign-out and return procedures that enable the firm to track files that get passed from one attorney to another and to follow up on files that aren't returned by the end of the day.

ANOTHER LOOK

Alpha-Block Numeric: The Best File Indexing Method?

Alpha-block numeric is considered "the best file indexing method" by the ABA Standing Committee on Economics of Law Practice for large or small firms, for its simplicity, accuracy, logic, suitability for use in bookkeeping and accounting, compatibility with computer use, and its expansion capabilities.

In the alpha-block numeric system, you simply assign numeric equivalents for the first letter in a client's name. For example, all names beginning with A begin with 01; B, 02; Z, 26. Because the system is numeric, it lends itself easily to computerized systems as well.

This is how it works: The first two digits are the numeric equivalents of the first letter of the client's name. The next three digits represent the matter sequence number of that client. For example, the sixteenth case for Joan Adams might have the number 01-033-016—the client's name begins with A, she is the thirty-third client beginning with A, and it is the sixteenth matter for this client.

This example illustrates the single-character alpha-block numeric system in its simplest form. A more sophisticated system, dual-character alpha-block numeric, keeps names in much closer alphabetical arrangements.

SOURCE: Charles R. Coulter, *Practical Systems: Tips for Organizing Your Law Office* (Chicago, Ill.: American Bar Association, Section of Law Practice Management, 1991): 21.

1. Describe one or two possible weaknesses you perceive in the alpha-block numeric system. When, if ever, might this system not work?
2. Establish a simple alpha-block numeric system for a set of personal files, such as bills or class notes or papers. How effective is your personal system?

File Location Monitoring Procedures. A firm may monitor the location of its files by using any of the following: checkout cards; file checkout indicator slips (left in place of a pulled file); in-out logs; or any other record that identifies personnel who remove files from the centralized location. As we noted earlier, bar codes provide a useful way of tracking files that have wandered from the central system.

Use Status. Files are not destined for perpetual existence. Though clients may return or remain with the firm over the years, many will use the firm's services only once. There are three general categories of client files, based on use: *active files*, for cases that are open and pending; *suspension files*, for cases that have become inactive; and *dead files* involving cases for which the firm has ceased to see or to expect client activity.

Maintenance of Active Files. The firm keeps active files according to its basic filing policies and procedures. If, for example, the firm utilizes an alphabetical file-index system, the most visible information on the file would indicate the client's name and matter, such as Chase v. Chase (Divorce). A numeric system would assign the file a file number, such as 93-1234, accompanied by additional information on the specific matter.

Disposition of Semi-Active Files. Semi-active files are either those that are awaiting a two-year court calendar or those that the firm has closed but retained for accounting purposes. The firm should keep these files separately, in an easily accessible location; store them; or convert them to space-saving microfiche or microfilm. For control purposes, within its centralized file system, the firm should assign these files new prefixes, such as S for suspension, H for holding patterns and retention, M for microfiche, W for warehouse, or A for archives. Space, like time, costs money. Some firms, comparing the prohibitive square-foot costs of downtown or central storage, find off-site storage advantageous, even when considering charges for storage services and for converting files to another medium, such as microfilm. Even despite additional issues, such as confidentiality, off-site storage is often worth consideration.

Termination of Dead Files. Dead files are those that no one expects to use. Files that have become inactive, according to the firm's definition of the term

1. **Numerical**
   a. Straight Numbering
   Organize your files by assigning a number to each file as it is opened, in sequence.
   b. Client/File Numbering
   Give each client a client number, and use subsequent numbers for files, such as 103/1, 103/2, or 103/267, etc.
   c. Calendar Numbering
   Assign a prefix to a client number, based on the year the case was opened, such as 88-1, 88-2, etc.
   d. Code Numbering & Color Coding
   Implement this system by using a predetermined letter code, by placing a prefix before the client number, or by using color codes based on elements such as case type or attorney.
2. **Alphabetical**
   a. Alphabetical
   This is the simplest of all filing systems. Keep all client files together, filing them according to the client's last name.
3. **Alphanumeric**
   a. Alphanumeric
   Organize your files according to letter-number combinations.
   b. Security Coding
   Assign security codes in access files to cases that require additional confidentiality, and regulate the access files.
   c. File/Tickler Combined
   To combine your filing system with a tickler system, visually cross-reference files with the attorneys who are responsible for them, reviewing schedules and critical dates.
   d. Computer Numbering
   Use computer software to formulate client/matter file designations and integrate the filing system with other computerized firm procedures, using billing and conflict-of-interest checks as time controls.
   e. Barcoding
   Barcode each client file and other important documents in the firm. Depending on its software, the firm may check materials in and out of a central location by scanning these codes, while attorneys and support staff may help the firm to audit the location of files by using light pens or other portable scanners to record the barcodes of files that turn up in offices, in conference rooms, or in warehousing areas.
4. **Geographical, Regional, Departmental, or Divisional**
   Organize your filing system according to the firm's interior or exterior subdivisions, such as departments or regional offices.
5. **Topical**
   Arrange files according to case types—for example, according to the area of practice or department that the case involves.

ANOTHER LOOK

Five Filing Systems*

---

*Based on Mary Ann Altman and Robert I. Weil, *How to Manage Your Law Office* (New York: Matthew Bender, 1988): 10.25–10.33; Vena Garrett, *Basic Law Office Management* (Lake Forest, Ill.: Glencoe, 1992): 53–55; and Kline D. Strong and Arben O. Clark, *Law Office Management* (St. Paul, Minn.: West Publishing Company, 1974): 274–77.

1. Which of these filing systems would you recommend for a small law firm? For a medium-sized firm? A large firm? Justify your choices.
2. Which of these systems do you think offers the greatest overall accuracy? Which seems most prone to failure—to lost or misplaced files? Explain how you might improve the filing system you consider to be least efficient.

(except for probate files and those in certain other categories, such as files of historical value), are considered dead files. The qualifying period of inactivity may range from five to fifteen years or more, and the firm can facilitate the termination or destruction of dead files by establishing clear criteria for file retention.

Guidelines for Retention of Files

Periodically reviewing the firm's adherence to file policies will prevent slipshod attitudes toward file maintenance. Although keeping files forever offers the path of least resistance, when files overflow, a firm is forced to reckon with the issue of file retention. Since very few laws mandate long-term record retention, a firm's retention policy is largely the product of discretion and judgment, as well as ethical consideration for whoever truly owns and is responsible for the documents. When the law firm works on behalf of special clients, such as those in the regulated utilities and trucking industries, federal or state regulations, available through sources such as the Federal Register or state agencies may govern retention procedures. Otherwise, as Mary Ann Altman and Robert Weil observe:

> There are very few matters which must be retained forever by a law firm. Among the few are binding contracts not of record, controls not of record, and controls setting base valuations on securities or property in estates subject to Federal Inheritance Tax. There are also a few areas of law where federal regulations provide that documents must be retained in their original condition. And, of course, a firm would want to retain files if it felt there might be a potential law suit.[26]

Considerations for keeping files should also include any applicable statutes of limitations; the year of majority for matters regarding minors; future needs information, such as for taxes; government laws and regulations; and time requirements for appeals.[27] The Association of Legal Administrators publishes a *Records Retention Guide* that provides a practical overview of retention time for law firm records.[28]

Guidelines for Confidentiality

A second and more elusive control issue is the "Big C," confidentiality. Lawyers may never knowingly divulge any client's "confidences or secrets," as described by one of the first sections in the Model Rules.[28] However, confidentiality is not just an obligation of lawyers. All members of the firm must honor this mandate. It extends to every aspect of a case, especially to client files. Even the disposal of files requires great care to preserve confidentiality. Not even the shredding of files is without risk. If the legal profession depends on client trust, and it does, lawyers and all those in the law firm who share that trust, in any capacity, must keep confidences. Client affairs must not be disclosed. Professionals should not only limit file accessibility and respect the ownership of the documents within those files, but should also be discreet in discussing their clients, even when everyone in the firm has read about cases in the news or has seen them on television. Whether it takes the form of whispering in the law firm lounge or careless slips made on the elevator or in restaurants, almost nothing can embody betrayal more precisely than professional gossip or disclosure.

THE CONTROL PROCESS

Within the law firm, the process of controlling workers and their activities involves comparing performance to carefully chosen standards.

Standards are criteria against which the firm measures its performance and productivity. A firm may base its standards on goals, on past performance, and on comparisons to industry standards, which may include standards for similar firms in the area, region, or nation, as well as rates and trends for the law firm industry or the economy.

Having established its criteria, the firm uses feedback in the form of regular reports to decide if its performance measures up to its standards. Such evaluations must be as objective as possible. When standards are open to interpretation, they are difficult to measure accurately.

Once the evaluation is complete, the firm must decide whether to continue its current standard of performance or to correct and, with luck and continued effort, improve it. A firm that is meeting its standards may simply decide to maintain its present course; unfortunately, many firms that operate inefficiently may do so out of a reluctance to change. In some firms, change occurs only when conditions become intolerable! (In Chapter 13, we will examine conditions, such as unsettling or discontent, that make a law firm ripe for change.) A firm that builds corrective action into its control system can make adjustments a normal part of its operations.

WORKERS AND CONTROLS

Do workers equate control with dictatorship? At worst, control rings of Stalinesque repression and secret police. Yet, the control of workers can also be akin to giving everyone the same song sheets and teaching them to sing together. The more enlightened firms benefit from different vocal qualities, as it were: workers who can harmonize their efforts while contributing their unique talents. At best, by providing safeguards and guidelines, control helps workers to coordinate their activities while working creatively and freely within the law firm environment.[30]

Resistance to Control

Despite a firm's best efforts to make control a harmonious, efficiency-promoting process, someone is bound to be unhappy. As Rosabeth Moss Kanter and Barry A. Stein point out, control is often especially chafing to lower-level personnel:

> ... the real sign of being at the bottom is the degree to which a person is controlled. Tasks are defined elsewhere, other people are giving orders, and those at the bottom do not, in turn, have the right to define tasks themselves or to develop commands. ... [H]ow little discretion, how little autonomy, how little influence remains. The worker, in short, is treated as if he were a child—or worse, a machine.[31]

Workers resist control for many reasons. They may fear overcontrol, subjective evaluation, narrow-minded supervisors and the restrictions they enforce, politics, and rigid systems of accountability.

Overcontrol

Although workers may have "a need to be controlled, directed, or structured by others," they also need both a certain sense of freedom and the ability to act at their discretion when they believe they should.[32] Sometimes controls can seem invasive: for no good reason (that workers can see), an organization may prohibit its personnel from wearing beards or placing knickknacks in their work spaces. A law firm should not confuse these kinds of restrictions, which have a sobering effect on the way workers view their organizations, with the type of control that creates an appropriate balance of power within the work environment. However, in professional settings, where autonomy is essential, it is especially difficult to obtain the right balance of independence and control. This presents challenges for law firm managers. For example, by overemphasizing rules and regulations in order to increase a firm's performance, management may in fact increase nothing but lawyers' contempt and refusal to cooperate.[33] As Tom Peters has wryly said, "About the best you can hope for is to get the herd heading roughly west."[34]

Subjectivity

Many organizational controls are subjective; that is, they establish no clear standards for worker evaluation. Employees who are uncertain how their organization wishes them to perform lose satisfaction in their jobs, which may lead, in turn, to poorer performance.[35]

Narrowness

Controls that are too tightly in place create an excessive sense of accountability, a personal or departmental myopia that leads to a disregard for broader organizational results.[36] It becomes commonplace for workers to say, "It's not my problem" or "That's not our department." Too tight a control encourages too narrow a focus. A firm must tailor its control system to its setting, to its workers, to its leadership, and to the work that it does.[37]

Politics and Arbitrariness

When the overwhelming urge to run a tight ship leads upper-level managers to despotism, subordinates often must focus their efforts on getting along with the powerful in order to survive and avoid trouble. When faced with demands from two different superiors, such workers often pay more attention to the needs of the superior who is the more manipulatively powerful. For example, a secretary may work for two attorneys, one of whom is a new associate and in no position of authority in the firm, while the other is a demanding and powerful senior partner. To avoid displeasing the senior partner, the secretary may attempt to accommodate his or her every need, at the expense of the new associate. Even the most honest employee may have few choices when facing potentially arbitrary and abusive treatment.

Accountability and Flexibility

To deprive professionals of flexibility is to create difficulties, since flexibility fosters innovation, adaptation, and change. Freedom and flexibility are not only good for professionals as people; they encourage good firm-wide results as well. On the other hand, poor performers don't like accountability, dreading the spotlight it will place on their shoddy work. Since control favors stability, accountability, order, and predictability, the question becomes a matter of balance: How can a law firm encourage flexibility without abandoning accountability, and vice versa?[38]

Overcoming Resistance

Law firm managers have a special role in balancing professionalism with controls, a balance they are most likely to achieve by involving the firm's other members in the control process itself. Attitude, atmosphere, communication, and participation are all part of this involvement.

Positive Attitudes

Managers can help overcome resistance to control by convincing workers, through their positive attitudes, of the firm's need to develop and meet (or exceed) standards for quality. To foster positive and productive attitudes, managers must care about workers while simultaneously promoting high expectations for the quality of their work. They are obliged to listen to employee concerns, to support their efforts and decisions, and to reward workers through a bread-and-roses approach that provides monetary rewards as well as a culture of appreciation that offers praise, positive feedback, recognition, honors, public releases and announcements, consideration, and well-deserved perks.

Supportive Atmosphere

A supportive atmosphere does not imply unconditional acceptance. In law firms, managers must have high expectations for workers, but must also be willing to give them the support they need to succeed. Many times, a simple "What can I do to help you?" can generate suggestions that improve working conditions and results not only for a single employee but for the entire firm. Managers who stay close to their workers foster employee comfort while keeping themselves usefully informed about the conditions in their part of the firm. Many of today's managers need to take time to talk and listen to employees, without making workers feel that walking into a manager's office is a center-stage event.

Communication of Dissatisfaction

Effective managers value open communications, knowing that to support good workers is a continued investment in the firm's human capital. In times of frustration, whether caused by seemingly impossible expectations or inequities, supervisors should encourage workers to communicate their problems as part of a mature and encouraging relationship. In Chapter 12, we will examine listening skills that can help managers to provide employees with feedback that is both honest and supportive.

Participation

Finally, overcoming resistance to control incorporates worker participation. For workers to accept standards as valid, they need to believe that such standards are fair. Employees who participate in setting standards not only feel a sense of ownership for such standards but are more likely to accept their validity and importance.

MEASURING EFFECTIVENESS

Two things help a law firm to measure its effectiveness: performance and productivity. Both depend on many factors, objective as well as subjective, not all of which are within the workers'—or the firm's—control. Management expert Rensis Likert, for example believes that these factors (which he identifies as *current conditions of the organization*) include an organization's overall commitment to its objectives, employee motivation and morale, and the skills of its leaders, particularly their skills in communication, conflict resolution, decision making, and problem solving. We will discuss these and other variables that affect organizational effectiveness in the following paragraphs.[39]

Measuring Individual Contributions

A law firm can observe and monitor only two aspects of its members' work with true objectivity: behavior and output. Measuring workers' performance, which usually involves appraising only the observable aspects of employee performance, is often far too subjective to assess productivity accurately.[40] Managerial control depends on the ability to measure effectiveness, both in order to foster good work attitudes and behaviors within personnel, to enable the organization, to establish equitable procedures, determine fair rewards and salary allocations, decide on promotions and terminations, and make informed decisions concerning personnel and training needs.[41] The indicators that law firms and other organizations commonly use to evaluate individual performance include absenteeism, tardiness, deadline adherence, interpersonal contributions, and performance appraisals. We will focus on methods for measuring worker performance in Chapter 8.

Quality Control

Effective organizations endeavor to provide quality products and services to their clients. Several recent theories for controlling work quality from which law firms may benefit place an international emphasis on high performance. In his work on Japanese **Theory Z** firms, Bill Ouchi, who was among the first to suggest that American organizations could increase the quality of their work by learning from Japanese culture, describes the open and accepting work climate within many Japanese firms, which he suggests is a result of trust, understanding, and respect for people's differences.[42] Many other cultures are now using **Quality Control (QC)** circles to implement Theory Z. The QC circle consists of a group of managers and employees who work together to address quality and coordination problems. In a law firm, for example, all of the members of the real estate department, from attorneys to the department's secretarial staff and registry of deeds personnel, might meet to discuss methods of reducing turn-around time for services. Another quality control concept is that of **Total Quality Control (TQC)**, also known as **Total Quality Management (TQM),** a brainchild of W. Edwards Deming. One of several American business professors invited to Japan in 1950 to teach Japanese industrial leaders about the quality control techniques developed in the United States just prior to World War II,[43] Deming greatly influenced Japan's rise to eminence in international business. First used in the Japanese manufacturing industry but now standard practice within manufacturing and service industries worldwide, TQM, a management philosophy based on the conviction that the responsibility for quality is part of every worker's job, stresses openness, leadership, and the total dedication of each member of the firm to improving service. In addition, TQM requires firms to establish objective and quantifiable standards for measuring the quality of each member's work. As part of this measurement process, leadership should replace arbitrary inspection, goals, and quotas, eradicating fear, building worker trust, and helping to inspire pride in workmanship, self-improvement, and the firm itself.[44] Those who doubt that TQM represents a viable quality control option for law firms should look to the United Kingdom, where firms earn TQM certification by meeting a code of quality management for solicitors established by The Law Society of England and Wales.

CRISIS MANAGEMENT

In the words of Steven Fink, a leader of Pennsylvania's crisis team at the time of the Three Mile Island nuclear accident, a **crisis** is "any unstable state of affairs in which a decisive change is imminent."[45] An unexpected problem that may lead to serious dangers or difficulties unless properly resolved, a crisis is any situation that is likely to intensify in terms of anger, hostility, or other negative emotions, to attract unwelcome public attention, to interfere with the firm's normal business, to jeopardize its image, or to impair its ability to make a profit. Crises, which can catch a law firm by surprise, are times of great stress. Crisis management is the process of analyzing a firm's vulnerable areas and using this analysis to formulate procedures to use in times of crisis.

Recognizing Symptoms

Prodromal periods are pre-crisis times that reveal symptoms of coming difficulties for a firm. However, some crises have no warning signs, and a firm must weather such problems with only its standard policies

ANOTHER LOOK

Are You Ready for Disaster?

A disaster plan should
1. Designate one person as the disaster recovery coordinator.
2. Define a "disaster."
3. List all the people on the disaster recovery team, including all information on how to reach them. Define each person's role, including liaisons with the public, insurance companies, financial agents and vendors, personnel, security, transportation, telecommunications, cleanup, salvage, restoration and rescue services, insurance companies, and a backup off-site disaster team.
4. Ensure that all necessary insurance coverage is provided for, even business interruption insurance, if possible.
5. Identify all vendors from whom the firm purchases equipment or supplies, listing emergency numbers.
6. Maintain a complete list of inventory.
7. Maintain a complete list of critical data and records, including their location and format.
8. Maintain a full index and sublisting of all computer software, including operating systems, software program data, and restoration procedures as well as contact numbers for critical computer support staff.
9. Outline operating procedures and determine which departments should have priority access to the computer, should part of the system fail.
10. Oversee ongoing security procedures for computer users, including backup procedures, document index printouts, and other systems.

SOURCE: Based on Randolph J. Burkhart and Linda R. Atkinson, "Disaster Plan Necessary for Equipment Failure," *The National Law Journal* (9 January 1989).

1. What kinds of "disasters" might seriously affect law firms?
2. Whose responsibility is it to prepare a firm for crises that may never happen?

---

for guidance. Establishing a crisis management team, composed of those in the firm who are most able to think and respond competently under pressure, is often an effective way to deal with the most unforeseeable crises.

Responses to Crises

The ability to respond well under pressure is a great asset, especially for a manager. The many law firm managers and members who can think their way through contingency situations commonly follow guidelines such as these:[46]

- They prepare for action by knowing as much as possible about all phases of an operation.
- They build a network of reliable sources to which they can turn in case of difficulties.
- They investigate crises firsthand whenever possible, defining the scope of the problem for themselves.
- They use their energy wisely, taking quick action only in situations that absolutely demand quick action.
- They test the validity of their responses with one or more key people whenever possible.
- They refuse to shirk a problem.
- They try to learn from every crisis.

The above Another Look lists specific steps that can help a law firm to prepare itself for crises.

TIME MANAGEMENT

For managers and other members of a law firm, control over time is one of the most difficult controls to achieve, especially since, as University of Michigan economists Juster and Stafford suggest, time may well be "the fundamental scarce resource."[47] Henry Mitzberg, a specialist on managerial behavior, notes that managers suffer frequent interruptions, rarely find time to spend on long-range activities, and consider their time to be constantly fragmented, dissipated, and controlled by others.[48] This is particularly true of managers in the law firm setting, which is known for its heavy demands on workers' time. The law firm presents special challenges in terms of time management, says management psychologist Marilyn Machlowitz, since "the realities of life in a professional service firm may conspire against practicing all of what time management teaches."[49] Each of us views time in a slightly different way; consequently, we each respond differently to being on time, behind schedule, or under pressure. Given these temporal idiosyncrasies, it may do little good to discuss rules for time management within a law firm unless people are aware of their own characteristics, such as a strong need for power, a penchant for focusing on details and the control of details, and a tendency to always take on too much work, always underestimating the time commitment involved.[50] In general, controlling time too tightly can, at times, be counterproductive, and wise managers realize that seeming time wasters such as idle chatter are actually essential (in moderation) to the social process within a firm. Socialization, which may be as simple as looking at snapshots of a secretary's new baby or as serious as sincerely expressing concern for a paralegal who may be suffering clinical depression, is invaluable in making workers feel at ease. Scheduling time to listen to workers' concerns and simply to let them know that they are important often can provide more long-lasting payoffs than the most carefully detailed production plan.

Time Control Strategies

A law firm manager's time falls into three categories: *boss-imposed time,* which the manager uses to fulfill requests of his or her superiors; *system-imposed time,* when system demands dictate the manager's activities; and *self-imposed time,* which encompasses the time that the manager spends meeting others' needs as well as whatever time is left over, a slim allocation of discretionary time that quickly vanishes when pressures mount.[51] In *The Time Trap,* Alec Mackensie lists the twenty activities and conditions most likely to gnaw away at a manager's time:

- Management by crisis,
- Telephone interruptions,
- Inadequate planning,
- Meetings,
- Paperwork,
- Leaving tasks undone,
- Inadequate staff,
- Attempting too much,
- Drop-in visitors,
- Ineffective delegation,
- Personal delegation,
- Lack of self-discipline,
- Inability to say no,
- Procrastination,
- Socializing,
- Confused responsibility,
- Poor communication,
- Inadequate controls,
- Incomplete information, and
- Travel.[52]

Controlling these time-consumers is a major accomplishment. Essentially, effective time management requires you, as a law firm manager, to establish priorities, to deal directly with difficult tasks, and to delegate.[53]

Establishing Priorities

This can be as simple as keeping an inventory of tasks in a spiral-bound notebook:

1. In one section of your notebook, list the tasks you must perform.
2. In a second section, list the things you would like to do.
3. Keep a log that describes the time you spend on your step 1 and step 2 activities.
4. Allot time each day for getting organized, doing busywork, answering phone calls, and opening mail.

Conquering Difficulties

Learn to deal with difficult tasks and to face them head on. Don't be too proud to ask superiors and subordinates for help, even if only to clarify a task in your own mind, to gain a different perspective on a tough job, or to engage the active support of your colleagues.

Delegating

As we discussed in Chapter 3, one of your primary jobs as a manager is to share the work load, to distribute it. Delegate routine tasks. Always ask: Can someone else be doing this job? Who? Then assign it. Work with that person closely, if you are concerned, but utilize your subordinates and their skills.

The following Another Look offers ten more suggestions for controlling time.

Workaholics[54]

A **workaholic** is someone who is literally addicted to work, who depends on work to define his or her very

ANOTHER LOOK

Ten Time Techniques

1. **Don't let others rule your life.** Arrive early but LEAVE ON TIME! Set aside time for interruptions, whenever possible, by listening to the first part of what someone has to say and inviting them back, if it makes sense. Meet office walk-ins by the door and make inviting them in *your* option.
2. **Control telephone interruptions.** Have secretaries screen and answer calls for you.
3. **Set limits to meetings.** Begin and end on time. Announce in advance how many minutes you can share for unplanned or unscheduled meetings.
4. **Control the THINGS in your office.** Have a place for everything and keep everything in its place.
5. **Don't touch any piece of paper more than once, unless it is absolutely necessary.** Decide instantly what to do with every document. Paper shuffling is one of the most common time wasters. Dispose of mail or paperwork instantly by responding to it, filing it, or passing it along to someone else.
6. **Be results-oriented.** It will feed your sense of accomplishment to cross off on your daily list the things you have taken care of.
7. **Set strict guidelines to ensure results of meetings.** Know and adhere to the agenda. Set a time limit for all meetings. Hold meetings at the end of the day, when time limits are easiest to enforce.
8. **Have subordinates suggest solutions for their problems.** Involve them in solutions. Don't let them put the monkey on your back. Always ask for *their* ideas.
9. **Control your personal space.** Have a place and/or a time where you can accomplish tasks without being interrupted.
10. **Keep your mind uncluttered.** Stress short-circuits the best of our talents and skills. Create a worry list. Instead of stewing over something, write it down. Thus validating your concerns not only clarifies them but keeps them from invading your consciousness and interfering with your thoughts as well.

---

1. Think of a manager or professor you have known whose office was always awash with clutter and one whose office was conspicuously neat. Of what importance is the ability to control the objects in one's office or other personal space? Is there a relationship between neatness and the organizational abilities that a manager or leader needs? How accurately do you think your own degree of neatness reflects your scholarly or professional abilities or your ability to manage time?
2. Analyze how time-conscious you are. How adept are you at managing time? Describe two or three time management techniques that you currently use. How effective are they?

---

identity and sense of self.[55] Not all people who work hard are workaholics, though they share a surface resemblance. Both workaholics and hard workers may arrive early, go home late, take work home, and skip long vacations. But hard workers work to reach goals, to achieve, to succeed. Workaholics put in long hours out of compulsion. Hard workers can find meaning outside of work. Workaholics can't. For them, work is the meaning of life. Ironically, workaholics may not be very productive workers. Although they often try to create the impression that they are highly productive and indispensable, workaholics often spend time spinning their wheels, shuffling through papers and redoing work already done. They frequently are unable either to delegate effectively or to work well with others. Unfortunately, the law firm environment, with its sharp emphasis on hard work and billable hours, may send mixed messages to workaholics. As Marilyn Machlowitz observes, ''Employers may say they want people with balanced lives and outside interests, they may pretend that workaholics are not welcome—but in fact they still encourage workaholic tendencies.'' [56]

ANOTHER LOOK

Checklist for Time Priorities

What I Do First:
    What I like/What I don't like
    What I know how to do/Whatever is new
    What is easiest/What is hardest
    What will take less time/Whatever will take a lot of time
    What has been scheduled/Whatever pops up
    What has been planned/What has not been scheduled
    What others demand/What I'd like
    What is urgent/What is important
    What advances my personal objectives/Whatever is politically expedient

What I Take Care of First:
    Crises and emergencies
    People according to their importance
    That which I have the best chance of finishing

What I Base My Decision On:
    Giving the squeaky wheel the grease
    Group consequences
    Personal consequences
    Deadlines
    The resources I have
    The order of their arrival
    The size of the job
    How tired I am
    My enjoyment of the job
    Options

SOURCE: Adapted from David A. Whetten and Kim S. Cameron, *Developing Management Skills* (Glenview, Ill.: Scott, Foresman, 1984): 104.

1. Which of the above indicates poor use of time?
2. Which items don't necessarily indicate either a good or a poor use of time?
3. Under What I Do First, how many of your answers fell to the left of the slash mark? How many to the right? What do you think this indicates about your management abilities?

Setting Limits

As a manager, determining the activities that represent the best and most legitimate use of your time will be one of your hardest tasks. First of all, concern for living up to high standards can make it difficult to say no, especially if you have convinced yourself that you alone can do a job well enough. However, as we have seen, a manager's responsibility includes allowing others to become involved, since a healthy and effective organization depends on the involvement of *all* its members. Secondly, you may be one of those people who simply cannot say no to others. Being unassertive is associated with low self-esteem. Realizing that your time and personal priorities are just as important as those of others is basic not only to your self-image but to your efficient performance within the firm. The third reason for difficulty in saying no is guilt. It is hard for many people to refuse requests for charity or from good friends or family members. However, your own values and needs constitute equally valid obligations. You may respect someone's cause and be honored by the fact that others value your services, but sometimes you may still need to say no.

The Another Look above can help you to assess your ability to effectively allot your time.

CONTROLLING GROWTH

A discussion of control necessarily includes the issue of growth. How do organizations grow? Kanter and

Stein observe that organizations "grow by adding parts, and that almost inevitably means adding people, as individuals or as members of ongoing groups." [57] Law firms, both in healthy economic times and in times of steady but hard-earned success, have witnessed many surges of growth and change. One consideration that controls those changes is the value that many American organizations, including law firms, place on size:

> We live in a society that stresses growth in size as a measure of success. It is easier to feel a sense of progress by seeking change that simultaneously involves growth rather than by holding a course.[58]

With growth comes growing pains, tensions that may alter an organization's very structure.[59] Weber, for example, believed that bureaucracy is inevitable with increased size. Growing firms must take care to ensure that inevitabilities, real and potential, don't take control of the growth process. Robert Gandossy and Allan Cohen describe twenty characteristics of law firms whose growth may be running wild. Among their warning signs are the following:

- The firm's turnover rate increases—or is unknown.
- Clients begin to accuse the firm of performing poor-quality work.
- Stress and burnout become common, especially among administrators and managing partners.
- Personal contact and relationships seem inadequate to manage the firm.
- The firm's overhead costs cut more and more deeply into its gross revenue.
- Costly mistakes occur—and no one will accept responsibility for them.[60]

How Growth Affects People

An organization's growth affects its personnel in many ways. Growing firms, according to Kanter and Stein, place more emphasis on formal procedures and training programs, more clearly define positions and the criteria for filling them, and add layers of managers and other personnel to their hierarchies. New personnel may feel at a special disadvantage, and even those who have long been part of the organization may be uncomfortable:

> [Even the] old timers may feel they are missing something—the spirit of pulling together, a voice in policy, the chance to create, a special and close relationship to the boss, ritualistic celebrations of first-time accomplishments—and resent its absence, though the organization may, objectively, still be a happy place to work.[61]

Changes in the Organization[62]

Growth changes an organization's operational needs, its culture, the numbers and types of decisions and crises that it faces, its internal dynamics, and its very structure. First, expanding operations often necessitate technological changes. The more technology, the more complexity. More machines translate into a need for physical growth and more office space, and may add layers of technical personnel to the hierarchy as well. This in turn creates a more complex coordination of work functions for everyone. While many organization members will work to make high tech part of their professional culture, those who feel strongly in touch with the organization's traditions may resist both the new technology and the change it represents. To make its own adjustments to change, the organization will need to create new structures from the top down, altering its status systems, reward systems, organizational expectations, and performance measures.

Stages of Growth

Because organizations are composed of people and because people need time to accustom themselves to change, organizational growth is often a slow and unpredictable process. Kanter and Stein note that organizations whose growth proceeds in stages create solid bases for later decisions.[63] Researcher Larry Greiner has proposed five stages of organizational growth, each of which terminates at a leadership crisis, which requires the organization to resolve issues of authority and to somehow shift the distribution of power within its structure.[64]

> Creativity. Creativity, the first stage of growth, is characteristic of organizations that are small, informal, and entrepreneurial.

> Direction. We find direction, the second stage of growth, in organizations that have begun to sense their need for "supervised supervision," an initial layer of management.

> Delegation. Delegation, the next stage, appears in organizations that need more indirect control of many of their functions.

Coordination. During coordination, the next stage, organizations attempt to create a formal balance between their centralized and decentralized activities.

Collaboration. Collaboration marks the fifth and last stage of growth, as organizations develop "teams and informal structures with sophisticated and interpersonally skillful members in a highly supportive context." [65]

Changes in Size

Although size is a conventional measure of success, small firms enjoy many benefits. Small-firm personnel are less likely to get trapped in routines and are more likely to perform their fair share of creative tasks as well as dull ones, work is easier to distribute, and employees at all levels share communications and information more effectively and directly. The small firm, relying less on bureaucracy than a larger firm might, makes accountability simpler to trace and its managers more accessible to their subordinates. For law firms, the idea that bigger is better is not necessarily true, even in economic terms. Larger organizations, by their nature, pave the way for more bureaucracy. The need for more controls and tighter organization creates a "variety of human and managerial dilemmas." [66] But law firms, when facing the issues that accompany growth, can always choose to control their size, even opting to be smaller. Smaller, younger organizations may not be as secure in today's competitive environment, but, ironically, such organizations often possess the internal conditions—the energy and the drive—that are essential to growth. What we should remember is that many factors influence a law firm's decision to be large or small. Size, in and of itself, does not dictate a firm's success.

QUESTIONS FOR DISCUSSION AND REVIEW

1. How do law firms set standards? What external and internal forces help to determine these standards?
2. What is the relationship between controlling and the other management functions?
3. Should performance be measured throughout the organization? Where should it be measured in the law firm?
4. Why is corrective action important? What does it entail? Who and what does such action correct?
5. What are the characteristics of effective control? Provide an illustration showing the controls that a law firm might implement to improve its below-standard performance in an area such as physical resources, human resources, or inventory.
6. What difficulties can managers encounter in setting standards?
7. Describe your own time management style.
8. What are the advantages of being a small organization? What risks does a firm take in deciding to significantly increase its size?
9. Research reactions to the ABA report, "At the Breaking Point," and discuss the following:
   a. Does greed motivate the legal profession?
   b. Are work pressures and time demands the result of the legal system or are they choices each lawyer makes?
   c. How can successful professionals, such as lawyers and paralegals, balance work demands with other aspects of their professional and personal lives?
   d. Respond to this statement: Law firms have a negative work climate that leaves little time for self and family.
   e. What special pressures do female and minority lawyers, paralegals, and support staff face in the law firm setting?

EXPERIENTIAL EXERCISES

I. Time: Are You in Control?

Read each statement and circle the number of the word that best describes your behavior. A scoring key follows the exercise.

```
                              A = Always
                              S = Sometimes
                              N = Never
A  S  N      1. I spend time looking for misplaced materials.
A  S  N      2. I shop at the supermarket without a list.
A  S  N      3. I buy my cards and gifts at the last minute.
A  S  N      4. I write out a to do list for my busy days.
A  S  N      5. I use off-peak hours to do easy jobs, like filing.
A  S  N      6. I shuffle through paper piles when I need to find things.
A  S  N      7. I break my jobs down into smaller sections.
A  S  N      8. I don't like to delegate.
A  S  N      9. I find I don't finish working on what I start.
A  S  N     10. I take notes on what I need to get done.
```

Scoring for items 4, 5, 7, and 10: A = +3; S = +1; N = −3.
Scoring for all other items: A = −3; S = −1; N = +3.
Results of scores: +16 to +30 = Excellent
                      0 to +15 = Good
                     −1 to −15 = Weak
                    −16 to −30 = Out of Control

If you scored +16 to +30, you are doing a superb job of managing your time, both at home and at work. If you scored 0 to +15, you are doing reasonably well, but could find areas to improve. If your scores fell between −1 and −15, try to initiate changes in your style, looking at how you can improve. If your scores bottomed out, you are nearly out of control! Seriously consider making some changes, paying attention to the advice of time management specialists.

II. Filing Proficiency: Vital Decisions

An effective filing system is indispensable to law firm operations. There are many approaches to organizing firm records. Analyze the filing procedures of an actual law firm by interviewing someone who works within the firm. Include information based on the following questions:

a. Who initiates files? When? How?
b. How does the firm organize its files?
c. Where are they located? Are all files in-house?
d. Who has access to files? For how long?
e. Are any files ever missing? What causes this? How are they located?
f. Who is responsible for the file system?
g. Are files ever weeded out? Are there active and inactive files? What criteria does the firm use to determine file retention and file status?

III. Timing Is Everything

Pick one of the following statements and discuss how it applies to the law firm setting.
1. To rest is to rust.
2. I become restless when I rest.
3. "Teach me to care and not to care. Teach me to sit still." (T. S. Eliot)
4. Sometimes I sits and thinks. Sometimes I just sits. (Unknown)
5. I have time on my hands.

6. "Oh, how full of briers is this working-day world!" (Shakespeare, *As You Like It*)
7. "Work expands so as to fill the time available for its completion." (Northcote Parkinson)
8. We like to hire workaholics.
9. You need to be a workaholic to be successful.

IV. Time on Your Hands

How do you distribute your time? Find out by creating two pie charts:

In the first chart, divide your 24-hour day into professional (or academic) time, family-dominated time (including the time you spend with significant others), and self-imposed time. Divide your self-imposed time into the time you spend fulfilling other obligations and whatever discretionary time remains.

In the second chart, analyze your time in a current or former job by dividing your pie into boss-imposed, system-imposed, and self-imposed time. Subdivide your self-imposed time into discretionary time and time dominated by the requests or needs of others.

What do these charts tell you about your ability to control and distribute your time?

PART TWO

Managerial Applications

CHAPTER 6

Managing Financial Resources

LEARNING OBJECTIVES

After completing this chapter, you should be able to:

- Discuss the basic components of financial management, identifying the basic reports used for financial data;
- Describe how the budget serves as a control, a guideline, and a planning tool;
- Explain the steps in the budgetary process;
- Identify the components of the accounting process;
- Trace the law firm's revenue stream;
- Discuss the value of time and the procedures involved in timekeeping;
- Describe the various forms of and managerial uses for financial reporting;
- Explain assets, liabilities, and the balance sheet; and
- Discuss partners' responsibilities in terms of financial management.

Long active nationally in the ALA, Mr. Fairchild serves as president of the association's Los Angeles chapter and chairs its Management and Administration Committee. He is a well-known writer on issues of law firm profitability and the challenges that confront the legal administrator. Mr. Fairchild is legal administrator of Cotkins, Collins & Franscell, with responsibilities for its offices in Los Angeles and San Francisco. A West Point graduate, he is one of many legal administrators whose service in the military has evolved into a distinguished career in the legal profession.

FOCUS FROM THE FIELD

James Fairchild: Good Advice as to the Future of the Firm

How has competition influenced your decisions?

We have a marketing program that is future-oriented for profit. I think that all law firms in this day and age must have a strong marketing program. We have a marketing assistant, and we have a marketing plan. We also have retreats once a year where all the partners, the shareholders, and I get together away from the office to plan for the next year. One of the things that we do is prepare a marketing plan for the next year. We try to market our skills within the firm. We also try to have the best, most qualified attorneys and to let the public know how well qualified the firm is and that we can do the job.

What is the most difficult part of dealing with financial planning?

The most difficult part of financial planning, from my perspective, is the fact that I can't and I don't know, at the beginning of the year, how much of what billing rate each attorney is going to bill. Each attorney in the firm may have two or three billing rates, depending on the type of work they are doing and which client they're working for. It's very easy to predict expenses for a given year but it's very difficult to predict the gross receipts and, therefore, net income. I don't think I've ever seen a good way of predicting that, short of the firm that has only one type of practice, only charges one or two billing rates—the billing rate for the junior attorneys and the billing rate for the senior attorneys—and they can pretty well figure their income. But in a firm like mine, that has a lot of different practice areas and a lot of different billing rates, it's tough to say ahead of time how much work in each area is going to be done during a given year. You can pretty well forecast from year to year, other than illnesses and unplanned absences, how many hours an attorney is going to put in. I try to take the number of hours an attorney will generally work, using historical information, and make an educated guess on the billing rate the attorney will use. I combine this information to try to predict the income for the year. Another very difficult part of financial planning, especially in this economic environment, is making sure that our clients pay us and that we work for clients that will pay us!

What do you see as a law firm administrator's most important role in firm finances?

Being able to tell the partners ahead of time that they are heading for problems, being able to give good advice as to the future of the firm. In other words, the most important role regarding financial planning is future-oriented. It has to be. The attorneys are looking at the present, at the work that they are doing now—that's where their interest is and that's where their interest must be. The firm needs someone to look ahead and tell it how to maintain or strengthen its profitability in the future.

How does a law firm reduce expenses?

There is a misconception that you increase your income by reducing expenses. That does not really work in a larger law firm setting. With about 75 percent of expenses in a law firm consisting of employee salaries and employee benefit programs, the only way to affect expenses is to cut back on employees. The real way you affect the bottom line in a law firm is to be very efficient in your work, in your billable hours. Maximize your billable hours and get those billable hours turned into bills, turn those bills into dollars, get them out the door, and get the money back, as quickly as possible. That's the key, the billing and collection program where you increase the bottom line and make the biggest difference, not by cutting out flowers in the reception area or the doughnuts on Friday morning, or not buying that extra piece of software. Those have minimal effect. Expenses are basically fixed in a law firm. Some people say, "Let's copy documents on two sides of the page and save paper. That saves paper." Well, it certainly does, but if you're doing it to improve the bottom line, it has no effect at all. The basic way to increase income is to work harder and bill more, and therefore, get more dollars in the door. The expenses are basically fixed in law firms so if you work more, it doesn't cost you very much more. Yes, you have the expense of overtime work for your employees, but that's about what it costs to do extra work. The extra work is just about all income, and very little of it is overhead. Part of the job of the legal administrator is looking ahead, predicting what's going to happen, and telling people how they can take action now to prevent bad things happening in the future, and how they can take action to cause better things to happen in the future.

Ideally, every manager should think like a small business entrepreneur whose own money is at risk and who has little of it at hand.
(Ames & Hlavacek, *Vital Truths*)[1]

Lawyers often assume being busy is being profitable. They also confuse growth with profit, not realizing that many partnerships that grow can rapidly go bankrupt if the growth gets ahead of the profit. Everyone in the firm may be busy, detailed time records kept, clients generally happy and many office systems automated; still, income per partner can go down and the firm can find itself in a constant "cash crisis."
(Holland & Turner, *Taking Your Firm's Pulse*)[2]

KEEPING TRACK OF FINANCES[3]

Do you remember your first report card? Organizations receive progress reports in the form of **financial statements,** summaries of financial data that help a law firm's management to evaluate the firm's progress and economic health and to make decisions based on its economic position. Generally, managers use these financial reports to understand the firm's profitability and solvency, to control, and to plan ahead.

Understanding Profitability and Solvency

Given the sobering examples of well-known and respected firms that have recently collapsed—New York-based Finley, Kumble, a firm encompassing the services of 680 lawyers;[4] Myerson & Kuhn, a Finley, Kumble offshoot; and Gaston & Snow of Boston, among many others—and the hundreds burdened with debt and uncollectible obligations, and at the mercy of a poor economic climate, today's law firms need few reminders of their need for a healthy bottom line. Understanding finances is one of the fundamental business skills necessary for running a practice. Management must know more than how much money has come into the firm. It must constantly deal with two major financial concerns: the firm's profitability and its solvency. **Profitability** is the firm's ability to increase its worth. **Solvency** is the firm's ability to pay its debts as they become due.

Controlling

Any organization that depends on money needs to track its revenues and its expenditures. This financial control function in an organization is called its **accounting,** the systematized keeping of financial records that enables a firm's management to make informed decisions based on the firm's financial requirements. The control that comes from an internal reporting system helps the firm to meet its payroll, to know its cash flow, to pay bills, to estimate its expenses, and to judge its ability to make major purchases. Accounting differs from bookkeeping, in that accounting goes beyond simply classifying and recording business transactions to analyze, summarize, and interpret the information it gathers. Many accounting methods and procedures have evolved from hundreds of years of business practices, and some of today's generally accepted accounting principles date back to fourteenth-century Europe.

Planning

By using financial reports, the firm can obtain a clear picture of its financial strengths or weaknesses, identify its areas of profit and loss, and, based on that information, can make sound decisions about its future operations. In planning terms, both data on revenues that the firm has received and information regarding bills that the firm has either failed to collect or has deemed uncollectible form the heart of financial statements, budget making, and reports to the firm's owners.

Finances and Workers

Why should someone new to the law firm care about its finances? For that matter, why should veteran law firm personnel who never deal with financial management understand how the firm converts energy into work and work into revenues, or how it analyzes, assesses, and records the whole process? The reason is simple: workers benefit from being informed. Although not knowing a process sometimes makes us feel comfortably absolved of responsibility for it, a worker who is solidly aware of his or her role in the financial process helps to create a sense of synergy within the firm, the feeling that each person's contribution, no matter how minor, leads to an organization that, in terms of efficiency and profitability, is greater than the sum of its parts. Such awareness need not involve formal training or an accounting degree. It may be as simple as knowing this: The client is income; the rest of us are overhead. This understanding makes client service the focus of the organization. Time becomes more valuable. As personnel acknowledge the connection between the firm's success and the success of each of its members, they become motivated not only in terms of contributing to the firm but in terms of understanding the consequences of their contributions. From the lowliest file clerk to the loftiest senior partner, the firm requires the work of every one of its people to ensure its financial health.

OPERATING BUDGETS

Not long ago, many law firms operated without budgets. Clients came to the door, brought their cases, most paid their bills, and legal life went on. With the complexities that accompanied the transformation of the practice of law into a business came additional financial risks. To reduce these risks, budgets became an absolute necessity for law firms. Now the principal form of financial control in the law firm, the **budget** sets the financial parameters for expenditures, based on income estimates for the coming year. A budget is a plan with a monetary focus. Like all plans, budgets should be flexible and objective. Although a firm's organizational goals largely guide the formation of its budget, input from managers and other members can make the budget more realistic, more equitable, and more effective as an organizational control. An **operating budget,** sometimes called a *revenues and expense budget,* classifies the firm's projected expenditures and balances them against its expected revenues. The operating budget may list these expected expenses by program, showing the estimated expenditures in various units or departments, or by line. Both detailed and relatively easy to understand, this latter *line item budget* lists, line by line, what the firm intends to spend for rent, utilities, equipment, salaries, and many other needs. A

IN THE NEWS

Financial Survival: Strategies for the Nineties

The Problem

We at Hildebrandt have serious concerns about the practice of law in the next few years. A number of factors are already converging that we believe may make 1990 and 1991 difficult years for our clients. Financial advisors are telling us that the nation's economy is flattening—perhaps even heading into a recession—so you need to be aware of the symptoms of the downturn and take steps to address the problems ahead.

The Symptoms

- Much of the profession is already experiencing slower economic growth.
- Many firms are not meeting their 1989 budgets, and are even less likely to meet their 1990 budgets. Associate salaries have risen dramatically in recent years. Even salaries for clerical staff have risen to unprecedented heights. Increasing retirement costs are also taking an ever-bigger bite out of firms' budgets. And firms are finding that they have to spend more money on business development than anticipated. In the past, firms may have been able to contend with these higher costs by increasing billable hours and raising hourly rates. But there are human limits to the number of hours that can be worked. And there is increasing client resistance to higher hourly rates.
- Corporate, real estate and tax are three practice areas that clearly are already on a downward swing. Mergers & acquisitions are down. Real estate practices are feeling the effects of the softening market nationwide. Building has slowed down, in part because increasing environmental concerns are making builders cautious. And real estate syndications have lost much of their appeal because of changes in the tax laws.
- Many firms have an ominously high debt structure. Some firms borrowed heavily to meet expansion plans and now must pay the often-crushing cost of higher debt service.
- Some firms have over-expanded. They over-hired and opened branch offices in an almost knee-jerk fashion without long-term planning.
- Clients are showing greater resistance to fees. Corporate clients are responding to higher fees by taking more work in-house. Few have shown any enthusiasm for premium billing or other forms of payment that are more lucrative to law firms than the standard fee structures. Many, in fact, are seeking discounts.
- Billable hours are lower than anticipated. Despite their high pay, attorneys are beginning to make

SOURCE: "Hard Times Ahead Demand Strong Actions, *The Hildebrandt Report* (February 1990): 5-6. Reprinted with permission, Hildebrandt, Inc., Somerville, NJ. Copyright © 1990.

---

firm's approval of an operating budget is tantamount to an unspoken agreement among its members that the items approved on the budget have received the go-ahead for purchase and for use.

Uses of Budgets

Why does a firm need a budget? A budget is necessary because, as the adage says, appearances can be deceiving. A law firm that looks well run and that has as many clients as it can handle may still be spending more money than it is bringing in. A budget helps a firm to trace its financial resources, going or coming.

Planning Finances

Budgets are indispensable for planning and for controlling a firm's finances. Just going through the budget preparation process forces the firm's management to think about the organization in depth.[5]

Controlling Finances

Budgets direct the use of resources by telling managers how much the firm expects to spend in particular areas, thereby providing formulas for future income and expenditures. In addition, by conducting periodic sensi-

CHAPTER 6 / MANAGING FINANCIAL RESOURCES

IN THE NEWS (continued)

more quality-of-life demands which may have an even greater negative impact in the years to come.

The Solutions

As you head into the new year and the new decade, you need to take a hard look at the way your firm is structured. As a first step, every partner should have an approved performance plan for 1990. We strongly suggest several other steps to help you weather the downturn and emerge in a strong position:

- Develop and implement a three-to-five-year strategic plan or re-examine your current plan in light of potential trends in the '90s.
- If your firm has underutilized or unproductive partners and associates, address these issues quickly and aggressively. Fill their plates or start thinking about out-placement.
- Reduce excess staff now; don't wait for the slowdown to arrive. Well-run firms can reduce their staffs without sacrificing productivity.
- Weed out problem lawyers and administrative staff at all levels.
- Reduce hiring goals for 1990–91 unless you have the work to support additional lawyers, or need to replace those who have left. Although admitting lateral partners can significantly improve firm economics, it is essential that you realistically evaluate each prospective lateral partner's potential contribution.
- Accelerate plans for improving technology and other systems that will heighten productivity. While technology can be expensive, technologically sophisticated clients are expecting their attorneys to keep pace. We are currently advising a number of clients on devising strategies to capture technology-related costs.
- Examine your practice management structure to insure that you can maximize the profitability and utilization of your lawyers and respond effectively to client needs.
- Accelerate the development and use of marketing programs. Focus available time more on business development than administrative matters.
- Re-evaluate your firm's practice areas. Talk to your clients and find out if—and how effectively—you are providing the services that they need.
- Alert partners now that their compensation expectations may be over-inflated.
- Watch realization rates. Falling realization rates may be a barometer of severe economic problems.
- Enforce stricter client selection procedures. Don't grow the firm on a weak client base.
- Admit new partners more selectively to guard against dilution.
- And, of course, minimize expenditures by controlling associate and staff salaries and watching space costs.

Although tougher times are ahead, there is no need to panic. We are recommending that you look at the current economic environment, readjust your thinking and take actions that will put your firm on a stronger footing. With these developments in mind, we are currently advising many firms on their strategic plans for 1990 and beyond.

---

tivity analyses that compare budget estimates with actual cash flow, managers can evaluate whether the firm's projections for income and expenditures are on target. In general, budgets help a firm to control constantly changing financial facts in amounts that would otherwise be unmanageable.[6]

Figure 6–1 summarizes how managers use the budget process to control a law firm's finances.

Characteristics of an Effective Budget

An effective budget establishes the proper kind of control for the organization's finances. It combines the realism and accuracy of projected figures with a specific time frame.

Realism and Accuracy

Budgets enable a firm to combine the financial plans of each of its units or departments with the financial plan for the entire organization. A firm usually prepares a budget for each of its major divisions, including specific financial information for each subdivision. The figures in each budget, as well as those in the firm's larger financial plan, should be realistic, based on the best estimates of each principal player in the budget

FIGURE 6–1
The Budget Process as a Managerial Control

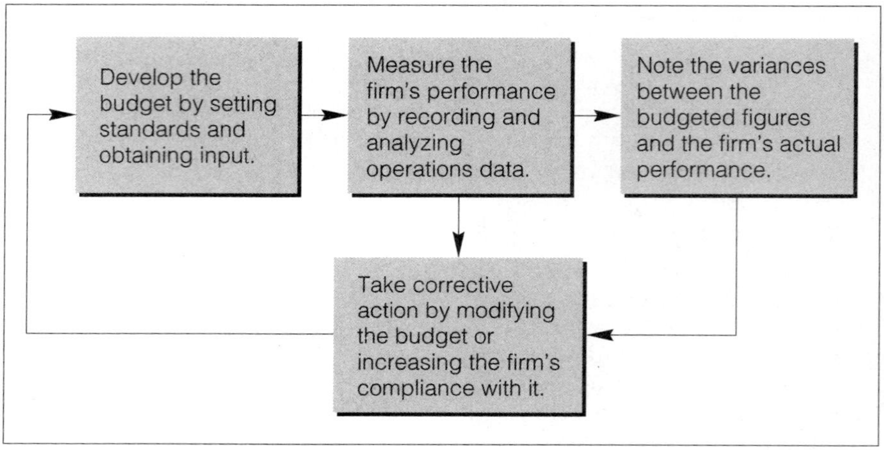

[Flowchart: Develop the budget by setting standards and obtaining input. → Measure the firm's performance by recording and analyzing operations data. → Note the variances between the budgeted figures and the firm's actual performance. → Take corrective action by modifying the budget or increasing the firm's compliance with it. → (loops back to Develop the budget)]

process, including those of people from the firm's main departments and divisions. Its estimates should be valid and reliable. Its overview should be balanced and flexible, clearly defining the latitude available to the firm in its planning.

Time Frame

Budgets cover specific periods of time, providing guidance for present expenditures and serving as a basis for expenditures in the years to come. Most budgets cover a full **fiscal year,** the twelve-month period that an organization establishes for tracking its finances. Fiscal years differ, depending on the type of organization and its preferences. Although companies tend to choose a fiscal year according to their peak times for doing business (schools, for example, consider graduation a peak time; their fiscal years commonly last from July 1 to the following June 30), most corporations and organizations time their fiscal year according to the calendar year, from January 1 to December 30. Law firms usually synchronize their fiscal year with the time frame that the government utilizes for tax reporting, January 1 to December 31.

THE STEPS IN THE BUDGETARY PROCESS

To formulate an operating budget that is both effective and acceptable to each department or division within the firm, budget makers must (1) focus on the firm's objectives; (2) prepare financial data by projecting the firm's revenues, estimating personnel costs, forecasting operating expenses, and analyzing the firm's costs of doing business; (3) obtain comparative data; and (4) present the proposed budget to the firm's decision makers for approval.

Focus on the Firm's Objectives

Here is where the budget process should begin. In studying the firm's challenges and opportunities, budget makers must balance wishes with reality. On one hand, the budget makers need to acknowledge how much money it will cost the firm to do what it would like to do. On the other hand, they need to estimate realistically how much money the firm will generate if it does in fact do what it would like to do.

Gather Input

In gathering information, the budget makers compile financial data in four specific areas: projections of the firm's revenues, estimates of personnel costs, forecasts of expenses, and a determination of the firm's hourly costs of doing business, or its operating margin per hour (its total expenses divided by its total billable hours for the year). These financial facts relate management decisions to the firm's ability to afford them. If only to offer an objective perspective on the budget makers' planning, legal administrators must be actively involved in the budget process. Without realistic funding, the best plans are only pipe dreams. Ideally, the budget process should furnish a forum in which managers can articulate their goals and see these goals approved in the form of plans that will benefit their departments and the firm itself.

Projecting the Firm's Revenues

This first step relies on the most basic component of law firm finances: the billable hour. In developing a budget, you must first estimate the number of billable or chargeable hours for the following year. Then you can estimate the firm's revenue for the year by multiplying the rate that the firm will charge for each hour that each of its attorneys, paralegals, and other timekeepers work times the number of hours that the firm expects each of those timekeepers to work. Table 6–1 presents a projected income budget for the fictitious firm of Snow & Owens, P.C. The first column lists expectations for possible billable hours in the following year for each of the firm's timekeepers, the second column presents the percentage of these hours that are actually likely to be billable hours, and the third column translates these percentages into hours. (Because timekeeper hours also indicate other services to the firm, such as firm management or marketing, not all of the hours in the first column translate into billable hours.) Column 4 lists the budgeted hourly rate for each timekeeper, and column 5 presents the projected income for each timekeeper, computed by multiplying his or her targeted billable hours times the budgeted hourly rate.

In preparing the billable hours part of the budget, you as a budget maker also must analyze the firm's professional staffing requirements, paying close attention to recent decisions regarding growth or cutbacks. The accounting firm Feeley & Driscoll suggests that budget makers obtain input from all of the partners in the firm for this analysis, since they can provide solid, experienced insights in terms of work estimates for the coming year.[7] Table 6–2a provides a sample projection of fee revenues, showing the current year's data and the projections that the partners in the firm have accepted for the next year.

TABLE 6–1
Sample Projected Income Budget

1994 Projected Income Budget

Snow & Owens, P.C.	Billable Hours	Targeted Billable % for 1994	Targeted Billable Hours for 1994	Budgeted Hourly Rate	Budgeted $ at Hourly Rate
Shareholders					
A. S. Snow	1800	90%	1620	$105.00	$170,100.00
R. B. Owens	1800	85%	1530	$130.00	$198,900.00
L. M. Stein	1800	95%	1710	$120.00	$205,200.00
G. R. Leiva	1800	90%	1620	$130.00	$210,600.00
L. P. Hurst	1800	95%	1710	$110.00	$188,100.00
Subtotal	9000		8190		$767,700.00
Associates					
P. R. Gomeau	1900	90%	1710	$100.00	$171,000.00
E. F. Epstein	1900	95%	1805	$95.00	$171,475.00
F. X. McCarthy	1900	75%	1425	$75.00	$106,875.00
Subtotal	5700		4940		$449,350.00
Paralegals					
J. Allaire	1600	95%	1520	$60.00	$91,200.00
S. Schwartz	1600	95%	1520	$50.00	$76,000.00
M. Donovan	1600	95%	1520	$50.00	$76,000.00
Subtotal	4800		3040		$243,200.00
Totals			16,170		$1,460,250.00

TABLE 6–2a
Projecting Fee Revenues

		Current Year (Actual)			
Level	**No.**	**Billing Rate**	**Billable Hours**	**Total Hours**	**Revenue**
Partners	6	$180	1,700	10,200	$1,836,000
Sr. Associates	2	130	1,800	3,600	468,000
Associates	5	100	2,000	10,000	1,000,000
Paralegals	4	75	1,800	7,200	540,000
Admin.	10	30	1,000	10,000	300,000
Total	27				$4,144,000

		Next Year (Estimated)			
Level	**No.**	**Billing Rate**	**Billable Hours**	**Total Hours**	**Revenue**
Partners	7	$200	1,700	11,900	$2,380,000
Sr. Associates	2	145	1,800	3,600	522,000
Associates	7	120	2,000	14,000	1,680,000
Paralegals	5	85	1,800	9,000	765,000
Admin.	11	40	1,000	11,000	440,000
Total	32				$5,787,000

SOURCE: "Smooth Operations: An Operating Budget for Your Firm," Feeley & Driscoll Newsletter: *Law Firm Management* (Summer 1990). Reprinted with permission.

After projecting the firm's fee revenues, the budget makers formulate two additional budgets: the **annual billing budget,** the amount of time for which the firm's attorneys, paralegals, and other timekeepers will bill in the coming year, and the **collections budget,** the amount of money that clients will actually pay the firm for the hours that it bills.

Estimating Personnel Costs

Once the budget makers have projected the firm's revenues, the next step is to estimate the firm's personnel costs for the coming year. Personnel costs vary greatly. A firm may include legal dues, insurance costs, and retirement plans under its personnel costs but may make similar costs, such as professional dues and activities, continuing education, professional development, and parking, part of its operating expenses. Generally, there are three major types of personnel costs: associates' compensation, nonlawyer compensation, and fringe benefits. To estimate these costs as accurately as possible, budget makers must obtain the firm's most current information on expected percentage increases and other projected growth in personnel costs. Estimating personnel costs helps budget makers to determine the operating expenses necessary for the work of the firm. Table 6–2b presents the projected personnel costs for a law firm, as suggested by the accounting and business consultation firm of Feeley & Driscoll.

Compensating Personnel.[8] The law firm is a labor-intensive business that relies on the services of "knowledge workers."[9] Because the contributions that these workers make can vary greatly in terms of complexity, responsibility, and experience, today's law firm must provide a variety of choices in terms of salary compensation. There are **equity partners** (or **full partners**), who own the firm, share in its profits and its losses, and vote on all partnership business; **nonequity partners** (or partners who have not contributed toward the firm's equity), who, in some firms, are entitled to salary, bonuses, or other benefits but can neither vote on partnership business nor claim entitlement to the profit distributions that equity partners share; salaried permanent associates or counsel; contract associates, both junior and senior; partners who opt out of partnership for contracts; staff attorneys; reduced-time or part-time attorneys; and paralegals,

TABLE 6–2b
Projecting Personnel Costs

	Current Year (Actual)	Next Year (Estimated)
Associates' Compensation		
Senior Associates	$ 160,000	$ 170,000
Associates	325,000	490,000
Nonlawyer Salaries		
Paralegals	160,000	315,000
Administrative	275,000	340,000
Fringe Benefits		
401(k) Plan	30,000	35,000
Payroll Taxes	75,000	82,000
Insurance Plans	70,000	90,000
Total	**$1,095,000**	**$1,522,000**

SOURCE: "Smooth Operations: An Operating Budget for Your Firm," Feeley & Driscoll Newsletter: *Law Firm Management* (Summer 1990). Reprinted with permission.

law clerks, and a wide range of support staff, both professional and technical. Compensation has become a great deal more complicated than the "splitting of fees" method that Abe Lincoln used. For example, law firms determine paralegal salaries through a process that begins with a review of the job analysis and description for the particular paralegal position and with a close examination of comparative data from similar positions in other firms. After base salaries are established, supervisors evaluate paralegal performance by focusing on productivity, accuracy, work attitudes, and attendance, and they award salary increases and bonuses both according to a paralegal's performance and the economic health of the firm.

Partnership Compensation. New business owners learn the advantages of regular salary and cash flow the first time they have too little cash on hand to pay themselves. Partners in a firm who must pay the firm's non-equity partners and support staff before they can pay themselves, risk similar shortages. Unlike other members of the firm, equity partners do not receive a set salary. Instead, the firm issues equity partners a monthly (or regularly scheduled) **partners' draw,** a payment made on the basis of the firm's current earnings; these partners also participate in a shared distribution of profits at the end of (or, when profits for a given period greatly surpass the firm's expectations, during) the fiscal year. Because draws and distributions depend on the firm's performance, equity partners prosper when the firm does. Conversely, during lean times, these allocations may be withheld to meet an urgent need for cash elsewhere in the firm. Typical compensation plans for partners include the following:[10]

The Lockstep Plan. This is a fixed salary, tied directly to seniority and billable hours, and based on the assumption that all partners are equally motivated. Other performance factors, such as success in recruiting new clients and contributions to firm management, are not considered.

Subjective Plans. The firm's managing partner, an executive committee, or a compensation committee establish compensation criteria and base each partner's salary on how well he or she meets these criteria.

Equal Distribution. The firm creates a total profit pool and allocates these profits according to partnership status.

Percentage of Profits. Partners agree to divide the firm's total profit according to percentages, such as a 40/30/30 split among three partners.

Bonus Pool. The firm allocates additional funds in the form of bonuses to partners who have made outstanding contributions.

Combinations of Salaries and Profits. The firm augments each partner's regular draw through a distribution of profits. Some firms calculate these distributions according to complex formulas that award percentage points for various contributions to the

TABLE 6–2c
Budgeting Operating Expenses

	Current Year (Actual)	Next Year (Estimated)
Occupancy Costs		
Rent	$ 400,000	$ 450,000
Amortization	50,000	55,000
Other Costs	60,000	60,000
Subtotal	$ 510,000	$ 565,000
General Business Expenses		
Equipment and Supplies	$ 240,000	$ 260,000
Repairs and Maintenance	20,000	20,000
Insurance	30,000	35,000
Library and Communications	58,000	60,000
Outside Services	72,000	80,000
Depreciation on Office Furniture	20,000	20,000
Uncollected Billings	30,000	30,000
Misc.	20,000	20,000
Subtotal	$ 490,000	$ 525,000
Professional Activities		
Dues	15,000	15,000
Subscriptions	5,000	5,000
Continuing Legal Education	35,000	40,000
Client Entertainment	50,000	60,000
Business Travel	30,000	30,000
Subtotal	$ 135,000	$ 150,000
Total	$1,135,000	$1,240,000

SOURCE: "Smooth Operations: An Operating Budget for Your Firm," Feeley & Driscoll Newsletter: *Law Firm Management* (Summer 1990). Reprinted with permission.

firm, such as a partner's outstanding achievements or his or her success in recruiting business (a process known as **business development**).

Tier System. This plan bases levels of salary compensation on such criteria as a partner's seniority and the business that he or she generates for the firm.

We will further examine partner and personnel compensation in Chapter 7.

Forecasting Operating Expenses

The third primary step in the budget-making process is to forecast the firm's other major expenses. These operating expenses fall into three categories: occupancy costs; the costs of doing business, such as equipment, supplies, repairs, insurance, furnishings, library and business communications, and uncollected bills; and the firm's professional activities, which include the dues that the firm pays for itself and for its members, subscriptions, continuing education and firm professional development, and client entertainment and travel expenses. Most firms now bill their office operating expenses back to the client through cost recovery systems such as those we examined briefly in Chapter 5. In estimating figures, budget makers can usually assume that payroll, benefits, occupancy and insurance will represent approximately three-fourths of the firm's expenses and that all other ordinary expenses will increase in the coming year. Table 6–2c provides an example of a law firm's attempt to budget its operating expenses.

The Firm's Hourly Costs of Doing Business

The last step in the budget process requires budget makers to calculate the firm's **operating margin per hour** by comparing its total expenses for doing business to its number of billable hours. By comparing operating margins from year to year, the firm's partners/owners can chart the direction its profitability has been taking annually.

A law firm calculates its operating margin per hour as follows:*

$$\frac{\text{Total collections}}{\text{Billable hours}} - \frac{\text{Total operating expenses}}{\text{Billable hours}} =$$

Operating margin per hour

Using the total hours and revenue figures from Table 6–2a, the equation would look like this for the current year:

$$\frac{\$4,144,000}{41,000} - \frac{\$2,230,000}{41,000} = 46.68$$

The equation would look like this for the estimated next year:

$$\frac{\$5,787,000}{49,500} - \frac{\$2,762,000}{49,500} = 61.11$$

Obtain Comparative Data

Once you and the other budget makers have finished compiling cost estimates for the new budget, you can obtain comparative data by balancing its estimates against past revenues and expenditures.

Present the Budget

Just as legislators spend hours debating and discussing a state's budget, this final stage of budget making is a momentous and often lengthy undertaking. The budget must gain the approval of the firm's top management according to whatever decision-making procedures that body has adopted, a process that by nature tests the soundness of the budget proposal. Involving the firm's decision makers in this stage of the budget-making process is essential not only for adopting the budget but for ensuring the commitment of those in the firm to its financial decisions in the coming year.

Budget Games

The budget process involves more than numbers. To some participants, it can resemble war games, with parties jockeying for turf and different interest groups protecting their concerns, particularly when resources are scarce. Aaron Wildausky, an expert on the political implications of the budgetary process, has described over two dozen kinds of budget ploys, from efforts to store monetary protective fat to attempts at enhancing existing programs.[11] The budget process needs to be as objective and as factual as possible. The more data that is based on solid comparisons and past performance, the easier it is to blow away the smoke and subterfuge concealing selfish interests.

THE REVENUE STREAM

Once the firm has determined how it will compensate its members for their services, the most central component of its financial structure is in place. Legal services equal fees, which the firm can convert into revenues, or capital. The law firm's financial process differs from that of other organizations in that a firm's income, which depends, often, not only on the firm's ability to win cases but on its ability to collect fees from its clients, is less fixed than that of other organizations. That a law firm deals exclusively in nontactile goods—in legal representation—doesn't help to stabilize its flow of income. A manufacturer, for example, can count its orders, adjust its production levels accordingly, and estimate its profits. A college can estimate its income by tallying its student body. By comparison, "The lawyer's time," as Abraham Lincoln is often quoted as saying, "is his stock in trade."

Throughout history, lawyers' fees have been an inexhaustible subject of debate and criticism. Geoffrey Furlonger, a New York attorney now living in England, traces the controversy back to three basic beliefs: that those gifted with intellectual skills should not trade such gifts for money, that clients are under no legal obligation to pay attorneys, and that any reward an attorney happens to receive should represent purely gratuitous recognition, a token payment for a debt of gratitude.[12] In early Rome, for example, legal services were free of charge, but as Roman law became more complex, practicing law required more skill, and lawyers began to charge fees, despite scandal that the practice caused, since being an advocate was supposed to be a reward in and of itself. Even after Emperor Claudius I prohibited lawyers from accepting money as gifts (in other words, as tips for legal services), lawyers—probably perceiving mere honor as scant re-

---

*The equations and figures which follow appear in "Smooth Operations: An Operating Budget for Your Firm," Feeley & Driscoll Newsletter: *Law Firm Management* (Summer 1990). Reprinted with permission.

ward for navigating Roman law—continued to expect fees for their services, and clients (not, after all, having much choice in the matter if they expected to receive quality representation) continued to "tip." William Forsythe, an English barrister in the late 1800s, expressed society's antipathy toward charges for legal services when he warned of the evils of bartering "the powers of intellect for money indifferently in the cause of virtue and of voice, . . . lest the profession degenerate into a mean and mercenary calling." [13] Even now, late in the twentieth century, comments Milton Zwicker, an innovative Canadian attorney and author, the lawyer's fee remains "one of the least understood aspects of practicing law, both within the profession and by the general public." [14] To offset the long-standing mistrust that surrounds the charging of fees for legal services, the American law firm has developed a fairly objective system for compensating lawyers for the exercise of their intellectual powers. Basically, the law firm tracks the number of hours during which lawyers use these powers, converts intellectual services into billable hours according to the lawyer's hourly rate, estimates any additional expenses the lawyer accrued while performing the services, and charges a fee. Ideally, there is a steady stream of revenues. This stream begins with the firm's decision whether or not to accept work, grows according to how much the service costs, turns service into bills, converts bills into cash through the collection process, and flows into revenues that culminate in the financial worth of the firm.

Accepting Work

One of the basic rules of conduct for lawyers is that they be competent enough to represent their clients. A lawyer's competency to handle a case is coupled with his or her ability to handle it. Not only must the lawyer and the law firm have the training and expertise that the case requires, but they also must be able to perform the work that the case involves, provide support services, and accurately assess the economic risk that the case represents to the firm. The firm also bases the decision to accept work on a case's being free of possible conflicts of interest and on many other factors, some of which appear in the Another Look which follows. When a firm actually accepts work, the client and the responsible attorney should clearly understand the fees involved. Confirmation of the fee arrangement should be in writing and should disclose the hourly rates or contingent fees, the billing frequency, the terms of payment, and whether the case will involve any premium billing.[15] This kind of record precludes possible confusion.

Selecting Billing Standards

Estimating the value of legal services and setting lawyers' fees involves many issues. The firm records in billable hours all of the services that it performs for the client. Even when charging fixed fees or contingency fees, the firm records all of its legal activities in order to determine its profitability. Some clients require detailed accounts of the time that law firms spend on their behalf; however, in a practice known as **value billing,** a firm may in actuality adjust bills either upwards or downwards, determining fees more according to the value of services than according to an equation involving rates and hours. (Nor, as we will see, are contingency fees based on billable hours, even though all of the time spent for a client on a contingency fee basis must be recorded.) No matter the firm's billing method, accurate billable hours information serves six essential purposes. It allows the firm to determine 1) the contributions of each of its attorneys and other timekeepers; 2) the costs for each matter; 3) the profitability of each matter; 4) the profitability of its various departments and areas of law; 5) the bases for client billing; and 6) the documentation that courts require when lawyers' fees are awarded pursuant to specific legislation, administrative requests, or court decisions. At the individual timekeeper level, we should note that lawyers who record their hours carefully each day may be able to bill up to 30 percent more than lawyers who are less records-conscious. In fact, attorneys who are scrupulously accurate with their timekeeping records can often record 80 to 90 percent of their time as billable.[16] Providing perhaps an even more convincing argument in favor of precise records, Mary Ann Altman and Robert Weil point out "that those lawyers who keep time records consistently *net* average incomes equal to the average *gross* of those who do not." [15]

Setting Fees

Donald Akins, senior vice president of Hildebrandt, Inc., management consultants, notes that more than twenty years ago, few lawyers kept time records and that billing was generally a haphazard process. Some attorneys billed annually, some requested their fees when a matter was completed, some billed when they

To determine its ability to accept a case, a law firm should ask itself questions such as these:

Are we able to handle the case based on the competencies of our present staff?

Do we have the resources we need to operate properly while the case is pending?

Can we afford to take this case?

What risks do we run, in terms of attorney sanctions, malpractice, and grievance actions?

What will the case cost and how will it be paid?

Can our staff handle the demands that this case will place on them?

What are our actual chances of collecting the fees?

Are there any conflicts of interests for us to deal with in this case?

Will we be able to work with the client long-term, based on issues such as honesty, cooperation, sincerity, and availability?

Have we given this client a clear understanding of what we can and can't do and of what will happen next?

SOURCE: William I. Weston, "Speaking of Ethics: When to Say No," *The Compleat Lawyer* (January 1991): 16.

ANOTHER LOOK

Accepting a Case

1. What problems can stem from accepting cases indiscriminately?
2. Discuss which of the above criteria, if any, conflict with your own sense of right and wrong.
3. Should firms accept only those clients who are able—and willing—to pay?

felt like it, and some obtained payment when the firm was short of cash. Pricing in those days could reflect any one of four factors: (1) a fee agreement between the attorney and the client, (2) the amount that the case involved, (3) the benefit and value of the legal services to the client, or (4) the attorney's hunch about the value of the matter and about the amount that the client could—or would—pay. Also about twenty years ago, surveys began to show lawyers that those who kept time records were more financially successful than those who did not. Naturally, these findings provoked many changes in law firm practices! Timekeeping became generally much more important.[18] However, Richard Reed, editor of *Beyond the Billable Hour*, believes that these surveys led some lawyers to overemphasize the billable hour while they lost sight of the fact that time records enabled them "to know *the cost of providing the service*," which was actually more critical to profitability. Conversely, Reed points out, "Perceptive lawyers recognize that hourly billing can penalize the efficient lawyer." To benefit clients and lawyers alike, billing standards today should emphasize the value of the service to clients and the benefits they receive.[19]

With this client-based focus in mind, firms now set fees in much the same way that commercial industries determine price—as a reflection of a good's value, expressed in dollars and cents. To determine an appropriate price for a given product, a manufacturer must consider all of the costs involved in producing the product: raw materials, labor overhead, advertising, packaging, and shipping, among others. A manufacturer may trace these operating expenses to a multitude of sources, including wages, benefits, utilities, maintenance, rentals, supplies, insurance, professional services, and depreciation. Setting fees and establishing billing standards in a law firm involves similar elements but is far more complex. Fee setting entails scores of inherently touchy issues, many of which center around establishing and maintaining client trust. While firms cannot absolutely guarantee that their fees will seem ethical to all clients, they must do their best to allay client suspicions (with luck, unfounded!) regarding practices such as bill padding or self-serving inefficiency. Most commonly, partners use detailed comparisons to determine costs for the services of the attorneys in their firms. They may base these comparisons on the fees set by other attorneys in the area and by those in similar practices, as well as on the reputation of their firm and of the individual attorneys. Above all, as Rule 1.5a of the Model Rules of Professional Conduct unequivocally states, "A lawyer's fee shall be reasonable." The rule provides eight criteria by which firms and clients may judge fees to be reasonable:

1. The time and labor required, the novelty and difficulty of the questions involved, and the skill requisite to perform the legal service properly;
2. The likelihood, if apparent to the client, that the acceptance of the particular employment will preclude other employment by the lawyer;
3. The fee customarily charged in the locality for similar legal services;
4. The amount involved and the results obtained;
5. The time limitations imposed by the client or by the circumstances;
6. The nature and length of the professional relationship with the client;
7. The experience, reputation, and ability of the lawyer or lawyers performing the services; and
8. Whether the fee is fixed or contingent.[20]

Kinds of Fees

Law firms may base payment for services on *contingency fees*, the *billable hour, fixed fees, retainers,* and any combinations of these or other arrangements that the attorney and the firm may determine.

Contingency Fees. Contingency fees, which are paid upon the completion of a matter, represent the usual method of payment for legal services in special kinds of cases, such as accident and other tort cases, and for collection of unpaid accounts receivable. The fee, as the word *contingency* suggests, depends on the outcome of the case, which is in itself uncertain. If a client's legal representatives are unsuccessful, they receive reduced payment or, in certain types of cases (commonly those involving personal injury), no payment at all. Contingency fees range from 25 to 50 percent of the total amount that the client recovers. In some instances, attorneys may charge flat fees plus a contingency fee, which depends on the results they obtain for the client. For instance, in *defense contingency* or *modified contingency* arrangements, the firm will receive a higher fee if the client pays less than a given amount of projected damages but will receive a lower fee if the client pays more than expected. (Although defense contingency and modified contingency normally differ in that the firm represents defendants in defense contingency arrangements and plaintiffs or those who file counterclaims in modified fee arrangements, law firms often use the terms interchangeably to indicate result-based fees.)[21] Some states have special laws controlling the use and amounts of contingency fees.

Billable Hours. Basing fees on time charges is one of the most common bases for billing—and controversial—methods of computing a client's costs for legal services. In defense of basing fees on billable hours, Geoffrey Furlonger comments that

> time-based billing methods were adopted with the best of motives. It was felt that the client preferred to be given a full account of the lawyer's activities. Thus, time billing was born, in part, of a desire to further the integrity of the legal profession.[22]

However, as Furlonger also comments, the billable hour practice has many flaws. In addition to its rewarding inefficiency and inexperience, the practice can put the interests of the client and those of the attorney in direct conflict, since the attorney receives more the longer the case takes. Furthermore, billable hours can result in client charges for costs that actually represented nonproductive uses of time. Thirdly, they allow the client no say over charges that the firm may add to his or her file; the practice requires no client approval for expenditures. Billable hours demand a client's blind trust in the professionalism of an attorney. Whereas experienced lawyers can achieve excellent results in little time, unscrupulous, less talented, or inexperienced lawyers may log enormous amounts of time on a case and bill accordingly. Jay Foonberg, a lecturer and writer on law practice management, reminds us that hourly billing, which represented a great departure from the "How big is the client? How big is the case? and How big is the lawyer?" method of fee setting, was originally intended to equalize the costs of legal services. But even with modern advances in cost recovery systems, the fees that many firms charge for billable hours still seem to be products of the "how big" method.[23] Properly handled, the fee process can help to reduce client anxiety and can also enhance the client/firm relationship.[24] The billable hour, which remains a valid (if not absolutely indispensable) tool for measuring profitability, analyzing performance, and improving service delivery, is no exception. By closely attending to its clients' needs for fair value, a law firm can use the billable hour to benefit its clients while maintaining its desired level of profits.

Fixed Fees and Percentage Fees. Many attorneys have developed flat rates for various services, a practice that traces its most notable historical roots to the 1600s, when the English legal system provided fixed-fee schedules for court, sheriff, and lawyer services. However, the use of fixed fees in those days was not related to today's consumer tendency to shop around. The price one pays for anything, even for legal services, often has but a tenuous and arbitrary link to actual value, and sensible clients question both fees and billing methods, carefully assessing the value of the services they receive. In terms of this assessment, Richard Reed notes that the value of a lawyer's services should neither be based primarily on hours spent nor simply on production. Value, for both client and firm, should reflect the responsibility that a lawyer exhibits through his or her expertise; through his or her accountability, reliability, and faithfulness to the client; and through his or her productivity, which in turn bespeaks the effort, timely performance, and delivery skills required for competency. Lawyer and client can base the negotiation of fixed fees on the value resulting from these three elements of responsibility.[25] In modern usage, **fixed fees**—which many firms consider the best alternative to hourly rates—are predetermined prices to be charged for legal services. Clients often see two variations on the fixed-fee theme: *modified fixed fees,* whereby a firm charges fixed fees for services in areas such as pleadings and depositions but charges hourly rates for legal activities such as trials, and *maximum-minimum ranges,* which entitle the firm to maximum rates for successful services but force it to make do with minimum fees when it fails.

All in all, even though basing the selection of an attorney on cost alone leaves much to be desired, law firms should realize that clients have few ways of assessing the value of a particular attorney's work. Even track records or reputation can sometimes reflect only luck, a fortuitous selection of cases, or impression management.[26] Comparing the value of work products from even the most seemingly uncomplicated of legal services is difficult. Consequently, firms normally develop fixed fees only for procedural activities and services, such as a fixed cost for arranging power of attorney, opening a file, or for being at interrogatories. Firms can also offer fixed rates, such as set percentages of amounts involved or recovered in the cases for which it provides services. For example, for settling an estate, a firm normally will charge a graduated fee based on the value of the estate.

Retainers and Alternate Payment Approaches.[27]
To address the many traditional problems in determining how to bill for legal services, some firms have adopted alternate payment arrangements, including retainers. Basically, a **retainer** is an amount that a client pays a firm in order to ensure continuing legal service. The client may place the amount in a trust or general account, out of which the firm will take payment for its services (and return any unused amount to the client); the client may pay the firm a nonrefundable amount in advance of services, thereby assuring counsel availability; or he or she may make periodic payments to the firm for continuing services (this amount is subject to regular review by the firm's collections committee, director of finance, a management team or finance committee, or another person or group, depending on the firm's organizational structure).

In addition to retainers, firms utilize other billing arrangements that reflect not so much their billing procedures as their choice of how much they wish to bill clients, based on their choice of service methods (and/or on the wish to simply charge less for a given service). These billing alternatives, many of which bear a sharp resemblance to marketing strategies, include small case programs that provide the client with the services of junior attorneys at reduced fees; loaned or rented counsel, by which a firm farms out work to out-of-office counsel at reduced rates; loss leaders, through which a firm operates at a loss in terms of one or two simple types of services in the hope that clients who take advantage of the bargains will use the firm's more expensive services as well; and modified contingency fees.[28]

Agreeing on Costs

Although Rule 1.5b of the Model Rules of Professional Conduct require lawyers to discuss fees and their billing practices with clients before (or only shortly after) initiating legal services,[29] many do not. Discussing fees with a client is often difficult, particularly when he or she might consider such fees to be exorbitant. Even attorneys whose fees are not excessive may dislike discussing their fees, out of a belief that the more commercial aspects of practicing law undermine the professional cooperation between lawyers and their clients.[30] Nonetheless, discussing fees openly with clients while they are anxious for the advice of counsel offers decided advantages, since time and a crisis neutralized or removed can easily make clients forget both their original, drastic need for help and their willingness to pay for it.

Cost Recovery and Billing

Through item-specific cost recovery systems, many firms pass along to the client all of the indirect costs that the firm has incurred in performing legal services for the client.

These costs, which vary according to factors such as the time pressures and demands that a case places on a firm, the auxiliary skills and services that the firm must recruit to complete the work, the technology and expertise that the case requires, and the amount of travel the matter involves, often include the following:

- Overtime, general overhead, and supplies;
- Postage, messenger services, and facsimile transmissions;
- Telephone and telex charges;
- Photocopying, binding, and document production and disposition;
- Food services, housekeeping services, and travel;
- Data base research, litigation support services, proofreading, and accounting; and
- Outside services.[31]

Collecting

Services that a law firm is performing or has performed fall into one of three categories: **work-in-process,** or work that the firm is still completing or for which the firm has not yet billed; **accounts receivable,** which represent services for which the firm has billed; and **write-offs,** the services that the firm has determined to be valueless for the purpose of collecting income.

Work-in-Process

By carefully tracking the work that it has yet to complete for which it has yet to bill, the firm can estimate its potential future revenue.

Accounts Receivable

Accounts receivable, which represent the legal services that a firm has billed to its clients, become revenue when clients actually pay for such services. Unfortunately, transforming accounts receivable into amounts received is often a touch-and-go proposition: Lawrence Bright, for example, estimates that 20 percent of the clients provide 80 percent of the case flow.[32] Those accounts that the firm has failed to convert into revenue after a length of time determined by the firm's management become "aging receivables." **Aging receivables,** which the firm still views as potential sources of revenue, represent the bills of clients who have the ability to reimburse the firm for services. The firm determines a retention period for its aging receivables, after which it must decide if and how it wants to collect the fees still owed it. These decisions may bring repercussions in terms of client retention, public relations, good will, and firm profitability. If the firm chooses to sue a client to recoup lost time and costs, for example, it should consider any and all consequences, including possible charges of malpractice, misrepresentation, and poor work and potential damage to its public image. In addition, the firm should ask whether a lawsuit would be worth the effort, in terms of time, energy, and money. It might be wiser to offer a nonpaying client an alternate method for paying his or her bill, possibly through minimal periodic payments. For unsatisfied clients who have refused to pay out of disagreement with the firm's charges, the firm might offer to reduce the final billing amount, since by carrying the bill, the firm has carried the costs of the services and has added to its expenses, besides suffering the loss of interest on the income. Finally, for valued clients, the firm might arrange discounts, thereby attempting to recoup its lost revenue as equitably as possible.

Write-Offs

On occasion, no amount of bargaining, rearranging, or threats will transform an aged receivable into income. On such an occasion, the firm must write off as a loss the billable hours that a case involved and accept the fact that it will receive no compensation for its attorneys' time and the costs it incurred during the course of the matter.

THE VALUE OF TIME

Accounting for time spent is one of the most indispensable law firm activities. To prevent valuable time from slipping by unbilled, attorneys and paralegals must keep time records on a daily basis and record activities as they occur, a practice requiring vigilance and discipline. In addition, the firm itself should periodically assess its financial health and activity through full-firm timekeeping reports. Earlier in this book, we looked at Abraham Lincoln's approach to keeping track. Like those of most lawyers of his time, Lincoln's system of record keeping was simple: he would jot notes on little scraps of paper and file the scraps in his tall hat. Hat styles may have changed, but, for some, record keeping has not noticeably varied. Some contemporary timekeepers, for instance, simply use a pink pad for phone messages and yellow legal pads for recording the details of the day. However, effective timekeeping becomes more complex on a department-wide or firm-wide scale. For many law firm managers, getting complete time records from timekeepers is a persistent problem. To accurately keep track of such things as phone calls, memos, pleadings, drafting, and dictations, timekeepers (or, in the case of some attorneys, their secretaries or receptionists) must record *what* takes place *as it happens*. The most common tools for keeping time in a law firm include time sheets, ledger sheets, and computerized timekeeping and billing systems.

Time Sheets

Although tallying manually kept time sheets may be too daunting a task for large firms, smaller firms often can use this uncomplicated method of recording time quite efficiently. Law firm time sheets commonly include the date on which a service was performed; the client's name and the name of the adverse party, since a firm may often represent a client in more than one case; the attorney's name, initials, or code; a brief reference to the matter involved; a code, checklist, or phrase describing the service rendered; and the time that the timekeeper spent on the activity, either in terms of the time of day (11:00 to 11:15 for example) or in multiples of whatever base time amount that the firm chooses to recognize. For example, a paralegal may record a two-minute phone call as a single multiple of a base time amount of ten minutes or as a minimal fraction of an hour, such as .2 or .25, depending on the policies of the firm (though we should note that decimal conversions of time often result in more accurate and simplified billing). Finally, a timekeeper may note estimated fees on a time sheet. In firms that use these forms as backup systems for newer timekeeping methods, time sheets are known as safeguard slips.

Figure 6-2a presents a customized time sheet that allows a firm's timekeepers to record their billable and nonbillable hours; Figure 6-2b defines some of the activity codes that can appear on the Figure 6-2a time sheet. (Note in the third column of the time sheet that the first two digits of the matter number indicate the year in which the matter was opened.)

Computer Timekeeping and Billing Systems

Because law firm timekeeping can be quite complicated, more and more firms are now using computer technology not only to track their use of time but to integrate their timekeeping and billing information with their accounting systems. More specifically, observes Mary Ann Mason, long active as a leader in law firm management,

> The advantage that computers offer over manual timekeeping systems is that they retrieve time entries at electronic speeds, by almost an unlimited number of criteria, and also perform complicated mathematical computations related to each individualized bill. In addition, a good computer program can generate financial reports regarding the productivity of each attorney, the entire firm, or any other measuring stick that is requested.[33]

Effective systems completely integrate time and billing, enabling a firm to avoid duplicate work and to simultaneously enter service costs in a client's account and in the firm's work-in-process account.[34] Several current timekeeping programs, such as *Timeslips III*, are usable in even the smallest firm. Whatever program a firm chooses should be able to accommodate the firm's information needs, reflect different fees for each attorney, minimize data entry by automatically applying to all of its functions any information change that the firm makes, facilitate the integration of its applications with the firm's general ledger accounting, thereby precluding duplicate accounting or billing efforts, and should be capable of producing a wide variety of management reports (some of which we will discuss in the following sections).

MANAGEMENT FINANCIAL REPORTING[35]

Financial reports represent the primary media through which partners receive information regarding the financial health of the firm. Such reports (sometimes referred to simply as *management reports*) are of many types, some of which partners use regularly and some of which they call for to address specific financial matters. Though, all in all, law firm reports may cover a multitude of topics, including the firm's programs,

FIGURE 6–2a
Sample Time Sheet

TIME RECORD FOR __VBR_____ ( ) Date: __1/21/93__
                                                      Page: __1__

Decimal Conversion
in 6 or 12 Minute Intervals Use:
  6 minutes = .1 hour   36 minutes = .6 hour
 12 minutes = .2 hour   42 minutes = .7 hour
 18 minutes = .3 hour   48 minutes = .8 hour
 24 minutes = .4 hour   54 minutes = .9 hour
 30 minutes = .5 hour   60 minutes = 1 hour

In 15 Minute Intervals Use:
 15 minutes = .25 hour
 30 minutes = .5 hour
 45 minutes = .75 hour
 60 minutes = 1.0 hour

CLIENT/MATTER

NAMES	CLIENT #	MATTER #	ACTIVITY WORK CODE#	TIME	COMMENTS
Firm Administration	99999	1	102	.5	Meeting: Mgmt. Partners & Litigation Practice Coordinator
American Textile ✓ Casey	15621	89-0029	122	.25	Requirement for filing with SEC
Thompson ✓ McGee	73125	93-0001	101	1.5	Obtaining facts Re: Forest Destruction
Flanagan ✓ Maples University	73198	93-0002	172	.5	Correspondence to University Re: Requests
Pro Bono	99999	3	122	.25	Smith v Smith with Clerk Re: Rescheduling
New Business Development	99999	6		1.5	Lunch Un. C. Bank & Trust Re: Loan Documents
Popkoski Purchase of 94 Pond View	73942	92-0689	250	1.5	Closing for Pond View Purchase
Carbery ✓ Kent	15851	91-1234	120	.25	Hearing
Edwards ✓ Bay	79632	92-0895	170	.5	Fax Documents on Commission Arrangements
Rose ✓ Rose	32165	90-6651	100	.5	Support Payments

TOTAL TIME FOR DAY: _____

SOURCE: Reprinted with the permission of Robinson, Donovan, Madden & Barry, P. C., Springfield, Massachusetts.

FIGURE 6-2b
Sample Timekeeping Codes

Billable Activities	**Nonbillable Activities**
100 Advice and Counsel to Client	A. Client #: Use 99999 for all FIRM activities.
101 Conference with Client	B. Matter #: Use codes 1 through 7.
102 Conference	1. Firm Administration
103 Conference with Clients	2. Legal Education/Professional Development
104 Telephone Conference with Insurer	3. Pro Bono
110 Conference for Client	4. Bar Association Activities
120 Telephone Conference with Client	5. Community Activities
121 Telephone Conference for Client	6. NEW Business Development/Marketing
122 Telephone Conference	7. EXISTING Client Development
140 Telephone Conference with Claimant Attorney	C. Work Codes #: When applicable, use the work codes listed above.
141 Telephone Conference with Defense Attorney	
142 Negotiation	
170 Receipt/Review of Correspondence from Client	
171 Correspondence to Client	
172 Correspondence for Client	
173 Correspondence to Claimant Attorney	
180 Prepare Memorandum	
190 Correspondence	
200 Legal Research	
210 Factual Investigation	
230 Examination of Records	
300 Review	

Note: Use Activity Work Code and Comments columns as you would with billable client matters. Be specific.

SOURCE: Reprinted with the permission of Robinson, Donovan, Madden & Barry, P. C., Springfield, Massachusetts.

---

management practices, trends, and performance, the most indispensable reports are those on finances. One report that managers commonly use to inform partners about a firm's finances is the *income budget report,* which compares the billable hours that the firm expects each timekeeper to contribute during the budgetary year with the total hours, billable and nonbillable, that each timekeeper actually contributes. Table 6–3 presents a six-month income budget report for the imaginary firm of Snow & Owens, P. C.

In determining the criteria for an effective report, function easily outweighs appearance, since even the most attractively formatted report is useless unless it is usable. A report must represent facts honestly, accurately, and thoroughly. To be reliable, a report must:

- Be complete. Incomplete reports are worse than invalid. They are misleading, counterproductive, and a waste of time.
- Reflect a single purpose. Reports should have a specific purpose. Too much data, particularly if it is disorganized and superfluous, can be distracting. Focused reports have more impact. To focus reports regarding the firm's finances, managers might, for example, utilize periodic **sensitivity analyses** to spot unacceptable budget deviations, such as surprisingly high library expenditures, and bring these problems to the attention of the firm's partners as necessary, following the principle of management by exception, in the form of deviation-specific reports.

TABLE 6-3
Sample Six-Month Income Budget Report

Snow & Owens, P. C.	Targeted Billable % for 1993	Targeted Billable Hours for 1993	Actual Total Hours	Actual Nonbillable Hours	Actual Billable Hours	Targeted Billable Hours	Over/Short Billable Hours	Value of Actual Billable Hours
Shareholders								
A. S. Snow	75%	1350	1379.8	310.6	1069.2	675.0	394.2	$100,782.00
R. B. Owens	80%	1440	768.6	229.0	539.6	720.0	−180.4	$80,198.00
L. M. Stein	85%	1530	948.3	98.1	850.2	765.0	85.2	$89,824.50
G. R. Leiva	85%	1530	955.9	169.1	786.8	765.0	21.8	$117,286.00
L. P. Hurst	90%	1620	1368.2	5.5	1362.7	810.0	552.7	$149,586.00
Subtotal		7470	5420.8	812.3	4608.5	3735.0	873.5	$537,676.50
Associates								
P. R. Gomeau	90%	1710	935.8	316.8	619.0	855.0	−236.0	$65,876.00
E. F. Epstein	95%	1710	1045.9	93.8	952.1	855.0	97.1	$86,560.50
F. X. McCarthy	75%	1425	1009.0	534.9	474.1	712.5	−238.4	$51,556.00
Subtotal		4845	2054.9	945.5	2045.2	2422.5	−377.3	$203,992.50
Paralegals								
J. Allaire	95%	1520	868.5	96.3	772.2	760.0	12.2	$46,332.00
S. Schwartz	95%	1520	924.5	99.0	825.5	760.0	65.5	$46,467.00
M. Donovan	95%	1520	839.0	54.4	784.6	760.0	24.6	$44,006.00
Subtotal		3040	1793.0	195.3	1597.7	1520.0	77.7	$92,799.00
Totals		15,355	9269.0	1953.1	8251.4	7677.5	573.9	$834,468.00

- Provide useful comparisons. Reports must provide comparisons that are adequate, valid, and appropriate. While the firm's financial data from the prior year often constitutes a focal point for comparisons, reports may provide comparisons based on information from other firms or on other areas within the firm, including resource use, productivity, and client demographics.
- Encourage action. Do partners use the reports they receive? A single short report that provokes a reaction is infinitely more valuable than any number of state-of-the-firm encyclopedias that lull partners into a sense of security—or to sleep. Graphs and concise summaries can emphasize the need for action.
- Indicate accountability. The information in the report can be of almost no use unless top management can link such information to the performance of specific individuals and units, accurately tracing the hierarchy of responsibility for a given act all the way from the firm's managing partners down to the lowest member of the support staff.[36]

AREAS OF FINANCIAL MANAGEMENT

"The good news," says Harvard professor David Maister, "is that the economics of professional service firms are very simple."[37] Despite the difficulty of determining the value of lawyers' services and the amount of detail that the entire process involves, managing a firm's financial resources seems to be a fairly straightforward activity. Firm members establish budgets, record services, send bills (and collect some, too), report to upper management, and make plans for next year. Like most simplified process descriptions, this summary merely skims the surface of law firm finances. To more fully understand the financial process in a law firm, we must understand the instruments with which the firm tracks the movement of its financial resources.

Financial Reporting Tools

Like other businesses, law firms utilize four principal periodic financial reports: (1) the income statement, (2) the statement of cash flows, (3) the balance sheet, and (4) the statement of retained earnings.

The Income Statement

Known by a number of names, including the statement of operations, revenues and expenditures, the statement of earnings, and, in older terminology, the profit and loss account, the **income statement** acts as a financial analysis of the firm's activities over a given time period, providing the most recent figures regarding its income, costs, expenses, and profits, and ending with the bottom line, or the firm's net profit. The **statement of operations,** a variation on the income statement, provides an overview of the finances involved in the firm's operations.[38] A second variation, the **financial report,** describes the firm's financial health over a specified time period, such as a month, a quarter, or the entire fiscal year, by summarizing all income the firm has received from fees and from other sources, such as interest from investments.

The Statement of Cash Flows

A **statement of cash flows** summarizes for a given reporting period (commonly the fiscal year) all the revenues that a firm has received (its receipts) and its spending or allocations of cash (its disbursements) in the areas of operations, firm investments, and financing. Once known as the *statement of changes in financial position* (a much broader report that described all of the financial changes that a firm experienced, including changes in value),[39] a cash flows statement tells the firm how much money is available to it, how much it will need, and whether it may make major expenditures. Analyzing a cash flow statement reveals a firm's **liquidity,** or its ability to convert its assets into cash. A company's liquidity is a sign of its financial health.

The Balance Sheet

The balance sheet, also called a statement of financial position, provides a picture of an organization's financial condition, a snapshot of the firm's assets and liabilities at a certain time. The **balance sheet** describes the law firm's assets, liabilities, and equity at a stated moment, thereby summarizing its status and value.[40]

Assets. **Assets** are the valuable property—monetary, tangible, and intangible—that a law firm owns. Usually, a balance sheet will show a subtotal for each of a firm's types of assets, as well as a grand total for all of its assets. (The sum of an organization's assets always equals the sum of its liabilities plus its net worth.) Assets are commonly of the following three types:

Current Assets. Current assets are cash and items which the firm expects to convert to cash within the fiscal year. They include the following:

- Cash Items. These equal cash on hand, as well as money in checking accounts, savings accounts, and short-term certificates of deposit.
- Marketable Securities. Although law firms usually do not count marketable securities among their assets, this category represents stocks, bonds, and other investments that the firm can easily convert to cash.
- Accounts Receivable. As we have seen in this chapter, accounts receivable equal the money that clients owe the firm.
- Notes Receivable. Although formal promissory notes are unusual, law firms will occasionally accept a client's written and signed promise to pay a specific amount of money on a specific date.
- Inventories. While, for most organizations, inventories usually represent a list of goods on hand, law firm inventories are more likely to include less tactile items, such as unbilled fees for legal services.
- Prepaid Expenses. These include amounts representing services for which the firm pays in advance, such as insurance or sometimes utilities or rents.

Fixed Assets. These include a firm's long-term assets, such as property, artwork, furnishings, and major equipment. A law firm's library also constitutes a fixed asset.

Intangible Assets. Of all the firm's assets, this last type is likely the most important. Intangible assets include the firm's client base and relationships, its personnel and its good will, as well as its location, market position, reputation, fee schedules, and referral sources.[41]

Liabilities. **Liabilities** are the debts and obligations that the firm owes to others. Current liabilities are those obligations that the firm must meet within the year. They include the following:

- Accounts Payable. **Accounts payable** are the obligations that a firm needs to pay within a certain amount of time, usually within thirty days. **Payables** are bills for such things as salaries, rent, insurance, goods, and utilities.
- Notes Payable. Written and signed obligations to pay a specific amount at a specific time, **notes payable** include, among other things, interest charges on money that the firm owes.
- Accrued Expenses. **Accrued expenses** are expenses for which the firm has yet to receive or record bills. These expenses include such things as the money that the firm knows it will have to pay in wages, taxes, health benefits, and interest charges.
- Long-term Liabilities. **Long-term liabilities** are debts that are not due until more than a year from the date of the balance sheet.
- Owner's Equity. **Owners' equity** is the amount left after the firm has deducted its liabilities from its assets.

Table 6–4 presents a sample balance sheet for the fictitious firm of Snow & Owens.

The Statement of Retained Earnings

Actually a part of the balance sheet, the **statement of retained earnings** describes the amount of profit that the firm keeps after all bills, salaries, bonuses, and partner distributions have been paid out.[42]

Other Finance-Related Reports

In addition to the four principal financial reports, law firms utilize a number of more minor reports in areas such as cash-receipts, billings, and billable hours, to assess their strengths and weaknesses and to base decisions. Often only one page long, these summarizations provide comparative data, monthly or yearly. We will discuss three of these secondary reports in the following paragraphs.

Accounts Receivable Statement

An *accounts receivable statement* lists by dollar value and age all bills for which the firm might receive payment. A firm should place these accounts into overdue categories (30 days, 60 days, 90 days, or 120 days, for

TABLE 6–4
Sample Balance Sheet for Snow & Owens, P. C.

Assets		Liabilities & Owners' Equity	
Financial Assets		**Current Liabilities**	
Cash	400,000	Accounts Payable	200,000
Clients Accounts Receivable	1,000,000	Accrued Expenses	100,000
Work-in-Process Inventory	2,000,000	**Total Current Liabilities**	300,000
Prepaid Expenses	200,000		
Total Financial Assets	3,600,000	**Owners' Equity**	
Tangible Real & Personal Property		Partnership Capital	4,700,000
Office Furnishings/Equipment	200,000	**Total Liabilities and Owners' Equity**	5,000,000
Computer Equipment	200,000		
Leasehold Improvements	200,000		
Total Real & Personal Property	600,000		
Intangible Real & Other Assets	800,000		
Total Intangible Real & Other Assets	800,000		
Total Assets	5,000,000		

example) and review them monthly until clients have paid in full. Such vigilance is essential: these accounts represent work that the firm has performed at its own expense. Because transforming receivables into revenues can sometimes seem, at best, an ongoing challenge, some firms create special billings and collections committees or hire professional collectors to perform the task.

Firm Utilization Report

A *firm utilization report* lists the billable and nonbillable hours of each timekeeper, computes the value of each timekeeper's billable time according to his or her fee rates, and indicates how each timekeeper spent his or her nonbillable hours. A law firm may assign nonbillable hours to categories such as firm administration, legal education, pro bono work, bar association and other community activities, new business and marketing, new client development, and existing client development. Like accounts receivable reports, work-in-process reports (discussed in the following paragraph), and many other reports of this type, firm utilization reports depend on thorough and accurate timekeeping and billing records.

Work-in-Process Reports

Work-in-process reports inventory work that the firm has performed or is performing and that it has yet to bill to clients. These reports enable the firm to analyze data regarding (1) the number of hours spent on behalf of each client, (2) the potential cash value to the firm of the time worked, (3) billing and collections, and (4) the status of work that has been done to date. The hours that represent money to the firm fall into these categories: realization (those for which clients have paid), write-offs (bills that the firm has determined will never be paid), work-in-process (cases that are still open and not yet fully paid or completed) and *accounts receivable aged* (unpaid bills that the firm still considers to be viable sources of revenue).

Figure 6–3 provides an overview of the financial management process in a law firm.

PROFITABILITY[43]

The main motivation behind the management of a law firm's financial resources, the goal on which the firm focuses its budget making, its billing system, and its financial reporting, is partner profitability. **Profitability** is net income per partner, the money that remains after the firm has paid all of its expenses and obligations.

"RULES" for Measuring Profitability

We can measure a firm's profitability according to five operating factors whose initials form the acronym RULES: (1) realization, (2) utilization, (3) leverage, (4) expenses, and (5) speed (of converting bills to payments).[44]

Realization

Realization is the actual percentage of time for which the firm both bills *and* collects.

Utilization

Utilization measures, in terms of chargeable hours per professional year, the use that the firm makes of its timekeepers' time.

Leverage

As an element of law firm profitability, **leverage** describes the ratio of nonpartner professionals to partners. A low-leverage firm is one that has a smaller ratio of nonpartners to partners. In general, the less leverage, that is, the more senior rather than junior partners a firm has, the more profitable it will be. Higher leverage reduces a firm's average billing rate, since relatively more junior partners bill at lower rates, and averaging in paralegal hourly rates (sometimes known as calculating a *blended hourly rate*) will reduce the rate even further. According to an Altman & Weil study, it takes approximately four years for a firm to make a profit on the average newly hired attorney. In fact, the average firm loses almost $45,000 during a newly admitted lawyer's first year of hire.[45] However, a new hire's law firm is apt to see an increase in its utilization: whereas senior partners usually spend more time bringing in clients, junior partners normally work more billable hours.

Expenses

Expenses, as a component of measuring profitability, refer to all of the costs, direct and indirect, that a firm

FIGURE 6–3
The Financial Management Process

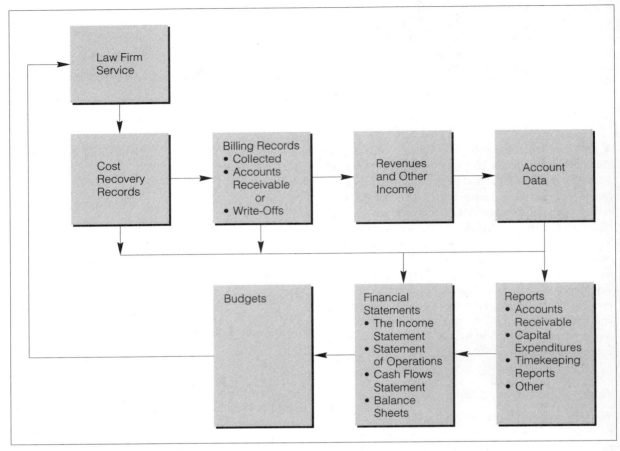

incurs while providing professional services. The more effectively a firm can control these costs, the more profitable it will be.

Speed of Collection

Speed is how quickly a firm receives cash for the legal services that it provides. The more quickly a firm can recoup its expenses, the higher its profitability will be.

Activity Centers

In assessing a firm's profitability, we can trace revenues and expenditures back to four **activity centers** within the firm. By linking revenues and expenses to their sources, managers can keep track of them. The units of activity to which we can trace expenditures and revenues in a law firm include (1) cost pools, (2) cost centers, (3) service centers, and (4) profit centers.

Cost Pools

Cost pools are sources of expenses that the firm cannot directly link to any one department or individual. Occupancy costs, including rent, depreciation, and the costs of furniture or fixtures, and employee benefits, such as Social Security and pensions, are examples of cost pool expenses.

Cost Centers

Cost centers are sources of expenditures that only indirectly produce revenue, such as the firm's administrative costs (including salaries, benefits, and other related administrative expenses) and the costs for accounting, reception services, and recruiting.

Service Centers

Service centers are sources of expenditures that one activity center creates in providing services to other activity centers. Examples of service centers include word processing, records management, duplicating, FAX and photocopying, and the firm's library.

Profit Centers

Profit centers are the units of activity in the firm that produce revenue directly. Examples of profit centers include lawyers, paralegals, and the departments or offices connected with clients and client matters, such as litigation, corporate law, and commercial law.

Law Firm Finances in the 1990s and Beyond

As we saw in the In the News article "Financial Survival" at the beginning of this chapter, law firms in the 1990s face increasing financial challenges. Law firms that recklessly created satellite branches, opened international offices, and hired scores of new associates in the 1980s and before now reap the sorry harvest of poor financial planning. The economic maelstroms that drown entire firms draw especially hard at specialty areas such as real estate law, corporate law, and tax law, even within firms that are relatively financially stable. Wary clients are less willing to pay fees they consider exorbitant, while many attorneys refuse to relinquish a single dollar of their diminishing draw. Watching billable hours fall, partners spend their meetings nervously discussing vanishing revenue, careful spending, and methods for increasing their own productivity. In times of scarce resources, all organizations are more susceptible to conflict and struggles, internal as well as external. Current economic demands on law firms have intensified especially their need for financial savvy and astute control of their existing and potential sources of revenue. Now and in the near future, firms will increasingly call on managers at all levels to offer advice on financial strategies and to help implement such strategies, in lean times as well as in profitable ones.

QUESTIONS FOR DISCUSSION AND REVIEW

1. What are the basic components of financial management?
2. Describe the basic reports that law firms use to control financial data.
3. Explain how the budget is a control, a guideline, and a planning tool.
4. Describe the steps in the budget-making process.
5. Discuss the financial management responsibilities of partners, associates, paralegals, support staff, and law firm managers.
6. Explain the economic value of paralegals and other nonlawyer personnel within the law firm. Should timekeeping practices be of equal importance to lawyers and nonlawyers? Why or why not?
7. Using national and local data, prepare a report on salary compensation for one of the following: partners, associates, paralegals, or other nonlawyer personnel. (You may find information for your report in publications of the AMA, ABA, and LAMA; in journals such as *Legal Assistant Today,* the *Journal of Paralegal Education, California Lawyer,* and *The National Law Journal;* or in newspaper articles such as "Is It the Beginning or the End for Paralegals?" in the *San Francisco Daily Journal* (21 January 1992) or "Paralegal Profession Alive and Kicking" in the *Los Angeles Daily Journal* (10 February 1992).

EXPERIENTIAL EXERCISES

I. Management Reporting

Arrange an interview with a legal administrator or an attorney who is familiar with one of the following:

- The timekeeping process,
- The budgetary process,
- The projection of revenues, or
- The fee-setting and collection process.

Below and on the following pages, you will find suggested questions to use in your interview. Remember that law firms adapt procedures to meet their particular needs and that, as a result, the procedures your interviewee describes are likely to be more organic than the ones we've examined in this textbook. Request samples of forms when appropriate, but be sure to assure your subject of confidentiality.

A. Timekeeping

1. Who are the timekeepers in the firm? (Lawyers, paralegals, others)
2. Who is responsible for time reports? Who is involved in the timekeeping process?
3. What timekeeping aids does the firm use?
    a. Manual forms? (Request sample forms)
    b. Automation? (If the firm uses a computer program, ask about the procedures the program involves. Do attorneys enter their own information? Does someone else enter information for them? Does the program utilize client numbers? Bar code scanning?)
4. What time categories does the firm use? (Billable and nonbillable hours, firm management, continuing education, firm marketing, pro bono, other?)
5. What kinds of time reports (such as missing time reports, billable hours reports, nonbillable hours reports, annual time expectations for partners, associates, and paralegals) does the firm utilize? Who prepares these reports? How often?
6. What is done about missing time reports?
7. What consequences do negligent timekeepers face?
8. What is the most difficult aspect of timekeeping in the firm?

B. Evaluating the Budget*

1. How detailed is the budget? Are the plans explicit?
2. How often does the firm consult the budget?
3. How flexible is the budget?
4. In what ways is the budget compatible with long range plans? How does it accommodate the expanding goals of the firm?
5. How does the firm monitor the budget?
6. What provisions does the budget make for the professional development of the firm's personnel?
7. Have the budget plans received the full support of the partners? If not, why?
8. In what ways do those affected by budget plans participate in the making of such plans?
9. What evidence shows that those affected by the budget understand its implications?
10. How does management use the budget as a tool?
11. In what areas does the budget reflect reasonable goals? In what areas might the budget's goals seem less realistic?

---

*Based in part on Wade Hampton, "The Budget Trainer," *Law Office Economics and Management* 23 (Winter 1988): 470–71.

12. Does the budget divide resources equitably?
13. What political pressures do budget makers face in this particular firm?
14. In what ways does the firm use the budget as a motivational tool?

C. Projecting Revenues

1. Describe the firm's primary and secondary sources of revenue.
2. How does the firm project its revenues for each budget?
3. How accurate is the projection?
4. Is revenue projection difficult? Why?
5. Through what procedures or activities (such as marketing) does the firm attempt to boost its revenue flow? How successful are these attempts?

D. Fees and Collections

1. Which types of fees does the firm use: contingency, billable hours, fixed fees, percentage fees, retainers, some other type, or a combination?
2. How does the firm set fees for attorneys and paralegals? What factors account for differences? Do fees differ from attorney to attorney? Paralegal to paralegal? What criteria does the firm use to establish differences in fees?
3. Describe the firm's billing process.
4. What costs other than legal services does the firm recover in client bills?
5. How are billing statements prepared?
   a. By whom? How often?
   b. How does the firm record nonbillable hours?
   c. What categories of nonbillable hours does the firm use?
6. Describe the firm's collection procedures.
   a. Who is responsible?
   b. What role do attorneys play in the collection process?
   c. Who follows up? How? How often?
7. What are the firm's write-off policies? What criteria does the firm use to distinguish between accounts receivable, aging receivables, and write-offs?

II. Current Economic Conditions

Using current newspapers, magazines, or professional publications, research the financial accomplishments or failures of a major law firm.** Using the advice given in the "Financial Strategies" article at the beginning of this chapter, analyze why the firm met—or failed to meet—its financial challenges.

III. Budget Time

After reviewing the steps in the budgetary process, 1) develop four financial reports (a projected income budget, projected fee revenues, personnel costs, and operating expenses) and 2) estimate the operating margin per hour for one of the following:

   a. A solo practitioner with two paralegals, a secretary, and a receptionist.
   b. A law firm partnership with five attorneys and a reasonable number of support staff.

**See, for instance, John H. Kennedy, "Death of a Law Firm/Gaston & Snow: A House Divided Against Itself," *The Sunday Boston Globe* (10 November 1991): A37, A40–A41.

c. A law firm partnership with twenty attorneys (ten of whom are partners), ten associates, five paralegals, five secretaries, a legal administrator, and an accountant.

IV. Timing Is Everything

Imagine that you are a legal administrator serving on the management committee of a 25-attorney law firm. The committee's task is to devise a new noncomputerized timekeeping system and form, and the committee chair has asked each member of the committee to submit a system description and a form mock-up at the next meeting.

1. Create a timekeeping form and write a brief report describing its merits.
2. Write a short proposal describing the timekeeping system you would suggest the firm use. Who will submit timekeeping forms? When? Where? Who will be responsible for collecting the forms and tallying the data they contain? How will the system account for omitted data?

CHAPTER 7

Managing Human Resources

LEARNING OBJECTIVES

After completing this chapter, you should be able to:

- Discuss the basic elements of human resources in the law firm;
- Explain what constitutes an effective use of human resources;
- Summarize the major human resource management activities;
- Describe the government's protection of workers and explain how these legal constraints control human resource activities;
- Explain the steps in the personnel selection process;
- Describe an effective interview;
- Discuss the criteria for an effective training and development program;
- Identify the components of compensation and explain the importance of ''psychic salary''; and
- Explain the four indications of an effective human resource program.

FOCUS FROM THE FIELD

Janis Bonvino: A Field to Be Proud to Work In

Janis Bonvino is office administrator in the New Britain, Connecticut, firm of Eisenberg, Anderson, Michalik & Lynch, P.C. She has long been active in educational programs, helping young people to explore careers in the legal field. She is an energetic and admired leader of Connecticut's Nutmeg Chapter of the ALA, having recently served as its president.

Why do law firm human resources differ from those in other organizations?

They are different because of the very nature of the work performed, the areas of confidentiality, ethics, deadlines, and pressures. It takes a special sort of person to handle all that. We look for varying degrees of specific talent that aren't necessarily used in the corporate or nonlegal world. We also look for people who are able to think rapidly on their feet, can work well autonomously, can take on varying degrees of responsibility and just handle the stress involved in working in a law firm, particularly when working in areas that impose tight deadlines. I think that this is very different from the basic corporate structure.

What do students new to law firm management need to know about human resource management?

I think that students going in to law firm management have to be taught very carefully because people skills are very, very important. I think that it would be good to have internships in law firms for students so that they could watch human resource departments in action. I consider it a very critical area.

Are there any trends that affect human resources in law firms?

Yes, there are many. For instance, single parents. Larger firms have worked toward flextime programs to help both the employee and the employer. I think that day care is a critical issue, to promote a lack of absenteeism. I think the new Americans with Disabilities Act is going to affect certain areas of the profession. I also think that there are many contemporary issues to be concerned about: drugs, alcohol, personal problems, and those types of situations. Many firms have structured personal assistance programs. These are the trends that definitely have an effect on today's society.

How can law firms use employment agencies?

I find employment agencies a valuable resource. Those who are very reputable, who specialize in law office personnel, and who have an established testing process and criteria, can be extremely helpful. They test the applicants for you; the bottom line, culling, is done within the firm itself. I find employment agencies very useful in finding applicants for a specific job. However, the interviewing process that is conducted by the employer is still most important in finding the right employees. I think that the interview process should be more structured and should involve better programs, such as testing for even the most basic skills, like spelling and writing.

What orientation procedures should law firms follow?

There should be a definite orientation period for all levels: support staff, management, and associates. When a new staff member comes in, I have specific individuals within the firm—who are expert in certain areas—spend time with the new employee. They take them through the various phases of the area in which they're going to be working. I have a set procedure. The first day a new recruit comes in, the forms are filled out. The benefits are explained. We go through things such as confidentiality, dress requirements, everyone gets introduced. They're given an outline of the building, who sits at what desk. The minimal things turn out to be the maximum things! I try to furnish new employees before they come in—at least a week before their start date—with a list of who is who and who does what. They have time to look at it, and I think some advance preparation prior to that first day in the office is very necessary. We all do everything we can to encourage longevity within the firm because it becomes very costly and very cumbersome to have turnover.

What approaches concerning human resources do you feel are lacking in the law firm setting?

There needs to be more of a "real world" approach that is lacking in applicants. It seems to start at both the high school and college levels. By "real world" I mean telling future members of law firms the truth. There are steps that must be taken into account. That goes for secretaries, paralegals, and attorneys. A strong work ethic must exist if one expects to succeed in his or her profession. The most important factor of a job is not the salary or the amount of vacation days given, as some people seem to think. It is whether or not the job is an interesting and challenging one that you have the ability to take on. The legal field is one of the most interesting and diverse professions. It is a field to be proud to work in. When you get into the area of human resources you get into such a broad area. In law firms today, there are so many more job titles and job specifications, such as legal secretary, levels one, two, and three. There are paralegals at different levels. There are file clerks, there are copy room supervisors. They say it's broadened so far that there's support at every level. There are many more positions available than legal secretaries and paralegals. There are many ways to expand the person's talents, in-house, but there also should be programs in schools that help develop a stronger work ethic, their work attitudes. In this era, there is that great "gimme-gotcha, let-me-have, I-want, I-take" syndrome. I've interviewed people who, before I could ask the first question, were asking me "How much vacation time? How many personal days? How many sick days? How many holidays? Do you give bonuses? How soon before the first raise?" Ultimately, it is the person who is the most qualified, the most trained, with the most initiative, and with the strongest work ethic who is going to get ahead. I've been in this field almost twenty-eight years myself, and it's one of the most interesting and diverse professions on the face of the earth and one of the most exciting in which to work. I think that has to be told to people, too. It's a field to be proud to work in!

In an information society, human resources is at the cutting edge.
(John Naisbitt, "What HR Professionals Can Do")[1]

Law firms traditionally had a short-term view of the need to manage their human resources. Human resource planning was considered a "soft" expense, not equal in importance to expenditures for equipment and facilities. Successful firms have awakened to the need for management and control of the firm's largest expenditure. Ensuring productivity is essential, and the proper matching of skills and personalities within the firm is, at best, a fragile mix.
(Dan DiLucchio, "Things They Never Taught You in Law School")[2]

THE HUMAN RESOURCE PROCESS

No decision is as important as a decision about human resources. Years ago, law firms considered loyalty to their members as sacred as the profession itself. The partners of a firm, once chosen, became part of a lasting brotherhood, committed not only to their profession but to the firm and to their shared ownership in it. Secretaries regularly made their work with a firm an exchange that was social as well as economic, expressing their loyalty through years of steadfast service, and firms carried their devotion to all of their members as far as they could afford to. Today, given the sharply competitive market for legal services, law firms still depend on the impeccable selection of competent workers. People are still the most important component of the delivery of legal services, and they are central to a law firm's profitability. No decision regarding law firm personnel can be made lightly.

Human Resource Management

Human resource management is the aspect of management that oversees, obtains, maintains, and develops the human assets of a firm. Basically, controlling human resources means recruiting the number and kinds of workers a firm needs, overseeing and arranging their compensation and their contributions, and coordinating their departures when the time comes. Although the activities we associate with human resource management date back to ancient times, not until the nineteenth century did employers develop a serious interest in the quality and well-being of their employees, and they often fostered less-than-altruistic motives for doing so. In the late 1800s, to dissuade workers from joining unions, big textile mills, factories, foundries, and other companies hired *welfare secretaries* (also known as *social secretaries*) to help employees with problems related to education, housing, and medical needs. In the early 1900s, this role expanded into human resource departments that were responsible for keeping wages at minimal levels, screening all job applicants, and handling grievances. After the Great Depression shattered the public's faith in the willingness of business to treat workers fairly, the government intervened, introducing laws that provided for unemployment compensation, Social Security benefits, minimum wages, and improved working conditions. Additional legislation guaranteed workers' rights.[3] Employers began appointing human resource managers (often former administrators whose loyalty to their companies compensated for their lack of human resources training) to find and screen applicants, process forms, and, in more liberal work places, to conduct worker attitude surveys! Though in the course of its development this field has been known by many other names, including personnel administration, personnel management, and industrial relations, human resource management seems best to reflect its philosophy: the belief that although all of an organization's resources are important, the key to its success is the wise use of its human resources, its most valuable capital.[4]

The Importance of Human Resource Management

The Human Investment

An overview of a law firm's budget reveals just how much firms spend on their human resources. Firms consider this spending to be an investment in **human capital** (or *social capital*): the talents, skills, knowledge, and positive attitudes of their members.[5] Of all a law firm's expenditures, none is as large or as critical as the expenditure for human resources, since the fair and encouraging treatment of personnel is an investment that offers generous returns in terms of productivity and profitability.

Costly Mistakes

Hiring the wrong people is a highly unprofitable activity. Mismatched workers don't last long, and once they leave, the firm wastes time and money trying to find and train suitable replacements. Effective human resource management not only can separate the wheat from the chaff in terms of screening applicants, but can transform new hires into highly productive personnel and help a firm to retain established personnel through programs that offer training, development, and personal and professional support.

Emotional Malpractice

Interaction with coworkers and superiors and with the work environment itself is often a source of great stress. Workers in certain fields have come to expect certain types of job-related stress. An emergency room nurse, for instance, knows the emotional demands that are part of the job. An attorney understands the high-paced, high-pressure expectations that accompany legal activities. However, employers now risk being held legally responsible for the setbacks and emotional pain that workers suffer as the result of inordinate stress. Human resource management can help to rectify working conditions that might otherwise lead to accusations of emotional malpractice.

Competition for Available Labor

The increasing competition for a shrinking pool of qualified workers, especially those who possess strong technical and secretarial support staff skills, has placed many law firms on shaky ground in terms of attracting and retaining quality personnel. Often out of economic pressures, modern law firms and many other employers are no longer as loyal to their employees as they once were, nor employees to their employers, and firms that have not treated their workers well are the first to feel the tight pinch of personnel shortages. Even in firms that handle their workers with care, the span of employment often seems to be largely the product of employee whim. Whereas legal colleagues once spent their professional lives upholding the reputation of a single firm, the mobility of law firm personnel is now commonplace. Through effective human resource management, a firm can attract the personnel it needs—and motivate them to stay.

Control of Human Resources

Controlling the human resource process requires a firm to continuously monitor its present personnel needs and to forecast future ones. In addition, the firm must establish criteria for spotting quality personnel at the point of entry into the firm and, in turn, for weeding out poorly qualified workers, even in areas where a declining labor pool increases the difficulty of finding high-quality recruits. Because people give a law firm its competitive edge,[6] finding and keeping good personnel is of major significance.

THE MAJOR ACTIVITIES OF HUMAN RESOURCE MANAGERS

Managers who are responsible for human resources perform these six major tasks: (1) staffing, (2) recruiting, (3) selecting employees, (4) orientation, (5) training and development, and (6) compensating.

Staffing

Providing the right people for the law firm is the primary function of human resource management, and the first step in this process is the activity known as **staffing.** Staffing, which affects recruiting, selection, and, later, training and development, is simply the process of providing workers for the firm when it needs them. More specifically, staffing involves estimating the number and types of workers a firm will need by studying its goals and objectives, reviewing its long-term plans, forecasting personnel supply and demand, and analyzing the jobs that the firm needs to fill.[7] Factors that affect staffing decisions include the creation of new jobs; openings brought about by promotions, transfers, terminations, and leaves of absence; restructuring; and resignations and retirements. Nonlawyer legal administrators are often fully responsible for staffing support service personnel and frequently facilitate the full staffing process in a firm.

Forecasting

Human resource staffing involves analyzing the firm's current needs, its resources, and its future directions, according to its top-level decision makers. **Forecasting** is the process of projecting the firm's personnel needs, in light of the supply of available workers and the demand for them. If, for example, the managing partners decide to create an environmental law department, they will estimate (often with the assistance of law office managers, personnel managers, or others with human resource expertise) the numbers and types of personnel the firm will need to staff this venture, study the needs and interests of current staff members, assess the available labor pool, and make recruiting decisions in keeping with the long-range goals of the firm. Forecasting a firm's personnel needs requires a clear understanding of the jobs that the firm needs to fill. This understanding is largely the product of the process of job analysis.

The Job Analysis

To clarify the jobs that a firm needs to fill and to locate people who possess not only the skills that those jobs require but the values and attitudes that will enable them to fit into the firm's culture, human resource managers rely on a type of research known as job analysis. The process of investigating the duties, responsibilities, and even the dynamics of a job, a **job analysis** is a study to determine the tasks that a job does or will involve and the skills, knowledge, and abilities that the jobholder must have to perform the job successfully.[8] Though job analyses may be external as well as internal, in larger firms, human resource managers or committees usually perform job analyses; in smaller firms, the responsibility normally goes to law office managers. Law firms and other organizations use information gathered through job analyses for a variety of human resource products and activities, including the following:

Job Descriptions. A **job description** is a written listing of all the tasks, duties, and responsibilities that a job involves. A law firm's job descriptions, which are usually from one to three pages long, should follow a consistent format (either paragraphs or listings of responsibilities are acceptable) and should include the job title, status (full- or part-time), location, and summary (the basic purpose of the job); the organizational relationships and reporting structures; working conditions; and detailed descriptions of all job duties and responsibilities.

Job Specifications. A **job specification** profiles the ideal mix of knowledge, skills, and abilities required for a job. When applicable, it also lists the education, training, and experience that are necessary, as well as specific job demands, such as interpersonal skills and regular overtime or travel.[9]

Figure 7–1 presents a job description for the position of paralegal coordinator. Note the job specifications in part IV.

Other Uses for Job Analysis Information. Besides using job analysis information to write job descriptions and specifications, human resource managers and other law firm personnel use analysis data to design or redesign jobs, establish job standards, determine and meet recruiting needs, select and place personnel, calculate reasonable compensation and benefits, and identify conditions that could threaten employee welfare. In addition, law firms use job analyses for orientation, training and development, performance evaluations, and career counseling.

Recruiting

Essentially, **recruiting** is the process of obtaining candidates for a firm opening by creating a pool of qualified applicants. We might say that recruiting has much in common with fishing: both involve going to the right places, using the right lures, and having the patience to wait until the big one takes the bait. While law firms use different recruiting techniques to fill different positions, most firms concentrate their recruiting efforts on obtaining the field's best prospects for new associates and legal administrators. Ideally, recruiting involves obtaining the best candidates with the least effort; however, reaching high-quality prospects is often a complex and costly endeavor. To recruit effectively for positions at any level, a law firm must be prepared to spend plenty of time on the process, must allow supervisors, position peers, and other line personnel to participate, and must stick to its criteria in terms of the qualities it is seeking in candidates.[10] From the lowest positions to the highest, a firm may recruit candidates from both internal and external sources.

Internal Sources

Hiring from within can benefit both a firm and its current personnel. Through internal recruiting, a firm's members enjoy an opportunity for professional growth; the firm, in turn, has been able to observe its potential candidates in action and to assess the quality of their work. A firm circulates official information about internal job openings by means of **job postings** that may include letters, memos, bulletin board notices, or other similar communications. Often, firms extend their internal recruiting by sharing leads, networks, and contacts with other firms.

External Sources

Effective external recruiting involves knowing where qualified candidates are likely to be.[11] When recruiting from without, law firms commonly utilize the services of private placement agencies and professional search firms. In using a placement agency, a law firm notifies the agency of its needs and the agency actively solicits candidates through its own advertising or from its pool of job seekers. The quality of the matching process differs widely: while some agencies carefully screen the candidates that they recommend to a firm, others simply provide a candidate pool. Either the law firm or the candidate pays the agency a fee, usually based on a percentage of the first year's salary, a set fee, or a fee roughly equal to a month's pay. Recruiting from external sources does present its share of risks. Besides

FIGURE 7-1
Job Description for a Paralegal Coordinator

Position: Paralegal Coordinator

I. Basic Purpose
   To manage and coordinate all functions of paralegal supervision, including work delegation, direct supervision, evaluation and training, work quality, and productivity.

II. Duties and Responsibilities
   A. Periodically assess needs for paralegal positions in all departments and report such needs to department heads and firm administrator.
   B. Prepare and update job descriptions for all paralegal positions.
   C. Assist in the preparation of advertising for all new paralegal positions in all departments.
   D. Review resumés and select applicants for interviewing.
   E. Participate in the interview process and make recommendations regarding applicants to the executive committee, department heads, and firm administrator.
   F. Review salary requirements and recommend salary ranges for paralegal positions to the executive committee.
   G. Conduct intensive paralegal training (utilizing lawyer and paralegal personnel) for the first six months of any new paralegal's employment.
   H. Assess and accommodate the continuing training needs of the firm's paralegals.
   I. Distribute task assignments through the firm's case management system.
   J. Participate with the department head in the evaluation process for each paralegal.
   K. Integrate evaluation results into a single report and participate in the evaluation meeting with the paralegal.
   L. Review monthly paralegal productivity reports, analyzing hours worked and hours billed.
   M. Supervise and coach paralegals in their job performance.
   N. Discipline paralegals as necessary in accordance with firm policies and procedures.
   O. Assist paralegals in interpreting the firm's policies and procedures.
   P. Prepare weekly, monthly, semiannual, and annual management reports that pertain to paralegals.
   Q. Direct and oversee paralegals' activities with a sense of responsibility for paralegal morale and job satisfaction.
   R. Serve as a liaison between paralegals and other firm management personnel as necessary.
   S. Provide leadership in the development and maintenance of highly professional paralegal services.
   T. Maintain and actively participate in the Western Massachusetts Paralegal Association and the Legal Assistant Management Association.
   U. Attend seminars and conferences relevant to the position.

III. Organizational Relationships
   The paralegal coordinator reports directly to the legal administrator, to the appropriate department heads, and to the executive committee for special management reports and services, when requested. The paralegal coordinator directly supervises all firm paralegals.

IV. Position Specifications
   Essential requirements include a bachelor's or master's degree in a management field and a degree or advanced certificate in paralegal studies plus a minimum of five years' experience as a paralegal. Candidate must possess outstanding abilities as a paralegal and must also have excellent interpersonal skills, as well as the ability to motivate people, supervise effectively, and work with the firm's attorneys and upper-level management. In addition, candidate must possess initiative, a cooperative work style, mature judgment, emotional stability, and leadership skills.

SOURCE: Robinson, Donovan, Madden & Barry, P.C., Springfield, MA. Adapted with permission.

simply having to deal with fees (which can be considerable for secretarial positions as well as for administrative ones), a firm risks encountering the rare unscrupulous employment agency that is far more interested in receiving its stipend than in providing quality personnel. On the other hand, the services of a conscientious placement agency can save the law firm time and money and provide expertise in employee selection. The services of professional search firms are more specialized services than those of placement agencies. Some search firms conduct active "headhunts" for candidates with specific kinds of talents by luring talented personnel away from a firm's competitors or "steal" a law firm's new recruits by offering them better positions with other firms—just after the first firm pays its placement fees. While some personnel professionals consider such activities unethical, others believe that mobility is simply freedom of choice.[12]

Table 7–1 lists some of the most common sources for external recruiting.

The Selection Process

Selection is the process of determining which candidate should be offered a position, based on his or her potential for meeting the needs and expectations of the firm. The selection process consists of (1) screening applications, (2) conducting an initial interview with a potential candidate, (3) reviewing the data on the candidate's application and confirming his or her suitability to work in the firm, (4) and inviting the candidate back for a final interview.

TABLE 7–1
Sources for External Recruiting

Source	Methods and Contacts
Advertising and Notices	Ads in publications, especially those in the target market.
Recruiters	Obtain and screen candidates.
Colleges	Sources of contacts: with career service offices (in law schools), paralegal programs, and specialized schools.
Placement Agencies	Match job seekers with openings.
Professional Recruiting Agencies	Actively solicit a limited number of qualified candidates, luring them from their present jobs.
Employee Referrals	Information from in-house workers about friends, professional contacts, colleagues or associates who may be qualified.
Professional Associations	Help members through placement activities.
Walk-ins and Write-ins	Job seekers who either visit the firm to inquire about work or who solicit your interest by mail.

Screening

Screening takes place after a firm has solicited and studied initial applications and resumés. In the screening process, the firm assembles a pool of candidates by weeding out those who fail to meet the minimal standards for a position and, conversely, by determining those who best meet the qualifications. Federal law limits job applications and other informational screening tools to inquiries concerning **bona fide occupational qualifications,** or BFOQs; that is, a firm may not ask a candidate questions concerning topics such as his or her age, gender, race, or religious beliefs unless it has a legitimate business reason for doing so. For example, a firm in the process of hiring a women's rest room attendant would be permitted to ask questions about gender; a firm hiring a new associate would not. So far, no court rulings have found an employer to be legitimately entitled to ask candidates questions concerning color or race.

The Interview

The interview is a challenge for the interviewer *and* the interviewee. Meeting a candidate in person yields information that would never appear on a resumé—as Tom Peters observes, "Great on paper is no guarantee."[13] An interviewer's initial impressions, while often hard to overcome, are rarely based on his or her perceptions concerning the interviewee's competency. Rather, they reflect what the interviewer values in candidates. In fact, the twelve most common reasons for rejecting candidates include, in order of their frequency among interviewers, the candidate's poor personal appearance, his or her overbearing and conceited attitude, an inability to communicate accurately and adequately, lack of career goals, lack of interest and enthusiasm, lack of confidence, an overemphasis on money, inadequate academic records, unrealistic expectations, excuses, lack of maturity and decisiveness, and lack of courtesy.[14] As an interviewer, you should look for three primary qualities in candidates: first, they should have a clear idea of what they want to do; secondly, they should know about your organization; and third, they should have some idea of what they can contribute to your firm. Since it is important for both parties to make a favorable impression, both the interviewer and interviewee do well to be thoroughly prepared.

Reviewing the Data

Studies have shown that few companies take the time to confirm the accuracy of applicant information, in spite of the fact that deception in the application process is not uncommon.[15] Resumé deception is perhaps the most usual. As consumers, we are accustomed to the "puffery" that advertisers use to sell products. Unfortunately, many professionals have adopted a similar type of exaggeration as part of their personal marketing style. No one involved in hiring can afford to be naive about the very real threat of "creative" resumé writing. In the interview process, you can test a candidate's validity through thoughtful probing questions (which we will discuss in more detail later in this chapter). Outside of the interview process, you can confirm a candidate's qualities by thoroughly examining his or her resumé, making careful personal contact with references, and verifying degrees and academic records.

Resumés. A resumé provides an overview of a candidate's education, experience, and interests, revealing who the candidate is and indicating his or her potential contributions. However, the picture that a resumé provides is, as Tom Peters and other business professionals would warn, only partial. As an interviewer, you should carefully examine the time sequence on a resumé, looking for steady patterns of employment and inquiring about time gaps or periods during which the applicant may have been out of work. Neither time gaps nor unemployment should prejudice a recruiter; instead, they should provide a basis for more accurate interpretations of a candidate's job history.

In the hands of an astute interviewer, the resumé is one of the most revealing communications an applicant can provide. Though never foolproof, a resumé allows an interviewer to glimpse an applicant's initiative and drive (as revealed by his or her choice of experiences), his or her attention to detail and sense of priorities, commitments and interests, and professionalism. As an interviewing tool, the resumé enables the interviewer to read between a candidate's lines. For example, if applicant A's resumé tells you of her great ability to work well with people, probe behind the abstraction by asking for details. Ask A to explain in detail how she worked with others and to describe the projects that she and her team accomplished, the procedures they used, and the part of the task for which she was actually responsible. Or, if the resumé reveals what seems to be a lack of professional focus (and/or a good deal of creative writing), find out if A really knows what the job is about by asking her to describe what she believes to be a typical day or what activities the position would ideally involve.

References. Be very wary of references. Remember that the person you are interviewing may be someone else's mistake: a current employer may be very happy to tell you what you want to hear in order to be rid of a problem employee. On the other hand, a past employer may sweeten his or her comments regarding your candidate out of a sincere belief that this person deserves a fresh start. One method for obtaining useful references is to ask the candidate for specific names of three people with whom he or she works or used to work, such as three present colleagues or his or her past three immediate supervisors. More than former or current employers, such people may be willing to give candid information. Then again, they may not!

People request and provide references for a variety of reasons, and delving into a candidate's references can reveal a tangled skein of motivation. First come the applicant's motives for selecting these references. While references often are simply those who know the candidate best, they are also likely to be those most apt to provide a potential employer with responses favorable to the candidate's job search. Employers, in turn, have, as we have seen, their own motives in providing references. Besides wishing to dump a poorly performing employee or seeking to secure a second chance for a candidate, employers, like most people, hesitate to communicate negatives about anyone, particularly about employees, and particularly in writing. An employer who is negative about a worker he or she would like to see advance risks being stuck with that worker. Worse, negative observations placed in writing may come back to haunt a former employer in the form of litigation! That is why, as a matter of policy, most employers' letters provide only the most basic information, such as dates of employment. Even when reading a glowing and utterly truthful letter about a worker, you would be wise to ask how many people the letter was written for. It is unlikely that you are its sole audience. Be especially wary of vague wording. Just as reading between the lines of a candidate's resumé takes talent, so does interpreting the wording of references. Lines such as "I am pleased to say that this candidate is a former colleague of mine," "I cannot say enough good things about this candidate," "In my opinion, you will be very fortunate to get this candidate to work for you," or "I would urge you to waste no time in considering this candidate" should, at the very least, inspire not only suspicion but a sincere need for clarification.[16] However, despite all these cautions, honest, reliable, and genuine recommendations *do* exist. Some employers are sincerely sorry to lose certain employees, but would not wish to hinder their professional advancement. When you doubt the sincerity, clarity, or accuracy of a reference, making personal contact with the person who provided it often can erase doubts—for better or, sometimes, sadly (as far as the applicant might see it), for worse.

Degrees. Degrees and credentials from the right school are often primary criteria for employment, but they never tell the whole story about a candidate. A paralegal who has completed only a short course of studies may prove to be more flexible and adaptable than one who has finished a substantive degree program. An associate from a top school may not have as much enthusiasm or be as unselfishly committed to the firm as someone who has completed an evening part-time program. Applicants can belie academic stereotypes in many ways, and those who screen and interview candidates must try to forego any biases they might harbor in favor of Ivy League graduates or against those who hold degrees from state universities or community colleges. In any case, verifying degrees can be a problem. As a policy, you should require only official records: ask applicants for official transcripts, to be sent to you directly from a college or university registrar's office. The presence of the school's official embossed seal provides some indication of a transcript's authenticity; you can verify unofficial records by calling the registrar's office of the institution directly, if need be. Do not place all your stock in grades, however. Poor grades may have resulted from factors other than ability and intelligence; remember that there are students (possibly even you) who have worked full-time jobs throughout college. Others may have suffered personal crises or encountered hard-marking professors. At any rate, research has yet to establish a definite correlation between high grades and workplace success.

Ranking

After you have screened candidates, conducted initial interviews, and reviewed the written data they have provided, the next step in the selection process involves ranking the applicants. To rank a field of candidates, many firms create categories based on their hiring criteria and provide each candidate a numerical rating within each category. Tallying each applicant's categorical ratings enables a firm to compare candidates objectively.

Inviting Candidates Back

Once ranking is complete, the firm invites the most promising candidates back for a second set of interviews. At this stage of the selection process, depending on the level of the position, human resource managers should involve other members of the firm, particularly those who authorize hiring. When a firm is hiring new attorneys, for example, partners (who provide final hiring authority for this level of recruit) and senior attorneys become involved at this stage. By comparison, when the firm is hiring for a non-attorney position, the person who is to be the candidate's immediate supervisor, who can best evaluate the candidate's potential contribution to the firm, should participate in this final interview, sometimes called the *supervisory interview.* Speaking with recruits gives the members of the firm a chance to talk realistically about their expectations, their sense of where the firm is headed and the challenges ahead. Final prehire interviews also allow candidates and current members to discuss realistic job expectations and any potentially unpleasant working conditions. These realism talks help to head off later job dissatisfaction and increase a candidate's likelihood of remaining with the firm.[17]

The Art of Interviewing

Although some human resource personnel pride themselves on their seemingly infallible ability to select the right candidate, successful selection more often resembles the ability to predict the future with a crystal ball. Achieving the alignment of intangible factors, such as organizational and personal goals, that enables a person to "belong" to the firm frequently seems a matter of chance or circumstance. Sometimes you are fortunate enough to find the right candidate because of strange twists of fate: the best candidate for your firm also happened to want to live in Colorado ski country, where your office is, or has recently become divorced and wanted to move to Dallas and saw your ad, or always wanted to be in on the ground floor of a New England law firm's new computer law department. Selecting the best candidate often takes much more than luck, however, especially if a firm wants to avoid expensive hiring mistakes. Determining whether an individual and an organization are truly suited for each other is the goal of the crucial and often difficult activity known as the interview.

The Interview Process

Interviewing is the process of obtaining information for a specific purpose by asking (and occasionally answering) questions.[18] Asking the right questions during an employment interview should provide information that will enable you, as an interviewer, to select a candidate who is compatible with your firm. Though most interviews attempt to cover a great deal of professional and personal detail in a limited amount of time, the interviewer must give the candidate a sense of rapport, consideration, and professionalism. This task is complicated by the fact that both parties are not only likely to feel anxiety toward the interview and its outcome but are likely to form lasting impressions during the first few minutes of the process. Therefore, as human resources consultant John Cogger observes,

> The heart of the interview process is rapport. Only in a relationship of mutual trust and comfort—a relationship largely free of anxiety—will a candidate talk freely. . . . No interview is without stress, however. . . . In view of this mutual anxiety, every effort should be made to allay the fears of both parties.[19]

Essentially, interviews are either directive or nondirective.

Directive Interviews. A **directive interview** makes use of a specific question format. The interviewer, who has control over the interview and who harbors a clear idea of the information that he or she needs to obtain, adheres to a specific list of questions.

Nondirective Interviews. During a **nondirective interview,** the interviewer operates according to specific objectives but allows the interviewee's answers to dictate the direction that the interview takes. Rather than utilizing a specific list of questions, the interviewer asks questions largely in response to the interviewee's answers, probing for clarification or more information.

Types of Interview Questions[20]

Open Questions. Generally, **open questions** are those which provide no advance indication of the interviewee's answer. Such questions require a detailed response revealing personal views. Answers to open questions can also illustrate a candidate's depth of knowledge and his or her ability to organize and articulate his or her thoughts. Examples of open questions might be "What makes a paralegal competent?" or "What kind of atmosphere do you like to work in?"; even more revealing queries might concern a candidate's values, ideals, or priorities: "What's the ideal relationship between a paralegal and a supervising attorney?" A **hypothetical question,** based on an assumed situation, is an open question that indicates how a candidate might act under certain job-related conditions. Here is an example: "Your computer has been giving you error messages all morning and files are being corroded. You've told your supervisor twice about the problem. However, she seems to think it might be because of your carelessness. Through no fault of your own, you lose a file again. What do you do?"

Closed Questions. Unlike their more open counterparts, **closed questions** confine an interviewee to very specific responses. Some examples of closed questions would be "When did you complete your paralegal studies?" or "How long did you work at Smith, Smith, and Jones?" A **leading question** is a closed question that, because of its wording, leads to a "correct" answer—that is, to the answer that the interviewer wants to hear. An example of a leading question would be, "You don't mind working overtime, do you?"; a corresponding question that is less confining would be "What are your views on working overtime?"

Informational Questions. Informational questions are designed to obtain specific information: "What legal specialty area do you prefer?" "How would you describe your work style?" "When are you able to begin work?" Through such questions, interviewers seek to identify collegial behaviors and attitudes that would benefit the firm, such as an emphasis on integration and teamwork, enthusiasm, commitment, self-discipline, and a tendency to welcome responsibility.[21]

Follow-up Questions. An interviewer uses follow-up questions to elicit additional information: "Is that your only preference?" "What do you mean when you say 'adequately responded'?" "How much time would you say is 'reasonable'?"

Probes. **Probes** are questions that explore topics that the interviewee mentioned only briefly in earlier answers. "You said working in the Registry was not easy. Why was that?" "What were those challenges you were talking about?" "You mentioned being 'uncomfortable' with your job demands. What were those pressures like?''

Nudges. **Nudges** are short comments or questions (''Yes?'' ''And then what happened?'' ''And?'') that encourage an interviewee to contribute more information concerning a particular subject.

Reflective Questions. A **reflective question** refers back to one of an interviewee's prior responses in order to clear up any inaccuracies or possible misunderstandings: ''Did you mean to say 1991 or did you mean 1990?'' ''Did you mean that your disliking your wills and estates professor led you to dislike the idea of working in that field?'' ''Did we clarify that it was firm policy to offer two weeks' vacation *after* the first full year of work?''

Clearinghouse Questions. At the end of an interview, **clearinghouse questions** allow the interviewer to obtain any other information that might be relevant and that the interviewee might want or need to provide: ''Is there anything else I should know about why you left your last job?'' ''Can you think of any other issues you might want to discuss before we sign this form?'' ''Are there any other expectations you have for us that you want to talk about now?'' ''Have we missed anything?''

The Parts of the Interview

A structured interview consists of a very simple and logical sequence of parts, each of which is designed to accomplish a specific purpose. These parts include the opening, the body of the interview, and the closing.

The Opening.[22] As an interviewer, you have two basic objectives in the opening minutes of an interview: to create a favorable rapport with your candidate and to describe what he or she can expect during the interview. In terms of the first objective, establishing a good rapport helps the applicant to participate more naturally in the interview. Your aim is to convey your good will and to reassure the candidate that you can be trusted. Small talk relaxes the newcomer and the atmosphere, and takes the pressure off both of you. Make it a point to include some talk about a specific resumé entry, such as, ''I notice you spent your junior year in England'' or ''The article you wrote for the review must have been quite a challenge.'' Regarding the second objective, previewing the structure of the interview helps to reduce the candidate's anxiety and lays the foundation for a two-way exchange of information. You might explain, for example, that you will first be asking questions about the candidate's previous experiences, that you will then inquire about his or her qualifications and other information the firm requires, and, finally, that the candidate will then have an opportunity to ask questions.

The Body. As an interviewer, you should observe two rules during the main part of an interview: look and listen and use open-ended questions. Your task is not to do all the talking, but to listen. Don't let your interviewee wander, but structure the interview, ask specific questions that expose strengths and weaknesses, interrupt if necessary, and probe answers that, upon reflection, say more than they seemed to at first. Talk about previous experiences and qualifications. Look for the commitment and enthusiasm that will make a good addition to the firm. Finally, explore the candidate's stability and resourcefulness, and, above all, his or her ability to be part of a team, even if you suspect that this recruit may in reality be a future ''star'' player.

Table 7-2 provides a list of typical interview questions.

The Closing. While you may validly think of the closing as an opportunity to take care of courtesies, the purpose of closure is to complete the time you have spent with the candidate in as respectful a way as possible. First, you must announce clearly that your interview has come to an end. Secondly, thank the interviewee sincerely for his or her help. The two of you have been at work, but only you have been paid. The applicant has *invested* his or her time. Your role as interviewer is to tell the candidate that you appreciate the chance to meet with and interview him or her. Third, provide some idea of the next step by telling the candidate, even if only in broad estimates, of when you expect to have a decision and how you will inform him or her of it. This gives the candidate the feeling that you will keep him or her in mind, that you were receptive, and that the interview was not a waste of time. All this creates in the candidate a positive lasting impression of you and your firm.

Of course, lasting impressions are a two-way street. The following Another Look offers wry advice for interviewees on how *not* to go about impression-building.

TABLE 7-2
Sample Interview Questions

Previous Experiences
    Tell me about your education. Is there anything you'd do differently?
    What areas (or courses) appealed to you the most? Why?
    Which work experience brought you the most opportunity for growth?

Qualifications
    In terms of quality, what kind of job will you do?
    What kind of feedback will you need from us regarding your job performance?
    Why do you believe you're right for our firm?
    What strengths do you have in _____? How did you develop these strengths?

Probing for Strengths and Weaknesses
    In what accomplishment do you take the most pride?
    What has been your biggest disappointment?
    Which superior has been the most helpful to you?
    Who has stood in your way the most? Why?
    Where do you feel your major competencies lie? Your inadequacies?
    Tell me about something you were asked to do that really challenged you.
    Have you ever had to say no to management or a superior? Why?
    What is your major motivational force?
    What work values are important to you?

Commitment and Enthusiasm
    Why did you choose your field?
    If you joined our firm, what would you like to see happen in the future?
    Do you have any additional career or professional plans?
    So far, have you been happy with your career choices? Explain.
    What do you do when you have a great deal to do and too little time?
    How have you reacted to time pressures? Did you work overtime? Were others involved?
    Tell me about a time when you dealt with a crisis.
    At your last job, were you able to get the support you needed? What could you have done to increase that support?

Stability and Resourcefulness
    What caused you to change colleges?
    Why are you considering a job change at this point?
    Do your career ambitions change? What causes these changes?
    Why was it that you didn't stay long at any of your previous places of employment?
    What is the hardest problem you've had to solve in the past few years? How did you do it?
    In what ways could your employer have helped you?
    What's your usual way of dealing with challenges at work?
    Who do you find most helps you to handle difficulties?

Ability to Be Part of a Team
    Do you prefer working with others or alone?
    What is the ideal work team (or committee) like?
    Should someone ever just give in and let others have their way? Why?

Socialization Processes

A new employee's first day on the job is always reminiscent of the first day of school. After completing all the requirements of the selection process, the applicant-turned-candidate undergoes both formal and informal socialization designed to teach the novice the rules for working in his or her new organization. For many newcomers, socialization is an uncomfortable time, some-

ANOTHER LOOK

How to Fail an Interview: The Tacky Ten

1. Don't make eye contact with your interviewer.
2. Ask only questions about salary, benefits, and vacations.
3. Dump on your current boss or employer.
4. Smoke, if you feel like it, without bothering to ask, or chew gum. It helps you relax.
5. Don't find out anything about the firm ahead of time. Who cares if they specialize in bankruptcies and you've avoided the field?
6. Be late for your appointment. Being late is a sign of power.
7. Don't worry about how you dress. They should be interested in your job skills, not your appearance.
8. If they insist on shaking hands, don't put much energy into your grip. If your hand reminds them of a dead mackerel, tough!
9. Talk as much as you like about whatever you want. After all, it's your interview.
10. Avoid those silly questions they ask about strengths and weaknesses; try humor instead.

SOURCE: Adapted from an original Recruiter's Elimination List developed by the Quaker Oats Company of Chicago.

1. From your own interview experiences, can you add further advice?
2. How prepared should the interviewee be for the interview?

---

times with good reason. Some organizations, such as the U.S. Marine Corps, certain fraternities, and some religious orders, maintain that demeaning, humbling, or debasing newcomers will "increase the perceived value of membership . . . and help them acquire the appropriate attitudes and behaviors."[23] Meanwhile, certain businesses believe that "a lowering of individual self-comfort and self-complacency promotes openness toward accepting the organization's norms and values,"[24] and many workers consider a certain amount of beginning discomfort part of paying one's dues. Nevertheless, not all workplaces believe in subjecting their newcomers to trials by fire. To teach members what behavior is acceptable, what the organization expects of them, and what its other members accept as their values, norms, and beliefs, law firms utilize three **socialization processes.** The first two, orientation and training and development, mostly apply to new employees (though we should keep in mind that continuing professional development is essential to top performance within a firm). The third process, performance appraisal (which we will examine in detail in Chapter 8), pertains to veterans and novices alike.

Orientation

Orientation is the process, often in program form, by which an organization introduces new members to their jobs and to the organization itself. The key to effective organization programs, which attempt to reduce adjustment anxieties and problems by creating a sense of security, confidence, and belonging, is moderation.[25] While those in charge of orientation should inform newcomers unequivocally about what the firm considers most important and provide them with position-specific instructions, effective orientation neither under- nor overwhelms with too little or too much information. Nor does an effective program overload the new arrival with forms to complete, and newcomers should receive assignments that are neither too hard nor too menial.[25] Finally, since the first impressions that an initiate forms in a new workplace are as potent as the ones he or she formed during the interview process and can have a lasting effect on his or her life within the firm, the entire staff should be prepared to participate in the orientation process. As Mary Ann Altman and Robert Weil note, introductions are essential to promoting a newcomer's comfort and sense of belonging:

> The first step is to introduce a new employee to the entire office, attorneys as well as clerical staff. Everyone should be as careful as possible to make the introduction to the office personnel cheerful and pleasant. If the size of the firm makes a personal introduction with all other employees impractical, a few key employees should meet the new staff member, and other employees should be instructed to make every effort to introduce themselves as time permits.[27]

For certain new hires, such as new associates, a firm might use a memo (see Figure 7–2) to supplement formal introductions and to inform those not in the newcomer's work unit of his or her arrival in the firm and what his or her role will be.

FIGURE 7–2
A Memo to Welcome New Hires

MEMORANDUM

TO: All RDM&B Personnel
FROM: Peter Kehoe, Executive Director
DATE: September 20, 1992
RE: New Hires

We are pleased to welcome Attorney Patricia M. Rapinchuk and Paralegal Kathy Olsen to RDM&B. I have enclosed both of their resumés for your review and invite your close attention. Both Pat and Kathy have exceptionally broad backgrounds which can benefit all members of the firm.

> Pat comes to us following a very prestigious clerkship with Chief Judge Antoinette L. Dupont of the Connecticut Appellate Court. Many of you remember Pat from her stint here with us as a law clerk, following her first year of law school. After her second year, she served as a legal intern in the Northwestern District Attorney's office in Hampshire County. Pat also worked for the Hartford firm of Blume & Elbaum where she worked in the areas of medical malpractice and civil rights. Of particular interest to the business lawyers is Pat's background with BayBank, where she began as a management trainee and worked her way up to assistant vice president in the Amherst branch. Her six years of practical, hands-on experience in banking will be of great use to many of our clients. Pat lives in Florence and helps us achieve two of our firm goals: a greater presence in Hampshire County, and a better means of servicing our Connecticut connections, since she has passed the bar in both Massachusetts and Connecticut.

> Paralegal Kathy Olsen has recently completed her master of science degree in geography at the University of Massachusetts in Amherst, where she specialized in land use policy. Her broad background in planning law, land and water policy analysis, intergovernmental relations and knowledge of state and federal funding sources can greatly benefit many of our business clients. She also has much to offer to our recent expansion of our environmental law services that we offer our real estate, business, municipal and other clients. Kathy has worked closely lately with Attorney Bob Cunningham to service our burgeoning condominium practice. She began her career as a secretary and has worked for several law firms in the Philadelphia area while she was earning her bachelor of arts degree, with honors, from Villanova University.

> I am confident that each of you will join me in welcoming them to the firm.

SOURCE: Reprinted courtesy of Robinson, Donovan, Madden & Barry, P.C., Springfield, Massachusetts.

Two additional elements that are essential to orientation in many firms are procedures manuals and handbooks, both of which provide newcomers (as well as established employees) with essential information and help to clarify the firm's expectations.

The Firm Procedures Manual. Often used in training, supervision, and evaluation, a procedures manual (previously discussed in Chapter 5) describes policies and methods for performing routine activities at all levels of a firm. The manual typically covers procedures for scheduling depositions, processing mail, filing, using office equipment, scheduling depositions, billing, docketing, making copies, using the firm's library, determining request priorities, word processing, and other activities. Besides describing procedures, the manual normally will outline the firm's policies regarding topics such as work overload and conflicts, social relationships, contact with the public, client relations, how to handle errors, and smoking. In addition, the manual may describe specialized procedures for conducting business in certain areas of the law and provide samples of forms specially adapted for the firm's use.[28]

The Firm Handbook. Unlike the procedures manual, which describes methods for performing typical firm activities, the law firm handbook outlines the firm's policies, rules, and procedures regarding employment and life within the firm. For example, a handbook section on personnel policies would include information on topics such as salary, vacation time and personal days, holidays, sick leave, bonuses, lunch and break periods, and outside employment. However, although most of the topics that the handbook covers apply to all employees, specific information within each topic typically will apply either to professionals or to support staff, and all members should observe these distinctions carefully. Larger firms may provide different handbooks for different groups of employees. A support staff handbook, for example, might describe regulations governing the operation of the firm's reception area and outline policies regarding overtime, working hours, tardiness, and absences for the firm's secretaries, clerks, bookkeepers, and other nonlawyer personnel.

Training and Development

Training and development is the process of teaching employees new skills and increasing their knowledge in order to improve their job performance. Although law firms traditionally have used both on- and off-the-job training to educate new members and to augment the skills and update the legal knowledge of support staff, training and development takes place on all levels.

General Training. Increasingly, firms are meeting their needs for people with nonlegal skills by training associates, partners, and nonlawyer personnel rather than hiring specialists or additional support staff. Training for professional and support staff personnel has always centered around professional development or continuing education, workshops, conferences, and training sessions in particular fields. Now, many firms also offer training programs to assist all of their personnel with professional, technical, and interpersonal skills, such as computer knowledge, writing skills, delegation and leadership skills, planning strategies, time management, stress management, interviewing, conflict resolution, negotiation skills (including strategies for dealing with difficult people), and marketing skills. Some firms assign newcomers to mentors in the form of junior partners, department coordinators or chairs, or the most competent personnel in the beginner's work unit, a contemporary practice based on the ancient Greek example of Mentor, a loyal friend of Odysseus, who taught and watched over Odysseus's son, Telemachus, while Odysseus was fighting and returning home from the Trojan War.

Training New Lawyers. In-house training for new associates presents two primary challenges for human resource managers and the law firm itself: that of providing suitably distinctive and respectful treatment for the new professional and that of developing a training program that is effective and affordable. Most firms are understandably wary of formal training programs for new associates. As Gerry Malone and Donald Akins note, such programs are apt to be a morass of

> ... law school professors on staff to handle the training programs, development of videotape programs, professionals being brought in to teach personal skills, innumerable nonbillable lawyer hours devoted to training, and astronomical budgets ...[29]

A firm can develop beneficial in-house training by accurately assessing and listing the qualities and skills it needs in a new associate, designing the training program to address its specific goals for the new associate, and devising a mechanism that can provide ongoing feedback regarding the new associate's contributions.

Training Paralegals. Many firms leave the training of paralegals to the paralegals' supervising attorney. Because of time and other pressures on supervising attorneys, such training often consists of nothing more than an open-door policy in which paralegals simply request of the supervising attorney whatever specific information their attorneys happen to need.[30] Law firms that employ paralegal coordinators, supervisors, or managers can provide more thorough training for paralegals while absolving harried supervising attorneys of the responsibility for such training. Some firms also hire training specialists or supplement their in-house training with the help of consultants, videos, seminars, and materials and advice from professional associations.

Compensating

Working necessitates an exchange between an organization and its members. In return for doing what the organization legitimately requests, workers agree to a certain type and amount of compensation. **Compensating** is the act of giving employees pay, incentives, and benefits in exchange for their time and productivity.

Workers attach three basic meanings to compensation. The first is economic: monetary compensation helps people to obtain necessities, as well as the luxuries and security they desire. The second meaning is psychosocial, arising from the sense of accomplishment that workers gain from pay and other work returns, such as title and status. The third meaning that workers associate with compensation is personal. For many people, compensation reflects achievement and indicates the success with which they have utilized their abilities. We all expect something for our labor, rewards that successful executive Max DePree calls the "participative premises":

> What is it that most of us really want from work? We would like to find the most effective, most productive, most rewarding way of working together. We would like to know that our work process uses all of the most appropriate and pertinent resources: human, physical, financial. We would like a work process and relationships that meet our personal needs for belonging, for contributing, for meaningful work, for the opportunity to make a commitment, for the opportunity to grow and be at least in reasonable control of our own destinies. Finally, we'd like someone to say "Thank you!"[31]

Since compensation is one of the primary functions of human resource management, those in charge of a law firm's human resources need to understand the kinds of rewards that workers expect for their contributions. We can divide these inducements into the intrinsic rewards known as *psychic salary* and the extrinsic compensation that consists of monetary rewards and employee benefits.

Psychic Salary

Though management experts cannot seem to agree on the role of monetary compensation in determining satisfaction and productivity, they do see a clear link between a worker's sense of on-the-job worth and his or her loyalty to an organization. We can loosely define **psychic salary** as the sense of satisfaction that results from a worker's perceptions of his or her personal worth to an organization, the value of his or her contributions, and the value that the organization places on its workers' morale and on the quality of the working environment, as revealed by the quality of relationships within the organization, especially those between superiors and their subordinates. We might say that the highest psychic salaries go to those who most honestly believe that their presence in an organization makes a positive difference. "The best people working for organizations are like volunteers," says Max DePree. "Since they could probably find good jobs in any number of groups, they choose to work somewhere for reasons less tangible than salary or position."[32] As we will see in the extensive discussion of motivation in Chapter 10, not all workers consider money a prime motivator. Those whose monetary needs are well taken care of are more apt to emphasize the importance of psychic salary and the voluntary nature of their association with an organization than those struggling to maintain a decent standard of living, honor important family responsibilities, or make backbreaking tuition payments.[33] Since retention is always less costly than turnover, the stability of a law firm depends on its ability to retain good help. Managers who wish to retain workers who are not simply slaves to monetary obligations must promulgate policies and programs that will promote worker satisfaction and provide the kind of psychic compensation that will enable them to attract, motivate, and keep good people.[34]

Extrinsic Compensation

Extrinsic compensation consists largely of the tangible rewards that organizations offer in the form of pay plans and fringe benefits. Pay plans are of two types. **Wages** are monetary amounts that the firm pays hourly workers for each hour they work. **Salaries** are set amounts of money that the firm pays non-hourly workers usually either weekly or biweekly. The effective management of extrinsic compensation enables a law firm to fulfill the following objectives:

To Acquire and Keep Competent Workers. Managing all aspects of employee pay is critical to attracting and retaining good workers. At the new hire end of the pay process, for example, carefully calculated initial salary offers represent some of the firm's most valuable bargaining chips, since potential newcomers who are shopping for a workplace consider salary offers as a sign of a firm's enthusiasm.

To Ensure Equity. As the primary form of extrinsic compensation, pay above all must seem equitable, internally as well as externally. Within the firm, workers need to perceive their pay as similar to that of other workers performing similar jobs. Externally, workers must believe that their pay is more or less in line with the going rate for people in like positions in other firms. When making pay decisions, human resource managers can gain a clear idea of the going rate by surveying wage and salary practices in similar firms nearby or within a given region, or by obtaining survey information from bar associations or professional groups, such as the Association of Legal Administrators. In addition, they can base equitable pay scales on the education that a position requires, the responsibility involved, a worker's years of service, performance evaluations, and any other criteria the firm considers important.[35] Again, equity is essential. Aside from the fact that seemingly arbitrary or otherwise unfair pay policies can cause poor morale, friction among workers, low productivity, and lower firm profits, law firms whose pay practices are judged unfair can be subject to severe legal sanctions. We will examine laws that regulate pay practices in law firms and other organizations later in this chapter.

To Reward Exceptional Work. Through effective compensation management, a law firm can offer the types of recognition and reward that not only encourage good workers to stay but inspire them to continue their top-notch efforts. To recognize the exceptional efforts of non-partner attorneys, for example, a law firm might establish new categories of attorneys and differentiate pay according to those categories, rather than lumping all nonpartner, non-associate attorneys under a single title at a single rate of pay. *The Lawyer's Almanac 1992* lists firms that have devised new attorney categories, such as staff attorney, permanent associate/senior attorney (also known as counsel or special counsel), non-equity partner, and provisional partner.[36]

To Control Costs. The careful management of compensation enables a firm to better track its expenditures and to judge more accurately whether it is getting its money's worth from its personnel.

Partner Compensation

Though the management of compensation for a firm's nonpartner personnel requires careful work, determining partner compensation is even more like walking on eggshells. As legal profession management consultants Bradford Hildebrandt and Jack Kaufman observe, the topic "that creates the greatest amount of debate, animosity, and upheaval in a large number of firms is profit distribution."[37] To satisfy partners (and to prevent nonpartners from crying foul), law firms follow four basic methods in distributing partner income:

Equal Distributions. Drawing on the belief that partners' contributions are approximately equal, this compensation technique, common among smaller firms, distributes profits evenly among a firm's partners.

Lockstep Systems. A firm can also base partner compensation on a system of lockstep increases by which partners in the same age group or at relatively the same level of experience receive identical percentage increases at the same time.

Seniority Systems. Another distribution method awards increases according to how long a partner has been with the firm. Those who have contributed the most time receive the largest shares of profit.

Formula Systems. Firms often create formulas to determine equitable allocations of profit. Under one such formula, a firm credits a partner with the hours for which he or she has billed and, after deducting overhead costs, allocates to the partner a percentage of the fees resulting from those billed hours. Other formulas combine lockstep and equal distribution systems, thereby allowing a firm to distribute profits and establish partner percentages at its discretion. Still other formulas take into account factors beside fees and profitability. One such formula credits partners for performing partner-approved work that benefits the firm, such as management or marketing activities; others consider a partner's efforts to attract new business, retain clients, assist the firm with technical concerns, and participate in bar association, community, and professional activities.

Fringe Benefits

Fringe benefits are financial benefits that employers offer in addition to salaries, wages, and incentives. Because of sizable increases in the costs of such benefits over the past few years, the term *fringe* is really no longer accurate. A 1986 study by the U.S. Chamber of Commerce showed that companies that paid an average yearly salary of $26,165 spent $10,283 on fringe benefits for each worker, well over one-third of total pay.[38] As the costs of health care benefits continue to rise, they represent an ever-increasing portion of an employee's total salary.

Mandatory Benefits. Some benefits, such as Social Security and unemployment insurance, are mandatory for all workers. Congress mandated unemployment insurance in 1935, providing benefits to those who lost their jobs through no fault of their own. In 1985, COBRA (the Consolidated Omnibus Budget Reconciliation Act) mandated that employers with over twenty employees must offer extended health care coverage to three groups, provided that the members of those groups pay the premiums for such coverage: employees who quit voluntarily or involuntarily, except those terminated for gross misconduct; the dependent children and widowed or divorced spouses of current or former employees; and retirees who, along with their spouses, have no other health coverage. The extended coverage lasts from eighteen to thirty-six months, during which time the employer cannot charge the former employee (or his or her dependents) premiums greater than 102 percent of the employer's costs for insuring a similar current employee. In addition to Social Security, unemployment insurance, and COBRA, legislation is currently being proposed that would make child care mandatory.

Insurance Benefits. Employees have come to expect insurance to accompany compensation, and although employers are under no obligation to do so, over 94 percent of U.S. firms offer some form of medical benefits. In 1990, over forty-seven percent of these employers offered full hospitalization, major medical, and surgical coverage, and fifty-one percent provided long-term disability coverage.[39] In addition, many employers offer life insurance, disability insurance, dental and eye care plans, and long-term care insurance.

Retirement Benefits. Increased life spans and a falling sense of obligation toward elderly family members have made putting money aside for one's postretirement years an ongoing concern of American workers in the twentieth century. Congress passed the Social Security Act of 1935 to help those who were unable to provide for their later years. Employers and employees make relatively equal contributions to this fund, and to date, at least, all workers who have adequately contributed are eligible for monthly payments in their later years. Employers or professional associations may also offer **retirement or pension plans** under which the employer or the association provides a certain amount of retirement income to workers or arranges to withhold income from an active worker's pay and to return the money in the form of periodic payments after he or she retires.[40]

Other Fringe Benefits. Just as they have come to count on insurance benefits, workers have come to expect vacations, sick time, personal days, and paid holidays; and even though they are not obliged to offer these time benefits (just as they need not provide medical coverage), many employers do. In 1986, workers received an average of 8.8 vacation days after one year of service; after 10 years, 15.8 days.[41] The number of days that firms allow employees for health concerns (either physical or mental) vary greatly; some firms have simply replaced "sick days" with "personal time/days" or "personal leave days," thereby removing the need to question whether someone who calls in sick really is sick, has urgent family or personal business to look after, or simply wants a day off. Other firms, adopting what human resources writer Frank E. Kuzmits identifies as no-fault absenteeism policies, define absences nonjudgmentally as "time missed from work."[42] Late arrivals and early departures are counted as half an absenteeism, and a failure to call entitles the firm to count one day of missed time as two. In terms of benefits in other areas, some firms offer their workers tuition funds for professional development, loans, personal computers, free legal services, parking reimbursement, and even sabbaticals and leaves of absence, during which the employee retains benefits and has the firm's guarantee that a position will be available upon his or her return. The firm's top members also receive a form of fringe benefits known as **perks,** or **perquisites:** benefits to which a person is entitled by reason of his or her status or position.

LEGAL CONSTRAINTS

Despite the efforts of those in business and industry to exclude it from their affairs, the government has become a major player in a process that was once a private dialogue between labor and management. James Ledvinka and Vida Scarpello, experts on federal regulations governing human resources, explain:

> Employee rights were not unheard of before the 1970s, but they were not commonplace. Employees covered by a union contract have always had certain rights, and government employees have enjoyed merit system protections for most of this century. But those exceptions accounted for only a minority of the work force, and the rights they had were more modest than the rights conferred in the past two decades. For the majority of employees before then, management power was nearly absolute, particularly in hiring and firing. Essentially, management had the right to discipline or discharge an employee "for good cause, for no cause, or even for cause morally wrong." Considered in that light, the changes brought about by recent legal developments are momentous indeed.[43]

Government regulations now control aspects of employment in all organizations. These legal constraints sometimes protect workers, sometimes organizations, and sometimes labor organizations. Labor law performs four major functions that are of significance to workers: it defends employee rights, protects them from discrimination, oversees their health and safety, and safeguards against sexual harassment.

Safeguarding Employee Rights

The government's gradual involvement in business dates back to the late 1800s. Less than twenty years after the Civil War, the United States Department of the Interior established the Bureau of Labor and the Bureau of Labor Statistics. In 1903, the Bureau of Labor became the Department of Commerce and Labor, which in turn became two departments, the present-day Department of Commerce and Department of Labor (which includes the Bureau of Labor Statistics), in 1913. The Great Depression gave rise to the first major legislation to provide for workers' rights, including the right to form unions and to bargain collectively, and, as we have seen, the Social Security Act of 1935 created a benefits system for retirees, as well as for their survivors and the disabled. Three years later, in 1938, the Fair Labor Standards Act established minimum wage provisions and required employers to pay workers one and one-half times their normal wages for work beyond their regular hours. In businesses large and small, this emphasis on workers' rights awakened a sense of caution that persists in the 1990s. In order to contend with the modern multitudes of federal and state laws that protect employee privacy rights (by governing, among other things, the use of lie detector tests, AIDS testing, drug testing, and the release of information from personnel files) and dozens of other prerogatives, human relations managers must handle employees with even more than reasonable care. As Ledvinka and Scarpello warn,

> . . . legal developments have made many of the traditional ways of handling people illegal. Managing people is something that most managers think they can do. Today, however, legal restrictions make it risky for managers to rely solely on their common sense; legal knowledge is necessary as well.[44]

Protecting against Discrimination

In the 1960s, civil rights activists paved the way for antidiscrimination legislation that would protect the rights of millions of workers. Throughout the sixties and seventies, Congress passed laws to provide equitable pay for women; to eliminate discrimination based on gender, race, religion, national origin, and age; and to safeguard the employment rights of veterans, women, and the handicapped. Table 7–3 summarizes the major U.S. employment laws, several of which we will examine in the following paragraphs.

Wages and the Equal Pay Act of 1963

Not until the late 1950s did women attain positions at the upper levels of law firms. The more women became visibly part of the legal practice, however, the more obvious became the pay inequities between male and female lawyers. In response to highly publicized cases that emphasized the plight of women receiving significantly less pay than their male counterparts for doing

TABLE 7-3
The Major Employment Laws and Mandates

Year	Law	Purpose
1963	Equal Pay Act	Mandates equal pay for men and women for jobs of comparable worth.
1964	Title VII of the Civil Rights Act	Prohibits discrimination on the basis of race, religion, color, gender, or national origin.
1965, 1967	Executive Orders 11246 & 11375	Prohibit discrimination based on race, color, religion, gender, or national origin; require affirmative action on the part of employers.
1967	Age Discrimination in Employment Act (amended in 1978 and 1986)	Prohibits discrimination against workers over the age of forty and restricts mandatory age requirements, except in cases where age is a bona fide occupational qualification.
1972	Equal Employment Opportunity Act	Amends Title VII of the Civil Rights Act of 1964 by providing for the Equal Employment Opportunity Commission, which oversees compliance with Title VII.
1973, 1974	Vocational Rehabilitation Act and the Rehabilitation Act of 1974	Prohibit discrimination against the handicapped.
1974	Vietnam Era Veteran's Readjustment Act	Prohibits discrimination against all disabled veterans with a 30 percent or more disability rating, veterans discharged or released because of service-related disabilities, and Vietnam-era veterans (on active duty at any time between 5 August 1964 and 7 May 1975).
1978	Pregnancy Discrimination Act	Prohibits discrimination against pregnant women.
1984	Retirement Equity Act	Assures retirement benefits to a divorced spouse.
1986	Immigration Reform and Control Act	Penalizes employers who hire illegal aliens and prohibits discrimination based on national origin or citizenship.
1986	Age Discrimination Amendment	Removed the age-seventy cap on mandatory retirement.
1990	Americans with Disabilities Act	Requires reasonable accommodations for the disabled.
1990	Older Workers Benefit Protection Act	Protects fringe benefits of older workers.

the same work, Congress passed the Equal Pay Act of 1963, which, like the Civil Rights Act of 1964, threatened law firms and other organizations with litigation if their pay and promotion policies were found to be discriminatory.

Although both the Equal Pay Act and the Civil Rights Act affected all fields, they had the greatest impact on professions that were traditionally male dominated. Specifically, the Equal Pay Act requires any organization with two or more employees to pay the same wages to women as it does to men for *substantially equal* work or for work that requires comparable skills, effort, responsibility, and working conditions. This concept of **comparable worth** stresses that an organization pay similarly for jobs that are of equal worth to the organization, as determined by the knowledge, skills, and competencies those jobs require. Pay differences can be based only on seniority, merit, or the quality or quantity of work. "Comparable worth pressure," writes Rosabeth Moss Kanter, "is just the tip of a quiet revolution occurring in pay practice."[45] In addition to federal legislation like the Equal Pay Act, many state and local laws now provide for pay equity.[46]

The Civil Rights Act of 1964

While the country was still mourning the death of John F. Kennedy, Congress passed the Civil Rights Act of 1964, also called *Title VII of the Civil Rights Act of 1964*. As amended by the Equal Opportunity Act of 1972, Title VII, which applies to almost all organizations that have fifteen or more employees, forbids discrimination in all areas of employer-employee relations. Section 703A of the act states that

> It is unlawful for an employer to discriminate against an individual with respect to his compensation, terms, conditions, or privileges of employment because of such in-

dividual's race, color, religion, sex, or national origin; or to limit, segregate, or classify his employees in any way which would deprive or tend to deprive any individual of employment opportunities or otherwise adversely affect his status as an employee, because of such an individual's race, color, religion, sex, or national origin.[47]

Compliance. Title VII lists unfair employment practices and provides specific guidelines regarding the employment practices that are exempt from its enforcement. These *bona fide occupational qualifications (BFOQs),* which we encountered earlier in the section on screening applicants, are the legitimate reasons (*bona fide* being Latin for "good faith") an employer can use to exclude from employment those whom the act would protect otherwise. The Equal Employment Opportunity Commission (EEOC), created by the Equal Employment Opportunity Act of 1972, oversees compliance with Title VII. In screening and interviewing potential employees, employers must be careful that the information they require on application forms and the questions they ask during interviews do not indicate discriminatory attitudes or practices. Only after the actual time of hiring (the **point of hire**) may the employer ask for information regarding topics that were prohibited earlier. For example, only after the point of hire may employers request photographs or information about the applicant's race, religion, or national origin. After obtaining this information, the employer should keep it in a separate file if there is any chance that it might be used in making discriminatory decisions, such as promotions.

Affirmative Action. Of all the policies resulting from Title VII, the most far-reaching is affirmative action. Mandated specifically by Executive Order 11246 of 1965 (which was amended by Executive Order 11375 in 1967 and updated in turn by Executive Order 11478 in 1979), **affirmative action** requires employers to take positive steps to hire and promote women, minorities, the handicapped, and workers in other protected classes in order to compensate for past discriminatory practices. Employers may establish affirmative action programs voluntarily; the courts can also order them to do so. Among other things, such programs may require employers to recruit employees from underrepresented groups, promote changes in management attitudes, remove obstacles that support discrimination, or provide preferential treatment (the most controversial form of affirmative action).[48]

Religion and Reasonable Accommodation(s). Title VII prohibits discrimination based on religion and entitles workers to "reasonable accommodation(s)" for their religious beliefs. What "reasonable accommodation(s)" actually means has proven difficult to determine, however; and since employers may not ask questions about religion prior to the point of hire, the specific accommodation(s) a worker might need may be impossible to guess. Broadly, Title VII does not require employers to allow workers complete religious freedom if doing so would interfere with normal business operations or especially if it would cause other workers "undue hardship." From another perspective, the word *reasonable* implies that accommodation(s) should subject an employer to little additional cost.[49] Although the standards are not yet clear, employers can accommodate workers' religious beliefs by allowing them some flexibility through regular work scheduling policies and by arranging compensatory time off that does not conspicuously disrupt the organization's everyday operations.

The Age Discrimination in Employment Act

An additional unfair practice that the federal government needed to confront was that of discrimination against the older worker. Through the Age Discrimination in Employment Act of 1967, Congress aimed to protect workers aged forty years and older from discrimination in hiring, promotion, discharge, pay decisions, qualification for fringe benefits, and other practices. A 1978 amendment of this law raised the age of mandatory retirement from sixty-five to seventy.

Laws Regarding Handicapped Employees

The primary laws regarding the treatment of handicapped employees are Section 504 of the Vocational Rehabilitation Act of 1973 and the Americans with Disabilities Act of 1990, both of which define as handicapped any individual

> ... who has a physical or mental impairment that substantially limits one or more of that individual's major life activities, has a record of such an impairment, or is regarded as having such an impairment—even if he or she does not, in fact, have such an impairment.

(An example of the latter would be a former cancer patient who is now considered cured.) Narrower in scope than the Americans with Disabilities Act and harder to enforce, Section 504 of the Vocational Rehabilitation Act obliges the Office of Civil Rights to protect from discriminatory employment practices any person who is physically challenged or impaired by some condition that "substantially limits" his or her ability to perform the "essential functions" of a job.[50] The Americans with Disabilities Act, by comparison, instructs employers of larger organizations to make "reasonable accommodations" for disabled workers, provided these accommodations don't cause the employer what the law recognizes as "undue hardship."[51] Hardship may result from many factors, all of which the courts nonetheless must examine and accept. For example, an employer may make a case for undue hardship based on the costs and nature of accommodating the handicapped person; the size, function, and structure of the workforce that the accommodation would affect; the number, type, location, and independence of the firm's facilities; and the impact on the financial and human resources of the firm. Despite the fact that the Americans with Disabilities Act specifically excludes a number of conditions, including homosexuality, transvestism, sexual disorders, compulsive gambling, kleptomania, pyromania, and psychoactive substance use disorders,[52] the law, as Margaret Hart Edwards, writing in the ALA News, indicates, is pervasive:

> Law firms should not assume that the ADA is for their clients, not them. Law students with disabilities will be looking at firms' compliance. In addition, the EEOC has approved the use of "testers," individuals who pose as applicants for employment. Finally, advocacy groups for individuals with handicaps will be active in the enforcement of the ADA.[53]

Laws Regarding Veterans

The Vietnam Era Veteran's Readjustment Act of 1974 prohibits employers from discriminating against all disabled veterans with a 30 percent or more disability rating, veterans discharged or released because of service-related disabilities, and Vietnam-era veterans (defined as those who were on active duty at any time between 5 August 1964 and 7 May 1975). Section 402 of the act requires organizations that accept federal contracts to provide evidence of affirmative action regarding Vietnam-era veterans, who are to receive job counseling, training, and placement services.

Laws Regarding Sex-Plus and Parenting Discrimination

One form of employment discrimination results not just from an employee's being a woman, but from some of the potential *consequences* of being a woman: pregnancy, childbirth, and related conditions. This *sex-plus discrimination*[54] leads employers to not hire or promote women because of their child care responsibilities, because their spouses might be moved, or because they are pregnant. The Pregnancy Discrimination Act of 1978 (PDA), an amendment to the Civil Rights Act, requires that women workers who are "affected by pregnancy, childbirth, or related medical conditions will be treated the same for all employment-related purposes."[55] The effect of this law is that employers use the same policies for women who become pregnant as they use for other kinds of personal leave or medical disabilities. This act also requires worker medical insurance to provide pregnant employees with the same kind of coverage available for those with long-term disabilities. In addition, some states require employers to provide maternity leave and to reinstate women in their jobs at the same pay when they return to work. For businesses with more than 50 employees, federal legislation now mandates up to three months of unpaid leaves of absence for parenting leaves for both mothers and fathers, for adoptions, and for sick care of family members. Some law firms, such as the Boston firm of Goodwin, Procter & Hoar, offer on-site back-up child care centers.[56] Other common accommodations include day-care consultants to help firm members research child care options, voucher systems for day-care costs, and flextime or part-time schedules for parents.[57] Table 7–4 lists the percentages of law firms providing certain types of parenting policies in 1989.

Worker Health and Safety

It is easier to think of the health and safety issues that affect workers in large industrial plants or settings that seem likely to present a physical threat. No work setting is immune from health and safety issues, however, not even the professional setting of a law firm. **Health** is a person's general state of physical, mental, and emotional wellness. **Safety** is the process of assuring physical security and protection. Providing a safe and healthy environment is an employer's obligation.

TABLE 7–4
Law Firm Parenting Policies

Percent	Policy
41	Provide paid maternity leave.
29	Allow additional unpaid maternity leave.
11	Are willing to arrange part-time work schedules for new mothers during the first year following the birth of a child.
8	Allow long-term, part-time schedules after one year following a birth.
32	Pay pregnancy-related health benefits, even if maternity leave itself is unpaid.
6	Allow paid paternity leaves.

SOURCE: "Parenting Policies in Law Firms," The 1989 Survey of Law Firm Economics, *The Altman & Weil Report to Legal Management* 15, no. 11 (August 1989): 1–2.

The Occupational Safety and Health Act

In 1970, contemporary and past examples of businesses scandalously ignoring health and safety standards led Congress to pass the Occupational Safety and Health Act, a law designed to "assure so far as possible every working man or woman in the Nation safe and healthful working conditions and to preserve our human resources."[58]

Enforcement. The task of enforcing the Occupational Safety and Health Act falls to the Occupational Safety and Health Administration (OSHA). OSHA holds employers responsible for knowing about and informing their employees of the health and safety standards that the agency promulgates, and OSHA agents investigate alleged health and safety violations. Employers may contest the administration's decisions through the Occupational Health and Safety Review Commission.

Hazards. The "right to know" standard of OSHA provides all employees with the right to be informed of any suspected threat to their well-being.[59] Under very specific conditions, workers also have the right to refuse unsafe work. Most OSHA guidelines seem to refer to industrial settings, but some areas of safety and well-being are universal. Technology, for instance, has brought with it a variety of office hazards. In law firms, word processors and computer operators have occasionally suffered *VDT (video display terminal) syndrome,* a malady that associates dizziness, eye strain, headaches, backaches, and muscle spasms with continuous computer use. Another ailment common among long-term computer users and others who perform continuous repetitive hand motions such as typing, tapping, twisting, or gripping is *carpal tunnel syndrome,* which can lead to inflammation and painful hard growths around the bones and tendons of the wrist.[60] User-friendly workstation designs and the proper pacing of work can help to alleviate these syndromes, the specific causes of which have yet to be determined.[61]

Employee Assistance Programs

Many law firms, aware of the role they play in their employees' well-being, now offer **employee assistance programs,** or **(EAPs),** which act as liaisons between professional counseling or social service agencies and employees with emotional, physical, or personal problems.

Benefits of EAPs. EAP can provide law firm management and their employees easy access to professional help and around-the-clock crisis intervention. Through EAPs, professional counselors can provide employees with short or long-term counseling services and educational programs.[62] When first established, EAPs primarily facilitated access to drug and alcohol abuse counseling. They now provide a wide variety of counseling services, such as help with occupational stresses, family and marital difficulties, substance abuse, eating disorders, and financial problems.[63]

Using EAPs. Even the best EAP is of no benefit if no one takes advantage of it, and employees sometimes seem stubbornly unwilling to seek help for their problems. Nonetheless, a law firm must be very careful in approaching a member's personal problem from a work-related angle, even when the problem is apparent. For instance, in holding a disciplinary conference with an employee who obviously has an alcohol problem, the law firm is not allowed to accuse the worker of alcoholism, to ask the worker if he or she has a problem with alcohol, or to state that the firm suspects that the worker has a problem with alcohol. The firm must base all of its comments on work-related observations and document these comments through performance records that reflect attendance problems, tardiness, and shoddy, careless, or uncompleted work.[64]

ANOTHER LOOK

Dealing with Sexual Harassment

Daniel Goleman, a writer for *The New York Times,* describes the picture emerging from research on sexual harassment:

> It has less to do with sex than with power. It is a way to keep women in their place; through harassment, men devalue a woman's role in the workplace by calling attention to her sexuality. "Sexual harassment is a subtle rape, and rape is more about fear than sex.... Harassment is a way for a man to make a woman vulnerable."

Writing in *The National Law Journal,* Rita Henley Jensen and Rorie Sherman comment:

> Many female attorneys who believe they are suffering sexual harassment at their workplace simply move out and keep quiet, just as Anita Hill testified she did. At least sixty percent of the 918 female attorneys in large law firms ... reported that they had experienced unwanted sexual attention. Yet only seven percent reported the incident to management and more than half of those said nothing had happened.

If harassment is related to power issues, where are the data that tell what happens to those in the bottom levels of the law firm hierarchy? If sixty percent of the women in relatively coequal relationships with male colleagues experience harassment, what happens to the women whose power is practically nonexistent compared to that of male workers? Cynthia Crossen, a staff reporter for *The Wall Street Journal,* believes that

> because men still hold so much power in business and politics—and women are trying so hard to get it—those relationships are often charged with fear or anger. Most women say that if men held no sway over them, it would be simple to dispose of their unwanted advances.

We can conclude that Anita Hill, who, in 1991, had remained silent for nearly a decade before confronting then-Supreme Court justice nominee Clarence Thomas with allegations of sexual harassment, is not unique: because of a lack of power or out of fear for their careers, few women are able to complain about sexual harassment. Most women blame themselves, thinking they may have done something to invite sexually oriented attention. According to Crossen, they remain silent also because they "feel a responsibility to be emotional managers of relationships and often want to keep things friendly."

Goleman cites ten observations from Dr. Louise Fitzgerald, a psychologist at the University of Illinois, regarding how women deal with on-the-job harassment. The victim of harassment might *detach* herself from the situation, thereby minimizing it. She might *deny* the harassment, *relabel* the behavior as flattering, or convince herself that she has somehow caused the situation and therefore *controls* it. She might *endure* the harassment quietly or try to *appease* the harasser; on the other hand, she might *confront* the harasser and make it clear that the behavior is unwarranted and unwelcome. The victim might *seek professional help* by reporting the harassment or look for *social support* among her friends. Finally, she might *avoid* further harassment by quitting her job.

SOURCE: Daniel Goleman, "Sexual Harassment: It's About Power, Not About Sex," *The New York Times* (22 October 1991): C1, C12; Rita Henley Jensen and Rorie Sherman, "More Female Lawyers Sue," *The National Law Journal* (28 October 1991): 13; and Cynthia Crossen, "Sex and Power in the Office: Are You from Another Planet or What?" *The Wall Street Journal* (18 October 1991): B1.

---

1. How has Anita Hill's testimony changed the workplace?
2. Some say that law firms are hotbeds of sexual harassment. Comment.
3. Are women responsible for sexual harassment? Explain.

EAPs as Managerial Tools. EAPs enable law firm supervisors and other management employees to obtain professional advice for working with troubled employees, from receptionists to partners.[65] Watching a subordinate deteriorate psychologically, physically, and professionally because of a problem outside the workplace can be very painful for a supervisor. EAP professionals can help supervisors to refer troubled employees, to arrange for their participation in the program, and to convince them that they risk termination if they cannot improve their work performance.[66]

Sexual Harassment

One of the issues to which human resource managers and other law firm personnel must be most sensitive in the 1990s is sexual harassment. **Sexual harassment** consists of insinuations regarding or requests for sexual favors or any other sexually oriented and unwelcome verbal or physical conduct that causes adverse employment conditions. Sexual harassment can occur between subordinates and their superiors, between coworkers and their colleagues, or between firm members and clients or other nonemployees who work with the firm.[67] Although, to date, most sexual harassment cases have involved women bringing charges against men, men have brought charges against women or other men, and women have accused other women. The allegations that Anita Hill brought against Clarence Thomas during the October 1991 Senate hearings to approve Thomas as a justice of the Supreme Court hammered home a sharp national awareness of sexual harassment as a hierarchical superior's use of status and position to badger and control a subordinate who is relatively powerless.

Law Firms and Sexual Harassment

In October 1990, the EEOC filed its first sexual harassment complaint against a major law firm. Among other signs of the growing recognition of harassment in the law firm setting are an increasing number of acknowledged complaints and a recent *National Law Journal* poll in which more than half of the women attorneys in the survey claim to have experienced sexual harassment.[68] David Margolick and others believe that several characteristics of the legal profession, including "the long hours, frequent travel, the autonomy of law partners, the entry of large numbers of women at junior levels and the increasing unwillingness of these women to put up with treatment their predecessors endured," aggravate the problem.[69] Since most law firm subordinates are women and most superiors are men, law firms must do more than publish a policy that condemns harassment. Like other employers, law firms are responsible if they know or should have known of any violations involving sexual harassment and unless they take immediate and appropriate corrective action. Essentially, the courts have found that Title VII violations have occurred "where an employer created or condoned a substantially discriminatory work environment, regardless of whether the complaining employee lost any tangible job benefits."[70]

Forms of Sexual Harassment

Harassment takes two forms: quid pro quo harassment and hostile work environments.

Quid Pro Quo Harassment. **Quid pro quo harassment** is a form of extortion that involves offering employment-related favors such as promotions, raises, and favorable performance evaluations in exchange for sexual favors.[71]

Hostile Environment. Though not necessarily leading to a loss of pay or benefits, a **hostile environment** is a harassment-engendered working atmosphere that impairs work performance or creates intimidating, unpleasant, or offensive working conditions.[72] Such an environment is generally not the product of a single derogatory comment or incident. The courts require evidence of "a continuous or repeated pattern" of unwelcome and sexually based offense prior to finding a violation. In addition, aggrieved employees typically must show that they were both actually offended by and not unusually sensitive in reacting to the challenged conduct[73] (which can be difficult, since women as well as men tend to believe that harassed coworkers are either overreacting or crying wolf). The following Another Look provides examples of behavior that can create a hostile environment.

Preventing Sexual Harassment

Educational programs to combat sexual harassment have been initiated in many work settings, including

ANOTHER LOOK

Sexual Harassment: What's Not to Be Endured

Suggestive comments on appearance or dress.
- Why don't all women look like you!
- Gee, that sweater really shows off your figure!

Offensive media prominently displayed.
- Lewd posters, pin-ups, cartoons, centerfolds, or publications.
- A pornographic word-processing program.

Repeated, annoying, and unwelcome invitations to get together after work.

Verbal expressions and physical gestures that are sexually explicit.
- Offensive sexual flirting and propositions.
- Degrading adjectives and verbal abuse with sexual overtones.
- Jokes in bad taste.

Suggestive looks and gestures.
- He says: I gave her a big smile, joked around a bit, and patted her on the shoulder.
- She says: He leered at me, propositioned me, and fondled me.

Unwanted touch and proximity.
- Nuzzling, fondling, pinching, or leaning closely over a worker.
- Examples: One boss put his arms on his secretary while dictating, another physically cornered a worker, and another "hugged" a secretary from behind at the Xerox machine.

SOURCE: Based on Brian S. Moskal, "Sexual Harassment," *Industry Week* (3 July 1989): 22–27; and David S. Machlowitz and Marilyn M. Machlowitz, "Preventing Sexual Harassment," *ABA Journal* (1 October 1987): 78–80.

---

1. How can workers tell when kidding, flattery, and flirting have crossed the line into sexual harassment?
2. Shouldn't women know how to take a joke? Why doesn't concern over some of the above behaviors and attitudes just show that the recipient lacks a sense of humor?
3. How can those in power *know* they are sexually harassing a subordinate if the subordinate never complains?
4. Comment on this statement: Since the modern workplace is often where one meets one's mate, it is difficult for both men and women to know when to draw the line.

---

those of the naval and military forces of the United States following investigations in 1992 of a convention attended by members of an association of Navy and Marine Corps fliers known as the Tailhook Association and incidents during the Persian Gulf War that revealed a pervasive pattern of harassment. While education is key to a lasting change in attitudes, employers must take care to involve both men and women in developing educational programs lest women consider their exclusion further evidence of the employer's insensitivity. The EEOC guidelines for preventing sexual harassment in the workplace offer the following suggestions:[74]

Develop a policy regarding harassment and ensure that all employees, from the top members of the organization down, receive a copy. A law firm can circulate such a policy through employee handbooks, personnel notices, and firm-wide memos.

Create a safe reporting process and a procedure for dealing with sexual harassment within the organization. Not only must the law firm create procedures by which workers can report incidents without embarrassment or fear of retaliation, but it must also create a climate in which the behaviors reported are clearly unacceptable. Although we could make a case for holding a law firm or any other employer liable only if "it has actual knowledge of the harassment," lack of actual knowledge does not get the firm off the hook, since we may also argue that an employer is liable if "the victim in question had no reasonably available avenue for making his or her complaint known to appropriate management officials."[75]

Communicate the importance of a harassment-free work environment. The firm must instill the need to avoid harassing behavior in all of its members, especially attorneys, managers, and others in positions of power. The 1991 Hill-Thomas confrontation highlighted the effects that alleged harassment can have on both accused and accuser. Those accused of harassment often do not believe themselves guilty; usually, they are convinced that no harassment occurred since the victim of harassment did not *seem* to protest while the alleged harassment was occurring. However, silence should never be interpreted to imply consent. We must remember that harassment is a power issue. The one being harassed, who is almost always in a position of lesser power, may risk losing his or her job, ruining his or her career track, receiving poor performance evaluations, and losing out on promotions should he or she complain. In addition, reporting harassment may serve to alienate the victim from the firm's circle of communications, removing his or her access not only to work-essential information but to job opportunities as well. Psychologists tell us that those who are sexually harassed have much in common with those who are sexually abused, since victims of harassment may actually believe that they have brought the harassment upon themselves, and their sense of guilt and shame keeps them silent. The stress from such experiences can have grave effects on a victim's health, some of which may require hospitalization.

Discipline offenders, quickly, through procedures such as verbal warnings, letters of reprimand, or termination.

Identify what constitutes offensive behavior. Defining harassment is difficult, since a message that a recipient considers offensive often is more a product of tone, facial expressions, and other body language than of actual (and, directly reportable) verbal content. New York City attorney David Machlowitz and his sister Marilyn Machlowitz, president of a consulting firm for corporations and professionals, observe that "victims and accused harassers may not disagree simply on the behavior that occurred, but on its intent and meaning."[76] Though male workers might determine whether their behavior constitutes harassment simply by asking themselves whether what they are doing or saying is something they would say or do to their mothers or sisters, a law firm must teach all of its members to recognize the symptoms of sexually offensive behavior.[77]

EVALUATING HUMAN RESOURCES

A team of Harvard experts suggest 4 C's for evaluating the health and effectiveness of a human resource program: (1) the overall competence of workers, (2) the degree of congruence between the goals of employees and those of the organization, (3) employee commitment, and (4) the cost-effectiveness of the organization's human resource management.[78]

Competence

Competence, which we can define as the state of possessing the skills, knowledge, and abilities requisite to performing a job, leads to profit, and overall profitability is the foremost indicator of the success of a law firm's human resource efforts.

Congruence

As we saw in Chapter 2, goal integration is the degree to which a worker's goals match those of the firm. When a worker can silently ask why he or she should work for a particular firm and provide him- or herself with a positive answer, goals overlap and **congruence,** or agreement between the firm and the workers, is strong. On the other hand, a worker who does not believe that a firm is meeting his or her personal and professional needs for such things as recognition and respect, equitable pay, reasonable consideration, and supportive relationships, is liable to shop around for a new job, if he or she is financially able to do so.

Commitment

There are two sides to commitment: on one side is the individual's loyalty to the firm; on the other is the firm's loyalty to its members. A law firm's effort to keep motivated and productive workers is called **retention**.[79] Because salaries rise when labor is scarce, law firms that manage to find valuable personnel know the importance of retaining them, especially given predictions that warn of substantial reductions in the number of employees available in specialized fields in the very near future. But money is only one aspect of the need for retention. "Beside the cost," write Linda Marks and Karen Rinquette, "still worse is the toll that turnover, continual training and uncertainty take on firms and their clients." [80]

Retention and the Process of Cultivating Commitment

A law firm focuses retention efforts on all of its members, from senior partners to secretaries and other support staff. Although managers have found that turnover is highest among highly skilled workers and unskilled workers at the bottom of the organizational hierarchy,[81] retaining good secretaries presents a special challenge for most firms. The secretarial career is a paradoxical combination of power-behind-the-throne responsibility and cellar-level status, and many secretaries escape into new careers, within the firm as well as outside of it, whenever the opportunity presents itself. (Ironically, firms that pride themselves on their efforts to cultivate their workers' professional growth often unwittingly encourage these "escapes.") Another factor increasing the tension among legal secretaries is the presence of the relatively new paralegal field. By virtue of on-the-job training, many legal secretaries have acted as paralegals, for all practical purposes; nonetheless, the insertion of a paralegal level into the law firm hierarchy has lowered the secretarial staff one notch in terms of hierarchical rank without, in many cases, reducing its slew of responsibilities. Understandably, cultivating commitment among legal secretaries can be a delicate and challenging task. To retain its secretaries—and its other personnel as well—a law firm should try to:

Improve Morale. Morale is a state of mind regarding the work environment, a composite of feelings and attitudes usually held in common by a group of workers.[82] It is a product of people's perceptions about the most important aspects of work: compensation, supervision, the nature of the work they do, the power they share, opportunities, equity, policies and procedures, working conditions, and other members of the organization.[83] While high morale is linked with job satisfaction, research has shown that one can like one's job and not like the job setting. Nonetheless, because demoralized workers are less committed workers, law firms should do their best to bolster the perceptions that produce morale.

Create a Sense of Belonging. Feelings of alienation and isolation, even in heavily trafficked work settings, are not uncommon: the presence of others is less important than the sense of being connected to those others in a manner that makes the worker feel valued. Law firms can create this sense of belonging in many ways. Through *professional bonding,* for example, many legal administrators have assumed the personal goal of making their coworkers and subordinates realize that they are a part of a team.

Cultivate Pride in the Firm. Executive Max DePree once suggested that organizations gauge their members' pride by asking how they felt about discussing their workplace and their coworkers with their families.[84] Occasional firm-wide activities shared can help to foster that sense of pride. Parties, family picnics, firm sports teams, and other get-togethers that welcome spouses, offspring, and significant others can build strong, friendly bonds between a firm's members.

Reduce Conflicts. One major reason for leaving a workplace is not being able to stand the pressures. Law firms are notorious for pressures. When interpersonal conflicts intensify these pressures, stress can spread beyond those who are immediately involved, sending shock waves through a whole department or the entire firm. "Stress as a part of the workload can be expected and sometimes treated as a challenge," writes Wenke Brandes, legal administrator for the Naples, Florida, firm of Harter, Secrest, & Emery. "However, stress as a result of negative feelings for or about another person is often intolerable and may justifiably cause valued employees to leave." Because of this risk, law firms have a "vested interest in creating harmony and mutual respect." [85] "Being a part of a law firm can be exciting and challenging," Brandes points out. "However, when everything seems to crumble due to unrealistic deadlines, stress, and crises, it is the foundation of our relationships with the team that wins the game. And winners are happy people." [86]

Cost-Effectiveness

The final test of an effective human resource program is its cost-effectiveness. Law firms do not have unlimited budgets for even the most essential activities or needs, and they must consider carefully the long-term effects of their chosen human resource expenditures. For example, despite the initial monetary strain they create, EAPs have been found to reduce worker compensation claims, improve work quality and productivity, reduce absenteeism and turnover, and improve employee morale. In many instances, replacement costs far surpass the money a firm invests in its human resources. Nonetheless, even retraining must be analyzed to see if its economic benefits exceed its costs or if the firm is simply offering it, with no real hope of economic return, out of a sense of social responsibility.[87] The cost demands of the human resource department should reflect a proper balance, and although these expenditures are solid investments in the future of the firm, they should receive the same scrutiny as expenditures originating in any other cost center.

QUESTIONS FOR DISCUSSION AND REVIEW

1. Explain what human resources are. Why is a law office manager's effectiveness in this area critical?
2. What are the six areas of responsibility in managing a law firm's human resources?
3. Explain what the effective use of human resources implies.
4. Describe the steps and tools involved in staffing.
5. Your law firm needs an environmental law paralegal for a newly created department. You have six applications before you. Explain the steps you will take next and the questions you will want answered at each step.
6. Write five to ten questions that you as an interviewer would want to ask candidates for one of the following positions:
    a. A full-time law firm receptionist.
    b. A management information systems (MIS) coordinator.
    c. A law firm messenger.
    d. A summer associate, to be working in the litigation department.
    e. An attorney for the Elder Law department.
    f. A paralegal coordinator for the real estate division.
7. In your view, what constitutes an effective law firm training and development program? Should law firms keep training and development in-house?
8. Explain how law firms compensate their members for their contributions. What is psychic salary? Why is it a critical component of repaying workers?
9. What are the objectives human resource managers must accomplish in order to manage compensation effectively?
10. Summarize the major areas of legislation that the government uses to protect workers. In your view, are these legal constraints guidelines or controls for human resource activities?
11. Explain what sexual harassment consists of and discuss whether law firm members may be particularly susceptible. Who is responsible for ending sexual harassment? What steps should they take?
12. How can a law firm tell if its human resource program is effective?

EXPERIENTIAL EXERCISES

I. Truth in Advertising

Unless a firm uses an agency or other recruiting methods, writing job notices is a much-needed skill.
  a. Write an ad for the position of paralegal supervisor, paralegal, or legal secretary. Before writing your ad, you need to determine the exact nature of the position and the qualifications required. You next need to decide where you will find the best pool of applicants. (Will the kind of people you are trying to reach read the publication in which the ad will appear?) Next, write the ad. It should be concise

CHAPTER 7 / MANAGING HUMAN RESOURCES

but complete, describing the nature and responsibilities of the job, the qualifications required, how and where to submit a letter of application, and any other requirements a job seeker should be aware of. Keep in mind that even blind ads that use a box number for replies rather than include the name of the firm must convey the firm's professional image (most firms hire professionals to design their ads, even those that are free of logos or other graphics) and that creative ads with catchy headlines and clever openings are not the usual law firm style.

b. In your local paper, regional or state legal publications, *Legal Management, Legal Assistant Today, The Wall Street Journal,* or similar publications, locate classified ads used to recruit applicants to law firms. Rate one of the classified ads you have found according to the following scale:

    5 = Excellent/Very effective
    4 = Good
    3 = Average
    2 = Poor
    1 = Very poor/Very ineffective

5 4 3 2 1 a. Visibility of the ad.
5 4 3 2 1 b. Clarity of information regarding the nature of the job and its required qualifications.
5 4 3 2 1 c. Clarity of information regarding the responsibilities of the job.
5 4 3 2 1 d. Clarity of information regarding how to contact the firm.
5 4 3 2 1 e. Suitability of the ad to the professionalism of the job.
5 4 3 2 1 f. Suitability of information about the employer.
5 4 3 2 1 g. Suitability of publication to target audience.
5 4 3 2 1 h. Success with which the ad language reflects equal opportunity, avoids stereotyping, and is nonsexist.
5 4 3 2 1 i. Success with which the ad provides a positive image of the firm.
5 4 3 2 1 j. Use of space in the ad.
5 4 3 2 1 k. Layout and design of the ad.

Critique the ad. What would you have done differently, if anything?

II. Do You Mind If I Ask?*

Place an **A** before any questions that are acceptable or legally permissible during a job interview or as part of a job application. Place a check mark before any questions that are not permissible. Place an asterisk before any that seem stupid or rude. Which questions would you, as an interviewer, feel most uncomfortable asking? Why? What qualities render the impermissible questions illegal?

Application
____ Date of birth.
____ Spouse's name.
____ Your maiden name.

---

*SOURCE: Based on Debra Cassens Moss, " 'Why Did You Go To Law School?' and Other Questions Not to Ask Job Applicants," *ABA Journal* (1 June 1987): 78–82.

_____ Your prior married names, if any.
_____ Any physical defects?
_____ Any illnesses?
_____ Any disabilities?
_____ Have you ever been arrested?
_____ Have you ever been convicted of a crime?
_____ Did you get an honorable military discharge?
_____ Who should we contact in case of emergency?
_____ Names of credit references.

Interview
_____ How old are you?
_____ Do you have a car?
_____ What year did you graduate?
_____ What church do you go to?
_____ What organizations do you belong to?
_____ Are you married?
_____ What does your husband/wife do?
_____ If s/he gets transferred, will you also move and change your residence?
_____ Do you have any children?
_____ How many?
_____ Do you plan to have any more?
_____ How old are your children?
_____ What are the names of your children?
_____ What is your spouse's name?
_____ What does s/he think of your working for us?
_____ How will s/he feel about your getting twice as much as s/he does?
_____ When can you start?
_____ Do you think you'll fit in around here?

III. Matching the Person and the Job**

Matching the right person to the right job is a difficult challenge. Each of us differs in what we like and dislike about our jobs. The following exercise will help you to analyze what you like about work. Listed below are twelve pairs of jobs. For each pair, you are to indicate which job you would prefer, assuming that everything else about the jobs is the same.

If you would prefer the job in the left-hand column (Job A), indicate *how much* you prefer it by putting a check mark in a blank to the left of the "neutral" point. If you prefer the job in the right-hand column (Job B), check one of the blanks to the right of "neutral." Check the "neutral" blank *only* if you find the two jobs equally attractive or unattractive. Try to use the "neutral" blank rarely.

Job A		Job B
1. A job where the pay is very good.	|___|___|___|___|___| Strongly Neutral Strongly prefer A prefer B	A job where there is considerable opportunity to be creative and innovative.

**SOURCE: J. Richard Hackman and G. R. Oldman, "The Job Diagnostic Survey: An Instrument for the Diagnosis of Jobs and the Evaluation of Job Redesign Projects" from Technical Report No. 4, Cambridge, MA, 1974. Reprinted with permission of J. Richard Hackman, Cahners-Rabb Professor of Organizational Behavior and Psychology, Yale University.

2. A job where you are often required to make important decisions.
   |⎯⎯⎯|⎯⎯⎯|⎯⎯⎯|⎯⎯⎯|
   Strongly   Neutral   Strongly
   prefer A   prefer B
   A job with many pleasant people to work with.

3. A job in which greater responsibility is given to those who do the best work.
   |⎯⎯⎯|⎯⎯⎯|⎯⎯⎯|⎯⎯⎯|
   Strongly   Neutral   Strongly
   prefer A   prefer B
   A job in which greater responsibility is given to loyal employees who have the most seniority.

4. A job in an organization which is in financial trouble—and might have to close down within the year.
   |⎯⎯⎯|⎯⎯⎯|⎯⎯⎯|⎯⎯⎯|
   Strongly   Neutral   Strongly
   prefer A   prefer B
   A job in which you are not allowed to have any say whatever in how your work is scheduled, or in the procedures to be used in carrying it out.

5. A very routine job.
   |⎯⎯⎯|⎯⎯⎯|⎯⎯⎯|⎯⎯⎯|
   Strongly   Neutral   Strongly
   prefer A   prefer B
   A job where your coworkers are not very friendly.

6. A job with a supervisor who is often very critical of you and your work in front of other people.
   |⎯⎯⎯|⎯⎯⎯|⎯⎯⎯|⎯⎯⎯|
   Strongly   Neutral   Strongly
   prefer A   prefer B
   A job which prevents you from using a number of skills that you worked hard to develop.

7. A job with a supervisor who respects you and treats you fairly.
   |⎯⎯⎯|⎯⎯⎯|⎯⎯⎯|⎯⎯⎯|
   Strongly   Neutral   Strongly
   prefer A   prefer B
   A job which provides constant opportunities for you to learn new and interesting things.

8. A job where there is a real chance you could be laid off.
   |⎯⎯⎯|⎯⎯⎯|⎯⎯⎯|⎯⎯⎯|
   Strongly   Neutral   Strongly
   prefer A   prefer B
   A job with very little chance to do challenging work.

9. A job in which there is a real chance for you to develop new skills and advance in the organization.
   |⎯⎯⎯|⎯⎯⎯|⎯⎯⎯|⎯⎯⎯|
   Strongly   Neutral   Strongly
   prefer A   prefer B
   A job which provides loss of vacation time and an excellent fringe benefit package.

10. A job with little freedom and independence to do your work in the way you think best.
    |⎯⎯⎯|⎯⎯⎯|⎯⎯⎯|⎯⎯⎯|
    Strongly   Neutral   Strongly
    prefer A   prefer B
    A job where the working conditions are poor.

11. A job with very satisfying teamwork.
    |⎯⎯⎯|⎯⎯⎯|⎯⎯⎯|⎯⎯⎯|
    Strongly   Neutral   Strongly
    prefer A   prefer B
    A job which allows you to use your skills and abilities to the fullest extent.

12. A job which offers little or no challenge.
    |⎯⎯⎯|⎯⎯⎯|⎯⎯⎯|⎯⎯⎯|
    Strongly   Neutral   Strongly
    prefer A   prefer B
    A job which requires you to be completely isolated from coworkers.

Scoring: Each of the 12 items utilizes a five-point scale. However, the direction of the scale is reversed for half the items. "Strongly prefer A" is scored 1, and "Strongly prefer B" is scored 5 for these items: 1, 5, 7, 10, 11, and 12. On the other six items (2, 3, 4, 6, 8, and 9) the scoring is reversed, so that "Strongly prefer A" is scored 5, and "Strongly prefer B" is scored 1. Compute your growth need strength score by averaging the numbers you indicated for all 12 items. To help you interpret your score, the authors of this instrument report that the mean growth needs scale score is approximately 3.0. Therefore, individuals who have growth need strength scores greater than 3.0 tend to prefer jobs where they have greater opportunities for personal growth and self-actualization.

1. What types of jobs have you performed? Does your growth need score appear to be related to your job satisfaction and productivity on these jobs?
2. Does your score seem intuitively right to you? Why or why not?

IV. Creating Job Descriptions and Job Specifications

Prepare a combination job description and job specification for one of the following:
a. Your present job.
b. A paralegal coordinator position.
c. A law firm marketing director.
d. A law firm librarian.
e. A law firm legal administrator.
f. A director of legal secretaries.

Include the following information:
a. Job title.
b. Names of supervisors or other reporting relationships.
c. Department or location of position.
d. General summary of position.
e. Chief duties and responsibilities.
f. Required knowledge, skills, and abilities.
g. Required education and experience.
h. Any comments that clarify the nature or requirements of the job.

CHAPTER 8

Supervision

LEARNING OBJECTIVES

After completing this chapter, you should be able to:

- Describe the challenges of supervising today's worker;
- Discuss supervision in the professional setting;
- Describe the skills effective supervisors need and the problems they face;
- Explain the role that trust plays in supervisor-worker relationships and describe the factors that enhance or weaken trust;
- Identify the characteristics of effective supervisors and the components of effective supervision;
- Explain and compare three supervisory styles that are common today;
- Describe the characteristics of effective performance appraisals and identify typical appraisal tools and techniques; and
- Discuss the meaning of discipline and explain the steps in progressive discipline.

FOCUS FROM THE FIELD

Deborah Thompson: Keep Your People Focused on the Big Picture

In 1979, Deborah Thompson joined the Washington firm of Jones, Day, Reavis & Poque. From her beginnings as a legal assistant, she became actively involved in the training and recruiting of legal assistants and eventually received promotion to an administrative position. She is currently the director of legal assistants at the law firm of King and Spalding in Atlanta, Georgia.

Does supervision in a law office setting differ from that in other offices?

Yes. Management is different in a law firm because you have much more crisis management. You have shifting needs and priorities that are client-driven. In a corporation, people can sit down and plan and project what they would like to accomplish in the next six months. In a law firm, it's a totally different ball game. Every day is different. That's what is so exciting about it. If you get a new client or a client has an emergency, you may have to redeploy people to meet that need. As a manager in a law firm, you have less control of your destiny on a day-to-day level.

How do you keep your legal assistants from burning out?

I think that people suffer from burnout if there are no career paths open to them, if their skills and job responsibilities never change. What a lot of firms have done is created career paths, a tier system, for legal assistants. They move into different levels as they gain experience and expertise.

How do managers deal with complaints from attorneys about follow-through and accuracy?

As a manager of legal assistants, you must have a good idea of the skills and talents of the legal assistants in your department. When you are making assignments, you must match them to the talents of a particular legal assistant. You, as a manager, need to know where your people's strengths lie. If there is a problem, you need to address that situation immediately. You must also closely monitor work assignments and provide feedback. People can't learn if they are not informed of their mistakes.

How does a supervisor develop a fire-in-the-belly enthusiasm?

I think that this type of enthusiasm is actually crucial for employees in a law firm setting. To get that enthusiasm, you need to display it yourself. You have to keep your people focused on the big picture and how important their contributions are. Your enthusiasm and commitment as manager will ultimately filter down to the people that you supervise.

What is the secret to good supervision in a law firm?

Flexibility and good organizational skills are the keys because you are dealing with shifting priorities. You need to identify the talents of the people that you supervise and develop each one individually. As a manager, you must also have a clear idea of the firm's goals. In the 1990s, goals are shifting constantly and you, as a manager, need to know what your firm expects of you and your people. You must constantly reevaluate the needs of your firm and make sure that your program is satisfying those needs.

CHAPTER 8 / SUPERVISION

> **A**lthough most top managements assert that their companies care for their people, the excellent companies are distinguished by the intensity and pervasiveness of this concern. . . . We are not talking about mollycoddling. We are talking about tough-minded respect for the individual and the willingness to train him, to set reasonable and clear expectations for him and to grant him practical autonomy to step out and contribute directly to his job.
> (T. Peters and R. Waterman, Jr., *In Search of Excellence*)[1]
>
> **H**ow do you humiliate and demean someone and then expect him or her to care about product quality and constant improvement?
> (Tom Peters, *Thriving on Chaos*)[2]

CHALLENGES OF SUPERVISION IN THE 1990S

The word *supervision* means to have vision over something or someone. **Supervision** is the process of overseeing, managing, and directing. Though all managers are responsible for the supervision of workers in some form or another, a **supervisor** is a manager on a first-line level who interacts directly with workers and who is responsible for short-range planning, for hiring workers or recommending the hiring of workers at his or her operational level, for representing the needs and concerns of workers to middle- and upper-level management, and for implementing the policies and decisions of the organization. Supervisors have close, continuous, and direct contact with the workers for whom they are responsible. **Supervisory skills,** required of managers at all levels, are the skills that enable supervisors to integrate managerial expertise with the ability to work well with people. Supervisors must have a balanced understanding of both workers and the workplace. They should be particularly sensitive to the many trends affecting today's working world, including demographics, technology, changing societal values, and the motivational needs of workers.

Demographics

Three irreversible trends that began in the 1960s have shaped the work force of the 1990s: workers are becoming better educated, more women are entering the work force, and people are choosing to wait longer before getting married and raising families.[3] Throughout the 1990s, dual income families will be the norm as more women continue to work outside the home and to choose careers in traditionally male-dominated fields. In the legal profession, more women will become and will remain practicing attorneys, and the number of women partners in law firms will continue to increase.[4] Workplaces in general will be more culturally and ethnically diverse.

Technology

Once producing changes that affected only business settings, technology now is transforming work settings of all kinds.[5] As technology continues to develop, knowledge becomes more specialized, and work demands, worker interactions, accountability, and supervisory roles continue to change. Law firms that hoped to avoid the brunt of the technological revolution have had to make major changes to keep pace with their technologically proficient competitors. Ours is an **information society** that requires workers to communicate, receive, and process on a daily basis information in quantities unheard of even twenty-five years ago.[6] Many of these workers, and the supervisors who oversee them, rely on computer technology to fulfill their everyday responsibilities. In coming years, supervisors will not only need to continue their technological adjustment but to facilitate their employees' adjustment as well, both psychologically and in terms of acquiring new technical skills.[7]

Changing Values

Changes as vast and powerful as waves rolling on the sea have rocked our society in recent years, writes John

Naisbitt in *Megatrends,* and some of our most basic values are still undergoing change.[8] Economic turmoil and unemployment have led American workers to question their sense of self and self-esteem, their view of authority, and their attitudes regarding loyalty and mobility.

Sense of Self

At the heart of employees' questioning of values and working conditions is the belief that they matter: that they are of value and that their contributions count. Modern employees expect to have a greater voice in decision making, especially regarding the decisions that affect their employment, and respecting this self-esteem has become an established trend among employers. Few modern employers would dare to say, "Take it or leave it," even in economically depressed times. Workers may indeed stay and "take it," but their resentment will surface in countless ways. We should note that efforts to undermine an organization are less often attempts at anarchy than efforts to maintain a balance of social power and that not even the most desperate worker is apt to believe that a job is worth abusive or inconsiderate treatment from an employer. Work is more than breadwinning, and employees expect meaningful returns, including personal satisfaction and equitable compensation. Professor Raymond L. Hilget of Washington University and Theo Haimann of St. Louis University note that workers in professional, technical, and supervisory positions seem especially likely to seek "personal involvement, a sense of achievement and satisfaction in the work they perform."[9]

Authority

How workers view supervision has changed drastically from the days when employees unquestioningly accepted authority and automatically respected those who exercised it, no matter how harshly they did so. Iron-fisted supervisory practices rarely work nowadays, and are often effective only as long as the supervisor is present. No matter where today's managers position themselves, observe Hilget and Haimann, "Authoritarian direction and close control usually will not bring about the desired results."[10] But the modern view of authority is more than a revolt against dictatorship. In our lifetimes, according to Joe Batten, chairman and CEO of the training and consulting firm of Batten, Batten, Hudson & Swab, Inc., we have

... witnessed a volatile series of changes in the way leadership is viewed in America.... The very nature of management must be perceived in a new way. In practical reality, management is an ever-changing, ever-dynamic system of interacting minds.[11]

With the social crises of the 1960s, write Hilget and Thaimann, came "radical changes in the values that many people held concerning morality, customs, and attitudes toward established authority." With the courts upholding the rights of workers, employees developed new attitudes about dress, behaviors, rights of redress, and many other work-related issues. As they have become more educated and have invested more in themselves and their careers, their expectations have risen. Employers, in turn, with the help of civil liberties advocates, have become increasingly sensitive to workers' rights. At the same time, however, they are concerned about the greater demands they must place on workers in terms of productivity and excellence in order to stay competitive.[12]

Loyalty and Mobility

Like monetary investments, employees go where they are assured of the best return, all other options being equal. Like that of stock dollars, our mobility is restrained by economic realities. In depressed economic times, when jobs become scarce, workers are more willing to stay put, take fewer career risks, and tolerate adverse conditions in order to survive economically. This does not imply that productivity and performance automatically improve during depressed times. As we will see in the following section, employers need to be conscious of the benefits of positive motivation, in good times and bad.

Employee Motivation

Many employers erroneously believe that high motivation is a direct result of good pay. There are several reasons for rethinking this belief. Each worker harbors personal dreams and differing expectations for fulfilling these dreams, based on his or her experience and effort. Work is only one aspect of these efforts at fulfillment, and salary is only one aspect of work. As Hilget and Haimann explain,

> Wages, benefits, and good working conditions are not the only influences on an employee's motivation and work performance. Of course, if these items are not satisfactory to employees, their morale will tend to be low and their

work performance will suffer. But even where wages and benefits are good or excellent, there is no guarantee that employees will be motivated to work beyond an average performance level. The never-ending task before supervisors is to supervise employees in a manner that is conducive to positive employee motivation and superior work performance.[13]

Supervisors may accomplish this task by repaying employees with the *psychic salaries* we encountered in Chapter 7, thereby fostering in them the sense that the firm respects and values them, that it is willing to listen to their ideas and recognize their input, and that it is willing to offer them opportunities to achieve and to grow professionally. A relatively sure method of ensuring loyalty and a degree of effort that can transform marginal results into superior ones, valuing workers is the key to a firm's success, especially in tight and volatile times, when funds for monetary salaries are scarce.

SUPERVISION IN THE PROFESSIONAL SETTING

Supervision in the law firm requires a supervisor to wear one or more of four different hats: one for partners, one for the firm's associates and other attorneys, one for paralegals, and one for the firm's support staff. The law firm presents a mixture of supervisory needs, from self-policing autonomy and the collegial supervision of new associates to the close professional supervision of paralegals by attorneys and the direct operational supervision of secretaries and support staff.

Supervision of Lawyers

Balancing autonomy with responsibility to the firm can be a challenge. At times, the expectations of a firm's management may clash, jarringly, with the expectations that partners and other professionals want to fulfill. **Operational autonomy** is the control a professional has over the matters in his or her area of professional operations. In law firms, this autonomy appears as the authority that lawyers exercise over their legal activities. Professionals cannot allow interference in this area; they will look to others in their field for whatever assistance they need. Law firm managers, for the most part, understand and accept this precept, and most professionals understand, in turn, the fact that management relies on them to set goals and to conform to the firm's policies. Both parties should realize that tight hierarchical control on the part of managers will directly conflict with the expert control, or expertise, that professionals must exercise without interference, to ensure the health of the firm.[14] For this reason, a nonlawyer manager who supervises professionals as well as support staff faces a contradictory and nearly impossible task. To experience any success, such a manager should have a deep respect for the professional aspects of legal activities and a clear idea of the limits of any supervisory jurisdiction. Because, as human resource professional Joseph Raelin points out, the very nature of the work of lawyers "predisposes them to resist organizational control," a nonlawyer manager who deals with lawyers should be prepared to face opposition from those who believe that a nonlawyer has neither the status nor the prestige necessary to command their cooperation. Rather than exhaust him- or herself trying to bring the firm's professionals to heel, the manager should remember that a supervisor's primary task is to coordinate the diverse functions of the firm so that all its members are accountable, no matter how differently they contribute.[15] A nonlawyer can best supervise a firm's partners by respecting their ability, through collegial responsibility and accountability, to supervise themselves.

Supervision of Associates

The supervision of associates also centers on collegiality. Like the other professionals in the firm, associates believe that they are best qualified to control and judge the quality of their own work.[16] This collegial monitoring extends to new associates, most of whom begin their careers with the firm under the watchful guidance of senior attorneys. Nonetheless, although some firms supervise their new associates carefully and formally evaluate their progress, others prefer a less structured approach. Law firm consultant Bob Bookman explains:

> In most law firms, it takes two to three years to develop the skills and legal knowledge necessary to be profitable for the firm. Often, however, senior lawyers give little thought to helping associates acquire these skills. Many firms simply play "survival of the fittest." They hire more associates than they can possibly make partner, and then watch to see who wins. But in this type of game, everybody loses.[17]

Some of the techniques that more attentive firms use to supervise new associates include coaching techniques that break work down into manageable assignments, regular partner-associate meetings that provide a forum for new-associate mentors, direct observation and pre- and post-work reviews, positive feedback, and constructive criticism. Those who supervise or who act as mentors for new associates should also encourage them to actively seek feedback concerning their effort and performance.[18]

Supervision of Paralegals

The third form of law firm supervision involves paralegals. A relatively new career, paralegalism has produced hybrid workers who are professionally prepared and oriented, but who do not have full autonomy and who are, therefore, still members of a support staff. Though many firms still think of paralegals as largely self-educated or as graduates of on-the-job training, most of today's paralegals hold degrees from substantive preparation programs and are, as Mary Ann Von Glinow observes in *The New Professionals,* typical of the "knowledge workers" of today, whose "currency of their trade is their brain power." [19] Because of their hybrid status, paralegals typically receive supervision from two sources: direct supervision from a practicing attorney (who might want to utilize techniques similar to those used to monitor and guide new associates) and more general supervision from the firm's supervisory management.[20]

Supervision of Support Staff

The law firm's support staff work for professionals and submit work to them, but these workers also are directly responsible to the firm's supervisory management. The supervision of support staff varies from firm to firm, ranging from settings in which supervisors work directly with their staffs only during crises to firms in which supervisors actively promote communication, offer support, and regularly evaluate their workers. Generally, support staff supervision involves overseeing routine tasks such as filing, entering time records in the computer, and updating tickler files. In addition, support staff supervisors provide for the equitable distribution of work assignments and monitor work quality and quantity.

BEING A SUPERVISOR

For many people, deciding to be a supervisor is often the first step toward a management career. For some, it is an easy decision to make. Becoming a supervisor is a rung up the career ladder. It represents professional growth, additional pay, status. It's an opportunity. Others, however, have doubts: Can I do the job? Can I tell others what to do? Will it be stressful? Will it cause me to lose friends? Will my people like me? Will I get cut out of the communications loop? Will I be strong enough to win respect? At one time or another, new supervisory managers, like all managers, will ask themselves these and a hundred other questions.

Skills Supervisors Need

Many challenges that supervisors face are in some ways more difficult than those confronting upper-level management. On the firing line, a supervisor is constantly responsible for and interacting with people. He or she often is acutely aware of their needs, concerns, stresses, and conflicts. And, as we saw in Chapter 1, first-line supervisors need to be adept at the job skills of their supervisees. They need to know what they are asking of those they supervise. Paralegal coordinators, for instance, who have not worked in real estate, may not understand all the time lines and the searches that working in this area involves. A word-processing coordinator who has not kept up-to-date with changes in equipment and in programs such as WordPerfect, has little hope of understanding what the word-processing staff is experiencing. Besides proficiency in their areas of expertise, all supervisors need superb communications skills and interpersonal skills. Instead of alienating and antagonizing, they need to work well with others, balancing the ability to treat workers with dignity and respect with the right to expect and to receive quality work.

Problems Supervisors Have[21]

Each manager knows almost instinctively that earning the respect and trust of their workers is half the battle. Although some new supervisors can create difficulties for themselves simply in trying to adapt to their new role, the following problems can plague neophytes and experienced supervisors alike:

Aloofness

In trying to stay objective and professional, many supervisors come across as—or actually are—aloof. Supervisors need to interact with workers, who appreciate concern and interest. On the other hand, workers also need breathing room, and some supervisors encroach far too much on their workers' space. In terms of personal and professional proximity, as with much else in life, supervisors should try to achieve a happy balance.

Lack of Empathy

In trying to be efficient and effective, supervisors may tend to focus on the work to be done while unconsciously ignoring the thoughts and feelings of their supervisees. To counter this tendency, supervisors need to develop **empathy,** the skill of understanding, being sensitive to, and experiencing vicariously the thoughts, feelings, and experience of others. Empathy requires strong appreciation of and respect for others, and to cultivate their empathic abilities, supervisors must actively seek to create a climate that not only allows but encourages feedback from their subordinates. It is far too easy for supervisors to label workers who come to them with feedback as "whiners" and "complainers." Supervisors should remember that unfair treatment, office politics, collegial jealousies, gossip, and slander can cause good workers tension and even anguish and that workers who are unable to discuss their frustration and dissatisfaction objectively and thoughtfully with their supervisors are likely to seek a more suitable work setting. Those who remain with the firm may become passive, alienated, and disinterested; on the other hand, they may choose to confront their tormentors directly, thereby escalating the conflict and enlarging the circle of repercussions. It is far better for supervisors to learn to listen, to confer with subordinates, and to intervene when necessary than to risk losing valuable workers or to endanger the working environment of the firm.

Lack of Initiative

Though some supervisors do their best work during disasters, others have a hard time even acknowledging crises, let alone admitting that they have a responsibility to do something about them. Ignored, small problems can rapidly grow into larger ones. Nipping troubles in the bud is essential, no matter how much one would like to believe that ignoring them will make them go away.

Indecision

Many supervisors have a hard time making decisions. Indecision wastes time and breeds aggravation. Most workers can accept the idea that a decision involving others will take time or that a supervisor may need to place a request on the back burner while he or she settles more pressing issues; what they won't accept is a supervisor who rudely fails even to acknowledge their queries. Simply indicating that a request has not been forgotten or that an answer is on the way can reduce worker anxiety and show a basic respect for the worker. Performing a **pocket veto** by setting a request aside until it dies from a lack of attention is a cowardly approach to decision making. A worker deserves to know the status of his or her request, even if the final response is no. Of all the possible ways of responding to workers, ignoring them is the worst.

The Tendency to Forget the Supervisory Role

To be a supervisor is to balance three essential tasks. First, a supervisor must act on behalf of his or her supervisees, representing them, presenting their views, and helping them to do their jobs better. Second, as a member of the firm's management, he or she must also act on behalf of the law firm. Part of acting on behalf of the firm is projecting an attitude of respect for its rules and policies. Failing to do so can have dire consequences. For one thing, taken together, seemingly inconsequential actions (such as overlooking a worker's tendency to take long lunches or to come in late) can create a pattern of inconsistency in the firm and destroy the supervisor's chances of establishing fairness and equity in his or her department. Second, an apathetic attitude toward upholding rules and policies can create havoc. Some personnel will be inclined to bypass a seemingly indifferent supervisor and go directly to the attorneys for whom they work to ask for favors and approval for their actions. The law firm supervisor must convince attorneys that, just as the supervisor is not to interfere with the attorneys' professional work, they should not usurp the supervisor's authority over his or her supervisees. To ensure the enforcement of standards, to avoid inequities, and to prevent office politics from interfering with productivity, support staff requests must be the province of a supervisor. A secretary or paralegal does not work for Attorney B or Attorney C; he or she works for the firm. Promoting this understanding is the supervisor's third task; without it, a support staff's concern for standards, quality, and highly professional work erodes. As Ben Franklin wrote, "For want of a nail, the shoe was lost; for want of a shoe, the horse was lost; and for want of a horse, the rider was lost." A little neglect breeds mischief. An effective supervisor is able to convince subordinates, superiors, and him- or herself of the wisdom behind the firm's policies and regulations.

The Role of Trust

Because it enables people to lower their guard and to deal openly with one another, trust is essential to work relationships, especially to the relationship between a supervisor and his or her supervisees. Workers continuously evaluate a supervisor's integrity, genuineness, and motives by studying his or her words and actions, both within the group and outside of it. Outside of the group, the supervisor is responsible for acting as liaison between his or her workers and the firm;[22] to gain trust when performing this role, he or she must present workers' needs candidly to the firm and accurately report its response back to the work group or to the individual who made the request. Within the group, trust in the supervisor depends on the consistency, honesty, and equity of his or her actions. To build trust is to ensure performance. As management expert William Ouchi explains, "To trust another is to know that the two of you share basic goals in the long run so that, left to your own devices, each will behave in ways that are not harmful to the other."[23]

How to Weaken Trust

A supervisor who has difficulty sensing a solid level of trust from his or her supervisees should take the time to examine his or her behavior from the supervisees' point of view. There are many ways of weakening trust. We will examine four of the most common.

Inconsistent Behavior. Workers who can't understand where a supervisor is coming from will hesitate to rely on that supervisor. Being all smiles one day and moody the next offers little assurance of dependability, as does openness that seems to change with the weather.

Manipulation. Supervisors who play one worker against another or who talk about employees behind their backs will win avid listeners while eradicating their own integrity. Supervisors must be candid when such candor is not at someone's expense, and they should be honest about their motives. Those who sow discord reap mistrust.

Lack of Dependability. It is perhaps only natural to want to trust people. Think of Charlie Brown kicking air and falling flat on his back time after time after Lucy says, "Trust me" and whips the football away at the last second. Supervisors who won't hold the ball in terms of department or group reliability spend a lot of time saying, "Trust me"—but, unlike Charlie Brown, workers are apt to become wise to the trick. They don't expect supervisors to perform miracles, but workers do count on supervisors to be dependable.

Authoritarian Leadership. Through their insistence on, rather than proof of, their right to authority and their tendency to ignore suggestions or to rebuke those who make them,[24] authoritarian supervisors are adept at evoking general mistrust in their subordinates. Placing rigid control in a guise of civility won't help to promote even a semblance of rapport: workers can see through a pleasant front. Only openness builds trust.

How to Build Trust

Saying that the only way to build trust is to be trustworthy seems redundant, but it's true. To communicate trustworthiness, a supervisor must in fact be trustworthy. Workers can be a supervisor's harshest (if least outspoken) critics, and once they think a supervisor isn't to be trusted, reversing that conviction, accurate or not, can take great effort. The deeper the sense of betrayal and hurt, the longer the damage takes to repair. Nonetheless, supervisors can create and increase trust in many ways.

Common Goals. Creating a team approach to reaching objectives builds trust. To simply delegate work is to give supervisees the impression that they work for or under you, not with or beside you.

Communications. Keeping workers informed reveals both a supervisor's interest in promoting positive, effective communication and his or her respect for workers. Workers know that information is power, and they are quick to spot managerial "mushroom philosophies" intended to feed them manure-like misinformation and keep them in the dark. Accurately informing workers whenever possible builds confidence and trust.

Openness. Effective supervisors know that on all organizational charts, hierarchical levels simply mark boundaries between those having different responsibilities. Each level represents real flesh and blood people, each of whom is entitled to respect. No matter the level they occupy, workers must believe that they are part of a larger team that supports its members and acknowledges the idea that each individual is important. Supervisors who use their status to render themselves unapproachable may dispel all doubt regarding who's in charge, but they do little to establish the rapport that is essential to mutual trust.

Genuine Interest. Workers are quick to see through illusory interest. Bosses who say "My door is always open" but who do not respect input or ideas deceive only themselves. Once they have good reason to be suspicious of invitations to share information, workers may come to be wary of participating in work groups and on committees. Effective supervisors know that worker trust relies on real interest and an honest use of worker input.

EFFECTIVE SUPERVISION

Being an effective supervisor places heavy demands on those who accept the role. In the following paragraphs, we will examine the characteristics of effective supervisors and four factors that influence supervisory effectiveness.

Characteristics of Effective Supervisors

Effective supervisors tend to be well-rounded people who balance their roles at work with outside interests. They are motivated and emotionally mature, and they are good communicators. These are all qualities and skills that can be learned and developed. As long as someone is interested in working with people and is willing to develop good interpersonal skills, he or she has the potential for becoming an effective supervisor.

Factors that Affect Supervision

As we have seen, effective supervision relies more on planning work and delegating special tasks than on becoming closely involved in the work. According to Rensis Likert, effective supervision is employee-centered, allowing workers to participate in those decisions that involve them and reflecting the supervisor's sincere interest in their needs and problems, not only in productivity.[25] Essentially, effective supervision depends on four factors: the quality of communications, group size, the kind of work being done, and the supervisor's attitude.

Communication Quality

Establishing two-way communication with workers is essential to good supervision, particularly if the supervisor works closely with his or her supervisees, as secretarial or office supervisors or paralegal coordinators commonly do. To keep communication channels clear, supervisors should avoid pulling rank. Almost nothing can block communication more effectively than actions that emphasize the hierarchical differences between supervisors and their workers.

Size of the Work Group

Group size and interaction determine the strength of a group and the influence that it has on a supervisor. Generally, the smaller the group, the easier it is to maintain personal relationships with supervisees. The larger the group, the more impersonal the interactions within it and the more a supervisor needs to delegate.

The Nature of the Work

The type of work that a supervisor oversees also affects the supervisory relationship. In a law firm, a single assignment can trigger a complex chain of interactions between many people at different levels, requiring supervisors not only to coordinate the efforts of their own people but to serve as negotiators, resource managers, representatives, and conciliators.

Supervisory Attitudes

Because supervisors must acknowledge the needs of those they supervise as well as the demands of their superiors and because they must act as liaisons between their supervisees and the rest of the firm, they need to balance concern with objectivity. When making decisions or setting standards for supervisees, a supervisor must broaden his or her attitude to include confidence in his or her abilities and the courage to stand by convictions. An effective supervisor knows that popular decisions are not always the most effective or the most appropriate. The following Another Look lists some of the characteristics that workers look for in effective supervisors.

STYLES OF SUPERVISION

The supervisory styles that managers adopt are nearly as numerous as the supervisees that such styles affect.

ANOTHER LOOK

What Workers Look for in Their Supervisors

Clear Direction
- Clear goals clearly communicated
- Efforts to involve others in setting goals
- Effective delegation

Two-Way Communication
- Honesty and candor in working with people

Support
- Willingness to act as a coach and to offer encouragement

Objective Recognition
- Willingness to praise good performance, not just to criticize failure
- Tendency to relate rewards to work well done

Reasonable Follow-up and Feedback
- Use of reasonable controls
- Ability to apprise workers of their progress clearly and impartially

Effective Selection of Other Staff
- A knack for choosing the right people for the firm

An Understanding of Financial Implications
- Ability to assess realistically the cost of a decision

Encouragement of Innovation
- A receptive attitude toward new and better ways of doing things

Good Decision Making
- Ability to make decisions thoroughly, clearly, and quickly

High Integrity
- Consistently ethical behavior

SOURCE: Survey Report of Harbridge House, *The Right Report* 2, no. 4 (Boston: Right Associates Management Consultants, Fall 1984).

---

1. Which characteristics would you most like to see in *your* supervisor? List the three characteristics that you consider most important.
2. Which characteristic would be most important for supervisors in the following settings?
   a. A hospital nursing supervisor
   b. A preschool teaching team
   c. A college faculty
   d. A financially troubled bank
   e. A corporate law department
   f. A law firm that specializes in criminal defense work
   g. A government law office for environmental affairs

In the following sections, we will examine three supervisory approaches in wide use today: counseling, coaching, and Ken Blanchard and Spencer Johnson's one-minute management.

The Supervisor as Counselor

Counseling is the process of listening to, understanding, and attempting to help a worker experiencing job-related problems. *Job-related* is the key phrase: a supervisor should not attempt to counsel an employee regarding *personal* problems, including marital, financial, mental, or emotional difficulties or problems involving chemical abuse. To do so may subject both the supervisor and the firm to legal liability for any negative consequences of such counseling. (Supervisors should not hesitate, however, to help troubled employees obtain counseling for personal problems through employee assistance plans.) We might say that the supervisor's first task as counselor is to decide whether to become involved. Once a supervisor determines that an employee's problem is work-related, he or she is obliged to help the employee. To trace the steps in the counseling process, let us use the following scenario:

Terry, a competent secretary under your supervision, has been under a great deal of stress. Yesterday, when Julie, the firm's receptionist, asked him to fill in for her during her lunch break, Terry flew into a rage. As his supervisor, you feel obligated to discover the reason for his behavior and to help him, if possible. To act as counselor to your supervisee, you should

1. Listen. Listening skills are invaluable for effective counseling. Let the story come out.
2. Understand the Facts. Ask questions. Do any homework you need to analyze the incident.
3. Get All Sides of the Story. A story has as many sides to it as it has participants. Ask Terry, Julie, and anyone else who is involved to interpret what has happened. Do this in confidentiality. Meet in a private setting and listen without interrupting.
4. Focus on the Facts. Realize that Terry must be experiencing strong feelings about what you are discussing. Try to discover what else may have led to the incident. Find out how often Terry receives last-minute notices. Discover how often he is taken from his other work, how long the interruptions take, and what consideration he receives for his trouble. Find out how the secretaries and receptionists rotate their stand-in duties. Take notes. Don't argue.
5. Express Your Concern. You should feel two types of concern regarding the incident: personal concern for Terry and his problem and professional concern for the effect on the organization. Avoid expressing moral judgments, such as "You were wrong to criticize Julie." Say instead, "I understand there were clients present" or "Attorney Adams heard you four offices away." Review the facts of the incident calmly but de-emphasize neither the gravity of the occurrence nor the idea that disciplinary action could result if it happens again.
6. Agree on the Cause. Explain again to Terry why his action was inappropriate and work with him to trace his problem to a specific cause. If you agree on the cause, it will be easier to agree on a solution, which is your next step.
7. Get Commitment to a Solution. Encourage Terry to suggest his own solution and to commit himself to working toward it, if the solution is within his control. Even if the solution requires help from others, you should establish an action plan with Terry.
8. Establish a Time Frame. Set a time to meet again, but be prepared to be flexible. Action plans are apt to require sudden revisions, and other difficulties similar to the original incident may arise.
9. Be Sure the Counseling Is Work-Related. Above all, make sure you are not overstepping the limits of your role. You are not a psychologist. If incidents interfere repeatedly with Terry's work or the work of others, you may need to obtain outside assistance.

The Supervisor as Coach

Coaching is job-related supervisory assistance that provides workers with professional encouragement and guidance. Whereas counseling seeks to improve employees performance by helping them to work through job-related problems, coaching aims to develop work competency.[26] As William Tracey, president of Human Resources Enterprises of Cape Cod, Inc., explains, informal coaching is part of the "continuing relationship between a manager and a subordinate. . . . Coaching involves a continuous flow of instruction, comments, and suggestions from superior to subordinate. It is day-by-day informal teaching done by the manager, involving precepts, demonstration, practice, observation, correction, feedback, encouragement, praise, reward, and above all, example."[27]

More formal coaching involves five steps. First, as supervisor, you analyze the worker's performance by observing them on the job and by scrutinizing his or her work results. Second, you determine the skills that the worker needs to improve. Third, you identify specific actions that the worker can take to improve his or her performance. Fourth, you assist the worker in making the improvements. Lastly, you periodically review the worker's performance.[28] Coaching differs from ordinary supervision in that coaching requires a supervisor to work alongside an employee to improve that employee's performance. In the process, supervisor and supervisee must agree on three things: what the job is, what it requires, and what the standards are for success.[29]

What the Job Is

Like an athlete and a coach discussing a training schedule in preparation for a big meet, both the supervisor and the worker must understand the demands of a job and the worker's interest in meeting those demands. More importantly, for a true coaching relationship to exist, the supervisor needs to know whether the worker is willing to be coached and how interested he or she is in succeeding.

Criteria for the Job

Just as a runner who wants to qualify for the U.S. Olympic team must know the times he or she needs to beat, an employee and his or her coaching supervisor know the firm's basic work criteria and the methods by which it evaluates those criteria.

Standards for Success

Beyond the criteria essential to basic job performance are standards for success. Making the team is one thing; winning the race is another. When an employee caps an open, communicative coaching relationship with excellent work, his or her supervisor can share proudly in the worker's success.

One-Minute Management

In their book, *The One Minute Manager,* Ken Blanchard and Spencer Johnson describe a very structured supervising strategy that enables a supervisor to communicate approval or disapproval directly and firmly within the space of a minute. Whether for offering feedback and praise or for making a one-minute reprimand, the authors suggest these steps:

Step 1. The Description. Tell the person exactly what he or she did well or poorly. Be precise, not dramatic, and look the worker in the eye.

Step 2. The Importance. Tell the worker why the behavior affects the entire organization. Explain why it is good for everyone or why it is harmful. Be as specific as you'd like about the benefits or disadvantages to the law firm.

Step 3. The Silence. Stop for a moment to let your words sink in. This brief silence focuses the employee's attention and forces him or her to wonder what you will say or do next.

Step 4. The Hopes and the Handshake. Encourage the performance you want to see. Then offer your supervisee a sign of your good will and caring by shaking hands or by offering a pat on the back, but only if you are certain that the employee will not interpret physical contact as sexual harassment and that the gesture won't seem patronizing. Like the rest of your one-minute management, your closing gesture must be genuine and natural.[30]

The acronym DISH can help to remind supervisors how to ''dish out'' one-minute management through (1) a description of the behavior observed, (2) its importance to the law firm, (3) the silence that allows words to sink in, and (4) the hopes and the handshake that close the exchange.

PERFORMANCE APPRAISALS

One of a supervisor's most important tasks, **performance appraisal** is the process of evaluating performance by measuring an employee's work activity and work product against the firm's established standards and expectations. Management uses appraisals for three essential purposes: to determine the efficiency with which employees are helping the firm to meet its goals, to improve employee performance by determining the areas in which an employee would benefit from training and further development, and to obtain information for decisions regarding retention, pay increases, and promotions.[31] Ideally, appraisals should benefit all members of the firm, not just supervisors and other management personnel. As training and development professional Ron Zemke explains,

> A good performance review system increases employee motivation and job-related communications between subordinates and managers. It provides a vehicle for discussing current performance, determining an individual's self-development and training needs, and for talking about advancement desires and opportunities.[32]

Accordingly, management should encourage employees to think of appraisals as an opportunity to receive (and offer) feedback, articulate their needs, and build a sense of teamwork between themselves and their supervisors. No employee should need to dread performance appraisals: from the top of the hierarchy to the bottom, members should regard evaluations as a chance to improve themselves and the firm.

Appraisals may be formal or informal. Informal appraisals, which constitute the core of the supervisor-worker relationship in some firms, commonly consist of the everyday feedback a supervisor offers an employee regarding his or her work. Formal appraisals, by comparison, often involve one or more evaluation tools, such as performance checklists or other forms, and occur according to a schedule. New workers, for instance, may be asked to participate in performance reviews every two weeks, at first, then every three months, then twice a year.

A 1990 survey of legal assistants provides a more detailed image of the appraisal process. In 45 percent of the firms surveyed, attorneys appraised the performance of legal assistants, with the help of office managers or personnel directors. In 72 percent of the firms, the first review took place after three months and then annually thereafter, unless problems in need of correction dictated more frequent appraisals. Some firms gave performance reviews after each assignment. Sixty-two percent of the firms provided legal assistants with copies of their evaluations, though many firms provided copies only to assistants who requested them; in 42 percent of the firms, the evaluations were primarily oral. Twenty-six percent of the firms gave annual raises to all workers, thereby rewarding seniority.[33] In addition, many firms give their members annual monetary bonuses, based on merit and firm profitability.

Criteria for Effective Appraisals

Possibly because the process seems too much like a trip to the dentist for a cleaning and a checkup, few workers look forward to formal performance appraisals. In addition, many employees—supervisors and supervisees alike—are aware of the potential inaccuracies in the appraisal process. Nonetheless, no matter the frequency with which they occur or the type or level of employee they involve, performance appraisals should be

Clear. An appraisal should not be a time for surprises. Both the supervisor and the supervisee should bring to the appraisal shared expectations and a thorough knowledge of relevant performance goals.

Fair. The entire firm should support an overall conviction that the appraisal process is fair and equitable. To ensure fairness, the appraisal system should allow workers not only to signify their participation in an appraisal by signing the appraisal form but to add their written views on the accuracy of the appraisal, if they choose to do so (see Figure 8–1).

Accurate. Performance appraisals are not easy. For the simple reason that supervisors are human and, as such, are apt to color their perceptions according to their personal limitations, expectations, and standards, appraisals can be inaccurate, subjective, and biased. Nonetheless, because an appraisal becomes part of an employee's permanent record and can create indelible impressions in the minds of his or her future managers, a supervisor should strive to make each appraisal as accurate as possible by recognizing his or her personal biases, using firsthand information whenever possible, and making sure that the qualities that the appraisal covers are professional, not personal. The fact that Nancy never smiles at work has no impact whatsoever on her top-notch word-processing skills or on her reliability.

Goal-Directed. All evaluations should refer to goals and objectives that benefit the firm and to the employee's efforts and success in achieving them. As we will see later in this chapter, this goal-directed focus is an innate part of the evaluation process in firms that practice management by objectives.

Positively Oriented. During an appraisal, a supervisor is always wise to accentuate the positive by focusing on a worker's particular contributions, development, and progress. An appraisal is not a time to vivisect an employee's shortcomings; instead, the supervisor should use the session to discuss the worker's opportunities for continued development and positive growth.

Mutually Beneficial. Imagine if every time an appraisal took place a supervisor asked, "What can I do to help you do your job better?" A team partnership philosophy would take root. All employee appraisals should be a two-way exchange, since supervisors can always improve their efforts to help their supervisees do a better job.

Privacy Issues[34]

Besides doing their best to ensure the accuracy of the appraisal information that enters employee files, supervisors should safeguard the privacy of such files and any other information regarding their workers. Law

---

FIGURE 8–1
Portion of Form Requesting Employee Response to Performance Appraisal

> By signing below, I indicate that I have read, participated in the development of, and have received a copy of this evaluation.
>
> Date: _____ Employee: _____
> _____ I DO NOT intend to attach a supplement.
> _____ I DO intend to attach a supplement.
>
> Date: _____ Supervisor: _____

SOURCE: Association of Legal Administrators, "Employee Performance Review." Copyright © 1991. Reprinted with permission of the ALA.

firms use employee files to retain personal data, salary records, performance evaluations, records regarding disciplinary actions, and, sometimes, employment test results, academic records, and medical and health data. Thirty-three states have privacy laws governing use of and access to employee records, and many states have laws for restricting third party access and for allowing employees access to their own files, as well. To avoid endangering their employees' right to privacy, managers should review files and eliminate materials that do not have a clear employment-related purpose. Next, they should establish a regular access policy and procedures that allow employees to review their own records to correct inaccuracies or to add personal statements to contested materials. Thirdly, they should ask employees to authorize in writing the use of any personal information or other materials from their files. Supervisors and management should understand the importance of limited file access. No medical information should be disclosed without an employee's permission. Job references should be given carefully; as we have seen, some company policies allow managers to provide only job titles and dates of service to a worker's prospective employer. Finally, subsequent employees should have no rights to materials or information in current employees' files.

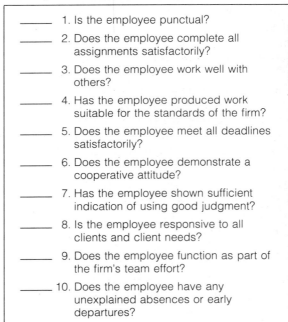

FIGURE 8–2
A Sample Checklist Evaluation

_____ 1. Is the employee punctual?
_____ 2. Does the employee complete all assignments satisfactorily?
_____ 3. Does the employee work well with others?
_____ 4. Has the employee produced work suitable for the standards of the firm?
_____ 5. Does the employee meet all deadlines satisfactorily?
_____ 6. Does the employee demonstrate a cooperative attitude?
_____ 7. Has the employee shown sufficient indication of using good judgment?
_____ 8. Is the employee responsive to all clients and client needs?
_____ 9. Does the employee function as part of the firm's team effort?
_____ 10. Does the employee have any unexplained absences or early departures?

SOURCE: Association of Legal Administrators, "Employee Performance Review." Copyright © 1991. Reprinted with permission of the ALA.

APPRAISAL TOOLS AND TECHNIQUES

Among the instruments and methods that supervisors use to evaluate subordinates are checklists, graphic rating scales, descriptive essays, the critical incidents technique, and management by objectives.

Checklists

Easy to use because it merely requires a supervisor to answer yes or no to questions based on his or her observation of a worker's performance, a checklist sets forth the expectations that a firm has established for a particular job. The simplicity of the checklist evaluation is an advantage as well as a disadvantage. Though the technique is objective and quick, the checklist form usually provides no room for comments, and doing a task isn't always as simple as it seems. Figure 8–2 illustrates a sample checklist evaluation.

Graphic Rating Scales

A **graphic rating scale** asks a supervisor to describe an employee's performance in a given area by choosing a verbal or numerical indicator on a graded performance scale. Those who devise rating scales should choose verbal indicators carefully. For example, say that a rating scale asks a supervisor to describe an employee's performance as inferior, average, good, or exceptional. Raters may not feel at ease classifying work as "exceptional," "outstanding," or "extraordinary"; categories such as "acceptable," "very good," or "superior" seem more attainable and more realistic. Also, too many choices can complicate a scale. Effective rating scales yield accurate and easily interpretable information. Most verbal scales utilize no more than five indicators; by comparison, numerical scales use a wide variety of ranges (for instance, 0 to 5, 1 to 10, or a scale from 1 to 100 that utilizes interior categories such as 1 to 20, 21 to 40, 41 to 60, and so on). Figure 8–3 provides an example of a graphic rating scale derived from the ALA's performance review for legal administrators.

FIGURE 8–3
Example of a Graphic Rating Scale

Indicate the level of competency or proficiency the administrator has achieved in each of the following areas and comment briefly on the performance of the employee relating to these skills. (You may add other skills that are not listed here.)

Ratings scale:
- **4 = Outstanding:** reserved for a select few who are consistently and uniformly excellent in their level of performance.
- **3 = Commendable:** for those who often exceed reasonable goals and objectives. They regularly exceed, sometimes far above, sometimes slightly above, established work standards.
- **2 = Satisfactory:** for those who normally fulfill the work requirements and who are able to establish and meet reasonable goals, even though sometimes they may fall short.
- **1 = Marginal:** for those who need significant improvement, who sometimes fail to fulfill the work requirements and who lack consistency in performance.
- **0 = Unsatisfactory:** for those who consistently fail to measure up to the requirement of this skill area.

	Circle One		Circle One
Job Knowledge	0 1 2 3 4	Personnel Management Skills	0 1 2 3 4
Verbal Communication	0 1 2 3 4	Financial Management	0 1 2 3 4
Written Communication	0 1 2 3 4	Team Cooperation	0 1 2 3 4
Planning	0 1 2 3 4	Delegation	0 1 2 3 4
Problem Solving	0 1 2 3 4	Leadership	0 1 2 3 4
Time Management	0 1 2 3 4	Initiative and Creativity	0 1 2 3 4
Responsiveness	0 1 2 3 4	Dependability	0 1 2 3 4

SOURCE: Association of Legal Administrators, "Employee Performance Review." Copyright © 1991. Reprinted with permission of the ALA.

Descriptive Essays

A **descriptive essay** provides a supervisor with a free-form tool for commenting on a worker's performance. Though the essay technique is less structured than the checklist or the rating scale, most firms ask supervisors to write in response to a focusing statement such as "Comment on the contributions of this individual during the past year," or "Discuss what you think this individual has contributed to the firm, describing both assets and your expectations for his or her future development." Writing an essay allows a supervisor not only to describe an employee's contributions but to discuss job-related areas in which he or she might develop. Because most people (supervisors included) enjoy offering their views on a particular topic, descriptive essays might seem easy to write. They're not. To write an accurate and objective essay, a supervisor must focus on an employee's observable behavior, recognize and sidestep personal biases, and avoid speculating on the employee's motives for acting as he or she does or did. A well-written descriptive essay is a true accomplishment.

The Critical Incidents Technique

Like the descriptive essay technique, the **critical incidents** technique allows a supervisor to evaluate an employee in a relatively unstructured essay format; unlike the descriptive essay, the critical incidents tool asks the supervisor to focus on the strongest and weakest aspects of the employee's performance. Though discussing another person's weaknesses is rarely easy, a supervisor can increase the objectivity and accuracy of his or her negative assertions (as well as his or her positive ones) by describing specific examples of the employee's behavior. The instructions for writing a critical incidents essay might ask a supervisor to "Discuss the employee's primary strengths and weaknesses," "Describe in detail the areas where this member of the firm would benefit from professional development," or "Describe an occasion during which the worker's contributions were positive and one in which they left something to be desired." For example, for an evaluation involving the performance of a law firm administrator, the ALA invites the evaluator to "comment on any aspect of the administrator's performance. In particular, if the administrator's performance is unsatisfactory in a specific area or overall, clearly indicate the firm's expectations and the period of time in which a satisfactory performance level is to be achieved."[35]

Management by Objectives

Management by objectives, which may be part of an annual review or may serve as an ongoing evaluative process, enables an employee and a supervisor to work together in setting specific goals for the employee that will benefit the firm. The ALA suggests that both the evaluator and the person being evaluated list future work objectives prior to an evaluation meeting. At the meeting, the evaluator will help the worker to select and finalize objectives that will become the focus of the next evaluation period.[36] In a firm that integrates MBO with its general planning, supervisors can help workers to select goals that will contribute to the firm's overall objectives, using the same kinds of goal-setting techniques that we examined in Chapter 2.

EMPLOYEE DISCIPLINE

In our personal lives and at work, we often think of discipline as the correction a person receives for deliberately ignoring rules. In a law firm, especially for supervisors, **discipline** is a systematic control: a work style that results from training based on self-control, order, character, and efficiency. Discipline is positive when firm members work together in an orderly way; discipline is poor or negative when work life is chaotic and inefficient, and when members basically disregard the rules that the firm has prescribed. Such an atmosphere can endanger a firm's operations, if not its existence. As George Odiorne observes, "In all organizations there are kinds of behavior that cannot be permitted because they keep the organization from going toward its objectives or interfere with the personal rights of its members. If such behavior occurs, some kind of disciplinary action must be taken."[37]

People sometimes confuse discipline with morale. As we have seen, morale is the result of shared feelings and attitudes. Discipline, by comparison, results from the acceptance of rules and procedures. Though we can often link poor discipline to high morale, the opposite may or may not be true. A high degree of discipline could stem either from high morale or from strict controls and intimidating supervision, which weaken morale. Discipline is at its best when workers accept it as a valuable standard and thereby incorporate it into the attitudes and feelings that comprise morale.

Self-Discipline

Law firm members who accept the standards and regulations of the firm are exercising **self-discipline.** Most workers honestly try to provide their employers with a fair day's work, to observe acceptable standards of behavior, and to cooperate and treat others ethically. In exchange, most ask only that their employers set fair and sensible rules, make these rules clearly known, and indicate in their treatment of their workers a belief in the basic goodness of people. As long as an employer honors this unspoken agreement, workers usually are willing to exercise the self-discipline necessary to place the firm's needs above their own. Should an employer treat workers unfairly, however, or should they believe that they are being treated unfairly, self-discipline can collapse, with disastrous monetary consequences. Worker theft from employers amounts to tens of billions of dollars annually. Many other forms of employee fraud and dishonesty can gnaw away at a firm as well, particularly *theft of company time* due to illicit absenteeism, late arrivals and early departures, long coffee breaks and lunches, making personal phone calls off-break, completing personal business on law firm time, and engaging in excessive, work-disrupting socializing. In 1989, employee theft and dishonesty was estimated to cost employers over 200 billion dollars a year.[38] Though few supervisors would want to mistrust their coworkers or their supervisees, only the most naive manager would believe that self-discipline is total and constant and that abuses never occur.

External Discipline

It is rare for a law firm to spend much time on issues such as the discipline of its members. Incompetent newcomers get weeded out quickly, simply because management has little time to waste converting the underzealous or trying to instill talent where none exists. In addition, most employment or placement agencies allow firms a trial period in which to determine the suitability of workers that the agency has provided. Although determining suitability never takes long, the opportunity to recoup often-steep placement fees encourages firms to decide quickly whether to keep new, agency-provided personnel.

Nonetheless, despite the trial periods and the weeding, even those workers whom the firm has deemed productive resources will produce their share of problems. Occasionally, even the best and most suitable employees will ignore the firm's rules. At such times, supervisors must decide whether—and how—to correct the transgressor's behavior. Whereas some firms will cut employees for the slightest offense, many others believe that modifying worker behavior helps a firm to retain good help and is always cheaper, in the long run, than recruiting and training new employees. When meting out discipline, a supervisor should consider the seriousness of the infraction, the frequency of its occurrence, and its effect on the firm, on other workers, and on productivity. In addition, the supervisor should consider the worker's track record with the firm. The facts about an offense should be completely documented, and the offense should be clearly the worker's fault, not something beyond his or her control. Finally, the supervisor should base disciplinary actions on obvious expectations with which the worker was or should be familiar, not on some obscure policy. Generally, a law firm will approach discipline in one of two ways: traditionally or developmentally.

Traditional Discipline. Advocates of traditional discipline believe that breaking a rule is an offense and that offenses must be punished. Unlike those who advocate developmental discipline, those who practice traditional discipline maintain that the primary purpose of discipline is to improve a worker's behavior, not to cater to his or her development, feelings, or sense of good will. Advocates of traditional discipline would not, for example, be comfortable suspending a worker with pay. Instead, they might place the offender on suspension for a period lasting from one day to one month, using the gravity of the offense to decide whether the offender should be paid during that period.

Developmental Discipline. Advocates of developmental discipline (also known as *discipline without punishment*) believe that discipline is not a punishment but a method of shaping a worker's behavior and that the key to discipline is to persuade the worker to change his or her behavior willingly. For example, in a firm that practices developmental discipline, a suspended employee is likely to receive a "decision-making leave," complete with pay. The phrase "decision-making" emphasizes the idea that the worker should use the time to reconsider his or her behavior; the pay not only signifies the firm's good will and interest in the worker but helps to eliminate the chance that the suspension will transform the worker's attitude into one of hostility. Nonetheless, developmental discipline is not infallible. A worker might return from suspension seemingly subdued, but harboring resentment rather than thoughts of improved performance.[39] We will examine the specific steps involved in progressive discipline later in this chapter.

Rules for Effective Discipline

When supervisors need to discipline employees, both parties enter conflict-laden territory. No one likes to receive correction, and even the most caring and empathic supervisor can inspire resentment. Of the approaches that endeavor to ensure effective, productive discipline, the most popular is probably the **hot stove rule**,[40] which suggests that effective discipline consists of four elements: advance warning, immediacy, consistency, and impartiality.

Advance Notice

Like a child reaching for the range top, workers are entitled to know the rules that govern their working environment and the consequences of ignoring or breaking those rules. To legitimately discipline a worker for failing to uphold a rule, the firm must have given the worker advance notice, in a handbook, memo, or other announcement, that the rule would be enforced.

Immediacy

Just as we feel instantly when we've burned ourselves, certain situations demand a supervisor's immediate re-

ANOTHER LOOK

When It's Time to Act

The following behaviors warrant immediate disciplinary action:

- Repeated or excessive absenteeism or tardiness
- Interfering with the work of other employees
- Abusive or inconsiderate treatment of clients or other workers
- Insubordination
- Failure to meet work standards and norms
- Violation of known rules
- Tending to personal matters during work hours
- Theft, destruction, misuse, or abuse of the firm's property
- Falsification of records
- Threats or acts of physical violence
- Use of drugs or alcohol on the job
- Leaving the work site without approval
- Striking a supervisor
- Fighting with other workers
- Spreading lies and maliciously misrepresenting work requests

1. Which offenses should warrant immediate suspension?
2. Aside from witnessing the event, for which offenses should a supervisor gather more facts before taking disciplinary action?
3. Which offenses seem most minor? Why?
4. For which offenses would the offender benefit most from progressive discipline?
5. Which offense might lead most easily to termination of law office employment?

sponse. Often, the more time that lapses, the less effective the discipline. Whereas a firm may justifiably subject a worker to immediate termination for hitting a supervisor, stealing, willfully damaging firm property, or falsifying records, suspension is a quick and certain disciplinary tool both as a last-straw technique for use with workers who have already received multiple warnings for lesser offenses and as an immediate response to a single serious infraction. Suspension prevents the offender from further disrupting the work environment (besides allowing him or her time to cool down, if necessary) and gives the supervisor time to ascertain the facts of the transgression. Even if the disciplinary action leads ultimately to demotion or discharge, suspension has the advantage of immediacy. "Unfortunately," observe Stephen Catt and Donald Miller, "a few employees simply fail to appreciate that certain behaviors will not be tolerated until they have been shocked by a suspension."[41] Behaviors warranting immediate suspension include fighting, the use of drugs or alcohol, criminal offenses, and insubordination (see the Another Look above).

Consistency

Just as we can depend on the fact that touching a hot stove will be as painful the second, third, or fourth time as it was the first, law firm members should be able to depend on their firm to establish sound rules and enforce them consistently. Any control that a firm establishes over its people must be grounded in the valid premise that a rule exists to help the organization or to protect the rights of others, and the firm must address each infraction. For members to perceive rules not only as fair but binding, the firm needs to demonstrate a clear, uniform interest in upholding those rules.

Impartiality

A stove will scorch whatever finger touches it, and discipline should be just as impartial. Because supervisors often work closely with those they need to discipline, however, impartiality can be difficult to achieve, especially when the offender is normally an outstanding worker. But workers are quick to perceive an unequal distribution of discipline—when, for instance, Dan gets suspended while Tami gets off with a warning for committing the same infraction, or when Bill, the supervisor's "pet," weasels his way out of trouble yet again. Supervisors who cannot discipline evenhandedly foster confusion, uncertainty, and poor morale among their workers; those whom they *do* discipline may regard the action as a personal attack. The most effective discipline is impartial, focusing on the offense, not the offender, and occurring in a context of professional caring and trust.

Progressive Discipline

Though disciplinary actions can be time-consuming and even counterproductive and though many firms would prefer to avoid disciplining workers altogether by hiring carefully and weeding out unsuitable newcomers, most firms inevitably need to develop a structured approach to discipline. The most successful firms try to work with offenders before problems escalate to a one-way, out-the-door solution that can damage both the firm and the employee. **Progressive discipline,** a process by which a firm not only can attempt to improve a worker's behavior but can prove its attempts to do so, should the need arise, consists of a series of documented and increasingly stern disciplinary measures generally divided into seven steps.

Informal Counseling

If the offense is not serious, talking to the worker is the first step in progressive discipline. Discussing the unacceptable behavior gives the worker a chance to tell his or her side of the story and allows the supervisor to convey the organization's concern. By calmly examining the effects that the unacceptable actions have had on the firm and on other workers, the employee and the supervisor avoid the tension that otherwise might have impaired their future communications.

Oral Warning

If the unacceptable behavior persists, the next step of the progressive discipline process consists of a verbal warning. The supervisor should always speak with the worker first, before administering the warning, to allow the offender another opportunity to clear up any misunderstandings or to talk about any extenuating circumstances. At this stage, the supervisor should remind the worker about the gravity of the problem and tell him or her clearly that further instances of the unacceptable behavior will provoke increasingly strict disciplinary actions. Training and development consultant William Tracey, who is known for his practical and effective suggestions for administering discipline in business settings, reminds supervisors always to give oral reprimands in private, out of respect for the worker, and to choose the time carefully. He also counsels not mincing words. He advises supervisors to be specific and direct, and to concentrate on the specific job-related behavior. By doing so, supervisors avoid criticizing the worker as a person or implying motives. When disciplining workers, supervisors should exhibit a very serious demeanor. Body language that conveys less than that, such as smiling, might imply that the supervisor's attitude is ambivalent or even accepting. The supervisor should listen to the employee, but refuse to accept excuses. Finally, the supervisor should end the discussion by saying that he or she usually appreciates the person's work (if this is true), but not this particular action. The supervisor should then drop the matter, not bear a grudge, and, above all, not speak of it with any other subordinate.[42]

First Written Warning

If the behavior reoccurs after the supervisor and the worker have spoken, the supervisor must respond as soon as possible. At this point, further discussion and sympathy are neither appropriate nor effective, and the supervisor should avoid being drawn into what could easily become a manipulative and subjective exchange. Instead, he or she should present the worker with a clear written warning that includes

- A statement describing what has happened, including when and where the unacceptable behavior took place;
- A listing of who was involved and who was present;
- An explanation describing why the firm considers the recurring activity a breach of expected behavior serious enough to warrant disciplinary action; and
- Precise instructions describing the behavior that the firm expects of the worker and the actions that the firm will take if the proscribed behavior reoccurs.

After reviewing this information with the worker, the supervisor should ask the worker to sign and date the warning form. The written warning should indicate that the worker

- Was asked to clarify any inaccuracies in the organization's version of what actually happened;
- Had an opportunity to add additional comments to the statement sheet; and
- Understood the contents of the disciplinary form.

Second Written Warning

If the behavior continues, the supervisor should provide a second written warning by repeating the procedures he or she used to give the first written warning.

Third Written Warning

The supervisor uses procedures the same as those he or she used in providing the first and second written warnings, but augments the third written warning with disciplinary action, usually suspension.

Suspension

The suspension that accompanies or follows the third written warning may be with or without pay, depending on the firm's philosophy. Verbally and in writing, the firm should tell the worker the reasons for and the dates of the suspension and warn the worker that any additional problems will result in termination.

Termination

After a verbal warning and a minimum of two written warnings, a firm may terminate a worker for continued or repeated infractions. Neither a supervisor nor anyone else in the firm, no matter how powerful, should make this decision lightly: given the modern tendency to question managerial authority (and to seek legal redress for workplace affronts), as well as the fact that a worker who has willfully caused his or her termination usually is ineligible to receive unemployment benefits, "the firing process, once a simple act, is now a potential landmine." [43] Although there is no way to make a termination pleasant, there are ways to avoid bungling the process. First, the supervisor should inform the worker of the decision quickly, preferably within the first two minutes of a meeting that should last no more than five minutes. Second, keeping in mind *Wall Street Journal* staff reporter Suzanne Alexander's warning that "the loyalty of those left behind can be diminished by callous treatment of former colleagues," [44] the supervisor should exhibit control and avoid showing anger, antagonism, or contempt for the employee or his or her abilities. Third, the supervisor should announce the decision clearly and with utter finality, allowing the employee to react but not to argue: at this point, after all the verbal and written warnings the employee has received, debate would only waste time and offer false hope. Next, the supervisor should ask the worker to sign a summary of the events leading to termination and allow him or her time to add comments to the form, which the firm will retain in the worker's personnel file. Finally, the supervisor should not discuss the termination with those not involved.[45]

Reluctance to Discipline

Because discipline is probably a supervisor's most difficult task, even the most seasoned managers would sometimes prefer to look the other way rather than confront a situation requiring disciplinary action. This reluctance to discipline manifests itself at all levels of law firm management. Top management may be reluctant to update policies or procedures, or to support the disciplinary actions of middle management, who may in turn fail to support management at the supervisory level. Finally, supervisors, who work closely with the firm's front-line staff, may avoid discipline out of fear of damaging their relationships with their workers, since few supervisors are trained to discipline effectively, without becoming emotionally involved, feeling guilty, or rationalizing the situation.[46] Managers at all levels dislike the emotionalism that can accompany discipline, as well as being seen as the "bad guy"; their reluctance to discipline also may arise from a fear of acting alone, a dislike for spending time on proper disciplinary procedures, or the threat of lawsuits.

With all this fear, dislike, and lack of training, it seems surprising that discipline happens at all. Fortunately, most law firm managers are wise enough to recognize not only that discipline is essential to a work environment that relies on order and on carefully followed procedures but also that evenhanded discipline promotes an image of the firm as a dependable, equitable, and fair place to work. In the final analysis, effective supervision relies on the quiet courage of managers who can discuss unsatisfactory performance without ridiculing or condemning a worker, who can be kind without sugarcoating or ignoring weaknesses and failings, and who care more about challenging their workers and communicating with them honestly, openly, and fairly than about winning their approval and affection. Supervisory practices administered with honesty and fairness do much to ensure the success of a firm.

QUESTIONS FOR DISCUSSION AND REVIEW

1. Supervising others has always been a challenge. Why do some say that supervising others is now harder than it used to be? Do you agree?
2. Why is supervising the members of a law firm different from supervising workers in other business settings?
3. Write your own ten commandments for increasing trust.
4. Think of a supervisor you have known and describe three characteristics that aided and three characteristics that impaired his or her performance as a supervisor.
5. Imagine yourself as supervisor in a law firm that has a busy, demanding and hostile environment. What would your three most difficult challenges be?
6. Describe the three supervisory styles that currently are in wide use. Which style do you think would be most effective in a law firm? Which style would you prefer to use?
7. Explain the critical components of successful evaluations, using examples from actual performance evaluations that you know about or have experienced.
8. Compose two short descriptive essays: one that evaluates the performance of a very inadequate secretary assigned to your department and one evaluating the performance of a hardworking and competent paralegal who is also under your supervision.
9. What are the characteristics of effective discipline?
10. Describe the steps involved in progressive discipline. What consideration should management have for a worker who reaches the last step, termination?

EXPERIENTIAL EXERCISES

I. Have You Looked at Your Work Values Lately?*

Read each of the following statements about work and decide the extent to which you agree or disagree with it. Circle the number that comes closest to indicating your true feelings.

	Strongly disagree		Neither			Strongly agree	
1. Being a dedicated worker makes you a better person.	1	2	3	4	5	6	7
2. A good indication of your personal worth is how well you do your job.	1	2	3	4	5	6	7
3. Work should be one of the most important parts of a person's life.	1	2	3	4	5	6	7
4. Rich people should feel obligated to work even if they do not need to.	1	2	3	4	5	6	7
5. Unproductive workers are not loyal to their country.	1	2	3	4	5	6	7
6. If I inherited a lot of money I would keep working: I work for reasons other than just to earn wages.	1	2	3	4	5	6	7
7. A worker should do a decent job whether or not the supervisor is around.	1	2	3	4	5	6	7

---

*Reprinted by permission of publisher from *THE WORK ETHIC*, by David J. Cherrington. Copyright © 1980 AMACOM, a division of American Management Association, New York. All rights reserved.

8. A worker should feel a sense of pride in his or her work. 1 2 3 4 5 6 7
9. An individual should enjoy his or her work. 1 2 3 4 5 6 7
10. Even if you dislike your work, you should do your best. 1 2 3 4 5 6 7
11. Getting recognition for my own work is important to me. 1 2 3 4 5 6 7
12. It's wrong to do a poor job at work just because you think you can get away with it. 1 2 3 4 5 6 7

Scoring: Of the preceding twelve statements, the first six measure the moral importance of work and the last six measure pride in craftsmanship. To compute your moral-importance-of-work score, add your responses to the first six items and divide by six. To compute your pride-in-craftsmanship score, add your responses to items 7 through 12 and divide by six. The average scores for 3,000 American workers were as follows: moral importance of work = 4.95, and pride in craftsmanship = 6.23.

II. What Kind of Supervisor Will You Make?

As we have seen in this past chapter, supervision requires a special set of values and a talent for understanding people. How will you measure up as a supervisor? Do you need to rethink some of your attitudes and practices or are you ready to be a superb supervisor right now? In the blank to the left of each of the following statements, write the number of the response that most closely matches your opinion: +5 = strongly agree; +3 = agree; 0 = neutral; −3 = disagree; −5 = strongly disagree.

_____ 1. A supervisor should be in touch with the views and feelings of his or her workers.
_____ 2. Supervisors should try to overlook as many infractions as possible in order to cut down on tension.
_____ 3. Supervisors should understand the technical skills that their supervisees use.
_____ 4. It's best to stay aloof from supervisees, so as not to become too close.
_____ 5. Sharing basic goals with workers and establishing a sense of teamwork is valuable for supervisors.
_____ 6. When workers are using the office for personal business, it's best to say nothing.
_____ 7. Even if a supervisor doesn't have the final answer for a decision, keeping the worker informed is essential.
_____ 8. Superiors who mistrust their workers are doing the right thing. Suspicion pays off.
_____ 9. Maintaining high standards may cause some tension at first but is necessary in a law firm.
_____ 10. Workers should inform supervisors about coworkers, even if the information they provide could be damaging.
_____ 11. When an attorney complains about a subordinate, the attorney is always right.
_____ 12. When faced with a request from a subordinate he or she dislikes, a supervisor is justified in setting the request aside.

___ 13. As supervisor, I am responsible for meeting the needs of my work groups.
___ 14. Superiors do better when their work groups are not close-knit enough to rally and rise up against them.
___ 15. Supervisors are responsible for and represent their subordinates; they should go to bat for them when the need arises.
___ 16. Superiors should try to be positive with subordinates by promising them whatever they want.
___ 17. When workers question superiors, it's a positive sign.
___ 18. It's much safer not to communicate openly with supervisees; the supervisor has less to explain and avoids having to answer to subordinates.
___ 19. Supervisors should think of subordinates not as those who work under them but as those who work alongside and with them.
___ 20. Superiors should encourage workers to suggest ways in which management can improve.

Scoring: Tally your responses for items 1, 3, 5, 7, 9, 13, 15, 17, 19 and 20. For items 2, 4, 6, 8, 10, 11, 12, 14, 16, and 18, change each negative response to a positive one and vice versa. For example, tally -3 as a $+3$ or $+5$ as a -5. Then add these numbers to the total for the first set of responses. You may estimate your supervisory potential as follows:

Superb potential:	+80 to +100	Little hope:	−41 to −80
Great promise:	+40 to +79	Time to explore	
The potential is there:	0 to +39	another career:	−81 to −100
After a lot of work:	−1 to −40		

CHAPTER 9

Leadership

LEARNING OBJECTIVES

After completing this chapter, you should be able to:

- Explain the meaning of and the need for leadership;
- Understand the competencies necessary to leadership;
- Discuss the attempts to define leadership;
- Explain the behavioral and traits theories of leadership;
- Explain the situational theories of leadership;
- Compare and discuss the future vision theories of leadership; and
- Identify leadership challenges as they apply to law office managers.

Harold A. Cort has been the executive administrator at the law firm of Halloran & Sage in Hartford, Connecticut, since 1980. Active in the Nutmeg Chapter of the ALA, Mr. Cort is a frequent lecturer and teacher of law office management. He is the author of numerous articles which have appeared in The ALA News, *a monthly magazine for legal administrators and attorneys.*

FOCUS FROM THE FIELD

Harold Cort: Leadership Is Being Placed in the Hands of Law Firm Administrators

Where is leadership found in law firms?

I strongly believe that firms go through an evolutionary process regarding their management. Small firms, with ten to twenty attorneys, are led by committees. At this point an administrator is usually hired. As firms grow and become more sophisticated, they are more inclined to appoint a managing partner, a lawyer who has overall control of the business direction of the firm. Today, law firms want to maximize their rate of return and are hiring professional managers to be administrators who have strong backgrounds with expertise in accounting, finance, computers, and long-range planning. I like to compare a law firm to a business with a corporate-style operation. The managing partner is likened to the chief executive officer. He or she is the one who has overall responsibility for the success of the business. The legal administrator has the role of the chief operating officer. He or she has overall responsibility for the day-to-day operations and long-range planning. Both the managing partner and the legal administrator need to be visionaries and risk-takers. Current and future leadership is being placed in the hands of law firm administrators who are equipped with strong accounting, finance, and management skills.

Does leadership in law offices take any special skills?

Beyond the obvious management technical tools that one should possess, I believe that someone in a leadership role must have two strong skills: communication and listening. Without them, I don't know how one could run a business, any business. The mark of a good leader is shown in one's ability to communicate without misunderstanding.

Is leadership of professionals difficult?

It's difficult because of the fact that you're working with lawyers, and they are not used to being managed. You have less of a problem communicating with and understanding support staff. Lawyers tend to dance to their own tune, and this creates some problems from time to time. It's just their nature as lawyers. They are very demanding and under tremendous pressure to service the clients as properly and as expeditiously as possible. There are times when their plans don't mesh with the firm's, so there is conflict. I think that a lot of it has to do with the philosophy that exists within the firm. If you, as an administrator, are supported by the partners, you tend to have fewer problems. When a problem does come up, it is managed appropriately. To be a leader, one must have the confidence of the people he or she is to lead.

What are some of the leadership challenges that law office leaders face?

One challenge is working with the diversified groups of people within the organization—partners, associates, paralegals, secretaries, and administrative and clerical personnel. Everyone has a different set of needs. One of the most challenging aspects of being an administrator is to make sure that all of those needs are satisfied. I think that another challenge is the barrage of new technology that has come into the marketplace. Administrators must be careful to bring the right technology into the firm. I think that you need to maximize the needs of the firm against the economic costs of technology to achieve the proper return on your investment.

What leadership styles seem to work best?

Along with communication and listening skills, a successful leader must guide and develop individuals to share more productively in group accomplishments. A successful administrator will generate the concept of working as a team. Here at Halloran & Sage, we work in teams specializing in different areas of the practice of law. This approach gives us more flexibility to handle any legal problem that a client brings to us, no matter how complex. All work is generated and completed within a particular unit. We have determined that this leads to job satisfaction. To summarize, the effective leader needs to be a combination of a human relations specialist and a productivity specialist. In addition, the effective leader will be able to understand group dynamics and will be able to understand people's reactions and know why they act as they do.

How do members of the firm know who the leaders are?

It's both the formal and informal pipeline, supported by top management, that gets the word out. People learn quickly as to the hierarchy within the firm. We spend a tremendous amount of time training new hires: lawyers, paralegals, secretaries, and administrative and clerical people alike. Everyone goes through two to five days of orientation. Our firm employs a training manager who has the responsibility and authority that such a position requires. By the time new hires walk out of the orientation process, they will know who is in control, whom to see for what problem, and the hierarchy of the organization. We have found that the time a new hire spends in orientation has been invaluable in providing positive reinforcement to the philosophy of the firm.

Does law firm management need to know about management theory in order to be effective? Isn't law firm management unique?

Yes. There isn't a day that goes by when I'm not craving to learn more about how to apply management principles and theory to the running of the law firm. I'm constantly trying to find books on management theory, accounting theory—anything of that nature so I can become a better manager with better leadership skills. However, one cannot just take a book off the shelf and apply it to the management of a firm. There's a lot more that goes on that one has to be concerned with. My philosophy and goal is to operate Halloran & Sage on a corporate-model basis. The ultimate goal, however, must always be to properly service the client in a timely manner.

These leaders are not born. They emerge when organizations face new problems and complexities that cannot be solved by unguided evolution. They assume responsibilities for reshaping organizational practices to *adapt* to organizational change. They direct organizational changes that build *confidence* and empower their employees to seek new ways of doing things. They overcome resistance to change by creating visions of the future that evoke confidence in and mastery of new organizational practices. . . . We do face an unsettling future but not one without vision. Vision is the commodity of leaders and power is their currency.
(Bennis and Nanus, *Leaders: The Strategies for Taking Charge*)[1]

> If you think about it, we love others not for who they are, but for how they make us feel. In order to *willingly* accept the direction of another individual, it *must* make you feel good to do so. . . . If you believe what I am saying, you cannot help but come to the conclusion that those you have followed passionately, gladly, zealously—have made you feel like *somebody* . . . . This business of making another person feel good in the unspectacular course of his daily comings and goings is, in my view, the very essence of leadership.
> (Bennis and Nanus, *Leaders: The Strategies for Taking Charge*)[2]
>
> Lives of great men all remind us
> We can make our lives sublime,
> And, departing, leave behind us
> Footprints on the sands of time.
> (Longfellow, "A Psalm of Life")[3]

THE SEARCH FOR LEADERSHIP

As children, most of us played Follow the Leader. Those who followed the best leaders found themselves in increasingly funny, crazy situations, and those who thought they could do better could persuade the leader to become a follower and take their turn at challenging the others. At the time, we were hardly aware that a game could illustrate the shifting dynamics between leaders and followers, the compelling nature of a leader's vision, the exchange of trust, a leader's skill at capturing attention, and many more of the aspects of leadership theory that we will examine in this chapter.

As adults, we are more discerning. We are more critical of leadership and of leaders themselves. In the twentieth century, neither political nor religious leaders may assume that their authority is sacrosanct, and, as we saw in Chapter 8, modern workers are far more apt than their earlier counterparts to question the authority of managers and other business leaders. Business writers, who also are quick to malign the current quality of leadership, observe that modern leadership is largely a case of the blind leading the blind through a maze of contemporary complexities. Educator, public servant and leadership scholar John Gardner writes of "the cry for leadership."[4] Management expert Warren Bennis wonders *Why Leaders Can't Lead*.[5] Abraham Zaleznik describes *The Leadership Gap*,[6] while John Kotter warns of a leadership crisis.[7] In his Pulitzer prize-winning work *Leadership*, James MacGregor Burns comments that "leadership rarely rises to the full need for it."[8]

Because such criticism can apply to any business setting, we should acknowledge the idea that career success in a law firm depends at least partly on a person's leadership abilities. Whatever your hierarchical level and whatever your method of contributing to the firm, the ability to influence others is not only valuable but essential. Unless they demonstrate leadership qualities, partners and new associates alike will never attract and keep new clients; secretaries will never be given positions of responsibility; paralegals will never advance to management positions; and law firm administrators will never stand the pressure. Law firms will always need members at all levels, who clearly recognize and advance the firm's goals and who can motivate others to do the same.

Unfortunately, many of us fail either to utilize or to develop our leadership potential. Like the people of Thebes waiting for Oedipus to solve the riddle of the Sphinx, we tend to endow leaders with a nearly superhuman ability to provide inspiration and answers, and we think poorly of those who fail to do so. As Bennis notes, we too often think of a leader as "the renegade, who magnetizes a band of followers with courageous acts," not realizing that what truly inspires us as followers is a leader's "deep respect for the aspirations of others"[9] and his or her ability to help us discover, through example, our own integrity, dedication, magnanimity, humility, openness, and creativity.[10] In this chapter, we will discuss the need for leadership and examine current theories that attempt to explain the behavior, traits, and abilities essential to those who hope to provide effective leadership, in law firms and elsewhere.

The Need for Leadership

As educated, thinking human beings, law firm members are capable of making worthwhile decisions. Further, by working within an organizational structure that clearly demarcates authority and responsibilities, each member knows the contributions he or she is expected to make. Why, then, is leadership necessary? We can trace the need for leadership to four factors: external and internal change, motivational needs within the firm, competition, and the fact that organizational structures are incomplete without human beings to coordinate the structure's human elements.

External and Internal Change

Few organizations can exist with their backs turned to the world. As the outside environment changes, the firm must change in order to keep up with the times and meet new demands. Leadership helps the firm to assess those demands and ensures that it remains responsive to change. In addition, leadership provides the direction and stability that enable a firm to accommodate the internal changes that must accompany external change. Finally, leadership helps a law firm to create an agenda for internal change by building a support network of motivated and committed workers.[11]

Motivational Needs

As a firm changes, leadership provides the continued support that encourages workers to continue to embrace the firm's goals and values and to foster this sense of commitment among newcomers.[12]

Competition

The competitive marketplace is the third factor that necessitates strong leadership. John Kotter explains:

> For the rest of this century, we shall probably continue to see a world of business that looks fundamentally different from the 1950s and 1960s. It will be a world of intense competitive activity among very complex organizations. It will be a world in which bureaucratic managers are increasingly irrelevant and dangerous. It will be a world in which even the best "professional" managers are ineffective unless they can also lead. In general, it will be a world in which the leadership factor in management will become increasingly important—for prosperity, and even survival.[13]

Once largely exempt from the competitive demands that plagued other businesses, law firms now face competition intense enough to resemble economic warfare. This explosive new need to compete has created urgent demands for leadership in all facets of a firm.

Incomplete Organizational Structure

No matter how perfectly planned, organized, directed, and controlled a law firm is, human elements are at work. Even the most mechanistic view of an organization must acknowledge that workers are not machines, ready to run perpetually once set in motion. Leaders create a human link between an organization's structures and its people and influence workers, singly and collectively, in the process of accomplishing organizational goals.

The Meaning of Leadership

Though, in the simplest terms, we can define a **leader** as one who directs, guides, or influences people in working toward a goal, little is actually known about leadership and the qualities of leaders. Despite the fact that thousands of articles and books have been written on the subject, tying leadership to an exact definition remains a perplexing problem. One reason for this confusion is the wide range of expectations that people have for leaders. Another stems from the many definitions given to the word "leadership."[14] (One study revealed over 350![15]) A third reason is the fact that many terms—"manager," "powerholder," "chief," and "boss," among others—are used interchangeably with "leader."[16] To understand leadership correctly, we must recognize it as a unique concept (an idea we will explore further in a later section that compares leadership and management). For our purposes, **leadership** is the process of influencing or directing the performance or activity of others. The leadership process consists of four components: a leader, his or her followers, the situation, and the leader's vision.

Leaders

Conceptually, leaders and followers cannot exist without each other, since a leader is not a leader without followers, nor are followers followers without a leader to lead them. As one half of a matched set, leaders are those who assume the responsibilities and challenges of leadership and who offer something of value to followers. Factors that affect the strength of the interdependence between a leader and his or her followers include the leader's legitimacy, credibility, competence, personality, and motivational forces.

Followers

Followers are those who cooperate with and accept the persuasion of a leader, offering support, belief or trust, and a willingness to be influenced in exchange for something they believe to be of value. Factors that affect a follower group's relationship with a leader include the followers' expectations, personalities, competencies, and motivation, as well as their willingness to trust the leader.

The Situation

The interaction between leader and follower, in which the leader convinces the follower to work toward a goal and the follower responds with support and cooperation, is also a product of context. Some situational factors that affect the leader-follower relationship are the kinds of tasks and resources, the social structure of the organization and its rules and norms, the size of the group, the internal and external environment, and the stability or uncertainty of the situation. Leaders need to fit their setting and the situation. We would expect, for instance, to find on a battlefield leaders different from those we might find in a university, a social service agency, or a law firm.

Vision: The Ability to Recognize Goals

The third element of leadership is the vision, or goals, that a leader can offer his or her followers. In this context, we can define "vision" as the ability to recognize the potential in a situation, convince others of that potential, and coordinate their efforts in fulfilling it. A vision's power depends on a leader's belief in and on followers' need for that vision. "Great vision," writes John Kotter, "emerges when a powerful mind, working long and hard on massive amounts of information is able to see (or recognize in suggestions from others) interesting patterns and new possibilities."[17] Though the word "vision" has almost a mystical ring to it, John Naisbitt and Patricia Aburdene point out that a leader needs both "the mental power to create a vision and the practical ability to bring it about."[18] In addition to a vision of what can and should be, leadership demands energy, thoroughness, dedication, sweat, and time, as well as practical strategies for making vision a reality.[19] Leaders who cannot offer vision soon fall into aimless step with those behind them and spend their careers waiting, like others who are unable to utilize their leadership potential, for someone to tell them where to go and how to get there.

LAW FIRM MANAGERS AND LEADERSHIP

When you assume any position in a law firm that places you in a supervisory or managerial role, you face the challenge of leadership. As a manager or supervisor, you now have subordinates. What you quickly learn is that all the authority in the world will not make you a leader unless your subordinates allow it! Conversely, if you are to be an effective manager, you must also acknowledge the fact that your subordinates, most if not all of whom will be highly trained knowledge workers, require a certain amount of freedom in doing their jobs. Clearly, there are managers who are leaders and leaders who are not managers. Most effective managers have learned also to be leaders—that is, they have learned to utilize both their personal and position power.

Essentially, leadership augments management by enhancing authority and, therefore, a manager's ability to persuade subordinates to work toward the firm's goals. Nonetheless, though the roles are complementary, they are also distinctly different. Each has its own functions and activities, and, as John Kotter notes, "Not everyone can be good at both leading and managing."[20] Management copes with the complexity of an organization, striving to maintain order, quality, and consistency. Managers organize staff, make plans that will guide the firm's financial progress, direct the use of resources, and control the firm's activities through problem solving, goal setting, and rewarding. By comparison, leadership copes with change. Leaders establish direction, align people, and guide the creation of coalitions. They motivate and inspire.[21] Finally, a leader's most basic task is to persuade followers that the goals toward which he or she has chosen to direct his or her managerial efforts are worthwhile. As Bennis and Nanus observe, "Managers are people who do things right and leaders are people who do the right thing."[22] We can trace the differences between managers and leaders to the compacts and contracts they make, to their commitments and focus, to their style, and to their philosophies.[23]

Compacts and Contracts

Leaders and followers are connected by *compacts* that bind them morally, intellectually, and emotionally in their search for mutual goals.[24] Managers, by comparison, use their power base to gain the support of subordinates and then link themselves to those subordinates through *contracts* that reinforce roles and positions.[25]

Commitments

Managers and leaders differ in their respective commitments. Managers are more committed to mustering the human and material resources necessary to perform a task, whereas leaders are more committed to convincing their followers that certain decisions are "right for the times, right for the organization, and right for the people who are working in it."[26] In terms of communication, managers are more committed to the process itself, while leaders commit themselves more to the content of that process, realizing that their effort to win support for the vision they believe in depends on the ideas that they communicate to followers. Both managers and leaders are committed to motivating their followers: leaders, to encourage their followers' personal development; managers, to increase their followers' productivity and efficiency.

Focus

Leaders focus on ideas. Managers focus on process. Managers concentrate more on how things get done; leaders pay more attention to what people think.

Style

Leaders tend to be more dramatic and unpredictable than managers; as Zaleznik observes, leaders bring creativity and imagination to their work, and they "tolerate chaos and lack of structure" in order to resolve issues thoroughly.[27] Managers are typically more practical people, fair-minded, hardworking, analytical, and tolerant, whose behavior is shaped by the responsibility of their position.

Philosophy

Leaders and managers also differ in terms of philosophy. Managers, Zaleznik observes, differ from leaders "in the very way they perceive life and relationships, adapting to environments rather than confronting them."[28] By comparison, leaders, he writes, have endured "major events that lead to a sense of separateness or, perhaps, estrangement from their environments."[29] In addition, as we noted above, leaders tolerate chaos and a certain lack of structure; managers, writes Zaleznik, "seek order and control and are almost compulsively addicted to disposing of problems."[30] When we combine a manager's concern for getting things done with a leader's concern for the meaning of events, we have an ideal mix.

WHAT MAKES A LEADER?

Why are some people leaders rather than followers? First, some people have unique competencies that suit them to the task of being a leader. Second, they are able to make leadership compacts with followers.

Leadership Competencies

Through a study based on interviews with ninety successful and recognized leaders, Bennis and Nanus identified four areas in which leaders develop competence: the management of attention through vision, the management of meaning through communication, the management of trust through positioning, and the management of self through careful deployment and thorough self-knowledge.[31]

The Management of Attention through Vision

The leaders in Bennis and Nanus's study captivated their followers, firing their emotions and imaginations by communicating the powerful potential of their vision through compelling agendas and ideas in which followers could recognize great promise.[32]

The Management of Meaning through Communication

Leaders are good communicators, able to articulate their visions in a way that makes those visions seem tangible, realistic, and worthwhile to followers.[33]

The Management of Trust through Positioning

As we saw in Chapter 8, one of the main components of trust is reliability. Simply by positioning themselves as leaders, leaders broadcast their willingness to stand for their unique visions, and through their constancy in working toward the goals they support, leaders earn and retain the confidence and trust of their followers.[34]

Management of Self through Self-Knowledge and Deployment

Lastly, the leaders in Bennis and Nanus's study showed that they understood who they were and what they stood for. They deployed themselves as leaders by choosing behaviors that were strategically appropriate for reaching their goals. They capitalized on their strengths, minimized their weaknesses, and learned from their mistakes. Through their healthy self-esteem and belief in their visions, they projected a contagious confidence and, most importantly, developed the sense of security necessary to empower their followers.[35]

Social Exchange and the Leadership Compact

Though the four competencies we just examined are essential to effective leadership, they are not in themselves sufficient to identify a person as a leader. The factors that distinguish a leader from a follower are external as well as internal, and the process that transforms a group of people into a leader and followers is difficult to define. Gary Yukl, who has documented nineteen categories of leader behavior, suggests that once a group's members initiate a pattern of exchange among themselves, they assume and assign to each other the roles of leaders and followers. The social exchange, or *leadership compact,* that accompanies this conferring of roles may involve benefits that are material or psychological. Material benefits commonly include favors and monetary or other tangible rewards; psychological benefits include recognition, approval, and psychic salary benefits such as status, esteem, and appreciation.[36] More specifically, a leader offers his or her willingness to exercise authority, make decisions (and accept responsibility for their consequences), and live with the fear of failure or rejection.[37] In addition, observes Yukl,

> Leaders are expected by group members to carry out a variety of leadership functions, such as organizing the work, distributing rewards, providing psychological support, representing the group in dealing with other groups, modifying the group's goals as circumstances change, and defining reality in a way that is consistent with the underlying needs and values of members.[38]

Followers, in turn, offer esteem, trust, a certain willingness to be influenced, and their commitment to the leader's vision in exchange for positive change, a sense of satisfaction and accomplishment, and personal growth. Above all, the leadership compact—and the strength of the leader/follower relationship itself—depends on the ability and willingness of the leader to present and promote his or her vision and the ability and willingness of followers to cooperate and offer support. In other words, the leader/follower compact ultimately exists only because people are willing to lead or be led.

LEADERSHIP THEORIES

Human beings have always been fascinated by the power that some people seem to have over others, and over the years many theories have attempted to identify the factors that comprise leadership. In the following sections, we will examine four schools of leadership theory: the **trait theories,** which ascribe leadership ability to certain personal characteristics; **behavioral theories,** which attempt to define leadership by analyzing how leaders act; **situational theories,** which trace leadership to environmental forces; **future vision theories,** which identify leadership as a product of charisma or the ability to inspire trust or bring about change.

Trait Theories

Widely criticized but still a springboard for leadership study and research, the **trait approach to leadership** assumes that we can associate leadership ability with certain specific physical, intellectual, and psychological characteristics. Early studies in support of this theory claimed that leaders showed a range of extraordinary abilities, such as tireless energy, uncanny foresight, penetrating intuition, and irresistible powers of persuasion.[39] Later studies have taken a more pragmatic approach by asking, first, if the ability to identify leadership traits would correlate with the ability to identify those who would make good leaders in organizations and, secondly, if people could cultivate leadership traits in order to become more effective leaders. Although their findings are as yet inconclusive, researchers continue to seek out universal leadership traits. As Shelley Kirkpatrick and Edwin Locke observe in defense of trait research,

IN THE NEWS

Camaraderie: Nancy Siegel and the People Side of Productivity

As executive director of Morrison & Foerster—the biggest law firm in San Francisco—Nancy J. Siegel often turns to small groups for the raw material that fuels her largest projects.

When she decides to restructure the way things are done in the 500-lawyer firm, she often will ask a few staff persons to provide options. "You want people who are performing a job to be involved in making the decisions that will affect them," said Ms. Siegel. "I've seen how easy it is to make mistakes when things come from the top down."

Ms. Siegel, who becomes president of the National Association of Legal Administrators during the group's annual conference at San Francisco's Moscone Center this week, runs the non-legal operation of Morrison & Foerster's 11 offices in the United States and overseas.

She has a reputation as one of the leading executive directors in the nation, and is among just a handful of women who manage large law firms. "She's one of the few women to bridge the discrimination gap," said Dru Ramey, executive director of the Bar Association of San Francisco. "She's paved the way in her field."

According to Kathleen V. Fisher, co-managing partner of Morrison & Foerster's San Francisco office, the key to Ms. Siegel's success revolves around her ability to motivate people. "In a sense she does what really good teachers or coaches do," Ms. Fisher said. "She has a fundamental respect for what each staff person does. And when she asks them to do something she does it in a way that gains their trust."

Ms. Siegel believes healthy law firms thrive on a simple principle: Keep employees happy and they will produce. "You try to create an environment where people are paid well, where they have good benefits, where they have respect and feel part of the team," she commented.

To accomplish that aim, Ms. Siegel asks her management staff to give even the newest employees a hand in decision making. She believes that "by involving various people in the levels of decisions, you keep the process dynamic."

As an example of the way she seeks participation in hashing out plans for new projects, when she decided new secretarial stations were needed, she gathered a group of secretaries to work with the architect. She asks, "Who would better know the needs than the people who would use them?"

In the last year, Ms. Siegel has formed 10 groups to approach such ideas as whether to hire a new psychological counselor or establish an office-wide copy service. One current task force is getting ready to select an in-house travel agent.

Although Ms. Siegel has been appointing task forces for years, she believes the method should be used much more than it has been by the ALA, where she hopes to phase in as many as a dozen in the next six months. . . .

Although Ms. Siegel may seem fully committed to her profession,

---

Leadership is a demanding, unrelenting job with enormous pressures and grave responsibilities. It would be a profound disservice to leaders to suggest they are ordinary people who happened to be in the right place at the right time. Maybe the place matters, but it takes a special kind of person to master the challenges of opportunity.[40]

Modern Trait Studies

Modern attempts to link leadership potential with innate characteristics have produced a number of relatively similar trait lists. In the early 1970s, Edwin Ghiselli, who studied leadership traits for over twenty years, identified these six leadership traits in business managers: (1) an ability to supervise and get the job done correctly, (2) a need for achievement at work, (3) intelligence, (4) decisiveness, (5) self-assurance, and (6) initiative.[41] Also in the seventies, Ralph Stogdill, an outstanding contributor to leadership trait research, conducted an extensive survey of leadership studies. This survey led Stogdill to suggest that leaders are superior to others in their groups in terms of characteristics such as intelligence, scholarship, dependability, activity and social participation, and socioeco-

IN THE NEWS (continued)

that was not the case when she came to the business 20 years ago. Born in New York and raised in Palo Alto, she graduated from San Francisco State University with a degree in English literature, and "I always thought that I'd be a writer and a teacher."

In 1969, when she began working as a part-time secretary at the San Francisco law firm then known as Lillick, McHose & Charles, she "was their resident hippie," she recalled. "I would come in with tie-dyed shirts and sandals."

However, a subtle transformation began taking place as she rose from secretary to paralegal to personnel manager and finally to office manager. She thought about becoming an attorney, but "I kept putting off law school until I put it off forever. I found that I liked management," said Ms. Siegel, who left Lillick in 1981 to join Morrison & Foerster.

Today, she commands a salary and benefits commensurate with those of the firm's partners and has much the same authority as chief executive officers of large corporations. "My job has very gradually changed as I've taken on more and more responsibility," she noted. "I've found that I've thrived on it. I like working with people."

Ms. Siegel has proven that she enjoys the social side of her work, said Ann Miller, a partner at Lillick & Charles. "She's a real people person," Ms. Miller added. "I think she has shown that her approach can be successful."

Commented Dru Ramey of the San Francisco bar association, "She has the ability to make you feel that the problem you come to her with has her full attention. She intuitively understands what makes people feel secure." . . .

At Morrison & Foerster, Ms. Siegel has instituted a number of personnel policies that she says have helped create a comfortable work environment. Secretaries are encouraged to apply for jobs in other departments or take advantage of job sharing. The firm has a flex-time policy that allows workers to begin as early as 8 a.m. or as late as 10 a.m. Employees can use sick-leave time to be with ailing family members, and new mothers are given three months of paid maternity leave, plus an additional three months unpaid. . . .

Because large law firms like Morrison & Foerster can expect continued growth and competition in the next decade, executive directors will be given more responsibilities to keep up, she predicted. "The office manager who is just concerned with the service staff and bookkeeping is a thing of the past," she said.

And because clients are shopping around for law firms more than ever before, executive directors increasingly will be asked to stay on top of new marketing and business development strategies, said Ms. Siegel. "Partners are not going to ask you just to manage the secretaries," she concluded, "they're going to look to you to move and manage the firm into the future."

SOURCE: Mark Blumberg, "New ALA President Believes in Involving Others in Decisions," *California Law Business* (2 April 1990): 12. Reprinted with permission.

---

nomic status.[42] (Table 9–1 lists leadership traits cited by Stodgill and by Gary Yukl.)

More recently, Kirkpatrick and Locke have suggested that leaders share certain traits in common. These traits include *drive,* which encompasses characteristics like achievement, motivation, ambition, energy, tenacity, and initiative; *leadership motivation,* or a willingness to assume the responsibility of leadership; *honesty and integrity,* which are essential for creating trust between leaders and followers; *self-confidence,* which in turn bolsters the self-confidence of followers; *cognitive ability,* at least sufficient to formulate strategies for enacting vision; and, lastly, a *working knowledge of the business* in which the leader is engaged. Traits, however, are only a precondition for effective leadership; as Kirkpatrick and Locke point out, "Leaders who possess the requisite traits must take certain *actions* to be successful (e.g., formulating a vision, role modeling, setting goals). Possessing the appropriate traits only makes it more likely that such actions will be taken and be successful."[43] John Kotter, a Harvard Business School professor of organizational behavior and human resource management, observes that leaders

TABLE 9-1
Overview of Leadership Traits

Physical Traits	Age Height Weight Athletic skills		
Demographics	Socioeconomic status Education Popularity		
Personality Traits	Dependability Initiative Persistence Energy	Aggressiveness Need to achieve Need to excel Stress tolerance	Self-confidence Emotional maturity Power needs Willingness to take risks
Intellectual Traits	Intelligence Alertness Verbal facility	Originality Judgment Memory for detail	
Social Skills	Cooperativeness Sociability Adaptability	Humor Activity Empathy	Tact Charm Attractiveness

SOURCE: Ralph M. Stogdill, "Personal Factors Associated with Leadership: A Survey of the Literature," *Journal of Applied Psychology* 25 (1974): 35–71; and Gary A. Yukl, "Managerial Leadership: A Review of Theory and Research," *Journal of Management* 15, no. 2 (1989): 251–89.

possess excellent communication skills, insight, and intelligence. More importantly, followers associate effective leadership with integrity and credibility. These perceived qualities, which a leader constructs through an impressive track record and a history of cooperative relationships, lead to a broad network of human and material resources.[44]

Behavioral Theories

Researchers who advance **behavioral theories of leadership** attempt to define how the behavior of effective leaders differs from the behavior of ineffective leaders. In the following sections, we will examine five notable studies that focus on leadership behaviors.

Studies Relating Leadership Behavior and Political Styles

In this series of studies, dating back to the late 1930s, social scientist Kurt Lewin and others used political governing styles to describe sets of leadership behavior.[45] They identified three such sets: autocratic, democratic, and laissez-faire.

Autocratic Leadership. **Autocratic** or **dictatorial leadership** is characterized by a leader's attempt to completely control the behavior of his or her subordinates. Autocratic leadership results initially in high productivity, which falls sharply when the leader is absent. Autocratic leaders often depend on their ability to coerce and reward. They issue orders frequently, give disrupting commands, and offer nonconstructive criticism. This leadership style, which also has been linked to worker aggression, features little two-way communication, and workers are expected to accept authority unquestioningly.

Democratic Leadership. **Democratic** or **participative leadership** is based on consideration and concern for followers. Democratic leaders allow workers to participate in the use of power and encourage them to offer suggestions, constructive criticism, and advice. Such participative leadership has a high correlation with productivity and satisfaction.

Laissez-faire Leadership. At worst, we associate **laissez-faire leadership** with a complete (or nearly complete) lack of intervention. Laissez-faire leaders abdicate their responsibilities and allow their followers inordinate freedom of action, often to mask a profound discomfort with supervising others. They set few, if any, rules, offer no instructions or constructive criticism, and rarely help their followers to organize work activities or direct those activities toward organizational goals. Ultimately, such leaders may be interested only in fulfilling **affiliative needs,** or needs for friendship, cooperation, and social interaction; studies link laissez-faire leadership with low production.

Under certain conditions, however, laissez-faire leadership can be productive or even essential; further, all three of these leadership styles may be applicable in the law firm setting. The key is discretion. A leader might successfully adopt a laissez-faire style in a stable, highly functioning work environment among professionals, such as attorneys, who are self-directing and whose work requires much freedom and little to no outside guidance. When working with competent support staff, the same leader might adopt a democratic style; in a time of crisis, he or she would be justified in exercising autocratic leadership.

Ohio State University Studies

Shortly after World War II, researchers at Ohio State University (including Ralph Stogdill, who is also known for his trait theory work) identified nearly two thousand items, divided into nine categories, that they could use to describe leadership behavior. They incorporated the items and categories into two questionnaires: a *Leadership Behavior Description Questionnaire (LBDQ),* with which peers, superiors, and subordinates would describe the behavior of leaders, and a *Leadership Opinion Questionnaire (LOQ),* with which leaders would describe their own behavior. Through the questionnaires, the OSU researchers identified two factors basic to leadership behavior: **consideration** and the **initiation of structure.**[46]

Consideration. Consideration describes the extent to which a leader shows concern for workers, by, for example, acknowledging their dignity and self-esteem, treating them as equals, expressing appreciation, and being approachable. Besides concern, these behaviors show trust and warmth.

Initiation of Structure. The degree to which leaders **initiate structure** describes the degree to which they establish order in their followers' work. Structure-initiating behaviors include insisting on standards, meeting deadlines, assigning tasks, planning work activities, and establishing and enforcing routines. Such behaviors show a concern for completion, accuracy, and the reliable performance of tasks.

The researchers at Ohio State plotted the two factors on a graph, the horizontal axis of which ranged from low consideration at far left to high consideration at far right and the vertical axis of which ranged from low structure-initiating behavior at the bottom to high structure-initiating behavior at the top. On the graph, the researchers identified four leadership styles: in the lower left-hand corner, *low initiating structure/low consideration;* at lower right, *low initiating structure/ high consideration;* at upper left, *high initiating structure/low consideration;* and at upper right, *high initiating structure/ high consideration.*

University of Michigan Studies

At the same time the OSU studies were underway, Rensis Likert and other researchers at Michigan State University were studying leadership behaviors through interviews with managers and workers in a wide variety of industries and organizations. They, like their OSU counterparts, identified two basic categories of leadership behavior: *production-centered behaviors* and *employee-centered behaviors.*[47]

Production or Job-centered Behaviors. Like the structure-initiating behaviors of the OSU studies, *production-centered behaviors* include activities such as giving instructions and orders, establishing goals, supervising and monitoring performance, and structuring work.

Employee-centered Behaviors. Similar to the consideration described in the OSU studies, *employee-centered behaviors* reveal a leader's concern for his or her followers. Such behaviors include efforts to show warmth and concern, establish supportive relationships and communications, and avoid punitive behavior.

Likert, applying these behavioral categories to leaders in a variety of industries, identified three basic leadership orientations: job-centered (those leaders who are deeply concerned with production and efficiency and who, as a result, practice close supervision); employee-centered (those leaders who are more concerned about their employees and who, as a result, practice participative, democratic supervision); or a combined job- and employee-centered orientation (those leaders whose concern for production and results equal their concern for their workers).

Rensis Likert's Four Systems of Leadership

As we saw in Chapter 3, Rensis Likert described four basic organizational designs, known as Systems 1, 2, 3, and 4, which range, in terms of the working environment, from rigidly bureaucratic to openly participative. Likert also identified four styles, or systems, of leadership, which essentially correspond to his systems of organizational design.

System 1: Exploitative Autocratic. The exploitative autocrat emphasizes fear, punishment, and compliance while offering only the slightest hope of reward.

System 2: Benevolent Autocratic. The benevolent autocrat also emphasizes compliance, but places less emphasis on punishment and fear.

System 3: Consultative. The consultative leader expresses interest in followers' ideas and allows subordinates to participate in goal setting and decision making. Like the System 4 leader, the consultative leader encourages mutual trust and two-way communication; both types of leader value their followers.

System 4: Democratic or Participative. The democratic or participative leader allows followers influence in determining tasks and work methods. Under such a leader, followers essentially make and take responsibility for their own decisions.[48]

The Managerial Grid®[49]

Organizational development experts Robert Blake and Jane Mouton proposed that leadership behavior consists of a variable mix of two concerns: *concern for task accomplishment* and *concern for people*. Using a questionnaire to gather information from executives in various fields, Blake and Mouton scored responses regarding each concern on a nine-point scale and marked the scores on an 81-square grid, plotting each respondent's concern for production horizontally and his or her concern for people vertically (see Figure 9–1). The results led them to identify five leadership styles: (Note: The first number indicates concern for people; the second number represents concern for production.)

1,1 Impoverished Management. This leader has minimal concern for both people and the job. This style is typical of those who abdicate their leadership positions. They no longer care; therefore, they are rarely, if ever, effective.

5,5 Organization Man Management. This leader has an average concern for both people and the job. (Unfortunately, average concerns and interests will not result in above-average results!)

1,9 Country Club Management. This leader has a high concern for people, is sensitive to their needs and wants, and is more concerned about their well-being than about reaching the organization's goals. Relationships are comfortable, caring, and social.

9,1 Authority-Obedience Management. This leader places work first and people a distant second. The job must get done and the schedule must be met, no matter what. High efficiency results from a combination of tight control and disregard for the problems and concerns of followers.

9,9 Team Management. This last style describes a leader who has a high degree of concern for both the job and the people. This leader is interested in meeting work demands, making deadlines, and maintaining high productivity, but is also concerned about the feelings, interests, and ideas of followers. Workers who follow this leader become committed to a team approach, supporting high standards through mutual trust and confidence.

Law firms and other organizations have used Blake and Mouton's work extensively to assess leadership styles and to encourage managers to become 9, 9 leaders—that is, leaders who promote high standards and supportive relationships. Like other measuring devices, however, the Managerial Grid® should be used carefully. Although the model accurately profiles leaders in both formal and informal groups, those who use it to assess leadership should realize that an organization consists of more than its leaders' attitudes toward production and people. The nature of the work, the certainty—or uncertainty—of the times, and the needs, values, competencies, skills, and attitudes of followers all contribute to the setting in which a leader must function. These environmental factors have become the focus of a third school of leadership thought: the **situational theories.**

Situational Theories

Situational theories of leadership emphasize the importance of context. In the minds of situational theorists, style is only one component of leadership. The other ingredients include followers, the organization itself, and external factors that directly and even indirectly affect the organization and its workers. Of the

FIGURE 9-1
The Managerial Grid®

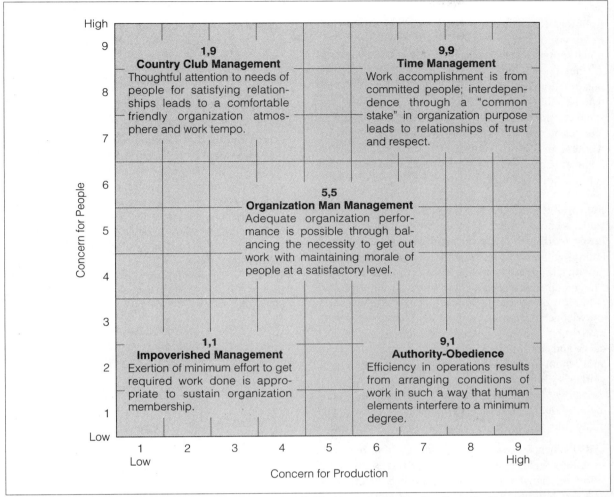

SOURCE: The Managerial Grid Figure from *The Managerial Grid III: The Key to Leadership Excellence,* by Robert R. Blake and Jane Srygley Mouton. Houston: Gulf Publishing Company. Copyright © 1985, page 12. Reproduced by permission.

many situational theories now available, we will examine two: Hersey and Blanchard's Life Cycle Theory of Leadership and Tannenbaum and Schmidt's Leadership Continuum.

Hersey and Blanchard's Life Cycle Theory of Leadership[50]

Like Blake and Mouton, who suggest in their behavioral theory that effective leaders balance their concern for tasks with their concern for people, organizational behaviorists Paul Hersey and Kenneth Blanchard build their Life Cycle Theory of Leadership on the careful weighing of environmental factors. To choose an appropriate style, they suggest, a leader must first assess follower readiness and the relationships and tasks that the work situation will entail.

Task Complexity and Leadership Behavior. *Task behavior* is the amount of supervision, guidance, and direction a leader provides his or her followers, depending on the complexity of the tasks they must perform. Hersey and Blanchard rank tasks on a continuum ranging from low to high. Low-level tasks require little explanation or supervision. High-level tasks, on the other hand, require detailed procedural descriptions and close supervision.

Follower Relationships and Leadership Behavior. *Relationship behavior* describes the amount of emotional support a leader must provide his or her workers. As they do with task behavior, Hersey and Blanchard rank relationship behavior from low to high. Followers who need high-level relationship behavior require personal consideration, active support, and a good deal of interaction with the leader. Low-relationship-behavior workers, in contrast, require little support, being confident enough in their abilities to perform well without pep talks or coddling.

Follower Readiness. Of the factors that determine a leader's choice of behavior, the most important is **follower readiness. Follower readiness** is the degree of ability, willingness, and confidence that followers exhibit in taking responsibility for their tasks and actions. This readiness consists of two types of maturity. *Job maturity,* or competence, results from a worker's knowledge and skills. *Psychological maturity,* or self-motivation and willingness, is the product of confidence and commitment. In this context, maturity is not an offshoot of biological age, but instead represents a worker's ability to perform a job independently, responsibly, and successfully. Hersey and Blanchard identify four levels of leadership behavior, corresponding to four degrees of follower maturity, or readiness:

> **R4.** When followers are confident and/or able and willing, and the task calls for low task skills and a low relationship level, the appropriate directive, or leadership, behavior is in the R4 category. For example, when dealing with partners and experienced associates, who are aware of their professional value to the firm, a leader need not provide personal encouragement, ego-stroking, or close supervision. Instead, he or she can concentrate on overseeing the flow and distribution of work, delegating, and coordinating activities.
>
> **R3.** When workers are able, but unwilling or insecure, and the task calls for low skills but a high relationship level, the appropriate directive behavior is in the R3 category. A leader who is working, for instance, with associates who are confident in their professional preparation might concentrate on teaching the more junior members the firm's norms and the importance of their being, as associates, contributing team players.
>
> **R2.** When the worker is unable but willing or confident, and the task calls for high skills and a high relationship level, the appropriate leadership behavior is in the R2 category. Close supervision, support, and continuing feedback would be behaviors appropriate to a leader who is working, for example, with newly trained paralegals, experienced secretaries who are new to the firm, or other relatively competent workers with adequate skills.
>
> **R1.** When the worker is unwilling, insecure, or unable and the task calls for high skills but a low relationship level, the appropriate directive behavior is in the R1 category. For example, a leader who is working with new or untrained employees such as receptionists or messengers might try to ease their anxiety or uncertainty by providing structure and close, task-focused supervision.

Leadership Styles. After assessing task complexity, relationship demands, and the level of follower readiness, the leader is ready to choose one of four leadership styles:

> **S-1: Telling.** When task requirements are high and relationship requirements and follower readiness are low (R1), a telling leadership style is appropriate. A leader adopts an S-1 style to deal with workers who are new, incompetent, unwilling, or prone to resist authority—in other words, workers who must be told what to do.
>
> **S-2: Selling.** This style is appropriate when task and relationship requirements are high and follower readiness is low-to-moderate (R2). A leader uses this style to "sell" followers on a task by clearly explaining decisions and directions and providing workers with an opportunity to ask for clarification.
>
> **S-3: Participating.** When task requirements are low, relationship requirements are high, and follower readiness is moderate (R3), a leader uses an S-3 style to encourage participation in decision making and in the task itself, rather than simply placing able but unwilling workers under close supervision.
>
> **S-4: Delegating.** When task and relationship requirements are low and follower readiness is high (R4), this fourth style is appropriate. Given secure, self-confident, and trusting followers and a straightforward task, a leader need provide neither close supervision nor excessive support.

Figure 9–2 illustrates the Life Cycle Theory of Leadership.

CHAPTER 9 / LEADERSHIP

FIGURE 9–2
The Life Cycle Model of Leadership

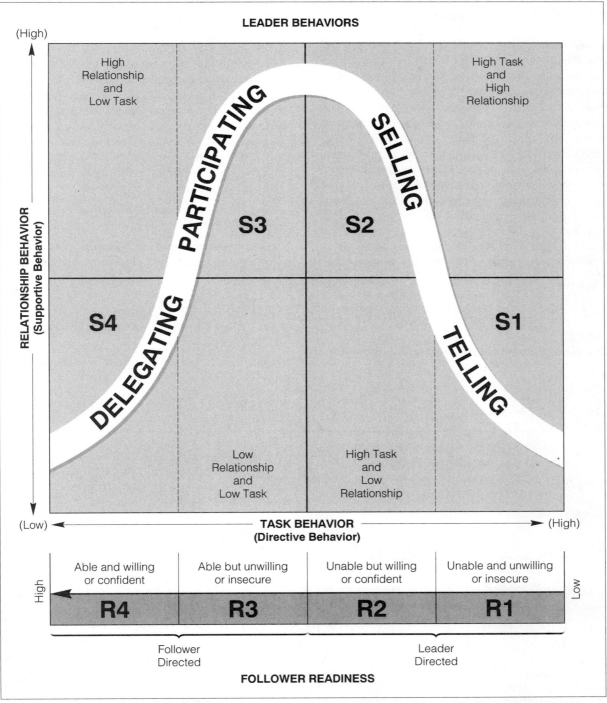

SOURCE: Paul Hersey and Kenneth H. Blanchard. Copyright © 1985, 1987 by *Management Leadership Studies, Inc.* All rights reserved. Used by permission of Prentice-Hall, Inc., Englewood Cliffs, New Jersey.

Tannenbaum and Schmidt's Leadership Continuum[51]

According to Robert Tannenbaum and Warren Schmidt, whose work provides possibly the best-known view of situational leadership, leadership is a process of analysis and adjustment. Leaders have always wondered when to direct their followers and when to consult with them, knowing that too much direction leads to autocracy and that too much consulting resembles an abdication of power. Tannenbaum and Schmidt suggest that effective leaders are primarily neither strong nor permissive but rather are adept at assessing followers and situations and adjusting their behavior accordingly. One of the first models to emphasize the importance of changing leadership behavior to accommodate environmental demands and the differing needs and abilities of subordinates, Tannenbaum and Schmidt's Leadership Continuum describes seven types of leadership behavior ranging from the authoritative practice of making a decision and announcing it to subordinates to permitting subordinates to function within defined limits (see Figure 9–3).

Future Vision Theories

In the 1990s, few organizations will avoid the impact of new technology, the global economy, and vast political and social changes. Consequently, a fourth school of leadership theory focuses on the need to meet the challenges that these changes will bring.[52] Focusing on motivation and the need to meet organizational goals, these future vision theories describe three types of leadership: charismatic leadership, transformational leadership, and transactional leadership.

Charismatic Leadership

The theory of **charismatic leadership** holds that certain people possess a combination of special abilities

FIGURE 9–3
The Continuum Model of Leadership Behavior

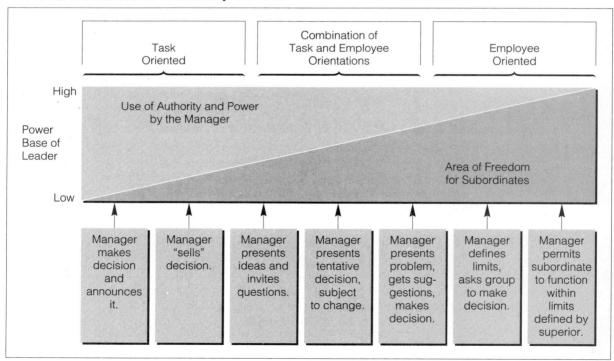

SOURCE: Adapted and reprinted by permission of *Harvard Business Review*. An exhibit from "How to Choose a Leadership Pattern" by Robert Tannenbaum and Warren H. Schmidt, May/June 1973. Copyright © 1973 by the President and Fellows of Harvard College; all rights reserved.

and appeal that inspires tremendous confidence, trust, and respect in followers, who may be prone to idolize the charismatic leader or to perceive his or her abilities as superhuman or spiritual. Among the theorists who have defined charismatic leadership is Max Weber. Though best known for his theories regarding bureaucracy, Weber identified charismatic leaders as people "endowed with supernatural, superhuman, or at least ... exceptional powers and qualities."[53] Charismatic leadership consists of a unique mixture of abilities, traits, and behavior.

Traits and Abilities of Charismatic Leaders.[54] Highly attractive and charming, charismatic leaders possess shrewd insight, sharp intelligence, a strong need for power, and a deep understanding of the situations in which they find themselves. They believe with wholehearted, awe-inspiring conviction that the visions they offer their followers are appropriate and correct. They identify and seize opportunities with hawklike speed and accuracy, and they seem able to persevere through even the most crushing setbacks and to overcome daunting limitations. Astutely sensitive to motivational needs and values, charismatic leaders inspire their followers to new heights of performance, all the while convincing them that their contributions are not only valuable but ennobling.

Behavior of Charismatic Leaders. Often most notable in times of crisis, the behavior of charismatic leaders tends to confirm their followers' expectations. Common charismatic behaviors include the following:

Managing Impressions. A charismatic leader will create for followers a picture of his or her competence and success, knowing that such images are potent motivational tools.

Offering Vision. To inspire workers, charismatic leaders offer visions that are novel without being disturbing.

Communicating High Expectations. A charismatic leader builds followers' confidence, igniting in them a high-intensity anticipation focused on realizing their hopes and meeting their goals.

Facing Risks and Making Sacrifices. Charismatic leaders are willing to risk money, status, and even membership in the organization in order to pursue their visions.

Setting an Example. Through model—and sometimes unconventional—behavior, charismatic leaders strive to enthuse their followers.

Followers' Response to Charismatic Leadership. Those who follow a charismatic leader tend to accept the leader unquestioningly and obey the leader willingly or even blindly. Followers place tremendous confidence in a charismatic leader. Their faith appears as emotional attachment, a tendency to idolize, or, as Weber notes, "devotion . . . , hero worship, or absolute trust. . . ."[55] (We should note that the tendency to perceive a charismatic leader as a superhuman or spiritual figure distinguishes charismatic leadership from transformational leadership, which we will discuss later in this chapter.[56]) Staunchly believing that the leader's views are correct, followers express their conviction as high-level performance; they are likely, however, to focus on the leader rather than on the work process or their role in it.

Pros and Cons of Charismatic Leadership in the Law Firm. Though it might seem as if a charismatic leader would be too independent (or even too eccentric) to operate effectively in a firm, charismatic leadership can become part of the operational style of almost any organization, especially those that have elected officers. When law firm partners select a managing partner, for example, they base their selection on their belief in the chosen partner's leadership abilities. A charismatic managing partner, in turn, can inspire trust and confidence and unite professionals whose goals might otherwise conflict. On the downside, some charismatic leaders flagrantly abuse their power over others, gorging their egos on adulation and personal loyalty while completely ignoring the needs of the firm. By focusing on their leader rather than on processes within the firm, the followers of a charismatic leader tend to become and remain dependent. If such dependence (or blind obedience) spreads, the entire firm could unravel, should the leader fall.

Transformational Leadership

Transformational leadership, observes James MacGregor Burns, is a leadership style in which "leaders and followers raise one another to higher levels of morality and motivation."[57] Transformational leaders change the attitudes and assumptions of their followers in order to build a collective commitment toward the organization, its goals, and its strategies. Their vision involves urging followers to forgo self-interests for the common good of the firm and its members and to become more aware of the value of their contributions as followers; by empowering his or her followers, the transformational leader not only increases their awareness but inspires them to greatness. At the same time, he or she faces the monumental task of revitalizing the firm itself. As Noel Tichy and David Ulrich observe,

> We call these leaders transformational leaders, for they must create something new out of something old; out of an old vision, they must develop and communicate a new vision and get others not only to see the vision but also to commit themselves to it.[58]

Involving leaders at all levels, transformational leadership consists of the following:

Charisma. Transformational leaders elicit enthusiasm and devotion in their followers, and allow themselves to be enthused by their followers in turn. Followers tend to perceive a transformational leader as a coach, mentor, or teacher who is concerned for their well-being.[59] Though essential to this leadership style, charisma is only one component of transformational leadership, and transformational leaders are less likely than purely charismatic leaders to use charisma to further their personal interests.

Intellectual Stimulation. Unlike charismatic leaders, who rely on their ability to manipulate their followers' feelings, transformational leaders appeal to their followers intellectually as well as emotionally. Such leaders encourage followers to see issues and problems from a wider perspective, informing them, encouraging two-way communications, and working with them to develop rational approaches to complex problems.

Individual Consideration. Transformational leaders are sincerely interested in the personal development of their followers and they express this interest through encouragement and support.

Empowering Others. As we saw in Chapter 4, empowerment is the process of strengthening people's belief in their own effectiveness. Transformational leaders empower their followers (and encourage them to empower others) by offering verbal and nonverbal support; creating a positive atmosphere, particularly in times of crisis or stress; rewarding workers by praising success, recognizing effort, and acknowledging hard work and commitment; and encouraging workers to take initiative and accept more responsibility, often by creating opportunities for success.[60]

Transactional Leadership

A form of transformational leadership, **transactional** or **exchange leadership** also focuses on organizational goals but emphasizes transactions rather than personal transformation. The transactional leader persuades followers to respond to his or her direction and work toward the organization's goals in exchange for material or psychological rewards; the leadership relationship lasts as long as the leader and followers satisfy each other's needs. Transactional leaders effect only minor changes in an organization's mission, structure, and human resource management; transformational leaders, by comparison, attempt to reshape not only those areas but the basic political and cultural systems of the organization as well.[61]

MEETING THE CHALLENGES OF LAW FIRM LEADERSHIP

For many reasons, being a leader in a law firm is demanding and even undesirable. First of all, law firms, like all organizations, harbor their share of difficult people, many of whom are well-meaning but unaware that being a good follower is a key component of ensuring good leadership. Further, law firms must follow rules and legal restrictions regarding hiring practices, and leaders sometimes find themselves caught between working with undesirable employees and the consequences of firing them. Finally, a law firm's policies often limit a leader's behavioral choices, in effect predetermining his or her leadership style. To accommodate these challenges and the challenges of an increasingly complex external environment, law firm leaders of the near future can attempt to share leadership with their followers by working with them to create a *zone of difference* and by helping them to develop their leadership potential.

Zone of Difference

A **zone of difference** combines similarity and diversity by recognizing followers' unique skills, qualities, and competencies while describing the areas in which their

ANOTHER LOOK

Keys to Successful Leadership

1. Trust your subordinates. You can't expect them to go all out for you if they think you don't believe in them.
2. Develop a vision. Some executives' suspicions to the contrary, planning for the long term pays off. And people want to follow someone who knows where he or she is going.
3. Keep your cool. The best leaders show their mettle under fire.
4. Encourage risk. Nothing demoralizes the troops like knowing that the slightest failure could jeopardize their entire career.
5. Be an expert. From boardroom to mailroom, everyone had better understand that you know what you're talking about.
6. Invite dissent. Your people aren't giving you their best or learning how to lead if they are afraid to speak up.
7. Simplify. You need to see the big picture in order to set a course, communicate it, and maintain it. Keep the details at bay.

SOURCE: K. Labich, "The Seven Keys to Business Leadership," *Fortune* (24 October 1988): 58.

1. Which key would you consider to be most important to followers? To leaders? Explain.
2. Think of a person under whose leadership you have worked. How many of these keys did that leader utilize? With what success? Which ones did he or she seem to disregard?

---

goals and attitudes overlap. "Difference," here, therefore implies "variation," not "dissent" or "disagreement." To create a zone of difference, a leader stresses the value of diverse roles, respects the leader/follower compact, and attempts to instill in his or her followers a uniform sense of commitment, all the while acknowledging them as people first and employees second. By emphasizing the importance of diverse roles, the leader helps followers to feel useful and important; by respecting the leader/follower compact (which is impossible to create in organizations where managers and workers treat each other as adversaries and isolate themselves within self-interests), the leader fosters mutual trust and a sense of common goals; and by working toward a uniform sense of commitment, the leader encourages followers to share pride in each other's success and in the success of the organization.[62]

Helping Others to Develop Leadership Potential

As the section describing the zone of difference implies, modern knowledge workers measure a leader's effectiveness by his or her ability to recognize others' competencies and thereby maximize their contributions. As described by Charles Manz and Henry Simms, Jr., this "superleadership" ability embodies the idea that "the most appropriate leader is the one who can lead others to lead themselves."[63] In law firms especially, successful leadership depends on the ability to acknowledge an employee's right to a certain degree of autonomy. As we have seen, attorneys must have freedom to perform their tasks; at the other end of the hierarchy, paralegals, secretaries, and even bookkeepers need to function independently in order to grow as workers in a professional setting.

Leadership is not the domain of a chosen few. Though a theory popular in the late nineteenth and early twentieth centuries suggested that leadership potential is inherited, there is no such thing as a "leadership personality" or genetically acquired leadership traits.[64] Further, leaders are not by definition heroes. Most effective leadership is an everyday thing. There is, nonetheless, an extraordinary need for ordinary managers to act as leaders for ordinary workers in ordinary places. All of us can—in fact, need to—learn leadership. As Bennis and Nanus observe,

> Biographies of great leaders sometimes read as if they had entered the world with an extraordinary genetic endowment, that somehow their future leadership was preordained. Don't believe it. The truth is that major capacities and competencies of leadership can be learned, and we are all educable. . . .[65]

QUESTIONS FOR DISCUSSION AND REVIEW

1. Why do all workers in a law firm need leadership skills? On the other hand, why is the ability to be a good follower essential to effective leadership?
2. To what extent can leadership be learned? To what extent does leadership quality or skill depend on predispositions and environmental factors?
3. What competencies does a leader need?
4. Outline the various leadership theories. Which of these theories seems most valid?
5. Discuss the principal behavioral theories of leadership. What do they have in common with the trait theories?
6. Using the situational theories of leadership, explain the conditions that enable people to become leaders.
7. Are leaders born or made? Explain.
8. Compare the future vision theories of leadership. Explain which theory would be most useful for a leader dealing with each of the following: a secretary; an environmental law paralegal; a paralegal in a government agency for low-income families; a new associate; a legal administrator; and the firm's senior partner.
9. What unique leadership challenges do law office managers face?

EXPERIENTIAL EXERCISES

I. Leadership Styles Questionnaire*

Leadership is very complex. Streams of research resulting from work in many behavioral sciences have led to agreement on two major dimensions of effective leadership. They are the orientation toward the task and the consideration toward people.

How do you evaluate your own leadership ability? More importantly, in what direction must your own leadership development take you? The T-P Leadership Questionnaire and Profile Sheet should help you to understand more clearly the answers to these questions. There is no correct score for the questionnaire. People vary considerably in their responses. Nor will this exercise provide you with all of the necessary answers about your abilities as a leader. However, it will serve as a point of departure from which you can become more aware of your present leadership style and your potential impact on group effectiveness.

The following items describe aspects of leadership behavior. Respond to each item according to the way you would act as the leader of a work group. Circle F if you would behave in the described way frequently; circle S if you believe that you would seldom behave that way.

As the leader of a work group . . .

F	S	_____	1. I would act as the spokesperson of the group.
F	S	_____	2. I would encourage overtime work.
F	S	_____	3. I would allow members complete freedom in their work.
F	S	_____	4. I would encourage the use of uniform procedures.

---

*SOURCE: G. H. Goldhaber et al., "Leadership Styles Questionnaire," *Instructor's Manual T/A Organizational Communication*, 4th ed. (Dubuque, Iowa: William C. Brown Publishers, 1986). Adapted with permission.

CHAPTER 9 / LEADERSHIP

F	S	_____	5.	I would permit the members to use their own judgment in solving problems.
F	S	_____	6.	I would stress being ahead of competing groups.
F	S	_____	7.	I would speak as a representative of the group.
F	S	_____	8.	I would strongly urge members to greater effort.
F	S	_____	9.	I would try out my ideas in the group.
F	S	_____	10.	I would let the members do their work the way they thought best.
F	S	_____	11.	I would work hard for a promotion.
F	S	_____	12.	I would be able to tolerate postponement and uncertainty.
F	S	_____	13.	I would speak for the group when visitors were present.
F	S	_____	14.	I would keep the work moving at a rapid pace.
F	S	_____	15.	I would turn the members loose on a job and let them go to it.
F	S	_____	16.	I would settle conflicts in the group.
F	S	_____	17.	I would get swamped by details.
F	S	_____	18.	I would represent the group at outside meetings.
F	S	_____	19.	I would be reluctant to allow the members any freedom of action.
F	S	_____	20.	I would decide what should be done and how it should be done.
F	S	_____	21.	I would push for increased production.
F	S	_____	22.	I would let some members have authority that I should have kept.
F	S	_____	23.	Things would usually turn out as I predicted.
F	S	_____	24.	I would allow the group a high degree of initiative.
F	S	_____	25.	I would assign group members to particular tasks.
F	S	_____	26.	I would be willing to make changes.
F	S	_____	27.	I would ask the members to work harder.
F	S	_____	28.	I would trust the group members to exercise good judgment.
F	S	_____	29.	I would schedule the work to be done.
F	S	_____	30.	I would refuse to explain my actions.
F	S	_____	31.	I would persuade others that my ideas would be to their advantage.
F	S	_____	32.	I would permit the group to set its own pace.
F	S	_____	33.	I would urge the group to beat its previous record.
F	S	_____	34.	I would act without consulting the group.
F	S	_____	35.	I would ask that group members follow standard rules and regulations.

Scoring Directions

A. Circle the item numbers for 8, 12, 17, 18, 19, 30, 34, and 35.
B. Write a one (1) in front of the circled items to which you responded "seldom".
C. Write a one (1) in front of the items not circled to which you responded "frequently."

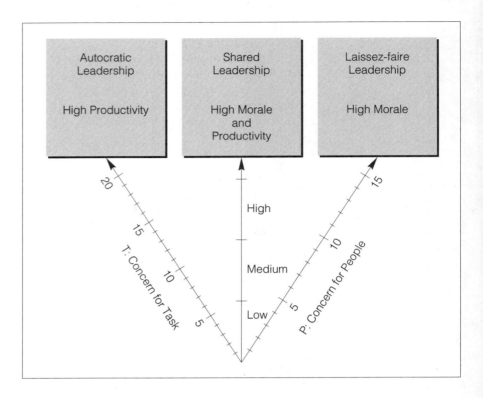

D. Circle the ones (1s) which you have written in front of the following items: 3, 5, 8, 10, 15, 18, 19, 22, 24, 26, 28, 30, 32, 34, and 35.

E. Count the circled ones (1s). This is your score for concern for people. Record the score in the blank following the letter P below.

F. Count the uncircled ones (1s). This is your score for concern for task. Record this score in the blank following the letter T below.

T score: _____   P score: _____

To determine your leadership style, mark your score on the concern for task dimension (T) on the left-hand arrow above. Next, move to the right-hand arrow and mark your score on the concern for people dimension (P). Draw a straight line that intersects the P and T scores. The point at which that line crosses the shared leadership arrow indicates your score on that dimension.

Shared leadership results from balancing concern for task and concern for people.

II. Placing Yourself in a Leader's Shoes

Do you see yourself as a leader? Though we tend to think that leadership exists only at the upper reaches of a law firm's hierarchy, leaders appear at all levels, in all positions. Discuss how you would use leadership skills to influence others in each of the following situations:

1. You are a paralegal in a small but growing firm, and you believe that the firm's increasing size justifies the creation of a paralegal coordinator position. You now need to find a way to present your idea to the firm's management committee.

2. You and other secretaries in your law firm have met to discuss the need for a policy change that would allow the secretarial staff to work flexible hours. The group asks you to present the policy change request to the secretarial staff coordinator and the firm's administrator.
3. You are a new paralegal coordinator, hired primarily for your expertise in workers' compensation defense. To your dismay, the paralegals under your supervision greet you with varying degrees of resistance.
4. As a freshly hired law firm administrator chosen for your expertise in computer applications (though you hold an M.B.A. and can boast successful—if limited—experience in a business setting as well), describe the problems you expect to encounter when dealing with the following groups: a) those who are older than you, b) those who have higher status, c) those who can boast many years of service with the firm, and d) those who have more education in specialized areas.

CHAPTER 10

Motivation

LEARNING OBJECTIVES

After completing this chapter, you should be able to:

- Understand the nature of motivation in the law firm;
- Identify the work-related characteristics of personality and the role that personality plays in motivation;
- Explain how needs, values, and attitudes influence the motivational process;
- Describe the basic motivational tools that managers use;
- Explain the behavior modification theory of motivation;
- Describe the theories that link motivation to meeting people's needs;
- Discuss theories that link motivation to cognitive processes;
- Understand the use of goal setting as a motivational tool; and
- Describe how the motivational process can differ for professionals and support staff.

Debra Greenberg is the manager of Paralegal Services at the law firm of Hale and Dorr in Boston, where she manages over seventy-five paralegals and case team assistants. Ms. Greenberg, who has been active in the legal assistant field since 1981, served as chairperson of the Legal Assistant Management Association Conference Committee in 1991.

FOCUS FROM THE FIELD

Debra Greenberg: Key Elements in Motivating People

What approaches to motivation are used in law firms?

The approaches I've seen that are most effective would include giving people recognition for a job well done, which is so often neglected. The law firm environment is so fast-paced and deadline-oriented that people tend not to take the time even to give constructive feedback, let alone positive recognition. I think that giving people responsibility to do their jobs and then recognizing the good job or giving instructions on how to do the job better are key elements in motivating people. I also think that feedback is more motivational if the person giving it is the same person who delegated the assignment, i.e., the attorney who gave the paralegal the assignment. Unfortunately, the responsibility for providing feedback often falls upon the administrator. Some people have an easier time giving positive or negative feedback than others. Attorneys seem to have a hard time with this.

What approaches do you think managers should use?

I think that a manager needs to know what his or her people are doing. When you recognize someone for something, you should be certain that the act was worth recognition. You really can't do that unless you're out there. It's very easy to sit in your office and lose touch with the people that you manage. To be visually active and aware makes the personal recognition that you give more valid. I would say that one needs to be visible and aware in ways that others know about, and to *know* when to praise and reward people. Some like to be rewarded in front of others while others may be horrified if they are singled out in a group. So part of the awareness is knowing what type of recognition is motivating to each member of the staff. Managers should also address problems up front. If you don't address problem behavior, even if the problem area is limited, it can affect the entire group, acting as a disincentive. Everyone in the group seems to know who works hard and who doesn't, so they are well aware of the problems that are or are not addressed.

What is the most difficult challenge you see in motivating your staff?

Because there are built-in limits to progression in a law firm, it can be difficult to get the sort of commitment and loyalty to the firm that the firm expects. Opportunities may be there for 90 percent of the support staff, but for the 10 percent that don't have it, you can't put it there. Paralegals never become partners, for instance. That's probably the biggest problem. It's a built-in disincentive to see certain people on the track when you're not. There are now legal assistant programs that have tiers, levels of built-in advancement, to provide the visible opportunity that the paralegals have been lacking. I think that, through the opportunities for gaining responsibility that exist in most firms, you have that possibility for progression, but there continues to be a need for visible distinctions among workers to show levels of expertise. I think that the tier programs are a positive move, since the paralegal profession is still defining itself. There will be more changes in the future.

> **W**ork should be and can be productive and rewarding, meaningful and maturing, enriching and fulfilling, healing and joyful. Work is one of our greatest privileges. Work can even be poetic.
> (Max DePree, *Leadership Is an Art*)[1]
>
> **M**anagers feel most motivated when they are realizing their potential—becoming what they have the capacity and desire to become.
> (M. Scott Myers, "Conditions for Manager Motivation")[2]
>
> **R**eputation is a key resource in professional careers, and the chance to enhance it can be an outstanding motivator.
> (Rosabeth Moss Kanter, "The New Managerial Work")[3]

MOTIVATION IN THE LAW FIRM

An organization consists of three elements: goals, structure, and people. As we have seen, goals guide the firm's progress and focus its energies, and structure provides the mechanisms for reaching those goals. But although goals and structure are essential to efficient operations, workers determine the firm's survival. No matter how great its goals or how solid its structure, without people and their commitment a firm is no more than office space and furniture. Consequently, managers must perform a kind of balancing act. To ensure the success of a firm, managers must push to meet its needs while treating their people with concern and respect. Achieving the perfect balance between productivity concerns and employee concerns is the goal of the process known as *motivation*. In this chapter, we will define motivation, discuss its importance in the law firm setting, and examine several theories that attribute motivation to personal factors such as needs, cognitive processes, and behavior. Motivating people, writes Max DePree, is "often considered from only one point of view: the manager's." But law firm management, like baseball, is a team proposition, and, as DePree notes, "In baseball and in business, the needs of the team are best met when we meet the needs of the individual person."[4]

The Importance of Motivation

For all managers, from the newest secretarial coordinator or paralegal supervisor to the most seasoned managing partner, motivating workers has always been a challenge. Nevertheless, to enable the firm to best utilize its human capital, managers must understand what motivates the workers who comprise that capital. In law firms, motivation is essential because direct managerial quality control is often impossible, given the constant need to delegate and the variety of individual tasks that workers perform. In addition, motivation compels people to accomplish not only their personal goals but those of their employing organization. "Individuals are willing," writes Nobel Prize laureate Herbert Simon, "to accept organizational membership when their activity in the organization contributes, directly or indirectly, to their own personal goals."[5] In short, motivated workers are productive and dependable—unlike unmotivated workers, who depress others, produce sub-quality work, and increase turnover, with all its attendant costs.

Definition of Motivation

We commonly think of motivation in terms of incentives. **Motivation** (from the Latin *movere,* "to move") is an inner force that influences behavior and drives people to reach their goals. Motivation results from the impulse, emotion, interest, or desire that moves one to act or not to act in a certain way. Understanding motivation is difficult, for many reasons. How can people even know, for instance, what causes their own motivation? Are they motivated to do something because of inner needs, some subconscious impulse, or external pressures? Understanding motivation is difficult; measuring it is even harder. We must infer motivation: only its results are visible. Strangely enough, we often hear people claim that they "know what buttons to push" to motivate others. Although they might know at a given moment what induces others to respond positively, it is impossible for them to know more than this.

This is because people change, and so do their motivators. People sometimes negate a motivational force by meeting or abandoning the need or desire that originally inspired it. In addition, times, needs, and the work environment change, as do people's perceptions of themselves, their jobs, and their personal and professional value as employees. Therefore, neither managers nor anyone else should believe that knowing what motivates people is easy. We are obligated to respect the mystery of who others are and, further, to accept the impossibility of fully understanding what motivates others.

Performance and Motivation

If motivation is a key to quality performance, managers must be convinced of their responsibility to motivate workers, like teachers who know that even limited students can do better with the right kind of interest and support. Managers who are convinced of their motivational responsibility act like coaches, encouraging, directing, and sustaining employee motivation. In contrast, managers who ignore their roles as motivators invite a host of trouble, including poor performance, increased absenteeism and turnover, and counter productive behavior.

Quality of Performance

Managers know that they can depend on motivated workers. But the factors that motivate workers to perform effectively remain a mystery. Researchers have yet to prove that worker satisfaction and happiness have anything to do with productivity, and even "too much support and understanding," cautions management consultant Robert H. Schaffer, "can keep expectations—and performance—unnecessarily low."[6] As Kanter and Stein observe,

> Perhaps what is important is not the development of strong worker-support groups that create meaning and involvement at work and do not function so much to boost productivity in the short run, but to make it possible for people to **survive their work** in the long run, to remain human and therefore, in fact, to have the energy to continue to come to work year after year—and to contribute to their families and society.[7]

Many office procedures, by their nature, are methodical and routine. For law firm employees who do not face intellectual or emotional challenges, aspects of work can become meaningless and boring. Much support staff work, for example, can become tedious. This may be due to an unavoidably weak job design that dictates a schedule heavy with humdrum details, which leads, in turn, to lack of motivation. Nonetheless, comment Kanter and Stein, "It is also clear that people may develop a strong feeling of commitment and involvement despite any objective sense in which their work is boring, meaningless, or demeaning. People want to invest in work and can make surprising investments in organizations that offer them very little in return."[8]

Absenteeism and Turnover

Irregular, undependable attendance, continual late arrivals, and early departures are red flags for motivational deficiencies. These behaviors show that a worker, for many possible reasons, is not interested in doing well at work. The interaction between job satisfaction and work pressures determines an employee's motivation to attend and to contribute; actual attendance depends on the motivation to attend plus an *ability* to attend.[9] We can trace turnover to a wider variety of causes: economic factors, the worker's personality, job satisfaction, and influences such as retirement, spouse's need to relocate, or disabling illnesses. But turnover also depends on the desire to stay or to leave. Employees who conclude that there is nothing in a law office to motivate them to stay will decide to leave, if the firm cannot or will not accommodate them in some way.[10]

Counterproductive Behavior

Experienced managers are not surprised by the hundreds of ways that workers "get even" with the organization. Workers who become disenchanted or unmotivated, who believe that they are receiving inequitable treatment, or who perceive that their employing organization considers them to be of little value get even in dozens of ways. Believing these conditions to be serious imbalances in the psychological contract they have made with an organization, disgruntled employees offset these letdowns through passive-aggressive behavior ranging from unconscious slowdowns to the deliberate formation of groups that threaten the organization or its leadership.[11]

Motivation and Workers

Being largely a product of personal factors, performance varies from worker to worker and, as we know

IN THE NEWS

Finding Common Ground between Growth and Morale at Hyatt Legal Services

On cue, Joel Hyatt leans across his desk and beams at the television reporter. With instincts honed by a decade of media attention, he deftly turns the interview into a polished pitch for his law firm. That night, he gets a boost that money couldn't buy: a two-minute plug on the local evening news for his firm's pre-paid legal-services plan.

Mr. Hyatt's marketing savvy has helped build the nation's biggest chain of legal clinics, Hyatt Legal Services, which boasts that it sees 22,000 new clients a month on matters ranging from traffic tickets to divorces. But managing the no-frills law firm has proved more difficult than getting its name on the air.

The 10-year-old firm has been plagued recently by management defections and firings, as well as by staff dissent. High turnover among Hyatt's 630 staff lawyers has delayed cases and left some in disarray. Although the firm says it now is profitable, losses in 1986 forced it to close seven of its 194 offices in December and January. Hyatt also cut its advertising by 13%, to $5 million.

"I've always thought the idea (of a chain of legal clinics) had a lot of potential, but as a business, the main question is making it pay," says Judith Scott, an analyst with Robert W. Baird & Co., Milwaukee. "Law is an intricate and time-consuming business. To me, the big question remains: Can you standardize the practice of law?"

Appealing to the Masses

Mr. Hyatt, who engineered his firm's spectacular growth, concedes that the expansion may have come too quickly. Moreover, efforts to control such an extended empire at times have taxed the firm.

Two years after graduating from Yale Law School, Mr. Hyatt founded the firm with two other lawyers in 1977. Their premise: legal services, like fast food, could be dished out profitably to a mass market if prices were cheap and volume high.

The 37-year-old Mr. Hyatt led the firm through its rapid growth mainly by flouting some old conventions of the legal profession. Hyatt was one of the first law firms to advertise on television, using commercials starring the boyish-looking Mr. Hyatt. The firm found a big market in blue-collar clients by opening offices in shopping centers and by offering low, standardized fees.

The firm devised a simple menu of legal services, shunning complicated business law felonies and cases that might go to trial. By streamlining procedures, the firm churned out a high volume of services at low prices—$20 for an initial half-hour consultation, $75 for a simple will, and $375 for an uncontested divorce.

By 1986, Hyatt had expanded to 200 offices in 22 states. The number of offices has shrunk to 187 now, but Hyatt remains well ahead of Jacoby & Meyers, the No. 2

---

from our own peaks and slumps, even within the same worker. In all organizations, we see a tremendous range of worker performance. At one end of the spectrum are the stars and achievers; at the other lounge the inevitable slouches and deadwood. In terms of motivation and performance, business management educator Robert Ullrich divides workers into three groups:[12]

Alienated Workers. Alienated workers show no commitment. A source of frustration for managers, they seem motivated neither to participate in the organization nor to work toward its goals. Often, an alienated worker is attempting to adapt to an unstimulating or dreary work setting or to cope with a boring, repetitive, and meaningless job.

Calculating Workers. Calculating workers fulfill their responsibilities in order to receive personal gratification in the form of power, money, or status. These workers often perform well as long as they receive adequate compensation for their efforts.

Committed Workers. Committed workers foster work-related values by believing in the organization, its goals, and their ability to contribute to its success. These organizational mainstays uphold performance standards and contribute energy and ideas.

Motivational Influences

If we had to guess, we would probably agree with Ullrich that "a predisposition to achieve and excel at

IN THE NEWS (continued)

legal-clinic chain, with 150 offices and 275 lawyers in six states.

As Hyatt has grown, however, it has faced increasing problems, most noticeably dissatisfaction among staff lawyers. The lawyers are under constant pressure to handle a large number of cases and are evaluated on their ability to sell additional services to clients attracted by the inexpensive initial consultation. Those who can't cut it are retrained or fired.

Still, because of the current glut of lawyers, Hyatt hasn't had trouble recruiting. Some lawyers are hired directly from law school. Training them can be a headache for some managers. One former manager even felt it necessary to hold one-hour law classes each morning.

The pressure and low pay—the average starting salary is about $23,000—have resulted in high turnover. Six-day workweeks and 14-hour days aren't uncommon in many offices. "Of the nine attorneys hired with me, eight left in the first year," says a recruit who quit in 1986 after working at Hyatt for about two years. "There was intense heat to bring in more money, money, money. Some stayed only a month or two, just long enough to generate a bunch" of cases, which had to be completed by other lawyers.

Revolt in Minneapolis

Staffers in seven Minneapolis regional offices revolted last year. Fourteen lawyers and legal assistants wrote a memo protesting the firm's emphasis on generating fees at the expense of quality legal work. "Employee morale is low, client complaints have increased," the memo read. "The only concern is for how much money we will make for (the firm)."

Mr. Hyatt fired the dissenters. Though the Minneapolis offices were big money-makers for the firm, "the region wasn't practicing law our way," Mr. Hyatt says. " 'Our way' refers to other things like service to clients and respect for peers." He declines to elaborate.

At the time of the dismissals, clinics in the region had 6,000 clients. Delays related to the firings kept the clinics from seeing new clients for three months, and several customers had to be given refunds for services that were never rendered. . . .

Growing Pains

Mr. Hyatt dismisses the firm's problems as growing pains. He says some of the people promoted during the firm's sharp expansion proved inept as managers. Now the firm is trying to smooth out its management and staff woes. To reduce turnover, for example, the firm plans to start awarding bonuses based on the revenue lawyers bring in.

SOURCE: P. B. Gray, "Hyatt Legal Services' Fast Growth Leaves Trail of Management Woes," *The Wall Street Journal* (6 May 1987): 25. Reprinted by permission of *The Wall Street Journal*, © 1987 Dow Jones & Company, Inc. All Rights Reserved Worldwide.

---

work may be a product of experiences going back to early childhood as well as a response to opportunities presented in the individual's immediate environment."[13] Most managers realize that life's patterns, including work attitudes, are deeply ingrained long before the worker arrives in the law firm setting. But they can still benefit from a basic understanding of the motivational process, no matter how predisposed workers are to act one way rather than another. Understanding the motivational options that are available is a good starting point for increasing the productivity of each employee. As Ullrich indicates, there's a lot of wisdom in recognizing the idea that "much of the employee behavior of which we approve or disapprove was learned long before these workers were old enough to work. For such behavior, managers can take neither credit nor blame."[14]

Motivational Mysteries

Motivation varies widely from firm to firm and from worker to worker, often for no immediately discernible reason. Managers who are insensitive to their role in motivating workers can only confound the problem. Despite the idea that people may be motivational mysteries even to themselves, it is imperative that managers acquire at least a basic understanding of the unique motivational needs of their subordinates. Such an understanding, teamed with a practical knowledge of motivational theory, can help managers to transform mysterious variations in performance into a more uniform and positive productivity.

Motivation and the Organization

Effective performance is the result of a minimum of four factors. For workers to perform well, they must (1) know the expectations for the job, (2) have the ability they need to do the job, (3) be motivated to do what the job requires, and (4) work in an environment that allows them to translate their intentions into performance. In recent years, researchers studying motivation have begun to focus not only on the worker but on the manager's role and on that of the organization as well.[15] Performance is considered a function of the motivation one has to do a job times one's ability to do that particular job, as *both,* motivation and ability, are affected by the work environment. This environment, which the manager can shape and control, is comprised of the components of the work setting, including the organization's formal and informal structures, its decision-making and reward processes, and its resources and culture. A deficiency in any element (ability, task-specific motivation, or environment), unless balanced by a surplus in terms of another element, creates a general deficiency in motivation.[16]

Motivational Levels

Managers often are concerned with the visible and controllable aspects of their subordinates' performance, including attendance, punctuality, obedience and accuracy in carrying out orders, and effort. Five categories describe the levels of motivation that managers can expect of good, reliable employees.[17]

Becoming Part of the Organization

An employee initially must be motivated to join an organization. A law firm, like all other organizations, needs the kind of reputation that attracts, in adequate numbers, workers who are capable of making useful contributions.

Remaining in the Organization

A firm not only must draw good workers to it but must motivate them to stay. An organization that fails to do so will lose its best people: talented workers are less likely to accept shoddy treatment, have more career mobility, and are more likely to shop around for employers who will appreciate them. Recruiting good personnel can be expensive, but the costs of turnover can be astronomical, both financially and in terms of lost stability.

Working Regularly

As we have seen, one of the most obvious signs of faltering motivation is a lack of regular, dependable attendance. Workers in whom a firm can cultivate and maintain a sense of personal involvement and responsibility are less apt to claim fraudulent sick days, arrive late, depart early, or fail to show up.

Performing Acceptably

In addition to ensuring attendance, the firm must be able to inspire quality performance and high output. Motivated workers are genuinely interested in doing good work—and a reasonable amount of it.

Contributing Self-Initiated Behaviors

We see the highest level of motivation in employees who exceed job expectations. Such self-initiated behaviors may in fact be a necessary survival tool in today's limited job market. "The new security," writes Kanter, "is not employment security (a guaranteed job no matter what), but employability security—increased value in the internal and external labor markets."[18]

PERFORMANCE AND INDIVIDUAL DIFFERENCES

If a paralegal supervisor in a real estate department were asked to decide which of two paralegals seemed most motivated, he or she would likely have a hard time deciding. It would not be simply a matter of selecting the paralegal who seemed most willing or the one who produced the highest volume of work. Because a worker's level of performance results from many factors, performance level alone does not accurately indicate motivation. Performance is the product of a worker's education, skills, experience, ability, and many other factors, including the work setting and the employee's attitude toward work. Performance levels vary from worker to worker and even, at times, within the same worker. People enjoy highly creative and productive peak phases, and they also struggle through slumps. Workers choose their behaviors from a wide range of options. Kurt Lewin suggested that behavior was a function of personality and the environment; that is, *behavior,* or what people do, is the result of how the *environment*—those realities that are part of each person's life—shapes and interacts with each person's *personality,* or the sum of who each person is, as determined by nature through genetic inheritance and shaped by nurture.[19] We will examine aspects of personality in the following sections.

Personality

Personality is the unique combination of characteristics and behavioral tendencies resulting from genetic inheritance and nurture, the social, cultural, and environmental influences that modify the expression of genetic traits.[20] Personality is stable and enduring. When we think of the people we know, it becomes obvious that each is unique because of the way he or she thinks, looks, and acts. It is also apparent that many people do not seem to change. We sometimes meet people we have not seen for years and are amazed by the lack of change we see in them. Even old acquaintances who have experienced hard times and upheavals in their lives seem remarkably the same. Our saying "You haven't changed a bit" does not mean, however, that we don't notice *some* surface changes. It merely shows that we appreciate the uniqueness of personality, which is the part of a person that endures through grey hairs, balding, and weight gained or lost. This uniqueness of characteristics and their stability are the two basic components of personality.

Work-Related Dimensions of Personality

Personality has both superficial and deeper aspects. Often, characters that we meet in real life or encounter in books seem like people we know or have known. We tend to develop categories for the personality types we encounter. Known as **stereotyping,** the practice of labeling a personality according to a single striking quality is both useful and dangerous. We use stereotypes to classify people, including the seemingly standard types such as the cheapskate, the tyrant, or the hard worker. These labels help us to simplify and predict a limitless range of personality types. But we should realize the danger of using superficial labels to describe something as complex as personality. Researchers, for all their effort, have yet to accurately assess the many dimensions of personality. Some of what they have learned remains theoretical; some has useful applications for management. Some work-related findings on the dimensions of personality include the following:

Locus of Control

One basic way in which people differ concerns a dimension of personality known as the **locus of control,** the degree to which people believe that the forces governing their lives are internal or external.[21]

External Locus of Control. Those whose locus of control is external believe that external forces, including other people, fate, and luck, determine what happens in their lives. Because such people resign themselves to thinking that the events in their lives are beyond their control, they can be difficult to motivate.

Internal Locus of Control. Those who have an internal locus of control believe that they govern their lives through their own abilities. Employees with an internal locus of control, who work hard to reach their goals and take full responsibility for their failings, are deeply aware of the role of motivation in effective performance and success.

Authority

Another dimension of personality is **authoritarianism,** a set of attitudes toward authority characterized by beliefs about the balance of power, the use of rules, and the roles of individuals. The earnest study of authoritarianism began shortly after World War II, when researchers attempted to find causes for the atrocities committed during the war. Those who are highly authoritarian believe, for example, that power is the sole domain of those in authority, that clearly defined status and hierarchical structures are the most essential components of organizational success, that all members of an organization should adhere strictly to conventional values, and that those in authority should receive unquestioning obedience. Other attitudes toward authority that closely resemble these basic beliefs regarding authority relationships and the absolutism of power include dogmatic, Machiavellian, and bureaucratic orientations.[22]

Dogmatic Orientation. Those who are highly **dogmatic** in terms of authority stick rigidly, even arrogantly, to their beliefs, ignore others' opinions and ideas, and reject those who will not accept their teachings, or dogma, all the while sharing with those who are highly authoritarian the belief that employees should not question organizational authority.[23]

Machiavellian Orientation. Machiavellian individuals believe in using power (which need not be based on authority) to overpower and control those around them. They manipulate others through deception, use false praise to get what they want, achieve goals through subversion rather than interaction, and think it unnecessary to reach decisions ethically.[24]

Bureaucratic Orientation. In sharp contrast to those who exhibit a Machiavellian orientation in their beliefs about authority, **bureaucratic** individuals willingly accept the authority of their superiors, comply strictly and unquestioningly with rules and directives, prefer impersonal relationships within a highly structured work environment, and thrive in rigid, clear-cut hierarchies.[25] (We should note that these bureaucratic, Machiavellian, dogmatic, and authoritarian orientations reflect extremes. Though they might lean toward one camp or another, most workers take a more moderate view of authority.) Table 10-1 summarizes the characteristics of those with authoritarian orientations.

Self-Concept

Self-concept, according to psychologist Carl Rogers, is the set of attitudes, values, and beliefs that result from the conclusions we draw regarding our behavior, abilities, appearance, and personal worth. Those around us shape and validate these self-perceptions, which in turn influence our perceptions of others.[26] People with positive self-concepts (or high *self-esteem*) are generally self-motivating. They also tend to be creative, independent, and spontaneous in their interactions with others. Because of their positive feelings about themselves, they can concentrate on original ideas and the issues at hand without worrying about how others perceive them. On the other hand, people with low self-esteem tend to feel overly concerned about others' opinions. This dilutes their ability to concentrate on problems and think creatively, which leads to a cycle of mistakes, failure, and even lower self-esteem. Under such circumstances, self-motivation can be next to impossible.[27]

Other Work-Related Dimensions of Personality

Many other dimensions of personality are work-related. Our different levels of tolerance for risk taking, the

TABLE 10-1
Characteristics of Authoritarian Orientations

Orientation	Characteristics
Dogmatic	■ Tends to reject the opinions and ideas of others ■ Adheres arrogantly, tenaciously, and sometimes blindly to beliefs ■ Believes that organizational authority is not to be questioned ■ Rejects those who do not accept their dogma, or teachings ■ Tends to be close-minded about issues
Machiavellian	■ Believes in using authority to overpower and control others ■ Attempts to manipulate others through deception ■ Believes in using false praise and flattery to achieve goals ■ Achieves goals through subversion rather than straightforward interaction ■ Enjoys manipulating people and situations ■ Finds excuses for deceit and thinks ethical decision making is unimportant
Bureaucratic	■ Believes in self-subordination to authority and in unquestioning compliance with rules and directives ■ Prefers a highly structured work environment and the security of a rigid, clear-cut hierarchy ■ Performs in a setting that promotes impersonal, formal relationships and strict conformity to rules

introvert-extrovert tendencies that color our interpersonal relationships, our social skills, and the Type A fervor or the Type B tranquility with which we act also influence our interactions in the work setting.

BEHIND THE SCENES: THE MOTIVATIONAL FRAMEWORK

To understand motivation, we must understand that motivation centers around needs, values, and attitudes and that, because of this, the behavior of people in organizations is sometimes perplexing. Rosabeth Moss Kanter, former editor of the *Harvard Business Review,* once wrote that "everyone in an organization, no matter how silly or irrational their behavior seemed, was reacting to what their situation made available, in such a way as to preserve dignity, control, and recognition from others."[28] In exploring motivation, the starting point is the individual.

Needs

Needs are perceived deficiencies that prompt people to seek something useful, required, or desired. The stronger the need, the stronger the drive to fulfill it. Needs may be physiological (for instance, the need for food or shelter), sociological (the need for interaction or a sense of belonging), or psychological (for example, the need for self-esteem). When our efforts to fulfill a need are successful enough to content us, we reach a state of *sufficiency.* This need-drive-action-sufficiency chain is a basic form of self-motivation. Let's say that Lynn, a paralegal, feels a need for more job responsibility. This need compels her to plan a course of action. She might ask her supervisor for more work, drop hints among the firm's attorneys that she is willing to increase her assignment load, or attempt to convince the firm's management of her competence by working harder. The last plan seems best, and Lynn starts to work more overtime and to treat every assignment with extra care. If her efforts succeed, and she receives enough additional responsibility to feel a sense of sufficiency, Lynn will be content until a new need arises. If the first plan of action fails, however, Lynn will reassess her options and try again.

Working to fulfill a need, or a goal, is, however, rarely so straightforward. As we have seen, most organizations expect employees to place the organization's needs before their own. Consequently, explains University of Chicago professor Mihaly Csikszentmihalyi, most people work toward goals they never had a chance to evaluate or choose.[29] Part of a manager's challenge involves helping employees to balance their efforts to fulfill organizational goals with their efforts to fulfill personal ones. Such concern, which allows employees to feel valued and important, is a prime motivator.

Attitudes

Predisposing us to think or act in certain ways, **attitudes** are our beliefs, feelings, and intentions regarding another person, an event, a task, or an organization.[30] Attitudes develop through experience, which shapes our beliefs and feelings about people and objects, situations, and concepts. Except for our most basic needs, such as those involving food or safety, our needs depend on the world about us, our immediate environment, and our attitudes toward it. A hungry person has a food deficiency, but a person who is motivated to go to an elegant restaurant is meeting a deficiency far different from the basic need for food. Our attitudes toward our environment can initiate the need-satisfaction cycle. For instance, one attorney's success can inspire others to achieve similar successes; one paralegal's highly enriching participation in advanced skills seminars may promote the interest of others in continuing education; one merit raise given a secretary for outstanding contributions may challenge others to improve their work. Attitudes toward these needs are key. If people consider the object in question—success, continuing education, or merit pay—to be of little consequence, they will feel no deficiency and no motivational drive in conjunction with that object.

The Components of Attitudes

Attitudes consist of three integral features: cognition, an affective component, and behavioral tendencies.

Cognition. The cognitive component of an attitude describes the perceptions, opinions, and beliefs that we hold about a person or a thing. This intellectual component is based on our knowledge regarding the object of the attitude. This information, which is generally descriptive, may rely less heavily on fact than on our perceptions.

Affect. The affective component of an attitude proceeds from our cognition of a person or thing to describe how we feel about that cognition. We learn and reinforce the emotional or feeling-based components of our attitudes through interaction with our parents, peers, and society.

Behavioral Tendencies. The behavioral component of an attitude describes our tendency to act, behave, or think in a certain way. This third component indicates only how we *intend* to act, based on our feelings toward a cognition of another person, task, event, or situation; we should realize that we do not always convert our attitudes into logically consequential actions.

Changing Attitudes

Some attitudes are remarkably stable; others are more ephemeral. Examples of rapidly changing attitudes include current fads and the fleeting dictates of high fashion. More stable attitudes include such solid considerations as respect for friendship and family values. The stability of attitudes depends on three factors: the situation and the environment, the nature of the attitude itself, and the individual. We change attitudes by altering their affective or cognitive components. Our feelings about objects change when new feelings take their place, and we alter our cognitions either by obtaining new information or by augmenting or modifying the information we already have. These changes can take place (1) through learning, which leads to new cognitions regarding the object of the attitude, (2) through moderate fear or punishment which leaves us more susceptible to change, (3) through a need to reduce cognitive tension that results from acting in a manner inconsistent with other attitudes and beliefs, and (4) through participation in group discussions and processes, which reinforces the need to change and provides support for the change itself.

Values

Once described as "the constellation of likes, dislikes, viewpoints, shoulds, inner inclinations, rational and irrational judgments, prejudices and association patterns that make up a person's view of the world,"[31] **values** are attitudes that carry a moral concern. "Our values," writes David Cherrington, "are the criteria we use in assessing our daily lives, arranging our priorities, measuring our pleasures and pains, and choosing between alternative courses of action."[32] We use values to determine what is desirable, good, important, and meaningful, as well as to decide what we should dislike, shun, avoid, or reject. Values, like attitudes, develop in a variety of ways. We learn most of our values from parents, teachers, and significant others, but society in general constantly reinforces the acceptable and appropriate values such as honesty, integrity, generosity, caring, and consideration.

Work Values

Family expectations and early life experiences reinforce work values, also known as the **work ethic.** The work ethic consists of two primary values: (1) the moral importance of work and (2) the pride that people take in what they do. The first value refers to the moral obligation that workers feel toward society and to their need to believe that their work contributes a useful service or product. The second value consists of the pride that workers take in their work. Most of us have been brought up to believe that working hard makes us better people and that we should always do our best, even at jobs we dislike. Nonetheless, the work ethic is only one of the many values that affect a worker's motivation and productivity.[33] Attitudes toward work are an important consideration in understanding motivational tendencies. For example, an employee for whom family involvement is a critical value will not easily be motivated to spend more time at work than is absolutely necessary. By comparison, a worker whose family values combine with a strong work ethic to create a third value—that of worker-as-extraordinary-provider—will log overtime, hone his or her skills, and pursue promotions and raises.

The Roles of Values

Values help us to shape our decisions and to theorize our behavior under hypothetical circumstances. But although they shape our vision of life, our values, like our attitudes in general, cannot predict with complete accuracy how we will act in a given situation. Values play the following roles:

- Values influence our perceptions regarding appropriate means and ends.
- Values enable us to organize our attitudes by providing us with categories of what we should and shouldn't do or be. They also help us to decide what we will have positive or negative feelings about. For example, if honesty is an important value to us, we will abhor deceit. If we consider justice important, we will champion equity and

fairness. Those who foster strong values regarding care for the deprived will adopt a whole range of attitudes about welfare, medical policies, the homeless, and the distribution of tax dollars.

- Values affect the motivational process, decision making, conflict resolutions, communications, evaluations, and many critical work-related areas.
- Values are deeply rooted and hard to change, and sharply differing values are often at the heart of interpersonal and intergroup conflicts.

Values vary according to setting and culture. For instance, the Persian Gulf conflict in 1991 exposed many Americans to a value system in which life centered around the family and the role of women in society was severely restricted. The image of American women actively serving in the allied military forces contrasted sharply with the Moslem world's refusal to allow women to drive or to appear in public without veils. Some values, such as the respect for life, are cross-cultural. Understanding the powerful roles that values play in our lives is essential for understanding interaction and motivation in the workplace.

THEORIES OF MOTIVATION

For centuries, people have attempted to explain motivation. Philosophers have analyzed motivation in order to better understand the qualities that make us human. Scientists have studied motivation to comprehend more fully the workings of the human mind. And businesspeople have studied motivation in order to increase productivity, work quality, and commitment among their workers. Motivation, however, continues to elude exact description. Scientists, philosophers, and businesspeople ascribe differences in performance between workers of equal ability to differences in motivation. The continuing attempt to discover the composition of these differences has produced dozens of theories regarding motivation, the most popular of which suggest that employers can motivate workers by modifying their behavior, understanding their needs, or acknowledging the cognitive processes that guide a worker's interaction with his or her environment. We will examine these behavioral, needs-based, and cognitive processes theories of motivation in the following sections.

Early Theories: An Overview

One of the earliest views of motivation centered on the concept of **hedonism,** which suggests that people are motivated instinctively to seek pleasure and to avoid pain, uncomfortable situations, and unpleasant activities. First suggested by writers in ancient Greece, hedonism figured prominently in the writings of many later seventeenth, eighteenth, and nineteenth century philosophers, notably John Locke and John Stuart Mill.[34] Hedonism is now largely considered invalid as a theory of motivation for the reason that it cannot explain, in the most literal sense, why people tolerate discomfort even as a means to a pleasurable end.

Another early view of motivation, set forth by William James, William McDougall, Sigmund Freud, and others in the late nineteenth and early twentieth centuries, suggested that **instinct,** the innate tendency to do certain things, explained motivation. Freud, for example, suggested that two of the most powerful motivators in human life were the instincts associated with sex and aggression, while English psychologist William McDougall identified twelve categories of instinctive (hence motivational) human behavior, including acquisitiveness, self-assertion, and gregariousness.[35]

Theories Based on Studies of Behavior

Behaviorism, an approach to motivation that focuses on observable actions rather than on inner states, has its roots in the studies performed by Russian physiologist Ivan P. Pavlov in the first decades of the twentieth century. His work strongly influenced the thinking of an American contemporary, psychologist John B. Watson, who believed that changes in behavior result from conditioning, a form of learning by which people associate responses with certain stimuli. In the 1930s, B. F. Skinner, an American behavioral psychologist, received much attention for a stimulus-response theory that drew heavily on the work of another American, educator Edward Thorndike, best known for his *law of effect,* which states that organisms are apt to repeat behaviors that lead to satisfying consequences.[36] In laboratory experiments with pigeons, Skinner attempted to encourage desired behaviors through a process involving reinforcement and punishment. We have come to know his principle of reinforcement by the term that describes its primary application: behavior modification.

Behavior Modification

Behavior modification is the process of altering behavior through the use of **reinforcement contingencies,** which consist of the situation that precedes a be-

ANOTHER LOOK

Three Motivational Parables

The First Parable: In Need of Carrots

Once upon a time there was a donkey standing knee-deep in a field of carrots, contentedly munching away. A farmer wanted the donkey to pull a loaded wagon to another field, but the donkey would not walk over to the wagon. So the farmer stood by the wagon and held up a bunch of carrots for the donkey to see. But the donkey continued to munch contentedly on carrots in the field.

A Second Parable: Carrots and Equity

Once upon a time there were six donkeys hitched to a wagon pulling a heavy load up a steep hill. Two of the donkeys were not achievement-oriented and decided to coast along and let the others do most of the pulling. Two others were relatively young and inexperienced, and had a difficult time pulling their share. One of the remaining two suffered from a slight hangover from consuming fermented barley the night before. The sixth donkey did most of the work.

The wagon arrived at the top of the hill. The driver got down from his seat, patted each of the donkeys on the head, and gave six carrots to each. Prior to the next hill climb, the sixth donkey ran away.

A Final Parable: Carrots and Goals

Once upon a time a farmer had six donkeys and a barn full of carrots, which she kept under lock and key. At the end of a day of wagon pulling, the farmer looked back over the day's performance of each donkey. To one of the donkeys she said, "You did an outstanding job; here are six carrots." To four of the others she said, "Your performance was average; here are three carrots." To the remaining donkey she said, "You didn't pull your share of the load; here is one carrot."

Another day of wagon pulling dawned. The top donkey, having been properly rewarded, began the day in high spirits. The thoughts of the remaining donkeys were consumed with how they might earn more carrots through their efforts that day. The farmer had carrots available, but they had to be earned.

SOURCE: Dale McConkey, "The 'Jackass Effect' in Management Compensation." Reprinted from *Business Horizons* (June 1974): 81–89. Copyright © 1974 by the Foundation for the School of Business at Indiana University. Used with permission.

1. When is a motivator not a motivator? How do attitudes, needs, and one's surroundings affect motivation?
2. In what ways is motivation a group process? An individualized process?
3. Describe your personal motivators. Which do you think are common? Which are unique? Explain.

---

havior (the *antecedents*) and the *consequences* which follow.[37] Those who apply behavior modification in the work setting encourage correct behavior by modifying the work environment and by responding to behavior in one of three ways:

Positive Reinforcement. Positive reinforcement occurs when an action produces a consequence that the actor considers desirable. A law firm librarian who arrives for work on time daily and whose attendance is excellent might receive positive reinforcement in the form of one extra day off for every six months of perfect attendance and punctuality.

Negative Reinforcement. Negative reinforcement occurs when an action triggers an undesirable consequence and the actor alters his or her behavior in order to eliminate or avoid that consequence. A chronically tardy receptionist who receives negative reinforcement in the form of thunderous complaints every time she walks in late is apt to alter her behavior by arriving on time.

Punishment. Punishment occurs when a behavior triggers an intensely unpleasant response. The effectiveness of punishment as a motivational tool is questionable; Lewin insisted that only positive or negative reinforcement could have a lasting, predictable effect on human behavior.[38] Though apt to extinguish undesirable behavior quickly, punishment may create resentment and damage motivation in the long run. Punishment falls into three categories:

- Natural Consequences. *Natural consequences* involve automatic or instinctive responses to unwanted behavior, such as when a worker who is rude and abrasive is shunned by other workers.
- Logical Consequences. *Logical consequences* are planned, appropriate responses to unwanted behavior. Requiring the firm's secretaries to sign out a rest room key because carelessness in locking the door has allowed vagrants to lodge there overnight would be an example of a logical consequence.
- Contrived Consequences. *Contrived consequences* are punitive responses that have no logical relationship to the behavior for which a worker is to receive punishment. Docking a worker half a day's pay for failing to dispatch a critical document to the state courthouse by overnight delivery, after he or she had been told specifically to do so, would be an example of a contrived punishment.

A fourth type of response is *extinction*, which relates to behavior modification but originates in classical conditioning. (We most commonly associate classical conditioning with the experiments by which Pavlov conditioned dogs to salivate in response to a ringing bell.)[39] Essentially, **extinction** is the process of stopping a behavior simply by ignoring it. A supervisor who completely disregards a paralegal's constant written complaints about her coworkers responds neither positively nor negatively to the behavior, and eventually the note writing stops.

Theories Based on Meeting Needs

Recall that needs are perceived deficiencies that induce people to seek something useful, required, or desired. The most popular school of motivational theory steps back from behavior to examine the needs that precede it. Incorporating the work of psychologists Henry Murray, Abraham Maslow, David McClelland, and others, the need-based theories of motivation contemplate individual needs and the forces that compel people to fulfill them.

Murray's Theory of Latent and Manifest Needs

Some of the earliest work linking needs and motivation was that of psychologist Henry Murray, also known for his studies of personality. In 1938, Murray proposed that a need exists in one of two states, depending on the need holder's attitude toward the object of the need. **Latent needs** involve objects, people, or activities of which the need holder is aware but about which he or she feels no immediate sense of deficiency. **Manifest needs,** in contrast, involve things about which the need holder feels an acute sense of deficiency; such needs usually motivate people to perform the activities necessary to fulfill them. (Murray suggested also that needs vary in *direction*—that is, in the object, activity, or person toward which they are directed. *Primary,* or *viscerogenic,* needs involve basic physiological functions. *Secondary,* or *psychogenic,* needs include psychological requirements in areas such as aggression, achievement, power, and affiliation.)[40]

What one person perceives as a manifest need may be a latent need for another. A newly practicing attorney who has come to depend on computers will feel lost without a PC; an attorney who has worked efficiently for years without a computer will feel no pressing need in terms of computers. The need for a given object can become manifest for a variety of reasons, however; and the second attorney might acquire a computer not out of dependence but out of a need for technology-related prestige or a desire to keep abreast of the latest innovations.

Maslow's Hierarchy of Needs

Approximately half a century ago, psychologist Abraham Maslow proposed that the highest motivational force is the drive to fulfill one's potential as a human being.[41] Accordingly, Maslow identified five categories of needs, which he arranged in a pyramid-shaped hierarchy. The pyramid shape represents a **prepotency of needs,** a continuum of predominance in which fulfilling needs at a lower level, or category, takes priority over fulfilling higher-level ones. Believing that people must meet needs at one level before moving up to the next, Maslow described the hierarchy of needs as follows:[42]

Physiological Needs. The lowest level of the hierarchy includes our most basic needs, such as those for food, drink, shelter, and relief from pain. In the work setting, these needs might translate into needs for pay, break periods, vacations, time off, sick days, light, heating and cooling, a comfortable environment, and ergonomic considerations. In hierarchy-related studies, Maslow estimated that 85 percent of the participants, who were American adults, had met their basic physiological and biological needs.[43]

Safety Needs. Safety and security needs occupy the next level of Maslow's hierarchy. This level encompasses security concerns and our needs for stability in daily life, without fear of harm to self, body, or psyche, as well as our need to protect and preserve our selves, our possessions, and our accomplishments. The objects of second-level needs in the workplace might include insurance, pension plans, job security, and tenure. Maslow estimated that 70 percent of the subjects in his studies had fulfilled their needs for safety and security.[44]

Belongingness or Social Needs. Social needs and the need to belong comprise the middle level on the hierarchy. This third level includes our need for a sense of connection to others and of being linked to the rest of life, connections we form through the intimacy and relationships we share with others. This level delineates our needs for affiliation, affection, love, and friendship. In the work setting, we would meet these needs by earning the acceptance of our coworkers and making friends. Maslow estimated that 50 percent of his subjects had fulfilled their social needs.[45]

Esteem Needs. The fourth level depicts the need for esteem, which includes our needs for being valued and appreciated, our needs for self-respect and self-esteem, and our needs for the respect and esteem of others. Obtaining power or receiving rewards, raises, and promotions fulfills esteem needs in the workplace. Maslow estimated that only 40 percent of his subjects had satisfied their esteem-related needs.[46]

The Need for Self-Actualization. Once we have fulfilled our lower-level needs, we can attempt to fulfill our potential as human beings. At the top of the hierarchy, Maslow placed the need for **self-actualization,** the drive to make the most of one's existence, abilities, skills, and personality. In the work setting, self-actualization might manifest itself in the consistent ability to produce excellent work. Maslow estimated, however, that a mere 10 percent of the people in his study had achieved self-actualization, a process that is unique for each of us.[47]

The hierarchy of needs has drawn its share of criticism, mainly from those who believe that the theory behind it is arbitrary and simplistic. Nonetheless, the hierarchy (pictured in Figure 10–1) illustrates how needs can become increasingly complex and, more importantly, how they motivate us throughout our lives. "Man," Maslow concluded, "is a perpetually wanting animal."[48] "The average member of our society," he believed, "is most often partially satisfied and partially unsatisfied in all of his wants."[49]

Alderfer's ERG Theory

Yale University professor Clayton Alderfer simplified Maslow's hierarchy by first consolidating motivational needs into a three-level hierarchy with no further divisions within the levels. He described the three levels of needs as follows:[50]

Existence Needs. At the base of Alderfer's hierarchy we find needs similar to the physiological and safety needs that Maslow described. *Existence needs* involve things, such as food, housing, and money, that are essential to physical survival and that exist in limited supply. At work, existence needs would focus on things such as decent surroundings, clean air and water, heat, a base salary or otherwise equitable compensation, retirement plans, insurance, basic amenities such as rest rooms, job stability, and health programs.

Relatedness Needs. We fulfill *relatedness needs* by experiencing intimacy and by sharing our thoughts and feelings with others. Alderfer's relatedness needs incorporate the needs that Maslow described as social needs, as well as the needs Maslow associated with safety and esteem. In the workplace, we fulfill relatedness needs through contact with effective supervisors and good colleagues, by working in productive teams, and by receiving positive social recognition and material bonuses such as merit pay.

Growth Needs. We meet *growth needs* by developing the abilities and capacities we consider important. At work, these needs, which are similar to the

FIGURE 10–1
Maslow's Hierarchy of Needs

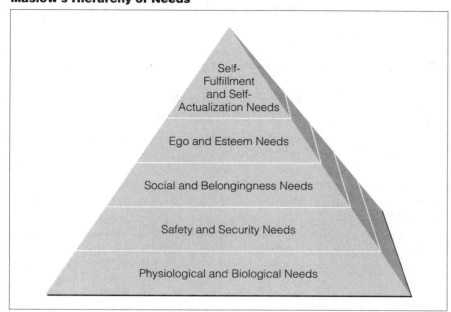

needs for self-esteem and self-actualization, center around creativity, success, participation, advancement, autonomy, responsibility, and accomplishment.

Alderfer next divided the process of meeting these needs into four phases. *Satisfaction-progression* occurs when people, after meeting needs at one level, progress to the level above it. *Frustration* sets in when people fail to meet their needs at a given level. Though frustration can drive people to increase their efforts, *frustration-regression,* or discouragement, can lead them to settle for success at a lower level. By comparison, *aspiration,* the fourth stage of the process, motivates people to seek additional opportunities for growth once they have satisfied their immediate needs.

McClelland's Learned Needs Theory[51]

Psychologist David McClelland suggested that through our experiences and learning, each of us develops a unique set of needs and that, consequently, the forces that motivate us differ enormously. Using a research tool he called the Thematic Apperception Test, which asked subjects to respond in writing to a series of pictures showing people engaged in various activities, McClelland identified three sets of need-related drives that workers try to satisfy in organizational settings:

the drive for achievement (n/ACH), the drive for affiliation (n/AFF), and the drive for power (n/POW).

n/ACH. n/ACH measures the need for success and positive recognition. Those who score high in n/ACH are task- and result-oriented, balancing an intense desire for success with an equally intense fear of failure. In their search for perfection, they prefer low-risk, low-stress environments. They work hard and resent interference. Not easily satisfied with their accomplishments, they place great importance on receiving feedback. Finally, out of fear of losing control of their projects and of missing out on recognition, they are reluctant to delegate.

n/AFF. n/AFF measures the need for intimacy, approval, and love. Those with high n/AFF like to work with others, balancing their drive for acceptance with their fear of rejection. Genuinely concerned about the needs of others, high n/AFF people readily offer compassion, consolation, help, and above all, friendship.[52]

n/POW. n/POW measures the need for influence and control. People who score high in n/POW tend to take charge. They are forceful, outspoken, stubborn, and demanding. They often seek leadership positions, welcome responsibility, and make formidable opponents. They are good conversationalists, enjoy teaching and making public presentations, and are often argumentative. Generally, those who score high in n/POW seek one of two types of power:

- Personalized Power. Personalized power is satisfaction in the control one has over others. The drive for personalized power, which is by nature self-serving, can conflict sharply with professional or organizational responsibilities.
- Socialized Power. Socialized power is power that one acquires in order to benefit others: an organization, a group, or society in general.[53]

Herzberg's Hygienes-Motivators Theory[54]

Through a series of studies in which he asked professionals, accountants, and engineers to describe the times at work when they felt either very good or very bad, Frederick Herzberg identified two categories of work-related needs: hygiene needs and motivator needs.

Hygiene Needs. Herzberg associated **hygiene needs** with the context in which work occurs. Such needs involve pay, working conditions, supervision, coworkers, interpersonal relationships, organizational policies, and administration. Herzberg nicknamed hygiene factors *dissatisfiers,* for although their presence in itself creates little or no satisfaction, their absence can lead to deep dissatisfaction.

Motivator Needs. **Motivator needs,** which relate to work content, involve factors such as the opportunity for achievement, recognition, advancement, growth, autonomy, responsibility, power, and appreciation. The presence of motivators, like psychic salary, creates a sense of satisfaction in workers. Herzberg found that motivators comprised 81 percent of the factors leading to job satisfaction.

We should note that Herzberg's findings are not as clear-cut as they appear. For example, hygiene factors (which respondents claimed constituted 19 percent of their positive job experiences) seem occasionally to act as motivators. Pay, especially, seems able to act both as a hygiene and as a motivator, depending on the needs, values, and attitudes of each worker, as well as on whether he or she perceives pay as equitable and linked to performance. Equitable pay is a reasonable work-context expectation, whereas bonuses and merit raises can motivate employees to perfect their attendance and work harder. Like the objects of latent and manifest needs, one worker's motivator can easily be another worker's hygiene factor, and vice versa.[55] Figure 10–2 presents the percentage frequencies with which certain factors act as hygienes and motivators in the work setting.

Theories Based on Cognitive Processes

Motivational theories based on *cognitive processes* reflect the idea that people choose to act as they do, rather than acting purely in response to their needs or their environment. In other words, motivation is the result of choice, not instinct, though many researchers believe that a majority of the needs we are motivated to fulfill stem from *learned instincts,* or drives that we have learned or acquired through conditioning and conscious interaction with our surroundings. We will examine two theories based on cognitive processes: the equity theory and the expectancy theory.[56]

Equity Theory

The **equity theory** proposes that motivation is a product of the fairness, or *equity,* that people perceive when they compare their efforts, or *inputs,* and results, or *outputs,* to the inputs and outputs of another person, or *referent.*[57]

Inputs. Inputs are contributions for which a worker will receive compensation. Inputs include status, seniority, education, experience, and technical or social skills, as well as qualities such as dependability, loyalty, and enthusiasm.

Outcomes. Outcomes refer to any results that people connect to their inputs at work, such as pay, appreciation, recognition, bonuses, honors, advancement, tenure, vacation time, perks, coveted office or department assignments, titles, and job assignments.

Central to the equity theory of motivation is **distributive justice,** the belief that each person should receive an equitable share of rewards.[58] A person whose inputs exceed his or her outputs will still perceive equity if his or her referent experiences a similar imbalance. On the other hand, an actual balance between inputs and outputs won't automatically negate a perception of inequity. If John, a paralegal, believes that fellow paralegal Nancy is receiving more compensation for completing the same amount of work, the inequality that he perceives might persist even if

FIGURE 10–2
Factors Affecting Job Attitudes: Hygienes and Motivators

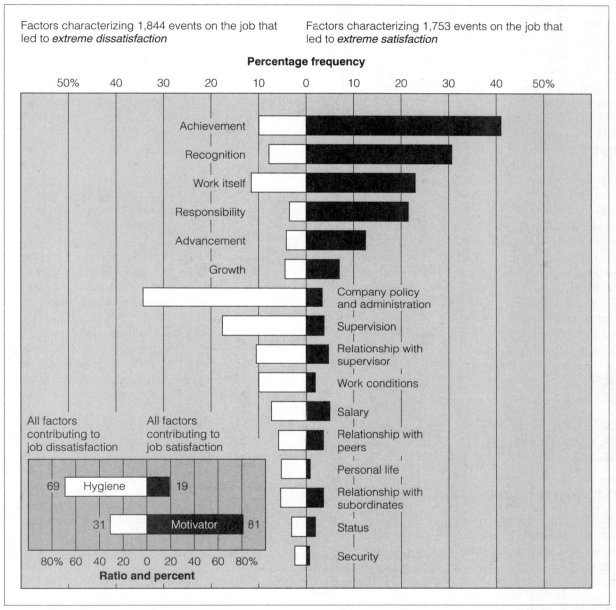

SOURCE: Reprinted by permission of *Harvard Business Review*. An exhibit from Frederick Herzberg: Factors Affecting Job Attitudes as Reported in 12 Investigations from "One More Time: How Do You Motivate Employees?" *Harvard Business Review* (September/October 1987): 112. Copyright © 1987 by the President and Fellows of Harvard College; all rights reserved.

he finds that Nancy's pay is identical to his. (We should note that a referent need not be a person: John might compare his compensation to that of a group of paralegals in his firm, or to national or regional statistics on paralegal salaries.) A worker who perceives an inequality will attempt either to receive an increase in outputs or to avoid further comparisons, even if such avoidance means leaving the work site.[59]

Expectancy Theory

First suggested by psychologist E. C. Tolman in 1932 and later developed as a theory of motivation by Victor

Vroom, a professor of organization and management at Yale University, the **expectancy theory** proposes that our motivational drives depend on (1) the perceived likelihood that our work will produce certain results and (2) the value (positive or negative) we place on those results.[60] Vroom suggested that the strength of our motivational drive (**force**) is the product of **expectancy** (the degree of success we foresee in our efforts) and **valence** (the value we place in an outcome).[61] We can think of expectancy in terms of percentages. For instance, you might harbor 0 percent expectancy regarding your chances of becoming a justice of the Supreme Court but 50 percent expectancy regarding the likelihood of your becoming a manager or administrator in a law firm. In a similar vein, Vroom measured valence in terms of outcome or reward, valence in terms of need, the degree of expectancy between effort and performance and between effort and outcome, and the strength of the instrumentality that a person perceives between outcomes and rewards, placing each of these five motivational factors on a scale ranging from -1.00 (highly negative) to $+1.00$ (highly positive). For example, promotion to a position as a director of paralegals might have a valence of outcome or reward score of $+.90$ for ambitious Alan; for Cathy, who's content in her current job, the possibility of promotion might carry a valence of only $+.20$.

GOAL SETTING AS A MOTIVATIONAL STRATEGY

Criteria for Effective Goals

People form intentions about what they mean to do. The more specific these intentions are, the more compelling they become. Intentions that people consciously decide to pursue are goals.[62] Though we tend to think of goals as the central element in the organizational planning process, they can be powerful motivators for employees at all levels. Especially in organizations such as law firms, which house dozens of independent activities, goals can create a sense of teamwork, focus, and cameraderie. Goals that both advance the firm and motivate its workers meet the following criteria:

Attainability

When forming a goal, whether for a work group, the entire firm, or yourself, you must carefully assess the people and resources at your disposal and tailor the goal accordingly. To act as motivators, goals should be challenging, but not overwhelming.

Clarity and Specificity

A goal must describe a specific action, and its wording should be concise. Most effective goals begin with an infinitive (a verb form, beginning with the word "to," that functions as a noun): "to achieve," "to produce," and "to improve" are examples.

Measurability

To determine your success in reaching a goal, you must specify a method for measuring the activity that the goal involves. Most measurements are quantitative; that is, they involve specific quantities of hard data such as a number of repetitions, an amount of money, or percentages. But goals involving qualitative, or subjective, data are measurable as well. Say, for example, that Helen, the firm's chief receptionist, adopts "To provide more courteous service" as a personal goal. Courtesy is not something you can count, weigh, or measure with a ruler. Nonetheless, by providing clients and other members of the firm with a measuring tool (possibly like the graphic rating scales we discussed in Chapter 8), Helen can determine her progress.

Time Frame

Information is essential to motivation, and goals should clearly state the progress the goal setter expects to see at a given time. Placing a goal on a schedule focuses workers' efforts to fulfill it and helps management to pace expenditures of money and other resources.

Description of Costs

The goal should delineate the amount of time and money as well as the types and amounts of resources the goal setter expects to expend in reaching the goal.

Goal Setting and the Expectancy Theory

One method of increasing the motivational power of goals is to apply the expectancy theory to the goal-setting process. Recall that the expectancy theory of motivation suggests that the strength, or *focus,* of a person's motivational drive is the product of confidence, or *expectancy,* and interest, or *valence.* When setting goals, managers can increase expectancy by providing realistic projections and by ensuring that workers hold valid expectations. Encouragement and constructive feedback will maintain expectancy when the goal-fulfillment process is under way. In terms of valence, defining outcomes that workers consider important, identifying results over which the manager has control, and providing rewards that seem relevant and valuable will increase or preserve employee interest in pursuing a goal.

NEW MOTIVATIONAL TOOLS

In this chapter, we have examined what motivates people in organizations. If managers can apply what they learn in terms of motivational theory, they'll have some powerful tools in their motivational tool kit. It becomes increasingly difficult to find the right one, however. Law firms that have experienced great spurts of growth are now experiencing the personnel demands that accompany expansion, while firms that are cutting back see insecurity, uncertainty, and resentment both in those workers who remain and in those who are left behind. Acquisitions and divestitures bring not only technical problems but hosts of people-related difficulties as well. Enormous pressure from competition, Rosabeth Moss Kanter observes, has left managers watching "traditional sources of power erode and the old motivational tools lose their magic." She notes that, in these uncertain times, "leaders need new and more effective incentives to encourage high performance and build commitment."[63] To transform alienated workers into team players committed to organizational goals, managers need to use new tools, such as allowing workers to participate in setting and controlling their own agenda, involving them in the creation of values, encouraging them to acquire new knowledge and skills, and helping them to build their reputations and reputation of the firm. "Pride," comments Kanter, "is often a better source of motivation than the traditional career ladder and the promotion-based reward system."[64] Law office workers in all areas can become more actively involved in client service, for instance, and developmental programs in hundreds of different areas can lead to better quality output from everyone, without detracting from the firm's productivity. Managers can often persuade top management to consider bright new motivational tools, which might include new approaches to old classics, such as flexible and enriched job design, leadership styles that complement the professional structures of the law firm, revamped versions of equitable compensation systems, the encouragement of growth, and the equalization of the power flow.

The Manager of Professionals

An equalization of the power flow occurs when a supervisor helps workers by becoming a mentor, a colleague, an adviser, and a coach. In workplaces that demand commitment and high performance, such as well-run law firms, there is a right and a wrong approach to motivating knowledge workers. As K. Kim Fisher advises managers in more technical settings, "Don't preach to, boss at, withhold information from, direct, or artificially limit technicians; do teach, coach, inform, facilitate and develop them."[65] In working with professionals, this is also the correct motivational litany.

The Manager as Motivator

Like Tom Peters in *A Passion for Excellence,* we can rightly define motivators as people who "find and nurture champions, dramatize company goals and direction, build skills and teams, and spread irresistible enthusiasm."[66] Managers should not underestimate their importance in the complex motivational process that affects workers. "Just as the manner in which a person is selected, trained, and assigned influences his image of the organization," writes Edgar Schein, "so the manner in which he is managed will influence this image."[67] Managers, then, become coaches, urging people to reach their goals. As we saw in the chapter on leadership, coaching entails many roles: educator, sponsor, counselor, and even confronter, when necessary. Coaching of this sort includes motivational roles that can improve workers' self-esteem, bring company philosophy to life, and generate a sense of teamwork and of belonging.[68] Managers who truly want to develop this kind of motivational relationship with workers must be willing to submit to an honest self-appraisal. They will need to ask themselves how genuine they are, how consistent in word and action, and whether they truly value relationships of integrity and trust. Managers need to work at and shape all these qualities in order to develop a motivational synergy between themselves and their workers.[69] By doing so, writes Kanter, they create "an excitement in mission and a share of the glory and gains of success."[70]

QUESTIONS FOR DISCUSSION AND REVIEW

1. Why is motivation essential in the law firm?
2. Identify the role personality plays in motivation and describe your own motivational profile.
3. Explain how needs, values, and attitudes influence the motivational process.
4. Can a manager's and a subordinate's motivational patterns conflict? Explain.
5. Of the motivational theories based on meeting people's needs, which seems to be the most useful for law firm management? Why?
6. In what ways is motivation a product of instinct? In what ways is it a product of cognitive processes and reasoning?
7. Compare the theories of Maslow, Alderfer, and McClelland. What similarities do these theories share?
8. How might a law firm manager motivate employees using the equity theory? The expectancy theory?
9. How does money motivate? What different motivational meanings do workers assign to "money"?
10. Discuss the different roles that a manager would assume as a motivator of professionals and of support staff.

EXPERIENTIAL EXERCISES

I. Measuring Your n/ACH, n/AFF, and n/POW Tendencies

Directions: Read each of the following statements. Using the scale on the right, circle the number of the response that most accurately describes your behavior when you are working.

4 = Always
3 = Almost always
2 = Usually
1 = Almost never
0 = Never

Need for Achievement

1. I do my best work when I have challenges.   4 3 2 1 0
2. I like to take moderate risks and think they are part of doing well.   4 3 2 1 0
3. I like to have feedback on what I've done.   4 3 2 1 0
4. I enjoy getting a handle on problems and solving them.   4 3 2 1 0

Total: _____

Need for Affiliation

5. I like to think others approve of what I'm doing.   4 3 2 1 0
6. I enjoy working with people and having people around.   4 3 2 1 0
7. Whenever possible, I'd rather go along with people than upset them.   4 3 2 1 0
8. I feel good when I think of the friends I've made.   4 3 2 1 0

Total: _____

Need for Power

9. I enjoy directing and organizing activities.   4 3 2 1 0
10. I usually find myself in charge or taking over.   4 3 2 1 0
11. I like to influence outcomes.   4 3 2 1 0

12. I like to influence and control not only people   4   3   2   1   0
    but the physical environment.

Total: _____

Scoring: To measure the strength of your needs for achievement, affiliation, and power, add the numbers you have circled in each section. Strong needs = 11 to 16; moderate needs = 5 to 10; low needs = 0 to 4.

II. Does Your Law Firm Play Fair?

Think of an organization that you know and rate each of the following statements, according to the scale below:

    5 = Always true
    4 = Almost always true
    3 = Sometimes true
    2 = Almost never true
    1 = Never true

_____ a. In my organization, pay raises are given according to fair rules.
_____ b. Promotions are based on competency.
_____ c. Vacation time is determined according to policies.
_____ d. People who have the same job are often paid less, even if they offer the same quality work and have similar education and experience.
_____ e. In this organization, managers offer preferential treatment to workers they like.
_____ f. Some employees are not required to meet deadlines whereas others who do the same job are.
_____ g. Some support staff workers are allowed to take a day off or leave early whenever they feel like it.
_____ h. If you flirt with, flatter or play up to managers, you get treated better.
_____ i. Managers in this organization don't play favorites.
_____ j. Some managers are known to give unpleasant and unrewarding jobs to people they don't like.
_____ k. Getting perks in this organization depends on who you are and who you know.
_____ l. All workers have the same opportunities to attend conferences and participate in professional development.
_____ m. Managers have their pets.
_____ n. The same standards for quality and hard work exist for all support staff.
_____ o. Evaluations depend more on "getting along and going along" than on good performance.

Scoring: *Step 1.* For items a, b, c, i, l, and n, add the numbers you have assigned each item. This is Total A. *Step 2.* For the remaining items, reverse the numbers you have assigned: if you have written a 5, change it to a 1; a 4, change it to a 2; a 2, change it to a 4; and a 1, change it to a 5. Items assigned a 3 remain the same. Add these numbers. This is Total B.

    Very equitable: 60 to 75
    Average: 45 to 59   Total A: _____
    Rather inequitable: 30 to 44   Total B: _____
    Very inequitable: 15 to 29   A + B = Score: _____

III. Writing Goals

A. Review the five criteria for effective goals. Then critique the following goals:
   1. To return all folders to their files at the end of the day.
   2. To answer all phone calls within the first three rings.
   3. To improve my absenteeism.
   4. To plan, communicate, and develop a comprehensive calendar for the probate paralegals.
B. Write a personal goal for each of these areas:[71]
   1. Client service.
   2. More positive interpersonal relations with colleagues.
   3. Stress management.
   4. Higher quality work.

IV. Assessing Your Assumptions about Motivation and People*

Individual differences play an important role in motivation, and the perceptions and behaviors of managers are critical in the motivational process. This exercise will help you assess your own assumptions about people and the motivational process. Ten sets of paired statements follow, and each pair is worth a total of ten points. Assign to each statement in each pair the number of points that indicates the strength of your belief in that statement. For example, a statement in which you believe strongly might rate a 7; its companion statement would then receive a 3 (7 + 3 = 10).

1. (a) It is only human nature for people to do as little work as they can get away with.   a. ____
   (b) When people avoid work it is usually because their work has been deprived of its meaning.   b. ____
       10
2. (a) If employees have access to any information they want, they tend to have better attitudes and to behave more responsibly.   c. ____
   (b) If employees have access to more information than they need to do their immediate tasks, they will usually misuse it.   d. ____
       10
3. (a) One problem in asking for the ideas of employees is that their perspective is too limited for their suggestions to be of much practical value.   e. ____
   (b) Asking employees for their ideas broadens the perspective of workers and results in the development of useful suggestions.   f. ____
       10
4. (a) If people do not use much imagination and ingenuity on the job, it is probably because relatively few people have much of either.   g. ____
   (b) Most people are imaginative and creative but may not show it because of limitations imposed by supervision and the job.   h. ____
       10
5. (a) People tend to raise their standards if they are accountable for their own behavior and for correcting their own mistakes.   i. ____
   (b) People tend to lower their standards if they are not punished for their misbehavior and mistakes.   j. ____
       10

---

*SOURCE: M. Scott Myers, "Management-Style Work Sheet: My Assumptions." Adapted from M. Scott Myers, *Every Employee a Manager,* 3d ed. (San Diego: Pfeiffer & Company, 1991). Used with permission.

CHAPTER 10 / MOTIVATION

6. (a) It is better to give people both good and bad news, because most employees want the whole story, no matter how painful it is.
   (b) It is better to withhold unfavorable news about business, because most employees really want to hear only the good news.

   k. _____
   l. _____
   10

7. (a) Because supervisors are entitled to more respect than are those below them in the organization, it weakens the prestige of supervisors if they admit that a subordinate was right and that they were wrong.
   (b) Because people at all levels are entitled to equal respect, the prestige of supervisors is increased when they support this principle by admitting that a subordinate was right and that they were wrong.

   m. _____
   n. _____
   10

8. (a) If you give people enough money, they are less likely to be concerned with intangibles such as responsibility and recognition.
   (b) If you give people interesting and challenging work, they are less likely to complain about things such as pay and supplemental benefits.

   o. _____
   p. _____
   10

9. (a) If people are allowed to set their own goals and standards of performance, they tend to set them higher than the boss would.
   (b) If people are allowed to set their own goals and standards of performance, they tend to set them lower than the boss would.

   q. _____
   r. _____
   10

10. (a) When people have more knowledge and freedom regarding their jobs, more controls are needed to keep those employees in line.
    (b) When people have more knowledge and freedom regarding their jobs, fewer controls are needed to ensure satisfactory job performance.

    s. _____
    t. _____
    10

Scoring: To assess your assumptions regarding people and motivation, add up the points you have assigned as follows:
The sum of a, d, e, g, j, l, m, o, r, and s = your x score.
The sum of b, c, f, h, i, k, n, p, q, and t = your y score.

Interpreting Your Scores: The work of Douglas McGregor, a well-known leadership theorist, is an extension of the Pygmalion theory, which proposes that subordinates behave as their managers expect them to behave. Interpreting your X and Y scores is an application of his research. Your X score indicates your degree of adherence to what McGregor called *Theory X* thinking, and your Y score indicates the degree of your *Theory Y* convictions, which encompass two sets of managerial beliefs about how followers act. If you score high in Theory X, you are apt to hold your subordinates in poor regard, believing that they dislike hard work, lack ambition, endeavor to avoid responsibility, and prefer being told what to do. Theory X managers believe that they must be strict and authoritarian and that they must use punishment and coercion to get their workers to accomplish organizational goals. They limit their subordinates' autonomy and discretion, exercise a great deal of control, and are very autocratic. On the other hand, if you score high in Theory Y, you are likely to believe in your subordinates. Theory Y managers are convinced that subordinates not only seek responsibility but welcome it and that they enjoy their work and take pride in their accomplishments. Such managers believe that workers, in general, exercise self-control, initiative, and discretion in accomplishing their work, which they see as part of the organization's success. As a manager, you can help to create a Theory Y environment by encouraging creativity, rewarding team work, and requiring high levels of skill and competence.**

**Douglas McGregor, *The Human Side of Enterprise* (New York: McGraw-Hill, 1960).

CHAPTER 11

Groups and Group Dynamics

LEARNING OBJECTIVES

After completing this chapter, you should be able to:

- Understand the concept of ''group'' and the function of groups in the law firm setting;
- Explain the major reasons for group formation;
- Distinguish between the different kinds of groups;
- Characterize the formal groups found in a law firm;
- Describe the stages of group development;
- Explain the criteria for a group;
- Define group norms, roles, and cohesiveness and explain their influence on members;
- Describe the function of roles and their effects on group and individual performance;
- Explain the stages of work group formation; and
- Define status and describe how status manifests itself in the law firm hierarchy.

FOCUS FROM THE FIELD

Deborah Wahl: Achieving Credibility and Respect with Coworkers

Deborah Wahl is manager of the legal assistant program at the Minneapolis, Minnesota, law firm of Robins, Kaplan, Miller & Ciresi. She also serves as the firm's legal recruiting administrator, manages the law library, and is a member of the firm's senior management team. Ms. Wahl supervises over seventy legal assistants in this national firm. Long active in the Legal Assistant Management Association, she currently serves as the association's national vice president, representing the Central Region. Ms. Wahl is a frequent lecturer and author in the field of legal assistant managers.

What special group challenges do members of a law firm face?

As a national law firm, it is sometimes difficult to conduct business as one unified organization rather than as several individual firms. That's a big challenge. Sharing similar philosophies and objectives is very important. Agreeing on common goals and acceptance standards (measures of success) is necessary. With the legal assistant profession, there tends to be little difference in the philosophies in each area of the country. The differences usually occur in the level of utilization and the level of financial contributions expected by the legal employer, and that, too, can differ among regional offices of the same organization. To operate on the same wavelength, being sure we are striving to accomplish the same end result, is definitely a significant challenge for managers in this type of environment.

What happens when the roles that people play in the different groups in the law firm are too tightly held?

From the individual's perspective, I think that employees may lose the opportunity to grow in the organization. Too often, I hear that there are no growth opportunities in private law firms. I really disagree. One thing I am acutely aware of is that legal assistants must have opportunities to pursue career paths within our firm. They can do this by transitioning into management positions or by getting involved with administrative functions in the legal assistant department, such as assisting with the interview process, acting as mentors, or assuming legal assistant education and training responsibilities. This adds an important and creative dimension to their day-to-day roles as legal assistants; it enhances the value of their jobs. On the other hand, if a law firm is too flexible with roles, ensuring maximum utilization and assessing staff needs may be more difficult. You tend to get too many individuals spread out in too many areas and accurately measuring productivity may become impossible. Firms are then not using staff efficiently enough.

How much status is healthy in a law firm?

To some extent, status is helpful in the personal and professional development of an individual. Most people find a natural link between expanded job responsibilities and increased awareness of their organizational status. Titles, however, really don't mean much in our organization. Achieving credibility and respect with coworkers is what matters. You accomplish that by your competence and your strong work ethic. Regardless of your title, you'll be known and remembered for your attitude and job performance. So I'm not sure that status is healthy or helpful. My own position is classified as senior management, yet I don't think that that alone gets me very far. People may listen more on occasion, but it does not get my ideas and proposals through any faster. I really think that it's you and your commitment to the firm or organization that matters in the long run.

CHAPTER 11 / GROUPS AND GROUP DYNAMICS

> **A** paradox: Many managers hate groups. They complain about them. They recall Fred Allen's definition of a committee as a "group of people who individually do nothing, but as a group decide that nothing can be done." They think of Milton Berle's comment that a committee "keeps minutes and wastes hours." But managers spend huge amounts of time in groups. They sit on committee and task forces, and they also create them. They go to meetings, and they call meetings for other people to come to. . . . Managers need groups for many different reasons. In a complex world of large organizations, people have to put their heads together to coordinate their efforts. Knowledge and information, widely dispersed in many heads, need to be brought together.
> (Leavitt et al., *Readings in Managerial Psychology*)[1]
>
> **G**roup life is difficult because it poses the often insoluble conflicts and challenges of rivalry, authority, and leadership. To skirt these issues, groups live in many kinds of "half-way houses." They may, for example, accept the authority of one person who introjects all the denied aggression of the group and then rules them like a king. They may simply prefer to operate as a nominal group in which relationships are shallow and cynicism shapes day-to-day life. Or they may struggle to create the image of a "good" group, the collegial and egalitarian group which creates good feelings by suppressing key differences, denying feelings of unfairness and entitlement and repressing aggression. . . . Professional organizations may face particular problems here.
> (Larry Hirschhorn, "Professionals, Authority, and Group Life")[2]

GROUPS AND THE ORGANIZATION

Organizations become workplace homes for many. They consist of groups of people who interact with one another, just as families do. As Larry Hirschhorn, a relationships consultant for professional organizations, points out in the above quote, professionals face unique challenges in the group life they live in these homes away from home. Lawyers in particular (and, therefore, all those who work with them) are affected by what Hirschhorn sees as a triangular relationship: lawyers as people, lawyers as practitioners of demanding professional skills, and lawyers as those who must respond to the demands of group life. The effects of these multiple relationships permeate the entire firm. Each member plays a different role as part of the groups in this "home." Understanding your role in the group, as part of a team, makes you a better player.

Organizations by definition are settings where groups of people interact. Each employee relates to others, playing from a repertoire of different roles. Few people, however, are totally free to choose their roles. Working with others means both give and take, conflict and consolation. Beneath the day-to-day activities of law firms we find the tensions and demands of working with people. In law firms, many groups have clearly defined territories, shaped by the nature of their work. The dynamics of group membership influence partners, associates, paralegals, and secretaries, even in the smallest firm. Both permanent and temporary groups are at the heart of each organization.[3]

Why Study Groups?

"Because organizations involve people working collectively toward some shared goals," note J. Richard Hackman, Edward Lawler, and Lyman Porter, **"relationships among people** always serve as the basic vehicle for carrying out the work, and for carrying on the organization."[4] The nature of these relationships and their effect has a profound impact on each individual. And if it is true that managers spend approximately 50 to 90 percent of their time in some form of group activity, then understanding groups is critical to the quality of work life.[5] Groups influence the entire organization. First, groups can affect attitudes, performance, and even how and what people think. Second, groups can be productive or counter-productive. They can be powerful forces in decision making and in setting norms for work activities. Groups of workers constitute collective forces that can create, shape, and influence decisions. **Group dynamics,** the set of forces that affect a group's performance,[6] explain much about how people interact. These forces are the result of a group's composition: its structure, its norms, the cohesiveness of its members, and the roles that they play in the groups. Identifying the dynamics of a given group can be a help in diagnosing conflicts and problems. Understanding group dynamics can also help to answer questions about individuals, about cooperating or competing groups, and about managers' use of groups.

The Meaning of "Group"

Members of a law firm department who share the goal of specialization in probate law represent a group. A set of newly arrived associates with the same interest in learning the ropes of a law firm constitutes a group. An office coffee klatch is a group. An executive management team is a group. A **group** is strictly defined as two or more people who interact on a continuing basis with each other, think of themselves as a group, and share a purpose or work toward a common goal.[7] This definition is much more restrictive than the usual idea of a group as a recognizable unit of persons or things. All four elements of the definition—two or more people, regular interaction, a common goal, and the members' belief that a group exists—must be present in order for a gathering to be a group; in addition, a group must be small enough for its members to communicate with and influence one another. A theater full of movie viewers would not constitute a true group. Nor would vendors, artisans, entertainers, and fairgoers at a street fair.

Types of Groups

We find two basic types of groups in organizations: formal groups, or those groups that the organization creates, and informal groups, or groups that the individual members initiate.

Formal Groups

Formal groups are groups that management and others in the organization create in order to reach organizational goals. They include functional groups, command groups, task groups, *ad hoc* and standing committees, boards, and commissions.

Functional Groups. A **functional group** is a formal group composed of employees who have the same area of responsibility or who perform the same kinds of tasks. The organization structures and approves the group's goals and procedures.

Command Groups. A **command group** is a formal group consisting of managers and their subordinates. The organizational chart, which illustrates the groupings to which the members belong, determines the group's membership.

Project Groups and Task Forces. A **project group** is a formal group established to accomplish a specific purpose. Once it achieves its purpose, the group dissolves. A **task force** is a group whose members perform similar tasks. Task forces can be groupings of workers who play similar roles within the organization, such as a legal activities work team composed of attorneys and paralegals, or can consist of representatives from different units, segments, or departments of the organization who together perform specific tasks, such as technological update and equipment selection or the development of new recruiting methods, public relations projects, office restructuring plans, or personnel training and development procedures.

Committees. A **committee** is a group of people charged with or assigned to fulfill a specific responsibility, such as generating ideas, developing policy, solving existing or potential problems, or investigating or acting on a matter that affects the firm. Committee work is often central to law firm operations. We classify committees according to the type of work they do and in terms of their degree of permanence. A **standing committee,** which is relatively permanent, performs specific tasks or fulfills certain responsibilities on an ongoing basis. Some examples would include a firm finance committee, a professional development committee, or a recruitment committee. An **ad hoc committee,** by comparison, is a short-term committee that exists to complete a single, specific purpose (*ad hoc* being Latin for "for this"). The members of an *ad hoc* committee might also see themselves as a team with a relatively long commitment to a specific project. A telephone system purchase committee or an office relocation committee would be examples of *ad hoc* committees.

Boards. A **board** is an elected or appointed group that is responsible for the upper-level management of an organization. The shareholders of companies that distribute stock choose boards of directors to represent their interests and to manage the operations of the organization.

Commissions. Usually found in the governmental structure, a **commission** is a group appointed to oversee compliance with a given set of regulations. The Securities and Exchange Commission, for example, is an independent federal agency that administers and enforces the federal laws governing the purchase and sale of stocks and bonds. Examples of other commissions include the Federal Communications Commission, the Nuclear Regulatory Commission, and the Federal Aviation Administration.

Informal Groups

Informal groups, which do not appear on organizational charts, form spontaneously around their members' shared interests, goals, needs, or political concerns. The organization does not arrange, regulate, or proscribe these groups, which are of three basic types: **interest groups,** composed of people in the firm who have a similar interest, such as in sports, card playing, religion, the outdoors, family activities or any other area; **friendship groups,** which can lay the foundations for effective work teams,[8] provide support, lessen the effects of stress, and make work a more enjoyable place to be; and **reference groups,** which provide a form of social comparison. This last type of group exists in the abstract, not as a group in the strict sense: a reference group represents a collection of people with whom an individual shares similarities and against whom the individual can compare him- or herself. For instance, a person might use a reference group composed of others in similar jobs to draw comparisons regarding salary or education. The National Paralegal Association, as well as the National Association of Legal Secretaries, can provide a reference base for those in the field who are seeking standards regarding educational preparation, certification, salaries, and professional advancement. The Association of Legal Administrators' annual salary data base is a rich source of information for those in that reference group. Corporate attorneys, as a referent group, provide similar information for that form of practice.

THE FORMATION AND EFFECTS OF GROUPS

Why Groups Form

As we have seen, firms generally create formal groups in order to fulfill organizational goals. Informal groups, however, come about for a variety of reasons. Socially, people form groups out of their need for affiliation, emotional support, and social validation, out of a desire to reach goals, or simply because of proximity.[9]

The Desire to Meet Needs and Accomplish Goals

People need others. Whether to build a deck, play touch football, or prepare for a bar exam, people join together to reach out to others for many reasons. In satisfying our needs, we commonly seek an equitable exchange of reciprocal benefits; that is, we enlist the help of someone who has a need that we can help to meet in turn. Many kinds of needs are suitable for this kind of exchange. We might fulfill safety and security needs, for example, by participating in a neighborhood crime watch committee, or attempt to meet economic needs by joining a union group that can help us to negotiate for better benefits and more equitable wages. In the work setting, the need to accomplish a shared goal, such as the completion of a special project or a tough case assignment, can create alliances between even the most seemingly dissimilar or incompatible people. The need to cope with or remove a source of conflict can unite people both within and outside of the workplace.[10] Table 11–1 lists examples of groups that form around mutual needs.

Affiliation

The opposite of alienation and isolation, **affiliation** (from the Latin *affiliare,* ''to adopt as a son'') is a sense of connection or association with others. As a product of group membership, affiliation constitutes a form of **ego extension** by making us feel we are part of something larger than ourselves with which we can identify. This feeling of belonging contrasts sharply with loneliness.

Emotional Support

The benefits of sharing feelings and experiences and of simply being with others in times of stress have been

TABLE 11-1
Types of Need-based Groups

Kinds of Needs	Examples of Groups
Interpersonal	
Proximity and attraction	Social clubs, sports teams, discussion groups, hobby clubs, neighborhood groups, gourmet clubs
Social needs	
Affiliation	
Individual	
Emotional needs	Support groups, counseling teams, education and training departments, study groups, panels, community crime watches, emergency squads, volunteer fire departments, investment clubs
Support	
Education	
Esteem	
Security and safety needs	
Economic and resource needs	
Organizational	
Group goals and management	Problem-solving task forces, committees, research teams, assembly line and construction crews, executive committees, consulting firms, advisers, boards

SOURCE: Based on Alvin Zander, *The Purpose of Groups and Organizations* (San Francisco: Jossey-Bass, 1985).

well documented.[11] Numerous support and therapy groups have come into existence because of these benefits. During times of crisis and stress, contact with people who have weathered similar troubles provides us with perspective and assistance. Group counseling, support sessions, expressions of caring, and acceptance can all help in difficult times.

Social Validation

Social validation is the process of confirming one's identity and worth through the expressed attitudes of others. The comments and opinions of those with whom we form groups serve as a psychological mirror that shows us what we really look like to others. As David Cherrington explains,

> The comments of peer group members generally have a great impact on our self-esteem because they come from people we respect. Because of our association with them, we have greater confidence in what they say; we can tell the difference between friendly sarcasm and serious crit-

icism. Their comments are also more credible because we assume they know us better and are concerned about our well-being. Sometimes, personal feedback is so threatening that it is useful only when it comes from close peers who can help us respond to the criticism.[12]

Proximity

In the work setting, proximity encourages group formation, simply because nearness allows employees more opportunities to meet and interact with one another. Office settings or divisions by branches, floors, or departments give rise to natural groupings. The paralegals in a separate litigation office are apt to form social groups that meet for after-hours get-togethers. A solo practitioner, simply because of the need to interact directly with his or her office staff, is more likely to think of them as people rather than subordinates. The attorneys in an environmental law section who interact frequently might develop a shared interest in golf or tennis into regular after-work matches or weekend tournaments. Studies link physical proximity not only to interaction but to feelings of friendship, affiliation, and attraction.[13]

Stages of Group Development

A group is a dynamic, evolving entity whose strength of performance depends on two factors: how well its individual members learn to function in the group setting and how well the group learns to function as a team,[14] a process of maturation that not all groups have time or motivation enough to complete. (Most groups, in fact, produce results without ever becoming "fully mature."[15]) In terms of development, suggest researchers Donald Carew, Eunice Parisi-Carew, and Kenneth Blanchard, all groups go through similar stages.[16] Of the models that propose to represent the stages of group development, the most popular is that of Bruce Tuckman, who divided **group development** into five stages: (1) forming, (2) storming, (3) norming, (4) performing, and (5) adjourning.[17]

Forming

At the forming stage, members become familiar with each other and with their task. They develop ground rules, define acceptable behavior, and assess their level of motivation. Informally, they examine their feelings regarding the group and who should assume its leadership. Perhaps most importantly, at this stage the members define the criteria for acceptance in the group and decide individually whether gaining acceptance is worth the effort. This stage is complete when the members think of themselves as a group.

Storming

Storming involves the struggle that comes with defining personal values, preserving one's identity in the group, and establishing roles. Group members know that group membership offers risks as well as rewards. Because of a group's collective strength, many people approach membership with profound ambivalence and anxiety.[18] Social commentator Marion McCollum explains:

> Ultimately, a group can threaten or damage members—for example, a group in which there is perpetual conflict, or a group that scapegoats individuals.... Because one does not know in advance what the group will be, one entertains a dull worry: if one joins, one may wind up a member of a group that one wants to be in; if one does not join, one may be rejected by a group that one wants to be in. [This shows] the deeper unconscious anxiety that all individuals carry about joining groups.[19]

At the storming stage, members stake out personal territory in the group and define the group's values. They resist and challenge those who would lead the group and push forth the issues they consider important. This stage ends in one of two ways: either the members resolve their conflicts, establish open communications, and accept their roles and the group's leadership or the group disbands partially or completely, as members withdraw physically or psychologically.

Norming

After the conflict of storming, the group begins to set goals and to develop and agree on standards and values, or **group norms.** At the norming stage, communication becomes more accurate and open. Relationships develop, and the members feel a camaraderie, confidence in their leader, and a sense of purpose that persists even when the group is not assembled. This stage is complete when the members not only think of themselves as a group but think of the group as "our group."

Performing

This stage consists of getting things accomplished. Leadership problems have been resolved, roles have been worked out, and the group is able and ready to work. Members relate well with one another and are dedicated to reaching the group's goal. The group has solved its interpersonal and structural problems—at least for the time being—and members share a sense of responsibility for reaching the group's objectives. This stage is complete when the group finishes its chosen task.

Adjourning

Groups with ongoing goals might continue to interact almost indefinitely, while groups whose members truly enjoy their interaction might request or even create new goals in order to continue their interaction. Some groups, however, cease to exist when they have completed their tasks, fulfilled their goals, and are no longer needed. Compromising, reaching consensus, and achieving a satisfying closure at the end of a complex litigation case provides an example of how a group adjourns.

The performing and adjourning stages of group development are not always trouble-free. Occasionally, a difficulty such as the sudden appearance of a critical problem, the addition of new members, or controversy regarding new ideas, policies, or procedures can cause feelings and behaviors from an earlier stage to resurface in the group. The need to reform by dealing again with such feelings and behaviors (which not all groups experience) proves not that a group has failed to mature but that it is, in fact, a dynamic entity. This stage is complete when the group has resolved its problems and can once again perform efficiently.[20]

Table 11–2 summarizes the stages in group development.

The Advantages and Disadvantages of Group Membership

Disadvantages

Most people realize that becoming part of a group involves trade-offs. The price of group membership might include having to give in to group demands and pressures, contend with overbearing members, and withstand demands to conform. Group membership implies sacrificing a certain degree of individuality and personal freedom. By seeking membership, you tacitly agree to subordinate your personal goals to the collective goals of the group. The group's success is a product

TABLE 11–2
The Stages of Group Development

Stages	Characteristics	Activities	Completion
Forming	■ Courtesy ■ Confusion ■ Caution ■ Commonality	■ Getting together ■ Learning about each other	When members think of themselves as a group
Storming	■ Concern ■ Conflict ■ Confrontation ■ Criticism	■ Testing limits of behavior ■ Preserving identity ■ Establishing roles	When the group has resolved its conflicts and has accepted its leaders
Norming	■ Cooperation ■ Collaboration ■ Cohesion ■ Commitment	■ Agreeing on standards, goals, and means	When the group has established its expectations and acceptable procedures for reaching its goals
Performing	■ Challenge ■ Creativity ■ Consciousness ■ Consideration	■ Accomplishing goals ■ Producing results	When the group finishes its task
Adjourning	■ Compromise ■ Communication ■ Consensus ■ Closure	■ Ending	When the group has met its goals and is no longer needed

SOURCE: B. W. Tuckman, "Developmental Sequences in Small Groups," *Psychology Bulletin* 63:384–99.

of each member's input. Being a member does not mean getting your way or launching off on your own; rather, it means having your ideas listened to (or ignored), altered, sold, rejected, or accepted. Groups do not always accept the most creative or brilliant idea, but tend to promote the idea that the majority considers most acceptable. Membership can therefore be a great test of patience. It is also time consuming. Participation in a group means finding extra time and energy, as well as tolerance for interpersonal irritations, political conflicts, and other inefficiencies of the group process. Finally, being a group member results in your being associated with the group, for better or for worse.

Advantages

After looking at the "price list" above, we might find it hard to believe that group membership offers more potential for personal satisfaction than working alone does. Nonetheless, in addition to providing a vehicle that is highly compatible with most of the work that law firms perform, groups and group membership offer these advantages:

- Membership satisfies important needs, including those for affiliation, collegiality, and a sense of purpose;
- Groups act as problem-finding tools by encouraging and supporting the honest expression of opinions and ideas;
- By providing a forum for varied and sometimes divergent ideas, groups often produce better decisions than solo decision makers do;
- Membership builds commitment in workers by encouraging them to feel a personal sense of responsibility for the group's outcomes;
- Group norms help to keep workers task-oriented by providing standards against which they can compare their behavior and the quality of their work;
- By illustrating the importance of individual contributions, groups prevent alienation and improve communication;

- Groups maximize positive social needs by channeling people's natural tendencies to want to be together.[21]

Characteristics of Effective Groups

Several characteristics distinguish effective work groups from ineffective ones. In a maturely functioning group, members communicate well with one another and seem close and friendly. They listen, share feedback on individual and group performance, and encourage equal participation. Members are empowered and seem motivated. The group divides labor equally, resolves conflict, and makes decisions by consensus. Its leadership is accepted and effective.[22]

THE STRUCTURE OF WORK GROUPS

Group structure is the combination of roles and relationships that distinguishes one group from another. Group structure influences the behavior of the individuals in the group and the results that the group produces.[23] Group structure is affected by the group's size, the composition of its membership, and factors such as the group's norms, the cohesiveness between its members, and their status.

Size

Size is the most easily determined aspect of group structure. A group can consist of as few as two individuals—a dyad—or can be composed of hundreds, as is the United States House of Representatives or an army battalion. Increasing size changes the nature of participation in a group, the degree to which members identify personally with the group's accomplishments, and the intensity of cohesiveness. For example, it is easier to express ideas and to provide equal opportunities to communicate in a class of only seven members; it is easier to feel personally linked with successful results when you are one of three members on a task force; it is relatively easy to think of being very close with a group of four other partners. In contrast, it is harder to speak and participate in a class of seventy students, assembled in a lecture hall. It is more difficult to feel personally responsible for the accomplishments of a sixty-member community group. Members of very large groups, such as a regional chapter of the Association of Legal Administrators, may have a sense of a common goal, but will be unable to feel tightly knit as a group. The cohesiveness of a solo practitioner's or three-partner law firm is entirely different from the cohesiveness in a large corporate firm. A sense of group belonging would seem almost impossible for "the collection of quasi-independent firms" known as Baker & McKenzie—which by the end of 1987 employed more than a thousand lawyers—or the great chain of clinics under the name of Hyatt Legal Services, which peaked at 674 lawyers in 195 offices in 1986–87.[24]

In determining the ideal size for a single work group, however, what is most effective becomes relative, though many believe that having more than twenty members reduces group satisfaction. Groups of five to seven members seem to be ideal. Members in a group consisting of fewer than seven members engage in more personal discussions, seem to have a better chance of increasing their cohesiveness, and have more opportunities to participate, interact, and share task responsibilities. Those in a group having more than seven members receive fewer chances to participate, are apt to be more inhibited in their interactions, and tend to split into subgroups. Larger groups tend to be more formal and less cohesive than smaller groups, and are more likely to be dominated by aggressive members.[25]

Although membership in a smaller group is generally more satisfying, all groups suffer **process losses** through time-wasting activities not directly related to accomplishing their goals. Group size intensifies these losses, which result from establishing procedures, making arrangements, engaging in nonproductive communications, and other inefficiencies such as interruptions, confusion, and late arrivals.

Composition of Membership

A group's makeup shapes its results. The potential of a group lies both in the personalities and in the abilities of its members. "An individual," observes organizational behaviorist Albert Shapero,

can substantially affect the way a group operates and the subsequent quality and quantity of the group's output....

Beyond the strictly technical [professional] aspects of work, an individual can make a substantial contribution through many kinds of social and professional interactions that include helping new and younger people; helping to create a positive atmosphere during tough or pressure-filled times; a willingness to work through the night to finish something on time without being asked; dealing well with clients or other groups; and, not least, making only limited demands on managerial time.[26]

The group's composition is an important factor in its performance. The potential of each member as well as the role he or she plays shapes the group's outcomes.

GROUP ROLES

The Concept of Role

A role is the set of actions or behaviors an individual is expected to perform in a given context or setting. As Robert Kahn and others observe, people's lives essentially consist of the collection of roles they play in the particular set of organizations and groups to which they belong. The characteristics of these groups affect the individual physically and emotionally. After all, the group determines how the individual is expected to act and how he or she actually acts. Our roles are the complex result of what others in an organization expect of us.[27]

Roles Played within the Group Process[28]

According to Kenneth Benne and Paul Sheats, group members tend to focus their energy and behavior in one of three different ways: they can be task-oriented, relations-oriented, or self-oriented.

Task-oriented Roles

Members who focus on the task to be accomplished act as initiator/contributors, those who offer solutions; information seekers, those who locate and contribute facts; opinion givers; and energizers, those who spur the group on.

Relations-oriented Roles

Participants who are concerned more with the people in the group than with the group's task or with their personal needs serve as harmonizers, those who mediate conflicts; compromisers; encouragers; and expediters, those who help the group to work more efficiently.

Self-oriented Roles

Occasionally, a member will use the group experience more to fulfill his or her needs than to help accomplish the group's task or to see that others receive a fair chance to participate. Such self-oriented members appear as blockers, those who resist any idea the group proposes; recognition seekers; dominators; and avoiders, those who withdraw, isolate themselves, and never fully contribute to the group.

GROUP NORMS AND STATUS

Norms

Norms are socially shared beliefs, consciously or unconsciously formed, regarding how members of a group should think and act. Through these informal, unwritten standards, groups communicate their expectations concerning behavior. Group members are sometimes unaware of the presence of these subtle behavioral guidelines. Norms exist for four reasons: first, they help to ensure the survival of the group; second, they render behavior within the group more predictable and productive; third, they help the group to avoid embarrassment and other negative experiences; and, fourth, they shape the identity of the group by expressing the values the group holds in common.[29] Group norms that are in keeping with the organization's goals lead to synergy—group efforts that equal more than the sum of each member's contributions—on an organizational scale. Groups establish their norms through debate or discussion, unspoken acceptance, or explicit norm setting; by unconsciously establishing behavior patterns; and by acknowledging precedents, traditions, and history.

Debate or Discussion. Norms arise from consensus regarding issues that the group has debated or discussed.

Unspoken Acceptance. A norm can simply be a manner of behaving that the group has never discussed, contested, questioned, or attempted to explain. Dress codes are often a product of unspoken acceptance.

Dominant Views. Norms can result when dominant members express opinions that no other members openly resist or question.

Behavior Patterns. Norms evolve through patterns of repeated, eventually predictable behavior. For example, clearing off desks fifteen minutes before closing

ANOTHER LOOK

Finding a Niche: Some Group Roles You May Play

The Company Enthusiast
The person who buckles down, wants to get the job done, and translates ideas into reality.

The Monitor/Evaluator
The person who thinks critically and evaluates the group's ideas, process, and progress.

The Team Worker
The person who makes team members his or her top priority by being concerned about the feelings, needs, and issues of the group and by building on the strengths of the group's members and downplaying their weaknesses.

The Resource Investigator
The person who uses a wide range of contacts and explores resources and ideas outside the group.

The Conscience
The person who keeps the group on track, on schedule, and attentive in terms of the details of its work.

SOURCE: Based on Philip R. Harris, *Management in Transition* (San Francisco: Jossey-Bass, 1985).

1. Which of these roles are you most likely to play in a group? To what extent is your choice determined by your personality? By your experience? By group or task requirements? By the nature or composition of the group?
2. To what extent are all five of these roles essential to an efficiently functioning group? Describe how the absence of one of these roles might affect a group.
3. What are the advantages and disadvantages of labeling the roles people actually or potentially play in groups?

---

time might become a behavior-pattern norm for a law firm's secretarial group. Unlike unconsciously accepted norms, behavior-pattern norms attract comments and sometimes necessitate explanation. The firm's secretarial coordinator might, for example, ask his or her subordinates to explain how they come to be milling around the coatrack ten minutes before the end of the day.

Precedents and History. Norms sometimes develop because of critical events in the organization's past. For instance, the anguish a lawyer causes a law firm for public betrayal of confidentiality may provoke that firm to instigate rigid norms regarding the disclosure of information.[30]

Types of Norms

Groups develop standards and expectations in many areas, but some of the easiest to identify are those norms that involve dress and appearance, social conduct, reciprocity, resource and reward allocation, and performance.

Dress and Appearance

Dress codes are a type of norm. Though some organizations specify what workers are to wear, most lawyers and paralegals model their style of dress on an unwritten code that reflects the formality of the legal profession. Few legal professionals are comfortable with deliberate deviations in terms of appearance, such as those of the late Gladys Towles Root, a flamboyant California attorney who chose outrageous costumes for her court appearances and who even dyed her hair to match her current client's favorite color![31] Defining the parameters of a group's dress code is often relatively easy: members are quick to note—and comment on—a style of appearance or dress that falls short of a norm.

Social Conduct

Norms govern a wide range of group behaviors, including the manner in which participants listen and express disagreement, the degree of caring and loyalty they exhibit toward and to others, and many other areas. Behavior in a professional setting to a great extent is a reflection of etiquette, or rules for correct social conduct. *Letitia Baldridge's Complete Guide to Executive Manners* stresses the need for understanding these conventions:

> ... [G]ood manners are cost-effective, because they not only increase the quality of life in the workplace, contribute to optimum employee morale, and embellish the company image, but they also play a major role in generating profit. An atmosphere in which people treat each other with consideration is obviously one in which a customer enjoys doing business. Also very important, a company with a well-mannered, high-class reputation attracts—and keeps—good people.[32]

Etiquette consists of socially accepted guidelines for maintaining civility, which we might define as a general attempt to curb conflict and interpersonal abrasion in an increasingly crowded and complex social setting. Most conduct-related norms, however, differ according to the setting. What is acceptable behavior in one department or group may be frowned on in the next. Rules regarding deference, for example—such as standing when a visitor arrives or knowing when to sit, when to use someone's first name, and when and how to initiate greetings—emerge in a host of highly context-specific practices. Whatever their form, behavioral norms allow a group to focus its energies on its task rather than on provocation, retaliation, and other forms of infighting. Highly considerate group norms create more desirable work settings.

Reciprocity

In some groups, reciprocity is a very strongly held norm. Reciprocity is the expectation that each action will lead to an equivalent, corresponding, or mutual action in return. In groups that value reciprocity, each member knows that favors are expected for favors and that accepting uncalled-for kindnesses creates an obligation to one's benefactors. For some, "What goes round comes round" is a meaningful standard. Others consider the notion selfish.

Resource and Reward Allocation

According to social psychologist Jerald Greenberg, group norms for the allocation of resources and rewards indicate one of three beliefs: a belief in equality, a belief in equity, or a belief in social responsibility.[33]

Equality. A norm reflecting a belief in equality translates into equal distribution of all rewards. For example, in a firm that espoused a norm of equality, each member of a given group (such as paralegals) would receive the same percentage increase in salary.

Equity. A norm of equity reflects the belief that rewards or resources should be allocated according to a fair assessment of the individual's contribution to the group. Those who believe in a norm of equity pay particular attention to the quality of performance and results, believing that those who contribute the most effort, have the greatest success, and add the most to the success of the group should receive the largest reward.

Social Responsibility. A group that distributes rewards according to a norm of social responsibility believes that allocations should be determined on the basis of need. For instance, in keeping with this norm, a widowed or divorced secretary with five children would receive better salary and health benefits than a childless, unmarried secretary. Social responsibility means just that: a group that espouses this norm is apt to extend its sensitivity to the handicapped and other disadvantaged groups in the larger social setting.

Performance Norms

In a series of studies beginning in 1924 at the Hawthorne plant of the Western Electric Company, near Chicago, Elton Mayo, Fritz Roethlisberger, and others examined aspects of group dynamics, especially norms for productivity and performance. They discovered that workers who participated in the studies developed higher performance standards because of the special attention they received, because of their heightened awareness of their own performance, and perhaps because of the novelty of the whole situation—a phenomenon now known as the *Hawthorne effect*. Subsequent researchers found that workers tend to establish an informal **zone of acceptance** regarding the level of performance they considered acceptable. Those group members who deviated from the group's performance standards in either direction met with varying signs of the group's disapproval. Members who exceeded the group's standards were called "rate busters" or "curve breakers," and those who underperformed were labeled "chiselers," "deadwood," or "sponges."[34] Groups produce three effects in the performance of their members: social facilitation, social inhibition, and social loafing.

Social Facilitation. **Social facilitation** is the positive effect that the presence of others has on work performance. People tend to perform better when they are working in a group than when they are working alone. This occurs even when those in the group are not actively involved in the same kind of work. One explanation for this is that people experience **evaluation apprehension,** the belief that those who are near us as we work naturally evaluate our performance. People will improve their performance in order to look good in the eyes of others—even if those others are, in fact, looking the other way![35]

Social Inhibition. **Social inhibition** is the negative effect that the presence of others has on performance. When performing complex or difficult tasks in the presence of others, some people become self-conscious and feel extreme anxiety regarding their performance, which suffers as a result. Managers need to be aware that some tasks and some workers are better suited to more isolated environments than others.[36]

Social Loafing. **Social loafing** (a term coined by B. Latane, K. Williams, and S. Harkins) refers to the reduced effort that sometimes occurs in groups that neither identify nor reward individual efforts. The larger a group, the less direct responsibility its members feel. Getting lost in the crowd provides anonymity. People who believe that their efforts will be combined with those of many others often relax their performance standards. "Many hands make light the work" is only true under certain conditions: that each member of a group senses his or her responsibility, that the group recognizes individual input, and that the group's performance expectations are high.[37]

The Negative Effects of Norms

The effects of group norms need not be positive and productive. Chris Argyris, an outstanding contributor to studies of organizational behavior, suggests that even norms regarding things such as high morale, satisfaction, and loyalty can become self-defeating if, in response to the organization's emphasis on these norms, workers forget their responsibility for reaching the organization's goals. Establishing norms that also emphasize learning, competence, and equity can counter the effort-diverting quest for satisfaction, loyalty, and morale and boost the quality of performance at the same time.[38]

Conformity with and Violation of Norms

Norms are standards that the majority of a group's members accept. Further, this majority shares an awareness regarding the legitimacy of the group's norms and knows that those norms will last only as long as members accept and uphold them. The group expects members to conform, and it rewards with acceptance those who live up to its expectations. Nonconformists meet with ridicule, criticism, exclusion, shunning, and rejection. The ultimate punishment for nonconformity to groups is banishment from membership, or, in employment terms, termination.

Idiosyncrasy Credits

Some group members are immune from the need to conform to all norms. A group commonly allows its leaders to deviate from certain norms as a way of acknowledging their status, and those who are high up in the firm's hierarchy or who have contributed unique, notable, or exceptional achievements often enjoy this privilege as well. The right to deviate is a product of what Dorwin Cartwright and Alvin Zander identify as **idiosyncrasy credits.** High-status members usually have garnered a safe store of credits, in the group's view, and are allowed to deviate more than low-status members.[39] A senior partner, for example, need not conform closely to the firm's norms, such as those regarding punctuality at meetings, proper dress, and even civility. In contrast, a new secretary who styles him- or herself as a nonconformist is apt to run into trouble.

GROUP COHESIVENESS

Cohesiveness is the degree to which members value a group and feel close to one another. David Maister, in describing the accounting and law firms which he calls "one-firm firms," found that "a remarkable degree of institutional loyalty and group effort" was the key to their success.

> In contrast to many of their (often successful) competitors who emphasize individual entrepreneurialism, autonomous profit centers, internal competition and/or highly decentralized, independent activities, one-firm firms place great emphasis on firm-wide coordination of decision making, group identity, cooperative teamwork, and institutional commitment. In most organizations, "Team Spirit" and a sense of "community" are highly valued.[40]

The way a group works together is important to its end results. Highly cohesive groups exhibit a sense of unity: members like one another, accept the group's goals, and work together to reach those goals. They communicate easily and get along well. Their degree of cohesiveness is a sign of satisfaction. Even if they disliked a particular task or even the organization itself, they would enjoy working together. In groups that are not at all cohesive, the opposite occurs. Members may even work to undermine the group's efforts.

Factors that Increase Cohesiveness

Group cohesiveness is the result of many factors: the group's frequency of interaction, its degree of interpersonal attraction, the kinds of dues its members pay, its goals, its track record, and the threats it may face from outside sources.

Frequent Interaction

The more often a group meets, the more consistent is its members' sense of themselves as a group and the easier it is for them to get to know one another. Smaller groups offer their members more opportunities to interact, and the more opportunities for informal relationships to develop as well.

Interpersonal Attraction

It is obviously easier to be with people whom one enjoys, trusts, and respects. The attraction between a group's members depends on how much fun they are to be with, how enjoyable or rewarding their interactions are, and their degree of similarity in terms of socioeconomic status, attitudes, values, and interests. It also depends on their personalities, including their supportiveness, their willingness to contribute, and their desire to be in the group.[41] Hewitt Associates, a professional service firm, looks for **SWAN**s in its recruiting efforts: those who are smart, hard working, ambitious, and most importantly, nice. Hewitt believes that those whose ego needs are too high can disrupt a law firm's work, which depends on cooperation and teamwork.[42] "Nice" folk are in demand: they lubricate a group's workings.

Membership Dues

The psychological price—and sometimes, the financial one—that people pay for membership in an organization helps to determine their initial assessment of its worth. Groups that have rigorous initiation practices are more highly valued by their members and, as a result, tend to foster more cohesiveness. Strict membership criteria, competition for entry, elections, and special competitive appointments all increase the prestige of being part of a group.

Group Goals

Group members exhibit more unity in reaching goals they think are valuable and worthy of the group's efforts.

> In today's world of professional megafirms composed of departments specializing in vastly different areas, one of the most significant dangers is that professionals in one area may come to view *their* area as somehow more elite, more exciting, more profitable, or more important to the firm than another area. Yet the success of the firm clearly depends on doing well in all areas....[43]

A group's private sense of responsibility for reaching goals is less important than its sense of place in terms of firm-wide effort. To function most effectively, a group must recognize the value of its contribution to the whole organization.

Track Records

The pride that members feel in a group's success increases their sense of belonging. Everyone likes to be part of a winning team. Even the group's positive reputation and its members' perceptions of themselves as successful, driven, contributing members fosters cohesiveness.

Outside Threats

Members of groups facing external challenges or threats tend to cooperate more. By pulling together to overcome a difficulty, they become more cohesive.

Factors that Diminish Cohesiveness

What pulls a group apart? Groups can attribute a loss of effectiveness or even complete collapse to many causes, including disagreements or personality conflicts among their members, domination by overbearing members, group size, and internal crises.

Goal Disagreement

Disagreement over a group's goals can lead to conflict and infighting. Members end up spending more energy arguing about objectives than on reaching them.

Domination

When one member of a group becomes domineering, the others generally become either submissive or hostile. A group that spends its energy controlling a dominant member's power plays loses its cohesiveness. Effective groups downplay the stardom mentality, observes Maister, who describes the atmosphere at the Los Angeles-based law firm of Latham & Watkins:

> As Clinton Stevenson, the firm's managing partner, points out: "We want to encourage clients to retain the firm of Latham and Watkins, not Clint Stevenson." Partner Jack Walker reinforces this point: "I don't mean to sound sentimental, but there's a bonding here. People care about the work of the firm."
>
> Above all else, the leaders, and more importantly, all the other members of these firms view themselves as belonging to an *institution* that has an identity and existence of its own, above and beyond the individuals who happen currently to belong to it . . . Loyalty to, and pride in, the firm and its accomplishments approaches religious fervor. . . .[44]

Increased Group Size

A group's increasing size decreases its members' chances of getting to know and accept one another. Growth thus reduces group cohesiveness.

Internal Crises

Group membership is sometimes a painful experience. Interaction between members who cannot trust one another ranges from uncomfortable and unpleasant to miserable and destructive. Internal crises such as betrayal can not only weaken (or destroy) a group's cohesiveness but can harm individual members or even the entire organization.

Personality Conflicts

When group life acts as a staging ground for a clash between abrasive and fragile egos or a continuous power struggle, all members suffer the consequences. Mutual efforts cannot exist amid rifts, tension, and selfish competition.[45]

Group Status

Status is the ranking we give to others based on our perceptions of their social or professional characteristics, such as age, education, socioeconomic level, skills, or gender. Status reflects how others rate us. The organization assigns formal status, which reflects the authority assigned the roles in the organization's hierarchy. Informal status is prestige that the organization does not formally assign. This status is not simply a product of hierarchical position. Status can reflect a person's standing in more than one group. An attorney who has already achieved high internal status within the firm might earn high external status as well, through his or her admirable work with the underprivileged in the community. In fact, lawyers who are active in community organizations automatically receive more deference and respect from community members than those who confine their activity to the law firm environment. Their professional status unlocks membership opportunities in community organizations and on various boards of trustees, school committees, and fund drives. In addition, each individual in the law firm can enhance his or her status through personal qualities beyond those that influence his or her contributions to formal organizations. Such qualities include education, special abilities, appearance, personal connections, and even the type of car a person drives.[46]

Status Symbols

Status symbols are the signs of personal and professional prestige that convey an individual's stature.

These symbols include the use of titles, prestige by association, higher pay and better fringe benefits, autonomy, personalized work spaces and privacy, and formal dress.

Interaction and Use of Titles

We usually show our deference to those of high formal stature by addressing them according to their titles. By comparison, we usually address those of equal or lower status by their first names. Women, members of minority groups, and children are more commonly addressed by first names. Given two or more people of differing status, those of higher rank are more likely to initiate interactions.

Prestige by Association

Secretaries who work for the firm's most senior partner enjoy higher status than those who work for a new associate, even if the work of the latter is more demanding and requires higher competency. Status reflects the professional company a person keeps, and we assign it by association.

Pay and Fringe Benefits

Pay and benefits are perhaps the most common indicators of status. Those with higher salaries typically have higher status, and may also have better health benefits, better insurance, and better retirement plans. Typically, they enjoy more of the extras, the privileges known as perquisites, or "perks."

Work Schedule Autonomy

High-status organization members determine their own schedules, pick their own arrival times, and work according to their own hours. Lower-status members enjoy less flexibility in terms of their schedules and in terms of punctuality.

Work Space

We often judge status according to the comfort, size, and privacy of working space. In a law firm, those with the greatest amount of status have larger desks, more elegant floor coverings, occasional pieces of original artwork, better furniture, windows, executive dining rooms, anterooms, and private bathrooms: often, they will claim the firm's coveted corner offices. Making all corner offices conference rooms is one of the few ways of short-circuiting the common debate over the right to corner-office occupancy.

Dress

Power ties and suits, "serious" attire, and formal dress are unspoken requirements for most legal professionals, unless their reputation is so strongly secured that they can deviate from the regular status symbols of dress.

We should note that the manifestation of status sometimes leads to problems. Respect and admiration are not always given to the most deserving but to those who have accumulated the most status symbols. This is a less-than-beneficial situation for a law firm.[47] If the aim of management is to foster a hardworking, cohesive team, a fixation on status symbols may create resentment, impair productivity, and stand in the way of collegiality.

MANAGERS AND GROUPS

Effective Management of Groups

Paradoxes abound in organizations. The Abilene Paradox, the decision of four relatives to drive in the Texas summer heat for a four-hour trip in an un-airconditioned old car, has become a classic example of the vagaries of group performance. Anxious to take care of the business assigned them, too polite to argue, or unwilling to wrestle with tough issues, group members often rush into agreement, consequently making decisions that no one believes in. The Abilene Paradox, which describes the tendency for group members to go along with ideas that they instinctively find absurd, illustrates that flaw in the group process. Management consultant Jerry Harvey, who, along with his wife and two in-laws, found himself literally on the road to nowhere out of a desire to be agreeable, explains:

> Here we were, four reasonably sensible people who, of our own volition, had just taken a 106-mile trip across a god-forsaken desert in a furnace-like temperature through a cloud-like dust storm to eat unpalatable food at a hole-in-the-wall cafeteria in Abilene, when none of us had really wanted to go. In fact, to be more accurate, we'd done just the opposite of what we wanted to do.[48]

Efforts to get along by going along are not uncommon. As we have seen, resistance to the group entails more energy, confidence, and time than cooperation. Passively accepting a group's decision is always easier. Managers concerned about group performance should understand when strong cohesiveness in a group can lead to high performance, when it can cause poor and unimaginative results (of the "A-camel-is-a-horse-created-by-a-committee" kind), and when it can enable a group to tyrannize individual members by not allowing them to deviate from the group's norms in any way. Strong cohesiveness can also lead to a phenomenon known as **groupthink,** the tendency of group members to become so concerned with unanimity that they no longer think impartially, critically, or even rationally when making group decisions.

Benefiting from Group Performance

As a manager, you can take the following steps to ensure work groups that are both cohesive and interested in high performance:

- Structure the group carefully. Keep in mind that members with similar attitudes, values, and backgrounds are more likely to get along with one another. Remember, however, that an element of difference or even of dissent is essential to good group work. A group that needs to work on creative and new types of decisions, for instance, would benefit greatly from a membership that offers a variety of views and skills.
- Maintain high standards for membership. Those who have survived an exhaustive search or interview process, or who have endured arduous training and orientation, will tend to have more respect for membership in a group, will be proud of having earned such membership, and will be more attached to the group.
- Keep the group small. Preserve the perception that membership in the group is selective. The smaller the group, the more critical members will feel their contributions to be.
- Help the group succeed. Build its reputation by providing good press and favorable publicity for its accomplishments. Being on a winning team helps members feel closer together.
- Be a participative leader. Utilize the group's input and make maximum use of its efforts.
- Present external challenges. Providing organizational deadlines, requiring the group to present its work before an outside audience, and allowing that audience to critique the group's work places the group's efforts in a larger, more realistic context and, conversely, helps the group to think of a manager as a facilitator and leader rather than as an assigner of arbitrary, meaningless tasks.
- Tie rewards to performance. Groups respond favorably to equitable rewards, just as individuals do.[49]

There are other avenues for getting the most out of work groups. Managers can arrange to heighten performance norms by adding hard workers to groups, by consistently supporting and rewarding excellent performance, and even by rotating membership. Several groups can be established to confront a critical issue worth the duplication, if a manager needs to increase participation and wants to prevent groupthink. Rosabeth Moss Kanter encourages managers to make debate a part of the group communication process, to ask members to act as "gadflies," and to "make confronters into heroes."[50] Because this is almost impossible if workers are afraid to express their opinions, Arthur Elliott Carlisle urges managers to create an atmosphere in which workers believe it essential to challenge the facts when necessary and in which the bearer of bad news is welcomed, not symbolically done in. Above all, he writes, do "not brand the dissenter as a loner, a troublemaker, or someone who is not a team player." A group, he notes, should not only tolerate and accept dissent, but should think of it as a professional responsibility.[51]

Stages for Creating Effective Work Teams[52]

The effectiveness of a work group such as a committee depends on the strength and efficiency of its structure. Such qualities are a product of the composition of the group's membership, the conditions under which the group is to perform, the process by which the manager forms the group, and the continued assistance and support that he or she provides. A manager who is thinking of establishing a committee or any other type of group should ask whether an existing group or subgroup has already worked on a similar type of task. If so, he or she should weigh the benefits of using that group as it currently exists, incorporating certain members of that group into an otherwise new group, or of forming an entirely new group. Whether already established or all-original, the group's membership should provide an optimal mix of technical and interpersonal skills. Table

11–3 outlines the stages for the creation of effective work teams.

Managing Committees

Committees are often at the heart of law firm governance. Usually, an administrator attends all meetings of firm committees, sometimes chairs committees, and creates them as needed. Committees consume enormous amounts of time; consequently, the administrator who is not convinced of the collaborative value of committees will dismiss the process of managing these groups as time-wasting, tedious, and irrelevant. Realistic managers, aware of time demands, form committees only when necessary and do not use committees when they serve only as a formality. (Though this seems like common sense, the average manager in business and industry serves on nine committees.[53]) Committees serve many purposes. For example, firms often divide their management functions among attorney committees that report their decisions to the firm's partnership, thus acting as vital governance links between the partners and the firm and as vehicles for collegiality and shared involvement. In addition, they provide a forum in which members from different levels of the law firm hierarchy can share conflicting views, thereby helping to establish policy, and can participate directly in the workings of the firm. In addition, committee work communicates knowledge and attitudes to new members and encourages them to involve themselves politically in the firm's operations.[54]

GROUP STATUS IN THE LAW FIRM

In examining group dynamics, an overview of the groups in a typical law firm may be helpful. In the following sections, we will discuss placement in these groups in terms of group interdependence, the position one occupies in the law firm hierarchy, and the status that results from membership in the major groups in the law firm.[55]

Interdependence of Groups

The law firm manager coordinates the interaction between groups in the firm. Directing and overseeing cooperative group efforts is among the most demanding of management challenges. The greater the groups' interdependence, the more important the coordination; however, the clearer the groups' identities, the more difficult that coordination becomes. To the degree that any group recognizes its relationship to another group as not only necessary but also capable of enhancing its identity and effectiveness, that group will work to safeguard and develop that relationship. In law firms, where the tasks performed by each individual as well as by each group are vital to the performance of the whole, the importance of the intergroup relationship to the firm and to both of the groups involved is well understood. To effectively coordinate groups, managers must ensure that each group understands its role in relation to the other group, communicates efficiently with the other group, recognizes and enhances the legitimacy

---

TABLE 11–3
Stages for Creating Effective Work Teams

Stage I. Prework

- Define the work that needs to be done and decide whether a group needs to do it.
- Determine the constituencies that the group should include, the authority that the group should have, and the group's goals.

Stage II. Create Performance Conditions

- Provide the necessary time, personnel, material, and equipment.

Stage III. Form and Build Team

- Establish boundaries (who is/is not in the group).
- Clarify the group's goals.
- Agree on the tasks to be performed.
- Decide if and how the tasks will be divided.
- Agree on the behavior that the group expects of members.

Stage IV. Provide Ongoing Support and Help

- Establish lasting communications.
- Track the group's progress.
- Intervene only to assist with problems, such as intractable members.
- Replenish and upgrade material resources as necessary.
- Replace departing members and consult with the group regarding the replacements, when appropriate.

SOURCE: Based on J. Richard Hackman, "The Design of Work Teams." In *Handbook of Organizational Behavior*, edited by J. W. Lorsch. Englewood Cliffs, New Jersey: Prentice-Hall, 1987: 315–42.

Position in the Hierarchy

People form perceptions of groups based on the hierarchical positions that the members of those groups occupy with respect to the members of other groups. Several distinctive groups exist within the law firm structure. They traditionally represent collections of partners, associates, nonlegal experts, paralegals, secretaries, and support staff. Members of these groups can participate in other groups within the firm, but their basic membership and resulting status reflect the roles they fill and the tasks for which they are responsible. Today's law firms in general have a more intensified hierarchy. There are more associates for every partner and new levels of superiors and subordinates, as well: permanent associates, senior attorneys, salaried partners, staff or contract attorneys, part-time and shared-time attorneys (two attorneys who share one role in order to have time for other responsibilities), paralegals, computer professionals, nonlawyer professionals (such as accountants, economists, doctors, and scientists) and nonlegal managers, finance personnel, and public relations and marketing specialists. The legal profession itself is increasingly stratified. As Richard Abel explains, "Many variables affect a lawyer's position in this hierarchy, including background (ethnicity, religion, class, gender, and race), education, and legal role (private practitioner, corporate counsel, civil servant, judge, and educator)." And each of these roles admits of further distinctions on the legal hierarchy.[57]

Status Levels

The complexity, importance, visibility, and profitability of a person's work, the quantity and quality of his or her contributions, and the formal roles that he or she fills are just some of the work-related criteria that determine the progression of status in the law firm. The highest levels of status belong to the firm's owners, or senior partners. As groups, junior partners, associates, and counsel claim the next highest levels. Status diminishes as we descend the ladder, until at the lowest but still vital levels we find support staff roles, including, at the very bottom, messengers, copy room assistants, and other similar positions.

The Status of Lawyers

Influence in an organization is based both on formal position and informal status, which is determined by the amount of education a person has, the social status of his or her profession, special skills, personal reputation, the importance of his or her work to the organization, and seniority. Partners, as owners, indisputably hold the highest status in a law firm. They enhance this status by holding degrees from prestigious schools, building seniority, becoming senior rather than junior partners, developing their fame, track records, or reputations (as evidenced by their skill), and acknowledging that their practice is critical to the entire organization.

Professional Identity. Richard Abel summarizes the unique identity of American lawyers as follows:

> Nearly 800,000 American lawyers constitute the largest legal profession in the world, both in absolute numbers and in proportion to population. They are also the wealthiest, particularly at the upper extreme but also on average. They may be the most politically powerful, dominating legislatures and executives, both national and state, more strongly than in any other country. Even culturally they are among the most prominent, ranging from mythic figures like Abraham Lincoln to the morally more ambiguous but perhaps even better known characters in the mass media, such as the television series *L. A. Law*....
>
> Most observers of American lawyers—even (perhaps, particularly) those who deplore their numbers, prominence, and alleged litigiousness—tend to take for granted the profession's exalted social, economic, political, and cultural standing.[58]

Educational and Economic Status. Lawyers progress through an educational preparation that culminates in the grueling experience known as the bar exam, a rigidly controlled certification process. Ongoing professional development is a way of life for attorneys, who need to keep abreast of the ever-changing legal system. Law school entrance is highly competitive, and firms across the nation compete heavily for the star graduates from the highest-ranked law schools. Nearly half of lawyers are employees rather than independent practitioners. Though generally, as Abel notes, the income of attorneys, neophytes as well as senior partners, provokes "awe and envy in most observers," lawyers who remain in solo practice or who are found in legal services, in governmental practice, and even in academia see many variations in salary.[59]

The Status of Nonlawyer Professionals[60]

Questions abound regarding the level of individual status nonlawyer professionals can hope to achieve, given the variety of professional and nonprofessional personnel with whom they must contend in the demanding context of the firm's culture and goals.[61] This is a critical issue for legal administrators nationally, whose presence—among the more significant changes taking place in the structure of law firms—reflects both the consideration of profit and managerial necessity: "Time expended by librarians, economists, accountants, engineers, nurses and doctors, lobbyists, experts in computer systems and public relations, financial planners, probate and trusts specialists and others adding their expertise to analysis and solutions of legal problems is being billed on client matters," notes Phyllis Weiss Haserot, president of the New York-based Practice Development Counsel, and firms are sorely in need of people who are capable of coordinating this nonlawyer expenditure of time. Such coordination becomes especially important if we believe, as Haserot does, that nonlawyer professionals are also potential "profit centers performing client services."[62] The question of how administrators and other nonlawyer professionals fit in the hierarchy concerns such issues as their status compared with that of attorneys. High-status professionals such as lawyers tend to think of administrators as being inferior in terms of status. "Hypothetically," notes management consultant John Seiler, "if there were an executive director in a law firm, who as a nonlawyer had achieved a legitimate organizational role of authority and responsibility over some or all of the professionals, the firm's attorneys would not view that executive director, no matter how capable or qualified, as legitimately able to control them, **even if the organizational chart shows the allocation of authority to those administrators.**"[63]

Clarifying the Status of Nonlawyer Professionals. To ensure that nonlawyer professionals receive the status equity that their professional credentials merit, law firms should provide these professionals with clear role descriptions and develop a fair formula for determining their professional equity and parity.

> Clarification of Roles. Well-written job descriptions will help to end role and status ambiguity for nonlawyer professionals. As professionals, they should have a clear idea of their role in business development and of the level of professional involvement that the firm expects of them. Their job descriptions should also demarcate the boundaries of their relationships with legal personnel and staff. Finally, the descriptions should provide specific performance evaluation criteria and define the ethical obligations of nonlawyer professionals in the firm, particularly in terms of confidentiality requirements.

Clarification of Parity. To integrate nonlawyer professionals into its hierarchy, a firm should develop a process for determining parity between nonlawyer professionals and lawyers at various levels. A firm wishing to establish parity might provide similar salary structures, perks, titles, and privileges for lawyers and nonlawyer professionals. "A senior level nonlawyer professional might be hired in a status comparable to that of counsel," Haserot suggests. "After a predetermined period, the firm can review accomplishments and compatibility and determine if a change in status and privileges is earned and desirable."[64] In addition, the firm might allow newly recruited nonlawyer professionals to participate in the same activities as other professionals who are accepted into the firm. For example, new nonlawyer professionals might receive an official orientation similar to that received by new attorneys, as well as the right to attend the firm's social events and any other appropriate functions.

The Status of Paralegals

Paralegals perform an important economic function by enabling a firm to perform professional-level work at lower costs. By using paralegals rather than associates to perform certain tasks, a firm may lower its salary costs and increase its market share by lowering its fees. As *National Law Journal* staff writer Rose D. Ors explains,

> Since a paralegal's time is billed to the client in the same way as an attorney's time, from a client's perspective, it makes economic sense for certain matters to be handled by a paralegal rather than an attorney. Clients, particularly corporate clients, are becoming more involved in the management of their cases by outside firms and are demanding cost controls. By staffing a large case with junior and senior paralegals, law firms can reduce their clients' fees.[65]

They need not consider paralegals for partnership, but many firms are establishing career paths for their paralegals, using tiers of seniority and accomplishment and providing appropriate compensation scales for each level and its subdivisions. In utilizing such a program, one West Coast firm also empowers its most experienced paralegals by awarding them eligibility for membership on the firm's leadership committee.[66] Rather than becoming unionized, paralegals have opted to stake their claims for fully recognized professional status, with the help of organizations such as the National Association of Legal Assistants and the National Federation of Paralegal Associations. The legal profession, however, has yet to recognize paralegals as full professionals. One reason for this is the relatively subordinate position that paralegals occupy on the law firm hierarchy.[67] Another is that the drive to professionalize, like paralegalism itself, is fairly new. Professional examinations and certification are still being debated, and the only workable indication of professionalization that is standardized to date is the American Bar Association's approval of colleges providing paralegal certification and education. Because they have traditionally trained many clerical workers to perform paralegal activities, not all attorneys are convinced of the value of a rigorous, thorough, and competitive educational preparation for paralegals. In 1990, there were an estimated 90,000 paralegals in the United States, and the number is expected to grow to approximately 167,000 by the year 2005.[68] Earning increasingly competitive salaries, paralegals have become a standard part of the practice of law, from their role in solo practitioner settings, corporate law departments, and smaller and midsize practices to their indisputable place in the mega-firms. Their economic contributions are undeniably sound. Nonetheless, status difficulties are likely to continue to confound paralegals, at least for the next few years. As paralegal expert William Statsky observes,

> Too many lawyers continue to perceive and treat paralegals as part of their furniture. The big four problems of low pay, underutilization, poor working conditions, and the lack of advancement continue to exist today because too many employers fail to grasp the fundamental principle that paralegals are people and not machines. They cannot, as some lawyers expect, reach peak efficiency immediately. They will come to resent conditions such as:
> —vague job descriptions
> —too many masters
> —unrewarding piecemeal work
> —in-house caste systems
> —"attorney-only" lunches and parties
> —conflict with secretaries.[69]

Paralegals are still carving out their professional niche. Schools across the nation that offer paralegal programs are finding that many bright and capable students are attracted to the field. Paralegalism has become a high-demand career track that can lead to other careers in the field: that of lawyer or law firm manager, for example. Given, in general, their intelligence, competence, and drive, paralegals as a group are likely to reach the status of fully recognized professionals in the near future, resolving the difficulties that now rightfully concern Statsky.

The Status of Secretarial and Support Staff

The status assigned those who perform these roles may be low within the legal setting itself but is high compared with the status of secretarial and support staff in business and industry. Like many subordinate positions, the secretarial role is often considered "women's work." It has carried with it the "only a secretary" stigma. Yet, the role of the secretary is critical to the legal profession. Although they do not interact constantly with the public, the members of a firm's secretarial staff exercise knowledge processing skills that create a base for the firm's legal activities. Today's emphasis on equal opportunity for women has had many effects on the secretarial field. In the past, when few fields were open to women, those who did not want to be teachers or nurses and who wanted a career in a challenging, stimulating field became legal secretaries. Such women were more than secretaries: often, they were administrators, paralegals, and financial controllers as well—in terms of function if not of title. Today, many women become lawyers themselves; coupled with other changes in the work force and in training programs, this has created a shortage of qualified secretarial and support staff personnel. Salaries have increased with the demand for talented secretarial staff, and law firm growth in the coming years will intensify the shortage of legal secretaries. Because of the usual practice of not billing secretarial costs directly to clients, many firms too easily blame secretarial salaries for high overhead costs. As a result, Abel observes, "efforts to keep salaries down have encouraged clerical employees to unionize." (Abel notes that, ironically, the first strike against a law firm was by clerical workers against a firm that represented unions!)[70] Other groups of support staff face similar problems in terms of low status and salary issues.

QUESTIONS FOR DISCUSSION AND REVIEW

1. Explain what a group is and what functions groups serve in organizational settings.
2. Define the characteristics of a group and identify the two most basic types of groups. How do they differ from one another?
3. For what reasons do groups form? What stages do they go through in their development?
4. Think of a group you know well. What norms does it have? What roles can you identify within the group? Describe its level of cohesiveness. Is this cohesiveness a positive or negative influence? Explain.
5. Identify the major characteristics of the different work groups in the law firm.
6. Describe the formal and informal elements of a class you are in. Are these elements mutually exclusive? Explain.
7. Describe a group you have belonged to that had difficulty working together. What group dynamics were at play?
8. Is being a team player beneficial in a law firm? If so, how can members of law firm groups, such as secretaries, paralegals, or associates, learn to be team players?
9. Identify the three sets of roles that members can play in the group process. What group roles do you presently fill?
10. How might an understanding of group dynamics help you to interpret the following circumstances?
    a. The silence of a paralegal coordinator's department members at weekly organizational meetings.
    b. The lasting conflict between a group of paralegals and a group of secretaries in a law firm.
    c. The lack of social communications between a firm's lawyers and paralegals.
    d. The competition between two paralegal departments.
    e. The grouping of lunch partners in the firm.
11. Why is inter- and intragroup cohesiveness essential to effective performance in an organization?
12. Comment on these statements:
    a. Successful law firms are made up of stars, not team players.
    b. Creative people don't need groups.
    c. Group work is a waste of time.
    d. Law firms have too many committees.

EXPERIENTIAL EXERCISES

I. How Does Your Group Measure Up?

An effective group credits its productive and mature functioning to many different factors. Think of the most effective group to which you have ever belonged and rate it according to the following dimensions. Then think of the worst group in which you have participated and rate it according to the same scale. Compare your results. Which factors most clearly seem to distinguish a good group from a bad one?

Scale: 5 = Very strong
        4 = Strong
        3 = Average
        2 = Weak
        1 = Very weak
        0 = Nonexistent

5 4 3 2 1 0   1. The group's understanding of the goals it wanted to reach.
5 4 3 2 1 0   2. The acceptance of goals by members.
5 4 3 2 1 0   3. The value placed on group membership.
5 4 3 2 1 0   4. The group's respect for its members.
5 4 3 2 1 0   5. The group's use of meeting time.

5 4 3 2 1 0   6. The value the group placed on positive contributions.
5 4 3 2 1 0   7. The appropriateness of the group's size.
5 4 3 2 1 0   8. The group's ability to communicate ideas.
5 4 3 2 1 0   9. The group's encouragement and acceptance of divergent thinking.
5 4 3 2 1 0 10. The degree to which all members participated.
5 4 3 2 1 0 11. The degree to which the group listened to and respected each member.
5 4 3 2 1 0 12. The degree to which members expressed feelings and accepted such expression as valuable to the group process.
5 4 3 2 1 0 13. How carefully the group assessed, analyzed, and understood problems before making decisions.
5 4 3 2 1 0 14. The trust and confidence the group's members had in one another.
5 4 3 2 1 0 15. The group's ability to consider new ideas, solutions, and approaches.
5 4 3 2 1 0 16. The amount of flexibility in the group.
5 4 3 2 1 0 17. The loyalty of the group's members to each other and their sense of ownership regarding the work that the group produced.
5 4 3 2 1 0 18. The members' acceptance of leaders and their willingness to assist in leadership when the need arose.
5 4 3 2 1 0 19. The group's ability to avoid or resolve internal power plays and power struggles.
5 4 3 2 1 0 20. The willingness with which members made and accepted the group's decisions.

Scoring: Total your responses and compare the sum to the scale below:
    0 to 20 = Barely functional.
    21 to 40 = Able to achieve consistent if average effectiveness.
    41 to 60 = Above-average effectiveness; sense of cohesiveness and teamwork.
    61 to 80 = Highly effective and cohesive.
    81 to 100 = Able to function consistently as a highly effective, mature team; regularly exceeds performance standards.

1. Was either of your scores particularly high or low? If so, why?
2. If you have been the leader of an ineffective group, what would you have done differently to make your group more effective?
3. Describe how the following factors improved or impaired the effectiveness of your two groups: (a) the work environment, (b) the group composition, (c) the nature of the task, (d) interpersonal relationships, and (e) the degree of group autonomy and authority.

II. Identifying and Eradicating Bias in the Law Firm

Status, titles, and the differential treatment of group members are issues about which managers should be sensitive. In law firms, those in the lower ranks still tend to be women or members of minority groups. Law firms, then, face a particular challenge in avoiding the perpetuation of sexist or racist attitudes, or other behaviors based on biased judgments regarding a person's membership in a particular group.

1. What law firm practices are apt to contribute to perpetuating sexist and racist practices? In a local or national newspaper, magazine, or law journal, locate an article that describes a court case involving biased and prejudicial practices in a law firm. How was the problem resolved, if at all? In what ways was the solution appropriate or inappropriate?
2. To which individuals or groups within a law firm are biased practices truly detrimental? Explain.
3. Study statistical information on the employment of women or members of a given minority group in the legal profession. How can managers change the treatment of women and minorities in the law firm?

III. The TORI Questionnaire: Self-Perceptions of Group Interactions*

Groups interact with different degrees of efficiency. In this exercise, you will assess the interactions of a group to which you currently belong by responding to a series of statements known as the TORI Group Self-Diagnosis Scale. The scale yields eight scores: four depicting how you see yourself in this group in terms of four core growth processes (trust, openness, realization, and interdependence—hence TORI) and four capturing your sense of the group itself on the same four dimensions. Think about a particular group of which you are a member. In front of each of the following items, write SD, D, A, or SA to indicate the extent to which that statement accurately describes the group itself and your feelings about it.

SD = Strongly disagree   D = Disagree   A = Agree   SA = Strongly agree

_____ 1. I feel that no matter what I might do, this group would understand and accept me.
_____ 2. I feel that there are large areas of me that I don't share with this group.
_____ 3. I assert myself in this group.
_____ 4. I seldom seek help from this group.
_____ 5. Members of this group trust each other very much.
_____ 6. Members of this group are not really interested in what others have to say.
_____ 7. The group exerts no pressures on the group members to do what they should be doing.
_____ 8. Everyone in this group does his or her own thing with little thought for others.
_____ 9. I feel that I have been very cautious in this group.
_____ 10. I feel little need to cover up things when I am in this group.
_____ 11. I do only what I am supposed to do in this group.
_____ 12. I find that everyone in this group is willing to help me when I want help or ask for it.
_____ 13. The members of the group are more interested in getting something done than in caring for each other as individuals.
_____ 14. Members of this group tell it like it is.

---

*SOURCE: J. R. Gibb, "Tori Group Self-Diagnosis Scale," *The 1977 Annual Handbook for Group Facilitators,* pp. 75–77. Reprinted from: J. William Pfeiffer and John E. Jones, (Eds.), *The 1977 Annual Handbook for Group Facilitators,* San Diego, CA: University Associates, Inc. Used with permission.

____ 15. Members do what they ought to do in this group, out of a sense of responsibility to the group.
____ 16. This group really "has it together" at a deep level.
____ 17. I trust the members of this group.
____ 18. I am afraid that if I showed my real innermost thoughts in this group, people would be shocked.
____ 19. In this group, I feel free to do what I want to do.
____ 20. I often feel that I am a minority in this group.
____ 21. People in this group seem to know who they are; they have a real sense of being individuals.
____ 22. Group members are very careful to express only relevant ideas about the group's task or goal.
____ 23. The goals of this group are clear to everyone in the group.
____ 24. The group finds it difficult to get together and do something it has decided to do.
____ 25. If I left this group, the members would miss me very little.
____ 26. I can trust this group with my most private and significant feelings and opinions.
____ 27. I find that my goals are different from the goals of this group.
____ 28. I look forward to getting together with this group.
____ 29. People are playing roles in this group and not being themselves.
____ 30. In this group we really know each other well.
____ 31. This group puts pressure on each member to work toward group goals.
____ 32. This group would be able to handle an emergency very well.
____ 33. When I am in this group, I feel very good about myself as a person.
____ 34. If I have negative feelings in this group, I do not express them easily.
____ 35. It is easy for me to take risks in this group.
____ 36. I often go along with the group simply because I feel a sense of obligation to it.
____ 37. Members seem to care very much for each other as individuals.
____ 38. Members often express different feelings and opinions outside the group than they express inside.
____ 39. This group really lets people be where they are and who they are.
____ 40. Members of this group like either to lead or to be led, rather than to work together with others as equals.

TORI Group Self-Diagnosis Scale Score Sheet

Instructions: The scoring is simple, even though it looks complicated. Look back at the items for one of the eight scales on the instrument to see how you responded. (The first scale shown below, for example, consists of items 1, 9, 17, 25, and 33.) On the score sheet, circle the number directly below your response for each item. Then sum the item scores for that scale. Do the same for each scale.

TRUST					OPENNESS					REALIZATION					INTERDEPENDENCE				
	Item Score					Item Score					Item Score					Item Score			
Item	SD	D	A	SA	Item	SD	D	A	SA	Item	SD	D	A	SA	Item	SD	D	A	SA
1.	0	1	2	3	2.	3	2	1	0	3.	0	1	2	3	4.	3	2	1	0
9.	3	2	1	0	10.	0	1	2	3	11.	3	2	1	0	12.	0	1	2	3
17.	0	1	2	3	18.	3	2	1	0	19.	0	1	2	3	20.	3	2	1	0
25.	3	2	1	0	26.	0	1	2	3	27.	3	2	1	0	28.	0	1	2	3
33.	0	1	2	3	34.	3	2	1	0	35.	0	1	2	3	36.	3	2	1	0

How I
See
Myself
in This   T ☐   O ☐   R ☐   I ☐
Group

	TRUST Item Score					OPENNESS Item Score					REALIZATION Item Score					INTERDEPENDENCE Item Score			
Item	SD	D	A	SA	Item	SD	D	A	SA	Item	SD	D	A	SA	Item	SD	D	A	SA
5.	0	1	2	3	6.	3	2	1	0	7.	0	1	2	3	8.	3	2	1	0
13.	3	2	1	0	14.	0	1	2	3	15.	3	2	1	0	16.	0	1	2	3
21.	0	1	2	3	22.	3	2	1	0	23.	0	1	2	3	24.	3	2	1	0
29.	3	2	1	0	30.	0	1	2	3	31.	3	2	1	0	32.	0	1	2	3
37.	0	1	2	3	38.	3	2	1	0	39.	0	1	2	3	40.	3	2	1	0

How I
See
This
Group   T ☐   O ☐   R ☐   I ☐

CHAPTER 12

Communications

LEARNING OBJECTIVES

After completing this chapter, you should be able to:

- Explain why effective communication skills are the most critical asset in any career;
- Describe the principal elements of the communication process;
- Define the value of words as symbols and of nonverbal communicators;
- Outline the three factors that determine if communication is persuasive;
- Discuss how to write, speak, and listen more effectively;
- Trace the flow of communication in an organization;
- Describe the barriers to effective communication and explain how to overcome them;
- Characterize effective communicators; and
- Explain how to run a successful meeting.

FOCUS FROM THE FIELD

Sherry Adelstein: Create a More Comfortable Environment

In 1979, following careers in teaching and in the insurance industry, Sherry Adelstein became a paralegal, specializing in pension and employee benefits. In 1985, she began her managerial career as legal assistant coordinator for the law firm of Kramer, Levin in New York and later became the first legal assistant manager at the law firm of Chadbourne & Parke in 1990. Ms. Adelstein currently manages its New York City staff of 42 paralegals and oversees additional staff in the Washington and Los Angeles offices of the firm. Along with Linda Katz and Lynda Wertheim, she coauthored the recent LAMA publication, The Manager's Manual: Setting Up a Legal Assistant Program.

What makes a legal assistant manager a good communicator?

A legal assistant manager should be able to express ideas either in writing or verbally in a concise and clear manner. It is most important to be able to clearly state problems, goals, and solutions. In order to be a good communicator, a manager must also have a good ability to listen, one of the most important aspects of communication. Listening enables you to assimilate information and respond to the issues at hand.

Are there any special challenges for communication in a law firm?

Law firms are service organizations; they operate on the basis of billing time. There are unique problems in this respect. Sometimes attorneys feel they do not want to devote their time to matters that are nonbillable. It must be impressed upon them that taking such time out from their own work for questions, explanations, etcetera is valuable time spent in properly serving the client. It is important for a manager to decide what issues should be absolutely discussed with attorneys, and to pursue those issues until they are appropriately addressed. A legal assistant manager must quickly learn how to cut to the bottom line so that time is not wasted and issues are presented clearly and concisely. The manager must then convey this bottom line to the staff.

Are there special communication challenges for legal assistants?

Legal assistants need to master communicating clearly with attorneys, since attorneys are the ultimate decision makers. Legal assistants are always under the direct supervision of attorneys, so they need directions on concrete projects as well as information on abstract issues. Legal assistants also need to communicate the status of work, as well as their questions or concerns. To a great extent, it is the manager's responsibility to create a suitable environment for this, impressing on both attorneys and legal assistants the importance of frequent and direct communication.

What approaches to communication seem to work?

One form of communication that you immediately learn in a law firm is the memorandum. Most internal communication, other than by phone, is handled in the form of memoranda. The writing of effective memos is an art form in terms of catching people's attention and communicating information. Another form of communication is the meeting. On the management level, if you don't have at least one meeting a day in some form, you are not doing your job. The meetings can be formal or informal. Formal meetings should always be planned with an agenda, which should be distributed in advance to the participants so that they can have an opportunity to add to it. Informal meetings may be one-on-one or with a group, but even then the reason for the meeting should be clearly spelled out before the meeting so that it does not result in a gripe session or chaos. One-on-one conferences are very useful both with attorneys and staff, because they provide an opportunity to listen closely to an individual's concerns and respond face-to-face. When there are problems to address, they're far more useful than trying to communicate over the phone. Manuals which include guidelines and procedures are important to distribute both to the staff and to the attorneys. They help create a more comfortable environment because the staff understands what is expected of them.

What can law firms in general do to improve how their members communicate?

Law firms should create an environment that encourages communication both on a formal and informal level. Employees should be encouraged to express their ideas on a continuing basis and in a legitimate forum. Legal assistant managers should create the type of environment in which the legal assistant staff can contribute to the program. This should be done through the vehicles previously mentioned, or through newsletters, or at social gatherings where the legal assistants can informally communicate with the attorneys. The attorneys should be encouraged to include the legal assistant manager in firm decision-making meetings and should include the legal assistants in case- or deal-related meetings whenever the situation warrants it. In summation, the most important thing for law firms to do is to include those involved in the firm's management whenever possible by providing them with an environment for expression.

Why is listening so important?

If you cannot listen, you cannot communicate! There are many skills to be learned in the legal environment. Much knowledge is gained by watching and listening. Since law is a service business and the ultimate responsibility is to serve the client, it is the firm's obligation to properly train its staff and closely supervise the work that is done for each client. A good legal assistant manager does not let someone sink or swim on their own. In order to be trained and to properly apply their knowledge, legal assistants must listen carefully and know when to ask questions. They must learn to avoid talking or being distracted while others give explanations. The most successful legal assistant is the one who can listen, follow directions, and execute.

If you had one communication rule for all those you supervise, what would it be?

It would be to learn to listen and respond to what is being said. It's important not to be afraid to ask questions or to give suggestions on how things should be done, but most important of all is gaining knowledge of the larger picture, in order to understand not only *what* is being done but *why*.

This asteroid has only once been seen through the telescope. That was by a Turkish astronomer in 1909. On making his discovery, the astronomer had presented it to the International Astronomical Congress, in a great demonstration. But he was in Turkish costume, and so nobody would believe what he said. . . . Fortunately, however, for the reputation of Asteroid B-612, a Turkish dictator made a law that his subjects, under pain of death, should change to European costume. So in 1920 the astronomer gave his demonstration all over again, dressed with impressive style and elegance. And this time everybody accepted his report.
(Antoine de Saint-Exupery, *The Little Prince*)[1]

> "**E**mpowering" really boils down to "taking seriously." No one denies where the answers are: on the firing line. How do we get people to come forth and give the answers, to take risks by trying new things even though they are bound to fail at times? Near the top of the list is listening—that is, taking people seriously by the act of listening per se, and making it clear that you do take people seriously by what you do with what you hear. Oddly enough, to listen, per se, is the single best "tool" for empowering large numbers of others.
> (Tom Peters, *Thriving on Chaos*)[2]

COMMUNICATIONS AND THE LEGAL PROFESSION

The work of accountants depends on numbers. The medical profession stakes its success on diagnoses and treatments. Lawyers rely on the power of language. Carefully chosen, accurately researched, and precisely interpreted and recorded words are the most basic resource in the legal profession. A lawyer's ability to persuade, to convince, and to induce others to follow a certain path in their decision making depends almost completely on his or her use of words. Communications in the practice of law are, however, subject to unique problems. Attorney Becky Klemt of Laramie, Wyoming, targeted one of these problems—legal pretentiousness—in a tongue-in-cheek letter that became the subject of an article in the *Wall Street Journal:* Pomposity? she noted wryly. "Most lawyers refuse to itemize it in their bills."[3] Yet it's relatively easy for lawyers to fall into using a pretentious tone—a tendency aggravated by the confusing terminology that abounds in law. This is nothing new. In 1817, Thomas Jefferson wrote:

> I should apologize, perhaps, for the style of this bill. I dislike the verbose and intricate style of the modern English statutes.... You however can easily correct this bill to the taste of my fellow lawyers by making every other word a "said" or "foresaid" and saying everything over two or three times so that nobody but we of the craft can untwist the diction and find out what it means.[4]

Words are key. "Words!" says poet Maya Angelou. "We are not respectful enough of their power. We have no idea of their power!"[5] But there is much more to communication than the use of words, as this chapter will explain. It doesn't matter whether the role you play in a firm is that of paralegal coordinator, executive director, or docket clerk. Your communication skills are the most critical component of your career success.

Managers and Communication

Communication is the process of exchanging ideas and information between one person or group, called the sender, and another called the receiver, through symbols, actions, or written or spoken words.[6] Management expert Chester Barnard insists that the very survival of an organization hinges on the ability of its members to communicate: that a manager's primary duty is, therefore, good communications.[7]

Communications Activities

Managers spend up to 80 percent of their time communicating. They speak or write to others, read messages, listen to ideas, arbitrate difficulties, and draw on dozens of other communication methods.[8] Mintzberg calls managers, who serve as information gatherers, monitors, disseminators, and spokespersons for the organization, "the nerve center" in communication processing activities.[9] One study on the uses to which managers in a variety of business and professional settings put their communication time showed that they spent 53 percent of their time on one-on-one exchanges and group meetings; 15.5 percent on writing; 14.9 percent reading; 8 percent telephoning; and 7.7 percent on other activities.[10] Another study found that talking occupied 30 percent of a manager's time; writing, 16 percent; reading, 9 percent; and listening, 45 percent.[11]

Communications and Managerial Success

Success as a manager results from the effective use of communications. Through their adept use of clear, positive messages, managers who are good communicators are better able to motivate workers. They are also better able to inform and influence workers and top management and to develop, articulate, and implement organizational goals. In addition, a proficiency in communication enables a manager to achieve and maintain control by reducing misunderstandings, ambiguity, and mistrust. By being accurate and clear, managers are able to convey work expectations, standards, and firm policies to subordinates. Finally, managers who are good communicators are more adept at revealing their integrity and imparting enthusiasm through the appropriate expression of emotion; more than that, they are genuinely interested in others and enjoy the communications they share.

Communications and Organizational Structure

How workers communicate in organizations is often a direct result of how the organization is structured. Territorial and competitive divisions can encourage secrecy. This in turn creates communication gaps.[12] Kanter describes communication in many organizations, including law firms, as

> A structure finely divided into departments and levels, each with a tall fence around it and communication in and out is restricted—indeed, carefully guarded. Information is a secret rather than a circulating commodity. Hierarchy rather than team mechanisms is the glue holding the segments together, and so vertical relationships dominate interaction. Each segment speaks only to the one above and the one below, in constrained rather than open exchanges. The one above provides the work plan, the one below the output. Preexisting routines set the terms for action and interaction, and measurement systems are used to guard against deviation.[13]

THE COMMUNICATION PROCESS

Getting ideas across to others is a complex process. It can be as easy as determining who says what, in what way, to whom, and with what results.[14] But, as we all know, words are often intended to mean one thing and heard to mean another. Messages are not only altered and distorted, but they also get lost in the process of our sending them and of others receiving them. Our messages are further complicated by the manner in which we send them, the setting in which we send them, and the people who hear them.

Elements of the Communication Process

A classic model divides the communication process into eight elements: (1) the sender, (2) encoding, (3) the message, (4) the medium, (5) the receiver, (6) decoding, (7) feedback, and (8) noise (see Figure 12–1).[15]

Sender

The **sender** is the origin of the message, the communicator, the initiator, the transmitter. Not all messages are intentional, however. A sender can communicate ideas through intentional messages, but he or she can also send a message unintentionally (for example, by accompanying words with a scowl or a frown).

Encoding

Encoding is the process by which the sender translates his or her ideas into a message consisting of symbols that will convey the sender's ideas to the recipient of the message. Words are perhaps the symbols with which we are most familiar, but senders can enrich messages through a wide variety of symbols, including nonverbal symbols such as gestures and the medium by which they convey those messages, which is a symbol in itself.

Message

The **message** is the actual idea that the sender wants to transmit. It is the information that the sender intends the recipient to receive.

Medium

The **medium** is the means or technique by which the sender transmits his or her message. Contemporary managers can choose from a variety of media in addition to person-to-person exchanges, including telephone calls, videos, facsimile transmissions, electronic mail, memos, policy statements, publications, and teleconferences. The choice of media influences the effectiveness of communication, as does the number of media that a sender uses to convey a message. **Rich media** describes the use of many forms of media to communicate one message. The use of rich media implies a personal focus and the use of face-to-face exchanges when possible. It allows immediate feedback,

FIGURE 12-1
The Communication Process

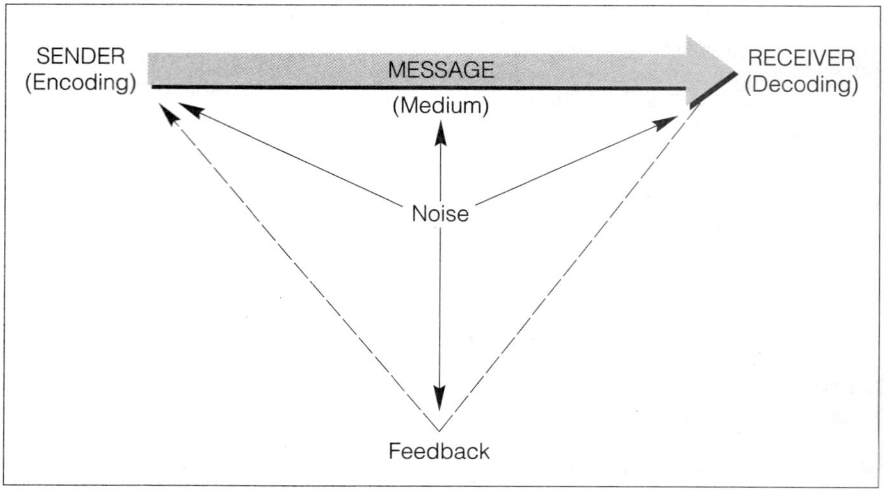

```
SENDER ──────── MESSAGE ────────▶ RECEIVER
(Encoding)      (Medium)          (Decoding)
       ▲           ▲           ▲
        ╲          │          ╱
         ╲       Noise       ╱
          ╲        │        ╱
           ╲       ▼       ╱
            ╲   Feedback  ╱
```

enabling both sender and receiver to use many verbal and nonverbal clues to convey and interpret the true content of a message. Rich media effectively communicate either routine or complex messages. **Lean media,** in contrast, describes the use of few media to communicate a message. Impersonal techniques such as memos, bulletin board messages, and notices, characterize the use of lean media, which provides no personal focus and allows little feedback.[16] Two schools of thought focus on the use of rich versus lean media. In one school are lean media managers, who are wary of communicating too much. Such managers control their messages carefully by avoiding the challenges of dialogue and accountability and by being ambiguous. They say little and decline putting their thoughts or wishes in writing, often by professing the desire to avoid potential litigation to justify their being managers of few words. In the other school of thought are rich media managers, who consider the use of multiple forms of media absolutely necessary for effectively working with others. Placing great store in multidirectional communication, such managers encourage exchanges from all stakeholders. They view written messages as an effective way of informing others: by specifying facts, such messages place greater accountability on both the sender and the receiver. Finally, these managers believe that the use of rich media helps them to reach and uphold standards of performance and production by allowing them to make quality standards, their expectations, and workers' responsibilities as clear as possible.

Receiver

Though the **receiver** is the recipient of a message, he or she need not be the person for whom the message was intended. Overheard conversations, for instance, are decoded messages in which listeners place a great deal of confidence: a sender will be less inclined to conceal information or in other ways distort a message to suit an audience of which he or she is unaware.

Decoding

Decoding is the process by which the receiver interprets the message. He or she must decode the message in order to understand it. As receivers, each of us has a complex decoding system resulting from our **frame of reference,** which encompasses our knowledge, perceptions, experiences, feelings, and beliefs. Through our unique frame of reference, each of us interprets what we perceive. It is as Tennyson wrote: "I am a part of all that I have met."[17] Each encounter and discovery augments our view of reality. As individuals, we are the evolving products of our family experiences, our socioeconomic realities, our work, our education, our culture and the extent to which it manifests itself in our lives and our needs, values, and attitudes. These elements form a perceptual framework that not only defines who we are and what is important to us, but also serves as a filter through which we see and experience new events. Our frame of reference is like a bubble that lies between us and our environment, acting as a lens through which we perceive our world.

Research has shown that a person calling your office forms an opinion about your company in the first four to six seconds. The person who picks up the phone represents the firm to the caller. Even if your office has a superb receptionist or secretary, there will be many times when you or other staff will answer the phone. Anyone who has a phone on his or her desk is responsible for maximizing the telephone's powerful potential. The following tips can help:

ANOTHER LOOK

Voices that Matter

1. When making a call, be prepared for the called party not to be there. *The Wall Street Journal* reports that only 30 percent of all business calls get completed on the first try. Learn to get value out of every call.
2. Answer the phone with your name. No one likes to be in the dark. This holds true for internal as well as external calls.
3. Be helpful, positive, and patient. The telephone link is one of today's most important connections.

SOURCE: Based on Nancy Friedman, "Telephone Tips," *Lawyers Monthly: A Supplement to Lawyers Weekly* (October 1990): 9.

1. What irks you about phone answering responses?
2. What is your reaction to being put on hold without agreeing to it? To "Who is calling, please"? To "Have a nice day"? To "phone music"? To telemarketers?
3. What "warms" a call and makes a caller feel valued, respected, and welcomed?

Feedback

Through **feedback,** the receiver expresses or clarifies his or her understanding of the message. Receivers can ask questions, comment, or respond. They can also provide feedback through facial expressions, through groans or nods of encouragement, or through written responses. For the sender, feedback illustrates the success or shortcomings of the communication attempt.

Noise

Noise consists of anything that interferes with or distorts the sender's intended message. Noise can consist of actual environmental sound, though it is just as likely to consist of psychological interference—such as an emotional state, an attitude, or a prejudice—internal to the sender or receiver. Time pressures that lead to hasty communications are a form of noise. A quantity of information sufficient to overload the communication process is another form of noise. Noise also exists on the printed page. A formal notice or memo that is smudged, filled with errors, and poorly duplicated interferes with the intended message. In oral exchanges, noise can consist of poor speech patterns, mumbling, mispronunciations, and the *er*'s and *uh*'s that we have been warned to avoid!

Communication Media

A variety of media is available to today's manager. Talks, meetings, conferences, and speeches accommodate the need to communicate face to face, and media such as memos, letters, reports, and announcements provide vehicles for written communication. To effectively utilize any medium, a manager must master the procedure or format relevant to that medium. Such requirements extend even to the use of relatively new media such as the telephone, electronic mail, and fax machines. Observing certain styles and formalities not only makes communication clearer and more uniform: such technological etiquette conveys the sender's respect for the receiver as well.

The Basic Forms of Communication

Whatever types of media we use, there are basically only two forms of communication: verbal and nonverbal. Verbal communication relies on the use of sounds and symbols to represent words, which are units of meaning that create a language. Verbal messages are easier to construct and to control than nonverbal messages, which depend on the receiver's ability to understand and interpret multiple levels of meaning, many of which the sender conveys subconsciously.

Nonverbal communications are more trustworthy than verbal ones. In becoming sensitive to a baby's gestures and cries, for example, parents learn the immediacy with which nonverbal messages communicate needs, emotions, likes, and dislikes. To better understand nonverbal communication, we will briefly examine paralinguistics, proxemics, and body language.

Paralinguistics

Paralinguistics is the study of how vocal cues and features of the human voice augment or otherwise modify the meaning of verbal messages. These features include pitch, rate, volume, and the timing and pauses the speaker uses in delivering the message.[18] To understand the importance of paralinguistics, we must realize that these features actually can change the meaning of words. Try saying "I am not the one you saw" several times, changing the volume, intonation, and emphasis of the words, the speed, pacing, or pauses between them, and the pitch or level of emotion in your voice. Listen carefully to yourself, and you will have a good idea of how a sender can enhance, alter, or even transform the meaning of words through paralanguage.

Proxemics

Proxemics is the study of the spatial separation that people maintain and of the effects that this separation has on communication and on other aspects of culture. We may describe the spatial separation between people in terms of physical distance and physical arrangement.

Distance. Researchers have found that the amount of space we maintain between ourselves and others when we communicate depends on our relationships with those others and on cultural differences. The amount of distance we leave between ourselves and others describes the degree of intimacy and openness between us, as well as our relative status. When we are with intimate acquaintances, our zone of comfortable proximity extends to about one and a half feet; when we are with friends or business associates, the zone ranges from one and a half to four feet; when conducting impersonal business, we tend to allow between four and twelve feet. The rules for personal proximity differ greatly in different cultures.

Physical Arrangements. Our use of space in office layouts and in office and meeting room seating arrangements says much about our use of and attitudes toward authority.

The Use of Space in Competitive Tasks. Managers and other law firm personnel most often conduct competitive tasks, such as negotiating for contracts, reprimanding subordinates, or even interviewing job candidates, in layouts that permit them to closely monitor nonverbal cues. Positioning chairs for office visitors directly across from your chair is a formal arrangement that tells your visitors that you are in charge. Seating visitors on the other side of your desk provides you with the security of a physical barrier and indicates your superiority in terms of power. Similarly, sitting at the head of a conference table conveys authority and power. Group members often try to balance the distribution of power between themselves and a dominant, head-of-the-table leader by gathering at the opposite end of the table.

The Use of Space in Cooperative Tasks. A more comfortable spatial arrangement, unless the need to work with subordinates prescribes formality, is to place chairs side-by-side. Seating committee members at a round table, for example, conveys a sense of equality.[20] Other cooperative tasks that utilize alternate seating arrangements might include luncheon meetings, office conferences with the participants seated on a sofa, or a brainstorming session with people seated in a cluster of comfortable chairs.

Body Language

Body language encompasses the physical movements and characteristics, including posture, gestures, and facial expressions that affect communication.[21] Twentieth-century communications researchers have placed a great deal of interest in this aspect of communication; Albert Mehrabian recently suggested that only 7 percent of the effect of a message comes verbally. The rest, he says, is nonverbal: 38 percent from paralanguage and 55 percent from facial expressions.[22] Communication researchers Paul Elkman and W. V. Friesen recognize five forms of body language: emblems, illustrators, regulators, adapters, and affect displays.[23]

Emblems. Emblems are gestures that convey attitudes, emotions, or conditions, such as the peace sign or the "thumbs-up" sign. The meaning of emblems may vary from culture to culture. Our thumb-and-forefinger "okay" sign is an obscene gesture in many South American countries, and Germans use "thumbs-up" to signify "one."

Illustrators. **Illustrators** are gestures that clarify a spoken message, such as the size of the fish that got away or the distance between your car and that of the rude driver who squeezed past you in a parking lot. Speakers often illustrate transitions between the points they are making by raising one finger for the first point, two for the second, and so on.

Regulators. **Regulators** are gestures that help to control the reception of a message, such as nodding your head to encourage others to continue, putting a finger to your lips to indicate the need for quiet, and cupping your hand behind your ear to indicate the need for more volume.

Adapters. **Adapters** are coping devices that help people adjust to tension or to new situations. We tend to be more unaware of our use of adapters, most of which we learned as children. Examples of these devices include jiggling one's foot, tapping one's fingers, or twisting a strand of hair.

Affect Displays. Through this final form of body language, we subconsciously communicate feelings or emotions. **Affect displays** include facial expressions, gestures, body positions and posture, and mirroring.

- Facial Expressions. Facial expressions mirror our emotions.[24] Our smiles provide encouragement and approval; raised eyebrows can show disbelief; frowns express displeasure; pursed lips, anger; lip biting, nervousness. The eyes are thought to mirror our thoughts: open pupils show acceptance, delight, and pleasure; hard, small pupils can reflect hatred and disapproval. Direct eye contact shows interest. Shifty eyes are a sign of avoidance.
- Gestures. Gestures can convey our emotions. Finger-jabbing expresses aggression; yawning and doodling communicate boredom; and clenched fists can signify belligerence or anger. Gestures can be fairly complex. One might express perceived or actual superiority, for instance, by leaning back during a conversation and putting one's hands up and behind one's head, particularly while smiling.[25]
- Body Position and Posture. Posture sometimes indicates our inner states. Watch how people slouch in defeat or strut in arrogance. Notice how a confident leader sits at a meeting. Try to read the defensiveness in the postures of colleagues who wrap their arms across their chests, cross their legs away from those whom they dislike, or turn their backs on certain people.
- Mirroring. Mirroring is a sign of emotional concord. Researchers have found that two or more conversationalists who share a solid rapport will start to mirror each other's gestures, shifting their body positions at approximately the same time and mimicking one another's arm and hand motions.

The Interaction of Verbal and Nonverbal Communications

As we have seen, nonverbal cues can augment the meaning of a verbal message. Sometimes, they serve as substitutes. A shrug of the shoulders or hands stretched out in welcome may have meaning, but such cues alone usually cannot communicate a message as specifically as words can. Nonverbal cues most often regulate and shape verbal communication by signifying attitudes or feelings such as approval, confusion, astonishment, boredom, and disbelief. When nonverbal cues seem to contradict a verbal message, we tend to trust the nonverbal communication.[26]

PERSUASIVENESS OF COMMUNICATIONS

Because their success depends on their ability to influence, we often think of those in the legal profession as experts in eloquence. Aristotle, who in his classic work, *Rhetoric,* described the characteristics of persuasive communication, believed that three factors—the speaker, the message itself, and the audience—determine how compelling and influential communication is.[27] These three elements are still critical to our attempts to persuade and to influence.[28]

Characteristics of the Source

First, unless the speaker as the source of the message is credible, the message will not be effective. The audience must believe that the speaker knows what he or she is talking about: it is imperative that the audience trust the speaker. Secondly, the audience must be able to relate to the speaker. In the opening of this chapter, you read of the Turkish astronomer who at first failed to persuade his audience because of his foreign appearance. He then earned acceptance not by changing the content of his message but simply by dressing like his European audience. If a speaker is too dissimilar from his or her audience, whether in appearance, intelligence, or views, the message is lost. Thirdly, favorable status automatically grants credibility to a speaker. If a secretary and an attorney were both to deliver the same message to the same audience, the listeners would likely grant greater credibility to the higher professional status of the attorney.

Characteristics of the Message

Four characteristics of the message itself play an important role in persuasion: form, substance, attractiveness, and primacy or recency.

Form

The form of the message is critical. The formality or informality of its structure, the quality of its construction or prose, and the degree to which the message suits its audience determine its ability to persuade. Much depends also on the speaker's or writer's ability to create a smooth balance between the complexity of the message and its format.[29]

Substance

Although the substance of most persuasive messages is a product of logic and reason, some messages persuade most effectively through the careful manipulation of emotions. Televangelists most often use emotional appeals, building on the needs, guilt, and fears of their listeners. Ironically, some of the same techniques surface in the austerely intellectual atmosphere of the law firm. Emotional appeals find their way into many law firm activities, including partners' committee meetings and support staff team sessions.

Attractiveness

Messages are more effective if they are given in attractive surroundings, by attractive people, in attractive ways. The producers of morning television programs such as "The Today Show" and "Good Morning, America" go to great lengths to achieve attractiveness in communication. The more pleasant a message, the more acceptable it is. We tend to reject information that is personally unappealing. Most listeners do not want to hear of their faults, their inadequacies, or their lack of good will.

Technological Considerations

Technological blunders will weaken even the most awesome message. People who utilize technology in their communications must ensure the quality of the technological application. A fuzzy video, the awkward use of a data display terminal, overheads shown out of order, and burned-out projector bulbs can all weaken the impact of a message.

Primacy or Recency

Some people believe that the first message an audience hears is more effective than the last; they believe, in other words, that primacy is more effective than recency. Others reverse the argument, and have yet to provide conclusive evidence one way or the other.[30]

Characteristics of the Receiver

Persuasion is not just a question of how good we are as speakers or how terrific our message is. In addition to the characteristics of the source and the message, there are always the characteristics of the audience to consider. In the end, the receiver or group of receivers, the audience, determines the success of our efforts to communicate. The persuasiveness of a message depends on three factors: the audience's intelligence, latitude of acceptance, and traits as a group.

Intelligence

First, the persuasiveness of a message always relies on a listener's ability to understand it. Highly complex or abstract messages are more likely to bore or offend than to persuade listeners of average intelligence. Conversely, highly intelligent listeners tend to outthink a message, thereby voiding its ability to persuade them. Such audiences are more resistant to influence.

Latitude of Acceptance

Next, to be effective, a message must reflect an audience's tendency to think conservatively, moderately, or liberally. Ideas that seem tame to a radical audience may offend or shock conservative listeners, whose *latitude of acceptance* is not as broad.

IN THE NEWS

Our (Un-) Lively Language: The Quest for Better Writing in the Law Firm

New York's Shearman & Sterling is again leading the pack in the legal community's pursuit of polished prose.

Next month the firm will dispatch a team of writing coaches to its Paris office, where they will help lawyers jump the hurdles they meet when working simultaneously in three languages: French, English and legalese.

Lawyers for whom English is a second language tend to get bogged down with unnecessary "herewiths" and "hereunders," says William L. Lee, Shearman's managing partner there. They want to fit into the professional culture, he observes, and seem to think legalese will add authenticity to their prose.

But it's not only for the French that Shearman has arranged to have Words/Worth Associates Inc. of Brooklyn, N.Y., work with its lawyers on the Avenue George V.

"We can all use it," says Mr. Lee, who adds that he also hopes to benefit from the Words/Worth teachers.

The trilingual tutorial is just one of the latest developments in a decade-long movement by U.S. law firms to hire consultants to improve their written communication.

Shearman was among the first of the big firms to say that even experienced, English-speaking attorneys could use outsiders' help in learning to write more clearly and effectively. In 1981, the firm hired a linguistics professor to coach all its attorneys—partners and associates alike.

Since then, a number of firms have followed suit. And a small industry of legal writing consultants has sprung up to provide videotapes and workbooks, private instruction and workshops.

Partners themselves aren't necessarily good writers, say consultants. Even if they are, they often are not good editors or teachers, they frequently don't have time to devote to associates' writing.

The net result is that associates waste time endlessly rewriting their own work. Partners squander hours endlessly rewriting associates. And the time lost, translated into billable hours, equals huge amounts of the firm's money wasted on an ineffective teaching method, according to the consultants who perhaps prefer that some of the money instead will be spent on them.

For, even with all this time, effort and money—"most lawyers write poorly," say Dean Goldstein and Prof. Lieberman. Their informal survey of 300 leading lawyers, judges, professors, writing instructors and journalists found a consensus that modern legal writing is "flabby, prolix, obscure, opaque, ungrammatical, dull, boring, redundant, disorganized, gray, dense, unimaginative." And that's not all.

Complaints about legal writing are nothing new. In fact, says Dean Goldstein, one of the most surprising findings in his research was that historically lawyers have been criticized for their writing style.

Why did some firms suddenly decide to do something about turgid prose? And what have they done about it?

Some attribute the new receptiveness to a general perception that the TV generation is less-schooled in the written word than its predecessors. Others say the plain English movement, begun in the 1970s, has been holding lawyers to a higher standard. Still others speak of the sudden growth of the megafirm, in which relations between all lawyers became more impersonal and the ability of partners to mentor associates was diluted.

Then there's the client-wooing theory: With the demise of the institutional "you are my lawyer for better or worse" relationship between firms and clients, attorneys suddenly had to become more competitive. And one of the best ways to get and keep clients is to impress them with writing that makes points quickly, clearly and eloquently.

SOURCE: Rorie Sherman, " 'Obscure, Opaque, Ungrammatical, Dull, Boring': That's What Writing Consultants Think of a Lot of Legal Writing." *The National Law Journal* (18 September 1989). Reprinted with the permission of *The National Law Journal.*

Traits as a Group

Each group of listeners is unique, and many factors determine what makes each audience different. These include an audience's motivation for being an audience. Captive audiences, such as college students in required courses, have little in common with receptive and enthusiastic fans at a rock concert. Other audience characteristics that affect a message's ability to persuade include the emotional state of an audience, the expectations and stereotypes that its members hold, and their collective needs, attitudes, and values. Persuasive communicators know that one of the keys to their success is knowing who their listeners are and what they want to hear.

WRITING EFFECTIVELY

Few people like to write. As political speech writer Peggy Noonan observes, "Writing is hard. It's like working out, only it's an intellectual workout."[31] This writing workout, when properly performed, produces a message that is correct, clear, complete, concise, and courteous.

Correct

An effective piece of writing is correct in terms of grammar and usage. In addition, the words you choose must be appropriate for the occasion. This implies that your language should be accurate, jargon-free, and nonexclusive.

Accuracy

Choose your words carefully, and use solid, plain, direct language. Why say "beg to advise" instead of "tell"? Why use "a viable alternative" instead of "possibility"? Some amusing errors have resulted from the improper use of "elegant" language: "Illiterate it from the records," "She was truly a child progeny," and "He was amused by her idiot-syncracies" are three real-life examples. Malapropisms such as these *will* entertain your listeners—at the expense of your message and your credibility. Similarly, using emotionally charged or haughty words is apt to create a barrier between you and your audience.

Jargon-Free

The best rule in writing is to avoid jargon. The business world is filled with buzzwords, clichés, and slang. For those in the know, who are familiar with the special terminology of a given group, jargon can simplify communication and create a sense of belonging or group identity. For those not in the know, however, the use of jargon in written or spoken communication creates confusion, frustration, and a sense of exclusion. It can be just as offensive to your readers as teenage slang is to those over 30![32]

Inclusive Language

Enlightened writers avoid the use of words that automatically exclude or imply the inferiority of one group of people because of gender, culture, religion, ethnicity, or race. Examples of words considered exclusive are chairman, gal-friday, and messenger boy. The potential exclusivity of language still excites debate. Some argue, for example, that the use of words such as "mankind" is generally understood to refer to women as well as to men. Others believe strongly that the use of words that specifically refer to one gender has a profound psycholinguistical effect. This means that word choice reinforces our perceptions and attitudes about the superiority or suitability of one group of people rather than another. On a larger, more philosophical scale, choosing to use inclusive language has far-reaching effects. Gender-free terms, for example, imply sensitivity toward the ongoing struggle of women for equity. On a smaller, more personal scale, avoiding exclusive language indicates sensitivity in general and a willingness to be open and fair with our coworkers.

Clear

To ensure that your writing is clear, you might try this procedure: First, list your ideas by answering these questions: What information do I need to get across? What do I need to say? How specific should I be? Secondly, write the words that best describe what you want to say. (They need not be in any specific order.) Third, try to isolate your major areas of thought, the themes for what you want to say. Fourth, based on these themes, establish headings in the order you want to use, leaving spaces under each. Next, write each of your ideas under the appropriate heading. This will help you to organize your thoughts into divisions or areas of content.

Complete

The content of your writing should communicate your message completely to your audience. To judge

In-house References	**Sports References**	**Military References**
He's a clubhouse lawyer.	Run it up the flagpole.	He was under the gun.
He runs a boutique firm.	I'm out in left field.	He's an outflanked manager.
She's a real pinstripe.	Let's try a team play.	We're talking corporate brass.
It's our flagship office.	Another end run?	We need to bite the bullet.
He's no rainmaker.	The ball's in your court.	Are you pulling rank?
	Touch base with the boss.	
	She's my pinch hitter.	
	Let's have a ballpark figure.	

ANOTHER LOOK

Law Firm Jargon: What Are They Talking About?

1. How might jargon simplify and shorten communication?
2. When can the use of jargon cause breakdowns in communication? Who is responsible?
3. Why does most jargon seem to come from sports and the military?
4. Try to add two or three law firm terms to the above list.

TABLE 12–1
Using Inclusive Language

Avoid:	Use instead:
mankind	human, people
salesman	salesclerk, sales associate
chairman	chair, chairperson
waitress	waitperson, server
foreman	supervisor
errand boy	messenger
man hours	work hours
man power	work force
workman's compensation	workers' compensation

SOURCE: For sensible ideas on avoiding sexist language, see Casey Miller and Kate Swift, *The Handbook of Non-Sexist Writing* (New York: Lippincott and Crowell, 1980).

whether your content is complete, ask yourself these questions: Have I included all of the points I wished to make? Have I answered all of the questions that might arise in my readers' minds? Have I provided enough information? What ideas are absolutely essential to this communication? Did I keep it simple? Often, you can write more clearly and logically simply by keeping in mind the idea that you wish to tell your readers a story.

Concise

Your writing should be concise. Readers have little patience for memos or reports that fail to come to the point. "Concise" does not necessarily mean "brief," however. A concise message uses words efficiently; a brief message has few words. Convey your message like a telegram or want ad, without wasting words.

Courteous

The last element your message should have is courtesy. Above all, you as a writer must give considerable thought to who your audience is, something you can do only by trying to take the reader's perspective, in terms of timing and of tone.

TABLE 12–2
Using Direct, Concise Language

Do I Say . . .	When I Can Say . . .?
arrive at a decision	decide
bring about an improvement	improve
as of this point in time	now
the most unique	unique
because of the fact that	because
in order to utilize	use
in that time frame	then
remunerate	pay
peruse	read
cognizant of	know

Timing

Have you considered when your message will be received? If there is information that requires a response, such as a meeting date or a deadline, have you allowed your reader enough time to make plans, to absorb the information he or she has received, and to respond? Do you schedule mandatory meetings a day before they take place? Do you demand detailed reports "tomorrow"? Do you make grueling requests right before long weekends or holidays and expect action the day of return? Timing also sets standards for your own responses to communications; never let a communication go unanswered. Make it a rule to reply within forty-eight hours, whether in person, by phone, or in writing. When someone takes the time to write, a reply is a necessity.

Tone

Tone conveys the respect you have for your reader. You should have consideration for your reader, even if you are conveying negative news. (If you are unsure of the tone of your writing, have someone read what you have written.) The tone you create must convey a positive attitude, respect, sincerity, and candor and be appropriate to your audience.

Positive Attitude. Assume the best of your reader. Avoid negativism. If you need cooperation, you will achieve nothing unless your tone implies that you think highly of your reader and his or her abilities, even if in fact you suspect the worst!

Appropriate Tone. The level of formality you use in your writing should be appropriate to your audience. Your friends would probably chuckle to receive a message written with the deference you show when addressing clients and superiors, who in turn would likely not be amused to receive announcements written in the commanding tone you use on subordinates.

Respect. Your choice of words reveals your attitudes toward your reader. Feel respect for your reader, and choose words—carefully—that reflect that feeling. By using the wrong combinations of words, you can come across as patronizing, arrogant, negative, mistrusting, and a host of other things. Avoid "fighting words" and words that are emotionally loaded. They will cause your reader to resist both you and your message.

Sincerity. Being genuine is important. Flattery, bragging, and even too much humility on your part can make your reader uneasy. This weakens trust.

Candor and Acceptance. Is your tone defensive and closed? Does it imply not only that your reader has somehow offended you but also that, whatever the subject of the disagreement, you could not possibly be at fault? Be open to what you might learn from criticism. Never write words to the effect of "No one has ever complained" or "You are the only one to ever find fault." Investigate the problems that your readers perceive and do not attack those who disagree with you. Always grant your audience the right to think differently from you.

SPEAKING EFFECTIVELY

Voice

Your voice, which can add to or detract from your message, may be as important as the words you choose.

Quality

Tape yourself in an actual exchange and listen carefully to the playback. (Don't be put off by what you hear: most people initially dislike how they sound on tape.) Listen to the pitch, speed, and general quality of your voice. Is it abrasive? Too loud? Weak? Do you mumble, or clip the ends off your words? Identify the qualities you value in other people's voices, and determine which of those qualities you would like to hear more clearly in your own, and practice, using the tape recorder, until you are pleased with the changes you hear.

Tone

What emotional qualities emerge in your voice? Do you sound warm? calm? reassuring? tired? enthusiastic? harsh? sarcastic? Is there happiness in your tone? Ask others what they hear.

Confidence

Do you hesitate or stumble over *er*'s and *uh*'s? On the other hand, do you reveal overconfidence and arrogance by overusing *I* and *me?* Do you race through your message, challenging your listeners to keep up, or do you allow them time, through pauses and considerate pacing, to absorb what you've said?

Message

Tailor your message to your audience. Whether your spoken presentations are for small groups or large ones, knowing your audience is essential to effective communication. Speaking before a group of any type or size is in effect a public performance. Your task is to connect with your audience and to convince them of the value of your message. To be important to your audience, your message must be important to you. As communications consultant Roger Ailes explains,

> When you know what your mission is in front of an audience, that sense of purpose automatically marshals your best natural resources as a speaker. You gesture purposefully and expressively with your eyes, face, voice, and body. We've all experienced these moments of deep commitment, when we were so excited about something or so immersed that we "forgot ourselves" and spoke very forcefully and expressively.[33]

Even if your presentation is merely the opening statement at a firm meeting, note David Whetten and Kim Cameron, "a cogent, stimulating, concise presentation provides a change of pace . . . broadens group participation, and is often the most efficient way to disseminate information. . . ."[34]

Oral Presentations[35]

As a supervisor, coordinator, or office administrator, or as anyone in a law firm who regularly must inform others about matters of concern, you often will be called on to make oral presentations. Managers, especially, spend much time talking to groups, and one managerial role in particular, that of representing the organization, suggests a need for managers who are experts at giving talks and addressing others. Audiences expect you, at the very least, not to waste their time. Giving effective presentations requires the following abilities: (1) to utilize your placement as speaker, (2) to convey confidence, (3) to connect with your listeners, (4) to arouse and keep your audience's interest, (5) to involve the audience, and (6) to handle possible challenges and hostility.

Placement

As a speaker, use your physical position to your advantage. Never stay seated if you want your message to receive full attention. The podium, if you use one, should have good lighting and be placed within a comfortable distance and in full view of your audience. If you are to give your talk in a conference room, always stand if you want your listeners to take you seriously. Move to a location that is easily visible to all present. On the other hand, make sure that your notes, whether cards or full-size sheets, are inconspicuous. Use them to stay on track, but do not allow them to come between you and your audience, particularly when speaking to smaller groups.

Confidence

By raising the expectations of the average listener, television has made oral presentations more difficult for all of us. As speakers, we are now expected to be as natural, as entertaining, and as informative as Jane Pauley or Johnny Carson! If you attempt to do too much, however, it is easy to have your speeches fall flat. If you are not yourself, if you try to be scholarly when you are not, if you aim to be humorous when you have trouble telling your jokes to your best friends, if you are too formal when the occasion does not call for it, you will weaken your attempt to communicate. Putting your audience at ease is important, for it enables you to open and smooth the channels of communication. This means, of course, that you must be—or at least **seem** to be—at ease. Almost all people, unless superbly confident, experience adrenalin surges when they realize that their listeners are not only listening but also are judging their message, their appearance, and them. In addition, listeners judge your credibility, which, as we saw earlier in this chapter, depends on the characteristics of the source, of the message itself, and of the audience. Your skill at seeming natural and at ease depends first on your confidence about what you are doing and, secondly, on your ability to channel your confidence into effective presentation skills. These include natural, logical gestures; a lack of nervous mannerisms; vocal control in terms of breathing, speed, and volume; eye contact with your listeners; and smooth use of your materials and equipment. Both factors, attitude and presentation skills, improve with practice, which in turn leads to confidence.

Connection

Reaching your audience by establishing a bond between its members and you is your biggest challenge as a speaker. You must be able to convince audience members that you respect them as individuals and that you care about what you are saying to them. Effective speakers link themselves to their audiences by observing and interpreting audience signals, such as facial expressions, which act as a nonverbal language through which an audience expresses its comprehension, agreement, and disagreement. Finding out in advance about your audience, as a group and as individual members, will enable you to be more responsive to its reactions. Discovering and referring to common ground helps a relationship to form between you and your audience. By thus connecting with your listeners, you bring a focus to your presentation that is audience-centered rather than self-centered. When this happens, you will have achieved your objective: to communicate.

Interest

When you have the opportunity, watch effective speakers. Attend public forums that invite outstanding speakers. Analyze how they win and keep the interest of their audience. A catchy opener may initially win an audience's attention, but if you don't offer enthusiasm and stimulating ideas throughout your presentation you may be one of those sleep-inducing speakers audiences dread. As a speaker, you must communicate variety, vigor, and vitality.

Involvement

Nothing stimulates an audience more than the ability to interact with a speaker and to participate in his or her presentation. Establishing a dialogue with your listeners involves them in your message and allows you a natural opportunity to respond to their questions and concerns. If you engage your audience in a question-and-answer session, keep these ideas in mind: [36]

- Avoid embarrassing anyone by calling on someone who has not volunteered.
- Limit answers to the information you want. Don't be led into areas you don't want to discuss.
- Ask friendly questions that won't create awkward silences.
- Avoid referring to your listeners' sore spots.
- Ask questions that are relevant to your listeners.
- Do not ask rhetorical questions.
- Structure open-ended questions that leave room for interpretation, new thoughts, and different ideas.
- Keep the exchange mutually satisfying.
- Show that you appreciate your listeners' input by referring to it, naming, whenever possible, the person who made the comment.
- Give respondents time to think. If they get stuck, summarize whatever they have contributed and ask whether anyone would like to add anything else.

Challenges and Hostility

If someone challenges your ideas or disagrees with you, don't over-respond. Be firm, not intimidated. If you don't, you may lose control of the situation.[37] Refuse to take negative reactions personally. If you convince yourself not only that each listener has the right to disagree but that dissenters are usually giving you the gift of honesty, then you will be less likely to react defensively to criticism. Try saying, "I appreciate your honesty," "I value this different perspective," or "You have the right to disagree." And then be sure to restate your own convictions. Not only do you have the right to your view, but you were formally asked to present it. On the other hand, it's impossible to know everything. Admitting honestly that you don't have an answer but are willing to find one will earn you credibility; hedging or avoiding an issue will not. Many people don't ask questions simply for the purpose of getting answers. They may be asking in order to attract attention, to lead the discussion toward their favorite topics, to test your knowledge, or even to assess you as a potential opponent or threat. Be open and honest in response to hostile questions.[38] Listen, get to the heart of the question, and empathize with the strong feelings of the questioner. Try to find some mutual ground, and phrase your response diplomatically as well as informatively. Remember that it is your talk. Rather than allow a belligerent questioner to take control of your time and your presentation, respond briefly and then, perhaps even while you are still replying, point to the next questioner and ask quickly for the next question. If all else fails, the final technique for accommodating a hostile questioner may be to respond with a simple, valid, "No comment."

LISTENING EFFECTIVELY

Most of us have had many occasions to admit "I wasn't listening." Listening is an art. To be a good listener, you must work actively to decode the messages of

Even when our message seems to have been well received, we always wonder how good we were after we finish giving a talk or presentation.

A checklist such as this one can help you to obtain feedback on your presentations.

I. Appearance:
  ___ 1. Positive impression.
  ___ 2. Mannerisms relaxed and natural.
  ___ 3. Good posture before and during presentation.

II. Voice:
  ___ 1. Audible and clear.
  ___ 2. Confident.
  ___ 3. Expressive.

III. Content:
  ___ 1. Appropriate and timely.
  ___ 2. Enthusiastic and interesting.
  ___ 3. Convincing and persuasive.

IV. Organization:
  ___ 1. Good opening.
  ___ 2. Coherent and logical organization.
  ___ 3. Satisfying conclusion.

V. Graphic Aids (if used):
  ___ 1. Easily visible.
  ___ 2. Relevant.
  ___ 3. Smoothly coordinated.

VI. Nonverbal Skills:
  ___ 1. Solid sense of connection with audience.
  ___ 2. Sufficient eye contact.
  ___ 3. At ease with the audience.

VII. Please comment on any of the above areas or on any other aspect of the presentation:

_____

1. How do you tend to respond to feedback or criticism? In what ways do you utilize feedback?
2. Describe your strengths and weaknesses at giving talks and presentations. Who do you think tends to be more critical of a speaker: the audience or the speaker him- or herself? Explain.
3. What items would you add to the feedback checklist?

ANOTHER LOOK

Was I Any Good?

---

senders. Such effort, explains *Fortune* columnist Walter Kiechel III, is essential to good management:

> Managers who like best to hear themselves talking, or who resent the time and energy it takes to listen well, run some real risks. Failed negotiations, poor interpersonal relations, and on-the-job encounters with unpleasant truths are among the likely consequences of a tin ear.[39]

Three types of skills are involved in good listening: attending skills, following skills, and reflecting skills.

Attending Skills

A good listener *attends* to what a sender is saying by making good eye contact and indicating through body language that he or she is paying attention. The listener tries not to let environmental detractors, such as noise or other conversations, interfere with the sender's message.

Following Skills

The listener *follows* not only by attending silently to the sender's message but by encouraging the speaker with words, sounds, and gestures ("Yes," "Mm hm," or a nod) and by allowing the speaker to ask pertinent questions.

Reflecting Skills

The listener *reflects* by verbally indicating to the speaker that he or she has heard and comprehended the message. A good listener will do this by repeating or paraphrasing the speaker's words and by giving brief summations along the way. Reflecting shows not only that the listener has heard the speaker's message correctly but that he or she understands the speaker's feelings as well.[40]

TABLE 12–3
Ten Rules for Good Listening

Listening Rule	Reasoning Behind the Rule
1. Stop talking	You cannot listen if you are talking
2. Put the person at ease	Help a person feel free to talk; create a permissive environment
3. Show the person you want to listen	Look and act interested; listen to understand, not to oppose
4. Remove distractions	Don't doodle, tap, or shuffle papers; shut the door if necessary to achieve quiet
5. Empathize	Try to see the other person's point of view
6. Be patient	Allow plenty of time; do not interrupt; don't start for the door or walk away
7. Hold your temper	An angry person takes the wrong meaning from words
8. Go easy on argument and criticism	Don't put people on the defensive and cause them to "clam up" or become angry; do not argue—even if you win, you lose
9. Ask questions	This encourages a person and shows that you are listening; it helps to develop points further
10. Stop talking	This is first and last, because all other guidelines depend on it; you cannot do an effective listening job while you are talking.

SOURCE: Adapted from Keith Davis, *Human Behavior at Work*, 5th ed. (New York: McGraw-Hill Book Company, 1977). Copyright © 1977 by Keith Davis. Used with the permission of McGraw-Hill Book Company.

COMMUNICATION IN THE LAW FIRM

The flow and direction of communication, as well as the informal communication that takes place through the organizational grapevine, rumors, and gossip, strongly influence law firm dynamics.

Communication Flow

In most organizations, the formal flow of communication follows the hierarchical chain of command. Those at the top usually direct and control communication, sending messages and information down through the organization; however, not all communication is one-way. Communication can be two-way as well, and can also be vertical, horizontal, or diagonal.

One-way and Two-way Communication

In some organizations, communication seems to travel in only one direction. In **one-way communication,** a sender conveys messages to a receiver who provides no feedback. In **two-way communication,** by comparison, the receiver responds to the sender's messages with feedback, and information travels in both directions. In both one-way and two-way communication, the sender may omit parts of or distort his or her message, sometimes accidentally and sometimes consciously. Subordinates, for example, may exclude information for a variety of reasons. First, they may wish to conceal their thoughts from managers whom they believe they cannot trust. Secondly, they may believe that managers are not interested in them and their problems. Thirdly, subordinates may see no advantage to upward communication, only complications and drawbacks. Fourth, they may be justifying their own communication inadequacies and inhibitions by blaming supervisors and managers for being hard to approach, too inaccessible, and unresponsive. Finally, many workers fear (often, unfortunately, with just cause) to be bearers of bad news. It is likely that neither the catastrophic explosion of the space shuttle *Challenger* in 1986 nor the launching of the Hubble space telescope with a badly flawed mirror in 1990 would have occurred had the managerial climate at NASA favored two-way communication. In both instances, engineers had been discouraged from bringing potential problems to the attention of their superiors. Even if bad news is unwelcome, the results of not knowing are significantly worse. Many organizations, including law firms, contribute to their own failure by refusing to reward honesty and full disclosure.[41]

Vertical Communication

Communication also flows upward and downward. **Downward communication** occurs when those at the top send information to those below them on the hierarchy. Much of this communication consists of information about work and is intended to direct the activities of workers in the firm. **Upward communication** results when someone from a lower hierarchical level communicates with someone at a higher level. Messages traveling upward are usually in the form of requests for information or help, reports, descriptions of work problems, suggestions, and feedback.[42]

Horizontal Communication

Horizontal communication takes place between those at the same hierarchical level. Sharing information with your colleagues about activities and events or coordinating work assignments with them constitutes horizontal communication. Written communications, directives, announcements, briefings, and bulletin board-type messages facilitate the flow of information between those on the same level. Horizontal communication is important for many reasons. For instance, through horizontal communication, paralegals might share information on job responsibilities, secretaries might develop interpersonal support systems, or associates might improve their cohesiveness by building on common interests and understandings. Horizontal communication also is useful in resolving conflicts and coping with change. A lack of horizontal communication results in a sense of separation and isolation among the members of a group. This in turn increases intragroup competition, weakens trust, and undermines the collegiality that creates a sense of pride in professionalism. In a law firm, where workers perform highly specialized tasks, people at the same level must share information and cooperate if they are to help the firm reach its goals. When workers are looking out only for their own interests, in the long run, everyone's interests suffer.

Diagonal Communication

Diagonal communication, which crosses hierarchical levels, provides a vehicle for coordinating activities in the organization. Such communication occurs in committees, task forces, and *ad hoc* groups composed of law firm workers from different areas, levels, or departments. A firm also may establish diagonal communication by designating one person to serve as a bridge or link between various groups. By belonging to two different work groups, this bridge person can keep each group apprised of the other's needs and concerns.[43]

The Grapevine

Not officially sanctioned by the law firm, the **grapevine** is the informal communication network that members use to spread news and unofficial information. People who are part of the informal communications network use the grapevine sporadically, whenever they need it, largely to meet their personal needs for information. Those in power in the hierarchy are often unable to control or influence use of the grapevine. Nonetheless, besides being quick, the grapevine is relatively accurate, contrary to what we might think.[44] One study found that over 80 percent of grapevine information tends to be business-related rather than personal.[45] Another study revealed that between 70 and 90 percent of the facts and details conveyed through the grapevine were accurate.[46]

Rumors

The grapevine can be quite destructive when used as a rumor mill.[47] The roles of rumors and gossip in organizations has intrigued many communications researchers. Rumors that are based on factual information that leaks out and spreads rapidly can be helpful if, for instance, they allow workers to prepare for difficult situations before the organization makes a full disclosure. Other rumors, however, can be costly, demoralizing, and anxiety-producing. They also may damage individual and organizational reputations. Rumors are of several types: (1) spontaneous rumors, which spring up in highly stressful times; (2) premeditated rumors, which the organization leaks intentionally in order to assess how workers will respond to certain information; (3) wedge drivers, created to cause dissension; (4) pipe dreams, which consist of wishful thinking; (5) bogeys, or rumors that feed on people's fears; and (6) self-fulfilling prophecies, which project an initially fictional situation that actually comes true. (Spreading a rumor that the organization will be closed the day before a holiday and then actually having that day off would be an example of this last type of rumor.) Squelching rumors takes skill. Three strategies are suggested: First, attack the rumor head on. Identify it, label it a rumor, address it, and ridicule it. Next, outflank the rumor. Rebut it, but don't repeat it. (Repeating a rumor allows it to gain credibility.) Last, postpone comment. Decline to glorify the rumor, but be ready to make a full disclosure if the rumor is true.[48]

Office Gossip

The grapevine also serves as a means for spreading office gossip, which is not always just idle talk about others' affairs. Though many of our experiences with gossip seem to be negative, gossip can play a very positive role as well. By providing a medium for passing along stories about the organization's heroes and legends, gossip helps to forge a firm's culture. It can also help naive or unperceptive workers to sharpen their observational skills, process social information and learn about people, as they share information on what motivates their colleagues. Kiechel says that workers can benefit from gossip since it can, "just possibly, refine their understanding of people." Finally, gossip can help less powerful members of the organization to deal with their lack of influence by providing an outlet for their frustration and by enabling them to know what those in power are up to. The best users of gossip, says Kiechel, are those who "pass along news likely to improve relationships in the organization or to burnish someone's reputation" but who are also likely to "stamp out gossip that might be harmful to reputations or personal ties."[49]

BARRIERS TO GOOD COMMUNICATION

Many people have never learned the skills involved in speaking, writing, and listening effectively, and the majority of work-related problems, researchers believe, are caused by poor communication skills. We can identify several types of communication problems. **Miscommunication** results when the message a receiver receives differs from the message that the sender intended. **Discommunication** occurs when a sender purposely distorts a message in order to confuse, distract, and undermine. Communication failures occur when people exchange little or no meaningful information. Statements like "That's not what I heard you say," "I never got that memo," or "I didn't think that's what you meant" are signs of communication failures. Organizational structure and members' communication habits and skills contribute to—or detract from—the quality of communication in the law firm. Because we form our communication habits over a lifetime of interacting with others, we often find people who are unaware of the quality of their own communication styles. Some are unwilling to communicate. Others choose to distort communication, for a variety of reasons. Though many communication problems are quite unintentional, people create most barriers to effective communications through (1) their frame of reference, (2) selective listening, (3) value judgments, (4) semantics, (5) omissions, (6) time pressures, (7) filtering, and (8) perceptual errors and bias.

Frame of Reference

People from different backgrounds see and hear things through different frames of reference. This perceptual filtering can result in conflicting expectations and interpretations.

Selective Listening

As listeners, we are apt to attend to what appeals to us and what we want to hear and to ignore the rest. We may spend up to 75 percent of every workday communicating, but within a week, we forget over 75 percent of what we've heard. Within three weeks, we remember only about 25 percent. What we do hear, we hear with only about 25 percent accuracy. These seemingly unintentional losses represent only part of the difficulties we experience in our personal communication patterns.[50]

Value Judgments

We tend to make quick initial judgments about communicators and about whether their messages are right or wrong. Afterward, we evaluate all the information that follows in light of that one initial judgment. For instance, if we don't approve of long hair on middle-aged males, we won't easily accept—in other words, find value in—messages from such people. Once we doubt a person's credibility, we tend always to doubt it, even if he or she later proves trustworthy and truthful.

Semantics

Once spoken, words assume a life of their own. A word heard by others means more than what we want it to mean. If you were to say, "That's just like a lawyer," *lawyer* to one person might imply someone who makes a leech-like living off of others' woes; to another, the word might connote a hard-working, dedicated person of intelligence and superb persuasive skills. Words are arbitrary symbols: as such, they can be ambiguous and abstract. A careless or inappropriate choice of words can create massive communication barriers.

Omissions

We often leave out parts of a message that would have resulted in more accurate communications. Sometimes this exclusion is intentional. It can also occur because of reasons such as oversight or carelessness.

Time Pressures

Time seems to be one of our most limited commodities. Not surprisingly, time pressures influence how we send and receive messages. Because we rarely have enough time, it seems only logical to conserve what we have by taking communication shortcuts. When this happens in a law firm, people who should be consulted are left out, messages are incomplete, and less-than-ideal communication is the result. Time pressures may force us to choose between communicating imperfectly or not communicating at all.

Filtering

Filtering is the process of manipulating the accuracy of communication by removing negative data from a message or by altering the message to suit one's needs. Downward communication filters information so that subordinates hear only what those at the top want them to hear. Upward communication does the same thing, usually by removing anything unpleasant or by presenting only information that places the communicators in a favorable light.

Perceptual Errors and Biases

As we have seen, perceptual errors and biases interfere with accurate communication in many ways. Even the most convincing perceptions harbor a great deal of room for error. By listening selectively, remembering inaccurately, and interpreting erroneously, we erect barriers in the process of communication.

IMPROVING COMMUNICATION

Improving communication requires us to attend more closely to its elements by more accurately encoding the messages we send, giving more thought to our choice of media, and more carefully decoding the messages we receive. Managers can improve communication by making more use of feedback, by controlling the flow of information, by speaking and writing more accurately, and by allocating adequate time for communication. We can identify effective communicators by their personality traits and their interpersonal skills.

Personality Traits

Two personality traits that are conducive to good communication are a strong self-monitoring ability and a healthy self-esteem.

Self-Monitoring

Self-monitoring is the ability to act according to the nature of one's social environment. People who are adept at self-monitoring more accurately decode nonverbal messages in their environment and more skillfully control their own nonverbal displays. Self-monitoring is a social skill that enables a person to read a situation and adapt their behavior accordingly. This interpersonal savvy is essentially the ability to behave according to people's expectations: highly self-monitored people are not always what they appear to be, and they sometimes prove to be masters of deception.[51]

Healthy Self-Esteem

The quality of our self-acceptance, wrote logistics expert, U.S. senator, and academic leader S. I. Hayakawa, "determines the character of the reality we see."[52] The esteem we have for ourselves shapes our interactions with others; what we know about ourselves helps us to interpret others. If we have confidence in our positive attitudes toward others and believe that we are honest and well-meaning, we tend also to believe that others think the same way. Our being open rather than defensive helps to overcome communication barriers. Those of us who also possess a rich and positive frame of reference enjoy a special advantage in terms of communication. Having a broader perspective strengthens self-esteem and enables people to draw from a wide range of experiences in interpreting new events and experiences.

Interpersonal Skills

Our ability to communicate successfully with others often hinges on two simple factors, both of which are signs of effective interpersonal skills: our ability to be direct balanced with our ability to empathize.

The Ability to Be Direct

Saying what you really mean is sometimes difficult. People who learn to be direct are able to speak for themselves and to describe how they personally experience reality. They honestly express their reactions and feelings, readily offer their interpretations, and say precisely what they feel and want. Instead of saying "You would have liked the luncheon meeting," they would say exactly what they meant: "I wanted you to hear that speaker and am disappointed you didn't follow my advice." Instead of saying, "You seem tired today," they would say, "I see you staring off into space and not working at that case today." Their listeners know exactly where such people are coming from.

The Ability to Empathize

Empathy is the ability to share in someone else's feelings and emotions. Three abilities in fact constitute the ability to empathize: the ability to accurately perceive the *content* of another person's communication, the ability to sense the unexpressed *core meanings* of what a person is saying, and the ability to *respond* as if the feelings were one's own.[53] Guides for empathic communication suggest that one listen to the speaker's full story, recognize his or her feelings and emotions, and try to put oneself in the other person's position. To do this, you should avoid making value judgments and question carefully, using prompts such as "Um-hum," "And then...," or "What did you do?" To test your understanding of what someone has said, try restating not only what the speaker has said but what you think he or she is feeling, by saying, for example, "You must have quite a few mixed feelings" or "You feel as though you have some heavy pressures to deal with."[54] This kind of perception encourages honest exchanges.

HOW TO RUN SUCCESSFUL MEETINGS[55]

Employees complain about few activities as much as group meetings. Law firms, in some cases more so than other organizations, should tackle their share of blame for the poor use of meetings, and those who conduct meetings should acknowledge their own culpability as well. Nancy Fredericks, human resources manager for the Los Angeles-based law firm of Buchalter, Nemer, Fields & Younger, explains:

> How you conduct a meeting often influences the way your firm views you. Although meetings may amount to only a small percentage of your day, they often reflect 100 percent of your partners' experiences with you. This is one of the few forums that will afford you the opportunity to highlight your business acumen simultaneously for all of your partners. Make sure they are seeing a coherent, focused, bottom-line oriented manager. There is no bigger time waster than meetings without strong leadership.[56]

Having a worthwhile meeting requires good communication skills of those who plan the meeting and of those who attend. The art of running effective meetings is based on some simple rules.[57] As a law firm member who is interested in getting full value out of a meeting, you need to consider (1) when to have the meeting, (2) whom to invite, (3) how to make the best use of time, (4) how to arrange and set up, (5) how to conduct, (6) how to manage meeting dynamics, and (7) how to end effectively.

When to Have a Group Meeting

Although meetings are essential to communication and decision making in organizations, most people agree with Mark H. McCormack, who says, in *What They Don't Teach You at Harvard Business School,* that "most [meetings] go nowhere, accomplish nothing, and waste everyone's time."[58] Knowing when a meeting would be an effective use of time is the first step.

TABLE 12-4
Ten Commandments of Good Communication

1. Clarify your ideas before communicating.
   Plan. Think ahead: Who will receive it and who will be affected?
2. Examine each communication's true purpose.
   What do you really want to accomplish: Information? Initiate action? Influence? Then prepare your message around that goal.
3. Consider the TOTAL physical and human setting.
   Meaning and intent are conveyed by more than words: Use timing, setting, climate.
4. To plan communications, CONSULT.
   Let others participate. Those who help you also support you.
5. Know that OVERTONES add to the content.
   Your tone of voice, expression, body language, energy, receptivity to listeners—all impact the listeners and the message.
6. Communicate what's valuable to the listener.
   Get in the habit of starting with that premise; look at the message from the other person's point of view.
7. Follow up your communication.
   Ask and encourage questions to see if you were able to get your message across. Allow time for feedback.
8. Communicate for tomorrow as well as for today.
   Try to serve long-term interests and goals as well as immediate needs. Putting off disagreeable communication complicates and intensifies the difficulty of the message.
9. Be sure your actions support your words.
   The most persuasive communication is not what you say but what you do. Don't let your actions contradict your words.
10. Be a good listener.
    When we start talking, we often cease to listen. Listening demands concentrating on what is being said, context, and overtones.

SOURCE: "Ten Commandments of Good Communication." Reprinted, by permission of the publisher, from *MANAGEMENT REVIEW* (October 1955). Copyright © 1955. American Management Association, New York. All rights reserved.

First, managers should ask themselves: Is this meeting necessary? If there are other ways to share information, worker time is too valuable to spend on a meeting. People who hold meetings simply for the sake of doing so are making counterproductive power plays by attempting to show who is in charge. Each meeting should warrant the expenditures of time, energy, and money that it entails. Estimate the hourly cost of having each person in attendance and determine whether the purpose of your meeting merits its costs. If it does, you should then decide the following:

- Do you need information from several people at once?
- Do you need to develop feelings of commitment to outcomes?
- Is there a complex decision that needs to be made by many people?
- Do you need a variety of skills and information in order to make decisions?
- Is there a need for an agreed-upon division of labor?
- Is there a need to develop and process ideas for better communication?

Answering yes to all or most of these questions would justify the decision to call a meeting.

Whom to Invite

Though the size of a meeting never indicates its effectiveness, usually the fewer the participants, the greater the productivity. Mark McCormack's rule is "A meeting's productivity is inversely proportionate to the number of people attending it." Meetings that become too large tend to be used more for informational purposes than decision making.[59] To determine the most effective and the most necessary constituency for a meeting, ask yourself these questions:

- Whom do you need to involve, either for their expertise or for political reasons?
- Do you have the right number of people for the task?

- Do you have the right representation for the task, in terms of departments, levels, and groups?
- Have you allowed three members for close work groups, five to seven for other tasks?
- Do your attendees share common goals or values?
- Have you planned a homogeneous group for solidarity and commitment or a heterogeneous group for diversity and creativity?
- Can you afford to have those you would like to have at your meeting?
- How much will your meeting cost in terms of time?

How to Prepare

You must know clearly what the meeting needs to accomplish, and you must communicate this knowledge to the others involved. To do so, you should prepare and circulate copies of an agenda before the meeting takes place.

Establishing an Agenda

Do not underestimate the power of an agenda. The agenda becomes the rule for controlling the meeting. It outlines the topics for discussion, shapes the flow of the meeting, clarifies responsibilities for and indicates the order of presentations and participation, helps to determine the amount of work to be done, sets time limits, and influences the effectiveness of the meeting. For attorney meetings and whenever appropriate, establish a process by which participants can include items on the agenda. This encourages people to be open and involved at the meeting and to take responsibility for the decisions and contributions they make.

Organizing Participation and Time

You should organize participation by arranging in advance those who will make presentations or present proposals. Communicate to all participants what the meeting is to accomplish. While the meeting is in progress, maintain boundaries between work groups; do not reward work that interferes with the work of other groups. Successful meetings come about not through happenstance but through planning. You shape in advance what actually happens at a meeting by carefully reviewing your objectives and by determining the most effective use of time. You should be sure also that the participants are clearly aware of the arrangements. Provide logistics for the meeting in writing, describing where the meeting will be, when it will be, and how long it will last. Establish and use policies for providing advance notice, and observe proper meeting etiquette. Choose workable times that respect the attendees' needs. Use early morning or late afternoon time slots to accommodate attorneys' and paralegals' schedules, if necessary. If yours is a firm that uses computers to integrate communication, there are software programs that can help you to schedule meetings at times when the firm's professional members and others are available. Table 12–5 outlines the process of preparing for a meeting.

How to Conduct a Meeting

Just as you would not think of driving without first learning how to drive, you must first answer certain questions before you can run a meeting effectively: Have you established ground rules for the meeting process and work rules for the participants' activities? Have you set policies that preclude duplication and interference between and among subgroups? How will the group make major decisions? By majority rule? A two-thirds vote? Consensus? In addition, you must make two decisions. First, you must decide whether to conduct the meeting formally and, in the case of a larger group, whether you should follow *Robert's Rules of Order*. Secondly, you must decide what reporting mechanisms to use in recording information from the meeting. Table 12–6 outlines procedures for opening and conducting a meeting.

Robert's Rules of Order. This classic set of rules for running meetings provides for the protection of the rights of the minority and of the majority. It ensures an orderly process by outlining procedures for responding to disagreement and political plays. Too many meetings are sidetracked by personal agendas or are dominated by aggressive members. *Robert's Rules* enables you to run a professional meeting that shows flexibility and concern for the entire group. For small groups, *Robert's Rules* offers modified procedures that safeguard participation.

Reporting Mechanisms. You should identify reporting mechanisms in advance and adhere to their use throughout the meeting. Such mechanisms include the written log-style format known as minutes and reports to the firm's executive committee, executive director, or other members of top management.

CHAPTER 12 / COMMUNICATIONS

TABLE 12-5
A Meeting Preparation Checklist

Have you arranged and distributed the agenda items,
- Being sure to put unimportant items last?
- Indicating work that participants should do in advance by scheduling report times on the agenda?
- Encouraging participants to add and suggest agenda items, if at all possible?
- Setting a time limit for the meeting that falls within a one and one-half hour maximum?

Have you done the advance work,
- Communicating with all major participants beforehand?
- Clarifying expectations for those who will give presentations?
- Notifying those with special responsibilities?
- Requiring those who cannot attend to notify you in advance?
- Having absentees arrange for replacements, when appropriate?

Have you made the proper arrangements,
Selecting meeting space that was
- Central or neutral?
- Isolated enough to minimize disturbances?
- Conducive to your goals?
- Suitable for your participants?

Overseeing the setup by
- Ensuring adequate and suitable seating and furnishings?
- Arranging the necessary equipment and materials?
- Providing refreshments, if customary or appropriate?

TABLE 12-6
Steps for Conducting an Effective Meeting

1. Begin on time.
2. Circulate an attendance sheet for each participant to sign.
3. Conduct the preliminaries:
   - Welcome the participants.
   - Introduce participants who are not known to the group.
   - Make any necessary announcements pertaining to the group's work.
   - Appoint someone to take minutes or notes, if necessary.
   - Assign someone the task of distributing any materials you were unable to distribute in advance.
4. Conduct the business of the meeting by
   - Adhering to the order set on the agenda,
   - Defining and restating the group's task,
   - Using time limits as guidelines, and
   - Summarizing group decisions and progress throughout the meeting.

How to Manage Group Dynamics[60]

Managing group dynamics is a true skill. Nonetheless, you need not be an expert in sociology or psychology to manage the forces that influence a group's performance. To give yourself an idea of how a particular group might interact, review the group's past progress, if it has met before. Then, during the actual meeting, follow these rules:

- As early as possible, request reports from all those to whom you preassigned work.
- Don't allow just a few participants to monopolize meeting time. Draw in contributors, if need be.

- Sustain the flow of the meeting and review progress.
- Clarify misunderstandings and misinterpretations.
- Do not allow interruptions.
- Do not deviate from the agenda or allow speakers to be sidetracked.
- Postpone for later all issues that are not on the agenda.
- Allow periods of silence, to allow participants time to think and to process information.
- Direct energy away from conflict and toward issues.
- Value dissent and divergence. Both are essential to quality decisions.
- Under no conditions, allow ANY sarcasm, personal attacks.
- Do not allow anyone to diminish or minimize the importance of the group's work.
- Review the progress of the group on each agenda item, from time to time.

How to Conclude Meetings and Follow Up

A meeting should not only begin on time, but it should also end at the finishing time specified in its agenda. Because events at a meeting usually affect more than the participants, the minutes of the meeting, its written record, are useful for many reasons, as Nancy Fredericks explains:

> Minutes are the long-term memory of the meeting. They become the tool for precisely delegating responsibilities. Minutes should concentrate on specific decisions made, responsibilities assigned for follow-up and deadlines for actions to be taken. They are also a vehicle for informing absent members about what went on at the meeting. They may occasionally be used to circulate information about procedures or policies at the firm.[61]

When concluding a meeting, summarize the group's decisions, assign follow-up where needed, review assignments and projected completion dates, and determine future meeting dates, if necessary. Thank the participants for their time and contributions, and remind them that they will receive minutes, a summary of responsibilities, assignments, and due dates, and information regarding future meetings, if any. If you complete these tasks, you've run your meeting well.

QUESTIONS FOR DISCUSSION AND REVIEW

1. Give examples of effective and ineffective managers you have known and describe their communication styles. How did their communication skills determine their success, or lack thereof?
2. Describe the elements of the communication process, using one of the following situations:
   a. The morning greeting you give the person who works next to you.
   b. A phone call home to check on your child or a sick roommate or spouse.
   c. The dirty look you give someone who has just lied to you.
   d. A letter from a lawyer to a client.
3. Explain why we consider words and nonverbal communication to be symbols. Give specific examples.
4. What factors distinguish persuasive communications from unpersuasive ones? Describe things you could do to increase your ability to be persuasive.
5. Analyze your effectiveness in writing, speaking, and listening. For each skill, choose an objective that would help you to improve your ability.
6. Analyze briefly the flow of communication in a specific organization. Is communication one-way or two-way? In what ways do members participate in a diagonal communication? How effective is communication in the organization as a whole?
7. What barriers to effective communication do you see as the most difficult to overcome? Explain.
8. What are the characteristics of effective communicators? Choose a communicator that you admire and explain how he or she exemplifies these characteristics.
9. Explain how, in a meeting, you would go about channeling participants' attention and energy away from conflict and toward the issues and work at hand.

EXPERIENTIAL EXERCISES

I. Reporting In

Choose a topic from the following list and write an outline for a report to be presented to the executive committee of a law firm.
1. A proposal for updating the firm's employee manual.
2. A plan for adopting a specialized form of computer software.
3. Strategies for implementing a continuing professional development program for paralegals.
4. A proposal outlining salary grades and merit increases for paralegals, based on professional preparation and certification, tenure with the firm, years of experience, and performance.
5. A plan for boosting firm morale.

Your proposal must include a cover letter, a table of contents, an abstract, and your recommendations. (Your instructor will supply you with a supplement on preparing reports, if you need one.)

II. Taking an Audience by the Ears

You have been asked to make a presentation at a meeting. It will be in the middle of the afternoon, and you are concerned not only that speeches at that time are difficult enough but also that yours is a potentially dull topic. Thinking back, you recall speakers you have heard who made instant connections with their audiences by grabbing their attention right from the start. You recall that many of those speakers brought their topic to life by using examples, humor, or stories or analogies that sometimes were factual and sometimes fictional. For each of the following situations, develop an "ear-opener," a story or analogy that would capture an audience's attention. Tape record the opener and the first few lines of your talk. You need not write and record an entire speech: just enough to show how your introduction leads into the main body of your talk.

   Example A. The local LAMA chapter has asked you to speak on employee evaluation.

   Example B. Your executive management committee has asked you to speak on the project management practices of the paralegal staff.

   Example C. The guidance counselors at a local high school have asked your firm to provide someone to speak to a select group of ten students about careers in law office management.

   When you finish taping the three sample openings, listen to the playback and critique your material and your vocal quality. In what ways do the openings seem effective or ineffective? What might you do to improve your speaking voice? Try your openers out on friends or classmates and ask for feedback. What do they hear in your voice or your message that you seem to have missed?

III. Feedback Skills Questionnaire*

For each item, circle the number that best describes your tendencies when giving feedback.

---

*SOURCE: M. Sashkin and W. C. Morris, *Experiencing Management* (Reading, Mass.: Addison-Wesley Publishing Company, 1987): 10–17. Reprinted with permission.

1. To what extent do you use terms like "excellent," "good," or "bad" when you give someone feedback?

1	2	3	4	5	6	7
always use such terms			sometimes use such terms			rarely or never use such terms

2. How often do you provide specific examples or concrete details when giving feedback?

1	2	3	4	5	6	7
rarely give specific details			sometimes give specific details			always give specific details

3. Do you generally first ask whether the other person wants feedback?

1	2	3	4	5	6	7
assume feedback is wanted			sometimes check to see if feedback is wanted			always check to see if feedback is wanted

4. When you give someone feedback, is it generally because you want to get a load off your chest?

1	2	3	4	5	6	7
generally I "unload" with feedback			sometimes I "unload" by giving feedback			I rarely "unload" when I give feedback

5. Do you generally give feedback as soon as possible or do you usually wait for an appropriate time, such as an appraisal session?

1	2	3	4	5	6	7
generally I wait for a good time			usually I give feedback close to the time of the behavior			I always give feedback immediately

6. When you give feedback, is it quite clear what that person could actually do to make effective use of your feedback?

1	2	3	4	5	6	7
feedback I give is not usually focused on applications			feedback I give is sometimes focused on applications			feedback I give is always focused on applications

Scoring: Helpful feedback is descriptive, not evaluative; specific rather than general; tuned to the receiver's needs, not those of the sender; requested, not imposed; immediately relevant, or follows as closely as is reasonable the behavior it addresses; and useful, not inapplicable. To estimate your skill at providing feedback, add the numbers you have circled and compare your score to the following scale:

> 31 and above = Very high skill
> 29–30 = Above average skill
> 24–28 = Average skill
> 22–23 = Below average skill
> 21 and below = Very low skill

CHAPTER 13

Change, Conflict, and Stress

LEARNING OBJECTIVES

After completing this chapter, you should be able to:

- Understand change and the causes of change;
- Describe techniques for controlling organizational changes;
- Explain the three phases of the change process;
- Define the role of the change agent;
- Understand resistance to change and how to overcome it;
- Describe the nature and causes of conflict;
- Explain strategies for effectively dealing with conflict;
- Identify the sources and symptoms of stress in the work setting;
- Discuss the effects of stress; and
- Develop strategies for dealing effectively with stress.

FOCUS FROM THE FIELD

Trudy Cashman: Change and the Ability to Prosper

Gertrude M. Cashman has been director of administration and human resources at the Boston, Massachusetts, law firm of Goodwin, Procter & Hoar, P.C., since 1985. She previously served as director of personnel at the firm from 1974 through 1978. Ms. Cashman, who holds an M.B.A. from the executive management program at Suffolk University, brings a depth of experience to her present position. Before joining Goodwin, Procter & Hoar, she served as president of the management consulting firm G.M. Johnson & Associates and as director of personnel at the Boston office of Arthur Andersen & Company, an international public accounting firm.

What kinds of changes do law firms face?

Law firms of the eighties differed from those same law firms in the sixties and seventies in terms of size, composition of staff, and management structure; in terms of how they recruited, trained, evaluated, and compensated legal and nonlegal staff; and in the way they produced their written product. The monumental changes experienced by law firms, their owners/partners, and their staff (associate, paralegal, administrative, and support) in the eighties will seem insignificant when viewed against the changes already experienced in the nineties and what we as legal administrators can expect to experience during the remainder of the decade.

Change is inevitable, but how can law firms manage the change process?

To a great extent, a law firm's ability to anticipate the need for change and then be able to plan for and control the change process will dictate its ability to prosper in the increasingly competitive environment in which it operates. Law firms face changes in location, size, governance, management structure, staff composition, and use of technology. Some of these changes can be planned for, all must be managed, and astute and capable managers will control the impact of each change as much as possible. Relocations, for example, can usually be planned for far in advance. But a needed downsizing may not have been anticipated. In fact, a number of national law firms implemented downsizing during 1990–91, but did not admit to their own staff that they were engaged in what could be considered a reasonable business response to a deteriorating economy. While those firms may not have been able to anticipate or plan for the needed downsizing, they could have better controlled the adverse publicity. They could have also allayed the apprehensions of their own staff by being honest and by effectively communicating their need to "rightsize" their firms.

What role has technology played?

The use of technology within law firms over the past twenty years has been responsible for more change, conflict, and stress than any other change agent. Large law firms traditionally armed attorneys with a lined pad, pencil or pen, a piece of dictating equipment, and a telephone. These tools and a good legal secretary provided all the support an attorney needed to practice law. In any modern law firm, an attorney has a PC to draft instruments, may schedule the calendar, and may access computerized data bases located in the firm or through outside sources such as WESTLAW®, LEXIS®, and NEXIS. The attorney also has a telephone, voice mail, access to fax equipment, and a secretary, often shared with one or more other attorneys. The secretary also has a PC with access to word-processing software. The attorney or secretary may input time directly and have access to recorded time summaries and/or billing information—all through their PCs and all immediate. The road from the first scenario to the present-day scenario has not been smooth in most cases, and most legal managers have had their share of failures. Any change in technology—whether a change in word-processing software or the process of moving from a centralized, highly controlled mainframe environment to a local area network requires lots of planning, communication, training and retraining where necessary, and an awareness of what is likely to create the most stress. A good administrator will learn from experience and know when to expand training, augment secretarial staff, or just when to call a halt on a Friday afternoon and spring for pizza.

Are there unique aspects to dealing with law firm change, conflict, and stress?

There are unique stressors in law firms that relate directly to each individual's position and level of responsibility within the firm and within the culture and management style of the firm. Partners are faced with the need to continually nurture and expand their client base in an increasingly competitive and hostile environment. Associates and paralegals need to demonstrate outstanding legal, interpersonal, and communication skills, with associates having the additional pressure of a generally faster-paced evaluation process. Secretaries and paralegals often work for more than one person, each of whom competes for the secretary's time. Administrators live with the additional dichotomy of trying to serve two constituencies—firm management and staff. Each of these groups is composed of individuals who all face the ordinary stresses of day-to-day living, such as sickness, death, divorce, a spouse's loss of a job, birth, weddings, care of children and parents, and on and on. Many of today's employees are part of two-income families and have all the problems associated with trying to balance work and family. Employees within law firms face all the usual life cycle stressors plus the stress of working in a fast-paced, intellectually stimulating yet demanding professional services environment.

What can firm management do to help employees deal with this stress?

Firm management has an obligation to provide a pleasant environment where all are treated with dignity and respect. It needs to recognize that there are times when employees and/or their families may be experiencing problems related to drug and/or alcohol dependency. To help them, the firm should have a vehicle in place, such as an employee assistance program. Firm management should also recognize and defuse possible excessively stressful conditions. Firm management must articulate its position in regard to its expectations as to how employees are to be treated, and talk to offenders. The difficult partner who goes through a number of secretaries should hear from the managing partner that he or she needs to learn how to retain a secretary. Firm management should provide opportunities for participatory management and should welcome suggestions from staff. It should also foster an environment which encourages mutual assistance between departments. It should encourage a propensity for praise. It is the wise lawyer or administrator who learns quickly to say "Thank you" often and loudly for a job well done.

Change is traumatic, even when you choose it. But change can also be thrilling. It is a chance to defy the unpredictability of life...
(Jane Pauley, interview on "The Today Show")[1]

> **W**hat people often mean by getting rid of conflict is getting rid of diversity, and it is of the utmost importance that they should not be considered the same. We may wish to abolish conflict, but we cannot get rid of diversity. We must face life as it is and understand that diversity is its most essential feature. . . . Fear of difference is dread of life itself. . . . Conflict may be thought of as not necessarily a wasteful outbreak of incompatibilities, but a normal process by which socially valuable differences register themselves for the enrichment of all concerned.
> (Mary Parker Follett, *Creative Experience*)[2]
>
> **H**ow we feel about ourselves, the joy we get from living, ultimately depend directly on how the mind filters and interprets everyday experiences. Whether we are happy depends on inner harmony, not on the controls we are able to exert over the great forces of the universe.
> (Mihaly Csikszentmihalyi, *Flow: The Psychology of Optimal Experience*)[3]

CHANGE

The Nature of Change

Changes affect people, the physical world, and all of society. We are not strangers to change. Each of us knows the opportunities and the reversals that change brings. We have all worked through changes at every point of our lives. What is change? **Change** is the process of evolving from one form or state to another. All of life is the process of evolving. We are born, we grow, and develop, physically and mentally, all within the context of a continuously changing environment. Life evolves, and not to evolve with it is to regress or to atrophy. Some of us see change as threatening, equating it with instability and personal losses. Others see change in terms of growth and opportunity. But almost everyone fears being unable to control the changes that he or she experiences. To change too quickly, for instance, is often to depend on fate and fortune, often without direction.

Some, like John Naisbitt and Patricia Aburdene, believe that change takes place in organizations only when there is a confluence of changing values and economic necessity.''[4] In this chapter, we will examine causes and effects of change, the barriers to constructive change, and the conflicts that arise because of change and difference. In addition, we will look at how we respond to forces that make demands on us to change and to become what we are not able nor choose to become. As the renowned psychologist Csikszentmihalyi observes, ''The universe was not designed with the comfort of human beings in mind. . . . There is not much we can do as individuals to change the way the universe runs.''[5] Nonetheless each of us can hope to contribute in some way to the order that makes our portion of the universe a better one. Managers can find in this hoped-for contribution a particular opportunity and calling.

Forces of Change

Change occurs because of the differing needs and values of employees, technological developments, business and economic forces, social forces, and organizational forces.

Needs and Values

The needs and values of workers, including those of owners as well as employees, influence all decisions in an organization. When their beliefs, particularly their most important values, differ, each side demands change. The conflict from strongly divergent personal values can transform the workplace, partially or entirely.

Technological Development

The discovery and adoption of new technologies continue to bring far-reaching changes to the law firm and a competitive market necessitates its keeping pace. Though the expression ''technological changes'' seems harmless nowadays, technology has almost single-handedly revolutionized the practice of law. Computer use has become commonplace in law firms, for activities ranging from the tracking of cases, costs, time, documents, and revenues to practice-specific applications in legal specialty areas, such as real estate, collections, and bankruptcy. Law practice research now depends on data bases like LEXIS® and WESTLAW®, and CD-ROM reference materials will soon change the traditional image of the law firm library. This technological progress has led to new kinds of conflicts and pressures. It has produced unique forms of stress which are intensified in the law firm because of the time and confidentiality issues that are at stake. In addition, all technology does not make life easier. All software is not user-friendly; in fact, observes *Wall Street Journal* staff reporter William Bulkely, sometimes "a combination of economic factors, technical difficulties, and the creative pride of software designers conspire to make software hard." [6] (Moreover, some of us simply don't catch on that easily.) In spite of its costs and challenges, law firm computer use has increased steadily, with over one out of three attorneys having workstations at their desks in 1989.[7] The result is that many firms are struggling to put procedures, policies, and systems in place that will reflect technology-related issues, such as new concerns about confidentiality, accuracy, and control and new forms of worker stress and inequity. For example, some firms allow workers the freedom of off-site computer work, which they may return to the office by modem or fax, while employees who do not own computers must work within the firm, under traditional supervision and standards of accountability. Technological change brings conflicts and challenges, and yet, as management consultants Joseph Stanislao and Bettie Stanislao note, "Change is inevitable if an organization is to survive in a world of developing technology and new consumer and employee demands." [8]

Business and Economic Forces

Many forces related to business and to the economy bring about change. Market drives and competition, the economic pulse with its downturns and upswings, and field-specific pressures all lead to change by increasing the demand for newer and better ways to provide services.

Social Forces

Social forces are among the prime movers and shapers of change. The rights of workers, the quality of work life, the effects of the economy on people, issues of equity and justice, and a concern for the environment and future conditions are only a few of the social forces that produce change.

Organizational Forces

Forces within the organization also lead to change. For example, a firm that chooses to grow and expand is apt to need new structures, new processes, and new kinds of workers. The firm's efforts to meet these needs will have a ripple effect on the existing organization, bringing changes to those who are already part of the firm. In addition, changes in laws or their interpretations result in changes and adjustments for those in the practice of law. **Organizational development** programs enable law firms to respond to changes by having problem-solving and renewal processes in place. By institutionalizing a collaborative approach to organizational development, a firm can be continually ready for and open to change. This kind of preparation becomes a requisite for success.[9]

Control of Change

Change without a sense of direction is change that is out of control. It can lead to chaos. To be effective, change needs to be well thought out, based on a vision for the future state of the organization, a philosophical commitment to a need or a desire for growth, and an appreciation for the constraints that lead to successful change.

Vision

To be successful, notes Warren Bennis, a CEO must create a "compelling vision of a desired state of affairs." The first step to controlling change is to project how that change will fit and work in a particular organization. The first ingredient, Bennis believes, is "a powerful vision—a whole new sense of where a company is going and how it is going to get there." [10]

Growth

Until the 1990s, American law firms experienced what Stephen Labaton has labeled as "twenty years of nonstop growth." [11] Figure 13–1 depicts growth rates between 1986 and 1990 for the top five New York law firms and the top five firms in five major cities. Firms everywhere have mirrored these patterns. Until recently, larger size has brought many economic advan-

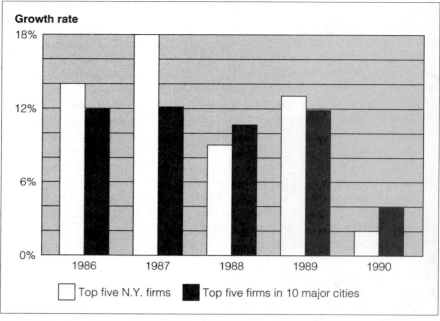

FIGURE 13-1
Average Growth Rate of Law Firm Employment

SOURCE: Stephen Labaton, "A Difficult Year, But with Potential," *The National Law Journal* (12 November 1990). Copyright © 1990, *The National Law Journal.* Reprinted with permission.

tages for law firm stakeholders. It also has created material prosperity and career opportunities for employees, which has, in many cases, resulted in good morale. To maintain the status quo is to stifle success, or so it appears. Expansion has always seemed more desirable than stagnation or decline, but many firms have learned that not all growth is healthy. For one thing, growth does not necessarily correspond to increased size. Being big goes along with the traditional American concept of success, but some law firms have learned—perhaps from Japan's Sei Shonagon, who wrote over a thousand years ago, "All things small, no matter what they are, all things small are beautiful"[12]—that "big" is not always better. Firms that choose to grow have found that growth brings additional challenges to members at all levels. Growth of any kind requires, for example, that managers adjust to changing procedures, methods, and equipment, as well as to new personnel requirements.[13]

Constraints

As mergers and acquisitions sometimes show, growth that serves only the interests of a few can lead to economic and personal disaster. Law firms that are considering growth must ask these critical questions: What kind of growth are we choosing? Will it benefit the entire firm? For how long? Growth can create good feelings, represent fulfillment of the American dream, and build optimism. As the tool of a greedy few, however, it can do just the opposite.[14]

Leadership Climate. The restrictions that promote successful change are a product of the law firm's leadership climate and its organizational climate. If the managing partners or those responsible for the firm's management are unreceptive to change, there is little chance for its success. A chilly reception for change-related proposals puts on ice any plans for progress, and inertia results. To function, to keep up with the competition, and to survive, a firm's leadership must be responsive to necessary change.

Organizational Climate. An organization's structure and its culture both shape the climate for change. Because being up-to-date is so imperative, change in the law firm is an extraordinary challenge. Major changes in the practice of law cannot help but affect each firm and each of its members, from the top down. Partners are fired for less-than-brilliant performance, firms merge, go international, set up satellites, and are restructured from the inside out. "In a tough legal environment, there is tremendous mobility that did not exist in prior years, and lawyers are moving more and more between law firms," says a partner at a prestigious Philadelphia firm.[15] One law firm consultant says, "From time immemorial, partnership was really a life commitment and problem partners were basically taken care of." Now, he observes, "we've trained our present management to be so bottom-line oriented that some may have become a bit hard-hearted and short-sighted."[16] Changes in how a law firm treats its people are far-reaching. Both major and minor changes of this type result from what is happening in the firm's formal and informal organizational structures and in the firm's climate. First, the formal organization promulgates policies and practices that either foster or inhibit change.[17] Though some firms have structures that welcome change, in others the very culture of the firm inhibits change. Law firm members who wish to bring about change need to approach the process with an ability to predict how the firm's partners will react to their proposals and an ability to listen patiently and thoughtfully to responses and feedback. They will also need a good support network and connections to the firm's decision makers. The firm itself must be able to build consensus among its members, an ability that is necessary not only for promoting a change-oriented environment but for ensuring in general the healthy functioning of a professional organization.[18] Secondly, the firm's informal structures either promote or hamper change. If the firm's culture and traditions run counter to change, it will be very difficult to overturn the status quo. In such a firm, change opposes the values and expectations of those who are able to influence it.[19]

THEORIES OF CHANGE

The Change Process

One of the most popular theories of change is Kurt Lewin's explanation, based on a law of physics which states essentially that the position of an object changes according to the forces being exerted on that object. Change will occur when the forces from one direction are stronger than the forces from another direction. Equilibrium results when both the restraining and the driving forces are equal and no new movement occurs. Lewin proposes that all change results from a **process of change** that consists of three stages: unfreezing, change, and refreezing. Imagine the status quo as a solid form, like a block of ice.

Unfreezing

In the change process, unfreezing occurs when the driving forces for change, triggered by some internal or external event or series of events, challenge the firm's equilibrium and status quo. This thawing of current values, attitudes, behaviors, and structures takes place when the restraining forces in the firm—all those factors that resist and hinder change—are weakened and overcome, leaving the firm open to change and ready for its benefits.

Change

When the driving forces of change have overcome the resisting forces protecting the status quo, the dynamics of change can occur, and the firm and its members are motivated to implement changes. The firm creates new structures, procedures, and policies in response to internal and external forces, and its members develop new values, attitudes, and behaviors.

Refreezing

Once the firm has adapted to the forces of change, equilibrium reappears. This period of refreezing stabilizes the change and solidifies the new patterns of being and doing. Refreezing will occur only if the firm's members accept the change, which will happen only if they can associate the change with positive experiences. Through refreezing, the change becomes the new status quo, which, in turn, will one day be known as the old way of doing things.

The Change Agent

A **change agent** is someone who provides ideas, approaches, and perspectives that help an organization to respond to challenges in new ways.[20] The role of the change agent may be filled by someone outside of the organization, such as a consultant; by someone new to the organization, such as a new and perhaps enlightened

ANOTHER LOOK

The Challenge of Office Changes

Gertrude Cashman of the Boston law firm Goodwin, Procter & Hoar sees a law firm's move to a new location as a major change. Cashman explains how the relocation of a law firm presents several challenges to an administrator, who sometimes must address competing needs.

BEFOREHAND: CLIENTS. Long before a move is accomplished, letterhead must be designed, printed, and available from day one at the new location. Announcements must be designed, mailed to clients and vendors, and run in local and national newspapers as well as professional journals. Some firms want to show off their new space to clients, and it is really the administrator and support staff who plan the function, develop an invitation list (with input from attorneys), develop and mail invitations, and arrange for a client open house.

PARTNERS. A relocation generally means an increase in expenses accompanied by the stress of trying to increase revenues accordingly. It is crucial that space needs be accurately planned for. Too little space means an inability to service clients appropriately or another move. Too much space means expenses are too high and partners' income suffers.

ASSOCIATES, PARALEGALS, AND OTHER LEGAL STAFF. Almost any change in office location means changes in secretarial assignments and, in some cases, ratios. Some firms use the move as an opportunity to improve existing ratios of legal staff to secretaries. Whenever a change of this magnitude occurs, conflicts arise and it is usually the administrator's job to lessen stress related to the move. One way to help reduce stress is to set up a stream of communications to the entire office relating to different aspects of the move.

OFFICE AND SECRETARIAL ASSIGNMENTS. Advise people as soon as possible. Publish information, but not before talking individually to all parties involved.

THE MOVE. Inform everyone of their role in the move. Inform them of the expected occupancy date. Let everyone know how on schedule the move is. Tell them if the space can be viewed or not. Communicate all expectations regarding packing, marking boxes, files, location of furniture, etc. Give information in detail and often. If you expect to move over a weekend, make sure that everyone understands that the office will close at noon on Friday and that movers will take over your space. Expect complications. There will be one packing box misplaced. One phone won't be working. Set up a help line. Staff it with individuals who will direct all messages to the appropriate parties. Arrange extra help for unpacking, hanging personal pictures, awards, etc.

LEADERSHIP. Any change brings a unique set of problems. Managing partners and firm administrators need to have thought through the possible repercussions of any specific change and planned accordingly. By the time a firm has moved, firm management will have held a series of meetings with representatives of various groups to determine their space needs and wants prior to designing the new space. It is even more crucial once a relocation has been accomplished to get early input as to the functionality and efficiency of the design. Even when it is not possible to modify the space, workers need to feel their input is sought and valued. In the case of a move, most experienced administrators will be able to anticipate conflicts that might arise just because the staff is packing or unpacking and will arrange for extra help. Even an experienced administrator might not anticipate a whole set of problems related to going from a smaller footprint to a larger one. In such a case it takes longer for secretaries to get to the mail/message center; it takes longer for them to go to the printer; secretaries are tired and unhappy; and attorneys are annoyed because secretaries are away from their desks for longer periods of time.

AFTERWARDS. After the physical move has been completed, meet each day with administrative staff to ensure that each person who has a problem has been contacted and knows where you are with regard to solving that problem. More importantly, give public credit to all those who assisted in the move. A pat on the back makes the recipient feel good, valued, and ensures continued cooperation.

SOURCE: Gertrude Cashman. Interview on change and conflict in the law firm, 26 April 1991.

1. Think of a move in which you've participated. Did you find it particularly stressful? Why or why not?
2. Describe the psychological effects that you think relocation is likely to have on a law firm's legal professionals and on support staff. For which group is moving apt to be more traumatic? Why?

manager or someone hired to be a catalyst; or by someone who has been part of the organization, understands it, and has a commitment to a new and possibly better way of doing things. All change agents realize that change, like leadership, consists of a process of influence. The use of power is necessary to bring about change. No matter how sophisticated and well designed the change is, leadership is the factor that will most enable workers to accept it. The change agent acts as an intervener, facilitating the process of unsettling the status quo and engineering the meltdown that clears the way for change.

Resistance to Change

"Change," observe Rensis Likert and Jane Gibson Likert, "almost always is accompanied by tensions, anxieties, resistance, and conflict."[21] Workers who don't accept changes may express their opposition in the form of sabotage, poor performance, unfounded grievances and complaints, and absenteeism. They will seem more remote, to colleagues as well as to supervisors. Their work will take more time to do and will have more errors, and somehow they will seem to have less time for doing "extras."[22] Though workers may resist change in hundreds of creative and not-so-creative ways, most of their resistance is based on fear: fear of loss, of instability, of the unknown, of being left out, and of damage to their self-interests.

Fear of Loss

At the heart of most resistance to change is a fear of some kind of personal loss. This loss may be as straight forward as the loss of some benefit, such as income, or more subtle, such as the loss of status or prestige, a loss of comfort, or a loss of trust and confidence in relationships with colleagues or superiors. Rosabeth Moss Kanter suggests that workers also may fear a loss of control, feeling that change is being done *to* them and not *by* them, or, thinking that the change would have been unnecessary had they performed their jobs correctly, they may fear to lose face. These performance doubts may trigger another fear in workers: that the change will render their current skills and talents useless or obsolete after the change.[23] Even a seemingly simple change, such as a change of desk location for a secretary, can trigger fears of loss. No matter how insignificant these fears may seem to others, they can be nerve-racking to the person experiencing them.

Fear of Disruption

For many people, traditions and life patterns are like the comfort and reassurance of a security blanket. After ten years, for example, you know how your boss acts. You've become accustomed to the people in your firm, to how things are done, to the unwritten rules, and to how much the firm expects of you. Change will leave you feeling unsettled or even unhappy, especially if the old ways were ones you liked.

Fear of the Unknown

No matter how good proposed changes seem, people will still be apprehensive. This "better-the-devil-you-know" uncertainty builds on the belief that change carries no guarantee of success.

Pressures from Others

Being around those who are opposed to change can sweep us into a ground swell of opposition in which we reinforce each other's fears and concerns as well as our perceptions of how senseless the change is or will be. Groups can oppose change in order to further their political interests and make power plays, to protect their values, to remove threats to the group or to its members, to protest their being uninvolved in the change process, or to profess genuine concern for the results the change will bring.

Fear of Exclusion

People are by nature social animals; as such, they fear being forgotten, isolated, or left out. At work, being kept in the dark about communications, being excluded from meetings that should have included you, and being the last to know that your paralegal position is the one scheduled for transfer to another area are not unlike the childhood crises that said to us, "You don't count." Besides reassuring people that they are important as individuals to the change effort as a whole, participation in the change process strengthens the support of those law firm members who are involved in it, builds responsibility and accountability, and fosters a team-effort mentality rather than a climate that promotes solo glory seeking.

Protection of Self-Interests

Fear of change automatically awakens a concern for protecting self-interests. The more insecure we are, the more intensely we feel this need for self-protection. At work, such concerns revolve around the fear of obsolescence, of new pressures and demands, of retraining, of the need to develop new skills, and of becoming incompetent in a professional sense. We may also fear change out of an interest in preserving the benefits of our present jobs. Those who enjoy having cushy jobs, for instance, are not likely to welcome changes that bring more demands. Change may also threaten one's comfort and convenience. It is often a bother to learn a new procedure, to get used to a new machine, or to learn the expectations of a new superior. Some people thrive on change and are the first to try all kinds of new experiences. Others base their lives on the philosophy "If it isn't broken, don't fix it." A wiser balance exists in the old rhyme: "Be not the first by which the new is tried, nor yet the last to set the old aside."

BRINGING ABOUT EFFECTIVE CHANGE

Recall, from our discussion of the planning process in Chapter 2, that activity in and around an organization is essential to effective planning. The same is true for bringing about effective change.

Responsive Leadership

Being in touch with the need for change helps a firm to prepare for it. Management needs to monitor the environment for trends, to be aware of impending problems, timing, and the firm's strengths, weaknesses, and capabilities, and to understand the kinds of change that the firm will need. Further, note Noel Tichy and David Ulrich, a firm's leadership must be able "to help the organization develop a vision of what it can be, to mobilize the organization to accept and work toward achieving the new vision, and to institutionalize the changes that must last over time."[24]

Overcoming Resistance to Change[25]

Of the many skills managers need for bringing about effective change, one of the most essential is knowing how to overcome resistance to change. Among the strategies available are these: education, participation and involvement, and managerial interventions.

Education

Those whom a change will affect are more likely to accept that change if they are thoroughly informed about it. Openly discussing a change and its implications facilitates the change process and reduces anxiety and uncertainty by giving workers a chance to learn from those in the know what the change will mean for them. Another critical factor in successfully implementing change is earning the support of those affected by the change. Managers can do this by involving affected workers in the change process. Those asked to implement a new idea should be assured of their continuing involvement in keeping managers informed on how the implementation is going. Managers can also give workers emotional support, encouragement, opportunities to complain and ask questions, and necessary training and work time. Sincere, empathic listening will help them to win workers' support and reduce their anxieties. Managers should also involve in group discussions those who are part of the change. By doing so, managers can provide information about the change and its rationale, thereby helping to ensure that attitudes toward the change will be positive and optimistic.

Information. Change is easier if managers keep workers informed, particularly through group discussions. All workers are not always entitled to all information in a firm, but whenever they will be affected by change, they should be well informed and part of the process. This minimizes the distortion of information as well as anxieties. Sharing information through discussions also airs the pros and cons of a proposed change and leads workers from passive consideration to a clear attitude of acceptance or rejection. Finally, because most people prefer to be seen as honest and genuine, speaking in a group encourages them to stand by what they say and not vacillate, which, of course, facilitates change.

Optimism. Enthusiasm, as successful teachers realize, is an important part of the educational process. Most changes directly affect workers' self-interests as well as their professional ones, and managers need to sell both the personal and the professional advantages of a change. Law firm members who hear of change as part of a group are less apt to feel that they are being singled out as targets of change. Knowing that change is organizationally based reassures workers that they will share in the firm's good fortune. This potential for mutual opportunities and benefits should serve to motivate members to accept change.

Participation and Involvement

Ownership of ideas in terms of change means that workers will buy into what they have helped to create. Workers who have helped to develop a change will not only be more committed to it but will encourage others to accept the change as well. Moreover, workers are quick to distinguish between sham participation and real participation. Law firms that opt only for surface involvement risk much in their managerial relationships. To acknowledge a worker's value by using his or her ideas is one way to encourage participation in the change process. Managers also can recognize worker input by acknowledging contributions, being open to recommendations, and expressing their appreciation for suggestions by including them in written reports and proposals. Most of all, managers can communicate a genuine respect for worker input by actively seeking their advice. All of this reinforces each worker's belief that he or she is worth listening to.

Political Strategies

Managers might need to consider political strategies when facilitating change. Those workers who are most likely to help others accept the change under consideration should be the target of such strategies. Enthusiasm is contagious, and working with small groups of representative workers who can spread acceptance among their coworkers, being selective about the distribution of information, and planting positive ideas can help to create a receptive climate for change. To some, such techniques may seem manipulative; often, in fact, managers persuade the leaders of resistance groups to participate (superficially) in change, in order to make them look as though they supported the change willingly if not eagerly. This often backfires, as few workers enjoy being exploited and few, if any, are easy to fool. Genuine involvement leads to genuine progress.

Managerial Interventions

Managers can use many tactics to overcome resistance to change. They include using negotiation and incentives, coercion, and the initiation of tentative changes.

Negotiation and Incentives. Managers should be willing to see if any trade-offs or incentives can encourage workers to accept significant changes. Especially when past changes have caused workers to suffer setbacks and personal and professional losses, bargaining strategies are worth consideration.

Coercion. Demanding compliance is unlikely to create a lasting commitment to change, but coercion is at times an organization's only alternative. When speed is critical and when change agents have considerable power, those in charge may be obligated to demand change. If resistance continues, workers can be threatened, nicely or otherwise, with transfers, fewer promotions and raises, and loss of jobs. Such tactics can be risky, if workers suffer poor treatment or resent those in power, and coercive measures have caused some long-lasting scars. Change can always be decreed, but like the ruler on the tiny planet in *The Little Prince* who only ordered sunsets when the time and conditions were right, wise managers understand the importance of using discretion when imposing their will on their subordinates.

Tentative Changes. To promote understanding, managers can set the stage for change by implementing change in stages. Pilot projects, for example, allow workers to try ideas on for size and enables them to experience a potential change, give feedback, and help market the change to the rest of the firm. For example, a manager who is considering new word-processing software might use this "toe-in-the-water" strategy by allowing a small department or even one or two members of the secretarial staff to experiment with a new program and involving them in its evaluation. The manager would then use this evaluation in choosing a software package; further, the evaluation might affect firm-wide software changes as well.

CONFLICT

Roughly, we think of **conflict** as a sharp disagreement, clash, or noncompatability of interests, ideas, needs, or values; Likert and Likert define it more precisely as "the active striving for one's own preferred outcome which, if attained, precludes the attainment by others of their own preferred outcome, thereby producing hostility."[26] Yet intrafirm conflict is more than a confrontation involving opposing interests. It usually (1) occurs as an ongoing process arising from continuing relationships and events, (2) involves people's feelings, ideas, and perceptions, and (3) stems from conditions and events that relate both to the firm *and* to individuals.[27] Some managers claim to spend over 20 percent of their time dealing with conflict and its effects.[28]

The Nature of Conflict

We usually think of conflict in terms of fighting, hostility, controversy, and aggression. Conflict, writes organizational development specialist Gordon Lippitt, is "an absolutely predictable social phenomenon" that almost always results from one basic thing: "unlike points of view." It can spring from disagreement about our perception of facts, the means we think we should use to reach our goals, our objectives, and our values. Lippitt believes that managers should take pains to see that conflict is creative and positive, whenever possible. Conflict can either be functional or dysfunctional.[29]

Functional Conflict

Conflict is not always negative, in spite of our natural aversion to it. **Functional conflict,** or conflict that benefits an organization, can help to clarify values and viewpoints, improve performance and drive, inspire innovative solutions to challenges, and force people to clarify issues and to communicate their feelings and views. Constructive conflict opens issues for discussion, improves problem solving, increases involvement, leads to spontaneity in communications, strengthens relationships, and helps to increase productivity. It can also increase creativity, effort, the availability of diagnostic information, and group cohesion.

Dysfunctional Conflict

Dysfunctional conflict harms an organization or hinders it from reaching its goals. Neither controlled nor channeled toward productive ends, it undermines the work setting by destroying morale, polarizing personal and group attitudes, deepening differences, obstructing cooperation, leading to irresponsible behavior, creating suspicion and mistrust, decreasing productivity, and causing lasting emotional scars both in people and in the company's culture. Dysfunctional conflict harms workers' physical and mental health, wastes resources, diffuses a firm's energies, and forces members to seek self-preservation rather than work toward the firm's goals. It sometimes causes irreversible harm.

Causes of Conflict

Conflict is a complex process. Once people are aware of the opposing interests of others, their thoughts and feelings begin to center on whether and how they should respond. There are two main sources of conflict: interpersonal, or sources that relate to other people and our relationship with them, and organizational, or sources that relate to organizational structures or processes.

Interpersonal Causes of Conflict

Conflict can come about because of perceived or real threats to one's personal worth, value, dignity, and sta-

No organization is perfect, but in some the combination of stressful work demands and personality needs can be explosive. Law firms are susceptible to this kind of spontaneous combustion, and smoldering conflicts can quickly ignite, affecting everyone. Here's one example from an article in *The Wall Street Journal:*

"As the summer rolled by, frictions in the firm became intense. Mr. Califano's temper became so fierce that he couldn't keep secretaries for more than a short time." (By one count, he went through eight secretaries while at the firm.) He also became the bane of younger lawyers at the firm, "nearly destroying some with sharp criticism." Their turning to another partner, Mr. Ross, for help caused another problem: "Ross was getting tired of putting all the pieces back together. He was beginning to feel like the office therapist. . . ."

Differences between Mr. Califano and the other partners over expansion came to a head. In a series of heated arguments during the summer—even during Mr. Califano's August vacation on Cape Cod—the partners made a final effort to talk Mr. Califano into bringing more talent into the firm. To no avail. Consequently, Ross and the firm's third partner, Mr. Heineman, left the firm.

"They didn't think they'd get 100 percent of what they wanted, they'd have settled for 60 percent, but Joe wouldn't give at all," said a friend of one of the other partners.

SOURCE: "Parting of the Ways: Law Firm Breakup is Tale of Dashed Hopes and Bitter Feelings," *The Wall Street Journal* (8 June 1983): 1, 16.

ANOTHER LOOK

When Tempers at the Top Get Hot

1. What responsibility does management have in alleviating personality-related stress at the firm?
2. What repercussions does the stress of those at the top of the firm have on those below them? What can be done? What can those at the bottom do about conflict and stress at the top?

---

tus. It can result from differences in personal and professional styles, such as an autocratic one versus a democratic one. In interactions with others, we often experience misunderstandings and personality clashes. Our differences in values and goals often create conflict. In addition, note Likert and Likert, "all the older causes remain unabated: struggles for power, the desire for economic gain, the need for status, and the exploitation of others." [30] Interpersonal conflict can be brought on by differing educations, backgrounds, and particularly by limited latitudes of tolerance. We often form a narrow range of expectations regarding how others are to treat us: psychologically we write rules for others, judge how well they follow these rules (which, unless they're psychic, they have no way of knowing!), and are offended when their actions fail to equal our expectations. In practice, the range of tolerance we create should be wide enough to allow others the freedom we would like them to allow us. Yet the range also should be narrow enough to preclude endangering or diminishing our work responsibilities and self-esteem. In addition to the friction between reality and our latitudes of tolerance, other causes of interpersonal conflict relate to (1) *faulty attribution,* our erroneously assigning to others motives for what they do, particularly in areas that affect us, (2) *faulty communications,* through which we unintentionally annoy or anger others, (3) *criticism* of the kind that damages our self-esteem and diminishes our feelings of efficacy, and (4) *grudges,* long-lasting negative attitudes and feelings of revenge toward those whom we believe to have injured us, especially those who have caused us to lose face.[31]

Organizational Causes of Conflict

Organizational causes of conflict relate to a firm's structures, policies, and processes. Such conflicts stem from disagreements over goals, performance criteria, and methods and procedures. Some of the more obvious causes of organizational conflict include (1) competition over scarce resources, when groups measure their importance to the organization by the resources they receive, (2) ambiguity over responsibility, which leads to disagreement over who has more power, (3) interdependence, when one person's poor performance reflects on his or her coworkers, disappointing and angering them, (4) reward systems in which individuals or groups perceive or experience inequities, and (5) differentiation, which occurs when those at differing levels of roles and responsibilities develop an us-versus-them mentality that labels others as outsiders and threats.[32] An organization's leaders are often unaware of their role in handling conflict and of "the impact of their status on the discussions and interactions in the problem-solving process." Likert and Likert explain:

> When members see their leader striving for status, they in turn compete for status: this pits subordinates against subordinates and creates hostile relationships. Confidences and trust, favorable attitudes toward other group members, loyalty to the group, candid communications, innovative and efficient problem solving, and efforts to minimize conflict are all appreciably poorer in groups where the leader seeks to use the power of status.[33]

Conflict is provoked by issues of responsibility, authority, and power. It is the fallout from differing values and perceptions. It results from organizational tensions, such as those between line workers or between members of a staff group such as paralegals. Organizationally, conflict is the consequence of lack of cooperation, of frustration and irritability, of competition for limited resources, and of a failure to comply with rules and policies.[34] Managers must walk a fine line between allowing conflict for its possible good effects and overcoming it because of the long-term problems it might bring:

> Diversity of orientation and differences of points of view—"fruitful friction"—are essential if one seeks creative and effective organizations. Differences, of course, can result in irreconcilable, costly conflict unless the interaction-influence network and the problem-solving processes of the organization channel the differences to productive and not destructive ends.[35]

Managing Conflict

Conflict, like all issues that involve emotions, can escalate, if left unattended. Since conflict is unavoidable, knowing how to resolve it is invaluable. Conflicts are often seen as power struggles: someone wins, someone loses. In resolving conflicts, therefore, managers have three alternatives: win/lose, where one party gains at the other's expense; lose/lose, where neither party wins and both suffer; and win/win, where both parties benefit. Achieving a short-term truce is less important than eradicating the source of a conflict and achieving lasting concord. To better understand how managers resolve conflict, we will examine five ways in which people respond to conflict, methods of intervention available to managers, and formalized conflict resolution processes.

Conflict Response Styles

People respond to conflict in five ways: (1) confrontation or forcing; (2) its opposite, avoidance; (3) accommodation; (4) collaboration; and (5) compromise. Each method reflects different degrees of assertion and cooperation.[36]

Confrontation or Forcing. **Forcing** is the process of resolving a conflict by simply forcing the other party to accept one's needs and wishes. It can consist of blatant rank pulling, outright hostility, threats, the dictatorial use of authority, or a refusal to acknowledge the other's needs.

Avoidance. According to Whetten and Cameron, **avoidance** is a nonresponse to conflict that "neglects the interests of both sides by ignoring or side-stepping the conflict."[37] Besides the impulse to fight conflict, another of our initial reactions is that of flight; and although avoidance does not eliminate conflict, it can ease the immediate effects and provide time for formulating a lasting solution. Avoiding conflict can range from concealing ideas or proposals under pocket vetoes to actually turning one's back on others. One common method of avoiding conflict is simply to ignore it. Like leaving a fire unattended, not addressing an issue may allow it to rage out of control. On the other hand, an unattended conflict may smoulder, die down, and eventually burn out. Avoidance of this type is accomplished by staying neutral, no matter what. A second method of avoiding conflict is through physical separation. Separating oneself from conflict is often as easy as physically removing oneself from the scene of an argument. Being present, by comparison, implies not only involvement but responsibility. Managers have little power as bystanders, but when and if they can convince themselves that it is better for an issue to be resolved at other levels or in other arenas, avoiding a conflict might be an effective strategy. A third avoidance technique is to ensure that workers are too busy to become embroiled, a strategy that weakens conflict by dissipating the energy that goes into it and downplaying its importance. However, conflict that centers on important issues may fester beneath a surface of seemingly benign activity, and management may lose its chance to resolve the conflict effectively.

Accommodation. **Accommodation** resolves conflict by stressing cooperation: the goal of the process is to keep the other side happy at your own expense.[38] Cameron and Whetten point out that this approach resembles Dale Carnegie's philosophy, which stresses that people should maintain friendly relationships within the context of the need to work with others and to achieve goals, even if they must sacrifice important issues and self-esteem to do so. By comparison, a manager arranging accommodation usually disregards this interplay between cooperation and sacrifice and settles for letting one party have its way and essentially sacrificing the needs of the other to the "winning" side. Smoothing is part of this process. The manager minimizes or denies differences in terms of the advantages and disadvantages that the solution will bring to either side, assures the ruling side that the solution is absolutely acceptable, and cajoles the losing side into accepting the solution, ostensibly for the common good.

Compromise. **Compromise** is the process of reaching partial agreement through a combination of assertiveness and cooperation, whereby both sides determine and accept areas of agreement by sacrificing some of their own goals. Neither side may be happy with a compromise solution, but both can agree that it may be the best solution they can reach under present conditions.

Collaboration. **Collaboration** occurs when each side fully accepts the other's objectives, and both parties work to determine the most mutually beneficial outcome. In order to collaborate, the parties must trust one another. Both sides are obliged to deal openly and honestly, which in turn builds more trust. The greater the trust, the greater the chance of an outcome that will benefit both parties. When resolving a conflict, it is almost impossible to speak of needs, wants, and priorities unless each party is convinced that the other is genuinely motivated to find a solution.[39]

Power Intervention Strategies

Managers have at their disposal the power and authority to intervene in and resolve conflicts in several ways: (1) through political maneuvering, (2) through managerial commands, (3) by restructuring appropriate parts of the organization, or (4) by restructuring the groups that are in conflict. First, through political maneuvering, managers can use their influence in talking to those who are able to arrange the resolution of a conflict. Secondly, by using managerial commands, they can decide issues by mandate. Because this method may provoke overt or covert resistance, a manager might formulate commands as diplomatic requests for regular or periodic reports, through which he or she can track the conflict in surreptitious detail. Thirdly, managers can resort to controlling conflict by restructuring work groups, reassigning responsibilities within them, and reallocating authority. A fourth tactic is to maneuver group composition by "stacking" committee membership or balancing a work group to produce the results the manager wants, or by reassigning members who are sources of conflict. In their efforts to control nonfunctional conflict, managers can also counsel and consult with workers, make lateral moves and transfers, or even terminate workers when no other alternative exists.

Conflict Resolution Strategies

Some conflicts, such as those involving matters of principle, are very difficult to resolve. The stakes are large, it is hard to prove losses or injury, and it is difficult to come to an agreement because values are at the heart of the issue. "Raising principles," explains management writer Leonard Greenhalgh, "makes conflict difficult to resolve because by definition one cannot come to a reasonable compromise: one either upholds a principle or sacrifices one's integrity."[40] Resolving conflicts is far different from suppressing them. Managers are compelled to seek solutions that will have the fewest negative side effects and to arrange win/win settlements whenever possible. In conflict resolution, both sides must work to establish facts and to identify areas of agreement and disagreement. This often is contrary to the adversarial instincts of lawyers, who are trained to focus on the facts that will best represent their clients, not the facts on which they and others can agree. A no-holds-barred approach to resolving conflicts offers few positive long-term results, particularly when ongoing relationships are involved. More productive conflict resolution strategies include (1) clarification activities, (2) negotiation, (3) intervention by a third party, and (4) superordinate goals.

Clarification Activities. The more objectivity, the easier conflict is to resolve, especially when both sides wish to reach an agreement. Emotions can cloud a conflict by padding the resolution agenda with irrelevant personal issues. There is an obvious necessity for sticking with the real issues and using factual information; as Likert and Likert note, "The greater the total amount of relevant facts available, the better will be the decision and the easier it will be to reach consensus even in situations where there is marked conflict."[41] When you experience interpersonal conflict, your own or others', remember that there are at least two sides to every story. As a manager, you are obligated to withhold your initial judgment. You are likely to hear many "facts" about the same incident. Like the five blind travelers who encountered an elephant for the first time and with their hands "saw" five different animals, participants in a conflict each perceive that conflict differently. As a manager, you should listen to all of the participants, each of whom contributes a different perspective and who can, perhaps, provide a solution to the conflict. You will discover that reality is usually a combination of perceptions. The truth usually will lie somewhere in the middle!

Negotiation. **Negotiation** is a formal form of compromise, a conflict resolution strategy that allows two sides to meet for the purpose of reaching an agreement by resolving or setting aside their conflicting interests. **Bargaining** is a form of negotiation in which opposing sides make offers, counteroffers, and concessions. Each side or its representatives bring proposals to the other for the purpose of discussing and acting on them.[42] Among the many negotiation tactics in use are these:[43]

- The Good-Guy/Bad-Guy Team. In order to direct outcomes, members of a negotiation team predetermine the roles they will play at a negotiation meeting. One will play the "bad guy," responsible for making weighty demands on the opposing side. The other team member, the "good guy," will be responsible for "rescuing" the opposing side from the inordinate demands of the "bad guy," thereby winning the opposing side's trust. Let's say, for example, that the executive committee's Attorney Bad-Guy informs the firm's paralegals that the firm is facing extraordinary economic times and is battling increased competition and declining revenues. The partners have been suffering, and now the paralegals must do their share as well. Henceforth, the firm will give no pay increases, will hire no new staff, and will require paralegals to increase their billable hours by 30 percent. Seemingly outraged, Attorney Good-Guy speaks on the paralegals' behalf, reminding Attorney Bad-Guy of how invaluable they are to the firm and insisting that there must be some way to recognize their many contributions. Grudgingly, Attorney Bad-Guy agrees. Apparently, Attorney Good-Guy has opened the door for concessions, but the final settlement will include a modified version of Attorney Bad-Guy's original offer. One member of the negotiation was responsible for making proposals that the team knew in advance were not going to be accepted. Their ultimate intention was to make an only slightly less undesirable offer look reasonable by comparison.
- The "Nibble." Members of a negotiating team, after reaching agreement on essentials, ask for a few additional minor concessions or perks to make the total resolution look good to their constituents.
- Joint Problem Solving. This win/win strategy builds its effectiveness on a realistic assessment of mutual benefits. Example: If the secretarial staff accepts the medical plan changes, the firm will provide a more open vacation schedule.
- Power of Competition. Losing to the competition is a valid concern of management, and any tactic that shows management realistically how its failure to concede to negotiation demands will help a competitor is apt to be effective. For instance, paralegals who ask for pay increases against the backdrop of an excellent job market are likely to get their wish. Given the financial and stability-related costs of recruiting and training new personnel, concerns about losing qualified help are always legitimate.
- Splitting the Difference. Because this tactic requires negotiators to know what the differences really are, it is not as easy as it sounds. If an opposing side offers to split the difference too soon, the other group may become suspicious, thinking perhaps that the opposing side already has gained more than appearances might suggest.
- Low-balling. In low-balling, one side holds out ridiculously low offers in order to lower the other side's expectations. Rather than becoming insulted

"Etiquette in law offices will make the workplace more pleasant and efficient, and could make it easier for someone in the legal profession to advance," writes Detroit news columnist Jeanne Whittaker, who notes that "etiquette helps ease tensions at law offices."

"Good manners build good relationships between people," she explains. "If employees feel appreciated, they work harder. They feel enthusiastic about their work, and good manners can make the stressful times bearable." The positive atmosphere that etiquette creates also may improve clients' perceptions of the firm.

Whittaker offers these hints for legal support staff in dealing with others in the law office:

- Be a gracious team player.
- Be tactful.
- Use good manners to express appreciation.
- Keep up confidence.
- Listen to everything but avoid becoming an office gossip.
- Admit your errors.
- Accept criticism.

SOURCE: Steve Harrington, "Etiquette Helps to Ease Law Office Tensions," *Michigan Lawyer's Weekly: Inside Today's Changing Law Firm* (31 July 1989): 8.

ANOTHER LOOK

Office Etiquette Is for Everyone

1. How idealistic is Whittaker's approach?
2. How might the law office courtesy quotient affect client perceptions?
3. In what ways might etiquette influence the bottom line? For instance, what impact might courtesy (or the lack thereof) have on productivity?

---

and breaking off communications, the side hearing the offer should discuss the difficulties of accepting it and diplomatically commit itself to further negotiations.

Third-Party Intervention. In some conflicts, barriers prevent either side from working effectively with the other. These barriers can consist of emotional issues, political influences, or personal factors such as intolerance, pettiness, and arrogance. If you have ever experienced this, you know that such barriers distort perceptions. People become irrational, illogical, uncommunicative, and more entrenched in their original ideas. They adopt unreasonable positions and indulge in personal attacks. Having a third party present, even if he or she does none of the talking, provides an immediate benefit. As Greenhalgh explains,

> People usually feel obliged to appear reasonable and responsible because they care more about how the neutral party is evaluating them than how the opponent is. The more prestigious, powerful, trusted, and neutral the third party is, the greater is the desire to exercise emotional restraint.[44]

In organizational conflict, a neutral third party tends to act either as a mediator or an arbitrator. A *mediator* has no formal power but helps to resolve disputes by being a facilitator, one who bridges the conflict gap and enables the opposing sides to come to an agreement. An *arbitrator* has the power to establish or to recommend the terms under which both sides must come to an agreement, whether by binding arbitration or other forms. This mediator or arbitrator is usually a person from outside the organization who can be chosen voluntarily by both sides or appointed either by the courts or according to an arrangement between the two sides. Other arrangements for selecting a third party can be made as long as both parties believe they will be fairly heard. The parties can communicate at the same time in the presence of the third party or can communicate through the mediator, if they so choose. A mediator identifies areas of agreement and disagreement between the parties and directs them toward solutions, having the location of a solution and listening to both sides as his or her primary objectives. The mediator has these responsibilities: to listen with understanding in lieu of evaluation; to clarify the issues rather than allowing the parties to become sidetracked; to ease emotional strain validating the feelings of each party; and to suggest procedures and ground rules that will help to produce a climate that is conducive to listening and resolving.[45]

Superordinate Goals. Superordinate goals are overall goals accepted by both groups that they can accomplish only by working together. In deciding on superordinate goals, both sides set aside their personal agendas (at least temporarily), suppress aspects of their own goals, and identify the goals they have in common. To do this, they must overcome past communication problems and disagreements. Groups determining superordinate goals often receive help from a conciliator, a go-between who interprets both sides' views, obtains information, and fills communication gaps.

Handling Conflict-Laden Communications

Newly appointed managers quickly wish that they had more opportunities to learn about the "people part" rather than the "paper part" of management. This wish is most fervent during conflict-laden communications. Essentially, managers learn five techniques to apply to conflict-heavy exchanges with subordinates: (1) evaluating, (2) confronting, (3) diverting, (4) probing, (5) reflecting, and (6) reinterpreting. In *evaluating,* the manager listens carefully to the worker's message, evaluates it, and expresses clearly the degree of validity he or she perceives in it. The manager then agrees or disagrees with the message, explaining his or her disagreement, if any. In *confronting,* the manager focuses on the facts by stating what he or she perceives as the truth. In *diverting,* the manager, faced with a conflict that could easily escalate, calms the subordinate and establishes common ground by discussing a more neutral related issue before leading gradually into the topic of the conflict. Through *probing,* the manager shows a genuine interest in listening to the worker and learning more about the conflict. Ineffective if done sarcastically or cynically, **probing** is the art of asking relevant questions in order to elicit additional information. By **reflecting,** the manager communicates respect for and thoughtful consideration of the worker's message by mirroring or reproducing it. Finally through *reinterpreting,* the manager restates the worker's message in his or her own words. Reinterpreting indicates not only that the manager is listening empathically but that he or she is able to forgo heated debate and is willing to communicate. In all conflict-laden communication, the choice of a resolution technique is only as good as the sincerity and genuine interest of the manager making that choice. It is easy to fall into an emotional verbal exchange, but it is much more beneficial to stay objective, calm, and rational. Some workers are adept at emotional manipulation, and they will repeat the process regularly once they know that a manager can't stand the heat.

STRESS

Stress is a reality of life. In a recent survey, over 80 percent of workers said their jobs were stressful, and over 64 percent of those workers said work was the most stressful part of their life. Home was the second most stressful environment, followed by public places such as highways and stores.[46] Few of us are new to stress, and the law office, with its unique pressures, expectations, and demands, brings its own intense forms of stress. Whatever its causes and however we respond, it is important to understand the impact stress has on our lives.

TABLE 13-1
Strategies for Handling Conflict

Interpersonal Response Strategies	Power Intervention Strategies	Conflict Resolution Strategies
Forcing	Political maneuvering	Clarification activities
Avoidance	Managerial commands	Third-party intervention
Accommodation	Restructuring	Negotiation
Collaboration	Changing the composition of the group	Superordinate goals
Compromise		

As office manager, you have asked one of the secretaries to replace the receptionist at noon time for the next two weeks. She glares at you and says, "I will never get my work done if I keep getting all these extra duties. I think you have something against me. You always find ways to get even." How should you respond?

Strategy	Example
Evaluating	Aim: to pass judgment, agree, or offer advice. "No, it's not getting even. This is part of our working together."
Confronting	Aim: to challenge the other to clarify the message. "Because I am asking you to cover for the receptionist does not mean anything punitive. I do not have anything against you."
Diverting	Aim: to change the focus. "I remember when I was first a paralegal and felt that way about the administrator. We became the best of friends after."
Probing	Aim: to get at the heart of what the other is saying. "Apparently you're upset because this is not what you'd like to be doing, but tell me what else makes you think this is getting even?"
Reflecting	Aim: to restate the message to get at the underlying cause. "There's no need to think I have something against you. I can see you're upset because you feel I haven't been aware of the demands on your secretarial work."
Reinterpreting	Aim: to let the person know you were listening carefully. "You think that this is getting even with you and that I have something against you. You are concerned about your regular duties."

ANOTHER LOOK

How to Handle An Angry Worker

1. How do you react to conflict? Under what conditions have you used responses similar to those described above? Were your responses effective? Why or why not?
2. Has anyone ever used any of these strategies on you? How did you respond?
3. Explain the importance of worker-considerate conflict resolution. Wouldn't it be easier to just put irate subordinates in their place?

The Nature of Stress

Stress has many meanings. We base our use of the term on what engineers and architects call stress: the pressure or forces placed on a structure. Long bridges, for instance, incorporate arches and spans that help to distribute weight and pressure. In the Middle Ages, builders began to construct flying buttresses, wing-like outer structures that would support the additional stress that the weight of stained glass windows placed on cathedral walls. The Notre Dame Cathedral of Paris is an outstanding example of the use of flying buttresses. In our own lives, stress has a similar meaning, and we need similar supports. **Stress** is an adaptive response to any external action, situation, or event that places excessive psychological and physical demands on a person.[47] It is the result of pressures that we feel from environmental forces. As the definition suggests, all people respond to stress differently. What constitutes excessive stress for one person may be nothing at all to another. Whether people feel stress depends on their individual makeup and on what is important to them. Surgeons, for instance, are under enormous life-and-death pressures. Many find, however, that their particular response to this stress is high-level responsiveness and a feeling of exhilaration at meeting the challenge. Dr. Hans Selye, who pioneered studies in stress research, emphasizes that not all stress is negative. **Eustress** (featuring the Greek prefix *eu-*, meaning "well" or "good") is a form of stress that constitutes a positive adaptive response to environmental pressures and forces. Eustress is "good" stress: it energizes us, spurs us on to higher levels of accomplishment, and helps us to operate at our maximum potential.

The General Adaptation Syndrome

In his research, Selye studied how people responded to environmental stressors. He learned that each stressor triggered a series of physical responses through which the body registered the presence of the stressor, responded to it, and readjusted. This defense reaction, which Selye called the **general adaptation syndrome (GAS),** consists of three distinct phases: an alarm reaction to stress, resistance to it, and the body's resulting exhaustion.

Alarm Reaction

The alarm reaction is the first stage of the general adaptation syndrome. When we perceive a threat in our environment, messages travel to our brains, giving our body systems biochemical orders to respond. This initial stage is highly similar to the adaptive mechanisms early humans used for survival. Like our ancestors sensing some monstrous predator lurking in the tall grass on a prehistoric plain, we respond to danger by going into physical overdrive. We breathe more rapidly, our pupils dilate, our adrenalin starts to surge, and our muscles tense. Though modern threats are less likely to involve large, hostile carnivores, our initial responses are still much like they were millions of years ago, depending on the intensity of the danger. Our systems charge up for battle and prepare to respond.

Resistance

In Stage 2, all of our reaction systems are engaged and we are intensely focused on fighting the threat that we have sensed. As Selye points out, however, humans have only finite sources of energy, concentration, and ability with which to resist stressors. While we are expending our reserves to meet one challenge, we are diminishing our ability to meet others. Consequently, we are often more prone to illness during periods of stress.[48]

Exhaustion

Exhaustion is the final stage of the syndrome. In resisting a stressor, we drain our supplies of energy. The systems fighting the stressor become depleted. As a result, we are exhausted, depending on the intensity and duration of the resistance we have put forth.

Major Sources of Stress

Responsible for eustress as well as negative stress, **stressors** are factors that cause people to experience anxiety, tensions, and pressures. Stressors come from three main sources: the environment, the organization, and the individual.

Environmental Sources

Stress is found everywhere, not only at home and at work. We pinpoint stress in the economy, greed, contemporary values, and the rat race. We are stressed by concerns about issues such as war, prejudice, disease, hunger, and the homeless. Changes in the world's environment and concern about global issues like pollution, toxic chemicals, and radiation are all sources of environmental stress. Our immediate environment abounds with stressors: crowding, standing in lines, insufficient or excessive light, questionably safe technology, excessive noise, unhealthy temperatures, polluted or smoke-filled air, hazardous drinking water, and the threat of communicable disease. Our personal aversions constitute another category of environmental stressors: certain kinds of music, particular perfumes, or specifically unpleasant body odors. In close quarters, even the nicest scents and people can cause us stress.

Organizational Sources

Stress within organizations comes from many sources. We may identify stresses related to work in general, as well as the fact that some jobs are more stressful than others.

Stressful Jobs. In order, from most stress to least, the five most stressful jobs are those of inner-city high school teachers, police officers, miners, air traffic controllers, and medical interns.[49] It is easy to see why some jobs are decidedly more stressful than others. Studies have linked the intensity of job-related stress to these factors: (1) making decisions, (2) constantly monitoring materials, (3) a repeated exchange of information with others, (4) unpleasant physical conditions, and (5) performing structured rather than unstructured tasks.[50]

Work-Related Stresses. What complaints about work are most commonplace? The foremost complaint is that work lacks variety and challenge. The second concerns the conflicts that workers have with other people on the job, particularly bosses. The third most familiar complaint about work involves the feeling of being burned out: as Csikszentmihalyi describes it, "too much pressure, too much stress, too little time to think for oneself, too little time to spend with the family."[51] This last complaint, he notes, is particularly troublesome to those at the top of the hierarchy, as burnout very often affects an organization's most talented, hardworking, and committed people:

> Thus we have the paradoxical situation: On the job people feel skillful and challenged, and therefore feel more happy, strong, creative, and satisfied. In their free time people feel that there is generally not much to do and their skills are not being used, and therefore they tend to feel more sad, weak, and dissatisfied. Yet they would like to work less and spend more time in leisure.[52]

Complaints about work should receive careful attention. Contrary to what we might think, such complaints do not automatically mean that people dislike what they are doing, since, as Csikszentmihalyi explains, "one can love one's job and still be displeased with some aspects of it, and try to improve what is not perfect."[53] Factors that create stress and other problems at work include (1) role conflicts, (2) ambiguity, (3) managerial failings, (4) time stressors, (5) responsibilities, and (5) environmental stressors.

- Role Conflicts. Role conflicts result from role overload (simply having too much to do) and from the need to fulfill often incompatible requests from two or more of the people to whom one must answer. Differing role expectations cause inevitable tensions: one or more of the answerees will obviously be displeased. Conflicting work obligations and responsibilities are common causes of stress. Demands that spouses, children, friends, and others place on workers intensify these stressors. Paralegals, for instance, may be justifiably stressed when the attorneys they work with have last-minute and overtime demands. Joe's supervising attorney, at the last minute, wants him to work overtime, and Joe has already solemnly promised his daughter that he would go to her basketball playoffs. Ann's been asked by her firm's attorneys to do some last-minute research; she needs to be with her aging father for his doctor's appointment. Role conflicts like these are often unavoidable, but they are always less stressful in work settings that employees consider to be supportive and caring.[54]
- Ambiguity. Uncertainty is one of the leading causes of stress at work. Between 35 and 60 percent of worker stress is caused by ambiguity regarding (a) job standards and expectations, (b) job priorities and the amount of time to be spent on responsibilities, and (c) accountability and reporting.[55]
- Management Failings. Poor management deprives workers of confidence and increases their anxiety. Badly formulated policies give rise to inequities and discontent, and performance appraisals and evaluations, which are stressful enough under good management, become increasingly pressured. Unskilled managers fare poorly at providing feedback, particularly negative feedback, which is hard for workers to accept from those they have little cause to respect.
- Time Stressors. Having too much to do and too little time in which to do it is the most pervasive form of stress for American managers. Although for some, work seems to expand to fit the time allowed it, time for many others seems to shrink and vanish. Many of us share a constant concern about time: with varying degrees of success, we balance our having too much to do with our inability to control time demands.[56]
- Responsibilities. A manager's responsibilities for his or her subordinates are significantly more stressful than his or her responsibilities for resources such as equipment, finances, space, and supplies. There are two reasons for this. First, in dealing with subordinates, a manager comes face-to-face with the effects of the stress that those subordinates feel, particularly those effects for which the manager is responsible. An especially onerous experience for many managers is seeing the tension and stress they bring to workers by delivering negative feedback. Secondly, a survey in-

TABLE 13-2
Pressures that Increase Worker Stress

Source of Stress	Percentage of Workers
Type of Work Done	64%
Lack of Communication	50
Understaffing	46
Employer Demands	44
Preoccupation with Work	38
Incompetent Supervisors	32
Not Allowed to Do a Good Job	32
Coworkers	32
Too Many Work Hours	31
Incompetent Subordinates	29

SOURCE: A. Miller, "Stress on the Job," Newsweek (25 April 1988): 43.

dicates that managers spend over 24 percent of their time dealing with interpersonal and organizational conflict.[57] Even managers who practice a policy of basic nonintervention pay a price in terms of being responsible for others at work. Confrontations, depression, unfairness, power plays, health changes and psychological problems, the home and family crises of workers, incompetencies and lost motivation, outcries, criticism, and complaints bear heavily on anyone who has the slightest bit of consideration for others. They all contribute to an intense source of stress for managers.[58]

Individual Sources

No matter how fortified and resilient a person is, stress can take its toll. In 1967, Thomas Holmes and Richard Rahe, psychiatrists at the University of Washington in Seattle, measured major stressors according to a tool they labeled the Social Adjustment Rating Scale; researchers R. S. Lazarus, A. Delongis, S. Folkman, and R. Gruen developed a ratings scale for minor stressors, or hassles, in 1985. Both major and minor stressors contribute to the work-related condition known as burnout.

Major Stressful Life Events. To measure the intensity of stressful events, Holmes and Rahe asked a large group of people to assign numerical values to a variety of life events (see Experiential Exercise III).[59] The respondents assigned the greatest number of points to the major difficult times of life, such as the death of a spouse or getting a divorce. They allocated fewer points to events like getting a traffic ticket and moving from one place to another. According to their numerical values on the scale, four Christmases can be as stressful as getting married, and retiring is almost half as stressful as the death of a husband or wife. Perhaps more importantly, the scale correlates stressful events with changes in personal health. Holmes and M. Masuda found that over 49 percent of those who accumulated more than 300 points on the scale in a single year experienced serious health problems.[60]

Minor Stressful Events, or Hassles. Most of the things that bother us daily are not on the Life Events Stress Scale. This does not mean that these problems fail to contribute to our stress levels, as we well know. If you were to list the dozens of minor irritations that you experience each day, you would perhaps include some that Lazarus, Delongis, Folkman, and Gruen placed on their list of daily hassles as sources of stress: (1) household hassles, such as preparing meals and shopping; (2) time pressure hassles, such as having too many responsibilities and too many things to do; (3) hassles that come from inner concerns, such as being lonely or in fear of confrontation; (4) environmental hassles, neighborhood deterioration, noise, and crime; and (5) financial hassles, including concerns about bills and about owing money and having financial responsibilities, particularly for someone who doesn't live with you.[61] **Hassles** are common events and happenings that, in combination with other regularly experienced events such as a lack of time, too many responsibilities, and other aggravations, are important causes of stress. The more hassle-related stress people report, the poorer their psychological health tends to be. Such stress also correlates highly to poor physical health.[62]

Burnout. One of the most common work-related symptoms of stress is burnout. **Burnout** is emotional, physical, and mental exhaustion in response to chronic job stressors.[63] There are many indications of burnout, one of which is a loss of respect, concern, or sympathy for the people with whom one works.[64] To burn out, according to H. J. Freudenberger, is "to fail, to wear out, or become exhausted by the organization making excessive demands on energy, strength, or resources. It is what happens when an organization member . . . for whatever reasons, and to all intents and purposes, becomes inoperative."[65] Burnout is a significant organizational reality. Its major behavioral symptoms are cynicism, apathy, and indifference. Some researchers believe that it results from a combination of work, social, and personal pressures and demands. Burnout affects too many workers to be dismissed as an ailment of the physically, spiritually, or psychologically weak. Without proper coping methods, any work that provides significant and reoccurring stress, conflict, pressure, and continuing frustration can contribute to burnout. Moreover, most people are not aware that burnout is happening until the condition is in its late stages. Some jobs and settings are more conducive than others to burnout, and that of the lawyer is among them. Burnout is contagious. Its effect on others, called the *singe factor*, results from the burned out worker's need to share his or her cynical perceptions and despair with others. Leading to the depletion of motivational drives, burnout is a well-established cause of poor work performance.

Stress and the Legal Profession

The legal profession is enmeshed in a high-stress environment. Today, the volatile legal marketplace and concerns for profit cause much additional stress in the law firm. Anyone who is part of the legal profession knows of the personal and professional conflicts it brings: "The profession of lawyering," notes David Margolick, "is by its nature an adversarial one. Not to be adversarial is economically unsound." Nonetheless, resolutions and negotiations are also important to lawyers, and, as Margolick points out, "Most individuals are not cut out to be adversaries all the time." [66] As a result, the fast-paced, innately adversarial, high-demand legal field places unique pressures on those connected to it. The culture of those at the top of the firm's hierarchy cannot help but influence the culture of those below. Stress issues for those in the upper echelons affect everyone, to some degree or another, and each of the firm's activities reflects to some extent the values and choices of those in charge.

Alcohol Abuse and Depression

Recent state bar association studies have uncovered some disturbing facts about their members. Studies in Washington State have shown that Washington lawyers as a group far surpass national percentages for rates of alcoholism and depression, with over 18 percent of lawyers in Washington State reporting alcohol-related problems. Among those who have practiced for more than 20 years, over 25 percent consider themselves to be "problem drinkers." A study by the Arizona bar showed that 18 percent of the lawyers in the study suffered from depression, three times the national average. The New York State bar reported that over 50 percent of the disciplinary cases it receives are linked to drugs or alcohol.[67] Finally, a national American Bar Association survey shows a growing malaise among lawyers. In 1984, 9 percent of male partners and 15 percent of female partners in private practice were dissatisfied. In 1990, the dissatisfaction grew to 22 percent for male partners and 42 percent for female partners. In solo practice, 43 percent of all men and 55 percent of all women were dissatisfied. The survey also discovered that, although teetotalism had been more in vogue because of an increasing health awareness, drinking was escalating at an astonishing rate among lawyers, particularly women. In 1984, less than half of one percent of those surveyed reported consuming six or more alcoholic beverages a day. By 1990, that figure had risen to 13 percent and included one in every five female lawyers. Ominously, the effects of malcontent and alcohol abuse, like the effects of burnout, are likely to spread within the legal profession. As Margolick observes,

> The increased stress of dissatisfaction and billable hours have disturbing and important implications for the profession. . . . These lie in the area of increasing social dysfunction or destructive behavior by lawyers and the impact of this behavior on themselves, their families, their quality of work and productivity, their firms, and their clients.[68]

Quality of Life Issues

The same ABA survey cited as causes of discontent the conflicts and stresses of the legal profession: "growing political intrigue and backbiting in the office, greater pressure to work longer hours and a concomitant decrease in personal time and time with families." In particular, the women in the survey believed that they were less challenged than their male counterparts. According to Margolick, they "found the office atmosphere less congenial, complained that they had fewer chances for advancement than men, were less likely to be judged on the quality of their work, and were more likely to feel they did not have enough time for themselves."[69]

EFFECTS OF STRESS

Stress reveals itself through symptoms that may be psychological, cognitive, physiological, or behavioral. The psychological manifestations of stress include anxiety, depression, tension, discouragement, apathy, fatigue, feelings of hopelessness and discouragement, and sadness. The cognitive signs of stress include poor concentration, mental blocks, sporadic memory recall, and cognitive short-circuiting (the temporary inability to remember the words or ideas you want to present). Cognitive symptoms of stress also include a tendency to misplace things, to confuse dates and appointments, and even to forget momentarily the names of those you know well, such as your best friend, your wife, or your son! The physiological symptoms of stress include increased blood pressure, headaches, chest pains, ulcers, allergies, a susceptibility to illnesses such as the common colds, and many other stress-related sicknesses. Among the behavioral signs of stress are low energy, moodiness, increased aggression, temper outbursts, compulsive eating, high anxiety, and chronic worry. Prolonged stress can lead to symptoms such as trembling, nervous tics, and twitches. Continued stress can encourage alcoholism, drug abuse, and increased smoking. Being accident prone is another common behavioral indication of prolonged stress.

DIFFERENCES IN RESPONSES TO STRESS

We all respond to stress differently. Moreover, each of us may find different stressors in the same organizational environment; as Csikszentmihalyi believes, "stress and pressures are clearly the most subjective aspects of a job." He writes that

> stress exists only if we experience it; it takes the most extreme objective conditions to cause it directly. The same amount of pressure will wilt one person and be a welcome challenge to another. There are hundreds of ways to relieve stress, some based on better organization, delegation of responsibility, better communication with coworkers and supervisors; others are based on factors external to the job, such as improved home life, leisure patterns, or inner disciplines like transcendental meditation.[70]

What makes a difference in how we respond to stress? The obvious answer lies in our personalities. Individual differences play a significant modifying role in how stressors affect people. Our approach to life, our attitudes, our outside interests, and our psychological resources, including our support systems, are four factors that make stress a challenge rather than a tragedy (or vice versa) for each of us.

Type A and Type B Behavior Patterns

Of the many studies seeking connections between behavior patterns and stress, the most significant involve the behavior patterns we have come to know as Type A and Type B. Each pattern manifests itself in certain tendencies and characteristics. Type A people are always in a hurry. (See Table 13–3.) They are impatient and often angry; research has shown that those who exhibit Type A tendencies such as cynical distrust, hostility, and chronic anger are more at risk in terms of suffering heart disease.[71] In contrast, those with Type B behavior patterns are easygoing, accepting, determined, and steady. They do one thing at a time, and they are patient and good listeners.[72] Recent studies have associated a third behavior pattern with stress. As described by Harriet Braiker, Type E behaviors are typical of women who not only try to do it all but who are compelled to do it well. It is not at all unusual for women who have been balancing careers, home life, and obligations to family, friends, and social groups to become disillusioned, resentful, frustrated, and burned out. Unlike Type A individuals, however, they direct their hostility not at others but at themselves. Type E women tend to direct their anger inward, and, as a result, they feel depression, guilt, and a sense of failure.[73]

TABLE 13–3
Type A Behavior Patterns

Psychomotor Signs

1. Facial and body tension
2. Fist clenching
3. Teeth grinding
4. Rapid blinking
5. Rapid speech
6. Finger tapping
7. Knee/foot jiggling
8. Sighs
9. Rapid head nodding when speaking, listening
10. Perspiration on forehead and upper lip

Behavioral Signs

1. Competitiveness
2. Compulsion to win
3. Need to dominate socially and in business
4. Touchiness and irritability
5. Obstinate on all topics
6. Difficulty in being happy for others
7. Difficulty in sitting still and doing nothing
8. Intense dislike of waiting in lines
9. Fast walking, eating
10. Polyphasic, doing several things at once
11. Hurrying others

Attitudinal Signs

1. Mistrusts others
2. Cynical
3. Hostile
4. Expects others to be perfect but caves in if criticized

SOURCE: Meyer Friedman and Diane Ulmer, *Treating Type A Behavior and Your Heart* (New York: Alfred A. Knopf, Inc., 1984); Karen A. Matthews, "Psychological Perspectives on the Type A Behavior Pattern," *Psychological Bulletin* 91 (1981): 293–323; and Earl Ubell, "The Deadly Emotions," *Parade Magazine* (11 February 1990): 4–6.

Attitudes

Attitudes also modify how stress affects people. The most stress-resistant outlook is one that combines the resilience of optimism, hardiness, and hope with the perspective that comes from outside interests.

Optimism

Optimists and pessimists approach stress differently. Optimists make lemonade when life hands them lemons. They plan how they will cope with stress, may avoid other activities until their stress is less intense, and actively seek advice from others. Pessimists try to ignore pressure, tend to give up when reaching their goals becomes too stressful, and spend more energy expressing their frustration than resolving their stress.[74]

Hardiness

Relatively few people become ill after periods of great stress.[75] This fact has led researchers to study resilience, the ability to handle stressful events. Suzanne Kosaba, who has written on positive coping skills, identifies this ability as **hardiness,** a resilient personality style built on three unique qualities. First, the hardy person has a sense of commitment, a belief in the truth, value, and importance of what he or she is doing. Secondly, he or she has a sense of control, believing that with enough determination, one can influence the outcome of events or one's reactions to them. Finally, the hardy person approaches changes and difficulties with a sense of challenge, based on the belief that taken creatively, challenges can stimulate personal growth. To such a person, change becomes more valuable than routine and stability. The hardy person believes that he or she can become a better person through coping with challenges. People who have this quality of hardiness keep life and its stressors in perspective, believe that they have the creativity and resources they need to deal with stressful events, and not only perceive such events as challenges rather than threats, but use them as opportunities to grow and develop.[76] As Csikszentmihalyi observes,

> The ability to take misfortune and make something good come of it is a very rare gift. Those who possess it are called "survivors," and are said to have "resilience," or "courage." Whatever we call them, it is generally understood that they are exceptional people who have overcome great hardships, and have surmounted obstacles that would daunt most men and women. In fact, when average people are asked to name the individuals they admire the most, and to explain why these men and women are admired, courage and the ability to overcome hardship are the qualities most mentioned as a reason for admiration.[77]

Hope

Psychologists recently have suggested that "hope plays a surprisingly potent role in giving people a measurable advantage in realms as diverse as academic achievement, bearing up in onerous jobs and coping with tragic illness." According to several studies, those who have higher levels of hope cope better with stress, and experience "fewer symptoms of burnout like mental exhaustion and emotional withdrawal."[78] Those who have hope share these characteristics: they turn more easily to friends for advice on reaching goals; they persuade themselves that they will succeed at what they want to do; they remind themselves in times of pressure that things will get better; they readily make alternate plans for reaching their goals when their initial plans prove unworkable; and they break larger goals into smaller, more accomplishable tasks. By comparison, those low in hope do none of these things. Because they are unable to see that reaching a goal, like taking a journey, consists of a series of steps, their goals tend to overwhelm and ultimately discourage them. Knowing this, managers might encourage law firm members not only to be more optimistic at work but also to focus on other aspects of their lives one piece at a time.

Outside Interests

One of our ongoing concerns as individuals is that of having a life outside of work. The relationship between the ability to handle stress and enjoying outside interests is well known. "Those who have a concern for other people and concerns beyond the self," observes J. E. Crandall, "have fewer stressful experiences, and stress has less effect on anxiety, depression, and hostility; they make more active attempts to cope with their problems."[79] An interest in other people, in other activities, and in life itself enables us to avoid the self-focus and myopic vision that seem to promote an inability to tolerate stressful events. Keeping one's sense of humor is always a sign of a positive yet realistic perspective. Humor breaks tension, helps establish rapport, and reminds us that things rarely are as bad as they first seem.

Social Support

Working in tandem with our personal resources are our social support systems, those who believe in us and who offer us strength and encouragement. People who know that others appreciate and value them more easily minimize and control the negative effects of stress.[80] **Social support** is the perception that others appreciate and care for us and that they are willing to help us in times of need. Family and friends, who often can provide care, material resources, and emotional help, are inestimable sources of support in times of stress.[81] Community support groups consisting of those who have had similarly stressful experiences are also helpful resources. Often, just being able to discuss how we might cope with pressure reduces the negative feelings that we associate with stress.[82]

COPING WITH STRESS

People cope with stress in a variety of ways and, as we might guess, with widely varying degrees of success. In the following paragraphs, we will examine effective methods for managing and reducing stress, individually and organizationally.

Individual Strategies

A personal stress reduction program incorporates a proper diet and physical exercise, relaxation responses, and the channeling activity known as transformational coping.

Diet and Exercise

Hundreds of studies document the benefits of healthy eating habits and exercise on stress control and reduction. A low-salt, low-fat diet that emphasizes fruits, vegetables, and fiber improves the body's ability to cope with the physiological signs of stress.[83] A strong, positive correlation also exists between regular exercise and lower rates of stress-related sickness.[84] A steady exercise program not only improves our physical fitness and sense of well-being, but also has a strong impact on our ability to manage stress.[85]

Relaxation

Constant stress can place heavy demands on people. Being able to relax plays an important role in stress management, whether by the simple use of relaxation techniques, by short breaks or changes in what one is doing, or by well-timed vacations. **Relaxation** is an adaptive anti-stress response that can have immediate positive physiological effects.[86] True relaxation depends on being in a quiet environment or on being able to mentally project a quiet environment. You might try to project such an environment by assuming a comfortable position, closing your eyes, and slowly repeating a calming mental device, such as a favorite word or phrase.[87]

Transformational Coping

By enabling us to utilize stress in spurring our personal development, transformational coping has the potential to become our most flexible stress management resource. Essentially, through transformational coping we channel into some positive activity the energy we would otherwise expend on negative stress. For instance, those who have just ended a poor marriage or who have lost a spouse might use these stressful events as motivation to start a new career, begin a new business, or return to college. Through such activities, they transform grief and loss into opportunity. The process is not always positive, however. A negative form of transformational coping known as regressive coping represents the need to run away from change and take comfort in the old ways. Most people use either transformational or regressive coping at different times and differ in their ability to utilize one approach or the other.[88]

Organizational Strategies

As we have seen, managers contribute significantly to the negative pressures that employees feel; for this reason and for others, management has a responsibility to help employees handle stress. "Part of a law firm manager's job is reducing the stress level in the firm," writes Lowell Forte, who points out that an effective work environment in a law firm depends on most lawyers wanting everything done not only immediately but thoroughly.[89] Organizational efforts to reduce stress can include health promotion and stress management programs, access to exercise equipment and reduced rates on memberships at fitness clubs, better selection and placement procedures, improved communications, comprehensive benefits, carefully planned job designs, flextime and other work schedule arrangements, sabbaticals, and employee assistance programs. Most of all, managers can try harder to recognize each worker as a unique person and to reward and challenge that worker supportively and effectively.

QUESTIONS FOR DISCUSSION AND REVIEW

1. What is change? Compare its positive and negative aspects. How do you view change?
2. Explain the forces that lead to organizational change. How does such change differ from personal change? Explain the manager's role in organizational change.
3. Describe the process of change and apply it to events in an organization with which you are familiar.
4. Describe the forces that constrain or limit change.
5. Discuss what a change agent is and what the change agent's role is. What particular challenges might a law firm change agent experience? What special skills might he or she need?
6. Give an example of a difficult change that you have experienced at work or have seen others experience. What made it difficult? Explain the sources of resistance to the change.
7. You are the legal administrator of a multi-branch law firm that has experienced serious financial losses in the past two years. Partners have defected, new associates have not been hired, accounts receivable have been left unpaid and are uncollectible, and the firm needs to make serious cutbacks in paralegal and support staff positions. You hold a meeting with the legal administrators from the three branches that will be most affected. What actions do you believe will be necessary to bring about effective changes?
8. Think of conflicts you have experienced that range in intensity from minimal to very intense. Give one example each of minimal, average, and intense conflicts and explain how each was functional or dysfunctional.
9. Describe a conflict in any work setting that you have experienced and discuss its causes. What conflict response styles, power intervention strategies, or conflict resolution strategies were, could have been, or should have been used?
10. Design a chart (pie, bar, or graph) that depicts your sources of stress. Design a second sheet showing your daily or weekly use of time. Include the time you allocate for stress reduction techniques. On a third chart, design your ideal stress reduction program. How does your ideal differ from your current efforts to reduce stress? What stress reduction techniques do you consider effective? Describe and explain your typical response to stress.

EXPERIENTIAL EXERCISES

I. Analyzing Problems in the Workplace*

Conflict often masks itself in covert resistance and passivity. Use the following exercise to analyze conflict and problems at a work site you know well. Circle the number that best represents your perception of life in that organization. Total your results and interpret your score according to the instructions below.

To what extent is there evidence of the following problems in your work unit?

	Low evidence		Some evidence		High evidence
1. Loss of production or work-unit output	1	2	3	4	5
2. Grievances or complaints within the work unit	1	2	3	4	5
3. Conflicts or hostility between unit members	1	2	3	4	5
4. Confusion about assignments or unclear relationships between people	1	2	3	4	5

*SOURCE: William Dyer, *Team Building*. © 1987 by Addison-Wesley Publishing Co., Inc., Reading, Massachusetts. Figure 4–1 on pages 42 & 43. Reprinted with permission of the publisher.

5.	Lack of clear goals or low commitment to goals	1	2	3	4	5
6.	Apathy or general lack of interest or involvement of unit members	1	2	3	4	5
7.	Lack of innovation, risk taking, imagination, or taking initiative	1	2	3	4	5
8.	Ineffective staff meetings	1	2	3	4	5
9.	Problems in working with the boss	1	2	3	4	5
10.	Poor communications: people afraid to speak up, not listening to each other, or not talking together	1	2	3	4	5
11.	Lack of trust between boss and members or between members	1	2	3	4	5
12.	Decisions made that people do not understand or agree with	1	2	3	4	5
13.	People feel that good work is not recognized or rewarded	1	2	3	4	5
14.	People are not encouraged to work together in better team effort	1	2	3	4	5

Scoring: 14 to 20 = Very positive conditions. Atmosphere promotes cooperation and teamwork. Few if any disruptive work-related problems.

29 to 42 = Good conditions. Though not perfect, your work site, in general, promotes a positive working atmosphere.

43 to 56 = Negative and counterproductive conditions. Extensive problems plague work teams. Atmosphere inhibits group performance.

Over 56 = Very unhealthy conditions. Sweeping problems prevent work units from completing tasks or reaching goals. Atmosphere is rife with disruptive conflict.

II. Stress on the Job? Ask Yourself*

Many jobs are stressful by their very nature. How we respond to job-related stressors gives us valuable insight about our coping skills. Before each of the statements below, write the number of the response that best describes your experience with stress.

1. Seldom True
2. Sometimes True
3. Mostly True

Determine your stress level by adding the numbers you've written to the left of each statement. Use the following scoring system to determine your level of stress:

20–29 You have normal amounts of stress.

30–49 Stress is becoming a problem. You should try to identify the source and manage it.

50–60 Stress is at a dangerous level. Seek help or it could result in worse symptoms, such as alcoholism or illness.

---

*SOURCE: "Stress on the Job? Ask Yourself," *USA Today* (16 June 1987): 7B. Copyright © 1987, USA TODAY. Adapted with permission.

_____ 1. Even over minor problems, I lose my temper and do embarrassing things, like yell or kick a garbage can.

_____ 2. I hear every piece of information or question as criticism of my work.

_____ 3. If someone criticizes my work, I take it as a personal attack.

_____ 4. My emotions seem flat whether I'm told good news or bad news about my performance.

_____ 5. Sunday nights are the worst time of the week.

_____ 6. To avoid going to work, I'd even call in sick when I'm feeling fine.

_____ 7. I feel powerless to lighten my work load or schedule, even though I've always got far too much to do.

_____ 8. I respond irritably to any request from coworkers.

_____ 9. On the job and off, I get highly emotional over minor accidents, like typos, spilled coffee.

_____ 10. I tell people about sports or hobbies that I'd like to do, but say I never have time because of the hours I spend at work.

_____ 11. I work overtime consistently, yet never feel caught up.

_____ 12. My health is running down. I often have headaches, backaches, stomachaches.

_____ 13. If I even eat lunch, I do it at my desk while working.

_____ 14. I see time as my enemy.

_____ 15. I can't tell the difference between work and play; it all feels like one more thing to be done.

_____ 16. Everything I do feels like a drain on my energy.

_____ 17. I feel like I want to pull the covers over my head and hide.

_____ 18. I seem off center, distracted—I do things like walk into mirrored pillars in department stores and excuse myself.

_____ 19. I blame my family—because of them, I have to stay in this job and location.

_____ 20. I have ruined my relationship with coworkers whom I feel I compete against.

III. How Are You Holding Up? Rating the Relative Impact of Stress on Your Life*

Calculating the impact that stress has on our lives can help us to better cope with it. The scale below measures the relative impact of common stressors. Place a check next to each stressor that you've experienced within the last twelve months and then use the scoring instructions below to estimate the effect of stress on your life.

Life Event	Point Values
Death of a close family member	100
Jail term	80
Final year or first year in college	63
Pregnancy (to you or caused by you)	60
Severe personal illness or injury	53

---

*SOURCE: Reprinted with permission from the *Journal of Psychosomatic Research,* 11: 213–18. T. H. Holmes and R. H. Rahe, "The Social Readjustment Rating Scale," © 1967, Pergamon Press, Ltd.

_____	Marriage	50
_____	Any interpersonal problems	45
_____	Financial difficulties	40
_____	Death of a close friend	40
_____	Arguments with your roommate (more than every other day)	40
_____	Major disagreements with your family	40
_____	Major change in personal habits	30
_____	Change in living environment	30
_____	Beginning or ending a job	30
_____	Problems with your boss or professor	25
_____	Outstanding personal achievement	25
_____	Failure in some course	25
_____	Final exams	20
_____	Increased or decreased dating	20
_____	Change in working conditions	20
_____	Change in your major	20
_____	Change in your sleeping habits	18
_____	Several-day vacation	15
_____	Change in eating habits	15
_____	Family reunion	15
_____	Change in recreational activities	15
_____	Minor illness or injury	15
_____	Minor violations of the law	11

Score: _____

Scoring: Total the point values to the right of the items you have checked. If your score is 300 or higher, you run a major risk of incurring a major illness within the next year. If your score is between 200 and 299, your risk is more moderate but is nonetheless real. If your score is between 150 and 199, your risk of incurring a stress-related illness is low.

IV. A Behavior Pattern Inventory*

When life hands you lemons, do you make lemonade or use them as projectiles? Using the scale below, rate each of the following items according to how you typically act. Then follow the scoring instructions to find whether your behavioral tendencies make yours a Type A or a Type B personality.

5. Always. This statement is true of me all the time.
4. Most of the time this is true of me.
3. Sometimes yes, sometimes no.
2. Once in a while I am like this.
1. Absolutely never. This is not like me at all!

a. _____ I like doing things that are very demanding.
b. _____ I am driven and compulsive.
c. _____ I probably work harder than the average person.
d. _____ I enjoy staying active.
e. _____ I often find myself doing two or more things at once.

---

*SOURCE: Adapted from Stephen J. Zyzanski and C. David Jenkins, "Basic Dimensions within the Coronary-Prone Behavior Pattern," *Journal of Chronic Diseases* 22 (1970): 781–95.

CHAPTER 13 / CHANGE, CONFLICT, AND STRESS

f. ____ I always push the elevator button more than once to make sure it comes.
g. ____ I tend to hurry while working, trying to get a lot done.
h. ____ I am a fast eater.
i. ____ I can never find time for haircuts and such things.
j. ____ When people talk very slowly, it drives me crazy.
k. ____ I bring home work from the office regularly.
l. ____ I often help people out when they talk, giving them words and ideas.
m. ____ I know I am competitive.
n. ____ I hate it when people beat me at anything, even sports.
o. ____ I'm often an officer, chair, or head of a committee.
p. ____ I like to take charge.
q. ____ Sometimes I think nothing is worse than waiting in lines.
r. ____ I find it very hard to sit still and not *do* anything.
s. ____ Most of the time, I can be very firm—some might say pigheaded.
t. ____ I'm one of those people who is a foot jiggler and/or finger tapper.
u. ____ I expect people to be perfect, but few are.
v. ____ I dislike it immensely when someone criticizes me.
w. ____ I sometimes find myself sighing when I'm overwhelmed.
x. ____ I often notice that I have my fists clenched.

Scoring: Total the ratings you have assigned to each item.

   100–120 = Hard-core Type A
   80–99 = Strong Type A
   60–79 = Low Type A
   40–59 = Low Type B
   24–39 = Strong Type B

CHAPTER 14

Clients and Marketing

LEARNING OBJECTIVES

After completing this chapter, you should be able to:

- Describe the role of marketing in the legal profession;
- Explain how the marketing of services differs from the marketing of goods;
- Appreciate the marketing concept and the marketing process as they apply to law firms;
- Explain the value of a marketing plan that is based on the right marketing mix;
- Describe how law firms can successfully promote themselves through advertising, public relations, and personal sales;
- Understand the manager's role in marketing, especially in planning and implementing marketing activities;
- Explain the strategies that firms use to attract and retain clients; and
- Understand how a law firm builds organization-wide involvement in marketing by creating a client service culture.

Merrilyn Astin Tarlton is the practice development director for the law firm of Holland & Hart in Denver, Colorado. She has been with the firm since 1984. Ms. Tarlton also currently serves as chair of the Education Board of the Law Practice Management Section of the American Bar Association. She is one of the founders and past president of the National Law Firm Marketing Association. Ms. Tarlton speaks and writes frequently on the marketing of legal services and other management issues.

FOCUS FROM THE FIELD

Merrilyn Astin Tarlton: A Contribution to the Bottom Line

How important has marketing become to law firms?

In the last five years, the number of marketing professionals engaged in law firms in the United States has grown from about twenty-one to almost seven hundred. We are seeing law firms around the country expand their support staff from a single marketing director to up to six or seven marketing staff members. We are also seeing that, even in this economic recession, many law firms are not reducing their marketing budget or their marketing staff. To me, this is an indication that law firms see that there is a contribution to be made to the bottom line.

Are there any characteristics that are unique to law firm marketing?

There are characteristics that are unique to marketing any professional services. Really what you're selling is the person who provides the service. Almost always, the person who provides the service sells the service. In other words, law firms don't hire salespeople to go out and sell their services. That makes law firm marketing somewhat unique. Another reason that it's unique is that lawyers, as a group, share some characteristics in common. They tend to be quite adversarial, by training or by nature, and so they are quicker to challenge marketing concepts than other professionals, such as engineers, who are more analytical. On the plus side, lawyers tend to be very bright and catch on rather quickly. As a result, they have gone through a very sharp learning period in a short time and have picked up client development skills that, five years ago, they never wanted or needed to learn.

How is marketing success measured?

I can't describe for you a science which we have developed to measure marketing success, but I can tell you that the most obvious way is by the bottom line. There is a tendency to want immediate results from particular marketing activities. There seems to be a lack of sophistication about what one can expect from an isolated activity. There is no scientific means of measurement. However, since the concept of marketing is still so new to the law firm setting, it is important to see whether or not the attorneys are comfortable with what is happening. One of the ways that I try to measure the success of a marketing program is by determining if there is a positive feeling about the marketing efforts on behalf of the professionals.

What background do you think is necessary to be a successful marketing professional in a law firm?

Statistics tell us that those people who are successful come from almost any background that you can imagine. We have people who have law degrees, no college degrees, public television experience, and backgrounds in education. It's difficult to pinpoint a specific kind of experience that's helpful in law firm marketing. I think that a very well-developed intuitive sense, a strong sense of motivation, and good diplomatic skills are very helpful. I also think that the greatest characteristic in a law firm setting is the ability to make other people the stars. That is sometimes difficult. Those who have been most successful in the field are the ones who are secure enough and comfortable enough with themselves to be able to do that.

What stage is the marketing field at today in the legal profession?

We are still in the development stages of marketing services in the legal profession. The changes that have occurred over the last few years have been phenomenal, but it's not over yet. Adding marketing to the concept of legal services is either a symptom of the change in law firms or it's a catalyst for what is going on with law firms. I think that within the next ten years, we will see radical changes in how law firms function as businesses. Marketing is going to change the way that lawyers behave in many respects, most or all of which, we hope, will benefit our clients.

As professionals possessing professional skills we still have not only the requirements, but the obligation of actively and energetically selling these skills. They won't sell themselves! We have to sell them. And, if we have to sell them, it is better that we do so on a conscious explicit basis rather than on an unconscious, implicit, hit-or-miss basis.
(Warren Wittreich, "Selling—A Prerequisite to Success as a Professional")[1]

An important thing we can do [in the 1990s] is to learn to market our services more effectively, not only to generate more work, but to generate the right kinds of work.
(Ward Bower, law firm consultant)[2]

MARKETING AND THE LEGAL PROFESSION

The Changing Legal Environment

Bates and O'Steen v. State Bar of Arizona was a breakthrough decision that revolutionized the legal world. In this famous 1977 case, the Supreme Court ruled that the blanket suppression of advertising by lawyers deprived them of the right to free speech guaranteed by the First Amendment.[3] Since that time, competition and marketing needs have led to radically different management activities in law firms across America. A 1990 survey in 44 states revealed that approximately 90 percent of law firms now participate in some form of marketing.[4] Throughout the 1990s, we will see how law firms continue to define the role of marketing, as well as how the legal profession overcomes its resistance to change. In this chapter, we will examine how far marketing has progressed from the days when lawyers and others perceived it as an activity that cheapened the legal profession. Will the "selling" of legal services ever sound dignified? Does it lower the loftiness of the legal profession? There are still lawyers who believe that marketing demeans the profession and that marketing activities are beneath their professional and even personal dignity. This attitude is compounded by the fact that lawyering is a profession that doesn't exactly thrive on humility. To some lawyers, notes Aubrey Wilson, a marketing consultant for professional organizations, to sell their services is to be "involved in an inferior activity."[5] Nonetheless, most firms today accept marketing as an obvious way to meet the demands of the marketplace and acknowledge that the phenomenon is here to stay. Though some lawyers are deeply unhappy about having to depend on marketing to deal with competition, law firms, notes Thomas Clay, "are spending more promotional dollars than ever before," and any that are resisting the trend are "at a terrible disadvantage."[6] Law firms are now learning effective marketing strategies. They are developing marketing plans and establishing computerized data bases of client information. Slowly but surely, they are working their way toward professional marketing expertise.

The Evolution of Marketing in the Legal Profession

Historical Changes

Prior to the 1900s, attorney advertising was commonplace. Among the more notable members of the profession to advertise was Abraham Lincoln. As a politician, Lincoln understood clients. A newspaper notice in *The Iroquois Journal* on 6 July 1853 informed prospective clients that "All business entrusted to them [Lincoln and then-current partner Thomas Herndon] will be attended to with promptness and fidelity." As a businessman, Lincoln understood competition and believed in bringing law to the people. He told his clients his fees in advance; he offered a fee structure sometimes built on ability to pay (which provoked other lawyers to complain that he undersold them); and he advertised not only his services but his whereabouts. In more modern terms, he offered low fees, timely service, and convenient locations. Lincoln had formed and dissolved several different partnerships throughout the years: Stuart and Lincoln, Logan and Lincoln, Lincoln and Lamon, and Lincoln and Herndon. This last partnership, which lasted sixteen years, continued all throughout Lincoln's presidency. "Give our clients to understand," he said, "that the election of a President makes no change in the firm of Lincoln & Herndon." [7]

Professional Perceptions

By 1908, when the ABA, in its Canons of Professional Ethics, expressed its official disapproval of solicitation through the distribution of printed materials, bar association members had decided that advertising was not in keeping with the lofty character of the profession. This attitudinal change reflected the strong views of those who believed that rules against advertising and solicitation would protect the practice of law from becoming commercialized. In a recent Supreme Court decision, Justice Sandra Day O'Connor's dissenting opinion seems to concur with early twentieth century views that advertising by its nature threatened the sanctity and dignity of the legal profession:

> One distinguishing feature of any profession, unlike other occupations that may be equally respectable, is that membership entails a special obligation to temper one's selfish pursuit of economic success by adhering to standards of conduct that could not be enforced either by legal fiat or through the discipline of the market. There are sound reasons to continue pursuing the goal that is implicit in the traditional views of professional life. Both the special privileges incident to membership in the profession and the advantages those privileges give in the necessary task of earning a living are means to a goal that transcend the accumulation of wealth. That goal is public service....
> In my judgment, however, fairly severe restraints on attorney advertising can continue to play an important role in preserving the legal profession as a genuine profession.[8]

Until 1977, bar associations viewed advertising almost as an avaricious evil that would promote economic self-interest as the motivating force of the legal profession. Consequently, they guarded the profession throughout those years with a variety of prohibitions that reinforced the notion that the advertising of legal services was vulgar and unworthy of the profession.[9] Placing a cap on advertising, however, produced side effects that the bar did not foresee. When lawyers began to perceive competitive practices for legal services as unprofessional, costs became secretive to the point of invisibility. As a result, clients were unable to understand fees and pricing for legal services. In addition, safe from competitive scrutiny, costs rose. Surveys now show a high correlation between lawyers' ages and their positive or negative views of advertising. Of those under 35 years of age, 85 percent find advertising acceptable under certain circumstances. The percentage shrinks with age. Of those lawyers over 55, fewer than 50 percent believe that advertising is acceptable, given the right circumstances; one-third of lawyers over 55 think that legal advertising is *never* appropriate.[10] Norman Carpenter, in his monthly book review column for *The Bench and Bar of Minnesota,* describes the impact of widening publicity and other changes on the legal profession:

> In the past two decades, our society, our legislatures, our courts, and we lawyers have seen, caused, and lamented change in the legal profession. The private practice is populated with law firms considered too large to be effective only a few years ago.... As private practice firms become larger and engage in marketing and public relations programs only recently considered ethical, they and their members acquire certain notoriety. Large cases create headlines and the firms involved become themselves the subject of coverage on the business pages and in the newly founded legal press.[11]

Accessing the System

In general, throughout early decades of this century, only those who could afford legal services had access to the justice system. Nonetheless, aware of the need for access to legal services, the legal profession stressed the provision of pro bono efforts. In the 1970s lawyers began to form Legal Clinics, hoping that the clinics would provide acceptable services at reduced costs. Yet legal clinics have not been prolific. Many low-income people still go without legal services because of prohibitive costs.[12] Nonetheless, legal clinics represent a form of competition to which traditional firms have had to respond, often by offering lower fees:

> Thus it is in the traditional law firm setting, if anywhere, that advertising, more efficient operating systems, standardized forms, routinized procedures, word-processing, paralegals working for lawyers and fixed-amount fees are going to increase access to justice for moderate-income people.[13]

Forms of Competition

Law clinics may have become an unexpected competitive factor, but the presence of larger organizations, such as franchised legal firms, have brought the greatest changes. They not only have challenged the fee structure of the ordinary practitioner but have also made consumers out of clients, thereby intensifying competition. The relatively competitive costs for services available through franchises are changing the face of law. Today's new look in the legal profession offers convenient locations well stocked with a variety of legal specialties. They offer standardized fees, legal insurance plans, and packaged services. Some competitors have even found a market niche by offering absolutely frills-free routine legal services.

Hyatt Legal Services. A leader in terms of new approaches to legal service is the Hyatt Legal Services chain, founded in Cleveland, Ohio, in 1977 by Joel Hyatt, Susan Metzenbaum Hyatt, and Wayne Willis. Hyatt speaks of his company's work as a mission. "I was not an entrepreneur when I started Hyatt Legal Services," he says. "I was challenged to make legal services available and affordable to people who did not have access to legal counsel."[14] Through the effective use of television advertising and highly visible yellow pages ads, Hyatt Legal Services offers easy access to local legal services supported by a high-tech network of computerized information. (See Another Look on page 409.)

Legal Services Benefit Plans. One of Hyatt's ventures, Hyatt Legal Plans, Inc., works with employer groups at large corporate firms such as AT&T, PepsiCo, and John Deere to provide prepaid legal service insurance coverage as an employee benefit. Under such plans, which may or may not require copayments of workers, employees are entitled to coverage in predetermined areas such as adoptions, real estate purchases, and simple wills.[15] There are several other employer-funded legal services group plans, some of which are administered by Midwest Legal Services of Des Moines; by Group Legal Services of Prudential Insurance in Roseland, New Jersey; and by the American Prepaid Legal Services Institute, a nonprofit group associated with the American Bar Association. These plans cover matters ranging from adoption to traffic violations and generally place no limits on employee's use of the service.[16] Maryland-based Advisory Communications Systems, Inc., offers a two-tier benefit plan: telephone access to legal advice and referrals and comprehensive employer-funded legal services in conjunction with The Travelers Companies.[17] Such plans have influenced law firms to rethink their service strategies and marketing approaches.

The Challenge of Marketing in Law Firms

Law firms have yet to universally embrace the marketing of legal services as a good business decision, and the practice still meets with opposition and criticism. In spite of the 1977 *Bates* ruling, some still believe that marketing spoils the traditions of the profession. Fixed fees are thought to imply reduced value. Most lawyers believe that it is almost always impossible to decide at a glance whether a legal matter is simple or not. For one thing, they know that complications abound in the practice of law. Second, they believe that fixed-fee services overlook the client counseling necessary to all legal transactions. They also know from experience that seemingly uncontested matters can quickly develop into conflicts of major proportions. As a result, many attorneys believe that lumping legal problems together in a category of generic fees dilutes the quality of legal services. Many critics also believe that certain forms of advertising—such as the televised advertisements of "auto accident attorneys" who promise financial windfalls for personal injuries—reinforce the public perception of attorneys as opportunists and provide consumers with misleading information. Some ads promise "free" initial consultation. The lawyer placing the ad then meets with a prospective client, assesses the opportunities that the

ANOTHER LOOK

Characteristics of Hyatt Legal Services

- Mission: to provide accessible legal services to median-income clients
- Over 114 offices in 22 states and the District of Columbia
- Services of more than 250 attorneys, not including those who work through Hyatt local partnerships
- More than 250,000 clients a year
- Low-price packages, such as $250 for uncontested divorces
- Expenditures of over $5½ million a year
- Fees sheets provided to all clients, with set fee schedules
- Establishment of Hyatt Legal Plans in 1990, offering legal coverage insurance
- Allows attorneys to become local partners after a capital investment
- Local partnerships give attorneys access to advertising, networking, and computer services
- Modest salaries for new lawyers
- Sole use of television and yellow pages advertising

SOURCE: Maurine Christopher, "More Lawyers Turning to TV for Advertising," *Advertising Age* (16 September 1985): 86; Tamar Levin, "Legal Advice: $6.75 a Month," *The New York Times* (3 February 1987): D1, D8.

1. What characteristics of Hyatt Legal Services best account for its success? Will its success continue? Explain.
2. If you were to need legal services, would you consider Hyatt? Why or why not?
3. In what ways might traditional law firms better respond to their clients' needs as consumers?

---

case might offer, and provides none of the advice that is central to the consultation process. Other ads emphasize "no costs unless we win," failing to mention the increased costs that the service will distribute to other consumers in the legal system. Such ads mislead the public as to the complexity of legal services. On the other hand, attorneys using public media marketing techniques maintain that they are making legal services available to people who otherwise could not afford them.[18] Competition has forced open law firm doors, and marketing is making itself at home. It has become a part of how professionals need to do business. The marketing challenge for law firms today is learning to adapt marketing expertise to the selling of legal services.

MARKETING

The Marketing Process

According to the American Marketing Association, **marketing** is the process of planning and putting into practice ways of selling the advantages of one's services in a mutually satisfying exchange of objectives with a consumer or client.[19] In the early part of the century, businesses thought of marketing simply as selling their products or services. Today's broader concept of marketing emphasizes a strategic approach built on analyzing and meeting client needs. Service marketing differs from the marketing of products or other goods in that a service is intangible, perishable, inseparable from its provider, and is by its nature unique and of differing quality.[20]

Intangibility

Goods are tangible, visible, and can be bought and physically owned by a consumer. By comparison, the services of the law firm are intangible. They involve acts, deeds, performances, and efforts which cannot be owned in the sense of purchasing, storing, or hoarding. The value that a consumer places on an intangible like a legal service depends on his or her experience with that service. Intangibility also means that the provider cannot display the service ahead of time, so that the client knows in advance exactly what he or she will receive. A lawyer can only describe the potential benefits of a legal service, what it will entail, and what the client might expect.

Perishability

Many goods have a shelf life of days, weeks, or even months; legal services, in contrast, are perishable, in that they can't truly be stored and used later. The effect of the service may last, but the specific service itself endures only for a limited time. Its value often depends upon the amount of time it takes to provide it; consequently, lawyers work within time restrictions. An attorney who loses time on Monday by attending a funeral will not be able to work with two clients simultaneously the following morning to make up for that lost time.

Inseparability from the Provider

Goods easily can be separated from their producers, being manufactured by one firm, distributed by another, and sold by yet another; but client service is inseparable from its provider, the attorney. The quality of a legal service depends entirely on an attorney's professional skills.

Differing Quality

Goods can be standardized and mass-produced, using quality control at each step of the process. In addition, similar goods are often interchangeable. Services differ immensely, even if the same attorney provides them. Many factors are beyond the attorney's control, and much depends on the number of people the service involves, the intensity of activity, the amount of information necessary and available, and timing.

The Marketing Concept

The **marketing concept** is a business concept which states that an organization, to be profitable, must understand, meet, and satisfy customer needs. Law firms that emphasize client satisfaction are practicing the marketing concept. This kind of marketing orientation has become the key to being profitable in an increasingly competitive legal environment. A **competitive advantage** is the ability to offer some aspect of service that is unique, desirable, or unattainable through other firms. A firm may obtain this competitive edge in two ways: through price and through uniqueness.

Price

A firm that can price its services lower than its competitors usually possesses an advantage. Some firms are able to charge lower fees because of their efficiency of operations or effective management. Essentially, firms base the pricing of services on the level of demand and the nature of the competition. But pricing is complex in that it is linked to people's perceptions of value. Some believe that, in a way, price indicates quality: "You get what you pay for." People tend to connect low prices with low value and high prices with high value; paradoxically, then, they may perceive a firm that charges reasonably low fees as less powerful, prestigious, and effective than one that charges high fees. (That firm, however, may find itself providing services only to those clients who believe they can afford them.) Studies have shown that the costs of legal services are not high on the list of why people choose one law firm rather than another.[21]

Uniqueness

Secondly, a law firm will have a competitive edge if it can persuade clients that it offers something that no other firm does. This is known as **product differentiation:** an organization's ability to build on the uniqueness of its particular brand of service. We can differentiate law firms in several ways. They can be distinct because of the expertise they offer in a particular area of the law, because of the genuine personal interest and attentiveness they convey in the delivery of legal services, and because of their style and reputation. Some firms, promising superb quality and results, build on their professional image and the respect that they command in the practice of law. Others proclaim their reliability and the utmost adherence to ethical behavior; still others promote their services through an image that combines aggression and wily know-how. Finally, firms can use accessibility to legal services as a selling point by promoting their low costs.

The Marketing Mix

To build its reputation, business, and profitability, a firm must be able to reach and meet the needs of clients. For each firm, the **marketing mix** consists of an appropriate blend of the four P's of marketing: product, price, place, and promotion.

Product

The result of an organization's efforts, a **product** is the good or service that the organization offers to meet the needs and wants of society. The uniqueness of the product contributes to its competitive advantage.

Price

Price is the amount of money asked or paid for something based on its perceived value or worth. A law firm determines the price of its legal services by proposing fees and establishing as prices those fee amounts that clients will pay.

Place

Place is the location of the law firm in relation to those who need and want its services. Since consumers determine the need for a given service, a law firm's placement helps to determine the kinds of services that the firm should provide. For example, legal specialties based on an expertise in technology laws would be in demand in intensely developed high-tech areas. In considering placement, law firms also must consider area competition, the legal and regulatory climate, social trends, and accessibility to clients.

Promotion

Promotion is any form or level of communication that an organization utilizes for the purpose of increasing the use of its services. Promotion is used for several purposes: to increase visibility, to persuade prospective clients, and to educate the public and reassure it that the organization is a positive presence, one that is interested in being of service. Firms promote themselves mainly through personal selling, public relations activities, and advertising, three techniques that we will examine later in this chapter.

Positioning

Positioning is the process of understanding consumer needs and of meeting those needs by offering a product that is distinctive enough to be markedly advantageous when compared to that of a competitor. It is carving out a unique niche for services. A law firm can achieve positioning through each of the four P's of marketing: by offering a singular service, by creating a distinctive value in terms of price, by finding an appropriate place, or by distinctively promoting its services. The process of positioning strengthens the effectiveness of these traditional marketing concepts.

The Marketing Plan

A **marketing plan** describes what actions the firm needs to take, why they are necessary, when the plan is to take place, and who will be responsible for the plan's actions, implementation, and coordination. A marketing plan is useless unless the firm is committed to the plan's value and implementation. Firm members can call on consultants to develop a marketing plan, but the firm itself is ultimately "the best architect" for its own marketing plan.[22] Marketing plans have five basic elements: (1) an analysis of the current situation, (2) the development of specific objectives, (3) the creation of strategies, (4) the implementation of those strategies, and (5) the monitoring and measuring of results.

Analysis of the Current Situation

An analysis of the current situation reveals where the firm is right now, where it is headed, and where it wants to be headed. Completely analyzing a firm's existing client base and the potential market will provide data on the types of legal activities that have proven to be the most profitable, on sources of business, and on financial reports that include specific client data.[23] The law firm needs to base its marketing decisions on solid, useful information. Analysis methods include in-house studies of management reports and other records, written questionnaires, telephone surveys, interviews, and special focus groups which obtain more specific information in areas of special interest.

Development of Marketing Objectives

In developing specific marketing objectives, management determines the firm's areas of strength or weakness, and the partners decide on the goals that the firm wishes to reach through its marketing plan. Some possible goals might include increased profitability, a greater emphasis on long-range strategies, and practice development.

Creation of Strategies

The creation of strategies focuses on methods for reaching the selected objectives. Marketing strategies traditionally include areas such as market penetration, market development, product development, and diversification. These strategies consist of the marketing tactics and tools the firm will use: brochures, resumes, advertisements, presentations, seminars, and television time. The firm will determine its choice of methods by assessing the costs, time requirements, and potential benefits of each.

Implementation of Strategies

In implementing strategies, which requires the development of specific tactics, the firm might focus on developing client commitment through a customer contact program, increasing the visibility of a new practice specialty through a marketing campaign, enhancing the firm's image through a program that targets increased community involvement, or increasing profitability through a campaign that involves the firm's attorneys more intensely in personal sales.

Monitoring and Measuring

The final part of a marketing plan is to monitor it as it progresses and to measure its results. This surveillance enables the firm to determine if its marketing objectives are being met through its marketing efforts. The law firm should ask how successful it was in meeting the goals it established and use the answer when making future marketing decisions.

PERSONAL SELLING

Personal selling is the use of persuasive techniques to convince potential buyers to use one's service. Being able to sell is to be able to persuade others by communicating a personal conviction regarding the value of what one is selling. Selling requires these basic qualities: confidence, a healthy ego, drive and the determination to go on trying, an outgoing personality, the ability to read both a situation and a prospect's reactions, good listening skills, and empathy.

FIGURE 14-1
Marketing and Organizational Objectives

Organizational Objectives
The goal of all marketing is ultimately to assist the law firm in reaching its organizational objectives.

Marketing Objectives and Strategies
The firm reaches its marketing objectives through effective use of the following strategies:
- Conducting Marketing Research
- Analyzing Data
- Planning a Firm Marketing Approach
- Implementing the Firm's Marketing Plan

The Four P's of Marketing
- **Product:** Services Offered
- **Price:** Fee Structure and Arrangements
- **Place:** Location and Accessibility
- **Promotion:** Sales Promotion, Public Relations, Personal Selling, and Advertising

The AIDA Process of Personal Selling

Those who have been successful in selling know that the communication between a buyer and a seller takes place in phases. The phases are described by the acronym AIDA: being aware of the buyers' needs, attracting their interest by describing how your product or service can meet those needs, responding to their desires by convincing them that what you are selling can in fact meet those needs, and by leading the buyers to act by purchasing your product or service. These four phases apply effectively to the selling of legal services. Sellers persuade clients to trust that the quality and competency of the yet-to-be-delivered and unseen legal service will meet their needs. The successful seller of legal services develops a buyer's faith by overcoming suspicion, asking the buyer to trust the firm's competence in delivering an intangible product that the buyer may or may not understand. The selling of services, therefore, evolves from the basic relationships established between a buyer and a seller, the law firm client and the service provider.

Proposals and Team Presentations

Proposals are devices that a firm uses to convince prospects of the competency of its products. They can range, notes Haserot, from the simplest of descriptions to complex assessments of "how the lawyers interpret the prospective client's situation, needs and objectives, and how they intend to solve the problems and achieve the goals."[24] Given an opportunity to make a proposal, a firm above all must convince the prospect of the value it has to offer. The proposal itself must be a carefully sculpted and persuasive communication. Within the time that the prospect is willing to allow, the firm's representatives must make a case for why their particular firm is uniquely able to assist the prospective client. The proposal, the personal meeting, and the presentation must inspire the prospect's confidence and trust, the keys to selling intangibles.[25]

Research

The main objective in selling is to meet the buyer's needs. To do this, presenters must perform substantial background work. This research will enable them to understand and to meet the expectations and needs of the prospective buyer, responding to them directly (see Table 14–1).

Format

The presentation's format will depend on the setting for the presentation, which can vary widely. Presentations can be as informal as an uncomplicated luncheon meeting, with a few influential partners meeting with one or two prospective clients, depending on whether the legal affairs involve individuals or organizations. At the other extreme, the presentation can take place in a boardroom or a conference room and reflect the strictest rules of formality and protocol.

Team Members

Members of the law firm must meet to plan the presentation in as professional a way as possible, according to their analysis of the prospective client. The first decision they must make is to determine who will make the presentation. Will the firm be more successful if they select one person or a team of attorneys, senior partners, or those in the specialty area only?

Written Presentation

For the written aspect of the presentation, those involved must carefully choose or prepare the materials and information that will best represent the firm.

Abstract. In a brief statement, the presenters should summarize their proposal. A few short, well-worded sentences are needed to assess the situation that the

---

TABLE 14–1
Questions to Answer when Preparing for a Presentation

When does the client want the information about the firm's skill and expertise?
Where and when will we meet?
Who will be present?
Who will make the decision to hire the firm?
Who else is the client talking to?
Why is the client interested in our firm?
Is there a particular case in question or is the client seeking general counsel?
What is the history of the situation?
Does the client want something in writing?

SOURCE: Merrilyn Astin Tarlton, "Business Presentations: A Brief Outline for Making the Best Pitch to Prospects," *Legal Management* (January/February 1989): 7.

client faces and the ways in which the firm can be of service.

Goals and Objectives. This section lists concisely what the firm's services will help the client to accomplish.

Scope of Services. This section, which contains the firm's proposed plan of action, is the heart of the proposal; and, as such, it should be the most fully developed. In this section, the presentation addresses the client's needs, showing what the firm can do to meet those needs, how it will do so, and when. This section must be measured and realistic: promising more than can be delivered is a serious mistake. In some marketing situations, such "puffery" is fairly harmless. Here, it represents an effort to mislead. The law firm risks damaging its credibility and its reputation.

Firm Capabilities and Policies. The proposal should contain information on the firm, a summary analysis of the prospective client's request, the firm's proposed staffing (complete with credentials of the principal players), its expertise in the type of work being considered, fee and billing policies, potential conflicts, if any, and an assurance of confidentiality. The firm's philosophy should reflect that of the client, to ensure a good working relationship.

Marketing Pieces. In addition to the preceding materials, the presentation packet might contain any other appropriate informative materials that emphasize the competency of the firm.

Rehearsal

A dry run will help to establish roles for each member of the firm's presentation team. Rehearsal allows the members to determine the verbal messages they wish to convey and to practice appropriate perception and image management. In addition, the team must decide who will open the presentation, who will lead it, what order it will have, what style will be used, and what specific aspects of the presentation will be summarized in the closing statements. Rehearsing builds confidence, reveals any gaps in the presentation, and displays the teamwork that prospective clients expect. The presentation showcases the firm's talents in an unobtrusive and professionally polished way.

Follow-Up

After the presentation, the lead attorney is responsible for telephoning the prospective clients to ask if they need any additional information and to thank them for meeting with the firm's representatives. The team members increase their skills as presenters by meeting to evaluate their strengths and weaknesses after each presentation.

PUBLIC RELATIONS

Public relations is the use of communications to promote prestige and good will; to maintain, correct, or enhance the firm's reputation; or to explain the firm's mission or purpose in serving the public. It is any communication that reputably increases the firm's visibility, enhances its image, or convinces the public of the competency and skill of its attorneys. Only lately, notes Edward Burke, law practice development consultant for, as well as a vice president of, Hildebrandt, Inc., have firms needed to come to grips with the consequences of visibility:

> It wasn't too long ago that public relations enjoyed a sleepy, comfortable existence in the backwater of law firm priorities—on a par with, say, what kind of flowers to have in the reception area. . . . Then came the legal press, and managing partners were suddenly besieged by reporters who not only had the temerity to ask tough questions but the cheek to actually expect an answer. After the initial shock, most firms settled back into a self-satisfied passivity, in the comforting assumption that this was of no consequence to their clients.[26]

Firms have realized as of late that good and bad press *do* make a difference. It is not only size that has made law firms more visible, but the amount of settlements, the number of cable networks that televise congressional hearings and courtroom proceedings, an increase in the number of legal publications other than the traditional law school journals, and the increased number of reporters assigned solely to legal coverage in general publications that reach millions of people have made a difference as well. *The Wall Street Journal* has eight legal reporters and two legal editors; *The New York Times* and the *Chicago Tribune* have weekly law columns and regular coverage of legal happenings of consequence; and national news magazines all have legal affairs reporters.[27] This has made law firms increasingly aware of the need for active public relations programs. Public relations differs from advertising in that it is not a service that a firm pays for, in terms of buying space in a magazine or printing and mailing fliers, for example. Public relations efforts center around specific tools: contacts with the press, visibility activities, communications, and image management.[28]

Use of the Media

Law firms utilize the popular media for public relations in many ways: through news releases, television and other media appearances, as on CNN or local stations, testimony at legislative hearings, and public speaking engagements or appearances. Working well with members of the media requires a firm to make special efforts, based on two-way exchanges. In being conscious of public relations, firm members should know when they should or should not speak to the press, the degree of availability they should provide, and how to contribute successful press releases. As part of its two-way exchanges with members of the media, the firm should offer information which provides glimpses into the firm's operations: all new hires, changes in association, promotions to management, the development of new specialties, and coverage of seminars. Whatever is happening that is of human interest can be used to place the firm's name in the public eye. A firm event—moving offices, for example, can be a cause for public celebration. To build good will, the firm might sponsor festivities for members of the local business community and for current and prospective clients. Personal contacts within the media also can benefit the firm. Building a respectful working relationship with members of the media provides access to the press when the firm needs it, although a law firm that persistently asks for favors and floods media contacts with trivia can easily be perceived as a self-serving pest.

Professional Public Relations

Many firms now are looking to professional public relations firms for their expertise. To date, this new relationship has presented some challenges in terms of incompatibility: public relations firms are eager to release articles on recent courtroom victories while the lawyers involved are just as anxious to protect client confidentiality. For many law firms, obtaining higher visibility without damaging their credibility—such as by obtaining newspaper coverage for lawyers by having them interviewed or quoted on issues, not on matters dealing with clients—is a tricky challenge.[29] Public relations firms also need to maintain tight communications with the law firms, in order to ensure that their information in legal areas is accurate and up-to-date.

In-house Public Relations Activities

Many firms have developed their own procedures and policies for working with the public media. One common system involves keeping an updated listing of media contacts that the firm can use to establish steady communications with the media. The database should include information on editors and their areas of responsibility, newspaper contacts, and news directors. The firm can use this information to generate personalized mailings for press releases, announcements, notices of seminars, and similar communications about firm activities of all types. The San Francisco-based firm of Morrison & Foerster, with offices in cities around the world, prepares a reference guide, targeted at the press, to provide regularly updated data about the firm. The guide contains information on the firm's size, areas of expertise, locations, members, and offices.[30] The guide also serves as a resource when media professionals are looking for specialists for opinions on current events. Both the media and the legal profession have needs. A relationship that is mutually beneficial is a profitable one.

Professional Activities

Becoming involved in professional and community activities enhances both the firm's reputation and the reputation of those members who are directly involved.

Community Involvement

Community involvement, besides its potential for good, also keeps firm members in contact with community leaders and activists. Such networking can increase visibility, create name recognition, and promote a socially responsive image of caring and involvement. Pro bono activities of this type can contribute to the local community, its civic and service organizations, its educational institutions, and its church groups. The American Bar Association reports that over 130,000 lawyers are part of 648 pro bono programs that the ABA and local associations have organized.[31] Lawyers can contribute their time and expertise to advisory boards, local civic and community groups, and boards of trustees of colleges and universities.

Professional Programs

Seminars, lectures, and workshops for clients have become public relations marketing techniques with which many professional firms feel at ease. They are currently the most commonly used professional marketing tools.[32] Seminars and lectures have proven effective both in boosting a firm's client base and in helping to develop a mailing list of present and prospective clients.[33] Effective public relations programs reflect the following traits:

Audience-Appropriate Content. A seminar, lecture, or workshop should focus on areas of current interest; such presentations seem to work best when they are tailored to a specific audience, such as small business owners. The presenters should prepare both an outline as well as a packet of materials that provides additional information.

Marketing Materials. Firms that capitalize on the time spent in presenting seminars know the advantages of including information on the firm, brochures, reprints of articles, newsletters, and comparable materials.

Educational Cosponsoring. A firm can offer seminars and lectures in conjunction with local colleges or universities, which often are willing to lend their expertise in offering educational programs as part of cosponsoring the event. Offering a seminar involves more than choosing a topic and extending invitations. The smoother and more professional the presentation, the more confidence attendees will have in the competency of the sponsoring law firm.

Carefully Chosen Attendees. Part of the knack for running effective seminars, workshops, and lectures lies in knowing who will attend. The right guests must be invited. To do this, a firm might maintain a data base of current and prospective clients from which it can cull mailing lists for target audiences consisting of clients who have similar needs. Members of a target audience are more apt to accept the firm's invitation if the seminar promises to address their specific needs. On the other hand, a firm that plans to address more general but hot topics can also send open invitations to prospective clients. This is another way to guarantee both successful attendance and an updated listing of prospects.

Image Management

Image is the perception that others have of an organization, based on its services, members, characteristics, and culture. For a law firm, image consists of the message that the firm communicates to the public regarding what it represents. Through impression management, the art of shaping others' perceptions, the firm creates a positive image for itself by enhancing and presenting publicly appealing qualities such as professionalism, success, and competence.[34] The more visual clues the firm can provide, the more convinced onlookers will be that the image is true. We expect law firms to follow the same kinds of rules for maintaining appearances as individuals do. Firms skilled at impression management embody these expectations in tastefully appointed spaces, well-dressed personnel, quality stationery, professionally published materials, and corporate-world etiquette. Occasionally, successful renegades set their own standards, but the general expectations for a law firm's professional image are quite demanding and restrictive. The image a firm creates is one of many ways in which firms can distinguish themselves from their competitors. For example, a law firm that advertises communicates its image through its selection of visuals. A professional but distinctive graphic image will help current and prospective clients to better understand the firm. The image of the competent law firm emphasizes dignity, success, and taste. In studies of client reactions to law firm advertising, advertisements that received positive ratings in general also received higher dignity ratings from both consumers and lawyers.[35]

ADVERTISING

Advertising is the use of printed or electronic media to bring the advantages of an available service to the public's attention. Some of these practices now in use by law firms include television advertising, yellow pages ads, law firm brochures, and newsletters.

Television

Television, notes Van O'Steen, a party to the 1977 landmark lawyer advertising case *Bates and O'Steen v. State Bar of Arizona,* is "the most effective advertising medium law firms have for reaching a broad segment of the general public." Though television advertising may not be cost-effective for all law firms, it can convey a firm's message to thousands or even millions of people.[36] Through its combination of aural and visual images, it also has great potential for conveying personality, emotions, and trust. Because these are critical elements in selling intangibles such as legal services, television advertising can be a remarkably valuable tool. Its effectiveness depends on understanding how the medium works and on arranging for and purchasing the right combinations of time. Studies have shown that the most persuasive television ads are those that show attorneys in professional office settings. Hyatt Legal Services, in working with a New York ad agency, recently developed a television ad campaign that combined visuals of the restored historical sites of Abraham Lincoln's law offices in Springfield, Illinois, with views of Hyatt offices. Speaking on-screen and in voice-overs, founder Joel Hyatt drew parallels between Hyatt's practices and Lincoln's: ''His fees were so low, they alarmed his fellow lawyers. And on top of that, Abraham Lincoln advertised.''[37]

The Yellow Pages

Many firms and some solo practitioners, in particular, have had successful results from the effective placement of yellow pages ads. The use of yellow page advertising by attorneys has increased dramatically over the past few years, to the point that some believe that finding a lawyer by perusing the yellow pages is now like looking for a needle in a haystack. Advertising experts claim that yellow page ads are relatively ineffective in isolation: they work best when used in tandem with advertising in other media. Clients who know an attorney's name from television advertising, for example, are more likely to consider using that attorney when they encounter his or her ad in the yellow pages. ''Unless the ad is supported by other creative advertising,'' O'Steen explains, ''it is unlikely to be effective unless it is very near the beginning of the attorney display ads or it is for a highly specialized type of practice (other than personal injury).''[38]

Newsletters

Newsletters have become one of the most popular vehicles for communicating law firm services. Many firms circulate three or four issues a year, often to small, select target groups, and at a cost of as much as $10 per copy, for small pressruns. A newsletter requires substantial commitments of time and money, and producing one is a continuing responsibility. It entails selecting subjects of interest, writing and editing the material, and overseeing production. It also requires firm members to maintain an up-to-date mailing list of clients and prospects (those who *want* to receive the newsletter) and to publish content that is up-to-date as well. A spring quarterly issue full of material written at the beginning of the year that is not printed until fall and not mailed until winter can do considerable damage to a firm's image. In addition to having out-of-date information, clients may perceive that their cases will receive the same shoddy treatment. Newsletters also can be overdone, and firms are advised to keep their publications short, readable, and in demand.

> In a world that considers advertising undignified but where the competition for business is intense, law firm newsletters are an increasingly popular marketing tool. The newsletters, often on expensive glossy paper with color graphics, are sent free of charge to clients and prospective clients.[39]

A firm wishing to produce a newsletter basically has two options. In the first, members can research, write, design, and print the materials entirely in-house. The second option is to purchase materials that have been professionally researched and written for the firm by an outside agency. The firm would then customize these materials by imprinting them with its name. Some perceive custom printing as more efficient and economical than in-house efforts; others believe that in-house materials represent a good investment of time and energy because they are more personalized and adaptable.[40] With a bit of help from the firm's communications experts, newsletters produced in-house often can convey the firm's message more directly and in a more up-to-date way than professionally produced materials. They also can target the unique needs of area clients without sounding canned.[41]

Brochures

Over 75 percent of the country's law firms provide some form of brochure that summarizes and explains the firm.[42] A typical brochure outlines services and includes biographies of the firm's principal members. Some incorporate material on the firm's associates, paralegals, and management as well. Brochures are best kept flexible. Some firms utilize modular units of information in their brochures, including inserts that the firm may change as necessary to update changes in its membership and specialization areas. Brochures can help a firm to cross-sell services, create positive impressions, change or reinforce its image, and present official statements. In addition, they can provide consumers with information to assist them in making informed decisions regarding legal services.[43]

Desktop Publishing and Computer Graphics

Used properly, desktop publishing and computer graphics permit a law firm to produce in-house publications that have the look and appeal of professionally printed materials. With a laser printer, a high-quality copier, and a software program such as, *PageMaker, Harvard Graphics, Applause,* or *WordPerfect's DrawPerfect* a firm can create a wide variety of materials. For instance, through the use of computer graphics, firm members can produce striking visuals in the form of slides, transparencies, and computer programs on data display terminals. In terms of printed matter, this use of new technology can turn out a host of materials quickly, efficiently, and (for extra effect) colorfully: regularly updated brochures, notices to clients regarding regulations and statutes, flyers advertising seminars, meeting luncheons, or special guest speakers sponsored by the firm, analytical and presentation graphs and charts, and informative materials for prospective clients.

PRACTICE DEVELOPMENT

Practice development relies on the continuing efforts of all members of the law firm to attain and sustain a suitable client base through marketing, public relations, and a well-founded and justified reputation for quality legal services.

Managerial Responsibilities

The firm's administration is responsible for its marketing principles. Top management must support marketing, with the conviction that it enhances the firm's values. The firm's management controls the marketing process and keeps it focused. Managerial marketing responsibilities include ensuring that expectations are realistic, allocating adequate resources for marketing efforts, and evaluating the efficacy of those efforts. When used from the marketing perspective, Mintzberg views the manager's contribution to the marketing process as part of interpersonal, informational, and decision-making roles.[44]

Interpersonal Roles

The first interpersonal role a manager fills is that of *figurehead;* as such, he or she visibly represents the firm and attends meetings on its behalf, with professional groups as well as with community and civic ones such as the chamber of commerce, Kiwanis, and Zonta. In the second role, that of *leader,* the manager coordinates and supervises the activities of the subordinates for whom he or she is responsible. In this role, the manager works at motivating firm members and involving them in the firm's marketing strategies. In the third interpersonal role, *liaison,* the manager keeps in touch with all stakeholders, sharing their ideas and representing them to others. In this role, the manager acts as the linking pin between groups, including outside constituencies and professional colleagues. As a liaison, a manager must maintain a positive image of the firm to outsiders.

Informational Roles

In the informational roles that a manager plays, he or she first serves as *monitor* of the marketing process, overseeing the firm's client data base, collecting information, and preparing reports. Developing a marketing plan may involve many of the firm's members, but monitoring the coordination and implementation of the firm's long- and short-term marketing strategies is a task best performed by one person. In firms without a marketer or a marketing committee, this responsibility goes to the firm administrator. The second informational role the manager plays is that of *disseminator.* In this capacity, in helping with marketing efforts, the manager distributes data, regularly sends information, and circulates memos, notices, or newsletters to all members of the firm, keeping the firm's marketing objectives before their eyes. The third informational role filled is that of *spokesperson.* As a spokesperson, the manager shares information about the firm with outsiders. He or she also speaks for the partners to the rest of the firm's members, communicating the directions they believe the firm should take in order to be responsive to new trends, ideas, and practices.

Decisional Roles

In this final set of roles, a manager first acts as an *entrepreneur* in terms of the firm's marketing plan, inspiring, motivating, overseeing, and coordinating lawyers' efforts. In addition, as entrepreneurs, they creatively interpret the directions the firm intends to take, come up with ideas that add to its marketing efforts, and facilitate the firm's marketing successes. In the capacity of decision maker, the manager also acts as a *disturbance handler*. Because he or she cares about the firm, its members, and its image, the manager helps to resolve inner conflicts related to marketing and also represents the firm to the press, polishing its image and quelling negative rumors, when necessary. In a third decision-making capacity, the manager acts as a *resource allocator*. As such, the manager proposes marketing expenditures, such as investments, and tracks their financial soundness. He or she pursues trends, data, and firm results and prepares management reports on the use of resources, knowing that the firm must preserve simultaneously its profitability and a certain operating style. For many law firms, cost-consciousness never used to be an issue. Today's economy, however, forces firms to differentiate legitimate from wasteful expenses. Finally, in the fourth decision-making role, the manager functions as a *negotiator*, collecting and disseminating data that will be used for resolutions. The manager works closely with attorneys in this role, seeing which of them have been asked and are willing to represent the firm and to participate in its marketing efforts. The manager also works with the firm's marketing committee to find ways to involve all members in the firm's marketing activities.

Overcoming Obstacles to Marketing

Managers must also work at helping firm members to understand the valid role of marketing within the firm, overcoming their concerns about the effects that marketing can have on professionalism by offering them reasonable marketing alternatives. The traditional individualism of members must also be transformed into a mutual concern about meeting competitive demands. In addition, managers can prepare informational reports that can help the firm's partners and committees to make sound and acceptable marketing decisions. Because successful marketing will involve each member of the firm, managers also should develop strategies for helping the firm members to cope with the changes that marketing will bring. Through strategies designed to overcome resistance to change, managers can develop an employee mentality that welcomes and is proud of marketing efforts.

Marketing Responsibilities

Traditionally, law firms entrusted the responsibility of bringing in business to one or more prominent members whose sterling contacts could cause work to rain like manna from clouds of prospective clients. Today, law firms continue to encourage and reward their rainmakers, but marketing responsibilities are beginning to pervade firm membership. Partners, for example, who once designed committees to meet all of their firms' marketing needs, are using time at partners' meetings to commit themselves to marketing roles. Most firms now realize that they need marketing efforts that are more vigorous, more professional, and still in keeping with the image of a professional organization. They realize, too, that this new breed of marketing is not within the traditional areas of legal expertise. All lawyers know that "the lawyer who represents himself has a fool for a client"; yet, notes O'Steen, "most lawyers who market their professional practices do it themselves, with virtually no expert assistance."[45] This has led to bemusement, shattered faith in marketing, and many costly advertising failures. Only an estimated 24 percent of firms in a national survey reported that they had formed and used marketing committees; 24 percent had hired marketing administrators; and another 24 percent had hired outside marketing consultants. (Of the remaining 28 percent, 18 percent seem to use informal or mixed marketing approaches and 10 percent perform no marketing activities at all.)[46] "Many firms are realizing that full-time business development efforts require full-time attention," writes Alan Levine, a consultant for Hildebrandt, Inc., "and few lawyers are prepared or eager to commit the necessary time and energy."[47] Some firms have invited marketing experts for in-house seminars, and others have hired outside consultants on a per-project or a part-time basis, but all realize that rainmaking is a firm-wide responsibility requiring specialized skills and a professional approach.

In-house Marketing Professionals

The use of in-house professionals offers law firms consistent help with their marketing needs. Some firms have found marketing experts within their ranks; those who are familiar with the firm and its activities have a marked advantage over those approaching the firm from outside. Some firms have hired consultants on a special project basis; others, on an ongoing part-time basis.

Marketing Committees

In any firm, the attorneys who are most interested in planning marketing strategies can become an effective marketing team. Many marketing committees have developed their expertise out of necessity. Committee members can look upon learning this new skill as a challenge and as part of their commitment to the future of the firm. Nonetheless, many attorneys, despite the potential payback from such contributions and the natural marketing skills these people may have, begrudge the time they spend on marketing committees as time taken away from practicing law. Marketing directors at law firms say that some lawyers have a knack for the sales aspects of legal services; others "must be coached so that they do not come across to potential clients as arrogant."[48]

Marketing Coordinators

Some firms promote a current member, such as a paralegal or long-time secretary, to coordinate the marketing efforts and to implement the decisions of the firm's lawyers and their marketing or management committees. Although providing members with opportunities is a valuable practice, in this instance it can be unfair both to the firm and to the individual. To be effective, the person filling the position needs marketing expertise, credibility, and leadership of the firm's professionals. These shoes are not easy to fill. Becoming a marketing coordinator may place almost impossible expectations on the shoulders of an ex-secretary, paralegal, or attorney, as talented as he or she might be.[49]

Consultants

Consultants can be welcome change agents. As outside marketing professionals, they have the potential for enabling the firm to consider and achieve goals it would never have considered otherwise. As Levine explains,

> Consultants can be tremendously effective in initiating marketing efforts, educating lawyers in marketing theories, training lawyers to function as business developers and carrying out discreet projects—from market research to putting together a public relations program. They bring objectivity, authority, and expertise to the firm.[50]

But consultants do not stay to implement plans or to maintain momentum in the firm when lawyers become re-engulfed in their professional work. They also do not have the sense of ownership in the firm that can shape marketing decisions.

Marketing Directors

Some firms, like Holland & Hart in Denver, have created positions for marketing professionals. Within the last five years, over 200 law firms have hired marketing directors. As nonlawyers, these people find themselves entering a new and sometimes resistant environment. Nonetheless, law firm marketing directors will grow in stature as their efforts bear fruit and as they forge lasting professional relationships of trust and mutual respect with other law firm members, particularly partners.

CLIENTS

A **client** is someone who depends upon another for services and skills that the client will use on his or her own behalf. Law firm clients depend on lawyers for their knowledge, conceptual skills, and communication skills. Those who study *consumer behavior* attempt to explain why people choose to spend their money in obtaining one thing rather than another, whether it be a product or a service. In other words, they attempt to determine the reasoning behind peoples' buying decisions. The intricacies of law have created the need for legal services. To answer the mutual dependency it represents, the client-lawyer relationship involves more than the provision of services: it requires trust, respect, consideration, and genuine concern on the lawyer's part. These relationships are the responsibility of every member of the firm, since the client is hiring not the attorney alone but the services of the entire organization. This takes more than efficient, austerely business-like dealings. "The key," notes Lowell Forte, "is to achieve efficiency and effectiveness while retaining an environment that's responsive to the client."[51] William Davidow, a general partner in a California high-tech venture capital firm, and Bro Uttal, a consultant with McKinsey & Co., explain further:

> The tools used to position customer service operations are the same communication tools any marketer uses—advertising, promotion, public relations and everything else that affects the all-important word of mouth. But sending messages about service is different from most forms of marketing communication. Since service is intangible, advertising has a special mission to dramatize service in ways that make the benefits clear and real.[52]

Clients as Consumers

As consumers, clients base their decisions on how much they need or want the services your firm can provide, on their willingness and ability to pay for what those services cost, and on their attitudes toward or perceptions of the value of those services. Among the factors that explain consumer decisions are rational and emotional motives, cognitive dissonance, and cultural factors.

Rational and Emotional Motives

Marketing experts say that consumers base their decisions on one of two types of motives. The first is the **rational motive,** prompted by a logical conclusion about the costs, dependability, and perceived usefulness of a particular product or service. The second type of motive is the **emotional motive,** which arises from one or more of these factors: the pleasure or emotional satisfaction that the client thinks paying for legal services will bring; fear, which involves the client's belief that legal services will protect him or her from a real or imagined threat to life, safety, security, or even ego; pride, in being associated with the prestige or status of a given firm's services; sociability, or doing the "in" thing in terms of obtaining legal services; and emulation, by which the client imitates those whom he or she admires or trusts in his or her choice of a service provider.[53] These motives can blend or overlap.

Cognitive Dissonance

In 1957, Leon Festinger suggested that people are motivated in general to resolve discrepancies between their attitudes and their overt behavior. More specifically, he defined cognitive dissonance as the intellectual discomfort or anxiety a person experiences when his or her attitudes, concepts, or perceptions of behavior are contradictory and inconsistent.[54] We might apply his theory to a client's choice of law firms. Let's say that Geri, after receiving advice from friends, associates, and colleagues, chooses Firm X to handle her personal injury suit. Once the case is settled, Geri will evaluate the services she has received. If she is satisfied—that is, if her experience with Firm X matches her expectations—she will be likely to call on the firm again, should the need arise. If she is dissatisfied, however, dissonance in the form of an intellectual discomfort or remorse will exist between her expectations and her experience, and Geri will be likely to take her future legal needs to a firm that can provide her with peace of mind. The ability to preclude or resolve cognitive dissonance in a client's mind is known as developing his or her loyalty. For products, we think in terms of brand loyalty; in terms of services, we think of loyalty as client commitment. With this in mind, a law firm should be aware of its role in forming realistic client perceptions and expectations. A client must not be deceived or even disappointed in the services that the firm provides, no matter what the outcome of the legal decision. The firm should make efforts to follow up, contact, or meet with the client, to reassure him or her of the firm's sincere interest in the client as a person and of its concern for the outcome of the work it performed on the client's behalf. A note or letter, sent apart from the bill and expressing the firm's appreciation for the opportunity to work with the client and to be of service, will help the client to evaluate his or her overall satisfaction. A surprising amount of return business can hinge on a firm's skill and sincerity in following up.

Cultural Factors

Many other factors affect the decision to purchase one service rather than another. Situational factors such as immediacy and convenience might lead people to choose a lawyer's services because hers was the first name they saw in the yellow pages, because of easy accessibility, or because they recognized the name of the firm. In addition to these simpler reasons, consumers make decisions that they think are in keeping with their social class, choosing between large, upscale firms known for their power and prestige, and down-to-earth solo practitioners with whom it is easy to work. People also make decisions because of their reference groups: they listen to the advice of people who are important or significant to them. They also make decisions based on the effect that they believe a given firm's services will have on their self-image, much in the same way that a consumer of goods contemplates the purchase of an article of designer clothing.[55]

Why Clients Choose Law Firms

Some of the reoccurring reasons for selecting law firms, according to a study of the motives of leading decision makers, are the following, in order from most to least common: (1) results of the firm's work; (2) the quality of counsel and advice; (3) expertise in a given area; (4) personal interest taken in the client's legal affairs; (5) the quality of written product; (6) keeping clients informed of work progress; (7) verbal skills; (8) fast turnaround on work; (9) personal interest taken in the client's business; (10) access to top people in the firm; (11) the firm's reputation in the community; (12) the ability to work with a specific lawyer; (13) the firm's representation of similar clients; (14) low costs; (15) the firm's size; (16) location of the firm's offices; and (17) the political connections that the client or the firm may have.[56] Other familiar reasons for selecting a law firm are the direct business contacts clients have had with members of the firm, the firm's reputation, and the reputation of a particular attorney. Other factors that influence the decision include referrals by friends, social or civic contact, and direct marketing.[57]

Selection Exclusivity

Most clients tend to use several firms, depending on the services they need. Firms that can provide multiple services for the same clients often see even the most satisfied clients take their needs elsewhere. This sometimes happens simply because a law firm has yet to develop skill at cross-marketing. To do so, the firm might establish a client retention program through which it would communicate the availability of other services. Clients also use other firms because of location, conflicts of interest, lower fees for routine matters, and a perception of more specialized expertise. In addition, they may utilize more than one firm because of company policies, political reasons, and personal contacts.

Defining Good Service

"Good service," note Davidow and Uttal, "has nothing to do with what the provider believes it is; it has only to do with what the customer believes is true. Good service results when the provider meets or exceeds the customer's expectations. Do less than the customer expects and the service is bad."[58] Understanding clients' perceptions of what law firms can do for them is essential to understanding their hopes and disappointments in terms of legal services. As Davidow and Uttal observe, "Great service providers inform customers about what to expect and then exceed the promise. Not all customers want or deserve high levels of service, but they are entitled to what they have been promised, explicitly or implicitly."[59]

Bonding

A firm's current client base is its richest source of future business. But client retention is often difficult. To preserve its clientele, a firm must be able to offer a full array of services and to lead each client to understand that real value exists in loyalty and bonding.

> Purchasers of legal services . . . are faced with a blurring of distinctions between one law firm and another. Increasingly, sizeable law firms provide similar arrays of services. So client "bonding" is dependent primarily on personal service—enhancing the perceived value by going the extra mile with added amenities, speed, accessibility, and attention to special protocol and to international cultural customs.[60]

Client Satisfaction

Law firms must make concerted efforts to understand the client as a consumer. Keeping current clients depends on client satisfaction. Most law firms agree that the loyalty of clients to an attorney or to a firm no longer resembles lawyer-client relationships of yesterday. Consumerism and escalating competition have pushed and pulled clients away from firms with which they were once deeply satisfied. Nonetheless, with effort, firms can still appeal to loyalty in retaining clients. "Some firms," write Phyllis Weiss Haserot and Brian Raftery,

> [report] that loyalty is bred by an honorable firm reputation, fairness, and respect, and the feeling that one is practicing with honorable people. Openness and goodness, frequent communications create loyalty. Interesting work and the example of hard work by the firm's leaders is significant, and the firm's leadership should set the style and pace. There should be a sense that all the attorneys are pulling their weight and that assistance will be supplied as needed. These factors spill over to client loyalty as well.

TABLE 14–2
Client Perceptions of the Most and Least Important Aspects of Legal Service

Most Important Aspects	Least Important Aspects
- Quality of work - Overall quality of available services - Attentiveness - Responsiveness - Timeliness - Aggressive representation	- Fees (before services are rendered) - Range of services

SOURCE: "Some Sample Queries and Responses," *The National Law Journal* (10 July 1989).

Most important is an attitude of superior client service conveyed by attorneys who are adept at human relations.[61]

Considering most people's natural tendency to avoid complaining out of fear of provoking a confrontation, complaints should be taken seriously whenever they are heard. **Service recovery** is the ability to listen carefully to complaints, act quickly and firmly, and turn angry, frustrated clients into contented ones. "Mistakes are a critical part of every service," write Hart, Heskett, and Sasser in "The Profitable Art of Service Recovery," but firms that have the good grace and the common sense to right a wrong and to go out of their way to respond to an unhappy client, thereby perfecting the art of service recovery, can create more good will than ever would have existed had the problem never occurred.[62] Consultant A. L. Jones points out that it is the "little things" that can "doom or save a client's future patronage. Most lawyer-client relationships," he writes, "are undone by the weight of accumulated minor irritations." [63] Everyone knows that to err is human. But few organizations have policies for dealing with errors that involve client rights and needs, and many manage to make their error-related problems worse. One manager, for example, after receiving a well-written and well thought-out complaint, wrote angrily in reply: "We have many, many satisfied clients. No one has ever complained about our services, except you." For each complaint that the firm hears, many more will reach other listeners. Only four or five percent of people will complain directly to a service provider if they are unhappy. They will, however, share their chagrin with an estimated eleven to seventeen others.[64] Understanding complaints is critical to the effectiveness of a firm.

Client Surveys

Many firms liken the marketing research they conduct with clients to keeping in touch with the hand that feeds them. No information is more important to a firm than the perceptions of those who not only use the firm's services but who do so regularly.[65] "Surveying clients," notes Sandra Yost,

> continues to be the hottest business development practice. The surveys often involve objective, outside consultants. Add to those surveys the efforts made by lawyers to know their client and to strategize according to what plays with the decision makers and you have the blueprint for the future.[66]

Perceptions

Surveys are a type of qualitative research. Through the use of surveys, firm members can obtain information about how their clients perceive the firm. As nationally recognized law firm consultants Susan Raridan and Donald Oppenheim explain,

> More and more law firms have come to realize the value of understanding clients' perception of their work product, service, staff, location, etc. Law firms are also realizing that they often do not have an accurate picture of clients' opinions or values.[67]

In an earlier chapter, we defined perceptions as interpretations of reality based on the interpreter's experiences, needs, and attitudes. Law firms should realize, therefore, that survey instruments are likely to collect unique, sometimes unexpected, and occasionally conflicting data. For example, clients taking part in a survey might perceive a firm's telephone receptionist as abrupt, cold, and haughty. The law firm members, on the other hand, might see that receptionist as someone who is kind, patient, and very polite. The clients and the members are neither right nor wrong in their perceptions. But their perceptions are based on different experiences: the clients' interactions with the receptionist are likely to have been more formal and very limited compared to interactions between the law firm members and the same person. In no way does this invalidate what the clients are saying. For a firm using surveys, a client's perceptions become the reality against which the firm measures its efforts. Client surveys are capable of achieving several objectives. They let the firm know what its clients are thinking. They also tell clients that the firm is not only interested in them but that it values their opinions. Most clients are not accustomed to providing feedback, and will not do so unless they are asked. Surveys, despite their variations in accuracy and reliability, provide information that a firm can use to make better-informed decisions improve client relations and obtain leads on broadening the services provided to current clients in areas such as improving services and meeting client needs. The most indicative survey questions involve service and satisfaction, but a firm can also use surveys to assess client needs and the use of associates and paralegals, to obtain feedback on billing practices and communications, and to analyze any other area that is of particular interest. Firms often form focus groups to interpret survey results, especially those that are vague or otherwise hard to understand.

IN THE NEWS

The Art of Interpreting Client Feedback

Few law firms ask their clients for feedback, so clients are favorably disposed to respond; and business clients survey their clients, too, and understand the value of this type of feedback.

Following are some of the questions used in client surveys, typical responses, and general comments regarding interpretation. . . .

Question: Why did you select (name of firm)?

Responses

Top reasons in order of priority:
(1) Direct business contact with member of firm.
(2) Reputation of firm.
(3) Reputation of particular attorney.

Interpretation

Reasons also include referrals, social or civic contact, and direct marketing. These results underscore the importance of professional and trade association involvement in the firm's markets, networking and high profile in organizations.

Question: How often have you used (name of firm) for legal services?

Responses

Once—14.2 percent.
2 to 5 times—22.5 percent.
More than 6 times—23.5 percent.
Routinely—41.1 percent.
Continuously since (fill in year).

Interpretation

Provides indication of cross-selling potential and client stability. For business clients, frequency of use of firm is higher.

Question: What are your feelings regarding the firm's use of associate lawyers to more cost-effectively handle appropriate aspects of your legal matters?

Responses

Average of 57 percent "like."
Average of 8.4 percent "do not like."
Average of 14 percent "don't care."
Average of 23.3 percent "have no experience."

Interpretation

In the comments following this question, clients indicate that use of

SOURCE: "Some Sample Questions and Responses." Reprinted with permission from *The National Law Journal* (10 July 1989), a publication of the New York Law Publishing Company. The survey results represent views of over 20,000 clients from more than 50 firms nationwide.

Survey Questions

In addition to providing feedback on clients' perceptions of the service they have received, survey questions can tell a firm why its clients selected it, how often they use its services, and how they feel about its use of associates and paralegals for its work. Such questions can also uncover clients' reasons for using other law firms.[68] Perfection in survey design isn't an absolute necessity, since follow-up studies are always an option. Nevertheless, questions should be simple, direct, and unambiguous. They should be directed toward only one issue or area at a time. The survey format itself should not be too lengthy or overwhelming. It should be easy to interpret, efficient, and flexible enough to encourage clients to provide further feedback or explanations for their responses. An invitation to use additional paper conveys that message. Finally, the firm can use information from its client data base to customize the mailing of the survey and the instrument itself. Figure 14–2 provides an example of a client survey.

The Client Commitment

All relationships are based on attraction and levels of commitment. Building a lasting professional relationship with a client has much in common with building strong relationships in personal life. Both processes progress from initial encounters, familiarization not unlike courting, and implicit or explicit agreements to culminate in well-developed, lasting interaction.

IN THE NEWS (continued)

associates is fine as long as they are well-supervised, are not "learning" at the client's expense and are not overstaffing matters. A common complaint is that the client "pays" for associates to get up to speed on a case the partner knows intimately. Comments from many clients indicate they do not understand the efficiencies and cost savings to be gained from effective use of associates.

Question: Do you use the services of other law firms in addition to (name of firm)?

Responses

An average of 72 percent of law firms' clients surveyed during the past three years responded "yes," and 28 percent responded "no."

Interpretation

Indicates the trend affecting law firms nationwide of clients using more than one firm and selecting lawyers on a transaction-by-transaction basis. Also indicates law firms need to have client maintenance/protection programs in place to prevent further client base erosion.

Question: If you use another law firm, what is the reason?

Responses

Primary reasons in order of priority:
(1) Geographic location.
(2) Conflicts of interest.
(3) Lower fees for routine matters.
(4) More specialized expertise.
(5) Formal or informal company policy.
(6) Personal contacts.

Interpretation

Provides a firm with valuable information on its clients' perceptions of its fees and areas of specialty.

Question: Have you referred others to (name of firm) for legal services?

Responses

An average of 77 percent of law firms' clients surveyed during the past three years responded "yes," and 23 percent responded "no."

Interpretation

Can indicate a more accurate level of satisfaction with the firm than some other questions. A follow-up question is frequently, "If no, why not?" The number of referrals can be lower if a firm has a highly specialized or technical expertise that is not in regular demand....

The Initial Encounter

As we saw in the chapter on group interaction, proximity increases our chances not only of finding others who share our interests but of encountering those who attract us. Increasing our prospects, then, means being aware of the role proximity plays. Many prospective clients are out there looking for the right kind of law firm service, and firms should realize that the same service doesn't appeal to everyone. Initial encounters between law firms and the prospective clients they wish to attract are therefore critical. At such times, a firm must prove to potential clients that it recognizes, understands, and appreciates their needs. Lawyers, notes Aubrey Wilson, have long since discovered that the world no longer "automatically takes expert and professional advice at its face value." Particularly when such advice is necessary but disagreeable, it will never be easy to sell legal services based on competency alone.[69] They must be accompanied by understanding and attentiveness.

Courting the Client

A firm must get to know its prospective clients, and they must come to know the firm. They must decide as well how they wish the firm to treat them. Taking the time to provide information reassures a new client and builds trust. This trust grows when the firm further reduces the client's anxieties by describing what he or she can expect from the firm.[70] At this stage, the firm will benefit from being persistent, positive, and confident.

FIGURE 14-2
Sample Client Survey Questionnaire

1. How long have you been a client of our firm?
   [ ] Less than 1 year   [ ] 1 to 3 years   [ ] 3 to 6 years   [ ] More than 6 years
2. How did you come to select our firm? Please check all that apply.
       [ ] Advertising
       [ ] Yellow Pages
       [ ] Firm's reputation in the area of _____
       [ ] Reputation of Attorney _____
       [ ] Recommendation of _____
       [ ] Advice of firm member _____
       [ ] Contact with attorney through the following:
           [ ] Civic/ Church/ Community Organizations
           [ ] Business Organizations/ Activities/ Associations
           [ ] Seminars/ Lectures/ Presentations
           [ ] Professional Organizations/ Activities/ Associations
           [ ] Social Activities
           [ ] Other:
3. What is your occupation?
   [ ] Executive   [ ] Business Owner   [ ] Professional
   [ ] Manager/Administrator   [ ] Homemaker   [ ] Retiree
   [ ] Other: _____
4. Please check the areas in which we have performed legal services for you.
   [ ] Estate Planning   [ ] Corporate & Partnership Law
   [ ] Estate Settlement   [ ] Real Estate Development/ Finance
   [ ] Wills   [ ] Zoning/ Environmental Law
   [ ] Real Estate   [ ] Bankruptcy/ Creditors' Rights
   [ ] General Business   [ ] Labor Law
   [ ] Business & Commercial Litigation   [ ] Workers Compensation
   [ ] Insurance & Casualty   [ ] Personal Injury
   [ ] Taxation   [ ] Administrative Law
   [ ] Other:
5. Based on the following scale, please rate your satisfaction with the legal services you have received.
       5 = Highly satisfactory
       4 = Quite satisfactory
       3 = Satisfactory
       2 = Somewhat unsatisfactory
       1 = Very unsatisfactory
      NA = Not applicable

   5 4 3 2 1 NA   1. How well the service met your expectations
   5 4 3 2 1 NA   2. The quality of the work the firm performed
   5 4 3 2 1 NA   3. The quality of the service you received
   5 4 3 2 1 NA   4. The responsiveness and attentiveness to your requests
   5 4 3 2 1 NA   5. The availability of firm members for your needs
   5 4 3 2 1 NA   6. The meeting of deadlines and the timeliness of service
   5 4 3 2 1 NA   7. The concern for your interest
   5 4 3 2 1 NA   8. How well you were kept informed
   5 4 3 2 1 NA   9. The information you received in advance regarding fees and costs
   5 4 3 2 1 NA   10. The success of your results
6. What could we have done to improve the quality of your service?
7. How would you describe your experiences with our firm?
8. Which firm members do you value the most? Please explain.

Prework Agreements

Like the partners to any personal relationship, law firms and new clients benefit from understanding clearly what they can expect from each other and from their professional relationship. Establishing realistic mutual expectations leads to closing the sale, the client's agreement to sign on with the firm.

The Lasting Professional Relationship

As we have seen, people judge the quality of services according to the expectations that they had for those services. Even if a firm knows that the client received superb services, the client will rate that service as poor if it fails to meet his or her expectations.[71] The importance of informing a client about the firm's capabilities before he or she commits him- or herself to the professional relationship cannot be overestimated. One can't promise the world and deliver nothing more than a fistful of dirt. A lasting relationship between a firm and a client is the product of realistic expectations, not false hopes.

BUILDING FIRM-WIDE INVOLVEMENT IN MARKETING

Every member of a law firm is part of its marketing efforts, and each can play a part in marketing. Not all members enjoy the back-slapping, hand-shaking socializing aspect of marketing; they can contribute in other ways. Firm-wide involvement in marketing results from personal marketing plans, training, and commitment to the creation of a client service culture.

Personal Marketing Plans

After establishing its marketing objectives, the firm might ask certain members to develop a personal marketing plan. Each plan should have as its objective the attraction and retention of clients, and each must reflect the overall marketing strategy of the firm. Before adopting a personal marketing plan, an attorney might ask, for example, if the plan is in line with the firm's goals, if it will help to sell the firm's more profitable services, and if it targets prospects who are likely to pay their bills. Each attorney has at least one talent that the firm can build on, and each one should be asked to contribute one or two personal objectives a year.[72] The firm's manager can suggest or assist other firm members with methods for participating in the firm's marketing efforts. According to Sandra Yost, practice development administrator with Coffield, Ungaretti & Harris in Chicago, support staff and paralegals can participate in law firm marketing by ''improving client relations, identifying client prospects from personal contacts; researching current or prospective clients and the marketplace; developing marketing tools and organizing activities; measuring marketing progress and results; automating the marketing function; and performing the administrative tasks of marketing.''[73] Management should convince each member of the firm of the importance of the role he or she is filling and should perform periodic evaluations based on the marketing objectives the firm has selected.[74]

Training

The formal education of a law firm member rarely includes areas of marketing such as client counseling, quality control, and service. Few attorneys, for instance, went to law school thinking that sales would be part of being a lawyer. Yet few lawyers today can practice profitably without addressing how each member in their firm participates in its marketing efforts. Because of this, most firm members can benefit from educational programs that develop marketing skills.

Creating a Client Service Culture

One executive in a service industry put in motion a blitz campaign of programs, policies, and presentations to remind his employees of their involvement with marketing. Every contact by any member of the organization with any client was designated ''a moment of truth.'' The members of this organization soon realized the importance of all the moments of truth each worker might have in any given day.[75] Service management, client-focused, client-driven approach to running an organization, suggests that two competencies are essential for any organization that depends on clients. The first is the ability to place the concept of service at the heart of the organization's planning, culture, and vision. The second is the ability to incorporate those ideas into the actual delivery of services.[76] There are simple ways to obtain feedback on the service a firm provides. Management might conduct a service audit, for example, by inviting an outsider to the firm, having the guest walk through, and watching how members

ANOTHER LOOK

Raindrops from Everyone

1. Celebrate your new ad campaign, product, or service with your staff. They'll be enthused and able to answer questions.
2. Report the results of marketing efforts to your team.
3. Send out press releases about all new hires. Include photos. It's good publicity that works two ways.
4. Have "Employee of the Month" awards. Give real gifts as well as recognition.
5. Educate your staff. Provide them with professional growth through seminars, conferences, and membership in associations.
6. Hold a writer's reception for all who have published in trade publications or journals. Distribute copies whenever possible.
7. Offer incentives for those who bring in new business.
8. Publish an internal newsletter that's interesting, light-hearted, and fun.
9. Hold management meetings with groups of staff members. Encourage them to speak about issues that concern them.
10. Ask all staff members to share what clients think about the firm's quality of service. *Reward* the messenger! Listen and act.

SOURCE: "Your Employees Can Provide Valuable Marketing Assistance," *Holland Shipes Vann Briefs on Practice Management* (November/December 1990): 3.

1. Which of these rainmaking suggestions seem to be off-limits to nonlawyers?
2. How can paralegals be involved in rainmaking? Members of the secretarial staff? Provide specific examples.

---

behave toward him or her. Do they smile, act courteously, step aside? People are the key to service. Every aspect of service that a client receives through a law firm must reinforce a perception of courtesy and competency. As a law firm member, you can help your firm to infuse its culture with client service through special training programs that address aspects of service with questions such as these: Do we offer clients coffee, something to read, a comfortable place to wait? Does information go out the same day a client requests it? Do clients ever think they are interrupting our work? They ARE your work.[77]

CREATIVE MARKETING APPROACHES

Public Partnerships

Marketing legal services has one major barrier: the marketing of the legal profession itself. Although the career is valued and respected, stereotypes label lawyers as avaricious, greedy, arrogant, dishonest, manipulative, opportunistic, and a host of other descriptions that might apply to those who aggressively earn a livelihood in the combative arena of persuasion and knowledge. In surveys less than a decade ago, the ABA discovered that its members' greatest concern was the legal profession's public image. Bar leaders believed that stricter lawyer disciplinary sanctions alone would not change the public's negative perceptions. The marketing strategy that they proposed to improve the image of the profession was simple: legal professionals must "deliver the message that lawyers and the legal system have as their primary goal the delivery of legal services and maintaining the rule of law in a free and just society." Lawyers, as part of this campaign, needed to "form close partnerships with the public, the media, schools, government and business to solve common problems." These common problems, said bar leadership, were those "in our society and community that deserve the response of the American public." A law firm that adopts the ABA's public partnership approach to marketing might combine *pro bono* involvement that addresses drug abuse, the homeless, the special needs of minority groups, and other outreach issues with "in-reach" involvement that addresses the problems of members of the legal profession.[78]

New Legal Specialties

In recent years, many firms have restructured their views of specialization through a careful examination of client needs.

Elder Law

We can best note this targeting of market audiences in a new specialty known as Elder Law, which focuses on the needs of elderly clients by blending traditional estate planning with the legal management of concerns connected with aging, such as long-term care, special tax considerations, complications of probate, and unwanted medical intervention. Law firms can assist elderly clients with questions about durable power of attorney, trusts, health care decision-making documents, incapacity, and many other issues that require trust and sensitivity.[79]

Preventive Law

Many firms are expanding their practices and increasing client loyalty through services that preclude legal difficulties. Preventive law, notes Thomas Harrison, editor of the national news magazine *Lawyers Alert,* emphasizes a firm's desire to serve a client's best interests: "What client wouldn't be highly grateful to be saved from a law suit, a regulatory fine, or a big tax blunder? Clients also appreciate—and are willing to pay for—being told that they are not in danger of any of these things." One common service that law firms perform as part of their preventive law practice is the legal audit, which analyzes a company's legal compliance program, much in the same way a physician checks a patient's physical health. Through an "Employer Legal Audit," for example, a firm can help a small business owner to have a handle on constantly changing federal statutes and court decisions, as well as on personnel laws and compliance, employee benefits laws, OSHA requirements, employees rights issues, estate planning, and trusts. Harrison observes that, in general,

> Legal audits have two big advantages. The first is that they tend to "wed" clients to the firm. If you can save a client from a lawsuit, a fine, or some other problem, the client will think of your firm as knowledgeable and concerned about the company. In addition, you can expose the client to the full range of your services, so that a business that hired you to represent it in a contract action, for example, may begin to look to you for advice on taxes and employee issues as well.
>
> Second, legal audits bring in fees from clients who otherwise wouldn't be retaining your services. Not only can you charge a fee for the audit itself, but also you will likely come up with additional work which no one would have known was necessary if the audit hadn't taken place.[80]

Technology

The power of computers, especially when coupled with desktop publishing and audience-pinpointing information from an actively maintained client data base, can result in fast, responsive, and professional mailings to clients. Computer-assisted mailings can inform clients about recent changes in the law, concerns to be aware of, new rulings, and new services that might be of interest. Through the use of computers and other forms of technology, a firm can facilitate both its understanding of its clients' needs and the marketing strategies it employs to meet those needs.

QUESTIONS FOR DISCUSSION AND REVIEW

1. How has law firm marketing changed in the later part of the twentieth century? What has caused these changes?
2. Explain how the "selling" of legal services is perceived both positively and negatively today.
3. Explain the four ways in which the marketing of legal services differs from the marketing of products or other goods.
4. What is the "marketing concept"? In what ways can a law firm attain the competitive advantage that is part of the marketing concept?
5. Create a fictitious law firm and describe the elements you would use to ensure that it has the right marketing mix.
6. How can a law firm develop an effective marketing plan? What areas does it need to consider?
7. Research an example of how a law firm has marketed its services through advertising, public relations, or personal sales. Explain why you think

the strategy was or was not successful.
8. In what ways is a firm's management responsible for its marketing process?
9. Why do clients choose one firm rather than another?
10. Through what strategies can a firm develop positive, lasting client relations?
11. What is meant by creating a service culture?
12. Explain how five of the following members of a law firm could be involved in marketing the firm's services.

a. Attorney Lamond Ferguson, senior partner
b. Mary Curley, receptionist
c. Dan McDowell, computer coordinator
d. Ellen Gallagher, firm librarian
e. Pat Bradley, new associate
f. Joe Moriarty, paralegal coordinator
g. Marian Sargent, title examiner

EXPERIENTIAL EXERCISES

I. Rate Your Professional Marketing Skills

Mark the following items using this scale:

SA = Strongly agree
A = Agree
O = No opinion
D = Disagree
SD = Strongly disagree

SA A O D SD 1. When clients say, "I can't afford your firm," that's what they really mean.

SA A O D SD 2. When hooking a client, it's best to talk about the most unpopular aspect of legal services—fees—first.

SA A O D SD 3. When clients are deciding to use your law firm's services, it's up to them to call you when they're ready to get in touch.

SA A O D SD 4. Lawyers are out of line if they think of working with a prospective client as "making a pitch," "asking for the order," and "closing the sale."

SA A O D SD 5. Firms should welcome opportunities to give group presentations to prospective business clients.

SA A O D SD 6. You either have credibility or you don't. There's no sense trying to establish it with prospective clients.

SA A O D SD 7. When inviting a potential business client to lunch, you should keep it strictly social and avoid talking business.

SA A O D SD 8. Effective lawyer-client relationships rely on little things, like sending clients congratulatory notes when they're promoted or honored.

SA A O D SD 9. Success with a client is due to your efforts and expertise in a particular field. Most clients don't care to hear about other ways the firm can help them.

SA A O D SD 10. When you feel awkward discussing how a prospective client might do business with your firm, it's a good idea to bring in another member of your firm who is good at making a sales pitch.

CHAPTER 14 / CLIENTS AND MARKETING **431**

SA A O D SD   11. There's not much sense in sending out law firm brochures to people who already do business with you.
SA A O D SD   12. Inviting clients to cosponsor or participate in civic or community events, or to coauthor an article, or to collaborate on special professional activities helps your firm to bond with prospective clients, who may think of your firm's name first when they need legal services.
SA A O D SD   13. Letting business and civic groups use your firm's facilities for special events or for emergencies only causes extra work and operational complications.
SA A O D SD   14. Getting together with clients socially is one of the most effective strategies for prospecting clients.
SA A O D SD   15. Keeping in touch with old friends and cementing the bonds of friendship with business associates effectively builds your network of contacts.

Scoring: For items 1, 2, 5, 8, 10, 12, 14, and 15: All SA responses receive +5, all A responses receive +3, all O responses receive 0, all D responses receive −3, and all SD responses receive −5. For items 3, 4, 6, 7, 9, 11 and 13: All SA responses receive −5, all A responses receive −3, all O responses receive 0, all D responses receive +3, and all SD responses receive +5. Add the scores for the two sets of items and compare your total to the following key:

Score	Comments
+50 to +75	Excellent. Your comprehension of quality marketing behaviors is admirable.
+25 to +49	Good. You possess a competent and reliable understanding of law firm marketing.
0 to +24	Fair. Yours is a basic understanding of marketing, with much room for growth.
−1 to −24	Weak. Your conception of marketing is flimsy and inadequate.
−25 to −49	Poor. You have an impoverished awareness of marketing activities!
−50 to −75	Substandard to nonexistent. Your grasp of marketing may be hopelessly deficient.

II. Rating Hot Ideas for Law Firm Marketing[81]

In a world of rapidly escalating competition, law firms are under increasing pressure to actively sell their services. Legal professionals new to the creation of marketing tactics find themselves wondering if image is more important than impact, if attracting specific clients is better than attracting many clients, if taste permanently supersedes shock value, and if originality is more often refreshing or ridiculous. Rate the effectiveness (E score) of each of the following items on a scale from 1 to 10, with 10 being the most effective. Then rate the appropriateness of each item (A score) according to the following descriptions:

VO = Very offensive
O = Offensive

N = Neutral
T = Tasteful
VT = Very tasteful

When you've finished, pick the ad that you think is best. Explain your choice.

E Score: _____ A Score: _____ 1. A California Invention: "Dial-a-Lawyer." A hot line referral service to full-time specialists who are prepared to discuss any legal question with you at the rate of $3 a minute, available 12 hours a day, with toll-free 800 and 900 numbers. All calls are recorded. Staff has access to an on-line data base that is updated constantly by research assistants. When callers think they know enough or have spent enough, they can simply hang up.

E Score: _____ A Score: _____ 2. "I Love My Lawyer" Ads. TV ads that show a woman sitting by a swimming pool as she happily describes the extraordinary settlement she received through the tireless efforts of her aggressive divorce lawyer.

E Score: _____ A Score: _____ 3. "Who Says You Can't Buy Love?" A Sacramento firm likes to market in any way "that creates personal contact." The firm likes to give "seminars for clients, tickets to sporting events and gifts whose labels and packaging identify the firm, in a memorable way."

E Score: _____ A Score: _____ 4. "Let Your Fingers Do the Walking." Some firms find yellow pages advertising particularly ineffective. Others, from Hyatt Legal Services to successful solo practitioners, find it very effective.

E Score: _____ A Score: _____ 5. "Music to My Ears." One firm sponsors Saturday symphonic broadcasts on public radio. Its management thinks that "the programs attract the targeted audience with the help of a format law firms typically overlook."

E Score: _____ A Score: _____ 6. "Sink or Swim." This television spot shows a scuba diver, who pops up from under the water, takes off his mask, and introduces himself as Attorney Adams, a lawyer who will go to any extent to protect you and your legal interests. As he leaves the water, he tells you how to contact him, someone who is not afraid to help you, no matter what.

E Score: _____ A Score: _____ 7. "Happy Holidays." A method used to benefit both civic and community organizations and the firm is to give holiday donations to select charities in the names of key clients or in lieu of sending holiday greetings. The charities can then inform the honorees of the gift given in their name or the firm itself can take out an ad in a local paper, notifying all of how it was able to celebrate the holiday season on its client's behalf.

E Score: _____ A Score: _____ 8. "Let's Do Lunch." A firm invites clients and potential clients to a series of in-house luncheon seminars, where they can interact with firm's attorneys in an informal, educational setting.

E Score: _____ A Score: _____ 9. "Conservative Cool." A TV ad opens with a picture of a conservatively dressed attorney, sitting at a highly polished and neatly organized desk. The walls are filled with what appears to be volumes of legal books. He says, simply, "You can rely on us for all your legal needs." A voiceover announces the name of the firm, and the name and phone number of the firm appear on the screen.

E Score: _____ A Score: _____ 10. "All You Deserve." You open the yellow pages, and there before you is a two-page ad: "Accident Hotline. Injured in an accident? Call to discuss the value of your case, at no cost whatsoever and with no obligation. No fee unless we are completely successful. We handle all personal injury matters. Let us help you collect the money you deserve. Know your legal rights." No names are given, only a toll-free 800 phone number.

III. A Brief Look at Client Perceptions*

Step 1. Estimate the importance that you believe clients in search of a law firm ascribe to the criteria below by labeling each with a 1 (very important), 2, 3, or 4 (unimportant).

____ Ability to work with a specific lawyer
____ Access to top people in the firm
____ Counsel and advice
____ Expertise in a specific area
____ Fast turnaround on work
____ Firm's reputation in the community
____ Keeping clients informed of the firm's progress
____ Location of the firm's offices
____ Low costs
____ Personal interest taken in client's business
____ Personal interest taken in client's legal matters
____ Political connections
____ Quality of written product
____ Representation of similar clients
____ Results of the firm's work
____ Size of the firm
____ Verbal skills

Step 2. Using your initial results, create four ranked sets of factors, with four factors in each of the first three categories and five in the last.

    First Set: Very Important
    Second Set: Important
    Third Set: Less Important
    Fourth Set: Least Important

Interpreting Your Results: A group of clients assigned the following order of importance to the seventeen items:

First Set: Very Important	**Third Set:** Less Important
1. Results of the firm's work 2. Counsel and advice 3. Expertise in a specific area 4. Personal interest in client's legal matters	9. Personal interest taken in client's business 10. Access to top people in the firm 11. Firm's reputation in the community 12. Ability to work with a specific lawyer
Second Set: Important	**Fourth Set:** Least Important
5. Quality of written product 6. Keeping the client informed of the firm's progress 7. Verbal skills 8. Fast turnaround on work	13. Representation of similar clients 14. Low costs 15. Size of the firm 16. Location of the firm's offices 17. Political connections

---

*Sally J. Schmidt, Questionnaire from "Clients and Research" in *What Clients Say: A Lawyer's Guide to Better Client Relations*. Copyright © 1989. Reprinted by permission of Sally J. Schmidt Consulting, Inc., Burnsville, Minn.

CHAPTER 15

Ethical Responsibilities

LEARNING OBJECTIVES

After completing this chapter, you should be able to:

- Define morality and three basic approaches to understanding ethics;
- Explain moral development and the characteristics of "good" people;
- Describe the role conflicts lawyers and those working with them in law offices have as people, professionals, and partners/owners;
- Express familiarity with the "laws of lawyering," including the Model Rules of Professional Conduct and other specific guidelines that apply to law offices and support staff;
- Determine what makes a "good" manager;
- Describe the characteristics of a "good" law firm and its obligations to its members and to society;
- Understand the kinds of obligations that people have to themselves and to society that create difficult ethical choices.

Geoffrey C. Hazard, Jr., is the Sterling Professor of Law at Yale University and director of the American Law Institute. A former reporter for the ABA's Kujak Commission, he contributed heavily to the development of the Model Rules of Professional Conduct. As a staff reporter for The American Lawyer, *Mary Morgan Stewart described him as "the country's leading expert on telling lawyers how to behave." In his efforts to promote respect for those in today's legal institutions, Hazard writes extensively on ethical decision making and on the role of ethics in the law firm.*[1]

FOCUS FROM THE FIELD

Geoffrey Hazard: Nonlawyers Have A Duty

How ethical are today's law firms?

There's a wide variation, probably wider than generations ago.

Have technology and new structures in law firms made ethical decision making more difficult?

Ethical conduct is more difficult because law is more complex, transactions take place faster, and society's values are more heterogeneous.

You were very influential in shaping the Model Rules of Professional Conduct. Are they largely ignored, as some critics say?

No. They've been widely adopted and are more fully in the consciousness of lawyers.

What do the Model Rules require of law firm management?

In a law firm or law department, the Model Rules require partners or managers to establish systems for achieving conformity to ethical requirements and require a lawyer with direct supervisory responsibility to take action when a violation can be corrected. There is a similar responsibility for the work of the paralegal staff.

What do you see as the most difficult challenge for the nonlawyer manager in a law firm?

Nonlawyer managers are faced with dealing with lawyers' assumptions that they are more perceptive and more intelligent than nonlawyers.

Can and should an employer try to ascertain "ethical skills" in hiring newcomers to the firm?

It is difficult to probe ethical sensitivity and discretion. However, these qualities should be looked for in hiring.

You wrote that lawyers play a vital role in the preservation of society. Is the magnitude of that responsibility linked to any sense of betrayal when we read of unethical practices?

Unethical behavior by a guardian of society inevitably causes a sense of betrayal.

How do ethical responsibilities spill over to the nonlawyers in the firm, the managers, paralegals, secretaries, and other staff members?

Nonlawyers have a duty to conduct themselves in ways compatible with and supportive of the lawyers' ethical responsibilities.

> **A** lawyer is a representative of clients, an officer of the legal system and a public citizen having special responsibility for the quality of justice. . . . Lawyers play a vital role in the preservation of society.
> (Preamble to the Model Rules of Professional Conduct)[2]
>
> **P**rofessionals in public and private service must be able to convince the general public that they are able to render difficult moral judgments and that they are not using their professional prestige to favor narrow interests.
> (Guy Benveniste, *Professionalizing the Corporation*)[3]
>
> **I** think that the hallmark of the ethical organization is that the individual abilities of people are magnified and enhanced by participation in it rather than suppressed in order to be members of it. [It is a place] where people don't feel that they have to sacrifice very much of who they are to belong.
> (William A. Kahn, "Toward an Agenda for Business Ethics Research")[4]

MANAGERIAL ETHICS

"Tell me a man is dishonest, and I will answer he is no lawyer," wrote Daniel Webster in 1847. "He cannot be, because he is careless and reckless of justice: the law is not in his heart, is not the standard and rule of his conduct."[5] In this last chapter, we will examine the law firm's most solemn challenge: ethical choices.

Lady Justice is a common image in legal publications: her blindfold represents impartiality in dispensing justice. That may be the only legal activity in which turning a blind eye is appropriate, however. All other decisions call for focused and discerning vision. Because of the nature of the legal profession, certain obligations in the law firm transcend what we ordinarily expect in terms of honesty and morality. "In law," comments ethicist Sissela Bok, "as in medicine and in other professions, the calling generates its own requirements that at times must override ordinary moral constraints." Only by intense efforts to be scrupulously honest do law firms "truly deserve the trust of their clients and thereby serve long-run societal interests."[6]

Learning Ethical Decision Making

Many believe that teaching adults to make ethical decisions is impossible, given the depth to which our value systems are entrenched by the time we reach maturity. Others are convinced that teaching ethics opens people's eyes, gives them food for thought, and helps them make informed decisions. There is considerable debate about whether or not values can be taught in a classroom setting. Many accept the idea that decision-making procedures, even those that involve values, can be learned. They particularly agree that we can learn different ethical approaches and reasons for respecting others' values. Attorney and former law professor Michael Josephson is among those who believe in teaching ethical concepts by showing people how to acknowledge their own value systems. He theorizes that adults build new values on their old ones. "You can teach ethics by confronting people with their own values and the consequences of their choices and by trying to inspire them to meet their own high standards," writes Josephson, who founded the Institute for the Advancement of Ethics for that very reason.[7] In addition, students can benefit from examining how ethical standards apply to the law firm setting. "Professional ethics can be effectively taught," he claims, if students have "first-hand observations of the ways in which the ethical problems of the lawyer arise and of the actual habits (the *mores*) of the bar."[8] Law firm members who master the unique ethical demands of the law firm setting will contribute both to the law firm and to society. In the following sections, we will examine the concepts of ethics and morality, society's expectations regarding lawyers and ethics, and the ethical responsibilities that managers and other members face in the law firm setting.

Ethics

There are many views on the meaning of "ethics." The word itself is akin to the Greek word *ethos,* which means "custom" or "character." In modern usage, ethos identifies the feelings, beliefs, and sentiments of a community of people. The ethos of a group distinguishes that group from another one: each group has unique characteristics, attitudes, and values. This kinship with ethos explains why we commonly think of ethics as rules for good behavior; we might, in fact, define **ethics** as the set of rules and standards people have for one another. "Ethical," then, would describe behavior that conforms to these rules and standards.[9] The concept of ethics encompasses four things: first, a standard for decisions; second, a sense of obligation; third, an agreement on what constitutes "right" and "wrong"; and, fourth, the underlying concept of justice.

Standards for Decisions

Our ethical systems provide an overview of what society thinks of as right or wrong. Ethics guides our decision making by helping us to determine "what one should do in a morally difficult situation."[10]

Obligations

Ethics incorporates the concept of obligation in that ethical norms are, as Hazard notes, "imperatives regarding the welfare of others that are recognized as binding upon a person's conduct in some more immediate and binding sense than *law* and in some more general and impersonal sense than *morals*."[11]

Right and Wrong

Generally, most people can agree on the "right" thing to do in a given situation. Life is often complicated, however; and that "right" thing can vary widely, according to what is at stake, who is involved, and what the outcomes of a response will likely be.

Justice

Ethics implies that we are working to ensure a just world. Ethical ideals safeguard and preserve justice. Society's ethical standards form around important beliefs we hold in common. One of the most fundamental concepts we share is the principle of justice, the staunch belief that what is fair for one is fair for another. The ethical rules that govern our conduct are those that all rational people would choose, if they realized that the rules they selected would ultimately apply to them.[12] One well-known version of this is the golden rule, "Do unto others as you would have them do unto you."

Fundamental Ethical Questions

We all can benefit from asking ourselves certain fundamental ethical questions: What is a good life? What values are worth pursuing? What do we owe one another? How can we act so that we promote a good life for all?[13] Those who participate in ethical decision making ask many questions. Who precisely will this decision affect? How? What are each person's interests and how would this decision benefit or harm those interests? Who has rights that might be affected here? What is the "decision rule"? (i.e., what basic rule would ensure the fulfillment of the decision makers' most critical objectives, such as keeping clients happy or maximizing owners' profits?)[14]

Morality

Mores is the plural of *mos*, the Latin word for custom. *Mores* has come to mean the customs or rules that one should follow for the welfare of society. These rules, which often develop the force of laws, serve as the basis for written codes of laws. Conduct described as **moral** conforms to generally accepted standards for what is right or good, and **morality** is a person's conformity to principles of right or wrong in conduct and decisions. The degree to which we conform to these principles determines our personal morality.[15]

Approaches to Ethics

How do we know what society thinks is right? On what basis do people determine what is good or evil? Many theories have attempted to explain how people determine what is ethical. Three of the more common are the utilitarian theory, the theory of rights, and the theory of justice.[16]

The Utilitarian Theory

Utilitarianism proposes that the purpose of all action is to bring the greatest happiness to the greatest number of people. Accordingly, utilitarianism would designate as most ethical the choice that brings the greater good to the greater number of people. Free enterprise decisions often are based on the utilitarian theory: competition keeps prices lower, and this is seen as a desirable condition. When people lose their jobs because of competition, supporters of free enterprise see their plight as an inevitable byproduct, insisting that it is the greater good that counts. Under the utilitarian view, creating the greatest good for the greatest number of stakeholders is the firm's highest priority.

The Theory of Rights

The **theory of rights** view proposes that ethical decisions reflect a moral belief in the fundamental rights of each individual. These basic rights are the natural liberties and privileges in society to which we should be entitled. According to this view, an ethical decision is not the one that benefits the greatest number of people but the one that protects people's rights, even when they are in the minority.

The Theory of Justice

The **theory of justice** maintains that decisions should ensure fairness, equity, and impartiality to all people. This theory is based on the conviction that all people have two basic rights: liberty and equity. The first right, described as the **liberty principle,** proposes that each person is entitled to be as free as any other person. The second right, equity, relates to the **difference principle:** when an inequity exists between the liberty and rights of different people, those who are disadvantaged should receive preference until the difference is eliminated.[17] This principle is at the heart of affirmative action efforts.

Individual Ethical Decision Making

Should you ever be in doubt as to the ethics of a decision you must make, ask yourself these three questions: Will my decision be legal? Will it be balanced? Will it lead to doing what I believe is right?

- Is it legal? If your decision is within the framework of the law, it has met the most basic standards for correct action.
- Is it balanced? Regarding both long- and short-term consequences, the action should be fair, rational, and equitable for all stakeholders.
- Does it reflect what I believe is right? In making an ethical decision, you must come to terms in advance with how the decision will make you feel about yourself. Deciding whether or not a decision is within one's code of behavior, even after the first two questions have been answered positively, is for most of us a valid indication of an action's ethical nature. Pride, self-esteem, and self-worth are at stake. In addition, decision makers faced with morally difficult situations should ask: How would I feel about this if my family were to find out, if it were to be in the paper, if the world were to know?[18]

Group Ethical Decision Making

Those who must confront ethical issues might try addressing their moral choices in a group setting. This can take place in a three-step process. First, those who are confronted with an ethical decision should meet to gather information about the issue. Second, they should arrive at a consensus about the right questions to ask. Third, after processing the ethical aspects of the questions, they should confront the issue to be decided. Kenneth Blanchard and Norman Vincent Peale suggest that each participant sit for a predetermined period, perhaps ten minutes or so, and search for the right answer from within.[19] The participants can then, as a group, reach some constructive certainty regarding the rightness of their decision.

GOOD PEOPLE

Being told to be "good" is probably one of the earliest admonitions we can remember. Our first moral awakenings involved simple struggles with the forces of good and evil. Being "good" is to be morally sound. The ways in which we are morally sound depend on our individual characteristics, universal values, and our development as moral individuals.

Individual Characteristics

Each person has different internal factors that shape his or her ethical choices. Their unique personalities, values, and beliefs are some of the factors that determine how people make moral choices. Each individual approaches life with a different set of skills, attitudes, and experiences. Our identities have a biological basis, but we continue to develop in many ways, as we respond to events in our lives. As we saw in Chapter 10, personality gives each person an identity, a meaning, and an attitudinal frame of reference for the decisions he or she makes regarding what is morally sound and cognitively comfortable. Three aspects of an individual's personality influence what he or she thinks to be right or wrong: values, ego strength, and locus of control.

TABLE 15-1
Key Terms in the Study of Ethical Standards

Values: Relatively permanent and morally weighted attitudes that represent what people desire and want to happen.
Rights: Entitlements that give people the freedom to take a particular action.
Duties: Obligations to perform specific actions.
Ethical: Conforming to codes and standards of moral principles.
Ethics: Moral rules and guidelines for behavior; such rules, which proscribe certain actions, apply to most situations under usual conditions.
Code of ethics: A formal statement of an organization or a group describing its most important values and standards, for the express purpose of regulating and encouraging the positive behaviors of its members.
Common morality: Unwritten rules, used by most people in a given community, that guide everyday situations such as keeping promises, not harming or injuring others, helping others if the personal costs aren't too great, respecting others and their property, and not manipulating or exploiting others.
Social responsibility: Management's social as well as economic obligation to uphold societal values.
Social responsiveness: Showing a moral leadership ethic by creating and implementing policies that anticipate and respond to the needs and demands of society.

SOURCE: R. Edward Freeman and Daniel R. Gilbert, Jr., *Corporate Strategy and the Search for Ethics* (Englewood Cliffs, N.J.: Prentice-Hall, 1988.)

Values

Each person accumulates a range of experiences that helps him or her to interpret and respond to life. The attitudes we develop about what is right and wrong constitute our values. Recall that values are attitudes with a moral component. They form the core of a person's moral character. We learned in Chapter 10 that an attitude consists of three basic parts: a cognition, an affect, and a tendency to act one way rather than another. What we say we will or would do, in keeping with our attitudes, is not always what we actually end up doing.

Ego Strength

Ego strength is a dimension of personality that describes how strictly people adhere to their convictions and values. Those who are high in ego strength are more likely to do what they believe is right, less likely to act on impulse, and more apt to be consistent than those with low ego strength.

Locus of Control

Recall also from Chapter 10 that **locus of control** describes the degree to which people believe that the forces governing their lives are internal or external. When making moral choices, those who believe highly in an internal locus of control—a sign that they feel responsible for determining what happens to them—will be more decisive in carrying out their moral convictions. Those who believe in an external locus will allow others and fate to determine the outcomes in their lives, even moral ones.

Universal Values

Most of us share many attitudes regarding what is good and desirable. As William Shaw and Vincent Barry, professors of business ethics, observe,

> The type of life each of us seeks to live reflects our individual values—whether following a profession, devoting ourselves to community service, seeking solitude, pursuing scientific truth, striving for athletic excellence, amassing political power, cultivating glamorous people as friends, or some combination of these and many other possible ways of living.[20]

We value love, innocence, and goodness. We try to show respect for others, their persons, their property, and their beliefs. We believe in fairness and justice. We cherish honesty, trust, and confidences. We believe in not harming others; as Sissela Bok points out, "Violence and deceit are the two most important ways by which human beings deliberately injure one another." Both, she notes, can do great harm, but "deceit, being surreptitious, often brings results that violence cannot muster."[21] That is why people need to be able to trust one another.

The Importance of Honesty

We abhor those who lie and deceive us. Nonetheless honesty is a value we cherish but find all too easy to neglect. A lie, in Sissela Bok's opinion, "is any intentionally deceptive message which is stated." Deception, which has a broader meaning than lying, consists of "messages meant to mislead through gesture, through disguise, by means of action or inaction, even though silence."[22] As Bok further explains,

> Deceit is tempting, moreover, since it comes so easily at first. One word spoken instead of another, a document back-dated so as to deflect inquiry, a false claim made in the process of negotiation, some figures altered in a tax document—these neither call for the same physical effort nor arouse the same immediate suspicions as, say, acts of violence. This ease makes lies not only more tempting but also peculiarly corrupting, especially as more and more concealment and deception may seem needed to keep up a false front.[23]

Not surprisingly, then, honesty is the quality that society cherishes most in its professionals. Honesty, which fosters trust, is the value most critical to the lawyer. However, even lawyers joke about "having a license to lie." Author and lawyer Scott Turow tells one of a new crop of discouragingly cynical lawyer jokes: "How do you know when a lawyer is lying?" The answer: "His lips move."[24]

Integrity

Integrity describes the moral constancy of those who are upright, honest, and sincere. "Integrity," notes business writer Tom Peters, "may be about little things as much as or more than big ones.... [Lapses in integrity] set a tone of disrespect for people, products, systems, customers, distributors, and relationships that can easily become pervasive.... There is no such thing as a minor lapse in integrity."[25]

How People Develop Morally

Some of the most widely recognized work on how people learn to make ethical decisions comes from Harvard professor Lawrence Kohlberg, who describes how people develop morally. Kohlberg suggests that people progress through several stages of moral development from early childhood to adulthood. In each stage, they use different criteria for making moral decisions, relying on different styles of **moral reasoning,** or a kind of reflective thinking about how to resolve ethical dilemmas. Kohlberg suggests that these stages of moral decision making begin at an early age. According to Kohlberg, most children first make ethical decisions out of *self-interest* based on a fear of punishment. Moral development eventually progresses to *caring,* or being able to make moral decisions out of concern about the effects of one's actions on other people, whether one actually knows them or just considers them to be real. The final stage of moral development is that of *principle,* when one makes moral decisions out of concern for humanity and for universal human rights. These stages of moral development, which may occur at any age and in any setting, affect decision making in every organization.[26]

GOOD LAWYERS

The word "good" has many meanings. A good lawyer may be a person who is morally sound. A good lawyer also may be someone who is effective in the courtroom, in resolving legal matters, or in advising clients. Finally, a good lawyer may be someone who does well by the profession and who, as a result, is economically successful. What does it really mean to be a good lawyer? Can someone who is good at delivering legal services also be good as a person? As Thomas Morgan, dean of the Law School at Emory University, and Ronald Rotunda, professor of law at the University of Illinois, wonder, "Is behavior that is morally acceptable for persons in general permitted or even required for persons who have assumed the mantle of attorney? Should a lawyer . . . be indifferent to the question of what kind of person he or she becomes?"[27] People struggle to understand not only how lawyers are entitled to excuse themselves from moral constraints that bind the rest of us, but how they are justified in doing so. Sissela Bok says that this has led to "the common perception that too many lawyers violate basic moral principles when it suits their purposes." For the lawyer who acts as a private individual, lying may be motivated by self-interest. For the lawyer who acts in his or her capacity as a professional, lying—whether by omission or concealment—may be part of a professional obligation to protect the client's interest. "Lawyers disagree among themselves," writes Bok, "about where to draw the line with respect to certain forms of deception, to confidentiality about the criminal activities of their clients, and to other forms of problematic behavior. . . ."[28] Lawyers and those who work with them need more than codes of professional responsibility in their attempts to accommodate multiple roles. Geoffrey Hazard describes how each lawyer's personal values and knowledge of what is going on often can be at odds with legal rules and "objective" facts. "The discrepancy," he notes, "can be a source of great personal distress, and sometimes serious professional and legal risk."[29] The person who becomes a lawyer enters a career that has inherent conflicts. The lawyer must respond to three types of ethical obligations: those of the lawyer as a person with ethical standards and responsibilities to others; as a professional with ethical responsibilities to clients; and as a partner/owner with business obligations to self and to others.

The Lawyer as a Person

The inner conflict that lawyers experience cannot be overestimated. It consists of being obligated at times to choose behaviors that are not in keeping with their personal standards of morality. This conflict of roles creates a unique set of stressors for those who happen to be lawyers and for those around them:

> And when lawyers choose or are forced to compromise their scruples by violating such constraints, their trust in themselves can be shaken, both as persons capable of a consistent moral stance and as individuals worthy of trust on the part of others. Some eventually set aside their doubts; others find themselves increasingly alienated from the profession.[30]

The Lawyer as a Professional

Society holds more responsible those whom it entrusts with loftier positions. Professional responsibility is based on the belief that power that comes from knowledge—professional expertise—brings with it a responsibility to society. The legal knowledge of lawyers and their role in the justice system have made society dependent upon them. Society, consequently, has entrusted lawyers with the responsibility of helping interpret its laws. This **fiduciary relationship** (a confidential one in which one person owes a duty of trust and loyalty to another[31]) creates ethical obligations for legal professionals.[32] In that those who rely on a fiduciary's services essentially place a part of their lives in that person's hands, society holds lawyers, in their fiduciary capacity, strictly responsible for looking after its well-being and its best interests. Their right as lawyers to be self-governing is accompanied by their duty to be socially responsible. Bok contends that when the public's trust is eroded in one part of the professional mosaic—among physicians, lawyers, or government officials, for example—the damage harms the fragile interconnections between all the other levels of society. That is why the role of the lawyer as a professional is of such importance to society. It matters greatly "that professionals see their activities in a larger social perspective" and that lawyers as well as other members of the law firm understand how the public's trust in them is a fragile "moral resource."[33] In this context, pro bono contributions become critically necessary to reassure society that lawyers understand the trust placed in them. Bok notes that society not only invests in its professions but also "invests *with* the professions and their institutions certain trusts, among them a trust that the professions will watch over the well-being of society."[34]

The Lawyer as a Partner/Owner

The lawyer who understands not only his or her personal responsibilities but the obligations of the legal profession as a professional service business faces a third set of values that brings additional conflicts. First, many lawyers still suspect that their profession has become tarnished and commercialized in recent years. Secondly, members of the business and corporate world are now obligated to institute programs that fight employment-related inequities and protect the rights of the individual. Thirdly, many law firms now face corporate-style obligations, simply because of their increased size, new structures, and larger circles of influence. Proportionately, then, they now owe more to society. Today's law firms—smaller as well as larger—now experience the same kind of public scrutiny and visibility that have long been commonplace for other businesses. Both the internal ethical climate and the external influence of the law firm, notes Bok, can pollute "the social climate of trust," much in the same way that other businesses can pollute the earth through environmental recklessness and ecological irresponsibility.[35] The lawyer/partner is responsible for setting the ethical tone for all workers in the law firm setting. As a businessperson, he or she must set standards, and the nonlawyers in the firm should see it as their obligation to believe in these standards, to support them, and to carry them out.

THE LAWS OF LAWYERING

Lawyers are indispensable to society. They are entrusted with interpreting the laws that society adopts to maintain as much justice as possible in an imperfect world. They are not, however, above or beyond the law. They are regulated by state laws, as administered by their respective state bar associations, under the authority and supervision of the state's highest courts. Regulations for lawyers are based on their own canon of ethics; when violations occur, state bar associations conduct investigations, hold hearings, and make preliminary decisions regarding sanctions such as official censure, suspension, or disbarment. Lawyers can appeal these decisions, according to procedures designated by their state's judicial system. Each person who directly assists the lawyers in a firm should be aware of the constraints under which lawyers work. "You should know," writes Bill Statsky to those who assist lawyers, "what ethical obligations are imposed on lawyers so that you can help your employing lawyers avoid charges of ethical improprieties." [36] In fact, lawyers are mandated by their own codes to give those assisting them "appropriate instruction" on ethical obligations.

Obligations to Clients

Basic to the ethical choices that lawyers make is the fact that lawyers offer a service to clients. In offering that service, a lawyer is under four obligations: he or she must be competent; the services he or she performs must be confidential; he or she must communicate to the client about what he or she is transacting on the client's behalf; and he or she must be committed, working loyally and diligently on the client's behalf. To deceive or mislead a client in any of those four areas betrays and cheats the client. The responsibility to clients governs the lawyer's decisions. Ethics in a larger sense may center around our obligations to others, but in a law firm, ethical obligations center around a client's right of access to the justice system, not around whether what the client did was right or wrong. Of the ethical considerations that govern a lawyer's office, Hazard comments:

> They are not universal because they give a preferred position to clients; the office of the lawyer begins with having to make distinctions among persons. At least in an immediate sense, they are not based on practical necessity, for no one is compelled to become a lawyer and, ordinarily at least, no lawyer is compelled to take a particular case. While in some situations a lawyer is supposed to act with perfect neutrality among others, a lawyer usually intervenes in relationships between others with a predisposition to treat the one who is his client with greater solicitude than he treats the other, regardless of the merits of their prospective positions.[37]

Outside the realm of legal ethics, he admits, this obligation does not make sense: "For the lawyer does not merely encounter choices between the conflicting interests of others but makes a business out of such encounters, and takes partisan positions for money. Thus, his vocation violates the concepts of ethics held both by philosophers and in folklore." [38] For a lawyer to be ethical by any standard definition, then, may be impossible; for he or she is obligated to the complete service of the client's legal needs, sometimes at the expense of his or her personal moral judgment.[39]

A Lawyer's Professional Obligations

The earliest formal ABA codes date to 1908, when the ABA Canons of Professional Ethics described thirty-two principles of traditional ethical conduct. Though the Canons had their earliest roots in canons of church law dating back to the Middle Ages, the ABA modeled them more specifically on the Alabama Code of Legal Ethics, drafted in the 1880s by Judge Thomas Goode Jones, who in turn had been inspired by *An Essay on Professional Ethics,* which Judge George Sharswood had published in 1854.[40] In 1970, the Canons of Professional Ethics were replaced by the Model Code of Professional Responsibility, which contained three divisions: an ethical code in nine canons, disciplinary rules, and ethical rules. In 1983, the ABA adopted a revision of this code, calling it the ABA Model Rules of Professional Conduct. It consists of eight model rules, followed by comments that describe and clarify the applications of the rules. Since membership in the ABA is voluntary, its codes by themselves are not binding. But each state relies on the ABA for its expertise and the role it plays in the self-governance of attorneys. Using the ABA codes as a model, each state considers proposals submitted by members of the profession and adopts as law the aspects of the ABA codes that it considers most suitable, a practice in keeping with the self-governing nature of the legal profession. Not all states, for example, have yet adopted new laws based on the 1983 Model Rules, but lawyers can still use the ABA's current codes as guidelines for their ethical conduct. A firm's partners may provide an ethical framework for all those who work with them, but each group within the firm operates under the guidance of codes developed by its own professional group or association. The Association of Legal Administrators has a special Ethics Task Force that concerns itself with an "ethics policy that reflects the responsibilities of the law firm executive" in areas such as confidentiality issues, escrow and trust fund procedures, stock ownership and trading, conflicts of interest, audit and opinion letters, and authority to sign for the firm.[41] The National Association of Legal Assistants has for its members a Code of Ethics and Professional Responsibility, adopted in 1975. Reminding legal assistants of their responsibility "To adhere strictly to the accepted standards of legal ethics and to live by general principles of proper conduct,"[42] it contains twelve canons that address topics such as the unauthorized practice of law, integrity, and unethical behavior. The National Federation of Paralegal Associations offers its members an Affirmation of Responsibility that recognizes its organization's "commitment to the realization of the most basic right of a free society, equal justice under the law." It offers guidelines for standards of professional responsibility, conduct, competence, and integrity; client confidences; support of public interests; and professional development.[43]

ABA MODEL RULES OF PROFESSIONAL CONDUCT[44]

The Model Rules of Professional Conduct constitute the current ABA guidelines for lawyers. Standards established to safeguard the ethical climate of the law firm, they offer clear-cut ethical guidelines in areas that are often very murky and complicated. These Model Rules of Professional Conduct are not designed for lawyers only. Because many of them apply directly to how the business of law is conducted, these laws of lawyering must be thoroughly familiar to nonlawyers as well. As Geoffrey Hazard emphasized in the opening interview, "Nonlawyers have a duty to conduct themselves in ways compatible with and supportive of the lawyers' ethical responsibilities."[45] Each of the eight sections of the Model Rules of Professional Conduct (outlined in Table 15–2) addresses a specific ethical concern. Each model rule is summarized in this text, but students of law office management are urged to consult the full text of the Model Rules for thoroughness and accuracy. The sections on which we will focus in this chapter pertain to conducting the business of law: they emphasize those aspects of the rules that are within a manager's jurisdiction and that the firm's nonlawyers are expected to help carry out. The Model Rules of Professional Conduct prescribe professional responsibilities in these eight areas: (1) the client-lawyer relationship, (2) the lawyer as counselor, (3) the lawyer as advocate, (4) transactions with persons other than clients, (5) law firms and associations, (6) public service, (7) information about legal services, and (8) maintaining the integrity of the profession.

Client-Lawyer Relations

The first of the Model Rules of Professional Conduct describes responsibilities in the following areas: (a) the kinds of competence that the lawyer must offer the client; (b) the scope of representation, or the lawyer's accurate representation of his or her expertise; (c) the diligence with which the lawyer should attend to the client's cause, since the lawyer must be able to deliver the promised scope of representation with perseverance and promptness; (d) the communications that the client must receive about matters that he or she has entrusted to the lawyer; (e) the lawyer's duty to establish reasonable fees and to inform the client of those fees in advance; and (f) the absolute need to conduct all transactions in the utmost confidentiality. "Breaching confidentiality" is defined as sharing any information "relating to the reputation of a client" with anyone unauthorized to receive that information. As part of their professional practices, lawyers often need to consult, but they must do so without committing any breach

TABLE 15–2
Overview of the Model Rules of Professional Conduct

Rule 1. Client-Lawyer Relations
Rule 2. The Lawyer as Counselor
Rule 3. The Lawyer as Advocate
Rule 4. The Lawyer and Transactions with Persons Other Than Clients
Rule 5. Law Firms and Associations:
- Responsibilities of Partners
- Responsibilities of Subordinate Lawyers
- Responsibilities of Nonlawyer Assistants

Rule 6. Responsibility for Public Service
Rule 7. Providing Legal Services
Rule 8. The Integrity of the Profession

of trust. Preserving the client's anonymity takes great restraint and discipline. Finally, this first of the Model Rules provides specific guidelines on what constitutes a conflict of interest for lawyers and for the law firm, how the property of the client is to be safeguarded, and when it is necessary to decline and/or terminate representation.

The Lawyer as Counselor

The second model rule provides guidelines for the scope and kinds of advice to which clients are entitled. As an adviser, the lawyer must serve the client candidly and fairly.

The Lawyer as Advocate

The third Model Rule of Professional Conduct describes the lawyer's responsibilities in acting as a spokesperson for his or her client. The client pays for the expertise, wisdom, and skills of the attorney, who should offer his or her services within a framework of appropriate impartiality and decorum.

The Lawyer and Transactions with Persons Other Than Clients

The fourth rule describes the kinds of communications in which the lawyer may participate when working with parties, other than the client, who are involved in the legal transaction.

Law Firms and Associations

The fifth of the Model Rules of Professional Conduct describes (1) the responsibilities of partners and supervisory lawyers, (2) the responsibilities of subordinate lawyers, (3) the responsibilities of lawyers regarding nonlawyer assistants, (4) the professional independence of lawyers, (5) the unauthorized practice of law, and (6) restrictions on the right to practice.

The Responsibilities of Partners and Supervisory Lawyers

This section addresses the special issues involved when a supervising lawyer obligates subordinate lawyers to act in accordance with his or her directions. The fifth rule specifically considers the responsibilities of lawyers with regard to nonlawyer assistants, asking lawyers to "make reasonable efforts to ensure that the firm has in effect measures giving reasonable assurance that the person's conduct is compatible with the professional obligations of the lawyer."

Responsibilities of Partners. Partners are obligated to set and monitor compliance with firm policies, to oversee continuing education, and to direct, help, and supervise subordinate lawyers.

Responsibilities of Subordinate Lawyers. Subordinate lawyers are under a singular type of ethical pressure: They must rely on their supervising attorney and accept his or her judgment instead of their own, in terms of "arguable ethical issues" even when those issues are ambiguous.

Responsibilities of Nonlawyer Assistants. A lawyer's supervisory duty must be "compatible" with his or her professional obligations. The firm is to determine compatible conduct, since it is the firm's duty to establish safeguards. It becomes the supervising lawyer's obligation to establish controls over the conduct of nonlawyer personnel, such as secretaries or paralegals.

The Responsibilities of Subordinate Lawyers

When making decisions, subordinate lawyers may at times be asked to submit their judgment to that of a supervising attorney, who takes the responsibility for the decision. However, no supervising attorney should ever ask a subordinate attorney to act knowingly against the Rules of Conduct.

Responsibilities Regarding Nonlawyer Assistants

Lawyers are responsible for those who assist them in the delivery of legal services, including managers, secretaries, interns, and paralegals. Attorneys are obligated to oversee and educate all personnel in the ethical dimensions of working in a law firm, particularly on issues of client confidentiality and professional standards. Many professional associations have developed additional, specific guidelines for their members, such as the NALA's Code of Ethics and Professional Responsibility and the NFPA's Affirmation of Responsibility.

Professional Independence of Lawyers

In order to protect the lawyer's independent professional judgment, the fifth rule also addresses the specific limitations placed on lawyers regarding fee sharing. This rule addresses the problems that may arise when ownership interests may be at stake. "Ownership interests" is a euphemism: the real issue is the fact that such fee arrangements, through which lawyers and nonlawyers combine to provide legal services, are fraught with potential conflicts and problems that may compromise the practice of law.

The Unauthorized Practice of Law

The fifth rule also provides guidelines for avoiding the unauthorized practice of law, which many states interpret as a criminal offense. The licensing of lawyers protects society by preventing those who are not certified as competent from victimizing the public. As is now being widely discussed in the press and in the courts, some tasks that have until now been strictly reserved for lawyers can be performed less expensively but equally as well by nonlawyers in several fields, but particularly by paralegals. In general, however, any practice of law by laypersons is unauthorized and should be prevented. This model rule warns that lawyers who are licensed in one state may not meet licensing requirements in another.

Restrictions on the Right to Practice

The rules recognize the idea that restricting a lawyer's right to practice after leaving a firm limits professional autonomy and restricts the ability of clients to choose their own lawyers. Because he or she has been privy to its operations, a lawyer who leaves a firm provokes issues of loyalty and confidentiality, and more basic concerns, such as the "theft" of clients. Yet the firm can't expect those who leave to abandon their rights to earn a livelihood. They should be able to serve some of the same clients, if those clients so request it! Though a client's choice of service providers should not be limited, there are rules that lawyers must observe in their efforts to attract clients. At one time, considering written contracts for such actions unseemly and unprofessional, law firms governed the departure of lawyers through gentlemen's agreements. While still at a former firm, lawyers still may not inform clients inappropriately of their new availability. Nonetheless, they often represent a formidable source of competition for many firms. Geoffrey Hazard and William Hodes explain:

> When lawyers leave a firm and seek to continue to serve clients they were serving while at the same firm, the free speech interests of the departing lawyers and the affected clients not only permit "solicitation" overtures to be made, but preempt any common law rights based on unfair competition that the law firm might otherwise have concerning the conduct of lawyers leaving the firm.[46]

Responsibility for Public Service

A lawyer has a duty to contribute to the improvement of the legal system and, by doing so, to the improvement of society. Though this sixth Model Rule of Professional Conduct is not enforceable, most lawyers consider it a moral duty. The rule suggests that lawyers contribute pro bono efforts in one of three ways: by offering reduced fees or no fees for professional service to those in need; by contributing services that will improve law, the legal system, and the profession; and by making contributions for legal services to organizations that help those of limited means.

Providing Legal Services

This seventh Model Rule of Professional Conduct offers guidelines for communications, advertising, direct contact with prospects, claims of competency in various fields, and the proper use of information about the firm.

Advertising

The seventh rule provides lawyers with safeguards for protecting the integrity of the sale of their services.

Responsible Attorney. Each advertisement must identify by name the lawyer who is responsible for the ad; in addition, the lawyer's name must appear on any communication that is published or used.

Gifts. A lawyer must give no gift of value in payment to those who recommend his or her services. All lawyers must pay whatever the usual charges are for advertising.

Retention. The lawyer must retain a copy of each advertisement for two years. This promotes truthfulness in advertising.

Other Attorneys. An ad may not compare one lawyer to another, since the practice of law involves more than the outcomes of cases.

Price Comparisons. Lawyers can make price comparisons if such comparisons are true, but to equate one fee with another is very difficult. Just as it is almost impossible to equate one "simple" will with another, for instance, it is just as difficult, if not impossible, to equate the fees for services regarding those wills.

Dignity. According to the seventh Model Rule, the legal profession can do little more than frown upon undignified ads. A lawyer emerging from a lake in a wet suit asking viewers who are "drowning in paperwork" to "let my office do your tax work" does not rate highly on the scale of good taste, but, according to the codes and the ruling of the Supreme Court, is allowed by law.

Unjustifiable Expectations. Creating false hopes is considered misleading. When advertising, an attorney or law firm may not claim a superb track record, since, once again, having successful outcomes involves many factors, not just skill. Reputation and referrals are thought to be the factors that most effectively attract clients. Those who advertise are often seen by other attorneys as *needing* to advertise.

Direct Contacts

The seventh rule places tight restrictions on the methods and conditions with and under which lawyers contact prospective clients. Lawyers cannot "in person or live telephone contact solicit" new clients. To **solicit** is to aim one's persuasive efforts at a specific prospective client in contemplation of having one's services hired for a specific legal matter, in order to make a profit. Nonetheless, the rule recognizes several forms of solicitation as commercial speech allowable under the First Amendment. They include the following:

Prerecorded Phone Calls. The rule protects prerecorded phone calls by attorneys as part of a telemarketing campaign. Technology allows lawyers to document the claims and promises that they make. "Live" calls, on the other hand, are not documentable. No existing safeguards can verify the content of a live call, the expectations that a lawyer raises during such a call, or the promises he or she makes. Besides warning prospective clients about the specific dangers involved in obtaining legal services through live phone solicitation, the rule allows them the option of hanging up on a caller who isn't live—a computerized telemarketing recording, perhaps—without fear of retaliation or of being rude. The rule neither allows nor protects live telemarketing calls.

Written Communications. Often, businesses make use of flyers and special mailings to reach a particular audience. The seventh rule allows attorneys to mail and distribute printed materials only when the mailing is not misleading and when it is sent to a general audience. The rule permits neither targeted mailing nor mailings sent to those known to be in need of specific legal services. A lawyer may not bother with advertising anyone who does not want to be bothered. What if, for example, after a mass disaster such as an airplane crash, a law firm used a targeted mailing list of the families of the deceased or injured to send a personalized letter offering its professional services? This would not only be insensitive and in poor taste, but it also would not be allowed.

Warning Labels. Lawyers can send general mail to prospects with whom they have had no prior relationship and who are not known to need a lawyer's services, provided that the material contains a plainly visible warning label containing the words "advertising material." If, for example, a law firm wants to advertise closing costs, by sending out a flyer to home buyers in general, it may do so, provided the flyer includes a warning label. The firm may not, however, send this material to a specialized targeted list, such as to people known to be in need of legal help with their home buying, no matter what warning the material bears.

Fields of Practice

Lawyers must be careful in advertising the kinds of business they will and will not accept. They may list their areas of practice, as this is protected as a form of commercial speech. But this must be done so as not to be misleading. An attorney just out of law school who is practicing alone cannot in good faith believe that listing twenty-five legal designations in a Yellow Pages will not mislead potential clients. A lawyer can use the word "specialist" or "certified" in an ad only if he or she is admitted to practice before the U.S. Patent and Trademark Office.[47]

Firm Names and Letterheads

Before the *Bates & O'Steen* decision in 1977, business/professional cards, letterheads, and office signs were the only permissible forms of self-promotion for lawyers. Only "dignified" announcements were acceptable. Now, the seventh rule provides guidelines to ensure the accurate, nondeceptive use of firm names, letterheads, and stationery.

Letterheads. Names and letterheads must accurately represent a firm's practice. A multistate office, for example, must state accurately the states in which its lawyers may legitimately practice, and no firm may imply that listed lawyers practice as partners, when in fact they only share office space, staff, and expenses with the firm's partners.

Elected Officials. If someone leaves the firm to serve in an elected office, leaving that person's name on the firm's letterhead implies that his or her services are still available. This is misleading and is, therefore, not allowed.

Shared Space. Two or more lawyers who share space and/or facilities cannot advertise together, as Smith & Allen, for example. This usage implies a partnership.

Use by Nonlawyers. The rules for firm names and letterheads create unique considerations regarding paralegals, to whom they also apply. For example, the states differ in their interpretations as to whether or not a firm can include the names of paralegals on its letterhead. In most states, however, paralegals can use the firm's stationery in communications to clients or opposing counsel, as long as the paralegal clearly states his or her nonlawyer status and as long as it is not an unauthorized communication or practice of law. Most states formerly prohibited firms from using the names of nonlawyers on their stationery, implying that the practice would diminish the dignity of the profession. Some states still do not allow law firms to permit their paralegals to use business cards. Others allow the use of business cards, provided that the firm has approved the format and content of the card and provided that its paralegals fully understand that they are subject to the same ethical guidelines and prohibitions as the firm's lawyers. Paralegals cannot use cards to solicit business for the firm, particularly if prospective clients do not request them. No state has yet authorized law firms to include paralegal names in the listings of attorneys at the firm's main entrance.

The Integrity of the Profession

In the eighth and last of the Model Rules of Professional Conduct, lawyers are reminded that they are no longer required to turn their backs on the communication methods of contemporary society. The use of media is a reality of contemporary life. After years of effort on the part of lawyers and the American Bar Association to regulate communication in the practice of law, restrictions have finally been lifted. As we saw in Chapter 14, the Supreme Court ruled in 1977 in *Bates & O'Steen v. State Bar of Arizona* that a lawyer's advertising is entitled to First Amendment protection as commercial speech.[48] The only permissible limitation is that such advertising not be false or misleading. Yet, law office personnel should be aware that there are still many applicable restrictions which cannot be ignored.

THE GOOD MANAGER

George Sharswood, credited with founding the field of legal ethics, wrote years ago that "No man can ever be a truly great lawyer who is not, in every sense of the word, a good man.... There is no profession in which moral character is so soon fixed as in that of the law; there is none in which it is subjected to severer scrutiny by the public."[49] And a legal administrator, a law firm manager, executive, coordinator, director, paralegal, secretary, or support staff member of any variety is subject to the same scrutiny and must assist the lawyer, as much as possible, in establishing an unpolluted ethical climate. This leads to the ideal law firm, one in which clients trust professionals: "Integrity," writes Tom Peters, "has been the hallmark of the superior organization through the ages."[50] Organizations, like people, have their own rules of ethics, and organization members share perceptions about what is right and wrong. Law firms are no exception. The only difference is the additional rules that exist for law firms. In deciding what its members should or should not do, a firm must answer several specific ethical questions. **Legal ethics** consists of two dictates: the set of legal rules that govern a lawyer's conduct and the lawyer's subjective assessment of his or her conduct in practicing law, including his or her personal values and knowledge regarding a given situation. "These personal values and perceptions," Hazard notes, "may be at odds with the legal rules and the objective facts, and the discrepancy can be a source of great personal distress, and sometimes serious professional and legal risk."[51] In the discussion of managerial roles, one pressing responsibility underlies all the others. That requirement is the need to make ethical decisions. The manager, in particular, must see ethical decisions in organizational terms not personal ones. Though the decisions he or she makes will inevitably be personal in some ways, the manager must realize that the manner in which he or she makes those decisions creates the ethical framework for the rest of the organization.

Administration and the Ethical Climate

A firm's moral climate starts with top management. Should those at the top dispense with ethical considerations, those at the bottom will likely do the same. Top management can, by looking the other way, subtly communicate not only its own unethical standards but its lack of interest in the unethical practices of workers, thereby establishing a dismal moral tone for the firm.[52]

Ethical Policy Statements

Top management should provide the rest of the organization with guidelines regarding the ethical decisions that the firm expects, accepts, ignores, or rewards. An ethical code or policy statement can provide written guidelines regarding what the firm considers important and what it expects of its workers.[53]

Managerial Ethics

Managerial ethics are principles by which managers ensure that their actions and decisions fulfill legal mandates and reflect the broader set of moral principles that guide society. Managerial ethics represent ethical decision making that conforms to the law but also is responsive to societal obligations.

ALA Code of Professional Ethics

In April 1991, the Association of Legal Administrators adopted a comprehensive Code of Professional Ethics, which urges ALA members to maintain public trust by adhering to high standards. The code sets forth guidelines for administration in all forms of legal practice, whether in private firms, corporate or government settings, or legal clinics. As the code states in its opening paragraphs,

> Legal administrators at all levels must become familiar with these standards and incorporate them into their every-day performance. They should also study and comply with all ethical guidelines of bar associations and law societies which apply in their own jurisdictions. Furthermore, they must take the lead in communicating relevant standards to staff personnel who may be less familiar than lawyers with the ethical guidelines of bar associations and law societies, and in communicating appropriate policies and procedures to lawyers.[54]

The Code of Professional Ethics (reproduced in Figure 15–1) offers guidelines in eight areas: (1) honesty, (2) integrity, (3) objectivity, (4) competence, (5) independence, (6) professional responsibility, (7) confidentiality, and (8) service.

Ethical Decision Making

Of all the challenges a manager faces, making ethical decisions is one of the most difficult. As a decision maker, the manager experiences conflicts from a human and personal perspective of values, from a business perspective of profit and success, and from a legal professional perspective, where what is ethical may not be legal, and where what is legal may not be moral. A manager must confront many ethical dimensions of leadership. In addition to being honest and truthful, a manager also needs to be aware of his or her ethical responsibilities, ensuring that ethical standards are in effect for the firm's operations. In this way, a manager can create a climate that encourages honesty and truthfulness in the implementation of policy and decisions. Ethical standards need to be integrated into all parts of a business, including its decision making, supervision practices, hiring policies and procedures, marketing decisions, personnel interactions, leadership influences, and compensation determinations, to name only a few.

Does Honesty Pay?

From those around us, we receive many messages about whether or not it pays to be ethical. On one hand, we hear that honesty is the best policy, that ethics is good business. On the other hand, many business cynics caution that virtue is its own reward. It's easy to agree with Harvard management professors Bhide and Stevenson when they tell us, "People aren't exclusively saints or sinners." They observe that "few adhere to an absolute moral code. Most respond to circumstances, and their integrity and trustworthiness can depend as much on how they are treated as on their basic character." As of yet, Bhide and Stevenson have

CHAPTER 15 / ETHICAL RESPONSIBILITIES

FIGURE 15-1
ALA Code of Professional Ethics

Principles and Rules of Conduct

Honesty
The professional legal administrator shall:
- Be open and honest in all relationships with attorneys, employees and others.
- Never compromise the reputation or good of the legal practice by dishonest or illegal behavior.

Integrity
The professional, legal administrator shall:
- Avoid actual or apparent conflicts of interest. Advise all appropriate parties of any potential conflicts.
- Never engage in activities that would prejudice the ethical performance of job responsibilities.
- Refuse any gift, favor or hospitality that would influence or appear to influence actions, unless such item is fully disclosed to and approved by management.
- Never solicit or accept any personal or family fee, commission, gift, gratuity, discount or loan for performing job duties or providing services to existing or potential clients.
- Pursue and promote fair and equitable employment practices and oppose discrimination which is based upon gender, age, race, religious creed, national origin, physical disability, marital, parental or veteran status.
- Endeavor to foster a work environment founded on respect and dignity and free of sexual harassment.

Objectivity
The professional legal administrator shall:
- Communicate all information fairly and objectively.
- Fully disclose all known information that would be material to a particular management or financial decision.
- Fully disclose all relevant information required for an intended user to understand management reports, employee communications, business recommendations and comments.

Competence
The professional legal administrator shall:
- Maintain an appropriate level of professional competence and enhance existing skills through ongoing professional education programs, peer group associations and self-training.
- Recognize and communicate professional limitations or other constraints that would preclude responsible judgment or successful performance of an activity.
- Ensure that delegated tasks are responsibly assigned and competently performed.
- Make every effort to ensure that subordinates have necessary skills and levels of competence.

Independence
The professional legal administrator shall:
- Ensure that all personal political activities are separated from the legal practice.
- Never make investments which would benefit from inside knowledge of the legal practice or its clients.
- Exercise prudence and restraint in personal financial affairs, including speculative investments and margin accounts, in order to avoid debts and other financial obligations which could compromise independence and professional judgment.

Professional Responsibility
The professional legal administrator shall:
- Promulgate a positive image of the legal practice to its clients and potential clients; attorneys and staff personnel; bankers, consultants and vendors; the press; governmental agencies; the legal community; and all other relevant audiences.
- Exercise reasonable diligence in gathering business data and information from internal and external sources and in reporting that information in a manner which facilitates informed decision-making.

Confidentiality
The professional legal administrator shall:
- Never disclose confidential information acquired in the course of employment, whether or not still employed by that legal practice, except when legally obligated to do so.
- Inform subordinates that confidentiality of information acquired in the course of their work is essential, and monitor their activities to ensure that confidentiality is maintained.
- Ensure that all confidential and proprietary information acquired in the course of duty is used solely for legal practice purposes, is not provided to unauthorized persons, and is not used for the purpose of furthering a private interest or making a personal profit.

(continued)

FIGURE 15-1 *(continued)*
ALA Code of Professional Ethics

> **Service**
> The professional legal administrator shall:
> - Perform business duties in good faith in a manner believed to be in the best interests of the legal practice.
> - Perform duties only within assigned authority.
> - Accomplish assigned tasks in a timely manner.
> - Promote and monitor guidelines for practice development and marketing activities to ensure that those activities are appropriate for the legal practice and conform with applicable professional guidelines.
>
> SOURCE: Reprinted with the permission of the Association of Legal Administrators. Copyright © 1991.

been unable to find any evidence to support the claims of economists, ethicists, and business experts who believe that honesty is the best business policy:

> To our surprise, our pet theories [regarding the role of ethics in business] failed to stand up. Treachery, we found, can pay. There is no compelling economic reason to tell the truth or keep one's word—punishment for the treacherous in the real world is neither swift nor sure. . . . Businesspeople do tell themselves that, in the long run, they will do well by doing good. But there is little factual or logical basis for this conviction.[55]

Instead of hard economic reasons, Bhide and Stevenson found only that businesspeople want to believe that honesty is the best policy. They also found that treachery often pays because businesspeople find it disadvantageous to fight power abuses and dishonesty. Nonetheless,

> The businesspeople we interviewed set great store on the regard of their family, friends, and the community at large. They valued their reputations, not for some nebulous gain but because they took pride in their good names. Even more important, since outsiders cannot easily judge trustworthiness, businesspeople seem guided by their inner voices, by their consciences.[56]

Ethical actions do have their staunch proponents. "We don't require honesty," Bhide and Stevenson conclude, "but we honor and celebrate it."[57] Managers admire ethical decision making. In an American Management Association survey, over 90 percent of the country's top managers agreed with this statement: "My organization is guided by highly ethical standards." William Tracey, a well-known management author and consultant, in assessing the study, commented on the values our country's top managers most admire:

> By no means is the profit motive the driving force behind managerial action, as some outside the business community may think. Nor is ambition number one on most managers' lists of admired qualities. In fact, it ranks well below responsibility, honesty, and imagination. Most respondents see a resurgence of basic values—commitment, responsibility, integrity, and the like—as a key to a better future and an improved quality of life.[58]

Others believe that ethical business does make good economic sense. As a token of his belief that this is so, John Shad, the former head of the Securities and Exchange Commission, contributed a $30 million grant to teach Harvard MBAs that "ethics pays." As Tracey observes,

> The word is getting out: ethical business is good business. . . . [It] contributes to success in the marketplace. A reputation for honesty and integrity attracts and holds customers, and will ultimately show up in the bottom line. Organizations that have strong ethical values and consistently display them in all their activities derive other benefits, too: improved top management control, increased productivity, avoidance of litigation, and an enhanced company image that attracts talent and earns the public's good will.[59]

In spite of our wanting to believe that there is a connection, however, no hard data proves as yet that "good" business is *good* business.[60]

Confidentiality Issues

Keeping one's own counsel is always difficult. Keeping the confidences of others is even harder. The issue of confidentiality is an ongoing major concern for those in law firms, as we can see in the Model Rules of

Professional Conduct. Law firm managers must clearly delineate support staff obligations and practical rules for confidentiality.

The Obligations of Support Staff. Members of a law firm's support staff share an important role in professional responsibilities. As keepers, processors, and recorders of knowledge, their main obligation is to safeguard confidential information, and they must uphold confidentiality with a commitment that approaches fanaticism. They *must* see theirs as a sacred trust. Even then, indiscretions and infractions will occur. Sometimes support staff, and professionals as well, unintentionally breach confidentiality by taking part in conversations that are unknowingly overheard, by carelessly leaving confidential documents and materials around the office, and by discussing cases with others who are not legitimately involved. Some law firms have required support staff members to sign confidentiality promises, to emphasize the importance of this responsibility. Managers should remember that only a firm's lawyers—and some fortunate paralegals—have formally learned the ethical obligations of their duties. Members of the support staff need additional training and assistance in learning the ethical expectations in the law firm setting and why those expectations are so critical.

Practical Rules for Confidentiality. In working with others, it is always difficult not to share information, particularly news about interesting or unusual happenings. Nonetheless, in a law firm, confidences must be inviolable. All members of the firm not only must receive instructions regarding but must be held responsible for the following obligations: no discussion of client matters outside the office or with unauthorized personnel within the office; discreet use of the telephone; complete and timely information given to clients; accurate and responsible document handling that leaves all documents readily accessible; and honesty in working with clients.

Why Good Managers Make "Bad" Decisions[61]

Even the best of managers can make a poor ethical decision. Good managers, Saul Gellerman suggests, make unethical decisions using the same rationalization patterns we use in our personal lives. The more common ethical rationalizations include these conclusions:

"This Isn't Really Illegal or Immoral." We are all familiar with ethical decisions that seem absolutely clear-cut. Charity is good. Killing is bad. Lying is wrong. Honesty is right. When it comes to the distinction between an ingenious decision and an immoral one, however, the black-and-white of an ethical choice merges to grey. In the grey zone, it is hard to tell if managers are being clever or if they are indulging in shady practices. Gellerman believes that when one manner of conducting business offers richer rewards than another and when the organization is more interested in an end than in the means to that end, then even the best of managers has a hard time making a purely ethical decision.

"This Is in Everyone's Best Interest." When we are convinced that the end result of an action will benefit everyone, we are more likely to minimize the wrongs involved. Gellerman observes that this happens when our view of the common good is narrower than we think. Managers who commit bribery or who falsify records to protect someone's reputation can erroneously persuade themselves that their actions are necessary to further the success of the firm.

"No One Will Ever Know." This rationalization is based on the mistaken idea that the wrongdoing is acceptable if no one finds out about it. Managers under pressure to perform often convince themselves that unethical events that go unnoticed have little chance of hurting anyone and, being harmless, aren't really wrong.

"The Organization Will Stand Behind Me No Matter What." Gellerman calls this last rationalization a form of "loyalty gone berserk." Managers who give an unqualified loyalty to an organization convince themselves that such loyalty is reciprocal. They foolishly believe that, even if they are caught red-handed, the organization will support them, no matter what. Gellerman observes that although organizations have a right to expect loyalty of their managers, no one is above the law, the codes of common morality, and the laws of society itself.

Managerial Responsibilities

A manager answers to multiple stakeholders. As we have seen, stakeholders are any constituencies within or outside of an organization that are affected by its decisions and policies. The range of a manager's responsibility toward stakeholders seems to be continually expanding: as businesspeople, owners and managers have a responsibility to minimize costs and maximize profits, but they are also responsible to those who are part of the firm. Managers are obliged to focus on human concerns. At this level of responsibility, managers must be aware that the firm interacts with the public. Though it takes from society, it must also give to society; and it is responsible to society as a whole. The law firm's business is of a public nature, and managers must contribute toward the public good. They can do this by actively promoting social justice, participating in activities that help the less financially fortunate to access justice, preserving the environment, supporting cultural activities, and making decisions that contribute to a stronger society. Managers encounter ethical decision making on a daily basis. Moral choices pervade every aspect of a manager's job. Many managers are quite aware of this and know the personal toll it can take. In struggling to resolve ethical aspects of daily on-the-job interactions, some managers believe they have been forced to become uncaring and insensitive to their workers. Other managers speak of their daily struggles with being direct and honest. Others tell of their conflicts with accepting kindnesses and small favors from workers, since they would like to accept their subordinates at face value and not concern themselves with whether or not workers are motivated by honest generosity or by a desire to manipulate. Many managers worry about becoming compromised by the demands of their job and about having to cut corners just to survive the pressures. These are seemingly uncomplicated ethical struggles. If we were to construct a continuum of ethical dilemmas, we might place daily and personal conflicts at one end, representing individual or microscale ethical issues, and juxtapose ongoing global concerns at the other, to represent societal or macroscale ethical issues.

GOOD LAW FIRMS

What makes a "good" law firm? In addition to its lawyers' competence in the areas of expertise that clients need, their ability to maintain confidentiality regarding their clients' affairs, the quality of their two-way communication about client-related matters, and their undiluted and total commitment to their clients, a "good" law firm is also aware of and responsive to the needs of society. This is **social responsibility,** a firm's obligation to make policies and choose courses of action that are in keeping with the values and needs of the larger social environment. Such responsibility is also known as social action, community involvement, and social concern. In examining the concept of social responsibility, we should understand that although it remains a much-debated issue, speaking out against social responsibility is like ridiculing yellow ribbons, the national flag, or apple pie. Those who debate the concept tend to take either the classical view or the socioeconomic view of social responsibility.

The Classical View of Social Responsibility

The *classical view* of social responsibility offers a stockholder model, stating that management has no other responsibility than that of maximizing profits for a firm's stockholders, its owners. Nobel Prize-winning economist Milton Friedman believes that holding the management of a firm responsible to both the owners and society creates a conflict of interest. He explains that the obligations imposed by social responsibilities are contrary to the primary duty of managers, which is to act for an organization's owners. Socially responsible actions also create additional costs, which are passed on to consumers as higher fees and costs. Some, like business ethics professors Robert Hay, Edmund Gray, and Paul Smith, see the spending of "money on nonbusiness philanthropic and community activities as synonymous with stealing from the owners. Excessive discretionary spending can also affect employees' pay and benefits, bringing negative effects to the very way the firm meets its objectives."[62] Friedman believes that "few trends could so thoroughly undermine the very foundations of our free society as the acceptance by corporate officials of a social responsibility other than to make as much money for their stockholders as possible."[63]

The Socioeconomic View of Social Responsibility

In contrast to the classical view of social responsibility, the *socioeconomic view* provides a stakeholder model, contending that all organizations are obligated, for the sake of those who have a stake in the organization, to contribute to the good of society. Most organizations are licensed or approved by the government, and lawyers are authorized by the state to practice law. Being thus subject to governmental authority, they are obligated to contribute to society. Because they must exist in a social setting, lawyers and law firms do not answer only to the profession. They are not independent of their surroundings. To maximize profits, then, notes Gellerman, is "a company's second priority, not its first. The first is ensuring its survival." [64] The leading voice speaking on behalf of this socioeconomic view is that of expert economist Paul Samuelson, who believes that "a large corporation these days not only *may* engage in social responsibility, it had damn well better try to do so." [65] Tom Peters offers further support for the socioeconomic view by explaining that the profit motive alone is not enough: "Integrity is not only absolute (stealing is bad, period), but it involves 'perceived equity.' That is, fairness is in the eye of the beholder. Paying bonuses to management and withholding worker bonuses in a problematic year is perceived to be unfair, regardless of the extenuating circumstances." [66]

A Continuum of Social Responsibility

Managers who are conscious of their larger role in society also know that their primary duty within the organization is to be an effective manager. Historically, managerial values have progressed from maximizing profits to being responsive to social concerns.[67] A. B. Carroll proposes a continuum of social responsibilities (see Figure 15–2) which divides into four phases the kinds of socially responsive decisions that organizations might make: economic, legal, ethical, and discretionary.[68]

Phase I: Economic

In the past, managers believed that their principal duty and the primary responsibility of the firm was to make money for the owners. It was also the firm's way of contributing towards a better—i.e., economically sound—society. Historically, the firm's duty at this first level of responsibility was to operate effectively and efficiently in order to provide society with the services it needed. Secondary responsibilities included concerns for workers and clients. For law firms that still subscribe to this phase of social responsibility, business depends on survival, which can happen only through profit.

Phase II: Legal

All organizations are obligated to observe not only civic and criminal laws but the regulatory laws that apply to businesses. In providing society with its services, a law firm must operate within the constraints of the law.

Phase III: Ethical

The ethical obligations of the third phase extend to areas that laws may fail to cover and mandate. After the activist days of the 1960s and 1970s, all organizations felt pressure to be socially responsible and responsive. Activists protested those groups whose practices harmed society, and organizations that were not responsive to quality-of-life issues received negative press. Consequently, law firms began to see socially responsive practices as good business. Avoiding profits made through social exploitation was not enough. To evade popular wrath, a firm needed to contribute affirmatively to society.

Phase IV: Discretionary

Discretionary responsibilities are those that are not mandated as duties, required by laws, or viewed as unethical if not acknowledged. These responsibilities are options; they are activities a firm can espouse voluntarily. As Hay, Gray, and Smith observe, we expect good organizations to be like good citizens, who "voluntarily assume the obligation to tackle some of the problems of society at large." [69] For law firm members, these voluntary activities can consist of working with social issues, such as the fight against drug abuse; participating in community activities, such as literacy programs; and taking part in public relations and community activities, possibly by sponsoring a YWCA House and Garden Tour, helping the Rotary run an essay contest on careers in justice, or serving on the mayor's Bicentennial Committee.

Arguments for Social Responsibility

Law firms, as organizations of professionals, exist in order to serve society. Why should they assume additional responsibilities, above and beyond fulfilling their mission of providing access to the system of justice? The answers include arguments ranging from the welfare of society to enlightened self-interest. "A manager who balances quality-of-life concerns with the firm's goals and objectives while making decisions," write Hay, Gray, and Smith, "is said to be motivated by enlightened self-interest." [70] A manager who understands the long-term value of being—and of being

FIGURE 15-2
The Continuum of Social Responsibility

Phase I	Phase II	Phase III	Phase IV
Economic Social Responsibilities	Legal Social Responsibilities	Ethical Social Responsibilities	Discretionary Social Responsibilities
Required by Organization	Required by Laws	Expected by Society	Desired for Respect

SOURCE: Based on A. B. Carroll, "A Three-Dimensional Model of Corporate Social Performance," *Academy of Management Review* (October 1979): 499.

perceived as—socially responsive knows the possible payoffs: the image of the law firm as caring and conscientious, a perception of trustworthiness, a stronger and more informed client base. All of these improve the firm's profitability. Caring organizations owe it to themselves to publicize their commitment to socially responsive issues to the individual, the community, and the larger social environment.

Arguments against Social Responsibility

Some who argue against the obligation to be socially responsible believe that such activities constitute nothing more than a drain on organizational resources, since an organization's primary purpose is to maximize profits. Further, they believe, socially responsible activities result in excess costs that the organization must pass on to clients. Others fear that socially responsible organizations will gain power over society, in proportion to the amount of money they contribute. Society, they worry, could easily become dependent on businesses and organizations, allowing them to assume the care of its most important issues. There is concern that business leaders are not equipped to deal with societal issues, since their primary interests are economic ones. Because they are not truly accountable to society for their decisions, social responsibility opponents argue, we have little guarantee that businesses involved in social responsibility programs will not, in the end, do more harm than good. Table 15–3 outlines the arguments for and against social responsibility.

Ways to Be Socially Responsive

Several studies have examined corporate responses to social issues, showing how law firms, businesses, and other organizations contribute to society.[71] Involvement assumes many forms. Some businesses stress environmental concerns by reducing waste, reusing materials, and recycling resources.[72] Others emphasize employee concerns, such as equal opportunity, health and safety, and quality of work life, or larger-scale human rights concerns, such as minority development and urban renewal. Some businesses accent their positive response to consumerism by promoting truth in advertising and fair credit practices. Others believe in contributing to their local communities through efforts to support education, health care, the arts, recreation, and civic involvement. Finally, there are those who point to their patriotism, highlighting their cooperation as good citizens dedicated to the common good. Law firm participation in socially responsive efforts continues to grow, in addition to the vocation's pro bono obligations.

ETHICAL CHOICES

Everyone agrees we need ethics. Nevertheless, few organizations before the 1960s gave much thought to social issues like racial discrimination, women's rights, opportunities for the physically challenged, and the environment. Realities may have been harsher in the days before social activism, but rarely were social issues the concern of management. Most either looked the other way or never saw what was happening. Few organizations ever considered contemporary innovations like an employee's Bill of Rights guaranteeing equity, respect for values, privacy, health, and safety. Government watchdog agencies are now assigned the almost impossible task of eradicating discrimination against the handicapped, older workers, minorities, and other protected groups. Most organizations try to give more than lip service to affirmative action programs, but the law firm, in spite of some progress, remains

TABLE 15-3
Arguments for and against Social Responsibility

Major Arguments for Social Responsibility

1. It is in the best interest of the business to promote and improve the communities where it does business.
2. Social actions can be profitable.
3. It is the ethical thing to do.
4. It improves the public image of the firm.
5. It increases the viability of the business system. Business exists because it gives society benefits. Society can amend or take away its charter. This is the "iron law of responsibility."
6. It is necessary to avoid government regulation.
7. Sociocultural norms require it.
8. Laws cannot be passed for all circumstances. Thus, business must assume responsibility to maintain an orderly legal society.
9. It is in the stockholders' best interest. It will improve the price of stock in the long run because the stock market will view the company as less risky and open to public attack and therefore award it a higher price—earning ratio.
10. Society should give business a chance to solve social problems that government has failed to solve.
11. Business, by some groups, is considered to be the institution with the financial and human resources to solve social problems.
12. Prevention of problems is better than cures—so let business solve problems before they become too great.

Major Arguments against Social Responsibility

1. It might be illegal.
2. Business plus government equals monolith.
3. Social actions cannot be measured.
4. It violates profit maximization.
5. Cost of social responsibility is too great and would increase prices too much.
6. Business lacks social skills to solve societal problems.
7. It would dilute business's primary purposes.
8. It would weaken U.S. balance of payments because price of goods will have to go up to pay for social programs.
9. Business already has too much power. Such involvement would make business too powerful.
10. Business lacks accountability to the public. Thus, the public would have no control over its social involvement.
11. Such business involvement lacks broad public support.

SOURCE: J. Monsen, Jr., "The Social Attitudes of Management," in *Contemporary Management*, ed. J. W. McGuire (Englewood Cliffs, N.J.: Prentice-Hall, 1974): 616. Reprinted with the permission of the author.

predominately a white male suit-and-tie stronghold. "One problem," notes Hazard, "is that the language and internal culture of the law still are male," and so are a majority of law faculties, alumni, examples in case books, and recruiters. "For example," he writes, "most law offices have a rigid status boundary between the lawyers and everyone else who works there. The lawyers are predominantly male, and everyone else is predominantly female."[73] The 1989 Survey of Law Firm Economics revealed that over 70 percent of firms ranging from 2 to 200 attorneys in size reported women in their ranks, but rarely are women found in the upper levels.[74] No one remains a passive rider on the ethical wagon train. We each contribute to the ethical climate of our work site, no matter what ethical tone those at the top may set. As Geoffrey Hazard points out, evasion of ethical responsibilities by a firm's senior partners is not only poor management. In an ethical setting riddled with indecision and weakness,

[T]here are bound to be differences among the junior lawyers and the nonlegal staff as to how to do the work, including how to resolve doubtful ethical issues. In default of resolution by responsible authority in the firm, the juniors will have to fight out these issues among themselves. They may try to dump the problems on the lowest level, which often will be the paralegals. They may try to pass the buck among themselves or share pretenses that there are no problems, techniques that involve systematic lying—all part of a condition that management and sociology literature calls negative firm culture.[75]

Each member of a law firm needs to confront any ethical issues involved in even the most mundane daily events. Partners and legal, writes business administration professor Kenneth Andrews, executives "must find in their own will, experience, and intelligence the principles they apply in balancing conflicting claims. Wise men and women will submit their views to others, for open discussion of problems reveals unsuspected ethical dimensions and develops alternative viewpoints that should be taken into account." Some issues, he notes, are bound to be "infinitely debatable."[76] Former NYNEX executive William Burns suggests that those who find themselves deadlocked on an ethical topic ask these simple questions:

Is it right?

Is it fair?

Who gets hurt?

Would you want your decision to appear in the *New York Times?*

What would you tell your child to do?[77]

ETHICAL DILEMMAS

An **ethical dilemma** occurs when two or more values conflict and a choice must be made between alternatives that offer differing personal or organizational benefits and represent differing ethical responses. An ethical dilemma occurs when two or more human values conflict. Managers frequently encounter ethical dilemmas, on both a small and a large scale. Like any other decisions, ethical decisions fall into two categories. The first category includes those decisions for which the issues seem black-and-white and which fall clearly within the firm's normal decision-making guidelines. The second category contains those "grey" decisions involving murky areas that have no clear and easy solutions. These harder ethical decisions require even the most astute among us to ponder alternatives and wrestle with possible solutions. An ethical decision that involves too many painful choices may remain a dilemma forever.

Workers and Their Moral Choices

The ethical problems that law firm members experience are different from those in any other work setting. Each associate, for example, has a fiduciary responsibility not only to his or her client but to the legal profession and to society as a whole. Beyond this, associates have an additional responsibility, that of obedience to the firm. They must answer to, meet the requests of, and submit to the professional authority of a supervising attorney. In addition, associates and other law firm workers face a daunting assortment of ethical questions: Is moonlighting a breach of ethical duty? What would happen to my loyalty, if I were to leave the firm? How do I respond to unfair assignments, given my duty to obey? What do I do when I receive unethical instructions? What is my duty to the client when the firm assigns me cases for which I have neither the time nor the expertise to serve the client fairly?[78]

Ethical Climate[79]

As we have seen, those at the top set the ethical climate in a law firm. John Cullen, Bart Victor, and Carroll Stephens suggest that an organization may establish one of five possible ethical climates, based on how it views its culture: an *instrumental climate* that centers around the importance the organization places on its self-interests and profitability; a *caring climate,* based on the importance of friendship, team interest, and social responsibility; an *independent climate,* centered around the importance of personal morality; a *rules-oriented climate,* shaped by a reliance on rules and standard operating procedures, and a *laws-and-codes climate,* which relies on the laws and kinds of professional codes the organization is obligated to observe. A laws-and-codes climate centers around considerations such as the importance of a profession's ethical code and primacy the organization places on making legal decisions. Each climate type reflects how members perceive the major emphasis in the organization's decision making. To be appropriate, an organization's ethical climate should complement its mission and ob-

- An office manager either must release materials she knows to be carelessly prepared or risk confronting the firm's management practices.
- A legal coordinator sees a new paralegal being asked to work on materials that are beyond his expertise.
- A director of finance is asked to make unrealistic budget projections.
- The firm asks its director of marketing to prepare copy for areas of expertise that the firm does not have.
- The firm's computer coordinator suggests to the director that they find the computer codes for work that a competitor has performed on an important case.
- The paper and forms supplier has offered the firm's purchaser a seven-day trip to Hawaii as a business appreciation gift.
- The law firm's secretary coordinator knows that the firm thought its client was not guilty and was engaging in organized efforts to prejudice testimony to win the trial by fabricating evidence, planting witnesses, and other activities.
- The office manager notes that his firm just happened to set up shop across the hall from a government agency that just happens to be staffed by friends who love to say, "By the way, there are some good lawyers right down the hall!"

ANOTHER LOOK

Ethical Dilemmas: What Is at Stake?

1. Think of an ethical dilemma in which you have been involved. How was it resolved? What repercussions did the solution bring?
2. Is ethical behavior equally important in all settings and under all conditions? Under what conditions is it all right to let unethical actions slide? Explain.
3. How many of the law firm members in the examples above do you think will confront the situations they see? For what reasons would they fail to do so?
4. What do you believe is the primary motivating force behind ethical behavior in the work setting? Are people motivated to behave ethically more out of a fear of punishment, of being discovered in their wrongdoings, or of hurting someone, or out of an honest desire to do what is right and fair?

---

jectives. Still, warn Cullen, Victor, and Stephens, each type of climate presents unique potential hazards:

> For example, a rules-oriented climate that plays down the importance of the employee's individual judgment could lead to misinterpretation or conflict between various rules and regulations. A climate that is low in caring could create an environment in which employees are treated in callous and potentially illegal ways; such a climate may lower motivation and increase the turnover rate.[80]

Because of the need to be governed by the codes of the profession and the laws of the legal system, a strong laws-and-codes climate is suitable for meeting the objectives of the law firm. A highly caring climate might not be appropriate. Understanding and confirming the compatibility of a predominant ethical climate results in organizational effectiveness.

Loyalty, Voice, or Exit[81]

What should a worker at any level in the law firm do if his or her personal ethical standards clash with those of the firm? Employees who find conflicts between what they think is ethical and the practices of their employing organization have three basic choices: loyalty, voice, or exit.

Loyalty. First, out of loyalty to the organization and its authority, the employees can simply comply, since compliance is a duty. If they decide to stay, they may need to mentally isolate themselves from the actions that conflict with their personal sense of right and wrong. This can be both lonely and very uncomfortable. Those who dissociate themselves are often rejected and shunned by others. But by subordinating their individual beliefs and convictions to the organization's authority they stand a good chance of preserving their moral integrity.

Voice. Secondly, the employees can voice their objections and try to make changes in the firm's ethical climate.[82] This may bring a wide range of consequences, depending on the organization's moral integrity. If the organization is committed to its workers and truly respects the role they play in the decision making process, it will perceive the protesting employee as a contributor, a person with sufficient independence and moral integrity to share his or her convictions. Only rarely, however, does an organization perceive a dissenter as a positive presence. More often than not, the employee who protests is seen as a problem: a dissident, a troublemaker, or a power seeker. An organization that has little respect for its workers or their opinions is unlikely to perceive a dissenter's contributions, let alone his or her cause for disagreement, in a positive light. Consequently, those who protest an organization's ethical choices often find themselves passed over for honors, promotions, and opportunities; in extreme cases, they may find themselves out of a job.

Exit. The third choice workers have is that of exit; they can leave the organization. If loyalty is the option with the most obvious benefit to workers and voice is the most risky, then exit may be the most difficult, initially. Workers who are unable to make themselves heard or to resign themselves to remaining loyal often persuade themselves that the option to leave is a valid choice for them and may be best for all involved. Nonetheless, this third alternative is a realistic option only for those who are financially and emotionally secure enough to seek a workplace with more compatible values. Those who opt to leave their organizations because of moral conflicts face many possible disadvantages. But exiting, in the long run, may be the best decision for those who are able to do so.

Whistleblowing

Through **whistleblowing,** an employee calls public attention to an organization's wrongful or illegal actions, often at great personal risk, so that greater issues of justice and equity are upheld. It is a difficult moral decision for a worker. As George Washington University professor Peter Raven-Hansen points out, whistleblowing involves many factors, most of which are potential sources of great pain for the worker. For one thing, whistleblowing forces an individual to choose between the obligation of reasonable loyalty to an organization and the dictates of legal, moral, or ethical standards. Moreover, it requires an employee to exhaust all possible avenues within the organization to resolve the problem and to face squarely the consequences of going public. "Blowing the whistle," especially when it means turning to the courts and the justice system, alienates both employer and colleagues, who distrust those whose actions seem to be self-serving. Even if the disclosure results in open hostility, the whistleblower must remain tactful. He or she must avoid name calling, slander, and engaging in mutual mud-slinging. Even when a particular individual is responsible for the illegal act, the whistleblower must view the issue in larger terms and stick to the facts of the disclosure.[83] Preserving ethical standards in this way brings great personal risks. To do so, a worker must overcome many roadblocks: the chain of command, the norms of his or her work group, and the ambiguity of the decision.[84] Perhaps most difficult is the worker's need to assure him- or herself that it was the right thing to do—that he or she had the right reasons for blowing the whistle.

The Chain of Command. Workers never can be sure who is covering for whom in an organization. Following the chain of command in order to address unethical and illegal issues entails many risks. Is it the immediate supervisor who is unethical? Is that supervisor acting on orders from above? Bypassing the chain of command can create even more professional risks, even when one's information is accurate.

Work Group Norms. Ethical and unethical decisions alike are bound up with personalities, and groups often are very protective of their bonds with those in authority. A worker who has had nothing but positive experiences in his or her relationship with an unethical manager will be likely to ascribe a whistleblower's accusations to nothing more than a personality clash with that manager. Such workers, who often take pride in their ability to get along with troublesome superiors, will perceive no problem unless the manager's unethical behavior causes them drastic personal losses or grief. Questioning the system is often seen as arrogant, self-serving, and destabilizing. Violating the norms of the work group results in social ostracism. Besides provoking punitive reactions from those in charge, the whistleblowing worker is shunned by other members of the organization, who ask, "Why can't you leave well enough alone?"

The Ambiguity of the Decision. Workers rarely have full access to information. Even when they are certain that unethical practices have occurred, they often are in the dark about the frequency of those practices, the degree of purposeful intent on the organization's part and its views regarding what actually constitutes right or wrong, as compared to the worker's perspective.

The Right Reasons for Whistleblowing. Whether it is anonymous, and the source of the information remains undisclosed, whether it is the act of alumni (those who have left the organization), or whether it originates with current staff, whistleblowing differs from mudraking and squealing in that it is usually done to disclose wrongdoings for moral reasons. The decision to protest is always difficult. Professor of philosophy Gene G. James suggests five guidelines for would-be whistleblowers:[85]

- A Serious Situation. Be sure that the situation involves illegal actions, harm to others, and violations of peoples' rights, and is not bound by rules of confidentiality. Furthermore, the whistleblower should have tried all available avenues within the organization to correct the wrong, if at all possible.
- Motives. The whistleblower should determine if the right motives are inspiring his or her actions.
- Facts. Can you find solid evidence to support your cause? Use only the facts. Emotions cloud the debate and the results.
- Nature of the Wrong. Determining the exact nature of the wrong, what law has been violated, will help to determine the proper agency for help.
- Personal Costs. Give considerable thought to what whistleblowing will cost you. Will you be able to tolerate the effects it will have on you as a person and on your career? Will it be worth the price you will have to pay, both for you and for the others that your action may affect?

QUESTIONS FOR
DISCUSSION AND REVIEW

1. What is meant by ethics and morality? Explain the three basic approaches to understanding ethics.
2. What makes a person "good"? How might you explain morality and moral development to a child or to a group of children? How might you explain to students newly arrived from another country the characteristics Americans have that help determine their particular kind of morality?
3. Explain the moral obligations and role conflicts that lawyers experience as people, professionals, and partners/owners.
4. What are the "laws of lawyering?" What enforcement power do they have?
5. How did the Model Rules of Professional Conduct originate?
6. Why do nonlawyers need to know about the Model Rules of Professional Conduct?
7. What are the specific guidelines that apply to law offices and support staff?
8. Discuss your criteria for a "good" manager. In your opinion, which ethical characteristic is most essential for a manager?
9. Interview members of one or two law firms informally. Ask them to offer their opinions regarding what creates a "good" law firm, to describe the kinds of ethical dilemmas or challenges they face most often, and to define what they see as the most important ethical obligation a law firm has to its members and to society.
10. Discuss why conflict is often caused by different values. In what ways can lawyers and other law firm personnel disappoint both their firm and society through poor ethical choices?
11. Describe a difficult ethical choice that you have heard of or experienced that involved lawyers, paralegals, managers, and/or other law firm members. Explain what made the choice difficult.

EXPERIENTIAL EXERCISES

I. Degrees of Right and Wrong

We might look at each of the following cases from four different perspectives: a strictly legal perspective, a moral and ethical perspective, an organizational perspective, or the individual's perspective. In each situation, what do you think is the right thing to do?

1. A very competent legal secretary from a nearby law firm has offered to come in and work for you Saturdays and Sundays to make a little extra money. She recently has been divorced and has three teenagers to provide for.
2. As a legal administrator, you notice that a senior partner routinely bills clients for twelve to sixteen hours of time when you are positive he actually has spent only one to two hours. He is nearing retirement, and both his efforts and his number of clients seem to be dwindling. You know that his saving face on the weekly all-firm time reports is very important to his pride.
3. Your bookkeeper is constantly late for work, sometimes by as much as a few hours. She works very industriously the rest of the day, but always seems to be sure to leave exactly on time. You discover that her husband is an alcoholic and that she is worried about her children. Occasionally, all goes well and her work seems very reliable. At other times, you find yourself dealing with serious errors that have occurred because of her work.

II. Making the World a Better Place

In a current publication such as *The National Law Journal, The Wall Street Journal, Fortune,* or *Newsweek,* find an article that addresses ethical issues in law firms. When you have read the article, complete the following chart:

Article Title: _____ Author(s): _____
Publication: _____
Date of Publication: _____ Page(s): _____
Summary: _____
_____

A. What kind of ethical question is involved? (Check all that apply.)
   _____ ■ Environmental issues: pollution, waste, recycling
   _____ ■ Worker issues: safety, rights, discrimination
   _____ ■ Policy, statements and codes of ethics
   _____ ■ Social responsibility activities
   _____ ■ Fraud deception, excess fees
   _____ ■ Breaches of the professional codes of ethics
   _____ ■ Treatment of individuals
   _____ ■ Marketing practices
   _____ ■ Other. Explain:

B. Who or what is affected? (Circle all that apply.)
   Microscale: Individual   Macroscale: Global
   <===>
   Self   Family   Law Firm   Local Community   Profession   Larger Community

	One or Few Individuals Affected		**Much or All of Society Affected**	
C.	Is the action economically effective?	Is the action legal?	Is the action ethical?	Is the action discretionary?
	Yes [ ] No [ ]	Yes [ ] No [ ]	Yes [ ] No [ ]	Yes [ ] No [ ]
	Economic Social Responsibilities	Legal Social Responsibilities	Ethical Social Responsibilities	Discretionary Social Responsibilities
	(Required by Organization)	(Required by Laws)	(Expected by Society)	(Desired for Respect)

Glossary

Accommodation. An approach to resolving conflict that stresses cooperation: the goal is to satisfy the other party's concerns while neglecting one's own.

Accounting. The systematized keeping of financial records that enables a firm's management to make informed decisions based on the firm's financial requirements.

Accounts Payable. The obligations that a firm needs to pay within a certain amount of time, usually within thirty days.

Accounts Receivable. Represent the firm's sources of potential revenue; consist mostly of legal services that the firm has billed to clients.

Accrued Expenses. Expenses for which a firm has yet to receive or record bills.

Activity Centers. Units within the law firm that are sources of revenue or expenditures: (1) cost pools, (2) cost centers, (3) service centers, and (4) profit centers.

Ad Hoc Committee. A temporary committee formed to fulfill a specific purpose.

Adapters. Subconscious coping devices, such as finger tapping, that help people adjust to tension or to new situations.

Administrative Management. Emphasizes discovering and understanding the principles and procedures that work best for each organization.

Advertising. The use of printed or electronic media to bring the advantages of an available service to the public's attention.

Affect Displays. Body language, including facial expressions, gestures, body position and posture, and mirroring, through which we subconsciously communicate feelings and emotions.

Affiliation. A sense of connection or association with others; the opposite of alienation and isolation.

Affiliative Needs. Needs for friendship, cooperation, and social interaction.

Affirmative Action. Legislation requiring an employer to take positive steps to hire and promote women, minorities, the handicapped, and other workers in protected classes in order to compensate for past discriminatory practices.

Aging Receivables. Sources of potential revenue consisting of the bills of clients who are able to reimburse the firm for services but who have not yet done so.

Annual Billing Budget. The amount of time for which the firm's attorneys and paralegals will bill in a particular fiscal year.

Assets. The valuable property—monetary, tangible, and intangible—a firm owns in these three categories: (1) current assets, (2) fixed assets, and (3) intangible assets.

Attitudes. Beliefs, feelings, and intentions regarding another person, an event, a task, or an organization that predispose people to think and sometimes to act in certain ways.

Authoritarianism. A set of attitudes toward authority characterized by beliefs about the balance of power, the use of rules, and the roles of individuals.

Authority. The legitimate right to tell other people what to do, to make decisions, and to use resources. The legitimate right to command or influence, based on one's place in the hierarchy.

Autocratic Leadership. Leadership is characterized by a leader's attempt to completely control the behavior of his or her subordinates.

Automated Records Management. Systems that provide an integrated technological approach to records management.

Autonomy. The degree of independence with which a worker may plan, schedule, and complete his or her assigned work. The greater the autonomy, the greater the responsibility.

Avoidance. The act of responding to conflict by ignoring or sidestepping it.

Balance Sheet. Provides an overview of the firm's assets, liabilities, and equity at a stated moment, thereby summarizing its status and value.

Bar Coding. The process of assigning a file or other piece of data an identifying mark consisting of computer-readable lines (similar to the universal product codes used on retail merchandise) for data integration and control.

Bargaining. A form of negotiation in which opposing sides make offers, counteroffers, and concessions.

Behavioral Leadership Theories. Examine how the behavior of effective leaders differs from that of ineffective ones.

Behaviorism. An approach to motivation that focuses on observable actions rather than on inner states.

Behavior Modification. The process of altering behavior through the use of reinforcement contingencies.

Board. An elected or appointed group that is responsible for the upper-level management of an organization.

Body Language. Physical movements and characteristics, including posture, gestures, and facial expressions, that affect communication.

Bona Fide Occupational Qualifications. Legal guidelines by which the government prohibits employers from asking otherwise qualified candidates questions concerning topics such as age, gender, race, or religious beliefs unless they have a legitimate business-related reason for doing so; also, the legitimate reasons an employer can use to exclude from employment those whom Title VII of the Civil Rights Act of 1964 would otherwise protect.

Bounded Rationality. Defines the personal limits within which we process information.

Brainstorming. A decision-making technique that asks members of a group to generate as many ideas as they can on a given subject.

Budget. A plan with a monetary focus which sets the financial parameters for the firm's expenditures, based on its income estimates for the year.

Budgets. Single-use financial plans that summarize the amounts of money allocated for resources and personnel.

Bureaucracy. A form of management that focuses on organizational structure and on the use of carefully determined roles, regulations, and functions.

Bureaucratic. An orientation regarding authority that advocates the unquestioning acceptance of authority, compliance with rules and directives, clear-cut hierarchies, structured work environments, and formal, impersonal relationships.

Burnout. Emotional, physical, and mental exhaustion in response to chronic job stressors.

Business Development. The activities through which a law firm's members attract new clients, thereby increasing the sources of potential revenue for the firm.

Buzz Sessions. Brainstorming sessions usually involving larger groups that subdivide, brainstorm, and report their ideas back to the larger group.

Centralization. Places authority with the central figures in the hierarchy, reflecting a structure in which responsibility rests with the few, usually the higher-level managers, rather than with the many.

Change. The process of evolving from one form or state to another.

Change Agent. Someone who provides ideas, approaches, and perspectives that help an organization to respond to challenges in new ways.

Charismatic Leadership. A combination of special abilities and appeal that inspires tremendous confidence, trust, and respect in followers, who may be prone to idolize the charismatic leader or to perceive his or her abilities as superhuman or spiritual.

Classical Management. A management style based on a concern for productivity, which seeks the most effective and most efficient ways to run organizations.

Clearinghouse Questions. End-of-the-interview questions which allow the interviewer to obtain any other information that might be relevant and that the interviewee might want or need to provide.

Client. Someone who depends upon another for services and skills.

Closed Questions. Questions which confine an interviewee to very specific responses.

Coaching. Job-related supervisory assistance that provides workers with professional encouragement and guidance.

Coercive Power. Power based on a leader's ability to punish, thwart, and dismiss uncooperative, disloyal, or poorly performing subordinates.

Cognitive Complexity. The ability to assimilate many dimensions of information when making a decision or when considering all the possible dimensions of an issue.

Cognitive Conflict. Structures different viewpoints and critical thinking into organizational decisions, especially those that involve different interpretations of common issues or problems.

Cognitive Dissonance. Intellectual discomfort or remorse resulting from a discrepancy between one's attitudes and behavior or between expectations and experience.

Cohesiveness. The extent to which members value a group and feel close to one another.

Collaboration. The process of resolving conflict by which each side fully accepts the other's objectives, and both work to determine the most mutually beneficial outcome.

GLOSSARY

Collections Budget. The amount of money that clients will actually pay the firm for the hours that it bills.

Collegiality. A form of self-governance based on the equality that the members of a profession share as colleagues.

Collegial Power. A form of collective position power usually found in organizations of professionals.

Command Group. A formal group consisting of managers and their subordinates.

Commission. A formal group, usually found in the governmental structure, appointed to oversee compliance with a given set of regulations.

Committee. A group of people organized to investigate or act on a matter that affects the firm.

Communication. The process of exchanging ideas and information between one person or group, called the sender, and another, called the receiver, through symbols, actions, or written or spoken words.

Comparable Worth. Stresses that an organization pay similarly for jobs that are of equal worth to it.

Compensating. Giving employees pay, incentives, and benefits in exchange for their time and productivity.

Competence. The state of possessing the skills, knowledge, and abilities requisite to performing a job.

Competitive Advantage. The ability to offer some aspect of service that is unique, desirable, or unattainable through other firms; achieved through price and uniqueness.

Compromise. The process of reaching partial agreement through a combination of assertiveness and cooperation, whereby both sides determine and accept areas of agreement by sacrificing some of their own goals.

Conceptual Skills. Skills that reflect the ability to observe, think, conclude, determine, and envision.

Conflict. A sharp disagreement, clash, or noncompatibility of interests, ideas, needs, or values; efforts to reach personally preferred outcomes which, if attained, prevent others from reaching their outcomes, thereby producing hostility.

Conformity. The attempt to maintain harmony by agreeing with the opinions and decisions of others.

Congruence. A state of agreement, in terms of goals, between a worker and a firm.

Connection Power. Power based on an individual's connections to, knowledge of, and positive relationships with people both inside and outside of the organization.

Consensus. A form of decision making based on general agreement.

Consideration. The extent to which a leader shows concern for workers.

Contingency Fees. Costs for legal services that depend on the outcome of the case, which is in itself uncertain.

Contingency Management. A management approach which stresses the need for managers to adapt to the situations and forces that are unique to each organization.

Control. The regulation of activities and results through direction, guidance, and the successful distribution and use of authority. The power to direct, regulate, and coordinate human and material resources.

Controlling. The process of regulating and overseeing activities to ensure quality performance and end results. The managerial activity that ensures that the organization is meeting its objectives.

Coordination. The process of ensuring, through the use of the principal coordinating elements, that different organizational divisions function together smoothly.

Cost Centers. Sources of expenditures that only indirectly produce revenue.

Cost Pools. Sources of expenses that a firm cannot directly link to any one department or individual.

Counseling. The process of listening to, understanding, and attempting to help a worker who is experiencing job-related problems.

Crisis. An unstable situation in which a decisive change is imminent.

Critical Incidents Technique. An evaluation method which asks a supervisor to evaluate an employee by writing an essay that focuses on specific strengths and weaknesses of his or her performance.

Decentralization. The sharing of authority and responsibility with many members of an organization.

Decision. A choice made from two or more considered alternatives.

Decisional Roles. The responsibilities managers have to make effective decisions.

Decoding. The process by which a receiver interprets a message.

Delegation. The process of transferring authority by assigning tasks and the necessary authority to subordinates, who accept responsibility for those tasks.

Delphi Method. A decision-making process that uses questionnaires to gather the written opinions of experts in a given field.

Democratic Leadership. A participative leadership style based on equal consideration and concern for followers.

Descriptive Essay. A free-form evaluation tool that asks a supervisor to comment on aspects of a worker's performance.

Departmentalization. The process of arranging work into logical divisions based on the organization's structural elements.

Devil's Advocacy Decision Program. A decision making program that builds programmed conflict into the decision-making process.

Diagonal Communication. Communication that crosses hierarchical levels and provides a vehicle for coordinating activities in the organization.

Dialectic Decision Method. A decision-making technique in which decision makers propose a plan that allows advocates of different points of view to propose and discuss assumptions in support of their ideas.

Difference Principle. A basic right which maintains that when an inequity exists in people's liberty and rights, those who are disadvantaged should receive preference until the differences are eliminated.

Directing. The process of staffing, influencing, and leading employees so that they attain organizational goals.

Directive Interview. An interview that uses a specific question format.

Discipline. A work style that results from training based on self-control, order, character, and efficiency.

Discommunication. A communication problem that occurs when a sender purposely distorts a message in order to confuse, distract, and undermine.

Distributive Justice. The belief that each person should receive an equitable share of rewards.

Divergent Thinking. The ability to think in ways that deviate from the norm or from previously expressed or commonplace ideas.

Division of Labor. The actual division of work into jobs that need to be done.

Docket Clerk. A person who oversees a centralized calendar control function in a large firm.

Docket Control Systems. Provide firm-wide information on all upcoming critical deadlines and responsibilities.

Document Retrieval System. Organized process for attaining legal briefs, legal opinions, articles for publication, speeches, other memoranda of law, and any other work products that a firm can use to provide future legal services.

Dogmatic. An orientation regarding authority characterized by a tendency to stick rigidly to beliefs, ignore others' opinions and ideas, and reject those who will not accept one's teachings, or dogma.

Downward Communication. Communication that follows the flow of messages from those at the top to those at the bottom.

Dysfunctional Conflict. Conflict that harms an organization or hinders it from reaching its goals.

Economic System. The process by which our society produces, markets, and distributes the goods and services that it wants and needs.

Effectiveness. The ability to reach intended results by determining appropriate objectives and accomplishing them.

Efficiency. The ability to obtain organizational objectives using the least amount of organizational resources.

Ego Extension. A form of affiliation resulting from group membership: the sense that we are part of something larger than ourselves with which we can identify.

Ego Strength. A dimension of personality that describes how strictly people adhere to their convictions and values.

Emblems. Gestures that convey attitudes, emotions, or conditions.

Emotional Motive. An influence on a client's choice of services that is based on one or more of these factors: pleasure, fear, pride, sociability, or emulation.

Empathy. Requiring a strong appreciation of and respect for others, empathy is the skill of understanding, being sensitive to, and experiencing vicariously the thoughts, feelings, and experiences of others. The ability, when communicating, to share in someone else's feelings and emotions.

Employee Assistance Programs. Liaisons between law firms and professional counseling or social service agencies to assist employees with emotional, physical, or personal problems.

Empowerment. The process of helping an individual to develop the power he or she needs to influence others, to function confidently within an organization, and to access the resources that he or she needs.

Encoding. The process by which a communicator, or sender, translates his or her ideas into a message consisting of symbols that will convey the communicator's ideas to a receiver.

Equity Partner. A partner who has contributed toward the equity of the firm, shares in its profits as well as its losses, votes on all partnership business, and is an owner of the firm; also called a **full partner.**

Equity Theory. A motivational theory based on the fairness people perceive when they compare their own efforts and results to the efforts and results of others.

Ethical Dilemma. A situation that occurs when two or

more values conflict and a choice must be made between alternatives that offer differing personal or organizational benefits and represent differing ethical responses.

Ethics. The set of moral rules and standards people have for one another. The adjective *ethical* describes conduct that conforms to these codes of moral principles.

Ethos. The feelings, beliefs, and sentiments unique to a community of people.

Eustress. A form of stress that constitutes a positive adaptive response to environmental pressures.

Evaluation Apprehension. Anxiety caused by the belief that those who are near us as we work are evaluating our performance.

Expectancy. The degree of success people foresee in their efforts.

Expectancy Theory. Proposes that motivational drives depend on the perceived likelihood that our efforts will lead to the expected outcomes.

Expenses. As a component of measuring profitability, expenses are all of the costs, direct and indirect, that a firm incurs while providing professional services.

Expertise Power. The influence an individual has based on his or her knowledge, expertise, or skills.

Explicit Strategy. A formally defined and articulated written plan.

Extinction. The process of stopping a behavior essentially by ignoring it.

Feedback. Information communicated back to the worker or the organization concerning the effectiveness and quality of work or performance. The process by which a receiver expresses or clarifies his or her understanding of a message.

Fiduciary Relationship. A confidential relationship in which one person owes a duty of trust and loyalty to another.

Filtering. The process of manipulating the accuracy of communications by removing negative data from a message or by altering the message to suit one's needs.

Financial Report. A report which describes the firm's financial health over a specified time period, such as a month, a quarter, or the fiscal year, by summarizing all income the firm has received from fees and from other sources.

Financial Resources Control. The use of financial reports to ensure the effective use of the firm's capital.

Financial Statements. Summaries of financial data that help the law firm's management to make decisions based on the firm's economic position.

Fiscal Year. The twelve-month period that an organization establishes to track its finances.

Fixed Fees. Predetermined prices to be charged for legal services.

Follower Readiness. The degree of ability, willingness, and confidence that followers exhibit in taking responsibility for their tasks and actions.

Force. The strength of a motivational drive.

Forcing. The process of resolving a conflict by forcing the other party to accept one's needs and wishes.

Forecasting. The process of projecting a firm's personnel needs, in light of the supply of workers available and the demand for them.

Formal Groups. Groups that management and others in the organization create in order to reach organizational goals.

Formal Organization. The official structures, work divisions, and processes that enable the organization to reach its goals.

Four Basic Managerial Functions. (1) Planning, (2) organizing, (3) directing, and (4) controlling.

Frame of Reference. The totality of perceptions through which we interpret our experiences and surroundings.

Friendship Groups. Informal groups that form from mutual attraction.

Fringe Benefits. Financial benefits that employers offer in addition to salaries, wages, and incentives.

Functional Conflict. Conflict that benefits an organization.

Functional Group. A formal group composed of employees who have the same area of responsibility or who perform the same kinds of tasks.

General Adaptation Syndrome. The defense reaction our bodies have when experiencing stress. It consists of three distinct phases: (1) alarm reaction, (2) resistance, and (3) exhaustion.

Goal Integration. An overlapping between individual and organizational goals.

Goals. Broadly stated long-term targets. Long-term directions.

Grapevine. The informal communication network, not officially sanctioned by the organization, that members use to spread news and unofficial information.

Graphic Rating Scale. An evaluation tool that asks a supervisor to describe an employee's performance in a given area by choosing a verbal or numeric indicator on a graded performance scale.

Group. (1) Two or more people who (2) interact with each other on a continuing basis, (3) think of themselves as a group, and (4) share a purpose or work toward a common goal.

Group Development. A dynamic process that consists of five stages: (1) forming, (2) storming, (3) norming, (4) performing, and (5) adjourning.

Group Dynamics. The set of forces that affect a group's performance. These forces are a result of a group's (1) structure, (2) norms, (3) cohesiveness, and (4) roles.

Group Norms. The standards and values that a group develops and agrees upon.

Group Structure. The combination of roles and relationships that distinguishes one group from another.

Groupthink. The tendency of group members to become so concerned with unanimity that they no longer think impartially, critically, or even rationally when making group decisions.

Hardiness. A resilient personality style built on commitment, control, and challenge.

Hassles. Common events and happenings that, in combination with other regularly experienced events such as a lack of time, too many responsibilities, and other aggravations, cause stress.

Hawthorne Effect. The tendency for workers to fulfill positive expectations when they receive favorable treatment or attention.

Health. A general state of physical, mental, and emotional wellness.

Hedonism. Concept which suggests that people are motivated instinctively to seek pleasure and to avoid pain.

Horizontal Communication. Communication between workers on the same hierarchical level.

Hostile Environment. A harassment-engendered working atmosphere that impairs work performance or creates intimidating, unpleasant, or offensive working conditions.

The Hot Stove Rule. Suggests that effective discipline consists of four elements: advance warning, immediacy, consistency, and impartiality.

Human Capital. A resource consisting of the talent, skills, knowledge, experience, and attitudes of an organization's members. Investing in human capital reflects a firm's realization that treating its members fairly is a true investment.

Human Relations Management. A management approach that emphasizes the equitable treatment of workers.

Human Resource Management. An aspect of management that oversees, obtains, maintains, and develops the human assets of the firm.

Hygiene Needs. Needs that are not directly related to work itself but to its extrinsic qualities, the context in which it occurs.

Hypothetical Question. A question, based on an assumed or imagined situation, that indicates how a candidate would act in a given job-related situation.

Idiosyncrasy Credits. The right, resulting from status, position, or achievement, to deviate from a group's norms.

Illustrators. Gestures that clarify a spoken message.

Image Management. The careful control of external symbols for the purpose of shaping the public's perceptions.

Implicit Strategy. An informally developed plan that responds to the firm's mission.

Income Statement. A financial analysis of the firm's activities for a stated time period, providing the most recent figures regarding its income, costs, expenses, and profits.

Influence. The ability to bring about change through the indirect use of power.

Informal Groups. Groups that form spontaneously around their members' shared interests, goals, needs, or political concerns. The organization does not arrange, regulate, or proscribe such groups.

Informal Organization. The unofficial structures, activity patterns, and processes that develop spontaneously in an organization, without formal planning.

Information Power. Power based on an individual's ability to share, conceal, or otherwise manipulate potentially valuable information.

Information Society. A social setting that requires workers to communicate, receive, and process on a daily basis information in quantities unheard of even twenty-five years ago.

Informational Roles. Roles through which managers control, disseminate, and process useful information.

Ingratiation. An attempt to benefit oneself by cultivating favor with powerful people or groups.

Initiation of Structure. The degree to which leaders initiate structure describes the degree to which they establish order in their followers' work. Structure-initiating behaviors include insisting on standards, meeting deadlines, assigning tasks, planning work activities, and establishing and enforcing routines.

Instincts. Innate tendencies to do certain things.

Integrated Expense Control and Recovery. An automated system that uses client codes such as bar codes to monitor the sources of service-related expenses.

Integration of Interests. A mutual answering of needs that enables people at all levels of an organization to coordinate their efforts to reach organizational goals.

Interest Groups. Informal groups that form around the mutual interests of their members.

Interpersonal Roles. Roles through which managers fulfill their responsibilities to act with, for, and on behalf of others.

Interpersonal Skills. The abilities that enable managers to understand others and to inspire them to contribute to the organization.

Interviewing. The process of receiving information for a specific purpose by asking (and occasionally answering) questions.

Inventory Control. A system that sets standards for the quality, kinds and amounts of supplies that the firm needs, provides feedback about the use of such supplies, and signals in advance the need for new supplies.

Job Analysis. The process of investigating the duties, responsibilities, and dynamics of a job.

Job Description. A written listing of the tasks, duties, and responsibilities that a job involves.

Job Postings. Methods for circulating information about internal job openings.

Job Specification. A profile of the ideal mix of knowledge, skills, and abilities required for a job. It may also describe the education, training, and experience that are necessary, as well as specific job criteria, such as interpersonal skills.

Laissez-Faire Style Leadership. A leadership style characterized by nonintervention and a lack of directions or rules.

Latent Needs. Involve objects, people, or activities of which the need holder is aware but about which he or she feels no immediate sense of deficiency.

The Law of Reciprocity. The process of persuading someone to do something by appealing to his or her expectation of reciprocal exchanges from peers, superiors, or subordinates.

Leader. One who directs, guides, or influences people in working toward a goal.

Leadership. The process of influencing or directing the performance or activity of others through interaction with those others.

Leading Question. A closed question that, because of its wording, leads to the answer that an interviewer wants to hear.

Lean Media. The use of few forms of communication media to convey a message.

Legal Ethics. Two dictates: (1) the set of legal rules that govern a lawyer's conduct, and (2) the lawyer's subjective assessment of his or her conduct in practicing law, including his or her personal values and knowledge.

Legitimate Power. Power based on a manager's role in the organizational hierarchy.

Leverage. The ratio of nonpartner professionals to partners in a law firm.

Liabilities. The debts and obligations that a firm owes to others.

Liberty Principle. A basic right that maintains that each person is entitled to be as free as any other person.

Linking Pin Roles. Managerial roles that connect managerial communications at different levels of the organizational hierarchy.

Liquidity. The firm's ability to convert its assets into cash.

Locus of Control. The degree to which individuals believe that the forces governing their lives are internal or external.

Long-Term Liabilities. Debts that are not due until more than a year from the date of a firm's current balance sheet.

Machiavellian. An orientation regarding authority that advocates the use of power, subversion, deceit, and manipulation to control others and achieve goals.

Management. Using an organization's resources in working with people, through planning, organizing, directing, and controlling, in order to reach organizational objectives.

Management by Exception. The policy of bringing to upper-level managers only those problems that are significant enough to warrant the decisions of top management.

Management by Objectives. The process, either as part of an annual review or as a form of evaluation in itself, by which an employee and a supervisor work together to set specific goals for the employee that will benefit the firm.

Management Science. A management approach based on the scientific method and the use of quantifiable data.

Manager. A person, assigned responsibility for the management process, who directs the efforts of others and who accesses and distributes the resources necessary for successful job performance.

Managerial Ethics. Principles by which managers ensure that their actions and decisions fulfill legal mandates and reflect the broader set of moral principles that guide society.

Manifest Needs. Involve things about which the need holder feels an acute sense of deficiency.

Marketing. The process of planning and putting into practice ways of selling the advantages of one's services in a mutually satisfying exchange of objectives with a customer or client.

Marketing Concept. A business concept which states that an organization, to be profitable, must understand, meet, and satisfy customer needs.

Marketing Mix. Consists of the appropriate blend of the four P's of marketing: product, price, place, and promotion.

Marketing Plan. A plan describing the marketing actions a firm needs to take, why they are necessary, when the plan is to take effect, and who is to be responsible for the plan's actions, implementation, and coordination.

Matrix Organizational Structure. A two-dimensional structure that combines functional and divisional forms of departmentalization to achieve better coordination and control.

Mechanistic Organization. A stable structure consisting of clear-cut divisions and roles, as specified by its rules, regulations, and hierarchical arrangements of responsibilities.

Medium. The means or technique that a sender uses to transmit a message.

Message. The actual idea that a sender wants to transmit.

Middle Management. The level of management that is responsible for subordinates in various areas but is also accountable to upper-level management.

Miscommunication. A communication problem that results when the message a receiver receives differs from the message that the sender intended.

Mission Statement. A written description of an organization's main purpose for existing.

Moral. Implies conformity to generally accepted standards of what is good or right in terms of conduct or character.

Moral Reasoning. A kind of reflective thinking about how to resolve ethical dilemmas.

Morale. A state of mind regarding the work environment, a composite of feelings and attitudes usually held in common by a group of workers. It is a product of people's perceptions about the most important aspects of work, including compensation, supervision, and the work they perform.

Morality. Conformity to principles of right or wrong in conduct and decisions.

Motion Studies. Detailed analyses of the different motions used to perform a task.

Motivation. An inner force that influences behavior and drives people to reach their goals.

Motivator Needs. Needs that relate to the intrinsic qualities associated with work, its content.

Needs. Perceived deficiencies that prompt people to seek something useful, desired, or required.

Negotiation. A formal form of compromise, a conflict resolution strategy that allows two sides to meet for the purpose of reaching an agreement by resolving or setting aside their conflicting interests.

Noise. Sound or anything else that interferes with or distorts an intended message.

Nominal Group Technique. The process of obtaining individual input as well as a group response on a particular topic from a given set of people.

Nondirective Interview. An interview in which the interviewer operates according to specific objectives but allows the interviewee's answers to dictate the direction that the interview takes.

Nonequity Partner. A partner who has not contributed toward the equity of the firm. May be entitled to salary, bonuses, or other benefits, but can neither vote on partnership business nor claim entitlement to the profit distributions that equity partners share.

Norms. Shared beliefs and standards, consciously or unconsciously formed, regarding how the members of a group should think and act.

Notes Payable. A firm's written and signed obligations to pay specific amounts at specific times.

Nudges. Short comments or questions that urge an interviewee to contribute more information on a particular subject.

Objectives. The specific short-range ends or goals that a person or group wishes to reach. Short-term targets that the organization establishes to help it reach its goals.

One-Way Communication. Communication in which a sender conveys messages to a receiver who provides no feedback.

Open Questions. Questions which provide no advance indication of the expected answer.

Operating Budget. A budget that classifies the firm's projected expenditures and balances them against its expected revenues. Sometimes called a revenues and expense budget.

Operating Margin Per Hour. An analysis of the firm's total expenses for doing business compared to its number of billable hours.

Operational Autonomy. The control a professional has over the matters in his or her area of professional operations.

Operational Plans. Short-term or standing plans for the day-to-day, monthly, or yearly operation of an organization.

Operational Controls. Controls that managers use to guide, monitor, and evaluate a firm's resources in four areas:

financial, human, physical, and information.

Organic Organization. A dynamic and responsive structure that can maximize its use of organizational processes and factors in both its internal and external environments.

Organization. A social system that is unified by a specific goal and is held together by the combination of the roles and activities of its members. Groups of people who engage in patterned activities for a particular purpose.

Organizational Chart. A graphic representation that depicts the managerial hierarchy and the roles and reporting relationships in an organization.

Organizational Consent. The voluntary give and take that occurs between workers and managers in the course of everyday management.

Organizational Culture. The perception of an organization that is formed by the shared beliefs and assumptions of its members.

Organizational Design. The process of matching an organization's structure, resources, and processes to its function.

Organizational Development. A long-range effort to respond to the forces affecting an organization by strengthening its problem-solving and renewal processes.

Organizational Structure. The system of logical and appropriate uses for activities enabling the organization to reach its goals.

Organizing. The process of allocating resources and work tasks so that the organization can reach its goals and objectives efficiently and effectively. The managerial activity that involves planning and deciding how to use resources to reach organizational goals.

Orientation. The process, often in program form, by which a firm introduces new members to their jobs and to the firm itself.

Owners' Equity. The amount left after the firm has deducted its liabilities from its assets.

Paralinguistics. The study of how vocal cues and features of the human voice augment or otherwise modify the meaning of verbal messages.

Partners' Draw. The payment made to an equity partner, based on the firm's present earnings. Partners may augment their draw by participating in a shared distribution of profits at the end of (or, when profits for a given period greatly exceed the firm's expectations, during) each fiscal year.

Payables. Bills that the firm owes for such things as salaries, rent, insurance, goods, and utilities.

Performance Appraisal. The process of evaluating performance by measuring an employee's work activity and product against the firm's standards and expectations.

Perks/Perquisites. The benefits to which a person is entitled by reason of his or her status or position in a firm.

Personal Power. Power that results from an individual's personality.

Personal Selling. The use of persuasive techniques to convince potential buyers to use one's product.

Personality. The unique and relatively stable combination of characteristics and behavioral tendencies resulting from genetic inheritance and nurture.

Physical Resources Control. The process of overseeing the use of the firm's material resources, including its equipment, its inventory of supplies, its library, and the use and upkeep of its space and facilities.

Place. The location of the law firm in relation to those who need and want its services.

Planning. The process of determining the future of an organization by establishing goals and objectives and by formulating a strategy to achieve them. The primary management function, involving the evaluation of information, the assessment of future outcomes, and the selection of a course of action in order to reach organizational objectives.

Pocket Vetoes. The act of setting a request aside until it dies from a lack of attention.

Point of Hire. The actual time of hire, after which the employer may ask the applicant questions involving topics (such as religion, race, and national origin) prohibited earlier by Title VII.

Policies. Standing plans that provide management with broad guidelines for making decisions and planning actions consistent with organizational goals.

Politics. The process of creating alliances, arranging obligations, manipulating others' behavior, exchanging influence, and engaging in other similar activities in order to influence or attempt to influence for the purpose of protecting self-interests or promulgating one's version of organizational goals.

Position Power. Power directly related to the power inherent in one's position in an organization.

Positioning. The process of understanding consumer needs and of meeting those needs by offering a product that is distinctive enough to be markedly advantageous when compared to that of a competitor.

Power. The ability to act, do, control, and influence.

Practices. Accepted methods for handling specific problems or situations, reflecting traditional interpretations of how things should be done.

Practice Development. A firm's continuing efforts to attain and sustain a suitable client base through marketing, public relations, and a justified reputation for quality legal services.

Prepotency of Needs. In Maslow's hierarchy of needs, a continuum of predominance in which fulfilling lower-level needs takes priority over fulfilling higher-level ones.

Price. The amount of money asked or paid for something based on its perceived value or worth.

Primary Purpose of Management. To help an organization reach its objectives effectively and efficiently.

Primary Responsibility of Management. To ensure that the organization does what it needs to do in order to reach its objectives.

Principle of Supportive Relationships. In the words of Rensis Likert, the principle of supportive relationships is followed when an organization's leadership and processes "ensure the maximum probability that in all interactions and in all relationships within the organization, each member, in the light of his or her background, values, desires, and expectations, will view the working experience as a supportive one which builds and maintains his or her own sense of personal worth and importance."

Probes. Questions that investigate topics that an interviewee mentioned only briefly in earlier answers.

Probing. The art of asking relevant questions in order to elicit additional information.

Procedures. Detailed guidelines for performing regularly occurring actions.

Process Losses. Inefficiencies that result when a group wastes time by performing activities not directly related to reaching its goals.

Process of Change. A theory by Kurt Lewin which suggests that change consists of three activities: unfreezing, change, and refreezing.

Prodromal Periods. Pre-crisis times that reveal symptoms of coming difficulties for a firm.

Product. The result of an organization's efforts; the goods or services the organization offers to meet the needs and wants of society.

Product Differentiation. An organization's ability to build on the uniqueness of its particular brand of service.

Professionals. Those whose careers call for expertise, relative autonomy in decision making, and commitment to a field that is governed collegially according to the agreed-upon ethical standards of its members.

Profit Centers. The units of activity in a firm that produce revenue.

Profitability. The firm's ability to increase its worth. The net income per partner, the money that remains after the firm has paid all of its expenses and obligations.

Programs. Large-scale single-use plans designed to achieve a specific goal.

Progressive Discipline. A process by which a firm not only can attempt to improve a worker's behavior but can prove its attempts to do so, should the need arise; it consists of a series of increasingly stern disciplinary measures generally divided into seven steps and culminating in termination.

Project Group. A formal group established to accomplish a specific purpose.

Promotion. Any form or level of public communication that an organization utilizes for the purpose of increasing the use of its services.

Proxemics. The study of the spatial separation that people maintain and of the effects that this separation has on communication.

Psychic Salary. The sense of satisfaction that results from a worker's perceptions of his or her personal worth to an organization, the value of his or her contributions, and the value that the organization places on its workers' morale and on the quality of the working environment, as revealed by the quality of relationships within the organization.

Psychological Organizational Contract. The expectations that the organization and the individual have for the other's behavior.

Public Relations. The use of communications to promote prestige and good will; to maintain, correct, or enhance the firm's reputation; or to explain the firm's mission or purpose in serving the public.

Quality Control Circles. Small groups of managers and employees who work together to address quality and coordination problems.

Quid Pro Quo Harassment. A form of extortion that involves offering employment-related favors in exchange for sexual favors.

Rational Motive. An influence on a client's choice of services that is prompted by a logical conclusion about the costs, dependability, and perceived usefulness of those services.

Realization. The actual percentage of time for which the firm both bills *and* collects.

Receiver. The recipient of a message in the communication process.

Recruiting. The process of obtaining candidates for a firm opening by creating a pool of qualified applicants.

Reference Group. An informal group, consisting of people with whom an individual shares similarities, that provides a form of social comparison.

Referent Power. Power based on association with those who have personal magnetism, powerful or pleasing personalities, or enviable resources.

Reflecting. The process of indicating respect for and thoughtful consideration of a message by mirroring or reproducing it.

Reflective Questions. Refer to an interviewee's prior responses in order to clear up inaccuracies or possible misunderstandings.

Regulators. Gestures that help to control the reception of a message.

Reinforcement Contingencies. In behavior modification, the situation that precedes behavior (the antecedents) and the consequences which follow.

Relaxation. An adaptive anti-stress response.

Restructuring. An effort to improve the organization by reorganizing or otherwise altering its structure.

Retainers. Fees that clients pay to a firm in order to ensure continuing legal services.

Retention. A law firm's effort to keep motivated and productive workers.

Retirement or Pension Plans. Benefit programs through which employers or professional associations provide retirement income to workers or arrange to withhold income for their retirement years.

Reward Power. Power based on a leader's ability to reward subordinates.

Rich Media. The use of many different forms of media to convey a message.

Rights. Entitlements that give people the freedom to take a particular action.

Role. The set of actions or behaviors an individual is expected to perform in a given context or setting.

Rules and Regulations. Written standing plans for specific actions that either are required or prohibited under certain conditions.

Safety. The process of assuring physical security and protection.

Salaries. Set amounts of money that a firm pays non-hourly workers, usually either weekly or biweekly.

Scalar Chain. The linkage of authority that begins at the top of the organizational hierarchy and descends.

Scenario Building. The process of envisioning what lies ahead.

Scope of Authority. The range of requests that a manager legitimately can make as well as the range of actions that he or she legitimately can perform.

Selection. The process of determining which candidate or applicant should be offered a position, based on his or her potential for meeting the needs and expectations of a firm.

Self-Actualization. At the peak of Maslow's hierarchy of needs, the drive to make the most of one's existence, abilities, skills, and personality.

Self-Concept. The set of attitudes, values, and beliefs that result from the conclusions we draw regarding our behavior, abilities, appearance, and personal worth.

Self-Discipline. The personal quality, often contingent on an employer's providing fair treatment and sensible rules, that enables a worker to accept the standards and regulations of an organization and to place its needs above his or her own.

Self-Monitoring. The ability to act according to the nature of one's social environment.

Sender. The origin of the message in the process of communication.

Sensitivity Analysis. A regular review of the budget in order to spot unacceptable deviations.

Service Centers. Sources of expenditures that one activity center creates in providing services to other activity centers.

Service Recovery. The ability to listen carefully to complaints, act quickly and firmly, and turn angry, frustrated clients into contented ones.

Sexual Harassment. Insinuations regarding or requests for sexual favors or any other sexually oriented and unwelcome verbal or physical conduct that creates adverse or hostile employment conditions.

Single-Use Plans. Operational plans designed to achieve specific purposes for specified or limited amounts of time.

Situational Leadership Theories. Emphasize the need to consider the context of where, when, and for whom one is a leader.

Skill Variety. The range of skills needed to perform a job.

Social Facilitation. The positive effect that the presence of others has on work performance.

Social Inhibition. The negative effect that the presence of others has on performance.

Social Loafing. The reduced effort that sometimes occurs in groups that neither identify nor reward individual efforts.

Social Responsibility. A firm's obligation to make policies and choose courses of action that are in keeping with the values and needs of the larger social environment.

Social Support. The perception that others appreciate and care for us and that they are willing to help us in times of need.

Social Validation. The process of confirming one's identity and worth through the expressed opinions of others.

Socialization Process. The training processes by which organizations teach members (especially newcomers) what behavior is acceptable, what the organization expects of them, and what other members accept as group norms, values, and beliefs. The three most common socialization processes include new employee orientation, training and development programs, and performance appraisal.

Solicit. To aim one's persuasive efforts at a specific prospective client in contemplation of having one's services hired for a specific legal matter, in order to make a profit.

Solvency. A firm's ability to pay its debts as they become due.

Span of Management. The number of subordinates for whom a manager is responsible.

Staffing. The process of estimating the numbers and types of workers a firm will need.

Stakeholders. All those who have a legitimate personal interest in the success of a company.

Standards. Criteria against which the firm measures its performance and productivity.

Standing Committee. A relatively permanent formal group that performs specific tasks or fulfills certain responsibilities on an ongoing basis.

Standing Plans. Operational plans that remain in effect over a considerable time.

Statement of Cash Flows. A financial statement that summarizes for a given reporting period all of a firm's receipts and its disbursement of cash in three areas: operations, investments, and financing.

Statement of Operations. An overview of the finances involved in the firm's operations.

Statement of Retained Earnings. Financial statement describing the amount of profit that the firm keeps after all bills, salaries, bonuses, and partner distributions have been paid out.

Status. The ranking we give others based on our perceptions of their social or professional characteristics, such as age, education, socioeconomic level, skills or gender.

Status Symbols. The signs of personal and professional prestige that convey an individual's stature.

Stereotyping. The practice of labeling a personality according to a single striking quality.

Strategic Plans. Long-range plans that determine the overall direction of an organization.

Strategy. A carefully crafted plan that describes how the organization will fulfill its mission and reach its objectives. There are two kinds of strategies: explicit and implicit.

Stress. An adaptive response to any external action, situation, or event that places excessive psychological and physical demands on a person.

Stressors. Environmental, organizational, or personal factors that cause people to experience anxiety, tensions, and pressures; cause both eustress and negative stress.

Structuring. The process of establishing groupings and patterns of work relationships and then coordinating them with an organization's resources.

Superordinate Goals. In negotiation, overall goals accepted by both groups that they can accomplish only by working together.

Supervision. The process of overseeing, managing and directing. All managers are responsible for supervision of one form or another.

Supervisor. A manager on a first-line level who interacts directly with workers and who is responsible for short-range planning, for hiring workers or recommending the hiring of workers at his or her operational level, for representing the needs and concerns of workers to mid- and upper-level management, and for implementing the policies and decisions of the organization.

Supervisory Management. The management level that directly oversees those who perform specific functions.

Supervisory Skills. Skills that enable supervisors to integrate managerial expertise with an ability to work with people.

Task Force. A formal group consisting of (1) workers who play similar roles within the organization or (2) representatives from different units, segments, or departments of the organization who together perform specific tasks.

Task Identity. The degree to which the worker can identify the finished product as being completely his or hers.

Task Significance. The importance of a task, as measured by its effect on others, inside or outside of the organization.

Technical Skills. A manager's ability to use knowledge, skills, and proficiencies necessary to perform tasks.

Theory of Justice. A view of ethics which maintains that decisions should ensure fairness, equity, and impartiality to all people, based on the conviction that all people have two basic rights: liberty and equity.

Theory of Rights. A view of ethics which maintains that

a decision is ethical when it reflects a moral belief in the fundamental rights of individuals.

Theory Z Organizations. Firms that create an open and accepting work climate built on trust, understanding, and respect for people's differences.

Tickler File. A file, arranged by upcoming calendar dates, that actively reminds law firm members of upcoming deadlines and required actions.

Time Studies. Scientifically designed analyses of the time used to complete a given task.

Total Quality Control. A management practice that stresses openness, leadership, and the total dedication of each member of the firm to improving service. In addition, TQC (also known as Total Quality Management) requires firms to establish objective and quantifiable standards for measuring the quality of each member's work.

Training and Development. The process of teaching employees new skills and increasing their knowledge in order to improve their job performance.

Trait Leadership Theories. Theories that propose a connection between leadership ability and physical, intellectual, and psychological characteristics.

Transactional Leadership. A form of transformational leadership that rewards followers in exchange for what they do for the organization.

Transformational Leadership. A leadership style in which leaders change the attitudes and assumptions of followers in order to build a collective commitment toward the organization, its goals, and its strategies.

Two-Way Communication. Communication in which the receiver responds to the sender's messages with feedback, and information travels in both directions.

Unity of Command. The issuing of orders by only one superior to a subordinate.

Universality of Management. The conviction that the same basic guidelines for organizational processes and structures are useful everywhere.

Upper Management. The management level that formulates major policies, determines directions and strategies, and makes the most important organizational decisions.

Upward Communication. Communication that occurs when someone from a lower level in an organization communicates with someone at a higher level.

Utilitarianism. An ethical theory which proposes that the purpose of all action is to bring the greatest happiness to the greatest number of people.

Utilization. Utilization measures, in terms of chargeable hours per professional year, the use that a firm makes of its timekeepers' time.

Valence. The strength of the positive or negative value a worker places on an outcome.

Value Billing. A popular contemporary billing practice by which a firm may adjust bills either upwards or downwards, determining actual fees more according to the value of services than according to an equation involving hourly rates and the number of hours billed.

Values. Relatively permanent and morally weighted attitudes; they represent what people desire and want to happen.

Vertical Communication. Communication that travels up and down the hierarchy.

Wages. Monetary amounts that a firm pays hourly workers for each hour they work.

Whistleblowing. The act of calling public attention to an organization's wrongful and illegal actions, often at great personal risk, so that greater issues of justice and equity are upheld.

Work Ethic. Values comprising the moral importance of work and the pride that people take in what they do.

Workaholic. Someone who is literally addicted to work.

Work-in-Process. Potential sources of firm revenue consisting of work that the firm either has yet to complete or has yet to bill to clients.

Work-in-Process Reports. Inventories of work that the firm has performed or is performing and that it has yet to bill to clients.

Write-Offs. Bills or services that the firm has determined to be valueless for the purpose of collecting income.

Zone of Acceptance. The level of performance that workers in a given setting consider acceptable.

Zone of Difference. Leadership strategy that recognizes followers' unique skills, qualities, and competencies while describing the areas in which their goals and attitudes overlap.

Endnotes

Chapter 1

1. James L. Hayes, *Memos for Management: Leadership* (New York: AMACOM, 1983): 3. **2.** Albert Shapero, *Managing Professional People: Understanding Creative Performance* (New York: The Free Press, 1985): ix. **3.** Thomas F. Gibbons, "Law Practice in 2001," *ABA Journal* (January 1990): 68–75. **4.** Henry Mintzberg, "The Manager's Job: Folklore and Fact," *Harvard Business Review* VI, 53 (July–August 1975): 61. **5.** Wayne K. Hobson, "Symbol of the New Profession: Emergence of the Large Law Firm," in *The New High Priests: Lawyers in Post-Civil War America*, ed. Gerard W. Gawalt, 1-27:6 (Westport Conn.: Greenwood Press., 1984). **6.** Gerard W. Gawalt, "The Impact of Industrialization on the Legal Profession," in *The New High Priests: Lawyers in Post-Civil War America:* 101. **7.** Gawalt, "The Impact of Industrialization": 101. **8.** Hobson, "Symbol of the New Profession": 3. **9.** Hobson, "Symbol of the New Profession": 6. **10.** Hobson, "Symbol of the New Profession": 3. **11.** Hobson, "Symbol of the New Profession": 6. **12.** Stephanie B. Goldberg, "Then and Now: 75 Years of Change," *ABA Journal* 76 (January 1990): 56–61. **13.** "Law Office Management," *ABA Journal*, (1 September 1986): 20. **14.** Mary Ann Altman, "Governing Structures: The Choices," *National Law Journal* (10 October 1988). **15.** William H. Rehnquist, "The State of the Legal Profession," *Legal Economics* 14 (March 1988): 44–49. **16.** R. Reed, "Comprehensive Management of the Firm's Professional Side," *Legal Economics* 24 (January/February 1985). **17.** Hobson, "Symbol of the New Profession": 6. **18.** "Do We Have Too Many Lawyers?" *Time* (26 August 1991): 54–55. **19.** John Naisbitt and Patricia Aburdene, *Re-Inventing the Corporation* (New York: Warner Books, 1988). **20.** Hobson, "Symbol of the New Profession": 6. **21.** "D.C. Ruling Opens Doors to Nonlawyer Partners," *Law Office Management and Administration Report* (April 1990): 13. **22.** *New York Law Journal* (27 February 1990): 1. **23.** "The Underlying Problem—Unsound Management Practices," in *At the Breaking Point: A National Conference on the Emerging Crisis in the Quality of Lawyers' Health and Lives—Its Impact on Law Firms and Client Services,* The American Bar Association (1991): 12. **24.** David B. Guralnik, ed., *Webster's New World Dictionary of the American Language,* college ed. (Cleveland: World Publishing Company, 1974): 859. **25.** Leonard Sayles, "The Unsung Profession," *Issues and Observations* (May 1984): 4. **26.** Peter Drucker, *The Changing World of the Executive* (New York: T. T. Times Books, 1982): xi. **27.** Robert Heller, *The Supermanagers* (New York: E. P. Dutton, 1984): 387. **28.** Peter Drucker, *Managing For Results* (New York: Harper & Row, Inc., 1964): 5. **29.** Peter Drucker, *The Practice of Management* (New York: Harper & Row, Inc., 1954): 341–42. **30.** Leonard R. Sayles, *Managerial Behavior* (New York: McGraw-Hill, 1964): 162. **31.** Robert J. Ambrogi, "Top Executive Resigns from Boston Firm," *Massachusetts Lawyers Weekly* 19: 52 (16 September 1991): 24. **32.** Naisbitt and Aburdene, *Re-Inventing the Corporation:* 53. **33.** J. Paul Getty, "The Fine Art of Being Boss," *Playboy* (June 1972): 143. **34.** Peter Drucker, *The Practice of Management.* **35.** Drucker, *The Practice of Management.* **36.** Peter F. Drucker, *Management: Tasks, Responsibilities, Practices* (New York: Harper & Row, 1974): xiii. **37.** Rosabeth Moss Kanter and Barry A. Stein, eds., *Life in Organizations: Workplaces As People Experience Them* (New York: Basic Books, 1979): 181. **38.** Shapero, *Managing Professional People:* i-x. **39.** Lawrence A. Appley, as quoted in *Management News* (November 1953): 1. **40.** Drucker, *Managing For Results:* 5. **41.** Henry Mintzberg, *Mintzberg on Management: Inside Our Strange World of Organizations* (New York: The Free Press, 1989): 21–22. **42.** Heller, *The Supermanagers:* 387. **43.** John F. Coburn, "The Legal Administrator of the 1990s: A New Breed," *Legal Economics* (January–February 1989): 36–44. Adapted from *Legal Administrator* (May/June 1988). **44.** Bradford W. Hildebrandt and Jack Kaufman, *The Successful Law Firm: New Approaches to Structure and Management,* 2d ed. (Clifton, N.J.: Prentice-Hall Law & Business, 1988): 91. **45.** Association of Legal Administrators, *Year in Review* (1989–90). **46.** Association of Legal Administrators, "Who Can Take the Steps to Higher Profits?" (May/June 1988): 34. **47.** Paul Manus, "The Evolution of the Legal Administrator," *Texas Lawyer* (8 January 1990). **48.** James Naisbitt, *Megatrends* (New York: Warner Books, 1984). **49.** Walter Kiechell. Interview by Randall B. Dunham and Jon L. Pierce in *Management* (Glenview, Ill.: Scott, Foresman & Company, 1989): 25. **50.** Harold Koontz, "The Management Theory Jungle Revisited," *Academy of Management Reviews*, no. 2

(April 1980), 175–87: 175. **51.** Koontz, "The Management Theory Jungle Revisited." **52.** C. George, *The History of Management Thought* (Englewood Cliffs, N.J.: Prentice-Hall, 1972). **53.** John K. Clemens, "A Lesson from 431 B.C.," *Fortune* (13 October 1986): 161–62. **54.** Exodus 18:13–26. **55.** Frederick C. Lane, *Venetian Ships and Shipbuilders of the Renaissance* (Baltimore: Johns Hopkins Press, 1934). **56.** Much of the material that follows has been based on various works, particularly Lyndall Urwick, *The Golden Book of Management,* written for the International Committee of Scientific Management (London, England: Newman, Neame, Ltd., 1956); and also Carl Heyel, ed., *The Encyclopedia of Management,* 3d ed. (New York: Van Nostrand Reinhold Company, Inc., 1982). **57.** Edwin A. Locke, "The Ideas of Frederick W. Taylor: An Evaluation," *Academy of Management Review* 7 (1982): 14. **58.** Frederick W. Taylor, *Principles of Scientific Management* (New York: Harper & Row, Inc., 1911): 36–37. **59.** Lillian M. Gilbreth, *The Psychology of Management.* (New York: Sturgis and Walton, 1914.) Reprint. Macmillan, 1921. **60.** Henry C. Metcalfe and Lyndale Urwick, eds., *Dynamic Administration: The Collected Papers of Mary Parker Follett* (New York: Harper & Brothers, 1940). **61.** Chester I. Barnard, *The Functions of the Executive* (Cambridge, Mass.: Harvard University Press, 1938): 286. **62.** Max Weber, *The Protestant Ethic and the Spirit of Capitalism,* trans. Talcott Parsons (New York: Scribner, 1958): originally published in German in 1905 and revised in 1920. **63.** Rensis Likert, *The Human Organization* (New York: McGraw-Hill, 1967) and *New Patterns in Management* (New York: McGraw-Hill, 1961). **64.** Chris Argyris, *Personality and Organization* (New York: Harper & Brothers, 1957). **65.** F. J. Roethlisberger and W. J. Dickson, *Management and the Worker* (Cambridge, Mass.: Harvard University Press, 1939). See also Roethlisberger and Dickson, *Industrial Worker,* 2 vols. (Cambridge, Mass.: Harvard University Press, 1938).

Chapter 2

1. Lewis Carroll, *Alice in Wonderland,* as quoted in Kenneth L. Lowe, "Long-Range Planning," *Legal Administrator* (Winter 1986): 24–27. **2.** Guy P. French, "The Payoff from Planning," *Managerial Planning* (September/October 1979). **3.** Ben Heirs, *The Professional Decision Thinker: America's New Management and Education Priority* (New York: Dodd, Mead & Company, 1987): 27–28. **4.** Samuel R. Certo, *Principles of Modern Management: Functions and Systems,* 4th ed. (Boston: Allyn and Bacon, 1989): 642. **5.** John R. Schermerhorn, Jr., *Management for Productivity,* 3d ed. (New York: John Wiley & Sons, Inc., 1989): 708. **6.** Kenneth L. Lowe, "Long-Range Planning," *Legal Administrator* (Winter 1986): 26. **7.** Leon C. Megginson, Donald C. Mosely, and Paul H. Pietri, *Management: Concepts and Applications,* 3d ed. (New York: Harper & Row, 1989): 91. **8.** Lloyd S. Baird, James E. Post, and John F. Mahon, *Management: Functions and Responsibilities* (New York: Harper & Row, 1990): 100, 702. **9.** John A. Pearce II and Richard B. Robinson, Jr., *Management* (New York: Random House, Inc., 1989): 12. **10.** William P. Anthony, *Practical Strategic Planning: A Guide and Manual for Line Managers* (Westport, Conn.: Quorum Books, 1985): 8. **11.** Rosabeth Moss Kanter, *The Change Masters: Innovations for Productivity in the American Corporation* (New York: Simon & Schuster, 1983): 294–95. **12.** Kenneth L. Lowe, "Long-Range Planning": 24–27. **13.** Lowe, "Long-Range Planning": 26–27. **14.** C. W. Roney, "The Two Purposes of Planning," *Managerial Planning* (November/December 1976): 1–6. **15.** "The Law Business in the Year 2000," *American Lawyer* (June 1989). **16.** David B. Guralnik, ed., *Webster's New World Dictionary of the American Language,* 2d college ed. (Cleveland: World Publishing, 1974). **17.** Anthony, *Practical Strategic Planning:* 76. **18.** P. Lorange and R. V. Vancil, *Strategic Planning Systems* (Englewood Cliffs, N.J.: Prentice-Hall: 1977). **19.** Based on Robert Tannenbaum, Irving Weschler, and Fred Massarik, *Leadership and Organization: A Systems Approach* (New York: McGraw-Hill, 1961): 277–78. **20.** Kjell A. Ringbakk, "Why Planning Fails," *European Business* (July 1970). **21.** Herbert Simon, *The New Science of Management Decisions,* 2d ed. (Englewood Cliffs, N.J.: Prentice-Hall, 1977). **22.** Peter Drucker, *The Practice of Management* (New York: Harper & Row Publishers, 1954). **23.** Paul C. Nutt, *Making Tough Decisions: Tactics for Improving Managerial Decision Making* (San Francisco: Jossey-Bass Publishers, 1989): xiii. **24.** Mervin Kohn, *Dynamic Managing: Principles, Process, Practice* (Menlo Park, Calif.: Cummings Publishing Co., 1977): 58–62. **25.** Silvia L. Coulter, Suzanne B. O'Neil, and Robert Poirier, "Administrators Face New Challenges as COOs," *National Law Journal* (8 May 1989): 26. **26.** Chester Barnard, *The Functions of the Executive (Cambridge, Mass.: Harvard University Press, 1938).* **27.** Based on James Gatza, Jugoslav S. Milatinovitch, and F. Glenn Boseman, *Decision Making in Administration: Text, Critical Incidents and Cases* (Philadelphia: W. B. Sanders, 1979): 16–18. **28.** Mark H. McCormack, *What They Don't Teach You at Harvard Business School: Notes from a Street Smart Executive* (New York: Bantam Books, 1984). **29.** Row Rowan, *The Intuitive Manager* (Boston: Little, Brown Publishers, 1986). **30.** Paul C. Nutt, "Types of Organizational Decision Processes," *Administrative Science Quarterly* 29 (1984): 414–50; and E. F. Harrison, *The Managerial Decision Making Process,* 3d ed. (Boston: Houghton Mifflin, 1987). **31.** Andrew D. Szilagyi, Jr., and Marc J. Wallace, Jr., *Organizational Behavior and Performance,* 5th ed. (Glenview, Ill.: Scott, Foresman/Little, Brown Higher Education, 1990): 451–54. **32.** H. M. Schroeder, M. J. Driver, and S. Streufert, *Human Information Processing* (New York: Holt, Rinehart & Winston, 1967). **33.** Randall B. Dunham and Jon L. Pierce, *Management* (Glenview, Ill.: Scott, Foresman & Company, 1989): 218. **34.** James G. March and Herbert A. Simon, *Organizations* (New York: Wiley & Sons, 1958): 11.

35. Daniel J. Isenberg, "Thinking and Managing: A Verbal Protocol Analysis of Managerial Problem Solving," *Academy of Management Journal* (1986): 775–88. **36.** Harold J. Leavitt, *Managerial Psychology: An Introduction to Individuals, Pairs, and Groups in an Organization,* 2d ed. (Chicago: The University of Chicago Press, 1964): 272. **37.** Richard A. Cosier and Charles R. Schwenk, "Agreement and Thinking Alike: Ingredients for Poor Decisions," *Academy of Management Executive* 4 (1990): 69. **38.** Harold Geneen, "Viewpoint: How to Make Winning Decisions," *For Members Only: American Express* (April 1985): 1. **39.** Ben Heirs, *The Professional Decision Thinker:* 62–63. **40.** Peter Drucker, *Management: Tasks, Responsibilities, Practices* (New York: Harper & Row, 1974): 465–80. **41.** Peter Drucker, The Practice of Management (New York: Harper & Row, 1954): 126–29. **42.** Irving L. Janis, *Crucial Decisions: Leadership in Policy Making and Crisis Management* (New York: The Free Press, 1989): 44. **43.** Cosier and Schwenk, "Agreement and Thinking Alike: Ingredients for Poor Decisions": 69–74. **44.** "The Rebel Shaking Up Exxon," *Business Week* (18 July 1988): 115. **45.** Nutt, *Making Tough Decisions:* 11. **46.** Robert E. Kaplan, "Creativity in the Everyday Business of Managing," *Issues and Observations* (Greensboro, N.C.: Center for Creative Leadership, 1983). **47.** John M. Keil, *The Creative Mystique: How to Manage It, Nurture It, and Make It Pay* (New York: John Wiley & Sons, 1985): 12–15. **48.** John M. Keil, *The Creative Mystique:* 12–15; 46. **49.** Keil, *The Creative Mystique*: 16. **50.** Michael Ray and Rochelle Myers, *Creativity in Business* (Garden City, N.Y.: Doubleday & Company, Inc., 1986): 4. **51.** Paul J. Stonich, "Formal Planning Pitfalls and How to Avoid Them," *Management Review* (June 1975): 5. **52.** Henry Mintzberg, "A New Look at the Chief Executive's Job," *Organizational Dynamics* (Winter 1973): 20–40. **53.** Rosabeth Moss Kanter, *The Change Masters*: 253–59. **54.** R. Edward Freeman, *Strategic Management: A Stakeholder Approach* (Boston: Pitman Publishing, Inc., 1984): 31–49. **55.** Ralph H. Kilmann, with Ines Kilmann, *Managing Beyond the Quick Fix: A Completely Integrated Program for Creating and Maintaining Organizational Success* (San Francisco: Jossey-Bass Publishers, 1989): 14–15. **56.** Olfa Hemler,"The Uses of the Delphi Technique in Problems of Educational Innovatings," *Rand Corporation,* no. 3499 (December 1966). **57.** Alex F. Osborn, *Applied Imagination* (New York: Charles Scribner & Sons, 1957). **58.** Andre L. Delbecq, Andrew H. Van de Ven, and David H. Gustafson, *Group Techniques for Program Planning: A Guide to Nominal Group and Delphi Processes* (Glenview, Ill.: Scott, Foresman & Co., 1975). **59.** Cosier and Schwenk, "Agreement and Thinking Alike: Ingredients for Poor Decisions": 69–74. **60.** Richard O. Mason, "A Dialectic Approach to Strategic Planning," *Management Science* 15 (1969): B403–B414; and Cosier and Schwenk, "Agreement and Thinking Alike: Ingredients for Poor Decisions": 73–74. **61.** Robert Whitfield, "Planning Essential for Law Firm Growth": 23, 26, *New York Law Journal* (24 September 1984): 23; and Whitfield, "Firms Should Develop Management Marketing Plans," *Chicago Daily Law Bulletin* (6 November 1990): 2. **62.** Heirs, *The Professional Decision Thinker*: 68. **63.** Cosier and Schwenk, "Agreement and Thinking Alike: Ingredients for Poor Decisions": 69. **64.** Janis, *Crucial Decisions: Leadership in Policy Making and Crisis Management*: 3–4. **65.** Nutt, *Making Tough Decisions*: 3. **66.** Herbert S. Kindler and Carol Phillips, "Deciding How to Decide," *Legal Administrator* (Summer 1986): 28. **67.** Joel A. Rose, "Planning and Conducting Retreats," *New York Law Journal* (22 July 1988): 4. **68.** Thomas S. Clay and Daniel J. DiLucchio, Jr., "The Successful Retreat," *Legal Economics* (September 1989). **69.** Thomas S. Clay and Daniel J. DiLucchio, Jr., "The Successful Retreat." **70.** Clay and DiLucchio, "The Successful Retreat." **71.** Joel A. Rose, "Planning and Conducting Retreats": 4, 6. **72.** Much of the material that follows is based on the work of Joel A. Rose, particularly on "Planning and Conducting Retreats," *New York Law Journal* (22 July 1988): 4, 6. **73.** Joel A. Rose, "Rediscover Purpose: Retreats Let Firms Face Themselves," *National Law Journal* (18 November 1985): 1, 15–16. **74.** Rose, "Planning and Conducting Retreats": 4. **75.** Rose, "Rediscover Purpose: Retreats Let Firms Face Themselves": 16. **76.** Donald S. Akins, "Do Not Retreat at a Retreat," *San Francisco Attorney* (June/July 1989). **77.** Rose, "Planning and Conducting Retreats": 4. **78.** Rose, "Rediscover Purpose": 15.

Chapter 3

1. Henry Mintzberg, *Mintzberg on Management: Inside Our Strange World of Organizations* (New York: The Free Press, 1989): 1. **2.** Elliot Jaques, "In Praise of Hierarchy," *Harvard Business Review* (January/February 1990): 127. **3.** Saul W. Gellerman, "In Organizations, as in Architecture, Form Follows Function," *Organizational Dynamics* (Winter 1990): 59. **4.** Randall B. Dunham and Jon L. Pierce, *Management* (Glenview, Ill.: Scott, Foresman & Company, 1989): 323. **5.** John R. Schermerhorn, Jr., *Management for Productivity* (New York: John Wiley & Sons, 1989): 174. **6.** John A. Pearce II and Richard B. Robinson, Jr., *Management* (New York: Random House, 1989): 296. **7.** Rosemary Stewart, *The Reality of Organizations* (New York: Doubleday & Company, Inc., 1972): xiv–xv. **8.** Samuel C. Certo, *Principles of Modern Management: Functions and Systems,* 4th ed. (Boston: Allyn and Bacon, 1989): 197–98. **9.** Peter M. Blau and W. Richard Scott, *Formal Organizations: A Comparative Approach* (San Francisco: Chandler Publishing, 1962). **10.** William G. Scott, "Organization Theory: An Overview and Appraisal," *Academy of Management Journal* (April 1961): 7–26. **11.** John M. Gaus, "A Theory of Organization in Public Administration," in *The Frontiers of Public Administration* (Chicago: University of Chicago Press, 1936): 66. **12.** Chester I. Barnard, *The Functions of the Executive* (Cambridge, Mass.: Harvard University Press, 1938): 752. **13.** Harold Koontz and Heinz Weihrich, *Essentials of*

Management, 5th ed. (New York: McGraw-Hill, 1990): 134. **14.** Henry Mintzberg, *Mintzberg on Management: Inside Our Strange World of Organizations*: 1–2. **15.** Daniel Katz and Robert L. Kahn, *The Social Psychology of Organizations,* 2d ed. (New York: John Wiley & Sons, 1978). **16.** Christopher A. Bartlett and Sumantra Ghosal, "Matrix Management: Not a Structure, a Frame of Mind," *Harvard Business Review* (July/August 1990): 140. **17.** Samuel C. Certo, *Principles of Modern Management: Functions and Systems,* 3d ed. (Dubuque, Iowa: Wm. C. Brown Company, 1986): 270. **18.** Keith Davis and John Newstrom, *Human Behavior at Work* (New York: McGraw-Hill, 1985): 308. **19.** Blau and Scott, *Formal Organizations: A Comparative Approach*: 2–8. **20.** David J. Cherrington, *Organizational Behavior: The Management of Individual and Organizational Performance* (Boston: Allyn and Bacon, 1989): 19. **21.** E. Jacques, *Equitable Payment* (New York: John Wiley & Sons, 1961); and Edgar H. Schein, *Organizational Psychology,* 2d ed. (Englewood Cliffs, N.J.: Prentice-Hall, 1972): 51. **22.** Cherrington, *Organizational Behavior: The Management of Individual and Organizational Performance*: 14–21. **23.** David Ewing, *Freedom inside the Organization* (New York: McGraw-Hill, 1977). **24.** Tom Peters, " 'Great' companies still make demands," *Springfield Union-News* (17 September 1990): 21. **25.** Chris Argyris, *Personality and Organization* (New York: Harper & Brothers, 1957). **26.** Samuel B. Bacharach and Edward J. Lawler, *Power and Politics in Organizations* (San Francisco: Jossey-Bass, 1980): 6. **27.** William G. Scott, "Organization Theory: An Overview and Appraisal," *Academy of Management Journal* (April 1961): 7–26. **28.** Adam Smith, "On the Division of Labor," from *An Inquiry into the Nature and Causes of the Wealth of Nations* (1776), in *Classics of Organization Theory,* ed. Jay M. Shafritz and Philip H. Whitbeck (Oak Park, Ill.: Moore Publishing Company, 1987): 8–9. **29.** Luther Gulick, "Notes on the Theory of Organization," in *Papers on the Science of Administration,* ed. Luther Gulick and Lyndall Urwick (New York: Institute of Public Administration, 1937): 3. **30.** J. R. Hackman and E. E. Lawler, "Employee Reactions to Job Characteristics," *Journal of Applied Psychology Monograph* 55 (1971): 269–86; J. R. Hackman and G. R. Oldham, "Development of the Job Diagnostic Survey," *Journal of Applied Psychology* 60 (April 1975): 159–70. **31.** William G. Scott, "Organization Theory: An Overview and Appraisal": 7–26. **32.** Stephen P. Gallagher, "The New Breed of Law Practice," *Law Office Economics and Management* (1989): 175. **33.** Scott, "Organization Theory: An Overview and Appraisal": 7–26. **34.** Saul W. Gellerman, "In Organizations, as in Architecture, Form Follows Function": 62–63. **35.** Richard Abel, *American Lawyers* (New York: Oxford University Press, 1989): 10. **36.** Stephen P. Gallagher, "The New Breed of Law Practice": 176–77. **37.** Herbert A. Simon, "The Proverbs of Administration," *Public Administration Review* 6 (Winter 1946): 53–67. **38.** James D. Mooney, *The Principles of Organization,* 2d ed. (New York: Harper & Brothers, 1947). **39.** Henri Fayol, *General and Industrial Management,* trans. Constance Storrs (London: Pitman Publishing, Ltd., 1949): 24. **40.** Herbert A. Simon, "The Proverbs of Administration," *Public Administration Review* 6 (Winter 1946): 53–67. **41.** Henri Fayol, *General and Industrial Management*: 37. **42.** James D. Mooney, "The Scalar Principle," in *The Principles of Organization,* 2d ed. (New York: Harper & Row, 1947). **43.** Lyndall Urwick, "Axioms of Organizations," *Public Administration Magazine* (October 1955): 348–49. **44.** Scott, "Organization Theory: An Overview and Appraisal": 7–26. **45.** Rosabeth Moss Kanter, *The Change Masters:* 209. **46.** Talcott Parsons, "Suggestions for a Sociological Approach to the Theory of Organizations," *Administrative Science Quarterly* 1 (June 1956): 63–85. **47.** Henri Fayol, *General and Industrial Management:* 19–20. **48.** Russell F. Moore, ed., *AMA Management Handbook* (New York: American Management Association, 1970). **49.** Philip Selznick, "Foundations of the Theory of Organization," *American Sociological Review* 13 (1948): 25–35. **50.** Scott, "Organization Theory: An Overview and Appraisal": 7–26. **51.** Mary Parker Follett, "The Giving of Orders," in *Classics of Organization Theory,* ed. Jay M. Shafritz and Philip H. Whitbeck (Oak Park, Ill.: Moore Publishing Company, 1987): 49. **52.** Fayol, *General and Industrial Management*: 19–42. **53.** Rensis Likert and Jane Gibson Likert, *New Ways of Managing Conflict* (New York: McGraw-Hill, 1976): 16. **54.** Rensis Likert and Jane Gibson Likert, *The Human Organization: Its Management and Value* (New York: McGraw-Hill, 1967): 11. **55.** Rensis Likert, *New Patterns of Management* (New York: McGraw-Hill, 1961): 103. **56.** Likert, *New Patterns of Management*: 103. **57.** Rensis Likert, *The Human Organization:* 51. **58.** Likert, *The Human Organization:* 51. **59.** Bartlett and Ghosal, "Matrix Management: Not a Structure, a Frame of Mind": 139. **60.** Stanley M. Davis and Paul R. Lawrence, *Matrix* (Reading, Mass.: Addison-Wesley, 1977): 11–24. **61.** Kenneth Knight, "Matrix Organization: A Review," *Journal of Management Studies* (May 1976): 111–30. **62.** Stanley M. Davis and Paul R. Lawrence, "Problems of Matrix Organizations," *Harvard Business Review* (May/June 1978): 131–42. **63.** Bartlett and Ghosal, "Matrix Management: Not a Structure, a Frame of Mind": 139. **64.** Tom Burns and G. M. Stalker, *The Management of Innovation* (London: Tavistock Publications, 1961): 119–25. **65.** Terrence E. Deal and Allan A. Kennedy, *Corporate Cultures: The Rites and Rituals of Corporate Life* (Reading, Mass.: Addison-Wesley, 1982). **66.** Edgar Schein, "The Role of the Founder in Creating Organizational Culture," *Organizational Dynamics* (Summer 1983): 13–28. **67.** Terrence E. Deal and Allan A. Kennedy, *Corporate Cultures: The Rites and Rituals of Corporate Life* (Reading, Mass.: Addison-Wesley, 1982), published in *The Manager's Bookshelf: A Mosaic of Contemporary Views,* 2d ed., ed. Jon L. Pierce and John W. Newstrom (New York: Harper & Row, 1990):

101–12. **68.** Edgar H. Schein, "Coming to a New Awareness of Organizational Culture," *Sloan Management Review* (Winter 1984): 7. **69.** Deal and Kennedy, *Corporate Cultures:* 107–8. **70.** Tom Peters, "Peters on Excellence: Major Challenges for '90s, Beyond," *Springfield Union News* (16 July 1990): 19, 20. **71.** "Inside Today's Changing Law Firm," *Massachusetts Lawyers Weekly Supplement* (July 31, 1989): 1. **72.** Rosabeth Moss Kanter, *When Giants Learn to Dance: Mastering the Challenge of Strategy, Management and Careers in the 1990's* (New York: Simon & Schuster, 1989): 32. **73.** Peters, Tom, *Thriving on Chaos: Handbook for a Management Revolution* (New York: Alfred A. Knopf, 1987): 27.

Chapter 4

1. John Gardner, "The Anti-Leadership Vaccine," *Carnegie Foundation Annual Report (1965).* **2.** Antoine de Saint-Exupéry, *The Little Prince,* trans. Katherine Woods (New York: Harcourt, Brace & World, Inc., 1943): 45. **3.** Mary Cunningham, *Powerplay* (New York: Simon & Schuster, 1984): 283. **4.** Richard Walton, "The Topeka Work System," in *Innovative Organization: Productivity Programs in Action,* ed. Robert Zager and Jerome Rosow (New York: Pergamon Press, 1982): 284. **5.** Hannah Arendt, "What Was Authority?" in *Authority,* ed. Carl J. Friedrich (Cambridge, Mass.: Harvard University Press, 1958): 82. **6.** William H. Wagel, "Information Technology and the Changing Workplace: An Interview with Shoshana Zuboff," in "Highlights of the AMA's 60th Annual Human Resources Conference and Exposition: Surveying the Past . . . Planning the Future," *Personnel* (June 1989): 26. **7.** Edgar A. Schein, *Organizational Psychology* (New York: Prentice-Hall, 1970). **8.** Abraham Zaleznik and Manfred R. F. Kets de Vries, *Power and the Corporate Mind* (Boston: Houghton Mifflin, 1975): 3. **9.** Gary A. Yukl, *Leadership in Organizations,* 2d ed. (Englewood Cliffs, N.J., 1989): 16. **10.** H. J. Reitz, *Behavior in Organizations* (Homewood, Ill.: Irwin, 1977): 468. **11.** Lawrence L. Steinmetz, *The Art and Skill of Delegation* (Reading, Mass.: Addison-Wesley, 1976): 4. **12.** Harold Koontz, Cyrill O'Donnell, and Heinz Weihrich, *Essentials of Management,* 8th ed. (New York: McGraw-Hill, 1986): 231–33. **13.** William H. Newman and E. Kirby Warren, *The Process of Management: Concepts, Behavior, and Practice,* 4th ed. (Englewood Cliffs, N.J.: Prentice-Hall, 1977): 39–40. **14.** Based on T. J. Erin, "How to Improve Delegation Habits," *Management Review* (May 1982): 59. **15.** Lawrence L. Steinmetz, *The Art and Skill of Delegation:* 82–95. **16.** Steinmetz, *The Art and Skill of Delegation:* 89. **17.** Based on Michael A. Nisbet, *Canadian Banker* 95 (September/October 1988): 35–39. **18.** D. Kipnis, S. M. Schmidt, and I. Wilkinson, "Intraorganizational Influence Tactics: Explorations in Getting One's Way," *Journal of Applied Psychology* 65 (1980): 440–52. **19.** Robert A. Dahl, "The Concept of Power," *Behavioral Science* 2 (1957): 201. **20.** Warren Bennis and Burt Nanus, *Leaders: The Strategies for Taking Charge* (New York: Harper & Row, 1985): 15–16. **21.** David McClelland, "The Two Faces of Power," *Journal of International Affairs* 24 (1970): 44. **22.** John P. Kotter, *Power and Influence* (New York: The Free Press, 1985): 136. **23.** Abraham Zaleznik, "Power and Politics in Organizational Life," *Harvard Business Review* 48 (May/June 1970): 47–48. **24.** John P. Kotter, *Power in Management* (New York: AMACOM, 1979): 16–17. **25.** David C. McClelland, *Power: The Inner Experience* (New York: Wiley & Sons, 1976): 258. **26.** Rosabeth Moss Kanter, *Men and Women of the Corporation* (New York: Basic Books, 1977): 166. **27.** Max Weber, *The Theory of Social and Economic Organization,* ed. and trans. A. M. Henderson and T. Parson (New York: Oxford University Press, 1947). **28.** David Mechanic, "Sources of Power of Lower Participants in Complex Organizations," *Administrative Quarterly* 7 (1962): 349–64. **29.** Abraham Kaplan, "Power in Perspective," in *Power and Conflict in Organizations,* ed. R. L. Kahn and E. Boulding (London: Tavistock, 1964). **30.** Samuel B. Bacharach and Edward J. Lawler, *Power and Politics in Organizations* San Francisco: Jossey-Bass, 1980): 42. **31.** John R. P. French, Jr., and Bertram Raven, "The Bases of Social Power," in *Studies in Social Power,* ed. D. Cartwright (Ann Arbor, Michigan: University of Michigan Press, 1959): 150–67. **32.** See John A. Pearce II and Richard B. Robinson, Jr., *Management* (New York: Random House, 1989): 506–7; 510. **33.** Rosabeth Moss Kanter, *Men and Women of the Corporation* (New York: Basic Books, Inc., 1977): 122. **34.** Gary A. Yukl, *Leadership in Organizations:* 44–45. **35.** Jay A. Conger, "Leadership: The Art of Empowering Others," *The Academy of Management Executive* 3 (February 1989): 18. **36.** Morgan McCall, Jr., "Leadership and the Professional" in *Managing Professionals in Innovative Organizations: A Collection of Readings,* ed. Ralph Katz (New York: Ballinger Publishing Company, 1988): 150. **37.** Jeffrey Pfeffer, *Power in Organizations* (Marshfield, Mass.: Pitman Publishers, 1981): 173. **38.** John P. Kotter, "Power, Dependence, and Effective Management," *Harvard Business Review* (July/August 1977): 128. **39.** Rosabeth Moss Kanter, "Power Failures in Management Circuits," *Harvard Business Review* (July/August 1979): 66. **40.** Jay A. Conger, "Leadership: The Art of Empowering Others": 18. **41.** Warren Bennis, *The Unconscious Conspiracy: Why Leaders Can't Lead* (New York: AMACOM, 1976): 18–29; 103–106. **42.** Gary Yukl and Tom Taber, "The Effective Use of Managerial Power," *Personnel* (March/April 1983): 43. **43.** Kanter, *Men and Women of the Corporation:* 180–84. **44.** Gary A. Yukl, "Managerial Leadership: A Review of Theory and Research," *Journal of Management* 2, 15 (1989): 255. **45.** Rosabeth Moss Kanter, "Power Failures in Management Circuits": 67. **46.** Samuel B. Bacharach and Edward J. Lawler, *Power and Politics in Organizations* (San Francisco: Jossey-Bass, 1980): 27–32. **47.** D. Kipnis, S. M. Schmidt, and I. Wilkinson, "Intraorganizational Influence Tactics: Explorations in Getting One's Way," *Journal of*

Applied Psychology 65 (1980): 440–52. **48.** D. Kipnis, S. M. Schmidt, and I. Wilkinson, "Intraorganizational Influence Tactics: Explorations in Getting One's Way": 440–52. **49.** Kotter, "Power, Dependence, and Effective Management." **50.** Allan R. Cohen and David L. Bradford, "Influence without Authority: The Use of Alliances, Reciprocity and Exchange to Accomplish Work," *Organizational Dynamics* 17 (Winter 1989): 4–17. **51.** Dale Carnegie, *How to Win Friends and Influence People* (New York: Simon and Schuster, Inc., 1936). **52.** James MacGregor Burns, *Leadership* (New York: Harper & Row, 1978): 444–47. **53.** Edward E. Jones, *Ingratiation: A Social Psychological Analysis* (New York: Appleton-Century-Crofts, 1964). **54.** Andrew M. Pettigrew, *The Politics of Organizational Decision-Making* (London: Tavistock, 1973): 240. **55.** Kotter, *Power and Influence.* **56.** Robert C. Benfari, Harry E. Wilkinson, and Charles D. Orth, *Business Horizons* 29 (May/June 1986): 12–16. **57.** Material in this section is based on David A. Whetten and Kim S. Cameron, *Developing Management Skills* (Glenview, Ill.: Scott, Foresman & Company, 1984): 247–58; and Rosabeth Moss Kanter, "Power Failures in Management Circuits": 65–75. **58.** David A. Whetten and Kim S. Cameron, *Developing Management Skills,* 2d ed. (Glenview, Ill.: HarperCollins Publishers, 1991): 292. **59.** Kanter, *Men and Women of the Corporation:* 180–81. **60.** J. Gantz and V. V. Murray, "The Experience of Workplace Politics," *Academy of Management Review* (April 1980): 237–51. **61.** Harold D. Lasswell, *Politics: Who Gets What, When, How* (New York: McGraw-Hill, 1936). **62.** Pfeffer, *Power in Organizations:* 7. **63.** Robert W. Allen, Dan L. Madison, Lymann W. Porter, Patricia A. Renwick, and Bronston T. Mayes, "Organizational Politics: Tactics and Characteristics of Its Actors," *California Management Review* 22 (1979): 77. **64.** G. Biberman, "Personality and Characteristic Work Attitudes of Persons with High, Moderate, and Low Political Tendencies," *Psychological Reports* (October 1985): 1303–10. **65.** R. W. Allen, L. W. Porter, P. A. Renwick, and B. T. Mayes, "Organizational Politics: An Exploration of Managers' Perceptions," *Human Relations* (February 1980): 79–100. **66.** Stephen P. Robbins, *Organizational Behavior: Concepts, Controversies, and Applications,* 5th ed. (Englewood Cliffs, N.J.: Prentice-Hall, 1991): 408–11. **67.** Harry Mintzberg, "The Organization as Political Arena," *Journal of Management Studies* 22 (March 1985): 134–39. **68.** David A. Whetten and Kim S. Cameron, *Developing Management Skills* (Glenview, Ill.: Scott, Foresman & Company, 1984): 251. **69.** Stanley Young, "Politicking: The Unsung Managerial Skill," *Personnel* (June 1987): 62–68. **70.** Allen, Madison, Porter, Renwick, and Mayes, "Organizational Politics: Tactics and Characteristics of Its Actors": 77–83. **71.** S. P. Feldman, "Secrecy, Information, and Politics: An Essay on Organizational Decision Making," *Human Relations* 41 (1988): 73–90. **72.** Colin McIver, "Use and Abuse of Consultants," *Management Today* (February 1986): 72–74. **73.** J. Greenberg, "Looking Fair vs. Being Fair: Managing Impressions of Organizational Justice," *Research in Organizational Behavior* 12, ed. B. M. Shaw and L. L. Cummings (Greenwich, Conn.: JAI Press, 1990). **74.** Conger, "Leadership: The Art of Empowering Others": 17–24. **75.** Kanter, *Men and Women of the Corporation:* 186. **76.** Kanter, "Power Failures in Management Circuits": 65. **77.** Kanter, "Power Failures in Management Circuits": 73. **78.** Kanter, "Power Failures in Management Circuits": 73. **79.** Kanter, "Power Failures in Management Circuits": 65–75. **80.** Albert Bandura, *Social Foundations of Thought and Action: A Social Cognitive View* (Englewood Cliffs, N.J.: Prentice-Hall, 1986): 400. **81.** Conger, "The Art of Empowering Others," 20–24. **82.** "Managing: 1960's Political Term Resurfaces in Business," *New York Times* (20 November 1989): B1. **83.** Robert A. Baron and Jerald Greenberg, *Behavior in Organizations: Understanding and Managing the Human Side of Work,* 3d ed. (Boston: Allyn and Bacon, 1990): 198–99.

Chapter 5

1. Thomas J. Peters and Robert H. Waterman, Jr., *In Search of Excellence: Lessons from America's Best-Run Companies* (New York: Harper & Row, 1982): 319. **2.** Peter Drucker, "Managing the Knowledge Worker," in *People and Performance: The Best of Peter Drucker* (New York: Harper & Row, 1977): 273. **3.** Joseph A. Litterer, "Elements of Control in Organizations," in *Organization by Design: Theory and Practice,* ed. Mariann Jelinek, Joseph A. Litterer, and Raymond E. Miles (Plano, Tex.: Business Publications, 1981): 439. **4.** Kenneth A. Merchant, *Control in Business Organizations* (Marshfield, Mass.: Pitman Publications, 1985). **5.** John R. Schermerhorn, Jr., *Management for Productivity,* 3d ed. (New York: John Wiley & Sons, 1989): 430. **6.** Robert H. Waterman, Jr., *The Renewal Factor: How the Best Get and Keep a Competitive Edge* (New York: Bantam Books, 1987). **7.** Charles R. Coulter, *Practical Systems: Tips for Organizing Your Law Office* (Chicago, Ill.: American Bar Association, Section of Law Practice Management, 1991): 6. **8.** Based on the ALA Planning Committee, "Challenges and Opportunities for Law Firms in the 1990's and Beyond: A Synopsis of Management Trends in the Legal Services Field," *ALA News* (October/November 1989): 2–6. **9.** Ronald W. Staudt, "Attorneys Make More Use of PCs," *National Law Journal* (23 March 1992): 25. **10.** Benjamin Wright, "Fax Facts," *Network World* (5 February 1990). **11.** "Case History: Robinson, Donovan, Madden & Barry, P.C., Springfield, Massachusetts. Making the Switch: The VoiceWriter 4800 Increases Efficiency 25–30 Percent," *Lanier Responds Newsletter* (Atlanta, Ga.: Lanier Worldwide, Inc., September 1991). **12.** Holley M. Moyer, "Libraries: A Diverse Role in Tough Times," *California Law Business* (19 August 1991): 39. **13.** Pamela Bluh, "Barcoding a Library Collection," *Law Library Journal* (17 February 1990): 727–36. **14.** Joan L. Axelroth, "Library Space Planning," *Legal Management* (January/February 1990): 15–22. **15.** Michael D. Harris, "Automated Legal Research Costs Closely Watched," *California Law Business* (15 July 1991): 13. **16.** Deborah Schwarz, "Law Librarians: More to the Job than Managing a Firm's Library," *California Law Business* (15 July 1991): 14. **17.** Holland Shipes Vann, P.C., "Simple Office Procedures that Avert Malpractice Woes," *Briefs on Practice Management* (September/October 1991): 1–2. **18.** Kline D. Strong and Arben O. Clark, *Law Office Management* (St. Paul, Minn.: West Publishing Company, 1974): 292–310. **19.** Mary Ann Altman and Robert I. Weil, *How to Manage Your Law Office* (New York: Bender, 1988): 10.15. **20.** K. Withgott and Austen G. Anderson, eds., *Webster's Legal Secretaries Handbook* (Springfield, Mass.: Merriam-Webster, 1981): 86. **21.** John Richardson, "Document Management Systems Add Efficiency," *National Law Journal* (17 February 1992): 40. **22.** Patricia Patterson, "How One Firm Automated Its Records Management," *American Association of Law Libraries Newsletter* 21, no. 8 (April 1990): 291–92. **23.** Geoffrey C. Hazard, Jr., "Checking for Conflicts," *National Law Journal* (30 October 1989). **24.** Hazard, "Checking for Conflicts." **25.** This information, as well as much of the material on effective systems for law firms, is based on the detailed work of Charles R. Coulter, *Practical Systems: Tips for Organizing Your Law Office* (Chicago, Ill.: American Bar Association, Section of Law Practice Management, 1991). **26.** Altman and Weil, *How to Manage Your Law Office*: 10.03. **27.** Demetrious Dimitriou, "File Retention Schedules," *Law Practice Management* (January/February 1990): 24–27. **28.** Association of Legal Administrators, *Records Retention Guide* (Vernon Hills, Ill.: 1987). **29.** *The Model Rules of Professional Conduct* (Chicago: American Bar Association, 1983). **30.** Waterman, *The Renewal Factor: How the Best Get and Keep a Competitive Edge*. **31.** Rosabeth Moss Kanter and Barry A. Stein, "Making a Life at the Bottom," in *Life in Organizations: Workplaces As People Experience Them,* ed. Rosabeth Moss Kanter and Barry A. Stein (New York: Basic Books, 1979): 177. **32.** David A. Whetten and Kim S. Cameron, *Developing Management Skills* (Glenview, Ill.: Scott, Foresman & Company, 1984): 55. **33.** Stephen P. Roberts, *Organization Theory: Structure, Design, and Applications*, 3d ed. (Englewood Cliffs, N.J.: Prentice-Hall, 1990): 269. **34.** Thomas J. Peters, "A Skunkwork's Tale," in *Managing Professionals in Innovative Climates,* ed. Ralph Katz (New York: Ballinger, 1988): 436. **35.** V. Govindarajan and Joseph Fisher, "Strategy, Control Systems, and Resource Sharing: Effects on Business Unit Performance," *Academy of Management Journal* 33, no. 2 (1990): 259–85. **36.** Charles D. Pringle, Daniel F. Jennings, and Justin G. Longenecker, *Managing Organizations: Functions and Behaviors* (Columbus, Ohio: Merrill Publishing Company, 1988): 451. **37.** Govindarajan and Fisher, "Strategy, Control Systems, and Resource Sharing: Effects on Business Unit Performance": 280. **38.** Stephen P. Roberts, *Organization Theory: Structure, Design, and Applications*, 3d ed.: 68–77. **39.** Rensis Likert, *New Patterns of Management* (New York: McGraw-Hill, 1961): 2. **40.** William Ouchi, "A Conceptual Framework for the Design of Organization Control Mechanisms," *Management Science* 25 (1979): 833–48. **41.** Neal W. Schmitt and Richard J. Klimoski, *Research Methods in Human Resource Management* (Cincinnati: South-Western Publishing, 1991): 157. **42.** William Ouchi, *Theory Z: How American Businesses Can Meet the Japanese Challenge* (Reading, Mass.: Addison-Wesley, 1981). **43.** Jeremy Main, "The Curmudgeon Who Talks Tough on Quality, *Fortune* (25 June 1984): 118. **44.** W. Edwards Deming, *Out of Crisis* (Cambridge, Mass.: MIT Press, 1986). **45.** Steven Fink, as quoted in Steven Markham, "Crisis Management: Preparing for the Inevitable," *The Manager's Bookshelf: A Mosaic of Contemporary Views,* 2d ed., ed. Jon L. Pierce and John W. Newstrom (New York: Harper & Row, 1990): 123. **46.** Based on Jack Stack, "Crisis Management by Committee," *Inc.* (May 1988): 26. **47.** Peter Passell, "Economic Scene: Time is Money and Other Things," *New York Times* (19 December 1990): D2. **48.** Henry Mintzberg, *The Nature of Managerial Work* (New York: Harper & Row, 1976). **49.** Marilyn M. Machlowitz, "Hints on Effective Time Management in Law Office Practice and Procedure," *New York Law Journal* (28 March 1988). **50.** Whetten and Cameron, *Developing Management Skills*: 104. **51.** William Oncken, Jr., and Donald L. Wass, "Management Time: Who's Got the Monkey?" *Harvard Business Review* 65 (March/April 1987): 19. **52.** Alec Mackensie, *The Time Trap: The New Version of the Classic Book on Time Management* (New York: AMACOM, 1990). **53.** Ellen James, "Time Management Techniques Can Help You Retain Your Job," *Los Angeles Times* (1 December 1990). **54.** David J. Cherrington, *The Work Ethic: Working Values and Values that Work* (New York: AMACOM Publishing Company, 1980): Chapter 12. **55.** Anne Wilson Schaef and Diane Fassel, *The Addictive Organization* (San Francisco: Harper & Row, 1988): 57. **56.** Marilyn M. Machlowitz, *Workaholics: Living with Them, Working with Them* (New York: New American Library, 1980). **57.** Kanter and Stein, *Life in Organizations:* 263. **58.** Kanter and Stein, *Life in Organizations:* 256. **59.** Kanter and Stein, *Life in Organizations:* 255. **60.** R. P. Gandossy and A. Cohen, "It's Out of Control: Growth at the Firm," *Legal Administrator* (Summer 1986): 18. **61.** Kanter and Stein, *Life in Organizations:* 259. **62.** George Downing, "The Changing Structure of a Great Corporation," in *The Emergent American Society: Large Scale*, vol. 1, ed. W. Lloyd Warner et al. (New Haven, Conn.: Yale University Press, 1967): 158–240. **63.** Kanter and Stein, *Life in Organizations:* 255. **64.** Larry E. Greiner, "Evolution and Revolution as Organizations Grow," *Harvard Business Review* 50 (July/August 1972): 37–46. **65.** Greiner, "Evolution and Revolution": 44. **66.** Kanter and Stein, *Life in Organizations:* 256. **67.** "The Underlying Problem—Unsound Management Practices," in *At the Breaking Point: A National Conference on the Emerging Crisis in the Quality of Lawyers' Health and Lives—Its Impact on Law Firms *and Client Services,* The American Bar Association (1991). **68.** Don Itkin, "Improving Attorney Job Satisfaction: How to Repair What's Broken in the Workplace," *Wisconsin Lawyer* (April 1992): 14–15.

Chapter 6

1. B. Charles Ames and James D. Hlavacek, "Vital Truths About Managing Your Costs," *Harvard Business Review* (January/February 1990): 147. **2.** L. Donald Holland and Paula F. Turner, "Taking Your Firm's Pulse," *Association of Legal Administrators: Financial Management Newsletter* 6, no. 3 (Fall 1988): 1. **3.** Anthony Phillips, John Butler, George C. Thompson, and Robert Whitman, *Basic Accounting for Lawyers,* 4th ed. (Philadelphia: American Law Institute, 1988): 1–10. **4.** Daniel Wise, "Final Approval for Finley, Kumble Bankruptcy Plan," *New York Law Journal* (25 February 1991): 1. **5.** Wade Hampton, "The Budget Trainer," *Law Office Economics and Management* 23 (Winter 1988): 473. **6.** Philip Bromiley, "Task Environments and Budgetary Decision Making," *Academy of Management Review* 6 no. 2 (April 1981): 277. **7.** "Smooth Operations: An Operating Budget for Your Firm," *Feeley & Driscoll Newsletter: Law Firm Management* (Summer 1990): 1–2. **8.** John G. Iezzi, "A Step Beyond the Checkbook," *Legal Management* (September/October 1989): 50–53. **9.** Peter Drucker, *People and Performance: The Best of Peter Drucker on Management* (New York: Harper & Row, 1977): 271–75. **10.** Carolee Morrison, "Confidential: To: Top Partners: Re: Compensation Allocation," *Lawyers Monthly, A Supplement to Lawyers Weekly* (June 1989): 9. **11.** Aaron Wildavsky, *The Politics of the Budgetary Process,* 2d ed. (Boston: Little, Brown, 1974). **12.** Geoffrey Furlonger, "Time for Business-Lawyers to Stop Billing Time?" in *Beyond the Billable Hour: An Anthology of Alternative Billing Methods,* ed. Richard C. Reed (Chicago: American Bar Association, 1989): 93. **13.** Geoffrey Furlonger, "Time for Business-Lawyers to Stop Billing Time?" *Law Office Economics and Management* 27 (1986/1987): 171. **14.** Milton W. Zwicker, "Legal Pricing Strategies," in *Beyond the Billable Hour: An Anthology of Alternative Billing Methods,* ed. Richard C. Reed (Chicago: American Bar Association, 1989): 117–18. **15.** Lawrence R. Bright, "Improving Your Profitability," *Legal Management* (January 1991): 21. **16.** Holland and Turner, "Taking Your Firm's Pulse": 1. **17.** Mary Ann Altman and Robert I. Weil, *Introduction to Law Practice Management,* 2d ed. (New York: Bender, 1987): 258. **18.** Donald S. Akins, "Client Acceptance of Alternative Pricing," *Legal Economics* (September 1989). **19.** Richard C. Reed, *Beyond the Billable Hour: An Anthology of Alternative Billing Methods* (Chicago: American Bar Association, 1989): 4–5. **20.** American Bar Association, *Model Rules of Professional Conduct* (Chicago: ABA, 1983). **21.** Barry Solomon and Rachel Gibbons, "Coming to Terms with New Billing Methods," *National Law Journal* (23 November 1992): 54–55. **22.** Geoffrey Furlonger, "Time for Business-Lawyers to Stop Billing Time?" in *Beyond the Billable Hour: An Anthology of Alternative Billing Methods*: 98. **23.** Jay G. Foonberg, "The Short, Happy Life of Hourly Fee Billings," in *Beyond the Billable Hour: An Anthology of Alternative Billing Methods,* ed. Richard C. Reed (Chicago: American Bar Association, 1989): 25. **24.** Kenneth Roberts, "The Hourly Fee is a Devilish System," in *Beyond the Billable Hour: An Anthology of Alternative Billing Methods,* ed. Richard C. Reed (Chicago: American Bar Association, 1989): 35. **25.** Richard C. Reed, "Responsibility, Expertise, Productivity: The True Measure of Value of a Lawyer's Services," in *Beyond the Billable Hour:* 79–82. **26.** Jay G. Foonberg, "The Short, Happy Life of Hourly Fee Billings": 25. **27.** Ezra Tom Clark, Jr., "Getting Out of the Hourly Rate Quagmire—Other Billing Alternatives," in *Beyond the Billable Hour: An Anthology of Alternative Billing Methods:* 183–86. **28.** Clark, "Getting Out of the Hourly Rate Quagmire": 186. **29.** ABA, *Model Rules of Professional Conduct* (Chicago: ABA, 1983). **30.** James W. McCrae, *Legal Fees & Representation Agreements,* Monograph Series Section of Economics of Law Practice (Chicago: American Bar Association, 1988): 7–10. **31.** Carol Vodra, "Survey of Cost Recovery Options," *Legal Administrator* (March/April 1988): 27–29. **32.** Bright, "Improving Your Profitability": 21. **33.** Mary Ann Mason, *Using Computers in the Law: An Introduction and Practical Guide,* 2d ed. (St. Paul, Minn.: West Publishing Co., 1988): 85. **34.** Brooks L. Hilliard, "Today's Practice Management Systems: What They Have to Offer that Your Present System May Not," *Arizona Attorney* (January 1992): 27. **35.** Based on Iezzi, "A Step Beyond the Checkbook"; Joel A. Rose, "Financial Planning for 1990," *New York Law Journal* (2 January 1990); Dennis M. Keefe, "You Don't Need Magic to Decipher a Financial Statement," *Legal Management* (September/October 1990): 36–40; and David J. Rachman, Michael H. Mescon, Courtland L. Bovee, and John V. Thill, *Business Today,* 6th ed. (New York: McGraw-Hill, 1990): 425–51; 481–505. **36.** Based on E. Joseph Kallas, "Advanced Management Reporting" (Paper presented at the A.L.A. Annual Educational Conference, Toronto, May 2–5, 1989). **37.** David Maister, "Profitability: Beating the Downward Trend," *The American Lawyer* (July/August 1984). **38.** Charles T. Horngren, *Cost Accounting: A Managerial Emphasis,* 5th ed. (Englewood Cliffs, N.J.: Prentice-Hall, 1982): 133. **39.** John A. Reinecke, Gary Dessler, and William F. Schoell, *Introduction to Business: A Contemporary View,* 6th ed. (Boston: Allyn and Bacon, 1989): 445–46. **40.** Phillips, Butler, Thompson, and Whitman, *Basic Accounting for Lawyers,* 4th ed.: 77–139. **41.** "What's Your Law Firm Worth?" *Law Firm Management* (Des Moines, Iowa: Ryun, Givens, Smith and Company, Spring 1991): 4. **42.** Phillips, Butler, Thompson, and Whitman, *Basic Accounting for Lawyers,* 4th ed.: 1–10. **43.** For the material on profitability, unless otherwise specified, the author is indebted to Robert J. Arndt of the Price Waterhouse Law/Firm/Law Department Services Group, "Identifying

Profits (or Losses) in the Law Firm'' (Presentation at the A.L.A. Educational Conference, San Francisco, 6 April 1990); and to E. Joseph Kallas, ''Advanced Management Reporting'' (Paper presented at the A.L.A. Annual Educational Conference, Toronto, May 2–5, 1989). **44.** Robert J. Arndt, ''Setting Billing Rates: A New (?) View,'' in *Beyond the Billable Hour: An Anthology of Alternative Billing Methods,* ed. Richard C. Reed (Chicago: American Bar Association, 1989): 111–13. **45.** Feeley & Driscoll Newsletter, ''Quarterly Tips'' (Fall 1990): 6.

Chapter 7

1. John Naisbitt, ''What HR Professionals Can Do to Assume New Leadership Roles,'' *Resource* (March 1986): 3. **2.** Dan DiLucchio, *Things They Never Taught You in Law School,* Human Resource Management, pt. 4 (Ardmore, Pa.: Altman & Weil, Inc., 1990). **3.** William B. Werther, Jr., and Keith Davis, *Human Resources and Personnel Management,* 3d ed. (New York: McGraw-Hill, 1989): 34–35. **4.** Marc G. Singer, *Human Resource Management* (Boston: PWS-KENT Publishing Company, 1990): 3–5. **5.** Michael Beer, Bert Spector, Paul R. Lawrence, D. Quinn Mills, and Richard E. Walton, eds., *Managing Human Assets* (New York: The Free Press, 1984). **6.** John Hoerr, ''Human Resources Managers Aren't Corporate Nobodies Anymore,'' *Business Week* (2 December 1985): 58. **7.** Beer, Spector, Lawrence, Mills, and Walton, eds., *Managing Human Assets* (New York: The Free Press, 1984). **8.** Division of Occupational Analysis, War Manpower Commission, *Training and Reference Manual for Job Analysis* (Washington, D.C.: U.S. Government Printing Office, June 1944): 7. **9.** Allan N. Nash and Stephen J. Carroll, Jr., *The Management of Compensation* (Monterey, Calif.: Brooks/Cole, 1975): 116–17. **10.** Tom Peters, *Thriving on Chaos* (New York: Alfred A. Knopf, 1988): 315. **11.** Steven L. Magnum, ''Recruitment and Job Search: The Recruitment Tactics of Employers,'' *Personnel Administration* (June 1982): 96–102. **12.** Kenneth J. Cole, *The Headhunter Strategy: How to Make It Work for You* (New York: Wiley & Sons, 1985). **13.** Peters, *Thriving on Chaos*: 382. **14.** Steven M. Ralston, ''Social-Communicative Anxiety and the Personnel Selection Interview: A Review and Synthesis'' (Paper presented at the International Convention of the American Business Communication Association, Salt Lake City, Utah, (19 October 1984). **15.** George M. Beason and John A. Belt, ''Verifying Applicants' Backgrounds,'' *Personnel Journal* (July 1976): 345. See also Jeremiah Bogert, ''Learning the Applicant's Background through Confidential Investigations,'' *Personnel Journal* (May 1981); Bruce D. Wonder and Kenneth S. Keleman, ''Increasing the Value of Reference Information,'' *Personnel Administrator* (June 1986): 129; and Carole Sewell, ''Pre-employment Investigations: The Key to Security in Hiring,'' *Personnel Journal* (May 1981). **16.** Based on Robert J. Thorntyon, ''I Cannot Recommend the Candidate Too Highly: An Ambiguous Lexicon for Job Recommendations,'' *The Chronicle for Higher Education* 33 (25 February 1987): 42. **17.** Bernard L. Dugoni and Daniel R. Ilgen, ''Realistic Job Preview and the Adjustment of New Employees,'' *Academy of Management Journal* (September 1981): 590. **18.** Charles J. Stewart and William B. Cash, Jr., *Interviewing: Principles and Practices,* 5th ed. (Dubuque, Iowa: William C. Brown, 1988): 3. **19.** John W. Cogger, ''Are You a Skilled Interviewer?'' *Personnel Journal* (November 1982): 840–43. **20.** Stewart and Cash, *Interviewing: Principles and Practices,* 5th ed.: 64–83. **21.** Based on Keith Davis, *Human Relations at Work: The Dynamics of Organizational Behavior,* 3d ed. (New York: McGraw-Hill, 1967): 480. **22.** Stewart and Cash, *Interviewing: Principles and Practices,* 5th ed.: 39–41. **23.** David J. Cherrington, *Organizational Behavior: The Management of Individual and Organizational Performance* (Boston: Allyn and Bacon, 1989): 336–40. **24.** Richard Pascale, ''The Paradox of 'Corporate Culture': Reconciling Ourselves to Socialization,'' *California Management Review* 27, no. 2 (1985). **25.** Madeline E. Cohen, ''Orientation—The First Step in Team Building,'' *Training and Development Journal* (January 1988): 20–23. **26.** William B. Werther, Jr., and Keith Davis, *Human Resources and Personnel Management,* 3d ed. (New York: McGraw-Hill, 1989): 223. **27.** Mary Ann Altman and Robert I. Weil, *How to Manage Your Law Office* (New York: Bender, 1988): 906. **28.** Donna Chevalier, National Association of Legal Secretaries, ''Why an Office Procedure Manual?'' *Law Office Economics and Management* 28 (Spring 1987): 27–29. **29.** Gerry Malone and Donald S. Akins, ''The 10 Commandments for Training New Lawyers,'' *American Bar Association Journal* 70 (June 1984): 58. **30.** Linda S. Jevahirian, ''More Firms Use Paralegal Managers,'' *National Law Journal* (25 February 1991): 23. **31.** Max DePree, *Leadership Is an Art* (New York: Doubleday, 1989): 21. **32.** DePree, *Leadership Is an Art*: 25. **33.** L. W. Porter and R. M. Sterns, ''Organizational, Work, and Personal Factors in Employee Turnover and Absenteeism,'' *Psychological Bulletin* 80 (1973): 151–76. **34.** E. A. Locke, ''The Nature and Cause of Job Satisfaction,'' in *Handbook of Industrial and Organizational Psychology,* ed. M. P. Dunnette (Chicago: Rand McNally, 1976). **35.** Louis A. Trosch, W. Douglas Cooper, and Robert B. Conrad, ''Wage & Salary Determination in a Law Firm,'' *Law Office Economics and Management* (Winter 1990): 419–30. **36.** *The Lawyer's Almanac,* 12th ed. (Englewood Cliffs, N.J.: Prentice-Hall Law & Business, 1992). **37.** Bradford W. Hildebrandt and Jack Kaufman, *The Successful Law Firm: New Approaches to Structure and Management,* 2d ed. (Clifton, N.J.: Prentice-Hall Law & Business, 1988): 151. **38.** Albert G. Holzinger, ''The Real Costs of Benefits,'' *Nation's Business* (February 1988): 30. **39.** David J. Rachman, Michael H. Mescon, Courtland L. Bovee, and John V. Thill, *Business Today,* 6th ed. (New York: McGraw-Hill, 1990): 255–56. **40.** James Ledvinka and Vida G. Scarpello, *Federal Regulation of Per-*

sonnel and Human Resource Management, 2d ed. (Boston: PWS-KENT Publishing, 1991): 261. **41.** *Employee Benefits in Medium and Large Firms, 1986,* U.S. Department of Labor, Bureau of Labor Statistics, Bulletin 2281 (June 1987): 7; 17. **42.** Frank E. Kuzmits, "Is Your Organization Ready for No-Fault Absenteeism?" *Personnel Administrator* 29, no. 12 (1984): 119–27. **43.** Ledvinka and Scarpello, *Federal Regulation of Personnel and Human Resource Management,* 2d ed.: 2. **44.** Ledvinka and Scarpello, *Federal Regulation of Personnel and Human Resource Management,* 2d ed.: 2. **45.** Rosabeth Moss Kanter, "From Status to Contribution: Some Organizational Implications of the Changing Basis for Pay," *Personnel* (January 1987): 12. **46.** Paul S. Greenlaw and John P. Kohl, "The EEOC's New Equal Pay Guidelines," *Personnel Journal* 61, no. 7 (July 1982): 517–21. **47.** Civil Rights Act of 1964, Title VII, Section 703A. **48.** James Ledvinka, *Federal Regulation of Personnel and Human Resource Management* (Boston: PWS-KENT, 1982): 118–19. **49.** TransWorld Airlines v. Hardison, 432 U.S. 63 (1977). **50.** Bonnie P. Tucker, "Section 504 of the Rehabilitation Act after Ten Years of Enforcement: The Past and the Future," *University of Illinois Law Review* (Fall 1989): 845–921. **51.** Albert R. Karr, "EEOC Clarifies Law on Rights of Handicapped," *Wall Street Journal* (28 February 1991): A4. **52.** Bonnie P. Tucker, "The Americans with Disabilities Act: An Overview," *University of Illinois Law Review* (Fall 1989): 923–39. **53.** Margaret Hart Edwards, "The Americans with Disabilities Act," *ALA News* (August/September 1991): 1; 4–7. **54.** James Ledvinka, *Federal Regulation of Personnel and Human Resource Management* (Boston: PWS-KENT, 1982): 62–63. **55.** Public Law 95-555, 92 Stat. 2076, 31 October 1978. **56.** "The Kids Are All Right," *Boston Business Journal* (12 February 1990): 29. **57.** "More Firms Take on Child Care Responsibilities," *Law Office Management & Administration Report* 90-9 (September 1990): 14–15. **58.** U.S. Department of Labor, Occupational Safety and Health Administration, *All About OSHA,* OSHA Pamphlet No. 2056 (Washington, D.C.: Government Printing Office): 3. **59.** W. J. Goldsmith, "Current Developments in OSHA," *Employee Relations Journal* 11(1986): 348–54. **60.** "No. 1 Work Hazards of the 1990's," *Omaha World-Herald* (7 June 1989): 2. **61.** W. Bellis, "How Safe Are Video Terminals?" *Fortune* (28 August 1988): 66; and D. Jordan, "VDT Health and Safety: A Summary of Medical Opinion," *Computer Dealer* (October 1988): 35. **62.** Deborah Bridwell, Jodie Collins, and David Levine, "A Quiet Revolution," *EAP Digest* (July/August 1988): 27–30. **63.** Lauren Behmer, "How Employee Assistance Programs Work in Law Firms" (Talk presented at the Association of Legal Administrators Conference, San Francisco, 5 April 1990). **64.** Karen Soehnlen McQueen, "Employee Assistance Programs," *Legal Management* (November/December 1989): 5–7. **65.** See "The Partner Problem," *Legal Administrator* (Spring 1986): 34. **66.** Richard Carlton, "EAP's: Support for Troubled Employees . . . and Managers," *Legal Management* (January/February 1989): 50–54. **67.** Robert L. Mathis and John H. Jackson, *Personnel/Human Resource Management,* 6th ed. (St. Paul, Minn.: West Publishing Company, 1991): 143–45. **68.** Teresa Sullivan, "Survey Shows Women Lawyers in Large Firms Still Experience Harassment," *National Law Journal* survey reported in *Chicago Daily Law Bulletin* (15 December 1989): 2. **69.** David Margolick, "Curbing Sexual Harassment in the Legal World," *New York Times,* (November 9, 1990): B5. **70.** Bundy v. Johnson, 641 F.2d 934 (D.C. Cir. 1981). **71.** Sheryl A. Greene, "Reevaluating Title VII Abusive Environment Claims Based on Sexual Harassment after *Mentor Savings Bank v. Vinson,*" *T. Marshal Law Review,* (Spring 1987–88): 29–65. **72.** Equal Employment Opportunity Commission, *1980 Guidelines* (Washington, D.C.: Government Printing Office, 1980). **73.** George W. Johnston, "Sexual Harassment: What It Is and How to Prevent It," *Legal Management* (September/October 1989): 10. **74.** O. A. Ornati, "How to Deal with EEOC's Guidelines on Sexual Harassment," *EEOC Compliance Manual* (Englewood Cliffs, N.J.: Prentice-Hall, 1980). **75.** Meritor Savings Bank (FBS) v. Vinson, 106 S.Ct. 57, *aff'd and remanded,* 106 S.Ct. 2399 (1986). **76.** David S. Machlowitz and Marilyn M. Machlowitz, "Preventing Sexual Harassment," *ABA Journal* (1 October 1987): 79. **77.** Machlowitz and Machlowitz, "Preventing Sexual Harassment": 79. **78.** Beer, Spector, Lawrence, Mills, and Walton, eds., *Managing Human Assets.* **79.** Fran Shellenberger, "Treat Them Well and They'll Stick Around," *Legal Management* (September/October 1990): 21–22. **80.** Linda Marks and Karen Ringuette, "New Ways to Attract and Retain Valuable Employees," *Legal Management* (September/October 1989: 18. **81.** Mary Ann Von Glinow, *The New Professionals: Managing Today's High-Tech Employees* (Cambridge, Mass.: Ballinger, 1988): 54. **82.** Raymond L. Hilget and Theo Haimann, *Supervision: Concepts and Practices of Management,* 3d ed. (Cincinnati: South-Western Publishing Company, 1991): 338–42. **83.** Jan P. Muczyk, Eleanor Brantley Schwartz, and Ephraim Smith, *Principles of Supervision: First- and Second-Level Management* (Columbus, Ohio: Charles E. Merrill Publishing, 1984): 200–203. **84.** DePree, *Leadership Is an Art*: 110–11. **85.** Wenke Brandes, "Building Blocks for a Strong Team," *Legal Management* (September/October 1990: 32–34. **86.** Brandes, "Building Blocks for a Strong Team": 32–34. **87.** William J. Heisler, W. David Jones, and Phillip O. Benham, Jr., *Managing Human Resource Issues: Confronting Challenges and Choosing Options* (San Francisco: Jossey-Bass, 1988): 23; 167–72.

Chapter 8

1. Tom Peters and Robert Waterman, Jr., *In Search of Excellence* (New York: Harper & Row, 1982): 239. **2.** Tom Peters, *Thriving on Chaos: Handbook for a Management*

Revolution (New York: Alfred A. Knopf, 1987): 382. **3.** Joe Schwartz and Susan Krafft, "Managing Consumer Diversity: The 1991 American Demographics Conference," *American Demographics* 13 (August 1991): 22–28. **4.** Joseph H. Boyett and Henry P. Conn, *Workplace 2000: The Revolution Reshaping American Business* (New York: Dutton, 1991). **5.** Norma Fritz, "Information Technology and the Changing Workplace: An Interview with Shoshana Zuboff," *Personnel* (June 1989): 26. **6.** John Naisbitt, *Megatrends* (New York: Warner Books, 1982): 250. **7.** Raymond L. Hilget and Theo Haimann, *Supervision: Concepts and Practices of Management*, 3d ed. (Cincinnati: South-Western Publishing Company, 1991): 9. **8.** Naisbitt, *Megatrends*. **9.** Hilget and Haimann, *Supervision: Concepts and Practices of Management*, 3d ed.: 12. **10.** Hilget and Haimann, *Supervision*: 3. **11.** Joe D. Batten, *Tough-Minded Leadership* (New York: AMACOM, 1989): 1–2. **12.** Hilget and Haimann, *Supervision*: 12. **13.** Hilget and Haimann, *Supervision*: 15. **14.** Joseph Raelin, "The Basis for the Professional's Resistance to Managerial Control," *Human Resource Management* 24, no. 2 (Summer 1985): 147–76. **15.** Joseph Raelin, "The Basis for the Professional's Resistance to Managerial Control": 147–76. **16.** Richard W. Scott, "Professionals in Bureaucracies—Areas of Conflict," in *Professionalization*, ed. Howard Vollmer and Donald Mills (Englewood Cliffs, N.J.: Prentice-Hall, 1966): 265–75. **17.** Bob Bookman, "Instruction Guidelines: Getting Associates' Best Effort," *National Law Journal* (28 October 1991): 19. **18.** Bob Bookman, "Instruction Guidelines: Getting Associates' Best Effort": 19. **19.** Mary Ann Von Glinow, *The New Professionals* (Cambridge, Mass.: Ballinger, 1988): 3–4. **20.** See William P. Statsky, *Introduction to Paralegalism: Perspectives, Problems, and Skills*, 3d ed. (St. Paul, Minn.: West Publishing Company, 1986): 184–85, for a comprehensive and useful "Checklist for Paralegal Supervision." **21.** Stephen E. Catt and Donald S. Miller, *Supervision: Working with People*, 2d ed. (Homewood, Ill.: Irwin, 1991): 14–16. **22.** Henry Mintzberg, *The Nature of Managerial Work* (New York: Harper & Row: 1977). **23.** "William Ouchi on Trust," *Training and Development Journal* 36 (December 1982): 71. **24.** J. Clifton Williams and George P. Huber, *Human Behavior in Organizations*, 3d ed. (Cincinnati: South-Western Publishing, 1986): 361. **25.** Rensis Likert, *New Patterns of Management* (New York: McGraw-Hill, 1967): 13–46. **26.** Thomas J. Von der Embse, *Supervision: Managerial Skills for a New Era* (New York: Macmillan, 1987): 331. **27.** William R. Tracey, *Leadership Skills: Standout Performance for Human Resource Managers* (New York: AMACOM, 1990): 264. **28.** Lynn McFarlane Shore and Arvid J. Bloom, "Developing Employees through Coaching and Career Management," *Personnel* 63 (August 1986): 36. **29.** Based on Richard D. Concilio, "Will Coaching Pay Off?" *Management Solutions* 31 (September 1986): 19–21. **30.** Kenneth Blanchard and Spencer Johnson, *The One Minute Manager* (New York: William Morrow & Company, 1982). **31.** H. H. Meyer, E. Kay, and J. R. P. French, Jr., "Split Roles in Performance Appraisal," *Harvard Business Review* 43 (1965): 123–29. **32.** Ron Zemke, "Is Performance Appraisal a Paper Tiger?" *Training* 22 (December 1985): 24. **33.** Pat Duran, "Survey on Administration of Legal Assistants," *AT Issue* (San Francisco Association of Legal Administrators: April 1990): 13. **34.** "Privacy: The Employee Relations Issue of the Decade," *Legal Administrator* (Winter 1986): 12–13. **35.** Employee Performance Review (Vernon Hills, Ill.: Association of Legal Administrators, 1991). **36.** Employee Performance Review (Vernon Hills, Ill.: Association of Legal Administrators, 1991). **37.** George S. Odiorne, *Strategic Management of Human Resources* (San Francisco: Jossey-Bass, 1984): 205. **38.** Banning K. Lary, "Why Corporations Can't Lock the Rascals Out," *Management Review* (October 1989): 51. **39.** David N. Campbell, R. L. Fleming, and Richard C. Grote, "Discipline without Punishment—At Last," *Harvard Business Review* (July/August 1985): 162–78. **40.** This rule is generally attributed to Douglas McGregor; the work in this section is based on Hilget and Haimann, *Supervision: Concepts and Practices of Management*: 385–88. **41.** Stephen E. Catt and Donald S. Miller, *Supervision: Working with People*, 2d ed. (Homewood, Ill.: Irwin, 1991): 436. **42.** Tracey, *Leadership Skills: Standout Performance for Human Resource Managers*: 190. **43.** "Wrongful Discharge under Massachusetts Law," brochure published by The Cambridge Institute (Cambridge, Mass.: 1988). **44.** Suzanne Alexander, "Firms Get Plenty of Practice at Layoffs, But They Often Bungle the Process," *Wall Street Journal* (14 October 1991): B1. **45.** Tracey, *Leadership Skills*: 192–93. **46.** Robert L. Mathis and John H. Jackson, *Personnel/Human Resource Management*, 6th ed. (St. Paul, Minn.: West Publishing Company, 1991): 466–67.

Chapter 9

1. Warren Bennis and Burt Nanus, *Leaders: The Strategies for Taking Charge* (New York: Harper & Row, 1985): 18. **2.** Irwin Federman, president and CEO of Monolithic Memories, Calif., as quoted in Bennis and Nanus, *Leaders: The Strategies for Taking Charge:* 62–64. **3.** "A Psalm of Life," *The Complete Poetical Works of Henry Wadsworth Longfellow* (Boston: Houghton, Mifflin and Company, 1922). **4.** John W. Gardner, *On Leadership* (New York: The Free Press, 1990): xi. **5.** Warren Bennis, *Why Leaders Can't Lead: The Unconscious Conspiracy Continues* (San Francisco: Jossey-Bass Publishers, 1989). **6.** Abraham Zaleznik, "The Leadership Gap," *The Academy of Management Executive* 4, no. 1 (February 1990): 7–22. **7.** John P. Kotter, *The Leadership Factor* (New York: The Free Press, 1988): 15. **8.** James MacGregor Burns, *Leadership* (New York: Harper & Row, 1979). **9.** Bennis, *Why Leaders Can't Lead*: 142. **10.** Bennis, *Why Leaders Can't Lead:* 116–20. **11.** Kotter, *The Leadership Factor*: 20. **12.** Daniel Katz and Robert L.

Kahn, *The Social Psychology of Organizations,* 2d ed. (New York: John Wiley & Sons, 1978): 530–35. **13.** Kotter, *The Leadership Factor:* 15. **14.** Burns, *Leadership:* 2–5. **15.** Bennis and Nanus, *Leaders:* 4. **16.** Burns, *Leadership:* 2–5. **17.** Kotter, *The Leadership Factor:* 29. **18.** John Naisbitt and Patricia Aburdene, *Re-Inventing the Corporation* (New York: Warner Books, 1985): 20–21. **19.** Kotter, *The Leadership Factor:* 20. **20.** John P. Kotter, "What Leaders Really Do," *Harvard Business Review* 68 (May/June 1990): 103. **21.** Kotter, "What Leaders Really Do": 104. **22.** Bennis and Nanus, *Leaders:* 21. **23.** Abraham Zaleznik, "Managers and Leaders: Are They Different?" *Harvard Business Review* (May/June 1977): 67–78. **24.** Zaleznik, "The Leadership Gap": 12–13. **25.** Peter L. Wright and David S. Taylor, *Improving Leadership Performance: A Practical New Approach to Leadership* (Englewood Cliffs, N.J.: Prentice-Hall International, 1984): 2. **26.** Bennis and Nanus, *Leaders:* 107. **27.** Zaleznik, "Managers and Leaders: Are They Different?": 131. **28.** Abraham Zaleznik, "The Leadership Gap": 7–8. **29.** Zaleznik, "The Leadership Gap": 7–8. **30.** Zaleznik, "Managers and Leaders: Are They Different?": 131. **31.** Bennis and Nanus, *Leaders.* **32.** Bennis and Nanus, *Leaders:* 27–33; 87–109. **33.** Bennis and Nanus, *Leaders:* 33–42; 110–51. **34.** Bennis and Nanus, *Leaders:* 43–55; 152–86. **35.** Bennis and Nanus, *Leaders:* 55–86; 187–214. **36.** Gary A. Yukl, *Leadership in Organizations* (Englewood Cliffs, N.J.: Prentice-Hall, 1989): 29. **37.** Bennis and Nanus, *Leaders:* 64–65. **38.** Yukl, *Leadership in Organizations:* 29. **39.** Gary A. Yukl, "Managerial Leadership: A Review of Theory and Research," *Journal of Management* 15, no. 2 (1989): 260. **40.** Shelley A. Kirkpatrick and Edwin A. Locke, "Leadership: Do Traits Matter?" *Academy of Management Executive* 5, no. 2 (May 1991): 48–60. **41.** Edwin Ghiselli, *Explorations in Management Talent* (Santa Monica, Calif.: Goodyear Publishing Company, 1971). **42.** Ralph M. Stogdill, "Personal Factors Associated with Leadership: A Survey of the Literature," *Journal of Applied Psychology* 25 (1974): 35–71; and Ralph M. Stogdill, *Handbook of Leadership: A Survey of Theory and Research* (New York: The Free Press, 1974). **43.** Kirkpatrick and Locke, "Leadership: Do Traits Matter?": 48–60. **44.** Kotter, *The Leadership Factor:* 29. **45.** Kurt Lewin, R. Lippitt, and R. K. White, "Patterns of Aggressive Behavior in Experimentally Created Social Climates," *Journal of Social Psychology* 10 (1939): 271–301. **46.** John K. Hemphill, *Leader Behavior Descriptions* (Ohio State Leadership Studies Staff Report, 1950); and Ralph M. Stogdill and Alvin E. Coons, eds., *Leader Behavior: Its Description and Measurement,* Research Monograph no. 88 (Columbus: Ohio State University Bureau of Research, 1957). **47.** Rensis Likert, *New Patterns of Management* (New York: McGraw-Hill, 1961). **48.** Likert, *New Patterns of Management.* **49.** Robert R. Blake and Jane S. Mouton, *The New Managerial Grid®* (Houston: Gulf Publishing Company, 1978); and Mouton and Blake, "How to Choose a Leadership Style," *Training and Development Journal* 36, no. 2 (February 1982): 38–45. **50.** Paul Hersey and Kenneth H. Blanchard, "Life Cycle Theory of Leadership," *Training and Development Journal* (May 1969): 26–34. **51.** Robert Tannenbaum and Warren H. Schmidt, "How To Choose a Leadership Pattern," *Harvard Business Review* (May/June 1973): 162–180. **52.** Much of the material in this section is based on Gary A. Yukl, "Managerial Leadership: A Review of Theory and Research, *Journal of Management* 15, no. 2 (1989): 269–79. **53.** Max Weber, *The Theory of Economic and Social Organizations,* trans. A. M. Anderson and T. Parsons (New York: The Free Press, 1947): 358–59; originally published 1921. **54.** Robert J. House, "A 1976 Theory of Charismatic Leadership," in *Leadership: The Cutting Edge,* ed. J. G. Hunt and L. L. Larson (Carbondale, Ill.: Southern Illinois University Press, 1977): 189–207. **55.** Weber, *The Theory of Economic and Social Organizations*: 358–59. **56.** Bernard M. Bass, *Leadership and Performance beyond Expectations* (New York: The Free Press, 1985). **57.** Burns, *Leadership.* **58.** Noel M. Tichy and David O. Ulrich, "The Leadership Challenge—A Call for the Transformational Leader, *Sloan Management Review* (Fall 1984): 59–68. **59.** Bass, *Leadership and Performance beyond Expectations:* 31. **60.** Alfred Bandura, "Self-Efficacy: Toward a Unifying Theory of Behavioral Change," *Psychological Review* 84, no. 2 (1977): 191–215; and Alfred Bandura, *Social Foundations of Thought and Action: A Social Cognitive View* (Englewood Cliffs, N.J., Prentice-Hall, 1986). **61.** Tichy and Ulrich, "The Leadership Challenge—A Call for the Transformational Leader,": 59–68. **62.** Abraham Zaleznik, "The Leadership Gap": 12–13; and Bennis and Nanus, *Leaders:* 8. **63.** Charles C. Manz and Henry P. Simms, Jr., *Super Leadership: Leading Others to Lead Themselves* (New York: Prentice-Hall Press, 1989). **64.** Peter Drucker, "Leadership: More Doing than Dash," *Wall Street Journal* (6 January 1988): 24. **65.** Bennis and Nanus, *Leaders:* 222.

Chapter 10

1. Max DePree, *Leadership Is an Art* (New York: Doubleday, 1989). **2.** M. Scott Myers, "Conditions for Manager Motivation," *Harvard Business Review* (November/December 1991): 159; originally published in January/February 1966 issue. **3.** Rosabeth Moss Kanter, "The New Managerial Work," *Harvard Business Review* (November/December 1989): 92. **4.** Max DePree, *Leadership Is an Art*: 27–30. **5.** Herbert A. Simon, *Administrative Behavior,* 2d ed. (New York: Macmillan Publishing Company, 1957): 110. **6.** Robert H. Schaffer, "Retrospective Commentary: Managers Must Establish High Performance Expectations and Demand Results," *Harvard Business Review* (March/April 1991): 146. **7.** Rosabeth Moss Kanter and Barry A. Stein, "Making a Life at the Bottom," in *Life in Organizations: Workplaces as People Experience Them,* ed. Rosabeth Moss Kanter and Barry A. Stein (New York: Basic Books, 1979): 183. **8.** Kanter and Stein, "Making a Life at the Bottom": 181. **9.** Richard M. Steers and Susan R. Rhodes, "Major Influences on Employee Attendance: A Process Model," *Journal of Applied Psychology* 63 (1978): 391–407. **10.** Richard M. Steers and Richard Mowday, "A Model of Voluntary Employee Turnover," in *Research on Organizational Behavior 3*, ed. L. L. Cummings and B. M. Staw (Greenwich, Conn.: JAI Press, 1981). **11.** Kanter and Stein, "Making a Life at the Bottom": 183. **12.** Robert A. Ullrich, *Motivation Methods That Work: How to Increase the Productivity of Every Employee* (Englewood Cliffs, N.J.: Prentice-Hall, 1981): 34–47. **13.** Ullrich, *Motivation Methods That Work: How to Increase the Productivity of Every Employee:* 33; 34–47. **14.** Ullrich, *Motivation Methods That Work:* 33. **15.** Terence R. Mitchell, "Motivation: New Directions for Theory, Research, and Practice," *Academy of Management Review* 7 (April 1982): 83. **16.** Victor H. Vroom, *Work and Motivation* (New York: John Wiley & Sons, 1964). **17.** Daniel Katz and Robert L. Kahn, *The Social Psychology of Organizations* (New York: John Wiley & Sons, 1966); and Thomas S. Bateman and D. Organ, "Job Satisfaction and the Good Soldier: The Relationship between Affect and Employee 'Citizenship,'" *Academy of Management Journal* 26 (1983): 587–95. **18.** Kanter, "The New Managerial Work": 92. **19.** Kurt Lewin, *Field Theory in Social Science* (New York: Harper & Bros., 1951). **20.** C. S. Carver and M. F. Scheier, *Perspectives on Personality* (Boston: Allyn and Bacon, Inc., 1988). **21.** J. B. Rotter, "Generalized Expectancies for Internal and External Reinforcement," *Psychological Monographs* 80, no. 609 (1975). **22.** T. W. Adorno, E. Frenkle-Brunswik, D. J. Levinson, and R. N. Sanford, *The Authoritarian Personality* (New York: Harper & Row, 1950). **23.** Milton Rokeach, *The Open and Closed Mind* (New York: Basic Books, 1960); and J. Garvey, "Deeper Than Emotions: The Guiding Role of Dogma," *Commonweal* 112 (21 June 1985): 357–58. **24.** F. Geis and T. H. Moon, "Machiavellianism and Deception," *Journal of Personality and Social Psychology* 41 (1981): 766–75. **25.** L. V. Gordon, "Measurement of Bureaucratic Orientation," *Personnel Psychology* 23 (1970): 1–11. **26.** Carl C. Rogers, *On Becoming a Person* (Boston: Houghton Mifflin, 1961). **27.** David J. Cherrington, *Organizational Behavior: The Management of Organizational and Individual Performance* (Boston: Allyn and Bacon, 1989): 109. **28.** Rosabeth Moss Kanter, *Men and Women of the Corporation* (New York: Basic Books, 1977): 291. **29.** Mihaly Csikszentmihalyi, *Flow: The Psychology of Optimal Experience* (New York: Harper & Row, 1990): 18. **30.** Randall B. Dunham and Jon L. Pierce, *Management* (Glenview, Ill.: Scott, Foresman and Company, 1989): 452. **31.** E. Spranger, *Types of Men* (Halle, Germany: Max Niemeyer Verlag, 1928), as quoted in V. S. Flowers et al., *Managerial Values for Working* (New York: American Management Associations, 1975): 11. **32.** David J. Cherrington, *Organizational Behavior: The Management of Individual and Organizational Performance:* 297. **33.** David J. Cherrington, *The Work Ethic: Working Values and Values That Work* (New York: AMACOM, 1980): 51. **34.** John Locke, "An Essay Concerning Human Understanding," Book II (1689), Chapters 7, 10, and 11 in *The Great Books*, no. 35; and John Stuart Mill, "On Liberty" (1859) and "Utilitarianism" (1863), in *The Great Books*, no. 43 (Chicago: Encyclopaedia Britannica, 1952). **35.** Robert B. Holt, *Freud Reappraised: A Fresh Look at Psychoanalytic Theory* (New York: Guilford Press, 1989); William McDougall, *An Introduction to Social Psychology*, 13th ed. (Boston: J. W. Luce & Co., 1918). **36.** Camille B. Wortman and Elizabeth F. Loftus, *Psychology* (New York: Alfred A. Knopf, 1981): 152–54. **37.** B. F. Skinner, *Science and Human Behavior* (New York: The Free Press, 1953); and B. F. Skinner, *Contingencies of Reinforcement* (New York: Appleton-Century-Crofts, 1969). **38.** John P. Campbell and Robert D. Pritchard, "Motivation Theory in Industrial and Organizational Psychology," in *Handbook of Industrial and Organizational Psychology*, ed. M. P. Dunnette (Chicago: Rand McNally, 1976): 68–69; 97. **39.** Wortman and Loftus, *Psychology:* 146–52. **40.** Henry A. Murray, *An Introduction to Motivation* (Princeton, N.J.: Oxford University Press, 1938). **41.** Wortman and Loftus, *Psychology:* 430. **42.** Abraham H. Maslow, "A Theory of Human Motivation," *Psychological Review* 50 (1943): 394–95. © 1943 by the American Psychological Association. **43.** Abraham H. Maslow, "A Theory of Human Motivation": 394–95. **44.** Maslow, "A Theory of Human Motivation": 394–95. **45.** Maslow, "A Theory of Human Motivation": 394–95. **46.** Maslow, "A Theory of Human Motivation": 394–95. **47.** Maslow, "A Theory of Human Motivation": 394–95. **48.** Maslow, "A Theory of Human Motivation": 370. **49.** Maslow, "A Theory of Human Motivation": 394–95. **50.** Campbell and Pritchard, "Motivation Theory in Industrial and Organizational Psychology": 97–98. **51.** David McClelland, *Power: The Inner Experience* (New York: Irvington, 1975). **52.** J. W. Atkinson and A. C. Raphelson, "Individual Differences in Motivation and Behavior in Particular Situations," *Journal of Personality* 24 (1956): 349–63; and R. C. DeCharms, "Affiliation Motives and Productivity in Small Groups. *Journal of Abnormal Psychology* 55 (1957): 222–76. **53.** David McClelland, *Power: The Inner Experience.* **54.** Frederick Herzberg, *Work and the Nature of Man* (Cleveland, Ohio: World, 1966). **55.** George S. Odiorne, "When Money Loses Its Motivational Power, What Else Can You Use to Motivate Your People?" *The George Odiorne Letter* (21 March 1986): 1–3; E. A. Locke, D. B. Feren, V. M. McCaleb, K. N. Shaw, and A. T. Denney, "The Relative Effectiveness of Form Methods of Motivating Employee Performance," in *Changes in Working Life*, ed. K. D. Duncan, M. M. Gruneberg, and D. Wallis (New York: John Wiley & Sons, 1980): 363–88. **56.** Campbell and Pritchard, "Motivation Theory in Industrial and Organizational Psychology": 74. **57.** J. Stacy Adams, "Inequity in Social Exchange," in *Advances in Experimental Social Psychology*, vol. 2 (New York: Academic

Press, 1965): 267–99. **58.** George C. Homans, *Social Behavior: Its Elementary Forms* (New York: Harcourt, Brace & World, 1961). **59.** Campbell and Pritchard, "Motivation Theory in Industrial and Organizational Psychology": 104–9. **60.** E. C. Tolman, *Purposive Behavior in Animals and Men* (New York: Appleton-Century-Crofts, 1932); and Victor H. Vroom, *Work and Motivation* (New York: John Wiley & Sons, 1964). **61.** Campbell and Pritchard, "Motivation Theory in Industrial and Organizational Psychology": 74–75. **62.** Campbell and Pritchard, "Motivation Theory in Industrial and Organizational Psychology": 110–12. **63.** Kanter, "The New Managerial Work": 85. **64.** Kanter, "The New Managerial Work": 91–92. **65.** K. Kim Fisher, "Managing in the High Commitment Workplace," *Organizational Dynamics* (Winter 1989): 33. **66.** Tom Peters and Nancy Austin, *A Passion for Excellence* (New York: Warner Books, 1985): 382. **67.** Edgar H. Schein, *Organizational Psychology*, 2d ed. (Englewood Cliffs, N.J.: Prentice-Hall, 1972): 79. **68.** Peters and Austin, *A Passion for Excellence*: 308. **69.** Peters and Austin, *A Passion for Excellence*: 382. **70.** Kanter, "The New Managerial Work": 92. **71.** For additional material on goal setting, see George Morrissey, *Getting Your Act Together* (New York: John Wiley & Sons, 1980): Chapter 7.

Chapter 11

1. Harold J. Leavitt, Louis R. Pondy, and David M. Boje, *Readings in Managerial Psychology*, 4th ed. (Chicago: The University of Chicago Press, 1989): 408. **2.** Larry Hirschhorn, "Professionals, Authority, and Group Life: A Case Study of a Law Firm," *Human Resource Management* 28, no. 2 (Summer 1989): 250–52. **3.** Edgar F. Huse and Thomas G. Cummings, *Organization Development and Change*, 3d ed. (St. Paul: West, 1985). **4.** J. Richard Hackman, Edward E. Lawler III, and Lyman W. Porter, eds., *Perspectives on Behavior in Organizations* (New York: McGraw-Hill, 1977): 322. **5.** Donald K. Carew, Eunice Parisi-Carew, and Kenneth H. Blanchard, "Group Development and Situational Leadership," *Training and Development Journal* (June 1986): 46. **6.** Connie J. G. Gersick, "Time and Transition in Work Teams: Toward a New Model of Group Development," *Academy of Management Journal* (March 1988): 9–41. **7.** D. L. Forsyth, *An Introduction to Group Dynamics* (Monterey, Calif.: Brooks/Cole, 1983). **8.** J. A. Pearce II and E. C. Ravlin, "The Design and Activation of Self-Regulating Work Groups," *Human Relations* 40 (1987): 751–82. **9.** William E. Scott, Jr., and Phillip M. Podsakoff, *Behavioral Principles in the Practice of Management* (New York: John Wiley & Sons, 1985): Chapter 7. **10.** Based on Leon Festinger, Stanley Schachter, and Kurt Back, *Social Pressures in Informal Groups* (New York: Harper & Brothers, 1950): 153–63. **11.** Stanley Schachter, *The Psychology of Affiliation: Experimental Studies of the Sources of Gregariousness* (Stanford, Calif.: Stanford University Press, 1959). **12.** David J. Cherrington, *Organizational Behavior: The Management of Individual and Organizational Performance* (Boston: Allyn and Bacon, 1989): 389. **13.** Marvin E. Shaw, *Group Dynamics: The Psychology of Small Group Behavior* (New York: McGraw-Hill, 1981). **14.** Colleen Cooper and Mary Ploor, "The Challenges That Make or Break a Group," *Training and Development Journal* (April 1986): 31–33. **15.** S. Long, "Early Integration in Groups: 'A Group to Join and a Group to Create,' " *Human Relations* 37 (1977): 419–27. **16.** Carew, Parisi-Carew, and Blanchard, "Group Development and Situational Leadership": 46. **17.** B. W. Tuckman and M. A. Jensen, "Stages of Small Group Development Revisited," *Group and Organization Studies* 2 (1977): 419–27; Bruce W. Tuckman, "Developmental Sequences in Small Groups," *Psychological Bulletin* (June 1965): 384–99; and M. F. Maples, "Group Development: Extending Tuckman's Theories," *Journal for Specialists in Group Work* (Fall 1988): 17–23. **18.** Kenwyn Smith and David N. Berg, *Paradoxes of Group Life: Understanding Conflict, Paralysis, and Movement in Group Dynamics* (San Francisco: Jossey-Bass, 1987). **19.** Marion McCollum, "Group Formation: Boundaries, Leadership, and Culture," in *Groups in Context: A New Perspective on Group Dynamics*, ed. Jonathon Gillette and Marion McCollum (Reading, Mass.: Addison-Wesley, Inc., 1990): 40–41. **20.** Dalmar Fisher, *Communication in Organizations*, 2d ed. (St. Paul, Minn.: West Publishing Co., 1993): 308–9. **21.** Leavitt, "Suppose We Took Groups Seriously," in *Readings in Managerial Psychology*, 4th ed.: 412–13. **22.** Douglas McGregor, *The Human Side of Enterprise* (New York: McGraw-Hill, 1960): 232–40. **23.** Dorwin Cartwright and Alvin Zander, *Group Dynamics: Research and Theory*, 3d ed. (New York: Harper & Row, 1968): 485–502. **24.** Richard L. Abel, *American Lawyers* (New York: Oxford University Press, 1989): 183; and Dan Margolies, "Hyatt Legal Offices Severing Ties, Will Be Hyatt No More," *Kansas City Business Journal* (2 October 1992): 1. **25.** E. J. Thomas and C. F. Fink, "Effects of Group Size," in *Readings in Organizational Behavior and Human Performance*, ed. L. L. Cummings and W. E. Scott, (Homewood, Ill.: Richard D. Irwin, 1969). **26.** Albert Shapero, *Managing Professional People: Understanding Creative Performance* (New York: The Free Press, 1985). **27.** Robert L. Kahn et al., *Organizational Stress: Studies in Role Conflict and Ambiguity* (New York: John Wiley & Sons, 1964): 11–12. **28.** Kenneth D. Benne and Paul Sheats, "Functional Roles of Group Members," *Journal of Social Issues* 4: 41–49. **29.** Daniel C. Feldman, "The Development and Enforcement of Group Norms," *Academy of Management Review* 9 (1984): 47–53. **30.** Based in part on Feldman, "The Development and Enforcement of Group Norms,": 47–53. **31.** Karen Berger Morello, *The Invisible Bar: The Woman Lawyer in America, 1638 to the Present* (New York: Random House, 1986): 186–88. **32.** Letitia Baldridge, *Letitia Baldridge's Complete Guide to Executive Manners* (New York: Rawson Associates, 1985): 3. **33.** Jerald Greenberg, "Equity, Equality, and the Protestant Ethic: Allocating Rewards Following Fair and Unfair Competition," *Journal of Experimental Social Psychology* 14 (1978): 217–26. **34.** Davis A. Nadler, J. Richard Hackman, and Edward E. Lawler III, *Managing Organizational Behavior* (Boston: Little, Brown, 1979); and Fisher, *Communication in Organizations,* 2d ed.: 318. **35.** Robert Zajonc, "Social Facilitation," *Science* 149 (1965): 269–74. **36.** Zajonc, "Social Facilitation": 269–74. **37.** B. Latane, K. Williams, and S. Harkins, "Many Hands Make Light the Work: The Causes and Consequences of Social Loafing," *Journal of Personality and Social Psychology* 37 (1979): 822–32. **38.** Chris Argyris, *Overcoming Organizational Defenses: Facilitating Organizational Learning* (Boston: Allyn and Bacon, 1990): xi. **39.** Cartwright and Alvin, *Group Dynamics:* 147. **40.** David H. Maister, "The One-Firm Firm: What Makes It Successful?" *Sloan Management Review* (Fall 1985): 3–14. **41.** A. J. Lott and B. E. Lott, "Group Cohesiveness as Interpersonal Attraction: A Review of Relationships with Antecedent and Consequent Variables," *Psychological Bulletin* 64 (1965): 259–309. **42.** Maister, "The One-Firm Firm": 5. **43.** Maister, "The One-Firm Firm": 12. **44.** Maister, "The One-Firm Firm": 5. **45.** Noel M. Tichy, "An Analysis of Clique Formation and Structure in Organizations," *Administrative Science Quarterly* (June 1973): 194–208. **46.** A. Mazur, "A Cross-Species Comparison of Status in Small Established Groups," *American Sociological Review* 38, no. 5 (1973): 513–30. **47.** Maister, "The One-Firm Firm": 3–14. **48.** Jerry B. Harvey, "The Abilene Paradox: The Management of Agreement," reprint and commentaries in *Organizational Dynamics* (Summer 1988): 17–43. **49.** Lott and Lott, "Group Cohesiveness as Interpersonal Attraction": 259–309. **50.** Rosabeth Moss Kanter, "An Abilene Defense: Commentary One," *Organizational Dynamics* (Summer 1988): 37–40. **51.** Arthur Elliott Carlisle, "An Abilene Defense: Commentary Two," *Organizational Dynamics* (Summer 1988): 37–40. **52.** J. R. Hackman, "The Design of Work Teams," in *Handbook of Organizational Behavior,* ed. J. W. Lorsch (Englewood Cliffs, N.J.: Prentice-Hall, 1987): 315–42. **53.** George P. Odiorne, *How Managers Make Things Happen* (Englewood Cliffs, N.J.: Prentice-Hall, 1982). **54.** Odiorne, *How Managers Make Things Happen.* **55.** Cartwright and Zander, *Group Dynamics:* 486. **56.** Robert R. Blake, H. A. Shepard, and Jane Mouton, *Managing Intergroup Conflict in Industry* (Houston: Gulf Publishing Company, 1964). **57.** Abel, *American Lawyers:* 10. **58.** Abel, *American Lawyers:* 4. **59.** Abel, *American Lawyers:* 4. **60.** Phyllis Weiss Haserot, "A Guide to Weaving the Non-Lawyer Professional Into the Law Firm Fabric," *National Law Journal* (April 1990): 10–11. **61.** Haserot, "A Guide to Weaving the Non-Lawyer Professional Into the Law Firm Fabric": 11. **62.** Haserot, "A Guide to Weaving the Non-Lawyer Professional Into the Law Firm Fabric": 10. **63.** John A. Seiler, "Diagnosing Interdepartmental Conflict," *Harvard Business Review* (September/October 1963). **64.** Haserot, "A Guide to Weaving the Non-Lawyer Professional Into the Law Firm Fabric": 11. **65.** Rose D. Ors, "Effective Paralegal Use Cuts Costs," *National Law Journal* (20 April 1992): 30–31. **66.** Ors, "Effective Paralegal Use Cuts Costs": 30–31. **67.** Abel, *American Lawyers:* 197. **68.** *Occupational Outlook Handbook,* 1992–93 Edition, U.S. Department of Labor, Bureau of Labor Statistics (May 1992): 11–12; 214–15. **69.** William P. Statsky, *Introduction to Paralegalism: Perspectives, Problems, and Skills,* 3d ed. (St. Paul, Minn.: West Publishing Co., 1986): 166. **70.** Abel, *American Lawyers:* 197.

Chapter 12

1. Antoine de Saint-Exupery, *The Little Prince,* trans. Katherine Wood (New York: Harcourt, Brace & World, 1943): 15–16. **2.** Tom Peters, *Thriving on Chaos* (New York: Alfred A. Knopf, 1988): 436. **3.** Ron Suskind, "A Lady Lawyer from Laramie Writes a Landmark Letter," *Wall Street Journal* (6 September 1990): A1–A8. **4.** Rorie Sherman, "Obscure, Opaque, Ungrammatical, Dull, Boring," *National Law Journal* (18 September 1989). **5.** Maya Angelou, interview on "Fresh Air," National Public Radio (13 July 1990). **6.** H. Sigband, *Communication for Management* (Glenview, Ill.: Scott, Foresman, 1969): 10. **7.** Chester I. Barnard, *The Functions of the Executive* (Cambridge, Mass.: Harvard University Press, 1938). **8.** J. J. Cribben, *Effective Managerial Leadership* (New York: American Management Association, 1972). **9.** Henry Mintzberg, *The Nature of Managerial Work* (New York: Harper & Row, 1973): 72. **10.** J. E. Baird, *The Dynamics of Organizational Communication* (New York: Harper & Row, 1977). **11.** Clark Caskey, "The Vision in Supervision," *Supervision* (August 1985): 3. **12.** Stephen P. Gallagher, "The New Breed of Law Practice," *Law Office Economics and Management* (1989): 175. **13.** Rosabeth Moss Kanter, *The Change Masters: Innovation for Productivity in the American Corporation* (New York: Simon & Schuster, 1983): 75–76. **14.** H. D. Lasswell, *Power and Personality* (New York: W. D. Norton, 1948): 37–51. **15.** Claude Shannon and Warren Weaver, *The Mathematical Theory of Communication* (Urbana: University of Illinois Press, 1948); Wilbur Schramm, "How Communication Works," in *The Process and Effects of Mass Communication,* ed. Wilbur Schramm (Urbana: University of Illinois Press, 1953): 3–26; and Lyman W. Porter and Karleen H. Roberts, "Communication," in *Handbook of Industrial and Organizational Psychology,* ed. Marvin D. Dunnette (Skokie, Illinois: Rand McNally, 1976). **16.** Robert H. Lengel and Richard L. Daft, "The Selection of Communication Media as an Executive Skill," *Academy of Management Executive* (August 1988): 225–32. **17.** Alfred, Lord Tennyson, "Ulysses" (1842) 1:6, in *The Poems of Tennyson,* 2d ed., ed. Christopher Ricks (Berkeley, Calif.: University of California Press, 1987). **18.** Philip V. Lewis, *Organizational Communications,* 3d ed. (New York: Wiley, 1987): Chapter 5. **19.** Phillip L. Hunsaker, "There's No Proxy for Proxemics," *Business* (March/April 1980): 41–48. **20.** Edward T. Hall, *The Hidden Di-*

mension (Garden City, N.Y.: Doubleday, 1986). **21.** R. H. Birdwhistle, *Kinesics and Context* (Philadelphia: University of Pennsylvania Press, 1970). **22.** Albert Mehrabian, *Silent Messages* (Belmont, Calif.: Wadsworth Press, 1971). **23.** Paul Elkman and W. V. Friesen, *Unmasking the Face* (Englewood Cliffs, N.J.: Prentice-Hall, 1975). **24.** A. Mehrabian, ''Communication without Words,'' *Psychology Today* (1968): 52–55. **25.** G. Neirenberg and H. Caler, *How to Read a Person Like a Book* (New York: Pocket Books, 1973). **26.** John Keltner, *Interpersonal Speech—Communication* (Belmont, Calif.: Wadsworth Press, 1970). **27.** Aristotle, *Rhetoric,* trans. W. Rhys Roberts (New York: Modern Library, 1954); and Annette N. Shelby, ''The Theoretical Base of Persuasion: A Critical Introduction,'' *Journal of Business Communication* 23 (Winter 1986): 5–29. **28.** The following material is based on David Cherrington, *Organizational Behavior* (Needham, Mass.: Allyn and Bacon, 1989): 569–72. **29.** S. Chaiken and A. H. Eagly, ''Communication Modality as a Determinant of Message Persuasiveness and Message Comprehensibility,'' *Journal of Personality and Social Psychology* 34 (1976): 605–14. **30.** N. Miller and D. Campbell, ''Recency and Primacy in Persuasion as a Function of the Timing of Speeches and Measurements,'' *Journal of Abnormal and Social Psychology* 59 (1959): 1–9. **31.** Roger Ailes with Jon Kraushar, ''How to Make an Audience Love You,'' *Working Woman* (November 1990): 119. **32.** S. I. Hayakawa, *Language in Thought and Action* (New York: Harcourt Brace Jovanovich, 1972); and J. C. Condon, *Semantics and Communication* (New York: Macmillan, 1966). **33.** Ailes and Kraushar, ''How to Make an Audience Love You'': 119. **34.** David A. Whetten and Kim S. Cameron, *Developing Management Skills* (Glenview, Ill.: Scott, Foresman, 1984): 472 **35.** Much of the following material is based on Whetten and Cameron, *Developing Management Skills*: 460–81. **36.** This next section is based on W. A. Mambert, *Effective Presentations* (New York: John Wiley & Sons, 1976). **37.** Whetten and Cameron, *Developing Management Skills*: 477. **38.** Mambert, *Effective Presentations.* **39.** Walter Kiechel III, ''Learn How to Listen,'' *Fortune* (17 August 1987): 107–8. **40.** R. Bolton, *People Skills* (Englewood Cliffs, N.J.: Prentice-Hall, 1979). **41.** J. Sharma, ''Organizational Communications: A Linking Process,'' *Personnel Administrator* 24, no. 7 (1979): 35–43. **42.** R. W. Pace, *Organizational Development: Foundations for Human Resource Development* (Englewood Cliffs, N.J.: Prentice-Hall, 1983). **43.** Pace, *Organizational Development.* **44.** Eugene Walton, ''How Efficient Is the Grapevine?'' *Personnel* (March/April 1961): 45–49. **45.** Keith Davis and John W. Newstrom, *Human Behavior at Work: Organizational Behavior*, 7th ed. (New York: McGraw-Hill, 1985). **46.** Donald B. Simmons, ''The Nature of the Organizational Grapevine,'' *Supervisory Management* (November 1985): 39-42. **47.** Keith Davis, ''Cut Those Rumors Down to Size,'' *Supervisory Management* (June 1975): 2–7. **48.** Row Rowan, ''Where Did That Rumor Come From?'' *Fortune* (13 August 1979): 13. **49.** Walter Kiechel III, ''In Praise of Office Gossip,'' *Fortune* (19 August 1985): 253–56. **50.** Robert Maidment, ''Listening—The Overlooked and Underdeveloped Other Half of Talking,'' *Supervisory Management* (August 1985): 10. **51.** M. Snyder, ''The Self-Monitoring of Expressive Behavior,'' *Journal of Personality and Social Psychology* (1974): 526–37. **52.** S. I. Hayakawa, *The Use and Misuse of Language* (New York: Fawcett World Library, 1962): 229. **53.** K. Heilman, *Empathy: The Construct and Its Measurement* (Ann Arbor, Mich.: University Microfilms International, 1972). **54.** J. Clifton Williams, Andrew J. DuBrin, and Henry L. Sisk, *Management and Organization,* 5th ed. (Cincinnati: South-Western Publishing Company, 1985): 402. **55.** Much of the following material is based on Whetten and Cameron, *Developing Management Skills*: 460–81. **56.** Nancy Fredericks, ''The Last Word: Meetings,'' *Legal Management* (March/April 1990): 96. **57.** Based in part on D. R. Siebold, ''Making Meetings More Successful,'' *Journal of Business Communication* (Summer 1979): 3–20. **58.** Mark H. McCormack, *What They Don't Teach You at Harvard Business School* (New York: Bantam Books, 1984): 222. **59.** McCormack, *What They Don't Teach You at Harvard Business School:* 222. **60.** Based in part on George Huber, *Managerial Decision Making* (Glenview, Ill.: Scott, Foresman, 1980): 179–88. **61.** Fredericks, ''The Last Word: Meetings'': 94.

Chapter 13

1. Jane Pauley, interview by Deborah Norville on ''The Today Show'' (13 March 1990). **2.** H. C. Metcalf and L. Urwick, eds., *Dynamic Administration: The Collected Works of Mary Parker Follett* (New York: Harper & Brothers, 1941). **3.** Mihaly Csikszentmihalyi, *Flow: The Psychology of Optimal Experience* (New York: Harper & Row, 1990): 9. **4.** John Naisbitt and Patricia Aburdene, *Re-Inventing the Corporation,* (New York: Warner Books, 1985): 26. **5.** Csikszentmihalyi, *Flow: The Psychology of Optimal Experience:* 8–9. **6.** William M. Bulkeley, ''Technology, Economics and Ego Conspire to Make Software Difficult to Use,'' *The Wall Street Journal Reports: Technology* (20 May 1991): R7. **7.** Ronald W. Staudt and Wan Hwang, ''Firm Computer Use Is Increasing Steadily,'' *National Law Journal* (April 1990): 26. **8.** Joseph Stanislao and Bettie C. Stanislao, ''Dealing with Resistance to Change,'' *Business Horizons* (July/August 1983): 74–78. **9.** Jane A. Gibson and Richard M. Hodgetts, *Readings and Exercises in Organizational Behavior* (Orlando, Fla.: Academic Press, 1985): 228. **10.** Warren Bennis, *Why Leaders Can't Lead: The Unconscious Conspiracy Continues* (San Francisco: Jossey-Bass Publishers, 1989): 116–20, as quoted in Naisbitt and Aburdene, *Re-Inventing the Corporation:* 20–21. **11.** Stephen Labaton, ''The Law: A Difficult Year But With Potential,'' *New York Times* (12 November 1990): B6. **12.** Tom Peters, *Thriving on Chaos: Handbook for a Management Revolution* (New York: Alfred A. Knopf, 1988): 14–15.

13. Stanislao and Stanislao, "Dealing with Resistance to Change": 74–78. 14. G. Ray Funkhouser and Robert R. Rothberg, *The Pursuit of Growth: The Challenges, Opportunities, and Dangers of Managing and Investing in Today's Economy* (Redmond, Wash.: Tempus Books of Microsoft Press, 1987): 6–7. 15. "Philadelphia Law Firm Suffers Partner Defections," *Wall Street Journal* (1 February 1991): B2. 16. David Margolick, "Pink Slips for Law Firm Partners as Tradition Bows to Tough Times," *New York Times* (24 December 1990): A46. 17. Russell L. Ackoff, "The Circular Organization: An Update," *Academy of Management Executive* (February 1989): 11–16. 18. "Optimism Prevails at ICLE Conference," *Law Office Management & Administration Report* 90–9 (September 1990): 7–10. 19. "Optimism Prevails at ICLE Conference": 7–10. 20. Louise Lovelady, "Change Strategies and the Use of OD Consultants to Facilitate Change: Part II," *Leadership and Organizational Development Journal* 5, no. 4 (1984): 2–12. 21. Rensis Likert and Jane Gibson Likert, *New Ways of Managing Conflict* (New York: McGraw-Hill, 1976): 4. 22. J. Goldstein, "A Far-From-Equilibrium Systems Approach to Resistance to Change," *Organizational Dynamics* (Autumn 1988): 16–26. 23. Rosabeth Moss Kanter, "Managing the Human Side of Change," *Management Review* 74 (1985): 52–56. 24. Noel M. Tichy and David O. Ulrich, "The Leadership Challenge—A Call for the Transformational Leader," *Sloan Management Review* (Fall 1984): 59–68. 25. Based on John P. Kotter and Leonard A. Schlesinger, "Choosing Strategies for Change," *Harvard Business Review* (March/April 1979): 106–14. 26. Likert and Likert, *New Ways of Managing Conflict*: 7. 27. K. W. Thomas, "Conflict and Negotiation Processes in Organizations," in *Handbook of Industrial/Organizational Psychology,* 2d ed., ed. M. D. Dunnette (Palo Alto, Calif.: Consulting Psychologists Press, 1989). 28. K. W. Thomas and W. H. Schmidt, "A Survey of Managerial Interests with Respect to Conflict," *Academy of Management Journal* 10 (1976): 315–18. 29. Gordon L. Lippitt, "Managing Conflict in Today's Organizations," in *Readings and Exercises in Organizational Behavior,* ed. Jane W. Gibson and Richard M. Hodgetts (Orlando: Academic Press, 1985): 234. 30. Likert and Likert, *New Ways of Managing Conflict*: 6. 31. Robert A. Baron and Jerald Greenberg, *Behavior in Organizations,* 3d ed. (Needham Heights, Mass. Allyn and Bacon, 1990): 461–65. 32. Baron and Greenberg, *Behavior in Organizations:* 460–61. 33. Likert and Likert, *New Ways of Managing Conflict:* 157. 34. Thomas and Schmidt, "A Survey of Managerial Interests with Respect to Conflict": 315–18. 35. Likert and Likert, *New Ways of Managing Conflict:* 6. 36. David A. Whetten and Kim S. Cameron, *Developing Management Skills* (Glenview, Ill.: Scott, Foresman, 1984): 407–10. 37. Whetten and Cameron, *Developing Management Skills:* 408. 38. Whetten and Cameron, *Developing Management Skills:* 408. 39. D. G. Pruitt, J. M. Magenau, E. Konar-Goldband, and P. J. Carnevale, "Effects of Trust, Aspiration, and Gender on Negotiation Tactics," *Journal of Personality and Social Psychology* 38, no. 1 (1980): 9–22. 40. Leonard Greenhalgh, "SMR Forum: Managing Conflict," *Sloan Management Review* (Summer 1986): 45–51. 41. Likert and Likert, *New Ways of Managing Conflict:* 162–63. 42. D. A. Lax and J. K. Sebenius, *The Manager as Negotiator* (New York: The Free Press, 1986): Chapter 1. 43. M. Zetlin, "The Art of Negotiating," *Success* (June 1986): 33–39. 44. Greenhalgh, "SMR Forum: Managing Conflict: 49. 45. Likert and Likert, *New Ways of Managing Conflict:* 168. 46. K. Maney, "Don't Let Stress Get the Best of You," *USA Today* (16 June 1987): B7. 47. James L. Gibson, John M. Ivancevich, and James H. Donnelly, Jr., *Organizations: Behavior, Structures, Processes* (Homewood, Ill.: Irwin Publishers, 1991): 224. 48. Hans Selye, *Stress without Distress* (Philadelphia: J. B. Lippincott, 1974): 5; and H. Selye, *The Stress of Life,* rev. ed. (New York: McGraw-Hill, 1956, 1976). 49. K. Maney, "Don't Let Stress Get the Best of You": B7. 50. J. B. Shaw and J. H. Riskind, "Predicting Job Stress Using Data from the Position Analysis Questionnaire," *Journal of Applied Psychology* 68 (1983): 253–61. 51. Csikszentmihalyi, *Flow: The Psychology of Optimal Experience:* 161. 52. Csikszentmihalyi, *Flow:* 159. 53. Csikszentmihalyi, *Flow:* 160. 54. T. J. Newton and A. Keenan, "Role Stress Reexamined: An Investigation of Role Stress Predictors," *Organizational Behavior and Human Decision Processes* 40 (1987): 346–68. 55. J. E. McGrath, "Stress and Behavior in Organizations," in *Handbook of Industrial and Organizational Psychology,* ed. M. D. Dunnette (Palo Alto, Calif.: Consulting Psychologists Press, 1976). 56. Whetten and Cameron, *Developing Management Skills*: 94–95. 57. K. W. Thomas and W. H. Schmidt, "A Survey of Managerial Interests with Respect to Conflict": 315–18. 58. A. A. McClean, *Work Stress* (Reading, Mass.: Addison-Wesley, 1980). 59. T. H. Holmes and R. H. Rahe, "The Social Readjustment Rating Scale," *Journal of Psychosomatic Research* 11 (1967): 213–18. 60. T. H. Holmes and M. Masuda, "Life Change and Illness Susceptibility," in *Stressful Life Events: Their Nature and Effects,* ed. B. S. Dohrenwend and B. P. Dohrenwend (New York: John Wiley & Sons, 1974): 45–72. 61. R. S. Lazarus, A. Delongis, S. Folkman, and R. Gruen, "Stress and Adaptational Outcomes: The Problem of Confounded Measures," *American Psychologist* 40 (1985): 770–79. 62. Lazarus, Delongis, Folkman, and Gruen, "Stress and Adaptational Outcomes: The Problem of Confounded Measures": 770–79. 63. Andrew J. Dubrin, *Human Relations for Careers and Personal Success,* 2d ed. (Englewood Cliffs, N. J.: Prentice-Hall, 1988): 82. 64. C. Maslach, *Burnout: The Cost of Caring* (Englewood Cliffs, N. J.: Prentice-Hall, 1982). 65. H. J. Freudenberger, "The Staff Burnout Syndrome in Alternative Institutions," *Psychotherapy: Theory, Research, and Practice* 12, no. 1 (1975): 73–82. 66. David Margolick, "At the Bar/More Lawyers Are Less Happy at Their Work, a Survey Finds," *New York Times* (17 August 1990): B5. 67. Lawyers Have High Rate of

Mental-Health Woes," *Wall Street Journal* (30 November 1990): B1. **68.** Margolick, "At the Bar/ More Lawyers are Less Happy at Their Work, a Survey Finds": B5. **69.** Margolick, "At the Bar/ More Lawyers are Less Happy at Their Work, a Survey Finds": B5. **70.** Csikszentmihalyi, *Flow*: 160. **71.** Meyer Friedman and Ray H. Rosenman, *Treating Type A Behavior and Your Heart* (New York: Alfred A. Knopf, Inc., 1984); Karen A. Matthews, "Psychological Perspectives on the Type A Behavior Pattern," *Psychological Bulletin* 91 (1981): 293–323; Earl Ubell, "The Deadly Emotions," *Parade Magazine* (11 February 1990) 4–6; R. B. Williams, *The Trusting Heart: Great News About Type A Behavior* (New York: Times Books, 1989); Timothy W. Smith and Mary K. Pope, "Cynical Hostility as a Health Risk: Current Status and Future Directions," in *Type A Behavior,* ed. M. Strube (Newbury Park, Calif.: Sage, 1991); and Harriet E. Braiker, *The Type E Woman—How to Overcome the Stress of Being Everything to Everyone* (New York: Dodd, Mead, 1986). **72.** J. K. Weintraub and C. S. Carver, "Coping with Stress: Divergent Strategies of Optimists and Pessimists," *Journal of Personality and Social Psychology* 51 (1986): 1257–64. **73.** Suzanne C. Kosaba, "Conceptualization and Measurement of Personality in Job Stress Research," in *Occupational Stress: Issues and Developments in Research,* ed. Joseph J. Hurrell, Jr., Lawrence R. Murphy, Stephen L. Sauter, and Cary L. Cooper (New York, Taylor & Francis, 1988): 100–09. **74.** Csikszentmihalyi, *Flow:* 200. **75.** Daniel Goleman, "Hope Emerges as Key to Success in Life," *New York Times* (24 December 1991): C1, C7. **76.** J. E. Crandall, "Social Interest as a Moderator of Life Stress," *Journal of Personality and Social Psychology* 47 (1984): 164–74. **77.** P. A. Thoits, "Social Support as Coping Assistance," *Journal of Consulting and Clinical Psychology* (1986): 416–23. **78.** C. Schaefer, J. C. Coyne, and R. S. Lazarus, "The Health-Related Functions of Social Support," *Journal of Behavioral Medicine,* 4, no. 4 (1981): 381–406. **79.** B. A. Winstead, "Positive and Negative Forms of Social Support: Effects of Conversational Topics on Coping with Stress among Same-Sex Friends," *Journal of Experimental Social Psychology* 24 (1988): 182–93. **80.** M. Davis, E. R. Eshelman, and M. McKay, *The Relaxation and Stress Reduction Workbook* (Oakland, Calif.: New Harbinger Publications, 1982). **81.** D. Girdana and G. Everly, *Controlling Stress and Tension: A Holistic Approach* (Englewood Cliffs, N. J.: Prentice-Hall, 1979). **82.** Johnathan D. Brown and Judith M. Seigel, "Exercise as a Buffer of Life Stress: A Prospective Study of Adolescent Health," *Health Psychology* (Winter 1988): 341–53. **83.** Herbert Benson, *The Relaxation Response* (New York: William Morrow, 1975). **84.** Michael T. Matteson and John C. Ivancevich, "Industrial Stress Management Interventions: Evaluation of Techniques," *Journal of Managerial Psychology* (Summer 1987): 24–30; Herbert Benson, *The Relaxation Response;* and D. Kuna, "Meditation and Work," *Vocational Guidance Quarterly* (June 1975): 342–46.

85. R. S. Lazarus and S. Folkman, *Stress, Appraisal and Coping* (New York: Springer Publishing Company, 1984). **86.** Lowell Forte, "The Pressure Is On to Reduce Lawyer Stress Levels," *California Law Business* (2 April 1990): 16.

Chapter 14

1. Warren Wittreich, "Selling—A Prerequisite to Success As a Professional," in Aubrey Wilson, *The Marketing of Professional Services* (London: McGraw-Hill, 1972): 17. **2.** Ward Bower, *The Pennsylvania Lawyer* (January 1990), as quoted in *Altman & Weil Client Advisory* (Spring 1990). **3.** Bates & O'Steen v. State Bar of Arizona, 433 U.S. 350 (1977). **4.** Sally Schmidt Consulting Company, "The State of Law Firm Marketing: 1990." **5.** Wilson, *The Marketing of Professional Services*: 16–17. **6.** Thomas S. Clay, *Lawyers Monthly* (February 1990), as quoted in *Altman & Weil Client Advisory* (Spring 1990). **7.** John Duff, *Lincoln: A Prairie Lawyer* (New York: Rinehart & Co., Inc., 1960): 104. **8.** Shapero v. Kentucky Bar Association, 486 U.S. 466 (1988). **9.** "Improving Consumer Access to Legal Services: The Case for Removing Restrictions on Truthful Advertising," Federal Trade Commission Report (November 1984). **10.** "Clients More Tolerant Than Lawyers of Legal Ads," *Law Office Management & Administration Report,* issue 90-11 (November 1990): 7. **11.** Norman R. Carpenter, "Times Are A-Changing . . ." *The Bench and Bar of Minnesota* (February 1991): 27. **12.** "Studies Have Shown that Legal Clinics' Techniques Have Filtered into Regular Law Firm Practice," *Tennessee Bar Journal* 27 (January/February 1991): 7. **13.** "Studies Have Shown that Legal Clinics' Techniques Have Filtered into Regular Law Firm Practice": 7. **14.** Sandra D. Atchison and Bruce Nussbaum, "Hyatt: A 'Mission' to Make Legal Services Affordable," *Business Week* (21 January 1985): 68. **15.** Gay Jersey, "Joel Hyatt," *The American Lawyer* (March 1989). **16.** Deborah L. Jacobs, "Managing: The Benefit of Legal Advice," *New York Times* (7 October 1990). **17.** "Group Plans Poised for Growth," *Employee Benefit News* 4, no. 1 (January 1990). **18.** Patricia Bellew Gray, "More Lawyers Reluctantly Adopt Strange New Practice—Marketing," *Wall Street Journal* (3 February 1987): D1, D8. **19.** "AMA Approves New Marketing Definition," *Marketing News* 1 (March 1985): 1. **20.** Joel R. Evans and Barry Berman, *Principles of Marketing,* 2d ed. (New York: Macmillan, 1988): 446–49. **21.** Sally Schmidt Consulting Company, "The State of Law Firm Marketing: 1990." **22.** Ward Bower, "Exploding the Myths," *ABA Journal* (May 1987): 109. **23.** Joel A. Rose, "Administrator's Role in Developing Marketing Plan," *New York Law Journal* (24 March 1987). **24.** Phyllis Weiss Haserot, "Clients Increasingly Seek Proposals from Lawyers," *New York Law Journal* (28 March 1988): 37. **25.** The material that follows is based on Haserot, "Clients Increasingly Seek Proposals from Lawyers"; and Merrilyn Astin Tarlton, "Business Presentations: A Brief Outline for Making the Best Pitch to Prospects," *Legal Management* (January/February

1989). **26.** Edward J. Burke, "The Force May Be With You: Time to Meet the Press," *Marketing for Lawyers* 4, no. 6 (October 1990): 4. **27.** Edward J. Burke, "The Force May Be With You": 1, 4. **28.** Don J. DeBenedictus, "A Better Public Image? Public Partnerships Are the Answer, Conference Told," *American Bar Association Journal* (April 1990): 107. **29.** Ellen Joan Pollock, "Lawyers Are Cautiously Embracing Public Relations Firms," *Wall Street Journal* (14 March 1990): B1, B5. **30.** Susan Raridon, "Getting Creative About Law Firm Marketing," *Legal Administrator* (November/December 1989): 42. **31.** Sandra L. Yost, "Staying Hot: Marketing Trends for 1991," *Marketing for Lawyers* 4, no. 7 (November 1990): 4. **32.** "Seminars #1 Marketing Tool in Nationwide Survey of Firms," *Marketing for Lawyers* 4, no. 7 (November 1990): 5. **33.** Steven H. Klinghoffer, "Smart Marketing: Strategies for Law Firm Growth," *Massachusetts Lawyers Weekly; Lawyer-to-Lawyer Referral Guide* (11 March 1991): 7. **34.** Joel P. Bowman and Bernardine P. Branchaw, *Business Communication: From Process to Product* (Chicago: The Dryden Press, 1987): 275–76. **35.** "Clients More Tolerant Than Lawyers of Legal Ads": 7–8. **36.** Van O'Steen, "Advertising As a Marketing Tool," *Legal Economics* (February 1986): 24. **37.** "Hyatt Legal Services: A Good Idea That Just Keeps Getting Better," *News from Hyatt Legal Services: Press Release* (26 November 1990). **38.** O'Steen, "Advertising As a Marketing Tool": 24–26. **39.** "Legal Publications: A New Growth Industry," *New York Times* (19 August 1988): B5. **40.** Steven H. Klinghoffer, "Smart Marketing: Strategies for Law Firm Growth": 6. **41.** Lynn L. Remly, "Marketing Adds Arrows to the Quiver," *Lawyers Monthly, A Supplement to Lawyers Weekly* (October 1990): 10. **42.** Victoria Arnold, "Setting Marketing Priorities," *Massachusetts Bar Association, Law Practice News Section* (Winter 1990): 2. **43.** Donna Greenfield, "How to Create a Firm Brochure" (Presentation at the ALA Annual Conference, San Francisco, 4 April 1990). **44.** Development of the ideas of Henry Mintzberg, "The Ten Roles of Managers," from *The Nature of Managerial Work* (New York: Harper & Row, 1977). **45.** O'Steen "Advertising As a Marketing Tool": 20. **46.** Sally Schmidt Consulting Company, "The State of Law Firm Marketing: 1990." **47.** Alan P. Levine, "Keys to Hiring a Marketing Director," *National Law Journal* (10 December 1990): 25. **48.** "New Partner in the Firm: the Marketing Director," *New York Times* (2 June 1989): B3. **49.** Levine, "Keys to Hiring a Marketing Director": 25. **50.** Levine, "Keys to Hiring a Marketing Director": 25. **51.** Lowell Forte, "Five Firms Describe Styles of Management," *California Law Business* (2 April 1990): 18. **52.** William H. Davidow and Bro Uttal, "Service Companies, Focus or Falter," *Harvard Business Review* (July/August 1989): 85. **53.** David J. Rachman and Michael H. Mescon, *Business Today,* 5th ed. (New York: McGraw-Hill, 1987): 275–76. **54.** Leon Festinger, *A Theory of Cognitive Dissonance* (Palo Alto, Calif.: Stanford University Press, 1957). **55.** David J. Rachman, Michael H. Mescon, Courtland L. Bovee, and John V. Thill, *Business Today,* 6th ed. (New York: McGraw-Hill, 1990): 306–9. **56.** Jackson, Brown, and Keith, "Business Executives' Evaluations of Various Aspects of Outside Legal Services," in *Services Marketing in a Changing Environment,* ed. Thomas Block et al. (New York: American Marketing Publications, 1985): 130–34. **57.** "Some Sample Queries and Responses," *Legal Economics* (October 1987); *National Law Journal* (10 July 1989). **58.** Davidow and Uttal, "Service Companies, Focus or Falter": 85. **59.** Davidow and Uttal, "Service Companies, Focus or Falter": 85. **60.** "Krazy Glue for Clients," *The Rainmaker's Quarterly* 1, no. 3: 11. **61.** Phyllis Weiss Haserot and Brian Raftery, "Problems of Perception Midsize Firms Seek for Solutions," *National Law Journal* (18 June 1990): 31. **62.** Christopher Hart, James Heskett, and W. Earl Sasser, "The Profitable Art of Service Recovery," *Harvard Business Review* (July/August 1990): 148–56. **63.** A. L. Jones, "Satisfied Clients Are a Law Firm's Biggest Asset," *Montana Lawyer* (March 1990): 3. **64.** Sally Schmidt Report, *Marketing for the Legal Profession* (Fall 1990): 1. **65.** Laurence M. Weinstein, "Customers Are the Best Consultants," *Fairfield Business Review* (Spring, 1990): 34. **66.** Sandra L. Yost, "Staying Hot: Marketing Trends for 1991," *Marketing for Lawyers* 4, no. 7 (November 1990): 3. **67.** Susan Raridon and Donald Oppenheim, "Client Surveys: Feedback Can Benefit Law Firms," *National Law Journal: Law Office Management* (10 July 1989). **68.** Raridon and Oppenheim, "Client Surveys: Feedback Can Benefit Law Firms." **69.** Aubrey Wilson, *The Marketing of Professional Services*: xii. **70.** James L. Heskett, *Managing in the Service Economy* (Boston: Harvard Business School Press, 1986): 23. **71.** James L. Heskett, *Managing in the Service Economy*: 35–36. **72.** Edward J. Burke and Justine Jeffrey, "Personal Best: Getting Started as a Rainmaker," *ABA Journal* (1 November 1987): 122–24. **73.** Sandra L. Yost, "The Support Staff Role in Marketing," *The Compleat Lawyer* (Spring 1992): 3. **74.** Burke and Jeffrey, "Personal Best": 122–24. **75.** Karl Albrecht and Ron Zemke, *Service America! Doing Business in the New Economy* (Homewood, Ill.: Dow Jones–Irwin, 1985). **76.** Albrecht and Zemke, *Service America! Doing Business in the New Economy.* **77.** Based on a flyer from Tuttle Newsletter, *Positive Impressions* (Winter 1990). **78.** Don J. DeBenedictus, "A Better Public Image?": 107. **79.** Michael Gilfix, "Gray Area of Practice: Building Legal Business with Elder Law," *Marketing for Lawyers Newsletter* 3, no. 6 (October 1989): 3–4; 6. **80.** Thomas F. Harrison, "Using Preventive Law to Build Your Practice," *Journal of Missouri Bar* (December 1989): 587–93. **81.** Examples in this exercise are based on Katherine Baker, "A California Invention: Dial-a-Lawyer," *New York Times* (28 December 1990): B6; Ellen Joan Pollock, "'I Love My Lawyer' Ads May Spread to More States," *Wall Street Journal* (7 December 1990); Carole Jordan, Donald Oppenheimer, and Charles Maddock, "Marketing That Works: Going for the Gold," *ABA Journal* (April

1990): 60; and Lynn L. Remly, "Marketing Adds Arrows to the Quiver," *Lawyers Monthly, A Supplement to Lawyers Weekly* (October 1990).

Chapter 15

1. Mary Morgan Stuart, "Ethical Dilemma? Dial H-A-Z-A-R-D (Geoffrey Hazard)," *American Lawyer* 9 (March 1987): 25. **2.** American Bar Association, *Model Rules of Professional Conduct* (Chicago: American Bar Association, 1983). **3.** Guy Benveniste, *Professionalizing the Corporation* (San Francisco: Jossey-Bass, 1987): 42. **4.** William A. Kahn, "Toward an Agenda for Business Ethics Research," *Academy of Management Review* 15, no. 2 (1990): 318. **5.** As quoted in David Margolick, "At the Bar/The Fleecing of the Client, a Cautionary Report about the Lawyer's Conflict of Interest," *New York Times* (4 May, 1990): B1. **6.** Sissela Bok, "Can Lawyers Be Trusted?" *University of Pennsylvania Law Review* 138 (1990): 914. **7.** Mark Thompson, "Ethics Entrepreneur Michael Josephson Wants to Talk. So Where, He Asks, Are the Lawyers?" *Student Lawyer* 17 (February 1989): 20. **8.** Jerome Frank, "Why Not a Clinical Lawyer-School?" *University of Pennsylvania Law Review* 81 (June 1933): 922. **9.** Geoffrey C. Hazard, Jr., *Ethics in the Practice of Law* (New Haven: Yale University Press, 1978): 1–3. **10.** Hazard, Jr., *Ethics in the Practice of Law:* 1–3. **11.** Geoffrey C. Hazard, "Legal Ethics," in *Looking at Law School,* ed. Gillers (New York: Penguin Press, 1990): 282–91. **12.** John Rawls, *A Theory of Justice* (Boston: Harvard University Press, 1971). **13.** R. Edward Freeman and Daniel R. Gilbert, Jr., *Corporate Strategy and the Search for Ethics* (Englewood Cliffs, N.J.: Prentice-Hall, 1988). **14.** Freeman and Gilbert, *Corporate Strategy and the Search for Ethics.* **15.** Robert C. Solomon, *Morality and the Good Life,* (New York: McGraw-Hill, 1984): 3. **16.** Gerald F. Cavanaugh, Dennis J. Moberg, and Manuel Velasquez, "The Ethics of Organizational Politics," *Academy of Management Review* (1981): 363–74. **17.** Lloyd S. Baird, James E. Post, and John F. Mahon, *Management: Functions and Responsibilities* (New York: Harper & Row, 1990): 564. **18.** Kenneth Blanchard and Norman Vincent Peale, *The Power of Ethical Management* (New York: William Morrow & Company, 1988). **19.** Blanchard and Peale, *The Power of Ethical Management.* **20.** William H. Shaw and Vincent Barry, *Moral Issues in Business,* 4th ed. (Belmont, Calif.: Wadsworth Publishing, 1989): 17. **21.** Bok, "Can Lawyers Be Trusted?": 916. **22.** Sissela Bok, *Lying: Moral Choice in Public and Private Life* (New York: Pantheon Books, 1978): 14. **23.** Bok, "Can Lawyers Be Trusted?":923. **24.** Scott Turow, "Law School v. Reality," *New York Times Magazine* (18 September, 1988): 52. **25.** Tom Peters, *Thriving on Chaos* (New York: Alfred A. Knopf, 1988): 518. **26.** Lawrence Kohlberg, *The Philosophy of Moral Development* (New York: Harper & Row, 1981). **27.** Thomas D. Morgan and Ronald D. Rotunda, *Problems and Materials on Professional Responsibility,* 4th ed. (Mineola, N.Y.: The Foundation Press, 1987): 12. **28.** Bok, "Can Lawyers Be Trusted?": 913–14. **29.** Geoffrey C. Hazard, Jr., "Legal Ethics,": 282–91. **30.** Sissela Bok, "Can Lawyers Be Trusted?": 913–14. **31.** Len Young Smith, Richard A. Mann, and Barry S. Roberts, *Business Law and the Regulation of Business,* 4th ed. (St. Paul, Minn.: West Publishing Co., 1993): 221; and Henry Campbell Black, with Joseph R. Nolan and M. J. Connolly, *Black's Law Dictionary,* 5th ed., s.v. "fiduciary or confidential relation," (St. Paul, Minn.: West Publishing Co., 1979): 564. **32.** William Lowrance, "Of Acceptable Risk," in *Ethical Theory and Business,* 2d ed., ed. Tom L. Beauchamp and Norman E. Bowie (Englewood Cliffs, N.J.: Prentice-Hall, 1983): 194. **33.** Bok, "Can Lawyers Be Trusted?": 920–21. **34.** Bok, "Can Lawyers Be Trusted?": 919. **35.** Bok, "Can Lawyers Be Trusted?": 925. **36.** William P. Statsky, *The Regulation of Paralegals: Ethics, Professional Responsibility, and Other Forms of Control* (St. Paul, Minn.: West, 1988): 54. **37.** Hazard, *Ethics in the Practice of Law:* 11–14. **38.** Hazard, *Ethics in the Practice of Law:* 11–14. **39.** Hazard, *Ethics in the Practice of Law:* 11–14. **40.** L. Ray Patterson, *Legal Ethics: The Law of Professional Responsibility,* 2d ed. (New York: Matthew Bender, 1984): 5–6. **41.** Betsy Kalb, "Ethics On My Mind," *ALA News* (February/March 1991): 9. **42.** *Code of Ethics and Professional Responsibility* (Tulsa, Okla.: National Association of Paralegal Assistants, 1975). **43.** *Affirmation of Responsibility* (Deerfield, Ill.: The National Federation of Paralegal Assistants). **44.** This next section and the material that follows are based on the American Bar Association's *Model Rules of Professional Conduct,* as presented and commented on by Geoffrey C. Hazard, Jr., and Susan P. Koniak, in *The Law and the Ethics of Lawyering* (Westbury, N.Y.: The Foundation Press, 1990). **45.** Geoffrey C. Hazard, interview with author, April 1991. **46.** Geoffrey C. Hazard, Jr., and W. William Hodes, *The Law of Lawyering; A Handbook on the Modern Rules of Professional Conduct,* vol. 2 (Englewood Cliffs, N.J.: Prentice-Hall Law & Business, 1990): 887. **47.** Peel v. Attorney Registration and Disciplinary Commission of Illinois, 58 U.S.L.W. 4684. **48.** Bates & O'Steen v. State Bar of Arizona, 433 U.S. 350 (1977). **49.** As cited in Lisa G. Lerman, "Lying to Clients," *University of Pennsylvania Law Review* 138 (January 1990): 659. **50.** Tom Peters, *Thriving on Chaos* (New York: Alfred A. Knopf, 1988): 518. **51.** Hazard, *Ethics in the Practice of Law:* 1–3. **52.** Harold L. Johnson, "Ethics and the Executive," *Business Horizons* 24 (1981): 53–59. **53.** Blanchard and Peale, *The Power of Ethical Management.* **54.** Association of Legal Administrators, *Code of Professional Ethics* (Vernon Hills, Ill.: ALA, 1991. **55.** Amar Bhide and Howard H. Stevenson, "Why Be Honest if Honesty Doesn't Pay?" *Harvard Business Review* (September/October 1990): 121–29. **56.** Bhide and Stevenson, "Why Be Honest if Honesty Doesn't Pay?": 127. **57.** Bhide and Stevenson, "Why Be Honest if Honesty Doesn't Pay?": 129. **58.** William R. Tracey, *Leadership Skills: Standout Performance for Human Resource Man-*

agers (New York: AMACOM, 1990): 308. **59.** Tracey, *Leadership Skills*: 308. **60.** "Harvard's $30 Million Windfall for Ethics 101," *Business Week* (13 April 1987): 40. **61.** Saul W. Gellerman, "Why 'Good' Managers Make 'Bad' Choices," *Harvard Business Review* (July/August 1986): 88. **62.** Robert D. Hay, Edmund R. Gray, and Paul H. Smith, *Business and Society: Perspectives on Ethics and Social Responsibility*, 3d ed. (Cincinnati: South-Western Publishing Company, 1989): 15. **63.** Milton Friedman, *Capitalism and Freedom* (Chicago: University of Chicago Press, 1962): 133. **64.** Gellerman, "Why 'Good' Managers Make 'Bad' Choices,": 89. **65.** Friedman, *Capitalism and Freedom*; and Paul A. Samuelson, "Love That Corporation," *Mountain Bell Magazine* (Spring 1971); both as cited by Keith Davis, "The Case For and Against Business Assumption of Social Responsibilities," *Academy of Management Journal* (June 1973): 312–22. **66.** Peters, *Thriving on Chaos:* 520. **67.** Robert Hay and Ed Gray, "Social Responsibilities of Business Managers," *Academy of Management Journal* 18 (March 1974): 135–43. **68.** A. B. Carroll, "A Three-Dimensional Model of Corporate Social Performance," *Academy of Managerial Review* (October 1979): 499. **69.** Hay, Gray, and Smith, *Business and Society: Perspectives on Ethics and Social Responsibility:* 14. **70.** Hay, Gray, and Smith, *Business and Society:* 15. **71.** Hay, Gray, and Smith, *Business and Society:* 14–15. **72.** Jonathan W. Rinde, "Several Ways to Save the Earth in Your Law Office," *ALA Management & Administration Section Newsletter* 9, no. 1 (Spring 1991): 1–3, 10–11. **73.** Geoffrey C. Hazard, Jr., "Traditional Legal Path Doesn't Work for Women," *National Law Journal* 11, no. 15 (19 December 1988): 2, 3. **74.** *Altman & Weil Report to Legal Management* 15, no. 11 (August 1989): 1–2. **75.** Geoffrey C. Hazard, Jr., "Firm Culture Sets the Tone on Behavior," *National Law Journal* 11 (20 February 1989): 15, 18. **76.** Kenneth R. Andrews, "Ethics in Practice," *Harvard Business Review* (September/October 1989): 104. **77.** William G. Burns, Commencement address, Duke University: The Fuqua School of Business (13 May 1989). **78.** Leonard Gross, "Ethical Problems of Law Firm Associates," *William and Mary Law Review* 26 (Winter 1985): 259–315. **79.** John B. Cullen, Bart Victor, and Carroll Stephens, "An Ethical Weather Report: Assessing the Organization's Ethical Climate," *Organizational Dynamics* 18, no. 2 (Autumn 1989): 50–62. **80.** Cullen, Victor, and Stephens, "An Ethical Weather Report": 60. **81.** Albert O. Hirschman, *Exit, Voice, and Loyalty* (Cambridge, Mass.: Harvard University Press, 1970). **82.** Blanchard and Peale, *The Power of Ethical Management.* **83.** Peter Raven-Hansen, "Do's and Don'ts for Whistleblowers: Planning for Trouble," *Technology Review* (May 1980): 30. **84.** James A. Waters, "Catch 20.5: Morality as an Organizational Phenomenon," *Organizational Dynamics* 6 (Spring 1978): 3–15. **85.** Gene G. James, "In Defense of Whistle Blowing," in *Moral Issues in Business,* 5th ed., ed. William Shaw and Vincent Barry (Belmont, Calif.: Wadsworth Publishing, 1992): 416–24.

Name Index

Abel, Richard, 337, 339
Aburdene, Patricia, 9, 14, 51n, 275, 376
Ackoff, Russell L., 46n
Adelstein, Sherry, 346–347
Advisory Communications Systems, Inc., 408
Aesop, 127
Ailes, Roger, 359
Ainge, Danny, 108
Akins, Donald, 75, 196, 228
Alderfer, Clayton, 308
Alexander, Suzanne, 266
Allen, Fred, 321
Altman & Weil, 6
Altman, Mary Ann, 152, 169n, 170, 196, 226
American Assembly of Collegiate Schools of Business (AACSB), 15
American Bar Association (ABA), 7, 8, 11, 339, 395, 405, 407, 408, 415, 428, 442, 443
American Law Institute, 435
American Management Association, 450
American Marketing Association, 409
American Medical Association, 15
American Prepaid Legal Services Institute, 408
Ames, B. Charles, 186n
Anderson, B., 28n
Andrews, Kenneth, 456
Angelou, Maya, 347
Anthony, William P., 41
Argyris, Chris, 37, 85, 331
Aristotle, 70, 353
Arizona Bar Association, 395
Arsenal of Venice, 33
Arthur Andersen & Company, 374
Association of Legal Administrators, (ALA), 6, 8, 9n, 15, 24–26, 230, 259n, 260, 260n, 261n, 262, 278, 322, 323, 327, 443, 448
AT&T, 408
Atkinson, Linda R., 174

Babbage, Charles, 35
Babylonians, 33

Bacharach, Samuel, 123
Baird, Lloyd S., 41n
Baker & McKenzie, 327
Baldridge, Letitia, 330
Bandura, Alfred, 135
Barnard, Chester I., 36, 56, 84, 347
Barry, Vincent, 439
Batten, Batten, Hudson & Schwab, Inc., 250
Batten, Joe, 250
Beatrice Foods, 108
Bellows, Paul, 7
Benne, Kenneth, 328
Bennis, Warren, 120, 272n, 273, 273n, 275, 276, 277, 289, 377
Benson, Doug, 45
Benveniste, Guy, 436n
Berkow, Robert E., 58n
Berle, Milton, 321
Bernstein, Leonard, 12
Bhide, Amar, 448, 451
Blake, Robert, 282
Blanchard, Kenneth, 256, 258, 283–285, 286n, 324, 438
Blumberg, Mark, 279n
Bok, Sissela, 436, 440, 441
Bonvino, Janis, 214–215
Bookman, Bob, 251
Booze, Allen & Hamilton, 55
Bowen, Donald D., 65n
Bower, Ward, 406n
Brandeis, Louis F., 5–6, 108
Brandes, Wenke, 241
Bright, Lawrence, 200
Brobeck, Phleger & Harrison, P.C., 94n
Brown, Jerry, 8
Brown, Rudnick, Freed & Gesmer, 116
Brubeck, Dave, 13
Buchalter, Nemer, Fields & Young, 366
Bulkely, William, 377
Bulkley, Richardson & Gelinas, P.C., 165, 165n, 166, 167
Bump, Ellen C., 3–4, 25
Burke, Edward, 414
Burkhart, Randolph J., 174
Burns, James MacGregor, 273, 287

Burns, Tom, 105
Burns, William, 456

Califano, Joseph, 385
Cameron, Kim S., 19n, 30n, 132, 177n, 359, 386–387
Carew, Donald, 324
Carlisle, Arthur Elliott, 335
Carlzon, Jan, 105
Carnegie, Dale, 127, 387
Carpenter, Norman, 407
Carrington, Coleman, Sloman & Blumenthal, 144
Carroll, A. B., 453, 454n
Carroll, Lewis, 40n
Cartwright, Dorwin, 331
Cashman, Gertrude, 374–375, 380–381
Catt, Stephen, 264
Certo, Samuel R., 41n, 83, 85n
Chadbourne & Parke, 346
Cherrington, David, 267n, 304, 324
Chiaiese, Beth E., 158n
Chinese, 33
Choate, Hall & Stewart, 108
Christie, Richard, 138n
Christopher, Maurine, 409n
Clark, Arben O., 151, 169n
Clay, Thomas, 406
Coburn, John F., 6, 24
Coffield, Ungaretti & Harris, 427
Cogger, John, 223
Cohen, Allan, 178
Conger, Jay, 123, 134n, 135
Cort, Harold A., 271–272
Cotkins, Collins & Franscell, 285
Coulter, Charles, 147, 168n
Crandall, J. E., 397
Crossen, Cynthia, 237
Csikszentmihalyi, Mihaly, 303, 376n, 392–393, 396, 397
Cullen, John, 456–457
Cuming, Pamela, 136n
Cummins, W. M., 110n
Cunningham, Bob, 227
Cunningham, Mary, 118

Dahl, Robert, 120
Davidow, William, 420

Davis, Keith, 362n
Delongis, A., 394
DeLucchio, Daniel, 6–7
Deming, W. Edwards, 173
DePree, Max, 229, 241, 296
Dickson, William J., 37
DiLucchio, Dan, 215n
Dodds, Anne, 144–145
Drucker, Peter, 11–12, 17, 49, 49n, 54, 63, 145
DuBrin, Andrew J., 61n
Duff, John J., 35n
Dunham, Randall B., 83, 131n
Dupont, Antoinette L., 227
Dyer, William, 399n

Edwards, Margaret Hart, 235
Egyptians, 33
Eisenberg, Anderson, Michalik & Lynch, 214
Equitrac, 160n
Ernst & Young, 58n

Facher, Jerome, 108
Fairchild, James, 185–186
Fayol, Henri, 35, 95, 96, 99, 100, 100n
Federal Aviation Administration, 322
Feeley & Driscoll, 191–192, 192n, 193n, 194n, 195n
Festinger, Leon, 421
Fink, Stephen, 173
Finley, Kumble, 186
Finnegan, Thomas J., Jr., 95n
Fisher, K. Kim, 313
Fisher, Kathleen V., 278
Fisk, Margaret Cronin, 7n
Fitzgerald, Louise, 237
Foley, Hoag & Elliot, 108
Folkman, S., 394
Follett, Mary Parker, 36, 99, 376m
Foonberg, Jay, 198
Forsythe, William, 196
Forte, Lowell, 53n, 398, 420
Fowler, Elizabeth, 13n
Fredericks, Nancy, 366
French, Guy P., 40n, 126
Freud, Sigmund, 305
Freudenberger, H. J., 394
Friedman, Meyer, 396
Friedman, Milton, 452
Friedman, Nancy, 351n
Fulbright & Jaworski, 7
Furlonger, Geoffrey, 195, 198

G. M. Johnson & Associates, 374
Galvani, Paul B., 108
Gandossy, Robert, 178
Gardner, John, 117, 273
Garrett, Vena, 169n
Gaston & Snow, 186
Gaston Snow & Ely Bartlett, 108

Gaston, Snow, Beekman & Bogue, 108
Gaus, John M., 84
Gawalt, Gerald, 5
Geis, Florence L., 138n
Gellerman, Saul, 82, 451
General Motors, 62
Gerhardt, John, 7
Getty, J. Paul, 14
Ghiselli, Edwin, 278
Gibb, J. R., 342
Gibbons, Thomas F., 5n
Gilbreth, Frank, 35
Gilbreth, Lillian, 35
Gold, Sandra S., 158n
Goldstein, Tom, 355
Goleman, Daniel, 237
Goodwin, Procter & Hoar, 108, 235, 374, 380
Gordon, George G., 110n
Gray, Edmund, 452, 453
Gray, P. B., 299n
Gray-Judson & Howard, Inc., 6, 24
Greece, 305
Greenberg, Debra, 295
Greenhalgh, Leonard, 387, 389
Greiner, Larry, 178
Group Legal Services of Prudential Insurance, 408
Gruen, R., 394

Haar, Jonathan, 108
Haberman, Meyer, 12–13
Hackman, J. Richard, 244, 321, 336n
Haight, Brown & Bonesteel, 44
Haimann, Theo, 250
Hale & Dorr, 108–109
Hall, Douglas T., 65n
Hall, Francine S., 65n
Halloran & Sage, 271–272
Hampton, Wade, 210n
Harkins, S., 331
Harrington, Steve, 389n
Harris, Philip R., 329n
Harrison, Thomas, 429
Harter, Secrest & Emery, 241
Harvey, Jerry, 334
Haserot, Phyllis Weiss, 338, 413, 422
Hay, Robert, 452, 453
Hayakawa, S. I., 365
Hayes, James, 4n
Hazard, Geoffrey C., 161, 435, 437, 441, 442, 443, 445
Heirs, Ben, 40n, 63, 71
Heller, Robert, 24
Hendel, Collins & Newton, P.C., 92n
Herndon, Thomas, 35, 407
Hersey, Paul, 283–285, 286n
Herzberg, Frederick, 310, 311n
Heskett, James, 423
Hildebrandt, Bradford, 230
Hildebrandt, Inc., 53, 188, 414, 419

Hilget, Raymond L., 250
Hill, Anita, 237, 238, 240
Hirschhorn, Larry, 321, 321n
Hlavacek, James D., 186n
Hodes, William, 445
Holland & Hart, 405
Holland, L. Donald, 186n
Holland Shipes Vann, 151, 428n
Holmes, T. H., 394
Hourihan, Patrick J., 165
Human Resource Services, Inc., 13
Human Resources Enterprises of Cape Cod, 257
Hyatt, Joel, 298–299, 408, 417
Hyatt Legal Plans, 408, 409
Hyatt Legal Services, 298–299, 327, 408, 409, 417
Hyatt, Susan Metzenbaum, 408

Institute for the Advancement of Ethics, 436
Interquest Inc., 12
Ireland, R. Duane, 61n

Jacobs, Neil, 108
Jacoby & Myers, 298
James, Gene G., 459
James, William, 305
Janis, Irving L., 60n
Jaques, Elliot, 82n
Jefferson, Thomas, 347
Jenkins, C. David, 402n
Jensen, Rita Henley, 237
John Deere, 408
Johnson, Spencer, 256, 258
Jones, A. L., 423
Jones, Day, Reavis & Poque, 248
Jones, Edward, 127
Jones, Thomas Goode, 442
Josephson, Michael, 436

Kahn, Robert L., 84, 328
Kahn, William A., 436n
Kalb, Elizabeth, 6
Kanter, Rosabeth Moss, 43n, 66–67, 111, 123, 125, 126, 133, 134, 171, 177–178, 233, 297, 300, 303, 313, 335, 349, 381
Kanungo, R. N., 134
Kaplan, Robert, 63, 123
Katz, Daniel, 84
Katz, Linda, 346
Kaufman, Jack, 230
Kehoe, Peter, 25, 55–56, 227
Keil, John, 64
Kennedy, John F., 233
Kennedy, John H., 211n
Kerr, S., 15n
Kets de Vries, Manfred, 119
Kiechel, Walter, 27, 361
King and Spaulding, 248

NAME INDEX

Kirkpatrick, James, 122
Kirkpatrick, Shelley, 277, 279
Klemt, Becky, 347
Koontz, Harold, 27, 84
Kotter, John P., 120, 124, 127–128, 128n, 274, 275, 279
Kramer, Levin, 346
Kuzmits, Frank E., 231

Labaton, Stephen, 377
Labich, K., 289n
Latane, B., 331
Latham & Watkins, 6, 44–45, 333
Lawler, Edward, 123, 321
Lazarus, R. S., 394
Leavitt, Harold, 62, 321n
Ledvinka, James, 232
Lee, William L., 355
Legal Assistants Management Association, 15, 26, 295
Levin, Tamar, 409n
Levine, Alan, 419, 420
Levy, M., 130n
Lewicki, Roy J., 65n
Lewin, Kurt, 280, 307, 379
Lewis, D'Amato, Brisbois & Bisgaard, 44
Lewis, Neil A., 10n
Lewis, Robert F., 44
Lieberman, Jethro K., 355
Likert, Jane Gibson, 381, 384–386, 388
Likert, Rensis, 37, 100–103, 112, 172, 255, 281, 282, 381, 384–386, 388
Lillick & Charles, 279
Lincoln, Abraham, 33, 35, 193, 195, 200–201, 337, 407, 417
Lippitt, Gordon, 384
Locke, Edwin, 277, 279
Locke, John, 305
Lowe, Kenneth L., 41n
Lurie, Sylvia, 6–7

Machiavelli, Nicolo, 33
Machlowitz, David S., 239n, 240
Machlowitz, Marilyn M., 175, 176, 239n, 240
Mackensie, Alec, 175
Macumber, Richard, 44
Mahon, John F., 41n
Maister, David, 204, 331
Malone, Gerry, 228
Mann, L., 60n
Manz, Charles, 289
March, James, 62
Marcus, Bruce W., 91
Margolick, David, 108n, 238, 395
Marks, Linda, 241
Mason, Mary Ann, 201
Massachusetts Mutual Life Insurance Company, 95n

Masuda, M., 394
Matthews, Karen A., 396
Mayo, Elton, 37, 330
McCall, Morgan, 123
McClelland, David, 120, 307, 309
McCollum, Marion, 325
McConkey, Dale, 306n
McCormack, Mark H., 56–57, 366, 367
McDougall, William, 305
McGregor, Douglas, 317–318
McKenna, Conner & Cuneo, 44
McKinsey & Co., 420
Megginson, Leon C., 41n
Mehrabian, Albert 352
Mentor, 228
Midwest Legal Services of Des Moines, 408
Mill, John Stuart, 305
Miller, Ann, 279
Miller, Casey, 357n
Miller, Donald, 264
Mintzberg, Henry, 12, 22–24, 23n, 82n, 84, 174
Mobil Chemical Corporation, 7
Monsen, J., Jr., 455n
Mooney, James, 94, 96
More, Sir Thomas, 33, 95
Morgan, Thomas, 440
Morris, W. C., 31n, 371n
Morrison & Foerster, 278–279, 415
Morton, Paul, 81–82
Mosely, Donald C., 41n
Moses, 33
Moskal, Brian S., 239n
Moss, Debra Cassens, 243n
Mouton, Jane, 282
Murphy, Evelyn, 116–117
Murray, Henry, 307
Myers, M. Scott, 316
Myerson & Kuhn, 186

Naisbitt, John, 9, 14, 27, 51n, 215n, 275, 376
Nanus, Burt, 120, 272n, 273, 273n, 275, 276, 277, 289
National Association of Legal Assistants, 339, 443, 444
National Association of Legal Secretaries, 323
National Federation of Paralegal Associations, 339, 443, 444
National Law Firm Marketing Association, 405
National Paralegal Association, 322
New York State Bar Association, 395
Nixon, Hargrave, Devans & Doyle, 8
Nixon, Richard M., 108
Noonan, Peggy, 356
Nordstrom and Dana, 105

Nuclear Regulatory Commission, 322
Nutter, McClennen & Fish, 105, 108

O'Connor, Sandra Day, 407
O'Steen, Van, 416, 417, 419
Odysseus, 228
Oedipus, 273
Oldman, G.R., 244
Olsen, Kathy, 227
Oppenheim, Donald, 423
Ors, Rose D., 338
Ouchi, Bill, 173
Overton, Lyman & Prince, 44
Owen, Robert, 35

Parisi-Carew, Eunice, 324
Pauley, Jane, 375n
Pavlov, Ivan P., 305, 307
Peale, Norman Vincent, 438
Pearce, John A., 41n, 83
PepsiCo, 408
Persian Gulf, 305
Peters, Thomas, 111n, 145, 147, 171, 249n, 313, 348n, 440, 447, 453
Pettigrew, Andrew, 127
Pfeffer, Jeffrey, 132
Phillips, Carol F., 57n
Pierce, J. L., 83, 131
Pietri, Paul H., 41n
Plato, 70
Porras, Jerry I., 28n
Porter, Lyman, 321
Post, James E., 41n
Prescott, Blane, 53

Quaker Oats Company, 226n

Raelin, Joseph, 250
Raftery, Brian, 422
Rahe, R. H., 394
Ramey, Dru, 278–279
Rand Corporation, 68
Rapinchuk, Patricia M., 227
Raridan, Susan, 423
Raudsepp, Eugene, 75
Raven, B., 126
Raven-Hansen, Peter, 458
Reed, Richard, 196
Reichman, W., 130n
Rinquette, Karen, 241
Robbins, Stephen, 110n
Robert W. Baird & Co., 298
Robins, Kaplan, Miller & Ciresi, 320
Robinson, Donovan, Madden & Barry, P.C., 3, 25, 93n, 153n, 162, 163, 202n, 203n, 227
Robinson, Richard B., Jr., 41n, 55, 83
Robinson, Rogers, Carl, 302
Roethlisberger, Fritz J., 37, 330
Romans, 33
Root, Elihu, 11

Root, Gladys Towles, 329
Ropes & Gray, P.C., 108
Rose, Joel, 39–40, 71, 74
Rosemont Forms, Inc., 155, 157
Rotunda, Ronald, 440
Ryan, Mary K., 108

Saint-Exupery, Antoine de, 118, 347n
Samuelson, Paul, 452
Sashkin, M., 31n, 371n
Sasser, 423
Scandinavian Airlines, 105
Scarpello, Vida, 232
Schaffer, Robert H., 297
Schein, Edgar, 108, 313
Schermerhorn, John R., 41n, 83
Schlichtmann, Jan, 108
Schmidt, Warren H., 286, 286n
Schriesheim, J., 15n
Scott, Judith, 298
Scott, William, 90
Securities and Exchange Commission, 323
Selye, Hans, 391–392
Shad, John, 450
Shapero, Albert, 5n, 327
Sharswood, George, 442, 447
Shaw, William, 439
Sheats, Paul, 328
Sherborne, Powers, & Needham, 81
Sherman, Rorie, 237, 355n
Sherry & Bellows, 7
Shonagon, Sei, 378
Siegel, Nancy, 278–279
Simms, Henry, 289
Simon, Herbert, 54, 62, 95, 296
Skadden, Arps, Slate, Meagher & Flom, 13
Skinner, B. F., 305
Skinner, Walter J., 108
Sloan, Alfred, 62
Smith, Adam, 33, 85
Smith, Paul, 452, 453
Smith, Ron, 45n

St.Clair, James, 108
Stalker, G.M., 105
Stanislao, Bettie, 377
Stanislao, Joseph, 377
Statsky, William, 339, 442
Stein, Barry A., 171, 177–178, 297
Stephens, Carroll, 456–457
Stevenson, Clinton, 333
Stevenson, Howard H., 448, 451
Stewart, Mary Morgan, 435
Stewart, Rosemary, 83
Stogdill, Ralph, 279, 280n, 281
Strong, Kline D., 151, 169n
Sumerians, 33
Summit Rovins & Feldsman, 6–7
Swift, Kate, 357n

Taber, Tom, 125
Tailhook Association, 239
Tannenbaum, Robert, 286, 286n
Tarlton, Merrilyn Astin, 405–406, 413n
Taylor, Frederick, 35
Telemachus, 227
Tennyson, Alfred, 350
The Travelers Company, 408
Thomas, Clarence, 237, 238, 240
Thompson, Deborah, 248
Thorndike, Edward, 305
Three Mile Island, 173
Tichy, Noel, 288, 382
Tolman, E. C., 311
Touche Ross & Company, 45
Tracey, William, 257, 450
Tuckman, Bruce, 324, 326n
Turner, Paula F., 186n
Turow, Scott, 440

Ubell, Earl, 396
Ulmer, Diane, 396
Ulrich, David, 288, 298, 299, 382
Uttal, Bro, 420

Van Oech, Roger, 65n
Vaughan, Jack, 7

Victor, Bart, 456–457
Von Glinow, Mary Ann, 15n, 252
Vroom, Victor, 311–312

Wahl, Deborah, 320
Walker, Jack, 333
Walker, John F. Jr., 6, 45
Waterman, Robert, 111n, 145, 147, 249n
Watson, John B., 305
Weber, Max, 36, 123, 287
Webster, Daniel, 436
Weick, Karl, 43n
Weihrich, Heinz, 84
Weil, Robert, 152, 169n, 170, 196, 226
Weissburg & Aronson, 44
Welch, Joseph, 108
Wertheim, Lynda, 346
Western Electric Company, 37, 330
Weston, William I., 197n
Whetten, David A., 19n, 30n, 132, 177n, 359, 386–387
Whyte, William Foote, 37
Williams, J. Clifton, 61n
Williams, K., 331
Willis, Wayne, 408
Wilson, Aubrey, 406, 425
Wittreich, Warren, 406n
Words/Worth Associates, Inc., 355

Yastrzemski, Carl, 108
Yost, Sandra, 423, 427
Young, Stanley, 132
Yukl, Gary, 125, 277, 279, 280n

Zaleznik, Abraham, 119, 120, 273, 276
Zander, Alvin, 324n, 331
Zemke, Ron, 258
Zinke, William, 13
Zuboff, Shoshana, 118
Zwicker, Milton, 196
Zyzanski, Stephen J., 402n

Subject Index

Abilene Paradox, The, 334–335
absenteeism, 87, 297
academic credentials, 222, 337
accommodation, 387
accountability, 100
accounting, 187
accounts payable, 206
accounts receivable, 200, 205
accounts receivable statement, 206–207
accrued expenses, 206
activity centers, 208–209
ad hoc committee, 322
adapters, 353
administrative management, 35
administrative services, 150
advertising, 416–418, 445, 446
 forms of, 408–409
 lawyers and, 407
advocate, 444
affect displays, 353
affiliation, 323
affiliative needs, 281
affirmative action, 234
agenda for meetings, 368
aging receivables, 200
AIDA process, 413
Alabama Code of Legal Ethics, 442
alcohol abuse and stress, 395
alienation of workers, 298
alternatives, 50, 57
ambiguity and stress, 393
American Bar Association, 7, 8, 11, 339, 442, 443
Americans with Disabilities Act, 234–235
annual billing budget, 192
appraisal tools, 260–262
 checklists, 260
 graphic rating scales, 260
 descriptive essays, 261
 critical incidents technique, 261–262
 management by objectives, 262
arbitrator, 389
assets, 205
associates,
 ratio to partners, 90

 retreats, 72–73
 supervising, 251–252
Association of Legal Administrators (ALA), 6, 8, 15, 24–26, 230, 260, 262, 278, 323
 Code of Professional Ethics, 448, 449–450
At the Breaking Point, 11
attending skills, 361
attitudes, 303
 and stress, 396
 components of, 303–304
 changes in, 304
attraction, interpersonal, 332
authoritarianism, 101
 forms of, 301
 characteristics of, 301
authority, 99, 101, 118–119, 250
 and influence, 126
 of nonlawyers, 338
 work-related attitudes, 301
autocratic leadership, 280
automated records management, 157
autonomy of professionals, 15
avoidance, 386

balance sheet, 205
bar codes, 157–160
barriers to communication, 364–365
barriers to planning and decision making, 71–72
Bates and O'Steen v. State Bar of Arizona, 406, 408
behavior modification, 305
behaviors, counterproductive, 297
behavioral theories of leadership, 280–282
behavioral theories of motivation, 305–307
belongingness (social) needs, 308
benefits, 87, 231–232, 334
Bill of Rights, workers', 454
billable hours, 198
billing,
 secretarial services, 339
 paralegal services, 338
billing, standards for, 196

boards, 323
body language, 352
bona fide occupational qualifications (BFOQs), 220
bonding, 422
 bounded rationality, 60
brainstorming, 69
brochures, 417
budget process, 190–195
budgets, 187–190
 as plans, 48
 characteristics of, 189–190
 games, 195
 uses of, 188–189
bureaucracy, 36, 101, 287, 302
burnout, 248, 394
business development, 194
buzz sessions, 69

calculating workers, 298
calendars and diaries, 152
Canons of Professional Ethics, 407, 442
careers,
 lawyers, 9
 paralegals, 338–339
 legal administrators, 5, 9, 18
 nonlawyers, 9
case index form, 157
CD Rom / compact disks, 150
centralization, 99
certification, paralegal, 339
chain of command, 458
challenges,
 from the contemporary environment, 41
 group, 320
 of law firm leadership, 271, 288
 of management, 14, 15
 of motivating others, 295
change, 376
 control of, 377
 education, 382
 effective, 382–384
 forces of, 376
 involvement in change, 383
 leadership climate and, 378

managerial interventions and change, 383–384
nature of, 376–383
organizational climate and, 378–379
participation in change, 383
political strategies and change, 383
process of, 379
resistance to, 381
responsive leadership and change, 382
technology and, 376–377
tentative changes, 384
change agent, 379–380
change(s), and law firms, 374
and technology, 374
coping with, 274
economy, 8–9
in the legal profession, 5–11
legal services, 10
societal, 5–8
size of law firms, 8
technology, 8
charisma, 125, 288
charismatic leadership, 286–287
checklists, 260
Civil Rights Act, 233–234
clarification activities, 388
classical management, 35
clearinghouse questions, 224
client files, 161–170
circulation and control, 167–168
codes for, 167
five kinds of systems for, 169
forms, 165–167
guidelines for retention of, 170
kinds of, 165
maintenance of, 168
opening, 164
procedures, 161
systems, 165–167
client service culture, 427–428
clients, 420–427
accepting, 97
and paralegals, 338
commitment, 424–427
contacting prospects, 446
law firm choice, 421–422
lawyer's obligations to, 442
satisfaction, 422
service, 422
service culture, 427–428
surveys, 423–424, 426
climate,
leadership, 378
ethical, 456
organizational, 378–379
coercive power, 124
cognitive complexity, 61
cognitive conflict, 63
cognitive dissonance, 421

cognitive theories of motivation, 310–312
cohesiveness, group, 331–333
collaboration, 387
collections budget, 192
collections, speed of, 208
collegiality, 15, 124
collegial power, 124
command groups, 322
commissions, 323
commitment of workers, 298
committees, 322, 336
in the law firm, 322, 336
collegial power and, 124
committees, 322, 336
executive committees, 20
management, 8
marketing, 420
communication, 348
and personality traits, 365–366
basic forms of, 351–352
improving, 365
management of meaning, 276
skills, 121
organizational, 101–103
communication process, 349–351
communications,
and managerial success, 348
and the organizational structure, 349
barriers to, 364–365
conflict-laden, 390
flow of, 362
improving in the law firm, 346–347
in the law firm, 362–364
interaction of verbal and nonverbal, 352
persuasiveness of, 352–356
community involvement, 415
comparable worth, 233
compensation, 229–232
intrinsic, 229
extrinsic, 229–230
paralegals, 338–339
partners, 230–231
competence, managerial, 449
competition, 185, 274, 408–409
competitive advantage, 410
compromise, 387
computers,
applications for law firms, 149
integrated hardware, 148–149
integrated software, 149–150
work stations, 149–150
conceptual skills, 22
confidentiality, 443–444, 449, 450–451
client files and records, 170
practical rules, 451
obligations of support staff, 451
conflict of interests, 160–161
check form, 167

systems, 160
requirements, 160
procedures, 160
conflict(s), 384–390
causes of, 384–386
in communications, 390
and law firms, 375
nature of, 384
managing of, 386–390
conflict resolution strategies, 387–388, 390
personality, 333
response styles, 386–387, 390
conformity, 62, 331
confrontation, 386
congruence, 240
connection power, 125
consensus, 63
consideration, 330
Consolidated Omnibus Budget Reconciliation Act (COBRA), 231
constraints and change, 378
consultants, marketing, 420
consumers, clients as, 420–421
contacts of clients by lawyers, 446
contingency fees, 198
contingency management theories (see situationalists), 37
control, 88, 145–171
areas of, 144, 147–170
levels of management and, 145
managerial responsibilites, 144
relationship to other functions, 146–147
reasons for, 147
process, 170–171
workers and, 144, 171
control mechanisms, 121
controlling, 20, 145–179
and other management functions, 146–147
of human resources, 148, 217
of financial resources, 148, 185, 187
of information resources, 151–170
of physical resources, 148, 149–151
coordination, 88, 94–95
coordinators, marketing, 420
cost centers, 208
cost pools, 208
cost recovery and billing, 200
costs, 339
counselling, 256
counsellor, 444
creativity, 63–64
in marketing approaches, 428–429
myths about, 64
power of, 65
role in decision making, 64
crises, 173
internal, 333

SUBJECT INDEX

crisis management, 173–174
critical incidents technique, 261–262
cultural factors and law firm selection, 421

dead files, 168
debt, 188
deceit, 440
decentralization, 99
decision makers, 60
decision making
  and personality, 61
  barriers to, 71–72
  cognitive traps, 60
  ethical, 448
  in law firms, 55–56
  involvement in, 64–68
  steps in, 54–60
  avoiding wrong choices, 57
decisions,
  definition of, 54
  as basic managerial activity, 54
  significance level of, 54
decisional roles,
  managerial, 23
  marketing, 418–419
decoding, 350
deference, 330
delegation, 99–100, 116, 119–122
  weaknesses in, 120–121
  styles of, 121
Delphi method, 68–69
democratic leadership, 280
demographics, 249
Department of Commerce, 232
Department of Labor, 232
departmentalization, 88, 90, 91–92, 94
  types of, 96
depression and stress, 395
descriptive essays, 261
  desktop publishing, 417
devil's advocate decision program, 70
diagonal communication, 363
dialectic decision method, 70–71
dictatorial leadership, 280
diet and exercise, 398
difference principle, 438
digital dictation, 150
directing, 19, 117–135
  and controlling, 146
directive interview, 223
directors, marketing, 420
disagreement, 63
discipline, 262–263
  rules for, 263–265
  progressive, 265
  reluctance to use, 266
discommunication, 364
discrimination, 232–235

age, 234
affirmative action, 234
BFOQs, 234
civil rights, 233–234
disabled, 234–235
equal employment, 234
equal pay, 232–233
religion, 234
sex plus, 235
veterans, 235
distributive justice, 310–311
divergent thinking, 62
division of labor, 88–90
docket control systems, 154
  document retrieval systems, 156
documentation, 151
dogmatism, 301–302
domination, 333
downward communication, 363
dress norms, 329, 334
dysfunctional conflict, 386

economic status,
  lawyers, 337
economy, 17
  and change, 377
  contributions of paralegals, 339
  current conditions, 188
education,
  lawyers, 337
  paralegals, 339
effectiveness, 17, 172–173
efficiency, 17
ego, 120, 439
ego extension, 323
emblems, 352
emotional malpractice, 216–217
emotional motive, 421
emotional support, 323–324
empathy, 366
Employee Assistance Programs (EAPs), 236
employment agencies, 214
employment laws, 232–236
  summary of, 233
empowerment, 133–135
  advantages of, 135–136
  empowering others, 288
  strategies for, 135
encoding, 349
enthusiasm, 248
entitlement, communal, 87
environmental stressors, 392
equal opportunity, 339
Equal Employment Opportunity Act, 234
Equal Employment Opportunity Commission, 234
Equal Pay Act, 232–233
equality, norm for, 330

equipment, control of, 148
equity, norm for, 330
equity partners, 192
equity theory, 310
equity theory of motivation, 309–310
ERG theory of motivation, 308–309
esteem needs, 308
ethical choices, 454–456
ethical climate, 448, 456
ethical decision making, 438
ethical dilemmas, 456–459
ethical responsibilities, 435
ethical skills, 435
ethics, 436–437
  and professionals, 15
  approaches to, 437–438
  lawyer's ethical obligations, 441–442
  learning, 436
  managerial, 15
ethos, 107, 437
etiquette, 330, 389
eustress, 391
evaluation,
  apprehension, 331
  of planning, 51
  of decision making, 58–59
  worker performance, 258–260, 260–262
excellence, criteria for, 111
exclusivity, 422
executive committee, 20
exercise and diet, 398
existence needs, 308
exit, 458
expectancy theory of motivation, 311–312
expenses, 207
  control and recovery systems, 160
  reducing, 185–186
expertise,
  managerial, 15
  power of, 125
explicit strategy, 47
external locus of control, 301
extinction, 307

Fair Labor Standards Act, 232
fax machines, 150
feedback, 89, 351
fees, 196–200, 408, 444
  and paralegals, 338
  billable hours, 188–189, 198
  client agreement on, 199
  collection of, 200
  contingency fees, 198
  fixed, 198–199
  Model Rules of Professional Conduct, 197–198
  percentage, 198–199

retainers, 198
  setting of, 196–198
fiduciary relationship, 441
filtering, 365
financial management, 186–209
  areas of, 205–209
  planning, 185
  reporting, 201–204
financial reporting tools, 205–207
  accounts receivable statement, 206–207
  balance sheet, 205
  financial statements, 186
  firm utilization report, 207
  income statement, 205
  statement of cash flows, 205
  statement of retained earnings, 206
  work-in-process reports, 207
financial resources, 148
firm names and letterheads, 446–447
firm utilization report, 207
fiscal year, 190
fixed assets, 205
fixed fees, 198–199
follower readiness, 284
followers, 275
following skills, 361
force, 312
forces, external and internal, 58
forcing (confrontation), 386
forecasting,
  human resource needs, 217
  operating expenses, 194
formal groups, 322–323
formal organization, 84
frame of reference, 350, 364
friendship groups, 323
fringe benefits, 231
functional conflict, 384
functional groups, 322
functions, managerial, 18
future,
  successful managers of, 24
  challenges of, 26–27
  financial survival strategies for, 188
  successful organizations in, 109–111
  organizational designs for, 81
  trends, 51
  vision theories of leadership, 286–289

general adaptation syndrome, 392
goal-setting,
  as a motivational strategy, 312
  and expectancy, 312–313
  criteria for writing, 312
  motivational theories of, 312–313
goals, 46, 48–49
  disagreement, 333
  group formation and, 323

law firms, 49
  integration of, 49
good law firms, 452–454
good people, 438–440
gossip, 364
governance, 8, 124
  and law firms, 8–10, 12–14
  and paralegals, 339
  role of committees, 322, 336
government watchdog agencies, 454
grapevine, 363–364
graphic rating scales, 260
group decision making, 54–75
  advantages and disadvantages of, 67
  techniques for, 68–71
group dynamics, 322–334
  managing of, 369
group membership,
  advantages and disadvantages of, 325–327
  costs of, 321
group(s), 321–339
  challenges, 320
  characteristics of effective, 327
  composition, 327–328
  development, 324–325, 326
  effective management of, 334–336
  ethical decision making, 438
  formation of, 323–324
  goals, 332
  hierarchical roles, 337
  influences of, 321–322
  interdependence of, 336–337
  law firm, 85
  managers and, 321
  meaning of, 322
  motivation, 297
  norms, 325
  performance, 335
  roles, 320
  size, 327
  status, 320
  structure, 327–334
  types of, 322–333
  work groups, 100–101
groupthink, 335
growth,
  effects of, 178
  control of, 177–179
  needs for, 308
  stages of, 178
  size, 179
growth rate of law firms, 378
guilt, 121

handbooks, 228
hardiness, 397
hassles, 394
Hawthorne effect, 330
hedonism, 305

hierarchy,
  inverted, 105
  law firm, 20, 337–339
  of needs, 307–308
hiring goals, 189
honesty, 440, 448, 449
hope, 397
horizontal communication, 363
hostile environment, 238
hostility, 360
human capital, 216
human relations management, 36–37
human resources, 215–242
  control of, 148, 217
  evaluation of, 240–242
  legal constraints, 232–240
  major activities of, 217–232
  management, 216
  process, 216–217
  trends, 214
  uniqueness of in law firms, 214
humanists, 37
hygienes, 310
hypothetical questions, 223

idiosyncrasy credits, 331
illustrators, 353
image management, 105, 416
impatience, 121
implementation,
  of decisions, 57–58
  of planning, 51
impression management, 416
inclusive language, 356, 357
income budget report, 203
income statement, 205
individuals,
  abuse by organizations, 87
  and organizations, 86–88
  differences in, 300–303
  sources of stress of, 394
  strategies and stress, 398
influence, 126–127
  tactics for, 126
informal groups, 323
information,
  power, 125
  resources, control of, 151–170
information society, 249
informational roles,
  managerial, 23
  marketing, 418
ingratiation, 127
initiating structure, 281
insecurity, 120
inseparability of services, 409
instinct, 305
insurance benefits, 231
intangibility, 409
intangible assets, 205

SUBJECT INDEX

integrated expense control and recovery, 160
integration of interests, 36
integrity, 440, 449
interest groups, 323
internal locus of control, 301
interpersonal roles, 23
   in marketing, 418
interpersonal skills, 22, 366
interviews, 220
   interviewing, 223
   parts of, 224–225
   process, 222–223
   questions, 223–224, 225
intuition, 61–62
inventories and supplies, 205
   control of, 150
   equipment, 148
inverted hierarchical structure, 105
involvement,
   in change, 383
   in decision making, 66–68, 101
   in marketing, 427–428
   in planning, 64–68

jargon, 357
job analysis, 217–218
job description, 217–218, 219, 338
job postings, 218
job specification, 218

knowledge workers, 339

laissez-faire leadership, 280–281
latent needs, 307
law,
   as a business, 5–9, 11
   as a profession, 11
   of reciprocity, 126
law firms,
   changes, 9
   communications in, 362–364
   "good," 452
   group status in, 336–339
   growth of, 377–378
   hierarchy of, 20–21
   internal culture, 455
   leadership challenges, 288
   leadership, 271–272, 275, 339
   marketing, 405
   mega firms, 8
   services of, 10
   sexism and, 455
   sizes of, 6–8
law office management, 5–8
   and leadership, 271–272
   changes, 5–8
   managerial job descriptions, 9
   new career, 5, 278–279
law offices, 14–15

law schools, 337
laws of lawyering, 442
lawyers,
   and marketing, 407
   billings, 8
   career options, 10, 16
   characteristics of, 14
   dimensions of work tasks, 89
   economic status, 337
   "good," 440–441
   hierarchical roles, 21
   managing of, 116
   number of, 8–9, 337
   power, 118
   professional status, 337
   public service, 445
   retreats, 72–75
   role in planning, 39
   status of, 337–338
   supervising, 251
leaders, 274–275
   commitments, 275
   compacts and contracts, 276
   focus, 276
   need for, 274
   philosophy, 276
   style, 275
   vision, 275
leadership, 273–289
   autocratic, 280
   charismatic, 286–287
   competencies, 276
   contemporary, 273
   developing potential for, 289
   dictatorial, 280
   laissez-faire, 280–281
   in law firms, 271–272, 275
   meaning of, 274
   need for, 274
   power, 119
   search for, 273
   styles, 272
leadership compact, 277
leadership theories, 277–280
   behavioral, 280–282
   future vision theories, 286–289
   situational theories, 282–286
   styles, 272, 284
   trait, 277–280
leading question, 223
lean media, 350
learned needs theory of motivation, 309–310
legal administrators (*see also* managers, nonlawyers), 338
   future changes in roles, 24
   hierarchical roles, 21
   job descriptions, 9
   professional status, 338
legal clinics, 408

legal ethics, 447
legal profession,
   as a business, 5
   and communications, 348
   and stress, 395
   changes in, 5
   changing environment, 406
   marketing, 406, 408
legal publications, 416
legal services benefits plans, 408
legal specialties, 429, 446
Legal Assistants Management Association, 15, 26, 295
legitimate power, 123
letterheads, 446–447
leverage, 207
liabilities, 205–206
liberty principle, 438
library, law firm, 150–151
   systems, 150
   technology, 151
   as a Clearinghouse, 151
Life Cycle Theory, 283–285
Likert's System, 1–4, 100–103, 282
limitations,
   of alternatives, 50–51
   organizational, 62
   personal, 60
line item budget, 187
linking pin roles, 101–103
liquidity, 205
listening effectively, 347, 360–361
locus of control, 301, 439
long-range planning, 44
long-term liabilities, 206
loyalty, 457

Machiavellianism, 302
management,
   and administration, 11–12
   as a science, 14
   as an art, 14
   as a profession, 14
   as orchestration, 12
   by exception, 146
   by objectives, 262
   contemporary theories, 27
   definition of, 16
   functions of, 16, 18–20
   in professional settings, 12–14
   levels of, 20
   of committees, 336
   primary purpose of, 17
   primary responsibility of, 16
   responsibilities of, 17
   teams, 8
   universality of, 16
management failings and stress, 393
management financial reporting, 201–204

management scientists, 37
management theories, 27, 33–37
  administrative theories, 35
  bureaucracy, 36
  classical theories, 35–36
  contemporary theories, 27
  forerunners of contemporary theories, 33–35
  human relationists, 36–37
  humanists, 37
  jungle, 27
  management scientists, 37
  of the ancients, 33
  scientific theories, 35
  situationalists (*see* contingency theories), 37
manager(s),
  and communication, 348
  as motivators, 313
  challenges of, 3, 81–82, 271
  definition of, 11
  ethical responsibilities, 449
  failures of, 24, 27
  financial planning role, 185
  future changes in roles, 24
  "good" managers, 447–452
  hierarchical roles, 21
  importance of, 11
  increased responsibilities of, 24
  interventions and change, 383–384
  law firm size and, 25
  levels, 20–21
  marketing roles, 418–419
  number of subordinates, 97
  of professionals, 17
  professional autonomy of, 15
  responsibilities and stress, 393
  roles of, 14, 16, 22–24, 25, 82
  skills of, 21–22
managerial ethics, 436–438, 448
Managerial Grid, 282–283
managing partners, 8, 20
mandatory worker benefits, 231
manifest needs, 307
manipulation, 127
marketable securities, 205
marketing, 409
  and the legal profession, 406–409
  challenges of, 408
  changes in, 406
  concept, 409
  evolution of, 407–408
  law firm, 405
  mix, 409–411
  obstacles to, 419
  plan, 411
  process, 409
  professionals, 405, 419–420
  success, 405
matrix organizational design, 103–105

mechanistic organizations, 105–106, 107
media, 349, 351, 417
mediator, 389
medium, 349
meetings, 366–370
  agenda, 368
  minutes, 370
megafirms, 8
membership dues, 332
message, 349, 359
middle management,
  control activities, 146
  skills and roles, 21, 22
minutes of meetings, 370
miscommunication, 364
mission statements, 43–46
  criteria for, 46
  sample mission statement, 47
Model Code of Professional Responsibility, 442
Model Rules of Professional Conduct, 435, 442, 443–447
  overview of, 443
moral, 437
  choices and workers, 456
  development, 440
  reasoning, 440
morale, 241, 330
morality, 437
motion studies, 35
motivation,
  and pay, 250–251
  and performance, 297
  and workers, 250–251, 297
  definition of, 296
  framework of, 303–305
  importance of, 296
  in law firms, 295, 296–313
  influences, 298–299
  levels, 300
  mysteries, 299
  new tools for, 313
  role of the organization, 300
  theories of, 305–313
motivational theories,
  behavioral theories, 305–307
  cognitive theories, 310–312
  early views, 305
  goal-setting theories, 312–313
  need theories, 307–310
motivators, 310
motives, rational and emotional, 421

National Association of Legal Assistants, 339
National Association of Paralegal Secretaries, 323
National Federation of Paralegal Associations, 339

National Paralegal Association, 323
need theories of motivation, 307–310
needs, 303
  group formation and, 323, 324
  motivational, 274
negotiation, 388–389
new matter reports, 161–162
  forms, 162–163, 165–167
newsletters, 417
noise, 351
nominal group technique, 69
nondirective interview, 223
nonequity partners, 192
nonlawyer assistants,
  repsonsibilites of lawyers for, 444
nonlawyer professionals, 90
  acceptance of, 24
  as partners, 10
  executive responsibilities, 10, 24
nonlawyers,
  and ethical responsibilities, 435
  managers, 435
  professional status, 338
  salaries, 338
  status of, 338
  roles of, 338
nonmanagerial positions, 21
norms, 328
  group, 328–331
  negative effects, 331
  types of, 329–331
  work group, 458
notes payable, 206
notes receivable, 205
nudges, 224

objectives, 17, 46, 49
  marketing, 412
Occupational Health and Safety Act, 236
office changes, 380–381
Ohio State Studies, 281
  omissions, 365
One Minute Management, 258
one-way communication, 362
open question, 223
operating budget, 187
operating expenses, 194, 207–208
operating margin per hour, 194–195
operational autonomy, 251
operational controls, 147
operational plans, 47
optical disk filing systems, 160
optimism, 397
oral presentations, 359
organic organizations, 105–106
organizations, 16, 84
  abuse by individuals, 87
  abuse of individuals, 86–88
  architecture of, 83–90

SUBJECT INDEX

concept of, 83–84
definitions of, 16, 84, 321
elements of, 296
formal, 84–85
informal, 84–85
workplace homes, 321
organizational charts, 91–95
organizational consent, 36
organizational culture, 105–109
  elements of, 106–107
  consequences of, 107–108
  law firms and, 108–109
  kinds of, 108
organizational design, 81, 90–105
  contemporary designs, 100–105
  successful designs of the 1990s, 109, 111
organizational development, 377
organizational forces and change, 377
organizational strategies and stress, 392, 398
organizational structure, 91, 274
organizing, 82–83
  and controlling, 146
  coordination elements of, 94–97
  control elements of, 97–100
  definition of, 19
  four activities of, 88
  guidelines for, 100
orientation, 214, 226–227
outside interests, 397
owners' equity, 206

paralegals,
  careers, 3–4, 25, 248, 295, 338–339
  compensation of, 338–339
  economic contributions, 339
  law firm hierarchy, 21, 339
  numbers of, 339
  planning roles, 39
  professional status, 338–339
  retreats, 72
  roles of, 16, 90, 339
  status of, 338–339
  supervising of, 252
paralinguistics, 352
parenting and sick care leaves, 235
parity, 338
participation in change, 383
participative management, 66–68, 101
partners,
  compensation of, 192–193, 230–231
  directing of, 13
  equity, 20, 192
  independence of, 13, 81
  management roles, 20–21
  nonequity, 192
  profitability and utilization, 189
  responsibilities of, 444
  retreats, 72–75

role in planning, 39–40
partners' draw, 193
partnerships, 10
  as an anachronism, 91
  categories of, 10, 90
  creation of, 5
  public, 428
  structure of, 91
payables, 206
percentage fees, 198, 199
perceptions, clients, 423, 433
perceptual errors, 62, 365
performance,
  and motivation, 297
  and individual differences, 300–303
  appraisals, 258–262
  criteria for appraisals, 259
  group, 335
  levels of, 300
  norms, 330–331
  quality of, 297
perishability, 409
perquisites (perks), 232
personal power, 124–125
  strategies for increasing, 127–129, 130
personal selling, 412–413
personality, 301
  work-related dimensions, 301–303
personalized power, 310
personnel,
  costs, 188, 192
  compensation of, 192–194, 337–339
persuasiveness, 352–356
physical resources control, 149–151
physiological needs, 308
place, 411
plans,
  definition of, 41
  marketing, 411
  operational plans, 47–49
  primacy of, 41
  purpose of, 42
  strategic plans, 42–47
planning, 40–53
  and controlling, 146
  barriers to, 71–72
  contemporary environment, 41
  definition of, 19
  financial, 187
  involvement in, 64–68
  long range, 44–45
  role of clients in, 39
  skills, 120
  steps in, 49–52
  styles of, 41–42
pocket veto, 253
point of hire, 234
policies, 48
political strategies and change, 383

politics, 131–132
  strategies, 132
position power, 123–124
  strategies for increasing, 129–130
positioning, 411
power, 122–126
  abuses of, 13
  balance of, 123
  definitions of, 123
  language of, 130
  law firms and, 118, 337
  managerial strategies for, 117, 127
  naivete and, 132
  personalized, 310
  powerful, 122–123
  powerless, 122–123, 133–134
  socialized, 310
  sources of, 123–126
power intervention strategies, 387, 390
powerplays, 122
practice areas, 48, 188
practice development, 418–420
practices, 48
Pregnancy Discrimination Act, The, 235
prepaid expenses, 205
prepotency of needs, 307–308
prestige, 334
price, 409, 411
primary (viscerogenic) needs, 307
primary purpose of management, 17
primary responsibility of management, 17
principle of supportive relationships, 101
privacy rights, 259–260
pro bono, 445
probes, 223
probing, 390
procedures, 48
procedures manual, 228
process losses, 327
  prodromal periods, 173
product, 409–410
profession of law,
  ethical obligations, 441–442
professional associations, 24–25
  Association of Legal Administrators, 24–26
  identification with, 15
  Legal Assistant Management Association, 26
  National Association of Legal Assistants, 339
  National Association of Paralegal Secretaries, 323
  National Federation of Paralegal Associations, 339
  National Paralegal Association, 323
professional autonomy, 445

professionals, 17
professionalism,
  characteristics of, 15
  collegial power and, 124
  ethical responsibility, 449
  integrity of, 447
  leadership and, 271
  of lawyers, 337
  of legal administrators, 338
  of paralegals, 339
  managerial, 15
profit centers, 209
profitability, 186–187, 207–209
programs, 47
project group, 322
projects, 47–48
promotion, 411
proposals, law firm, 413
proxemics, 352
proximity, 324
psychic salary, 229, 251
psychological organizational contract, 86
public relations, 414–416
  in-house activities, 415
  professional firms, 415
  programs, 416
public service, 445
punishment, 306

quality control, 145–147
  of services, 409
quality of life issues and stress, 395
Quality Control Circle (QCC), 173
quid pro quo sexual harassment, 238

rational motive, 421
realization, 207
receiver, 350
reciprocity, 330
reciprocity, law of, 126
records management, 156
recruiting, 218, 220
reference groups, 323
references, 220
referent power, 125
reflecting, 390
reflecting skills, 361
reflective question, 224
regulators, 353
reinforcement contingencies, 305–306
  positive, 306
  negative, 306
relatedness needs, 308
relationships, 321–322
relaxation, 398
religion and reasonable accommodation, 234
resistance to change, 381
  overcoming, 382–383

resistance to controls, 171–172
responsive leadership and change, 382
restrictions on the practice of law, 445
restructuring, 90
resumes, 220
retainers, 198, 199
retention of workers, 250–251
retirement benefits, 231
retreats,
  agenda preparation, 73
  data packets, 74
  facilitator, 75
  general preparation, 74
  ground rules, 74
  hidden agendas, 75
  participants, 72
  potential problems, 75
  purpose of, 72–73
  site selection for, 73
revenues,
  projection of, 191–192
  revenue stream, 195–200
revenues and expense budget, 187
reward allocation, 330
reward power, 124
rich media, 349
rights, 438
Robert's Rules of Order, 368
role conflicts and stress, 393
roles, 328
  group, 320, 328
  nonlawyers, 338
  paralegals, 339
  support staff, 339
rules and regulations, 48
rumors, 363–364

safety, 235
salaries, 230
  lawyers, 337
  nonlawyers, 338
  paralegals, 339
  secretaries and support staff, 339
scalar chain, 96
scenario building, 68
scientific management theories, 35
scope of authority, 119
screening of applicants, 220
secondary (psychogenic) needs, 307
secretaries, 339
  status of, 339
  law firm hierarchy, 339
selection process, 220
selective listening, 364
self-actualization, 308
self-discipline, 262
self-esteem, 302, 365
  self-knowledge and management of self, 277
self-monitoring, 365

semantics, 365
semi-active files, 168
sender, 349
sensitivity analysis, 203
service, 422
service centers, 209
service recovery, 423
sexism, 232–235, 455
sexual harassment, 237, 238–241
  dealing with, 237
  forms of, 238
  law firms and, 238
  preventing, 238–239
single-use plans, 47
situational theories of leadership, 282
situationalists, 37
size of groups, 327, 333
skills variety, 89
social (belongingness) needs, 308
social conduct, 330
social facilitation, 331
social forces and change, 377
social inhibition, 331
social loafing, 331
social responsibility,
  arguments for and against, 453–454, 455
  classical view, 452
  continuum of, 453
  norms for, 330
  socio-economic view, 452–453
social responsiveness, 456
social support, 398
social validation, 324
Social Security, 231
socialization process, 225–226
socialized power, 310
soliciting business, 446
solvency, 186–187
space, 334
  planning, 151
span of management, 97
speaking effectively, 358–360
staffing, 217
stakeholders, 66
standards, 170
standing committees, 322
standing plans, 48
statement of cash flows, 205
statement of operations, 205
statement of retained earnings, 206
status,
  group, 320, 328–331, 333, 336–339
  hierarchical levels, 337–339
  lawyers, 337
  nonlawyers, 338
  paralegals, 338–339
  secretaries and support staff, 339
  symbols, 333–334
stereotyping, 301

SUBJECT INDEX

strategic management, 58–59
strategic plans, 42–43
strategy, 46–47
stress, 390–398
   alcohol abuse and stress, 395
   ambiguity and, 393
   and law firms, 375
   attitudes and stress, 396
   depression and stress, 395
   differences in response to, 396
   effects of stress, 395–396
   hassles, 394
   individual strategies, 398
   individual sources of, 394
   legal profession and, 395
   management failings and, 393
   managerial repsonsibilites and, 393
   management strategies, 375
   nature of, 391
   organizational strategies, 398
   quality of life issues and stress, 395
   role conflicts and, 393
   sources of, 392–395
   stressful life events scale, 394
   time pressures and, 393
stressful life events scale, 394
stressors, 392
   environmental stressors, 392
   organizational stressors, 392
   work-related stressors, 392, 393
structures,
   formal and informal, 85
   group, 327–334
structuring, 90
subordinate lawyers,
   responsibilites of, 444
super leadership, 289
superordinate goals, 390
supervision, 21, 249–255
   challenges of, 249
   control activities, 146
   effective, 248, 255
   of professionals, 17, 248, 251
   confusion about, 27
   responsibilities, 17
   skills and roles, 21, 22
   styles of, 255–258
supervisors,
   as coaches, 257–258
   as counsellors, 256–257
   expectations of supervisees, 256
   problems of, 251–253
   trust and, 254–255
   skills, 252
supervisory lawyers,
   responsibilities of, 444
supervisory management, 21
supervisory skills, 249, 252, 256
support staff,
   confidentiality, 451

delegating, 116–117
dimensions of work tasks, 89
guidelines for, 10
hierarchical roles, 21
law firm hierarchy, 339
motivation of, 295
retreats, 72
roles of, 16
status of, 339
supervising of, 252
work load inequities, 152
supportive relationships, principle of, 101, 102
Supreme Court, 406, 407
surveys, 423–424, 426
systems manual, 147–148

task force, 322
task identity and significance, 89
team presentations, 413
   teams, effective, 335–336
technical skills, 22
technology, 148, 189, 249, 435
technology and marketing, 429
   desktop publishing, 417
telecommunications, 148
television, 416
theories, managerial, 27
theory of justice, 438
theory of rights, 438
Theory X and Theory Y, 317–318
Theory Z, 173
third-party intervention, 389
tickler (or monitor) systems, 9, 152–155
   critical dates, 154
   procedures, 154
   sample form, 155
time,
   lawyers, 337
   nonlawyers, 338
   paralegals, 338
   secretaries, 339
   theft of, 87
   time sheets, 201
   timekeeping and billing systems, 200
   value of, 200–201
time management, 174–175
   techniques for, 176
time pressures, 365
time stressors, 393
time studies, 35
   timekeeping and billing systems, 200
titles, 334
top (upper) management,
   control activities, 145–146
   skills and roles, 20–21, 22
Total Quality Control, 173

Total Quality Management, 173
training and development, 228–229
training for marketing, 427
trait theories of leadership, 277–280
transactional leadership, 288
transformational coping, 398
transformational leadership, 287–288
trust, 254–255
   management of, 276–277
turnover, 297
two-way communication, 362
Type A and Type B behavior patterns, 396

unauthorized practice of law, 445
unions, 339
uniqueness of services, 409
unity of command, 95
universality of management, 16
University of Michigan Studies, 281–282
upper (top) management,
   control activities, 145–146
   skills and roles, 20–21, 22
upward communication, 363
urgency, 121
utilitarianism, 437–438
utilization, 207

valence, 312
value billing, 196
value judgements, 364–365
values, 304, 439
   changing, 249
   role of, 304–305
   universal, 439–440
   work related values, 304
vertical communication, 363
vision,
   and change, 377
   and management of attention, 276
   and planning, 41
   of leaders, 275
Vocational Rehabilitation Act, 234–235
voice, 358, 457–458

wages, 229
wealth and lawyers, 337
whistleblowing, 458–459
work assignments, 152–153
work environment, 278–279
work ethic, 304
work group norms, 458
work-in-process, 200
   work-in-process reports, 207
work-related stressors, 392, 393
workaholics, 175–177
workers,

alienated, 298
and moral choices, 456
benefits, 87, 231–232
committed, 298
calculating, 298
equity, 230
insurance benefits, 231
labor pool, 217
loyalty, 250
mandatory, 231
mobility, 250
motivation, 250–251, 297
retention, 230
retirement benefits, 231
rights, 87, 232
secretarial shortage, 339
sense of self, 250
Workers' Bill of Rights, 454
working,
    conditions, 87
    inducements for, 86–87
    motives for, 86
    schedule autonomy, 334
write-offs, 200
writing effectively, 356–358

yellow page advertising, 417

zone of acceptance, 330
zone of difference, 288–289